Media Arabic Vocabulary

Book 3

lingualism

ISBN: 978-1-962752-00-8

website: www.lingualism.com

email: contact@lingualism.com

Written by Ahmad Al-Masri and Matthew Aldrich
Edited by Hend Khaled and Matthew Aldrich
Cover design by Matthew Aldrich

Disclaimer:

This publication is designed exclusively as a language educational resource. The contents of this book, which include sentences and texts, typically do not reflect or comment on real situations, whether historical or contemporary. When real events, individuals, or organizations are referenced, the specifics may not always uphold factual accuracy.

Where certain names or trademarks may appear, they are used strictly for educational purposes. They do not imply any affiliation with or endorsement by the respective rights holders and should not be considered as infringement.

Opinions expressed in the content are ascribed to fictional characters and journalists and do not necessarily reflect the views of the book's contributors or publisher. These opinions are included solely to mimic realistic language use in media settings and do not intend to endorse, critique, or influence real-world ideologies.

By using this book, readers acknowledge that it is for language education, not a source of reliable real-world information. Any errors or inaccuracies are unintentional and do not detract from the book's purpose as a language-learning tool.

Table of Contents

Introduction

Media Arabic Vocabulary is a series specially designed to bridge the gap between **intermediate** learning and reading real-world Arabic news articles. These books are intended to make the often-daunting journey into Arabic media literacy not only accessible, but engaging and enjoyable.

In our experience, many learners find themselves stuck in a language learning plateau, where they can handle classroom scenarios but are left feeling overwhelmed by the complexity of authentic, native-speaker materials, such as news articles. That is exactly where this book series comes in. Each volume is structured to help you scale that seemingly daunting wall by presenting carefully selected vocabulary and controlled texts that emulate the style and complexity of real-world Arabic media.

In this third book of the series, we will navigate through three distinct units: Military, Religion, and Weather. Each unit is further broken down into manageable sections and subsections. Subsections introduce you to key vocabulary in context, helping you understand not only the meaning of the words but also their appropriate use. As an additional aid to word recognition and correct pronunciation, all Arabic content in the book contains **diacritics** (tashkeel). You will find **English translations** for all Arabic content, which allows for better comprehension and learning, plus **audio tracks** to help you get a firm grasp on pronunciation and listening comprehension.

This dynamic approach, combining the introduction of **topical vocabulary** with **example sentences** and end-of-section practice **texts**, ensures you are not just memorizing words, but actively learning to use them in context. Over time, this exposure will greatly increase your confidence and proficiency in reading actual media Arabic-style texts.

While the volumes are numbered, they are not incremental in learning level. They simply cover different topics. Feel free to pick any book from the series that aligns with your interest in a particular theme or topic. We hope you find this approach as empowering and rewarding as we do.

Acknowledgments

This series would not have been possible without the dedicated work of some exceptional individuals. I would like to express my deepest gratitude to Ahmad Al-Masri for his invaluable contributions in compiling the extensive vocabulary list and crafting the example sentences and texts. Ahmad's insights and expertise in the Arabic language have been fundamental in shaping this book.

Likewise, I would like to extend my heartfelt thanks to Hend Khaled for her meticulous editing and proofreading of our materials. Her thoughtful feedback and suggestions have significantly elevated the quality and usability of this series. Likewise, her diligence and dedication have been indispensable in shaping the final product.

–Matthew Aldrich

How to Use This Book

Media Arabic Vocabulary is a versatile, flexible tool that can adapt to your personal learning style, immediate needs, and specific interests. Here's how to make the most of it:

Follow Your Interests

The organization of the book allows you to chart your own learning path. Feel free to delve into any unit that piques your interest or aligns with your immediate learning needs. There is no strict order to follow; every path leads to enrichment.

Understand the Structure

Vocabulary Lists: Vocabulary lists serve as your first contact with the topic-specific words and phrases. Each underline vocabulary item appears on the right-hand side, while its English translation appears on the opposite side. Sometimes you will notice word forms between them, preceded by a large dot. These are irregular plurals of nouns or verbal nouns (masdars) of verbs. Following each vocabulary item, in a shaded box, is an example sentence to demonstrate its use in context. Dozens of note boxes appear throughout the book with lexical and grammatical notes, learning tips, and references to other vocabulary items.

End-of-Section Texts: Following the vocabulary lists, you'll encounter different kinds of texts, including mini-articles, news reports, interviews, and more. These texts aim to immerse you in a variety of real-world contexts, further reinforcing the vocabulary and enhancing your reading proficiency.

Engage in Self-Discovery

We've consciously decided not to include traditional exercises such as multiple-choice or true-false questions. Instead, we promote a self-discovery approach, empowering you to actively engage with the material.

To effectively analyze the texts, try to identify the vocabulary from the lists in the actual context. Notice how these words interact with each other, what collocations they form, and how they contribute to the overall meaning of the text. As you progress through the content, you may notice that the English translations for certain vocabulary items in the example sentences and texts sometimes differ from those presented in the vocabulary lists. Far from an oversight, this is an intentional aspect of the methodology. Our aim here is to encourage you to ponder more deeply on the meanings of words and the nuances in their usage.

Lingualism offers a series of notebooks designed for recording Arabic vocabulary, all with beautiful covers:

www.lingualism.com/vocabulary-notebooks

As for vocabulary organization, we encourage you to keep a dedicated notebook. Classify and group words according to logical categories that make sense to you – be it themes, synonyms, antonyms, or even roots for Arabic words. This personalized lexical resource will greatly aid your recall and application of vocabulary.

Utilize the Audio Tracks

The accompanying audio tracks can be used in conjunction with the text or separately for additional listening practice. You can listen before, during, or after reading the texts, depending on your individual preference. They are designed to help improve your listening comprehension and pronunciation. Each section in the book is preceded by its track number.

Visit www.lingualism.com/audio, where you can find the free accompanying audio to download or stream (at variable playback rates).

Expand Your Vocabulary

One of the key strengths of this book is the wealth of vocabulary embedded within its pages beyond the given lists. Each section is filled with relevant vocabulary items not explicitly listed as vocabulary items. These additional vocabulary treasures can be found within the example sentences and texts. We encourage you to be an active explorer, seeking them out and adding them to your notes. The more you interact with the texts, the more you will uncover additional topical vocabulary to bolster your Arabic language repertoire.

Happy Learning!

Remember, the journey of language learning is not a linear one. It's a process of exploration, discovery, and personal growth. We hope this book will serve as your faithful companion on this fascinating voyage into the vibrant world of Arabic media.

Unit 7
Military and Conflict

This unit offers an exploration of various facets of military engagement, covering traditional warfare to modern asymmetrical conflicts, all within the context of media Arabic. As you progress, you'll grasp the nuances of language used in discussing military strategies, defense technologies, and security concerns, which are prevalent themes in news coverage.

We start with a focus on traditional warfare, including ground, naval, and air operations. Through vocabulary, example sentences, and articles, you'll acquaint yourself with terminology related to military units, ranks, and maneuvers, acknowledging the potential variations across countries.

Advancing further, we delve into modern and asymmetrical warfare, touching upon topics such as terrorism, cyber-terrorism, and special operations. Here, you'll encounter terminology associated with insurgent tactics, counter-terrorism endeavors, and the roles of special forces in contemporary conflicts.

Moreover, we explore defense and security matters, scrutinizing military strategies, equipment, and technology. From discussions on defense budgets to analyses of emerging security threats, you'll gain a comprehensive grasp of the language used in addressing defense and security issues within media discourse.

It's essential to note that the terminology associated with military ranks, units, and operations may vary from one country to another. Therefore, as you engage with this material, we encourage you to remain flexible and open-minded, recognizing the diversity of linguistic expressions within the Arabic-speaking world.

By immersing yourself in this unit, you'll not only enhance your Arabic language proficiency but also deepen your comprehension of military and security issues, given their frequent coverage in the news. This vocabulary proves invaluable given the unfortunate prevalence of military conflicts, making this unit especially relevant and useful.

7.1 Traditional Warfare

Track 1

war • حُروبٌ   حَربٌ

تَدورُ حُروبٌ عِدَّةٌ في مَناطِقَ مُختَلِفَةٍ حَولَ العالَمِ.

Several wars are taking place in various regions around the world.

> Note that the noun حَربٌ is feminine, as demonstrated by the adjectives in the following expressions.

civil war   حَربٌ أَهلِيَّةٌ

اِندَلَعَت حُروبٌ أَهلِيَّةٌ في عِدَّةِ دُوَلٍ نَتيجَةً لِلاِنقِساماتِ الدّاخِلِيَّةِ.

Civil wars broke out in several countries due to internal divisions.

world war   حَربٌ عالَمِيَّةٌ

شَهِدَتِ الحَربُ العالَمِيَّةُ الثّانِيَةُ مُشارَكَةَ العَديدِ مِنَ الدُّوَلِ.

World War II saw the participation of many countries.

ally • حُلَفاءُ   حَليفٌ

تَمَّ التَّوَصُّلُ لِاتِّفاقٍ بَينَ الحُلَفاءِ لِتَنسيقِ الهَجَماتِ.

An agreement was reached among the allies to coordinate attacks.

weapon • أَسلِحَةٌ   سِلاحٌ

تَمَّ تَطويرُ سِلاحٍ جَديدٍ يُمكِنُهُ إِصابَةُ الأَهدافِ مِن مَسافاتٍ بَعيدَةٍ.

A new weapon was developed that can hit targets from long distances.

enemy • أَعداءٌ   عَدُوٌّ

اِستَخدَمَتِ القُوّاتُ الخاصَّةُ تَكتيكاتٍ مُتَطَوِّرَةً لِمُواجَهَةِ العَدُوِّ في المِنطَقَةِ الحُدودِيَّةِ.

Special forces used advanced tactics to confront the enemy in the border region.

military عَسْكَرِيٌّ

اِجْتَمَعَ المَسْؤُولونَ لِمُناقَشَةِ الاِسْتِراتيجِيَّةِ العَسْكَرِيَّةِ الجَديدَةِ لِلدِّفاعِ عَنِ الحُدودِ.

Officials met to discuss the new military strategy for defending the borders.

> Note that the term عَسْكَرِيٌّ رَجُلٌ ('military man') can refer to anyone in the military, while عَسْكَرِيٌّ as a noun (see page 8) is an official rank.

7.1.1 Ground Forces

Track 2

prisoner of war أَسيرٌ • أَسْرى

تَمَّ الإِفْراجُ عَنِ الأَسْرى بَعْدَ مُفاوَضاتٍ طَويلَةٍ.

The prisoners were released after lengthy negotiations.

to command أَمَرَ • أَمْرٌ

أَصْدَرَ الجِنْرالُ أَمْرًا بِالاِنْسِحابِ مِنَ المِنْطَقَةِ.

The general issued an order to withdraw from the area.

security أَمْنٌ

باتَ أَمْنُ المِنْطَقَةِ تَحْتَ السَّيْطَرَةِ بَعْدَ عَمَلِيَّةٍ ناجِحَةٍ.

The security of the area came under control after a successful operation.

to halt أَوْقَفَ • إيقافٌ

أَوْقَفَتِ القُوّاتُ العَسْكَرِيَّةُ العَمَلِيّاتِ لِإِجْراءِ مُفاوَضاتِ السَّلامِ.

The military forces halted operations to conduct peace negotiations.

supplies إِمْداداتٌ _pl._

تَمَّ قَطْعُ الإِمْداداتِ عَنِ القُوّاتِ المُحاصَرَةِ.

Supplies were cut off from the besieged forces.

occupation

اِحْتِلالٌ

بَدَأَ الاِحْتِلالُ بَعْدَ هَزِيمَةِ الجَيْشِ المَحَلِّيِّ.

The occupation began after the defeat of the local army.

front

جَبْهَةٌ

فُتِحَتْ جَبْهَةٌ جَدِيدَةٌ فِي الحَرْبِ، مِمّا سَبَّبَ تَوَتُّرًا إِقْلِيمِيًّا.

A new front opened in the war, causing regional tension.

wounded (person)

جَرْحَى • جَرِيحٌ

تَمَّ نَقْلُ الجَرْحَى إِلَى المُسْتَشْفَيَاتِ المَيْدانِيَّةِ.

The wounded were transported to field hospitals.

soldier, private

جُنُودٌ • جُنْدِيٌّ

سَقَطَ عَدَدٌ مِنَ الجُنُودِ فِي الهُجُومِ الأَخِيرِ.

Several soldiers fell in the latest attack.

general

جِنِرالٌ

فِي اعْتِقادِ الجِنِرالِ، هُناكَ حاجَةٌ لِتَعْزِيزِ الدِّفاعاتِ حَوْلَ المَدِينَةِ.

In the general's opinion, there is a need to bolster the defenses around the city.

army

جُيُوشٌ • جَيْشٌ

تَحَدَّثَ قادَةُ الجُيُوشِ عَنْ ضَرُورَةِ التَّعاوُنِ الدَّوْلِيِّ لِمُكافَحَةِ الإِرْهابِ.

Army leaders talked about the need for international cooperation to combat terrorism.

alert status

حالَةُ تَأَهُّبٍ

أَعْلَنَتِ القُوّاتُ المُسَلَّحَةُ حالَةَ التَّأَهُّبِ القُصْوَى بَعْدَ التَّفْجِيراتِ.

The armed forces declared a state of high alert after the bombings.

state of emergency

حالَةُ طَوارِئَ

فُرِضَت حالَةُ الطَّوارِئِ في البِلادِ بَعْدَ الهُجومِ عَلى العاصِمَةِ.

A state of emergency was imposed in the country after the attack on the capital.

trench warfare

حَرْبُ خَنادِقَ • حُروبٌ

كانَتْ حَرْبُ الخَنادِقِ مُرْهِقَةً وَكَلَّفَتِ الكَثيرَ مِنَ الأَرْواحِ.

The trench warfare was exhausting and cost many lives.

civil protection

حِمايَةٌ مَدَنِيَّةٌ

تَمَّ تَنْفيذُ عَمَلِيّاتِ حِمايَةٍ مَدَنِيَّةٍ لِإِجْلاءِ السُّكّانِ المَحَلِّيّينَ.

Civil protection operations were carried out to evacuate local residents.

map

خَريطَةٌ • خَرائِطُ

اِسْتَخْدَمَ القادَةُ الخَرائِطَ لِلتَّخْطيطِ لِلْعَمَلِيّاتِ القادِمَةِ.

The leaders used maps for planning upcoming operations.

front line

خَطُّ الجَبْهَةِ • خُطوطٌ

كانَ خَطُّ الجَبْهَةِ مُتَقَلِّبًا بِسَبَبِ الهَجَماتِ المُتَكَرِّرَةِ مِنَ الطَّرَفَيْنِ.

The front line was fluctuating due to repeated attacks from both sides.

battle line

خَطُّ قِتالٍ • خُطوطٌ

نَشَأَ خَطُّ قِتالٍ ثابِتٌ بَيْنَ القُوّاتِ المُتَقابِلَةِ عَلى طولِ الحُدودِ.

A stable battle line formed between the opposing forces along the border.

defense plan

خُطَّةُ دِفاعٍ • خُطَطٌ

أَعَدَّتِ القُوّاتُ خُطَّةَ دِفاعٍ مُحْكَمَةٍ لِحِمايَةِ المَدينَةِ.

The forces prepared a robust defense plan to protect the city.

attack plan
خُطَطٌ • خُطَّةُ هُجومٍ

وُضِعَتْ خُطَّةُ هُجومٍ لِاقْتِحامِ قاعِدَةِ العَدُوِّ في الفَجْرِ.

An attack plan was made to storm the enemy base at dawn.

trench
خَنادِقُ • خَنْدَقٌ

كانَ الجُنودُ يَحْفِرونَ خَنادِقَ لِلْحِمايَةِ مِنَ القَصْفِ العَنيفِ.

The soldiers were digging trenches to protect themselves from heavy shelling.

tank
دَبّابَةٌ

تَمَّ اسْتِدْعاءُ الدَّبّاباتِ لِاقْتِحامِ خُطوطِ دِفاعِ العَدُوِّ.

Tanks were called in to break through enemy defense lines.

patrol
دَوْرِيَّةٌ

فَتَّشَتِ الدَّوْرِيَّةُ المِنْطَقَةَ بَحْثًا عَنْ نَشاطٍ مَشْبوهٍ.

The patrol searched the area for suspicious activity.

ammunition
ذَخائِرُ • ذَخيرَةٌ

نَفِدَتِ الذَّخائِرُ، مِمّا أَثَّرَ عَلى قُدْرَةِ الجَيْشِ عَلى مُواصَلَةِ القِتالِ.

The ammunition ran out, affecting the army's ability to continue fighting.

major
رُوّادٌ • رائِدٌ

تَمَّ تَرْقِيَةُ الرّائِدِ إلى عَقيدٍ بَعْدَ عَمَلِيَّةٍ ناجِحَةٍ.

The major was promoted to colonel after a successful operation.

marksman
رُماةٌ • رامٍ

كانَ الرّامي مَسْؤولًا عَنِ التَّصْويبِ الدَّقيقِ خِلالَ المُهِمَّةِ.

The marksman was responsible for precision shooting during the mission.

convoy

رَتْلٌ • أَرْتَالٌ

تَوَجَّهَ رَتْلٌ مِنَ العَرَبَاتِ المُدَرَّعَةِ نَحْوَ الجَبْهَةِ لِدَعْمِ القُوَّاتِ هُنَاكَ.

A convoy of armored vehicles headed toward the front to support the forces there.

sergeant

رَقِيبٌ • رُقَبَاءُ

أَصْدَرَ الرَّقِيبُ أَوَامِرَ لِفَرِيقِهِ لِلتَّحَرُّكِ نَحْوَ الهَدَفِ.

The sergeant issued orders for his team to move toward the objective.

uniform

زِيٌّ عَسْكَرِيٌّ • أَزْيَاءٌ

يَرْتَدِي الجُنُودُ أَزْيَاءً عَسْكَرِيَّةً مُمَوَّهَةً لِلْعَمَلِيَّاتِ فِي الغَابَةِ.

The soldiers wear camouflage military uniforms for operations in the forest.

company

سَرِيَّةٌ • سَرَايَا

قَامَتِ السَّرِيَّةُ بِتَنْفِيذِ مُهِمَّةٍ اسْتِطْلَاعِيَّةٍ خَلْفَ خُطُوطِ العَدُوِّ.

The company carried out a reconnaissance mission behind enemy lines.

infantry

سِلَاحُ المُشَاةِ • أَسْلِحَةٌ

اِنْخَرَطَ سِلَاحُ المُشَاةِ فِي مَعْرَكَةٍ شَرِسَةٍ لِلسَّيْطَرَةِ عَلَى الجِسْرِ الاِسْتِرَاتِيجِيِّ.

The infantry engaged in a fierce battle to control the strategic bridge.

> The term سِلَاحٌ has two meanings in Arabic: The more common meaning is 'weapon' (see page2).
> However, سِلَاحٌ can also refer to a specific branch or sector within the military, such as infantry,
> artillery, or cavalry. This usage is more specialized and context-dependent, typically associated with
> military or defense language.

to launch (an attack)

شَنَّ • شَنَّ

شَنَّ الجَيْشُ هُجُومًا مُفَاجِئًا عَلَى مَوَاقِعِ العَدُوِّ.

The army launched a surprise attack on enemy positions.

officer   ضُبّاطٌ •   ضابِطٌ

يَجْتَمِعُ الضُّبّاطُ لِمُناقَشَةِ اسْتِراتيجِيَّةِ الحَمْلَةِ الجَديدَةِ.

The officers are meeting to discuss the strategy for the new campaign.

bullet   طَلْقَةٌ

اسْتَخْدَمَ الجُنْدِيُّ آخِرَ طَلْقَةٍ في مُسَدَّسِهِ لِتَحْييدِ التَّهْديدِ.

The soldier used the last bullet in his pistol to neutralize the threat.

armored vehicle   عَرَبَةٌ مُدَرَّعَةٌ

تَمَّ نَشْرُ عَرَباتٍ مُدَرَّعَةٍ لِتَأْمينِ الطُّرُقِ المُؤَدِّيَةِ لِلْمَدينَةِ.

Armored vehicles were deployed to secure the roads leading to the city.

corporal   عُرَفاءُ •   عَريفٌ

حَصَلَ العَريفُ عَلى وِسامٍ لِشَجاعَتِهِ في المَعْرَكَةِ.

The corporal received a medal for his bravery in battle.

soldier, private   عَساكِرُ •   عَسْكَرِيٌّ

قامَ العَساكِرُ بِتَنْفيذِ تَدْريبٍ مُكَثَّفٍ اسْتِعْدادًا لِلْحَمْلَةِ القادِمَةِ.

The soldiers conducted intensive training in preparation for the upcoming campaign.

> عَسْكَرِيٌّ can also be used as an adjective (see page 3). عَسْكَرِيٌّ, as a noun, is synonomous with جُنْدِيٌّ (see page 4).

military personnel   *pl.*   عَسْكَرِيّونَ

شارَكَ عَسْكَرِيّونَ مِنْ مُخْتَلِفِ الفُروعِ في التَّدْريبِ المُشْتَرَكِ.

Military personnel from various branches participated in the joint training.

colonel   عُقَداءُ •   عَقيدٌ

تَوَلّى العَقيدُ مُهِمَّةَ تَنْظيمِ الدِّفاعاتِ حَوْلَ القاعِدَةِ.

The colonel took on the task of organizing the defenses around the base.

brigadier general

عَمِيدٌ

• عُمَداءُ

تَمَّ تَعْيينُ العَميدِ كَمُديرٍ لِلأَكاديمِيَّةِ العَسْكَرِيَّةِ الجَديدَةِ.

The brigadier was appointed as the director of the new military academy.

squad

فِرْقَةٌ

• فِرَقٌ

تَلَقَّتْ فِرْقَةُ القُوّاتِ الخاصَّةِ تَعْليماتٍ لِلانْضِمامِ إلى العَمَلِيَّةِ اللَّيْلِيَّةِ.

The special forces squad received orders to join the night operation.

lieutenant general

فَريقٌ

• فُرَقاءُ / أَفْرِقَةٌ

اِجْتَمَعَ الفَريقُ مَعَ قادَةِ الوَحَداتِ لِمُناقَشَةِ الاِسْتِراتيجِيَّةِ.

The lieutenant general met with unit commanders to discuss strategy.

platoon

فَصيلَةٌ

• فَصائِلُ

اِنْضَمَّتْ فَصيلَةٌ مِنَ القُوّاتِ الخاصَّةِ لِلعَمَلِيَّةِ.

A platoon of special forces joined the operation.

commander

قائِدٌ

• قادَةٌ / قُوّادٍ

تَمَّ تَعْيينُ القائِدِ الجَديدِ لِلقُوّاتِ المُشْتَرَكَةِ بَعْدَ مَراسِمِ تَنْصيبٍ رَسْمِيَّةٍ.

The new commander of the joint forces was appointed after an official inauguration ceremony.

to fight

قاتَلَ

• قِتالٌ / مُقاتَلَةٌ

قاتَلَ الجُنودُ بِبَسالَةٍ لِلدِّفاعِ عَنِ النُّقْطَةِ الاِسْتِراتيجِيَّةِ.

The soldiers fought valiantly to defend the strategic point.

combat, fighting

قِتالٌ

كانَ قِتالُ الشَّوارِعِ هُوَ الأَكْثَرَ شَراسَةً في المَعْرَكَةِ.

The street fighting was the most brutal in the battle.

casualty	• قَتْلى	قَتيلٌ

تَسَبَّبَتِ المُواجَهَةُ في عَدَدٍ كَبيرٍ مِنَ القَتْلى مِنَ الجانِبَيْنِ.

The confrontation resulted in a large number of casualties on both sides.

sniper	• قَنّاصَةٌ	قَنّاصٌ

اِسْتَخْدَمَ القَنّاصُ مَهارَتَهُ لِإِسْقاطِ عَدَدٍ مِنْ جُنودِ العَدُوِّ.

The sniper used his skills to take down several of the enemy soldiers.

rules of engagement	*pl.*	قَواعِدُ الْاِشْتِباكِ

وُضِعَتْ قَواعِدُ الِاشْتِباكِ لِلتَّحَكُّمِ في اسْتِخْدامِ القُوَّةِ خِلالَ العَمَلِيَّةِ.

Rules of engagement were established to regulate the use of force during the operation.

battalion	• كَتائِبُ	كَتيبَةٌ

تَمَّ نَشْرُ كَتيبَةٍ مِنَ القُوّاتِ البَرِّيَّةِ لِتَأْمينِ المِنْطَقَةِ.

A battalion of ground forces was deployed to secure the area.

brigade	• كَتائِبُ	كَتيبَةٌ

تَمَّ نَقْلُ كَتيبَةٍ كامِلَةٍ لِتَعْزيزِ الجَبْهَةِ الشَّماليَّةِ.

An entire brigade was transferred to reinforce the northern front.

to reveal, uncover	• كَشْفٌ	كَشَفَ

كَشَفَتِ الِاسْتِخْباراتُ عَنْ مَواقِعَ مُحْتَمَلَةٍ لِلْعَدُوِّ.

Intelligence revealed potential enemy locations.

major general	• لِواءاتٌ	لِواءٌ

أَصْدَرَ اللِّواءُ أوامِرَ لِبَدْءِ الهُجومِ عَلى العَدُوِّ.

The major general issued orders to commence the attack on the enemy.

allied مُتَحالِفٌ

دَعَمَتِ الدُّوَلُ المُتَحالِفَةُ الحَمْلَةَ بِالْمَوارِدِ وَالعَتادِ.

Allied nations supported the campaign with resources and equipment.

explosives pl. مُتَفَجِّراتٌ

تَمَّ العُثورُ عَلَى مُتَفَجِّراتٍ في مَخْبَأٍ بِالْقُرْبِ مِنَ الحُدودِ.

Explosives were found in a hideout near the border.

advanced (as in position) مُتَقَدِّمٌ

تَقَدَّمَتِ القُوّاتُ إلى مَوْقِعٍ مُتَقَدِّمٍ لِلسَّيْطَرَةِ عَلَى الجِسْرِ.

The forces advanced to an advanced position to take control of the bridge.

recruit, conscript مُجَنَّدٌ

تَمَّ اسْتِدْعاءُ المُجَنَّدينَ لِلْخِدْمَةِ العَسْكَرِيَّةِ في ظِلِّ الأَزْمَةِ.

Conscripts were called up for military service amid the crisis.

bunker, hideout مَخابِئُ • مَخْبَأٌ

اِكْتَشَفَتِ القُوّاتُ مَخابِئَ تُسْتَخْدَمُ لِتَخْزينِ الأَسْلِحَةِ.

The forces discovered hideouts used for storing weapons.

armored مُدَرَّعٌ

اِسْتَخْدَمَ الجَيْشُ عَرَباتٍ مُدَرَّعَةً لِتَأْمينِ المَناطِقِ الحَسّاسَةِ.

The army used armored vehicles to secure sensitive areas.

> The feminine adjective مُدَرَّعَةٌ can also function as a noun meaning 'armored vehicle,' without the need for the noun عَرَبَةٌ ('vehicle'), so عَرَباتٌ مُدَرَّعَةٌ is synonymous with مُدَرَّعاتٌ ('armored vehicles').

artillery (large-caliber guns) مَدافِعُ • مِدْفَعٌ

تَمَّ اسْتِخْدامُ المَدافِعِ لِدَعْمِ الهُجومِ عَلَى القاعِدَةِ المُعادِيَةِ.

Artillery was used to support the attack on the enemy base.

mortar مِدْفَعُ هاوِنْ • مَدافِعُ

اِسْتَخْدَمَ الجَيْشُ مَدافِعَ هاوِنْ لِتَدْمِيرِ مَواقِعِ دِفاعِ العَدُوِّ.

The army used mortars to destroy enemy defense positions.

artillery (military detachment) مِدْفَعِيَّةٌ

أَطْلَقَتِ المِدْفَعِيَّةُ النّارَ عَلى مَواقِعِ العَدُوِّ لِفَتْحِ الطَّرِيقِ لِلْمُشاةِ.

The artillery fired at enemy positions to clear the way for the infantry.

> An artillery can also be referred to as سِلاحُ مِدْفَعِيَّةٍ.

infantry مُشاةٌ
pl.

تَقَدَّمَ المُشاةُ بِبُطْءٍ تَحْتَ غِطاءِ النّيرانِ.

The infantry advanced slowly under covering fire.

field marshal مُشِيرٌ

أَصْدَرَ المُشِيرُ تَوْجِيهاتٍ اسْتِراتِيجِيَّةً لِلْعَمَلِيّاتِ القادِمَةِ.

The field marshal issued strategic directives for upcoming operations.

hostile مُعادٍ

بَدَأَتِ القُوّاتُ المُعادِيَةُ في التَّحَرُّكِ نَحْوَ الحُدودِ.

The hostile forces began moving toward the border.

lieutenant colonel مُقَدِّمٌ

اِسْتَقْبَلَ المُقَدِّمُ وَفْدًا دَوْلِيًّا لِبَحْثِ سُبُلِ التَّعاوُنِ.

The lieutenant colonel received an international delegation to discuss avenues of cooperation.

lieutenant

مُلازِمٌ

تَمَّتْ تَرْقِيَةُ المُلازِمِ إِلَى رُتْبَةِ مُلازِمٍ أَوَّلَ بَعْدَ عَمَلِيَّةٍ نَاجِحَةٍ.

The lieutenant was promoted to first lieutenant after a successful operation.

mission

مُهِمَّةٌ • مَهامٌّ

أَتَمَّتِ الوَحْدَةُ مَهامَّها دونَ خَسائِرَ كَبيرَةٍ.

The unit completed its missions without significant losses.

battlefield

مَيْدانٌ • مَيادينُ

اِحْتَدَمَتِ المَعارِكُ في مَيادينَ مُتَعَدِّدَةٍ عَبْرَ الحُدودِ.

Battles raged in multiple fields across the border.

field- (as in field operations)

مَيْدانِيٌّ

أُسْتُخْدِمَتِ التَّكْتيكاتُ المَيْدانِيَّةُ بِفَعالِيَّةٍ ضِدَّ العَدُوِّ.

Field tactics were effectively used against the enemy.

to deploy

نَشَرَ • نَشْرٌ

نَشَرَ الجَيْشُ قُوَّاتٍ إِضافِيَّةً في المِنْطَقَةِ الحُدودِيَّةِ.

The army deployed additional forces in the border region.

to ambush

نَصَبَ كَمينًا • نَصْبٌ

نَصَبَ الجُنودُ كَمينًا لِلْعَدُوِّ في الغابَةِ.

The soldiers set an ambush for the enemy in the forest.

captain

نَقيبٌ • نُقَباءُ

عُيِّنَ النَّقيبُ كَقائِدٍ لِلْوَحْدَةِ الجَديدَةِ.

The captain was appointed as the commander of the new unit.

ambush	هُجومٌ مُباغِتٌ

شَنَّ العَدُوُّ هُجومًا مُباغِتًا وَلَكِنَّ القُوّاتِ كانَتْ مُسْتَعِدَّةً.

The enemy launched a surprise attack, but the forces were prepared.

unit	وَحْدَةٌ • وَحْداتٌ / وَحَداتٌ

انْضَمَّتْ وَحْدَةٌ خاصَّةٌ لِلْعَمَلِيَّةِ لِتَقْديمِ الدَّعْمِ.

A special unit joined the operation to provide support.

7.1.1.1 Mini-Articles

Track **3**

تَمَكَّنَ الجَيْشُ مِنْ شَنِّ هُجومٍ مُباغِتٍ عَلى خَطِّ الجَبْهَةِ الشَّماليِّ الماضِيَةِ اللَّيْلَةِ مُسْتَخْدِمًا الدَّبّاباتِ وَالمِدْفَعِيَّةِ الثَّقيلَةِ. اعْتَقَلَتِ القُوّاتُ العَسْكَرِيَّةُ عَدَدًا مِنْ جُنودِ العَدُوِّ في عَمَلِيَّةٍ خاصَّةٍ. وَقَدْ أَظْهَرَتِ الخَريطَةُ المَيْدانِيَّةُ تَقَدُّمًا مَلْحوظًا عَلى هَذِهِ الجَبْهَةِ. وَقَدْ أَمَرَ العَميدُ مُحَمَّد أَحْمَد بِتَعْزيزِ خَطِّ الدِّفاعِ وَتَأْمينِ المِنْطَقَةِ.

The army managed to launch a surprise attack on the northern front last night, employing tanks and heavy artillery. The military forces detained a number of enemy soldiers in a special operation. The field map showed significant progress on this front. Brigadier General Muhammad Ahmed ordered the fortification of the defense line and securing the area.

أَعْلَنَتِ الوَحَداتُ العَسْكَرِيَّةُ حالَةَ الطَّوارِئِ في المَدينَةِ الجَنوبِيَّةِ بَعْدَ اسْتِشْعارِ حَرَكَةٍ مَشْبوهَةٍ عَلى الحُدودِ. كَشَفَتْ دَوْرِيّاتُ الجَيْشِ عَدَدًا مِنَ المَخابِئِ الَّتي اسْتَخْدَمَها المُتَمَرِّدونَ لِتَخْزينِ الذَّخيرَةِ وَالمُتَفَجِّراتِ. هَذا وَتَعْمَلُ الحِمايَةُ المَدَنِيَّةُ جَنْبًا إلى جَنْبٍ مَعَ الجَيْشِ لِضَمانِ أَمْنِ المُواطِنينَ في المِنْطَقَةِ.

Military units declared a state of emergency in the southern city after sensing suspicious activity on the borders. Army patrols uncovered several hideouts used by the rebels to store ammunition and explosives. Civil defense works alongside the army to ensure the safety of citizens in the region.

أَعْلَنَ الرّائِدُ أَحْمَد سالِم عَنْ إجْراءِ تَدْريباتٍ مَيْدانِيَّةٍ لِلْجَيْشِ الوَطَنِيِّ في مِنْطَقَةِ الصَّحْراءِ الغَرْبِيَّةِ. تَهْدُفُ هَذِهِ التَّدْريباتِ إلى زِيادَةِ كَفاءَةِ الجُنودِ وَالتَّأَكُّدِ مِنْ جاهِزِيَّةِ الأَسْلِحَةِ. وَتَمَّ تَنْظيمُ هَذِهِ التَّدْريباتِ بِالتَّعاوُنِ مَعَ الشُّرَكاءِ المُتَحالِفينَ لِتَبادُلِ الخِبْراتِ وَتَطْويرِ قَواعِدِ الاشْتِباكِ.

Major Ahmed Salem announced field exercises for the national army in the Western Sahara region. These exercises aim to enhance the soldiers' proficiency and ensure weapon readiness. They were organized in cooperation with allied partners to exchange expertise and develop engagement rules.

في تَطَوُّرٍ جَديدٍ لِلْأَحْداثِ، تَمَكَّنَ فَصيلٌ عَسْكَرِيٌّ مِنَ احْتِلالِ مِنْطَقَةٍ اسْتراتيجِيَّةٍ في الشَّرْقِ. اسْتَخْدَمَ الفَصيلُ المُشاةَ وَالعَرَباتِ المُدَرَّعَةِ في هَذِهِ العَمَلِيَّةِ. أَكَّدَ العَميدُ مَحْمود سامي أَنَّ هَذِهِ الخُطْوَةَ تُعْتَبَرُ نُقْطَةَ تَحَوُّلٍ في الحَرْبِ، وَأَنَّ القُوّاتِ قَدْ تَقَدَّمَتْ بِنَجاحٍ، مَعَ الاحْتِفاظِ بِعَدَدٍ مِنَ الأَسْرى.

In a recent development, a military faction managed to occupy a strategic area in the east. The faction employed infantry and armored vehicles in this operation. Brigadier Mahmoud Samy confirmed that this move represents a turning point in the war, and that the forces have successfully advanced, capturing a number of prisoners.

بِنَجاحٍ باهِرٍ، نَصَبَتْ وَحْدَةٌ مِنَ الجَيْشِ كَمينًا في مِنْطَقَةِ غاباتٍ، مِمّا أَسْفَرَ عَنِ اعْتِقالِ مَجْموعَةٍ مِنَ القَنّاصَةِ الَّذينَ كانوا يُهَدِّدونَ المِنْطَقَةَ لِأَسابيعَ. قامَتِ الوَحْدَةُ العَسْكَرِيَّةُ بِمُصادَرَةِ مَجْموعَةٍ مِنَ الأَسْلِحَةِ وَالذَّخيرَةِ. وَقَدْ أَشادَ الجِنْرالُ يوسُف مَحْمود بِالعَمَلِ المُتْقَنِ الَّذي قامَتْ بِهِ الوَحْدَةُ.

With remarkable success, an army unit ambushed in a forested area, resulting in the arrest of a group of snipers who had been threatening the area for weeks. The military unit confiscated a batch of weapons and ammunition. General Yusuf Mahmoud praised the impeccable work of the unit.

وَقَعَتْ سِلْسِلَةٌ مِنَ التَّفْجيراتِ اليَوْمَ اسْتَهْدَفَتْ رَتْلًا عَسْكَرِيًّا في الطَّريقِ الرَّئيسِيِّ لِلْمَدينَةِ. أَسْفَرَتِ الهَجَماتُ عَنْ مَقْتَلِ وَجَرْحِ عَدَدٍ مِنَ الجُنودِ. حَذَّرَ قائِدُ الفِرْقَةِ اللِّواءُ سامي سالِم القُوّاتِ وَأَمَرَ بِإِعْلانِ حالَةِ تَأَهُّبٍ قُصْوى. تُعْتَبَرُ هَذِهِ الهَجَماتُ الأولى مِنْ نَوْعِها في المِنْطَقَةِ خِلالَ الشُّهورِ الأَخيرَةِ.

A series of explosions occurred today targeting a military convoy on the main road of the city. The attacks resulted in the death and injury of several soldiers. The division commander, Brigadier Sami Salem, cautioned the forces and ordered maximum alertness. These attacks are the first of their kind in the region in recent months.

7.1.1.2 Historical Account: A Surprise Attack on Berlin

Track **4**

الجَيْشُ الأَحْمَرُ يَشِنُّ هُجومًا مُباغِتًا عَلى بِرْلينَ في نِهايَةِ الحَرْبِ العالَمِيَّةِ الثانِيَةِ

في الأَشْهُرِ الأَخيرَةِ مِنَ الحَرْبِ العالَمِيَّةِ الثانِيَةِ، اسْتَعَدَّ الجَيْشُ الأَحْمَرُ لِشَنِّ هُجومٍ ضَخْمٍ عَلى بِرْلينَ، عاصِمَةِ الرّايخِ الثالِثِ. كانَ هَذا الهُجومُ جُزْءًا مِنْ خُطَّةِ هُجومٍ اسْتراتيجِيَّةٍ وَضَعَتْها القُوّاتُ المُتَحالِفَةُ لِإِنْهاءِ الحَرْبِ.

اسْتَخْدَمَ الجَيْشُ الأَحْمَرُ العَديدَ مِنَ المُدَرَّعاتِ وَالدَّبّاباتِ لِتَحْقيقِ تَقَدُّمٍ سَريعٍ عَبْرَ خُطوطِ الدِّفاعِ الأَلْمانِيَّةِ. تَمَّ دَعْمُ هَذا الهُجومِ بِإِمْداداتٍ مُسْتَمِرَّةٍ وَذَخيرَةٍ ضَخْمَةٍ لِضَمانِ التَّقَدُّمِ المُسْتَمِرِّ وَتَحْقيقِ النَّصْرِ.

وَقَدْ تَقَدَّمَتِ الْقُوَّاتُ السُّوفِيتِيَّةُ بِسُرْعَةٍ، حَيْثُ كَشَفَتِ الْخَرَائِطُ الْمَيْدَانِيَّةُ عَنْ تَقَدُّمِهِمِ السَّرِيعِ نَحْوَ مَرْكَزِ الْمَدِينَةِ. واجَهوا مُقَاوَمَةً شَرِسَةً مِنَ الْوَحَدَاتِ الْأَلْمَانِيَّةِ الَّتِي كَانَتْ تَحْتَ إِمْرَةِ ضُبَّاطٍ مُتَمَرِّسِينَ، وَلَكِنْ تَمَكَّنوا مِنْ شَنِّ هَجَمَاتٍ مُتَتَالِيَةٍ وَاسْتِعَادَةِ الْمَوَاضِعِ الِاسْتِرَاتِيجِيَّةِ.

تَمَّ أَسْرُ الْعَدِيدِ مِنَ الْجُنودِ الْأَلْمَانِ، بَيْنَما قَاوَمَ الْبَعْضُ الآخَرَ حَتَّى الْمَوْتِ. في الْمُقَابِلِ، واجَهَتْ قُوَّاتُ الْجَيْشِ الْأَحْمَرِ خَسَائِرَ كَبِيرَةً، حَيْثُ سَقَطَ الْكَثِيرُ مِنَ الْجُنودِ جَرْحى أَوْ قَتْلى.

في نِهَايَةِ الْمَطَافِ، مَعَ انْكِسَارِ خُطُوطِ الدِّفَاعِ الْأَلْمَانِيَّةِ وَاقْتِرَابِ قُوَّاتِ الْحُلَفَاءِ مِنَ الْغَرْبِ، كَانَ مِنَ الواضِحِ أَنَّ نِهَايَةَ الْحَرْبِ قَدِ اقْتَرَبَتْ. تَمَّ احْتِلالُ بِرْلينَ بِالْكَامِلِ مِنْ قِبَلِ الْجَيْشِ الْأَحْمَرِ في مايو 1945، مِمَّا وَضَعَ نِهايَةً فِعْلِيَّةً لِلْحَرْبِ الْعالَمِيَّةِ الثَّانِيَةِ في أوروبّا.

The Red Army launches a surprise attack on Berlin at the end of World War II

In the final months of World War II, the Red Army prepared to launch a massive assault on Berlin, the capital of the Third Reich. This attack was part of a strategic offensive plan devised by the Allied forces to end the war.

The Red Army utilized numerous armored vehicles and tanks to achieve rapid progress through German defense lines. This attack was bolstered by continuous supplies and vast ammunition to ensure sustained advancement and achieve victory.

The Soviet forces advanced swiftly, with field maps revealing their rapid progress toward the city center. They faced fierce resistance from German units commanded by seasoned officers, but managed to launch successive attacks and recapture strategic positions.

Many German soldiers were captured, while others resisted to the death. In contrast, the Red Army forces experienced significant losses, with many soldiers injured or killed.

Ultimately, with the breaking of German defense lines and the approaching Allied forces from the west, it became evident that the end of the war was near. Berlin was fully occupied by the Red Army in May 1945, effectively marking the end of World War II in Europe.

7.1.1.3 Historical Account: The Naksa

Track **5**

الحَرْبُ العَرَبِيَّةُ الإِسْرائيليَّةُ 1967: النَّكْسَةُ

في يونيو مِنْ عامِ 1967، انْدَلَعَتْ حَرْبٌ خاطِفَةٌ بَيْنَ إِسْرائيلَ وَثَلاثِ دُوَلٍ عَرَبِيَّةٍ هِيَ: مِصْرَ، سوريا، وَالأُرْدُنِّ. وَقَدِ اسْتَمَرَّتِ الحَرْبُ لِسِتَّةِ أَيّامٍ فَقَطْ، لَكِنَّها أَسْفَرَتْ عَنْ تَغْييراتٍ جيوسياسِيَّةٍ كَبيرَةٍ في المِنْطَقَةِ.

كانَتِ القُوّاتُ المِصْرِيَّةُ في حالَةٍ تَأَهُّبٍ قَبْلَ بَدْءِ الاشْتِباكاتِ، حَيْثُ كانَتْ قَدْ نَشَرَتْ قُوّاتِها عَلى طولِ خَطِّ الجَبْهَةِ في سَيْناءَ. وَقَدْ قامَتْ مِصْرُ بِطَرْدِ قُوّاتِ السَّلامِ الدَّوْلِيَّةِ مِنْ سَيْناءَ وَقامَتْ بِإِغْلاقِ مَضيقِ تيران أمامَ المِلاحَةِ الإِسْرائيلِيَّةِ.

رَدًّا عَلى ذَلِكَ، شَنَّتْ إِسْرائيلُ هُجومًا مُباغِتًا، تَمَكَّنَتْ خِلالَهُ مِنْ تَدْميرِ مُعْظَمِ الطّائِراتِ المِصْرِيَّةِ عَلى أرْضِها. تَبِعَتْ ذَلِكَ مَعارِكُ شَرِسَةٌ في سَيْناءَ، حَيْثُ اسْتُخْدِمَتِ الدَّبّاباتُ وَالمِدْفَعِيَّةُ بِكَثافَةٍ. واجَهَتْ قُوّاتُ الجَيْشِ المِصْرِيِّ صُعوباتٍ كَبيرَةً، وَبَدَأَتْ في الانْسِحابِ إلى الغَرْبِ.

وَفي الوَقْتِ نَفْسِهِ، شَهِدَتِ الجَبْهَةُ الشَّمالِيَّةُ قِتالًا عَنيفًا بَيْنَ إِسْرائيلَ وَسوريا. في حينِ بَدَأَتِ المَعارِكُ عَلى الجَبْهَةِ الشَّرْقِيَّةِ بَيْنَ إِسْرائيلَ وَالأُرْدُنِّ.

خِلالَ الأيّامِ السِّتَّةِ، تَمَكَّنَتْ إِسْرائيلُ مِنَ احْتِلالِ سَيْناءَ بِأَكْمَلِها، وَالضِّفَّةِ الغَرْبِيَّةِ، وَالقُدْسِ الشَّرْقِيَّةِ، وَهَضْبَةِ الجولانِ. وَقَدْ تَرَكَتْ هَذِهِ الحَرْبُ ميراثًا مِنَ الأحْزانِ وَالخَسائِرِ لِلعَرَبِ، مَعَ أسْرِ العَديدِ مِنَ الجُنودِ العَرَبِ وَتَكَبُّدِ خَسائِرَ كَبيرَةٍ في الأرْواحِ وَالمُعَدّاتِ.

وَقَدْ أُطْلِقَ عَلى هَذِهِ الحَرْبِ اسْمَ "النَّكْسَةِ" في العالَمِ العَرَبِيِّ، ما يُعَبِّرُ عَنِ الصَّدْمَةِ وَالخَيْبَةِ الَّتي أَحْدَثَتْها.

The Arab-Israeli War 1967: The Naksa (The Setback)

In June of 1967, a swift war erupted between Israel and three Arab nations: Egypt, Syria, and Jordan. The war lasted only six days but resulted in significant geopolitical changes in the region.

The Egyptian forces were on alert before the hostilities began, having deployed their forces along the front line in Sinai. Egypt expelled the international peacekeeping forces from Sinai and closed the Strait of Tiran to Israeli navigation.

In response, Israel launched a surprise attack, successfully destroying most of the Egyptian aircraft on the ground. This was followed by intense battles in Sinai, where tanks and artillery were heavily used. The Egyptian army faced significant challenges and began to retreat westward.

Simultaneously, the northern front witnessed fierce combat between Israel and Syria, while battles began on the eastern front between Israel and Jordan.

Over the six days, Israel managed to occupy the entirety of Sinai, the West Bank, East Jerusalem, and the Golan Heights. This war left a legacy of sorrow and loss for the Arabs, with many Arab soldiers captured and substantial losses in lives and equipment.

In the Arab world, this war is referred to as "Al Naksa" (The Setback), expressing the shock and disappointment it brought about.

7.1.2 Naval Forces

to sail
إبْحارٌ •
أَبْحَرَ

أَبْحَرَتِ السَّفِينَةُ الحَرْبِيَّةُ نَحْوَ المِياهِ الدَّوْلِيَّةِ لِتَنْفِيذِ مُهِمَّتِها.

The warship sailed toward international waters to carry out its mission.

fleet
أَساطِيلُ •
أُسْطُولٌ

تَمَّ نَشْرُ أُسْطُولٍ بَحْرِيٍّ لِلرَّدِّ عَلَى التَّهْدِيداتِ المُحْتَمَلَةِ.

A naval fleet was deployed to respond to potential threats.

to launch
إطْلاقٌ •
أَطْلَقَ

أَطْلَقَتِ الغَوّاصَةُ صَوارِيخَها تُجاهَ الهَدَفِ المُعادِي.

The submarine launched its missiles toward the enemy target.

to sink
إغْراقٌ •
أَغْرَقَ

أَغْرَقَتِ البَحْرِيَّةُ السَّفِينَةَ المُعادِيَةَ لِمَنْعِها مِنَ الوُصُولِ إلى المِياهِ الإقْلِيمِيَّةِ.

The navy sank the hostile ship to prevent it from reaching territorial waters.

> This verb is transitive; it takes an object. Compare to its intransitive counterpart on page 21.

maritime rescue
إنْقاذٌ بَحْرِيٌّ

تَمَّ تَنْفِيذُ إنْقاذٍ بَحْرِيٍّ لِلرُّكّابِ الَّذِينَ تَعَرَّضُوا لِحادِثٍ بَحْرِيٍّ.

A maritime rescue was performed for passengers involved in a marine accident.

maritime law
قَوانِينٌ •
القانُونُ البَحْرِيُّ

تَمَّ تَطْبِيقُ القانُونِ البَحْرِيِّ لِمُعالَجَةِ حادِثِ القَرْصَنَةِ.

Maritime law was applied to address the piracy incident.

بَحْرِيٌّ

maritime, sea-, naval

تَحَمَّلَتِ الشَّرِكَةُ البَحْرِيَّةُ المَسْؤُولِيَّةَ عَنْ حادِثِ تَسَرُّبِ النَّفْطِ.

The maritime company took responsibility for the oil spill.

بَحْرِيَّةٌ

navy

شارَكَتِ البَحْرِيَّةُ في مُناوَراتٍ عَسْكَرِيَّةٍ لِتَعْزيزِ الأَمْنِ البَحْرِيِّ.

The navy participated in military exercises to enhance maritime security.

بَعيدُ المَدى

long-range

تَمَّ تَطْويرُ طائِراتٍ بَعيدَةِ المَدى لِلْعَمَلِيّاتِ البَحْرِيَّةِ.

Long-range aircraft were developed for naval operations.

جُنْدِيٌّ بَحْرِيٌّ • جُنودٌ

sailor

خَدَمَ الجُنْدِيُّ البَحْرِيُّ في عِدَّةِ مَهامَّ عالِيَةِ الخُطورَةِ.

The marine served in several high-risk missions.

حادِثٌ بَحْرِيٌّ • حَوادِثُ

maritime incident

تَعامَلَتِ القُوّاتُ البَحْرِيَّةُ مَعَ حادِثٍ بَحْرِيٍّ كَبيرٍ بِكَفاءَةٍ.

The naval forces efficiently dealt with a major marine accident.

حامِلَةُ طائِراتٍ

aircraft carrier

أَرْسَلَتِ البِلادُ حامِلَةَ طائِراتٍ لِتَعْزيزِ الأَمْنِ البَحْرِيِّ.

The country sent an aircraft carrier to bolster maritime security.

حَرْبٌ بَحْرِيَّةٌ • حُروبٌ

naval warfare

لَقَدْ شَهِدْنا تَصاعُدًا في الحُروبِ البَحْرِيَّةِ في العَقْدِ الأَخيرِ.

We have seen an escalation in naval warfare in the past decade.

naval blockade

حِصارٌ بَحْرِيٌّ

فَرَضَتِ القُوّاتُ حِصارًا بَحْرِيًّا لِمَنْعِ وُصولِ الإمْداداتِ لِلْعَدُوِّ.

The forces imposed a naval blockade to prevent supplies from reaching the enemy.

right of passage

حَقُّ المُرورِ • حُقوقٌ

ناقَشَتِ الدُّوَلُ حَقَّ المُرورِ في المِياهِ الإقْليمِيَّةِ.

The countries discussed the right of passage in territorial waters.

maritime supply line

خَطُّ إمْدادٍ بَحْرِيٌّ • خُطوطٌ

تَأْمينُ خُطوطِ الإمْدادِ البَحْرِيَّةِ كانَ أَوْلَوِيَّةً لِلْأَميرالِ.

Securing maritime supply lines was a priority for the admiral.

to defend by sea

دافَعَ عَبْرَ البَحْرِ • دِفاعٌ عَبْرَ البَحْرِ

دافَعَتِ البَحْرِيَّةُ عَبْرَ البَحْرِ لِمَنْعِ التَّهْديداتِ القادِمَةِ مِنَ المِياهِ.

The navy defended by sea to prevent threats coming from the waters.

to dock

رَسا • رُسُوٌّ

رَسا الزَّوْرَقُ في المِيناءِ بَعْدَ مُهِمَّةٍ ناجِحَةٍ.

The boat docked at the port after a successful mission.

patrol boat

زَوْرَقٌ دَوْرِيَّةٍ • زَوارِقُ

شارَكَ زَوْرَقُ الدَّوْرِيَّةِ في عَمَلِيّاتِ البَحْثِ وَالإنْقاذِ.

The patrol boat participated in search and rescue operations.

coastal

ساحِلِيٌّ

وَقَعَ الهُجومُ السّاحِلِيُّ قُرْبَ مَدينَةٍ ساحِلِيَّةٍ كَبيرَةٍ.

The coastal attack occurred near a major coastal city.

ship

سَفينَةٌ • سُفُنٌ

تَعَرَّضَتِ السَّفينَةُ لِهُجومٍ مِنْ قِبَلِ قَراصِنَةٍ.

The ship was attacked by pirates.

navy

سِلاحُ البَحْرِيَّةِ • أَسْلِحَةٌ

نَفَّذَ سِلاحُ البَحْرِيَّةِ عَمَلِيَّةً لِإغْراقِ سَفينَةٍ مُعادِيَةٍ كانَتْ تُهَدِّدُ المِياهَ الإقْليمِيَّةَ.

The navy executed an operation to sink an enemy ship that was threatening territorial waters.

naval officer

ضابِطٌ بَحْرِيٌّ • ضُبّاطٌ

أَصْدَرَ الضّابِطُ البَحْرِيُّ أوامِرَ لِتَفْتيشِ السَّفينَةِ المَشْبوهَةِ.

The naval officer issued orders to inspect the suspicious ship.

naval helicopter

طائِرَةٌ مِرْوَحِيَّةٌ بَحْرِيَّةٌ

شارَكَتِ الطّائِرَةُ المِرْوَحِيَّةُ البَحْرِيَّةُ في عَمَلِيّاتِ إنْقاذٍ بَحْرِيَّةٍ.

The naval helicopter participated in maritime rescue operations.

transcontinental

عابِرٌ لِلْقارّاتِ

تَمَّ اسْتِخْدامُ صَواريخَ عابِرَةٍ لِلْقارّاتِ في التَّدْريباتِ البَحْرِيَّةِ.

Intercontinental missiles were used in naval exercises.

to dive

غاصَ • غَوْصٌ

غاصَتِ الغَوّاصَةُ الحَرْبِيَّةُ لِتَجَنُّبِ اكْتِشافِها مِنْ قِبَلِ القُوّاتِ المُعادِيَةِ.

The war submarine dove to avoid detection by hostile forces.

to sink

غَرِقَ • غَرَقٌ

تَعَرَّضَتِ الغَوّاصَةُ لِلْغَرَقِ بَعْدَ حادِثِ تَصادُمٍ.

The submarine sank after a collision incident.

submarine غَوّاصَةٌ

تَمَّ اسْتِدْعاءُ الغَوّاصَةِ لِتَقْدِيمِ الدَّعْمِ في المِياهِ العَمِيقَةِ.

The submarine was summoned to provide support in deep waters.

frigate فَرْقاطَةٌ

أَصْدَرَتِ الفَرْقاطَةُ تَحْذِيرًا لِلسُّفُنِ القَرِيبَةِ مِنَ المِنْطَقَةِ الخَطِرَةِ.

The frigate issued a warning to ships near the hazardous area.

> This word can also be pronounced فِرْقاطَةٌ.

naval base قَواعِدُ • قاعِدَةٌ بَحْرِيَّةٌ

نُقِلَ الجُنودُ إلى القاعِدَةِ البَحْرِيَّةِ لِلتَّدْرِيبِ المُكَثَّفِ.

The soldiers were transferred to the naval base for intensive training.

to patrol قِيامٌ • قامَ بِدَوْرِيَّةٍ

قامَ الزَّوْرَقُ بِدَوْرِيَّةٍ في المِياهِ الإقْلِيمِيَّةِ لِلتَّأَكُّدِ مِنَ الأَمْنِ.

The boat patrolled in the territorial waters to ensure security.

naval peacekeeping force قُوَّةُ حِفْظِ سَلامٍ بَحْرِيَّةٌ

تَمَّ نَشْرُ قُوَّةِ حِفْظِ سَلامٍ بَحْرِيَّةٍ لِضَمانِ حُرِّيَّةِ المِلاحَةِ.

A naval peacekeeping force was deployed to ensure freedom of navigation.

waters (jurisdiction) مَجالاتٌ • مَجالٌ مائِيٌّ

تُعَدُّ حِمايَةُ المَجالِ المائِيِّ جُزْءًا مُهِمًّا مِنَ اسْتِراتيجِيَّتِنا الدِّفاعِيَّةِ.

Protecting the aquatic zone is an important part of our defense strategy.

destroyer مُدَمِّرَةٌ

كانَتِ المُدَمِّرَةُ جُزْءًا مِنَ الأُسْطولِ المُتَّجِهِ نَحْوَ العَدُوِّ.

The destroyer was part of the fleet heading toward the enemy.

The destroyer was part of the fleet heading toward the enemy.

maritime surveillance   مُراقَبَةٌ بَحرِيَّةٌ

تَمَّ تَفْعِيلُ أَنْظِمَةِ المُراقَبَةِ البَحرِيَّةِ لِلكَشْفِ عَنِ الأَنْشِطَةِ غَيْرِ المَشْروعَةِ.

Maritime surveillance systems were activated to detect illegal activities.

harbor   مَرافِئُ •   مَرْفَأٌ

جَرى الإِشْرافُ عَلى تَحْميلِ البَضائِعِ في المَرْفَأِ.

Cargo loading was supervised at the harbor.

boat   مَراكِبُ •   مَرْكَبٌ

اِنْطَلَقَ المَرْكَبُ في رِحْلَةِ بَحْثٍ وَإِنْقاذٍ بَعْدَ الإِبْلاغِ عَنْ حادِثٍ.

The boat embarked on a search and rescue mission after an incident was reported.

naval battle   مَعارِكُ •   مَعْرَكَةٌ بَحرِيَّةٌ

فازَ الأُسْطولُ في مَعْرَكَةٍ بَحرِيَّةٍ مِحْوَرِيَّةٍ ضِدَّ العَدُوِّ.

The fleet won a pivotal naval battle against the enemy.

port   مَوانِئُ •   ميناءٌ

نُقِلَتِ البَضائِعُ الثَّقيلَةُ عَبْرَ الميناءِ الرَّئيسِيِّ.

The heavy goods were transported through the main port.

to transport by sea   نَقْلٌ •   نَقَلَ عَبْرَ البَحْرِ

نُقِلَتِ المُعَدّاتُ العَسْكَرِيَّةُ عَبْرَ البَحْرِ لِدَعْمِ العَمَلِيّاتِ.

Military equipment was transported across the sea to support operations.

to attack by sea   مُهاجَمَةٌ •   هاجَمَ عَبْرَ البَحْرِ

هاجَمَتِ القُوّاتُ عَبْرَ البَحْرِ لِلاسْتيلاءِ عَلى مَوْقِعٍ اسْتِراتيجِيٍّ.

The forces attacked by sea to capture a strategic location.

في اسْتِراتِيجِيَّةٍ جَديدَةٍ، قامَتْ قُوّاتُ العَدُوِّ بِفَرْضِ حِصارٍ بَحْرِيٍّ عَلَى المَوانِئِ الرَّئيسِيَّةِ لِلْوَطَنِ، مِمّا أَدّى إلى تَعْطيلِ خُطوطِ الإمْدادِ البَحْرِيِّ وَشُحٍّ في المَوارِدِ. القُوّاتُ الوَطَنِيَّةُ تَسْعى لِكَسْرِ الحِصارِ، حَيْثُ تَتَجَهَّزُ الغَوّاصاتُ وَزَوارِقُ الدَّوْرِيَّةِ لِمُواجَهَةِ هذا التَّحَدّي وَضَمانِ اسْتِمْرارِيَّةِ نَقْلِ المَوارِدِ عَبْرَ البَحْرِ.

In a new strategy, enemy forces imposed a naval blockade on the nation's main ports, disrupting maritime supply lines and causing resource shortages. National forces are trying to break the blockade, with submarines and patrol boats gearing up to face this challenge and ensure the continuous transport of resources by sea.

وَقَعَ حادِثٌ بَحْرِيٌّ مَأْساوِيٌّ اليَوْمَ في ميناءِ العاصِمَةِ، حَيْثُ غَرِقَتْ سَفينَةٌ تِجارِيَّةٌ بَعْدَ أَنِ اصْطَدَمَتْ بِفَرْقاطَةٍ تابِعَةٍ لِلْأُسْطولِ الوَطَنِيِّ. غَرِقَتِ السَّفينَةُ بِسُرْعَةٍ، مِمّا أَدّى إلى إطْلاقِ عَمَلِيَّةِ إنْقاذٍ بَحْرِيٍّ كُبْرى. تَعاوَنَتِ القُوّاتُ البَحْرِيَّةُ مَعَ الأَجْهِزَةِ المَحَلِّيَّةِ لِإنْقاذِ جَميعِ الرُّكّابِ وَأَفْرادِ الطّاقَمِ.

A tragic maritime accident occurred today in the capital's port where a commercial ship sank after colliding with a frigate of the national fleet. The ship quickly submerged, leading to the launch of a major maritime rescue operation. Naval forces collaborated with local agencies to rescue all passengers and crew members.

في السّاعاتِ الأولى مِنَ الصَّباحِ، هاجَمَتْ غَوّاصاتٌ مُعادِيَةٌ قاعِدَةً بَحْرِيَّةً اسْتِراتيجِيَّةً تابِعَةً لِلْوَطَنِ. أَطْلَقَتِ الغَوّاصاتُ عِدَّةَ صَواريخَ بَعيدَةِ المَدى، مِمّا أَسْفَرَ عَنْ أَضْرارٍ جَسيمَةٍ لِلْمَرْفَأِ وَإغْراقِ عِدَّةِ سُفُنٍ. تُحاوِلُ القُوّاتُ البَحْرِيَّةُ حالِيًا تَقْديرَ الخَسائِرِ وَتَنْظيمَ خَطِّ دِفاعٍ جَديدٍ.

In the early hours of the morning, aggressive submarines attacked a strategic naval base belonging to the nation. The submarines launched several long-range missiles, causing significant damage to the port and sinking several ships. The naval forces are currently assessing the losses and organizing a new defense line.

أَعْلَنَ سِلاحُ البَحْرِيَّةِ عَنْ تَنْظيمِ تَدْريباتٍ بَحْرِيَّةٍ واسِعَةِ النِّطاقِ في المَجالِ المائِيِّ الوَطَنِيِّ خِلالَ الأُسْبوعِ المُقْبِلِ. سَيُشارِكُ في التَّدْريباتِ حامِلَةُ طائِراتٍ وَغَوّاصاتٌ وَزَوارِقُ دَوْرِيَّةٍ. الهَدَفُ مِنْ هَذِهِ التَّدْريباتِ هُوَ تَعْزيزُ قُدُراتِ الضُّبّاطِ البَحْرِيِّينَ وَتَحْسينُ الاسْتِعْدادِ لِأَيِّ حالَةِ طَوارِئَ.

The navy announced a large-scale maritime training exercise in the national waters next week. An aircraft carrier, submarines, and patrol boats will participate in the exercises. The goal of these exercises is to enhance the skills of naval officers and improve readiness for any emergency.

جَدَّدَتِ الحُكُومَةُ التَّأْكيدَ عَلى احْتِرامِ القانونِ البَحْرِيِّ وَحَقِّ المُرورِ في المِياهِ الإقْليمِيَّةِ. جاءَ هَذا بَعْدَ تَقاريرَ عَنِ المُراقَبَةِ البَحْرِيَّةِ المُشَدَّدَةِ لِلسُّفُنِ الأَجْنَبِيَّةِ الَّتي تَعْبُرُ المَجالَ المائِيَّ الوَطَنِيَّ. أَكَّدَتِ الحُكُومَةُ عَلى أَهَمِّيَّةِ التَّعاوُنِ الدَّوْلِيِّ لِضَمانِ أَمْنِ المِلاحَةِ البَحْرِيَّةِ.

The government reaffirmed its commitment to respecting maritime law and the right of passage in territorial waters. This came after reports of strict maritime surveillance of foreign ships passing through national waters. The government emphasized the importance of international cooperation to ensure maritime navigation security.

بَدَأَتْ قُوّاتُنا البَحْرِيَّةُ حَمْلَةً هُجومِيَّةً عَبْرَ البَحْرِ بِهَدَفِ فَتْحِ جَبْهَةٍ جَديدَةٍ في الحَرْبِ. أُسْتُخْدِمَتِ المُدَمِّراتُ وَالفَرْقاطاتُ لِضَرْبِ مَواقِعِ العَدُوِّ عَلى السّاحِلِ، بَيْنَما قامَتْ طائِراتٌ مِرْوَحِيَّةٌ بَحْرِيَّةٌ بِتَوْفيرِ الدَّعْمِ الجَوِّيِّ. أَكَّدَ ضابِطٌ بَحْرِيٌّ أَنَّ العَمَلِيَّةَ تَسيرُ وَفْقَ الخُطَّةِ، وَأَنَّ القُوّاتِ مُسْتَعِدَّةٌ لِأَيِّ مَعْرَكَةٍ بَحْرِيَّةٍ قادِمَةٍ.

Our naval forces began an offensive sea campaign aiming to open a new front in the war. Destroyers and frigates were used to strike enemy positions on the coast, while naval helicopters provided aerial support. A naval officer confirmed that the operation is proceeding as planned and that the forces are ready for any upcoming naval battle.

7.1.2.2 Historical Account: The October 1973 War

Track 8

الأُسْطولُ المِصْرِيُّ خِلالَ حَرْبِ أُكْتوبَرَ 1973

في حَرْبِ أُكْتوبَرَ 1973، قامَ الأُسْطولُ المِصْرِيُّ بِدَوْرٍ حَيَوِيٍّ في تَأْمينِ الجَبْهَةِ البَحْرِيَّةِ. عَلى الرَّغْمِ مِنْ أَنَّ الحَرْبَ كانَتْ تُرَكِّزُ بِشَكْلٍ أَساسِيٍّ عَلى القِتالِ البَرِّيِّ، فَقَدْ لَعِبَتِ القُوّاتُ البَحْرِيَّةُ دَوْرًا مِحْوَرِيًّا في تَأْمينِ خُطوطِ الإمْدادِ البَحْرِيِّ وَمَنْعِ أَيِّ تَدَخُّلٍ بَحْرِيٍّ مِنَ العَدُوِّ.

في بِدايَةِ الحَرْبِ، نَجَحَ الأُسْطولُ المِصْرِيُّ في إطْلاقِ عَمَلِيّاتٍ ناجِحَةٍ ضِدَّ السُّفُنِ الإسْرائيلِيَّةِ، أُسْتُخْدِمَتْ فيها الغَوّاصاتُ وَالفَرْقاطاتُ. وَقَدْ ساعَدَ هَذا في تَعْزيزِ مَرْكَزِ مِصْرَ الاسْتِراتيجِيِّ في البَحْرِ الأَحْمَرِ.

كَما قامَتْ زَوارِقُ الدَّوْرِيَّةِ المِصْرِيَّةِ بِتَنْفيذِ هَجَماتٍ ضِدَّ القُوّاتِ البَحْرِيَّةِ الإسْرائيلِيَّةِ، مِمّا أَدّى إلى تَعْطيلِ مُحاوَلاتِ إسْرائيلَ لِلتَّدَخُّلِ في خُطوطِ الإمْدادِ البَحْرِيِّ المِصْرِيِّ.

حِمايَةُ المِياهِ الإقْليمِيَّةِ المِصْرِيَّةِ كانَتْ أَمْرًا أَساسِيًّا خِلالَ الحَرْبِ، وَقَدْ أَظْهَرَ الأُسْطولُ المِصْرِيُّ جَدارَتَهُ وَقُدْرَتَهُ عَلى الدِّفاعِ عَنِ السَّواحِلِ المِصْرِيَّةِ وَضَمانِ أَمْنِ المِلاحَةِ في المَجالِ المائِيِّ.

بِالرَّغْمِ مِنَ التَّحَدِّياتِ الَّتي واجَهَتْها مِصْرُ خِلالَ حَرْبِ أُكْتوبَرَ، فَإِنَّ جُهودَ القُوّاتِ البَحْرِيَّةِ المِصْرِيَّةِ أَسْهَمَتْ بِشَكْلٍ كَبيرٍ في تَحْقيقِ التَّوازُنِ الاسْتِراتيجِيِّ وَدَعْمِ الجُهودِ البَرِّيَّةِ لِلْجَيْشِ المِصْرِيِّ.

The Egyptian Fleet during the October 1973 War

During the October 1973 War, the Egyptian fleet played a vital role in securing the maritime front. Although the war primarily focused on ground combat, the naval forces played a pivotal role in securing maritime supply lines and preventing any naval intervention from the enemy.

At the beginning of the war, the Egyptian fleet successfully launched operations against Israeli ships, utilizing submarines and frigates. This helped strengthen Egypt's strategic position in the Red Sea.

Egyptian patrol boats also executed attacks against Israeli naval forces, disrupting Israel's attempts to intervene in Egypt's maritime supply lines.

Protecting Egypt's territorial waters was a primary concern during the war, and the Egyptian fleet proved its worth and ability to defend Egypt's coasts and ensure maritime security in its waters.

Despite the challenges Egypt faced during the October war, the efforts of the Egyptian naval forces significantly contributed to achieving strategic balance and supporting the ground efforts of the Egyptian army.

7.1.3 Air Forces

Track **9**

supersonic   أَسْرَعُ مِنَ الصَّوْتِ

تَمَّ اخْتِبارُ طائِرَةٍ جَديدَةٍ تَتَمَيَّزُ بِسُرْعَةٍ أَسْرَعَ مِنَ الصَّوْتِ.

A new aircraft that features supersonic speed was tested.

to shoot down   • إِسْقاطٌ   أَسْقَطَ

أَسْقَطَ الدِّفاعُ الجَوِّيُّ طائِرَةً مُسَيَّرَةً كانَتْ تَقْتَرِبُ مِنَ المِنْطَقَةِ المَحْظورَةِ.

The air defense shot down a drone that was approaching the restricted area.

to take off   • إِقْلاعٌ   أَقْلَعَ

أَقْلَعَتْ طائِراتُ النَّقْلِ لِإيصالِ المُساعَداتِ الإِنْسانِيَّةِ.

The transport planes took off to deliver humanitarian aid.

distress signal   إِشارَةُ طَوارِئَ

أَرْسَلَتِ الطّائِرَةُ إِشارَةَ طَوارِئَ قَبْلَ فُقْدانِ الاِتِّصالِ.

The aircraft sent an emergency signal before losing contact.

to collide

اِصْطِدامٌ •

اِصْطَدَم

اِصْطَدَمَتْ طائِرَتانِ في الجَوِّ وَأُجْرِيَ تَحْقيقُ كَوارِثَ لِمَعْرِفَةِ الأَسْبابِ.

Two planes collided in the air, and a disaster investigation was initiated to determine the causes.

air interception

اِعْتِراضٌ جَوِّيٌّ

تَمَّ اعْتِراضُ الطّائِرَةِ المَشْبوهَةِ جَوِّيًّا بِواسِطَةِ الطّائِراتِ المُقاتِلَةِ.

The suspicious aircraft was intercepted by fighter jets.

to intercept (an aircraft)

اِعْتِراضٌ •

اِعْتَرَضَ

اِعْتَرَضَ الطَّيَرانُ الحَرْبِيُّ الطّائِرَةَ المَدَنِيَّةَ لِلتَّحَقُّقِ مِنْ هُوِيَّتِها.

The military aviation intercepted the civilian aircraft to verify its identity.

aviation security

تَأْمينُ الطَّيَران

تَمَّ تَأْمينُ الطَّيَرانِ لِلرَّئيسِ خِلالَ زِيارَتِهِ الدَّوْلِيَّةِ.

Aviation security was provided for the president during his international visit.

air alliance

تَحالُفٌ جَوِّيٌّ

شَكَّلَتْ دُوَلٌ مُتَعَدِّدَةٌ تَحالُفًا جَوِّيًّا لِمُواجَهَةِ العَدُوِّ.

Multiple countries formed an air coalition to confront the enemy.

to crash

تَحَطُّمٌ •

تَحَطَّمَ

تَحَطَّمَتِ الطّائِرَةُ العَسْكَرِيَّةُ في مِنْطَقَةٍ نائِيَةٍ وَنَجا الطَّيّارُ.

The military plane crashed in a remote area, and the pilot survived.

crash

تَحَطُّمٌ

حَدَثَ تَحَطُّمٌ أَثْناءَ هُبوطِ الطّائِرَةِ، لَكِنْ لَمْ يَكُنْ هُناكَ إِصاباتٌ.

A crash occurred during the plane's landing, but there were no injuries.

crash investigation

تَحْقيقُ كَوارِثَ

تَمَّ فَتْحُ تَحْقيقِ كَوارِثَ لِمَعْرِفَةِ سَبَبِ تَحَطُّمِ الطّائِرَةِ.

A disaster investigation was opened to determine the cause of the plane crash.

to evade

تَفادٍ • تَفادى

تَفادى الطَّيّارُ الصَّواريخَ بِمَهارَةٍ عالِيَةٍ.

The pilot skillfully evaded the missiles.

air superiority

تَفَوُّقٌ جَوِّيٌّ

حَقَّقَ الجَيْشُ التَّفَوُّقَ الجَوِّيَّ بَعْدَ إِسْقاطِ عَدَدٍ مِنْ طائِراتِ العَدُوِّ.

The army achieved air superiority after shooting down several enemy planes.

air tactic

تَكْتيكٌ جَوِّيٌّ

اُسْتُخْدِمَ تَكْتيكٌ جَوِّيٌّ مُعَقَّدٌ لِإِلْهاءِ العَدُوِّ.

A complex aerial tactic was used to distract the enemy.

wing

جَناحٌ • أَجْنِحَةٌ

تَضَرَّرَ الجَناحُ الأَيْمَنُ لِلطّائِرَةِ بَعْدَ الِاصْطِدامِ.

The right wing of the plane was damaged after the collision.

aerial, air-

جَوِّيٌّ

شُنَّ هُجومٌ جَوِّيٌّ عَلى مَواقِعَ اسْتِراتيجِيَّةٍ.

An aerial attack was launched on strategic locations.

aviation accident

حادِثُ طَيَرانٍ • حَوادِثُ

وَقَعَ حادِثُ طَيَرانٍ فَوْقَ البَحْرِ وَنُفِّذَتْ عَمَلِيَّةُ إِنْقاذٍ جَوِّيَّةٌ.

An aviation accident occurred over the sea, and an aerial rescue operation was carried out.

air emergency

حالَةُ طَوارِئَ جَوِّيَّةٍ

تَمَّ الإعْلانُ عَنْ حالَةِ طَوارِئَ جَوِّيَّةٍ بِسَبَبِ العاصِفَةِ.

An aerial emergency was declared due to the storm.

aerial warfare

حَرْبٌ جَوِّيَّةٌ • حُروبٌ

شَهِدَتِ المِنْطَقَةُ حَرْبًا جَوِّيَّةً طاحِنَةً.

The region witnessed intense aerial warfare.

to soar

حَلَّقَ • تَحْليقٌ

حَلَّقَتِ الطّائِراتُ فَوْقَ المَدينَةِ في تَشْكيلَةٍ.

The planes flew over the city in formation.

to defend from the air

دافَعَ عَبْرَ الجَوِّ • دِفاعٌ / مُدافَعَةٌ

دافَعَتِ القُوّاتُ الجَوِّيَّةُ عَنِ المِنْطَقَةِ عَبْرَ الجَوِّ بِاسْتِخْدامِ طائِراتٍ مُقاتِلَةٍ.

The air forces defended the area by air using fighter aircraft.

radar

رادارٌ

تَمَّ رَصْدُ الطّائِرَةِ المُعادِيَةِ عَلَى الرّادارِ.

The hostile aircraft was detected on radar.

pilot's license

رُخْصَةُ طَيَرانٍ • رُخَصٌ

حَصَلَ عَلَى رُخْصَةِ طَيَرانٍ بَعْدَ دَوْرَةٍ تَدْريبِيَّةٍ مُكَثَّفَةٍ.

He obtained a flying license after an intensive training course.

to monitor (as in air traffic)

رَصَدَ • رَصْدٌ

يَجْري رَصْدُ الحَرَكَةِ الجَوِّيَّةِ بِاسْتِمْرارٍ لِلْحِفاظِ عَلَى الأمانِ.

Air traffic is continuously monitored to maintain safety.

air force   سِلاحُ الطَّيَرانِ = سِلاحُ الجَوِّ = القُوّاتُ الجَوِّيَّةُ   • أَسْلِحَةٌ

سَيَتِمُّ تَجْديدُ أُسْطولِ سِلاحِ الطَّيَرانِ هَذا العامَ.

The air force fleet will be renewed this year.

sky   سَماءٌ   • سَماواتٌ / سَمَواتٌ

ظَهَرَتْ سُحُبٌ مُظْلِمَةٌ في السَّماءِ قَبْلَ الهُجومِ الجَوِّيِّ.

Dark clouds appeared in the sky before the aerial attack.

air-to-ground missile   صاروخُ جَوّ - أَرْضٍ   • صَواريخُ

أُطْلِقَ صاروخُ الجَوِّ - أَرْضٍ عَلى الهَدَفِ بِنَجاحٍ.

The air-to-ground missile was successfully launched at the target.

air-to-air missile   صاروخُ جَوّ - جَوّ

تَمَّ إِطْلاقُ صاروخِ جَوّ - جَوّ لِاِعْتِراضِ الطّائِرَةِ المُعادِيَةِ.

An air-to-air missile was launched to intercept the enemy aircraft.

aircraft   طائِرَةٌ

تَمَّ تَطْويرُ طائِرَةٍ جَديدَةٍ لِلْعَمَلِيّاتِ الخاصَّةِ.

A new aircraft was developed for special operations.

reconnaissance aircraft   طائِرَةُ اسْتِطْلاعٍ

حَلَّقَتْ طائِرَةُ الاِسْتِطْلاعِ عَلى ارْتِفاعٍ مُنْخَفِضٍ.

The reconnaissance aircraft flew at a low altitude.

drone   طائِرَةٌ بِدونِ طَيّارٍ

اُسْتُخْدِمَتِ الطّائِرَةُ بِدونِ طَيّارٍ لِجَمْعِ المَعْلوماتِ.

The drone was used for gathering information.

fighter jet

طَائِرَةٌ مُقاتِلَةٌ

تَصَدَّتِ الطَّائِرَةُ المُقاتِلَةُ لِلْهُجومِ الجَوِّيِّ.

The fighter jet repelled the aerial attack.

transport aircraft

طَائِرَةُ نَقْلٍ

تَمَّ تَحْميلُ طائِرَةِ النَّقْلِ بِالمُعَدّاتِ الطِّبِّيَّةِ.

The transport plane was loaded with medical supplies.

to fly

طَيَرانٌ • طارَ

طارَ الطَّيّارُ في مُهِمَّةٍ اسْتِطْلاعِيَّةٍ.

The pilot flew on a reconnaissance mission.

emergency-

طَوارِئُ • طارِئٌ

نَجا الطَّيّارُ مِنْ حالَةٍ طارِئَةٍ بِمَهارَةٍ.

The pilot skillfully survived an emergency situation.

pilot

طَيّارٌ

تَمَّ القَبْضُ عَلى الطَّيّارِ بَعْدَ هُبوطِهِ الطّارِئِ.

The pilot was captured after his emergency landing.

tactical aviation

طَيَرانٌ تَكْتيكِيٌّ

اُسْتُخْدِمَ الطَّيَرانُ التَّكْتيكِيُّ لِضَرْبِ الأَهْدافِ المُعادِيَةِ.

Tactical aviation was used to strike enemy targets.

air rescue operation

عَمَلِيَّةُ إِنْقاذٍ جَوِّيٍّ

نُفِّذَتْ عَمَلِيَّةُ إِنْقاذٍ جَوِّيٍّ ناجِحَةٌ لِلْمُسافِرينَ المُحْتَجَزينَ في الجِبالِ.

A successful aerial rescue operation was carried out for the passengers stranded in the mountains.

raid غارَةٌ

شَنَّتِ الطّائِراتُ غارَةً عَلى مُعَسْكَراتِ العَدُوِّ السِّرِّيَّةِ.

The planes launched a raid on the enemy's secret camps.

bomber (aircraft) قاذِفَةُ قَنابِلَ

أَقْلَعَتْ قاذِفَةُ القَنابِلِ مِنَ القاعِدَةِ الجَوِّيَّةِ لِتَنْفيذِ مُهِمَّةٍ اسْتِطْلاعِيَّةٍ.

The bomber took off from the air base to execute a reconnaissance mission.

air base قاعِدَةٌ جَوِّيَّةٌ • قَواعِدُ

أُغْلِقَتِ القاعِدَةُ الجَوِّيَّةُ لِأَعْمالِ الصِّيانَةِ وَالتَّحْديثِ.

The air base was closed for maintenance and upgrades.

to bomb قَصَفَ • قَصْفٌ

تَمَّ قَصْفُ مَواقِعِ العَدُوِّ بِنَجاحٍ كَجُزْءٍ مِنَ العَمَلِيَّةِ العَسْكَرِيَّةِ.

Enemy positions were successfully bombed as part of the military operation.

airspace مَجالٌ جَوِّيٌّ

اِنْتَهَكَتْ طائِرَةٌ مَجْهولَةٌ المَجالَ الجَوِّيَّ لِلْبِلادِ.

An unidentified aircraft violated the country's airspace.

engine مُحَرِّكٌ

تَعَطَّلَ المُحَرِّكُ الأَيْسَرُ لِلطّائِرَةِ خِلالَ الرِّحْلَةِ.

The left engine of the plane malfunctioned during the flight.

flight investigator مُحَقِّقُ طَيَرانٍ

بَدَأَ مُحَقِّقُ الطَّيَرانِ في فَحْصِ أَسْبابِ الحادِثِ الجَوِّيِّ.

The aviation investigator began examining the causes of the air accident.

runway مَدْرَجٌ • مَدَارِجُ

هَبَطَتِ الطَّائِرَةُ عَلَى المَدْرَجِ بِسَلامٍ.

The plane landed safely on the runway.

air traffic control مُراقَبَةُ الحَرَكَةِ الجَوِّيَّةِ

تَمَّ تَعْزِيزُ مُراقَبَةِ الحَرَكَةِ الجَوِّيَّةِ لِلتَّعامُلِ مَعَ الحالاتِ الطَّارِئَةِ.

Air traffic control was enhanced to handle emergency situations.

aerial surveillance مُراقَبَةٌ جَوِّيَّةٌ

أُجرِيَتْ مُراقَبَةٌ جَوِّيَّةٌ لِكَشْفِ أَيِّ نَشاطٍ مَشْبوهٍ في المِنْطَقَةِ.

Aerial surveillance was conducted to detect any suspicious activity in the area.

helicopter مِرْوَحِيَّةٌ

أَنْقَذَتِ المِرْوَحِيَّةُ النَّاسَ المُحْتَجَزينَ بَعْدَ الفَيَضانِ.

The helicopter rescued the people trapped after the flood.

parachute مِظَلَّةٌ

فَتَحَ الجُنودُ مِظَلّاتِهِمْ بِمُجَرَّدِ القَفْزِ مِنَ الطَّائِرَةِ.

The soldiers deployed their parachutes as soon as they jumped from the plane.

air corridor مَمَرٌّ جَوِّيٌّ

تَمَّ تَحْديدُ مَمَرٍّ جَوِّيٍّ آمِنٍ لِلطَّائِراتِ التِّجارِيَّةِ.

A safe air corridor was designated for commercial aircraft.

no-fly zone مِنْطَقَةُ حَظْرٍ جَوِّيٍّ • مَناطِقُ

أَعْلَنَتِ الحُكومَةُ مِنْطَقَةَ حَظْرٍ جَوِّيٍّ فَوْقَ المِنْطَقَةِ المُتَنازَعِ عَلَيْها.

The government declared a no-fly zone over the disputed area.

anti-aircraft system	أَنْظِمَةٌ / نُظُمٌ •	نِظامٌ مُضادٌّ لِلطّائِراتِ

تَمَّ تَفْعِيلُ النِّظامِ المُضادِّ لِلطّائِراتِ لِصَدِّ الهُجومِ الجَوِّيِّ.

The anti-aircraft system was activated to repel the air attack.

to attack from the air	مُهاجَمَةٌ •	هاجَمَ عَبْرَ الجَوِّ

هاجَمَتِ الطّائِراتُ المُقاتِلَةُ عَبْرَ الجَوِّ وَدَمَّرَتِ الأَهْدافَ.

The fighter planes attacked by air and destroyed the targets.

to land	هُبوطٌ •	هَبَطَ

هَبَطَتِ الطّائِرَةُ في مَطارٍ بَديلٍ بِسَبَبِ الظُّروفِ الجَوِّيَّةِ السَّيِّئَةِ.

The plane landed at an alternate airport due to bad weather conditions.

aerial attack	هُجومٌ جَوِّيٌّ

نَفَّذَ الجَيْشُ هُجومًا جَوِّيًّا عَلى مُعَسْكَرِ العَدُوِّ.

The army carried out an aerial attack on the enemy camp.

civil aviation authority	هَيْئَةُ الطَّيَرانِ المَدَنِيّ

جَرى تَطْبيقُ قَواعِدَ جَديدَةٍ مِنْ قِبَلِ هَيْئَةِ الطَّيَرانِ المَدَنِيّ لِزِيادَةِ الأَمانِ.

New rules were implemented by the Civil Aviation Authority to increase safety.

7.1.3.1 Mini-Articles

وَقَعَ حادِثُ طَيَرانٍ مَأْساوِيٌّ اليَوْمَ حينَ اصْطَدَمَتْ طائِرَةُ نَقْلٍ عَسْكَرِيَّةٌ بِطائِرَةِ اسْتِطْلاعٍ في السَّماءِ فَوْقَ مِنْطَقَةِ الحُدودِ. فَوْرَ تَلَقّي إِشارَةِ الطَّوارِئِ، باشَرَتْ وَحَداتُ الإِنْقاذِ الجَوِّيِّ بِالتَّدَخُّلِ، وَتَمَّ تَأْمينُ مِنْطَقَةِ الحادِثِ. يَجْري حالِيًّا تَحْقيقُ كَوارِثَ لِمَعْرِفَةِ أَسْبابِ التَّصادُمِ وَتَقْييمِ حَجْمِ الأَضْرارِ.

A tragic aviation accident occurred today when a military transport aircraft collided with a reconnaissance plane in the sky over the border area. Upon receiving the emergency signal, aerial rescue units immediately intervened, and the accident site was secured. An aviation disaster investigation is currently underway to determine the causes of the collision and assess the extent of the damage.

أَعْلَنَتِ الْقُوَّاتُ الْجَوِّيَّةُ عَنْ تَنْفِيذِ غَارَاتٍ جَوِّيَّةٍ نَاجِحَةٍ ضِدَّ مَوَاقِعَ مُعَادِيَةٍ اسْتَهْدَفَتْ قَوَاعِدَ عَسْكَرِيَّةً. اُسْتُخْدِمَتْ طَائِرَاتٌ مُقَاتِلَةٌ مُتَطَوِّرَةٌ قَادِرَةٌ عَلَى التَّحْلِيقِ بِسُرْعَاتٍ تَتَجَاوَزُ الصَّوْتَ. أَكَّدَتِ الْمُرَاقَبَةُ الْجَوِّيَّةُ تَفَوُّقَ الْجَيْشِ وَتَمَكُّنَهُ مِنْ تَأْمِينِ مَمَرَّاتٍ جَوِّيَّةٍ أَسَاسِيَّةٍ.

The air force announced successful air raids against hostile sites targeting military bases. Advanced fighter jets capable of flying at supersonic speeds were utilized. Air surveillance confirmed the army's superiority and its ability to secure vital air corridors.

أَطْلَقَتْ هَيْئَةُ الطَّيَرَانِ الْمَدَنِيِّ مُبَادَرَةً جَدِيدَةً لِتَعْزِيزِ الْأَمَانِ فِي الطَّيَرَانِ الْمَدَنِيِّ. وَقَدْ تَمَّ تَجْدِيدُ نِظَامٍ مُضَادٍّ لِلطَّائِرَاتِ فِي الْقَاعِدَةِ الْجَوِّيَّةِ الرَّئِيسِيَّةِ. بِالْإِضَافَةِ إِلَى ذَلِكَ، تَمَّ تَحْدِيثُ أَنْظِمَةِ الرَّادَارِ لِرَصْدِ الطَّائِرَاتِ وَالتَّأَكُّدِ مِنْ حَالَةِ الطَّوَارِئِ الْجَوِّيَّةِ. وَتَأْتِي هَذِهِ الْخُطُوَاتُ فِي إِطَارِ الرَّغْبَةِ فِي تَوْفِيرِ بِيئَةِ طَيَرَانٍ آمِنَةٍ لِجَمِيعِ الرُّكَّابِ.

The Civil Aviation Authority launched a new initiative to enhance safety in civil aviation. An anti-aircraft system at the main airbase has been updated. Additionally, radar systems have been modernized to monitor aircraft and ensure aerial emergency preparedness. These steps come in line with the desire to provide a safe flying environment for all passengers.

7.1.3.2 Informative Article: No-Fly Zones

Track **11**

مَنَاطِقُ الْحَظْرِ الْجَوِّيِّ: كَيْفِيَّةُ عَمَلِهَا وَأَهَمِّيَّتُهَا الِاسْتِرَاتِيجِيَّةُ

تُعْتَبَرُ الْمَنَاطِقُ الْمَحْظُورَةُ جَوِّيًّا مِنَ الْأَدَوَاتِ الِاسْتِرَاتِيجِيَّةِ الْمُهِمَّةِ الَّتِي تُسْتَخْدَمُ فِي السِّيَاسَةِ الدَّوْلِيَّةِ وَفِي الْمُوَاجَهَاتِ الْعَسْكَرِيَّةِ. تُعْرَفُ هَذِهِ الْمَنَاطِقُ عَلَى أَنَّهَا مِسَاحَاتٌ مِنَ الْمَجَالِ الْجَوِّيِّ يُحْظَرُ أَوْ يُقَيَّدُ فِيهَا الطَّيَرَانُ، سَوَاءٌ كَانَ طَيَرَانًا مَدَنِيًّا أَوْ عَسْكَرِيًّا.

كَيْفَ تَعْمَلُ مَنَاطِقُ الْحَظْرِ الْجَوِّيِّ؟

عِنْدَمَا تُعْلِنُ دَوْلَةٌ أَوْ تَحَالُفٌ مِنَ الدُّوَلِ عَنْ مِنْطَقَةِ حَظْرٍ جَوِّيٍّ، فَإِنَّهَا تَقُومُ بِتَحْدِيدِهَا جُغْرَافِيًّا وَتُحَدِّدُ الِارْتِفَاعَاتِ الْمَحْظُورَةَ. تُعْتَبَرُ مُرَاقَبَةُ نُظُمِ الرَّادَارِ الْحَدِيثَةِ وَالْحَرَكَةِ الْجَوِّيَّةِ أَدَاتَانِ أَسَاسِيَّتَانِ لِمُرَاقَبَةِ هَذِهِ الْمَنَاطِقِ وَضَمَانِ عَدَمِ انْتِهَاكِهَا. فِي حَالِ اخْتِرَاقِ أَيِّ طَائِرَةٍ لِهَذِهِ الْمِنْطَقَةِ، قَدْ تَتَعَرَّضُ لِاعْتِرَاضٍ جَوِّيٍّ أَوْ حَتَّى يَتِمُّ إِسْقَاطُهَا بِوَاسِطَةِ الصَّوَارِيخِ الْجَوِّ - جَوٍّ.

الْأَهَمِّيَّةُ الِاسْتِرَاتِيجِيَّةُ لِلْمَنَاطِقِ الْمَحْظُورَةِ جَوِّيًّا:

1. ضَمانُ الأَمانِ: يُمْكِنُ لِلْمَناطِقِ المَحْظورَةِ جَوِّيًّا أَنْ تَكونَ وَسيلَةً لِحِمايَةِ المَدَنِيِّينَ وَمَناطِقَ مُحَدَّدَةً مِنَ الهَجَماتِ الجَوِّيَّةِ أَوِ القَصْفِ.

2. إِرْسالُ الرَّسائِلِ السِّياسِيَّةِ: قَدْ يُعْلَنُ عَنْ مِنْطَقَةِ حَظْرٍ جَوِّيٍّ كَرِسالَةٍ سِياسِيَّةٍ لِلضَّغْطِ عَلى دَوْلَةٍ أَوْ كَتَحْذيرٍ لَها مِنْ مُواصَلَةِ سُلوكِيّاتٍ مُعَيَّنَةٍ.

3. التَّحَكُّمُ في المَجالِ الجَوِّيِّ: مِنْ خِلالِ فَرْضِ مَناطِقِ حَظْرٍ جَوِّيَّةٍ، تُحافِظُ الدُّوَلُ عَلى التَّفَوُّقِ الجَوِّيِّ، مِمّا يُقَلِّلُ مِنْ قُدْرَةِ العَدُوِّ عَلى شَنِّ الهَجَماتِ أَوْ نَقْلِ المَوارِدِ.

4. تَفادي النِّزاعاتِ: في بَعْضِ الحالاتِ، قَدْ تُساعِدُ مَناطِقُ الحَظْرِ الجَوِّيِّ في تَجَنُّبِ تَصْعيدِ النِّزاعاتِ، حَيْثُ تُقَلِّلُ مِنَ احْتِماليَّةِ وُقوعِ حَوادِثِ طَيَرانٍ بَيْنَ الدُّوَلِ المُتَقاتِلَةِ.

تُعْتَبَرُ مَناطِقُ الحَظْرِ الجَوِّيِّ مِنَ الأَدَواتِ الدِّبلوماسِيَّةِ وَالعَسْكَرِيَّةِ الَّتي تُسْتَخْدَمُ لِضَمانِ الأَمانِ وَتَحْقيقِ التَّوازُنِ الاِسْتِراتيجِيِّ في المَجالِ الجَوِّيِّ. وَعَلى الرَّغْمِ مِنْ فَعاليَّتِها في بَعْضِ الحالاتِ، فَإِنَّ تَطْبيقَها قَدْ يَتَطَلَّبُ تِكْنولوجيا مُتَقَدِّمَةً وَدَعْمًا دِبْلوماسِيًّا واسِعَ النِّطاقِ.

No-Fly Zones: How They Work and Their Strategic Importance

No-Fly Zones are important strategic tools used in international politics and military confrontations. These zones are defined areas of airspace where flight is prohibited or restricted, be it civil or military aviation.

How do No-Fly Zones work?

When a country or a coalition of countries declares a no-fly zone, they geographically delineate it and specify the prohibited altitudes. Modern radar systems and air traffic monitoring are essential tools to oversee these zones and ensure they are not violated. If any aircraft breaches this zone, it may face aerial interception or even be shot down by air-to-air missiles.

Strategic Importance of No-Fly Zones:

1. Ensuring Safety: No-Fly Zones can serve as a means to protect civilians and designated areas from aerial attacks or bombings.

2. Political Messaging: A no-fly zone might be declared as a political gesture to pressure or warn a country against continuing certain behaviors.

3. Control Over Airspace: By imposing no-fly zones, nations maintain aerial supremacy, reducing an enemy's ability to launch attacks or transport resources.

4. Conflict Avoidance: In some instances, no-fly zones can help in de-escalating conflicts as they reduce the chances of aerial incidents between warring nations.

No-Fly Zones are both diplomatic and military tools used to ensure safety and achieve strategic balance in the airspace. While effective in certain scenarios, their implementation may require advanced technology and broad diplomatic support.

7.1.3.3 Historical Account: The American Invasion of Iraq

Track 12

الغَزْوُ الأَمْرِيكِيُّ لِلْعِراقِ 2003: تَحْلِيلٌ لِلْعَمَلِيّاتِ الجَوِّيَّةِ

في عام 2003، شَهِدَ العِراقُ تَدَخُّلًا عَسْكَرِيًّا كَبِيرًا بِقِيادَةِ الوِلاياتِ المُتَّحِدَةِ الأَمْرِيكِيَّةِ. كانَ هذا الغَزْوُ جُزْءًا مِنْ "الحَرْبِ عَلَى الإِرْهابِ" الَّتي أَطْلَقَتْها الوِلاياتُ المُتَّحِدَةُ بَعْدَ هَجَماتِ 11 سِبْتَمْبَرَ. وَقَدْ لَعِبَتِ القُوّاتُ الجَوِّيَّةُ الأَمْرِيكِيَّةُ دَوْرًا حاسِمًا في الهُجومِ عَلَى العِراقِ.

مَعَ بِدايَةِ الغَزْوِ، شَنَّتِ القُوّاتُ الأَمْرِيكِيَّةُ قَصْفًا ضَخْمًا جَوِّيًّا اسْتَهْدَفَتْ فيهِ البِنْيَةَ التَّحْتِيَّةَ العِراقِيَّةَ، وَخُصوصًا مَواقِعَ الرّادارِ وَأَنْظِمَةَ الدِّفاعِ الجَوِّيِّ. اُسْتُخْدِمَتْ طائِراتٌ مُقاتِلَةٌ مُتَطَوِّرَةٌ قادِرَةٌ عَلَى التَّحْليقِ بِسُرْعاتٍ أَسْرَعَ مِنَ الصَّوْتِ وَكَذَلِكَ طائِراتٌ بِدونِ طَيّارٍ لِلاسْتِطْلاعِ وَجَمْعِ المَعْلوماتِ.

كانَتْ قاذِفاتُ القَنابِلِ الأَمْرِيكِيَّةُ تُهَيْمِنُ عَلَى السَّماءِ، مُطْلِقَةً مَجْموعَةً مِنْ صَواريخِ جَوٍّ - أَرْضٍ عالِيَةِ الدِّقَّةِ عَلَى أَهْدافٍ اسْتِراتيجِيَّةٍ. وَقَدْ أَسْقَطَتِ القُوّاتُ الجَوِّيَّةُ العَديدَ مِنَ الطّائِراتِ العِراقِيَّةِ الَّتي حاوَلَتِ التَّصَدِّيَ لِلْغَزْوِ. تَمَكَّنَتِ الوِلاياتُ المُتَّحِدَةُ مِنْ تَحْقيقِ التَّفَوُّقِ الجَوِّيِّ سَريعًا، مِمّا مَهَّدَ الطَّريقَ لِقُوّاتِها البَرِّيَّةِ لِلتَّقَدُّمِ بِسُهولَةٍ نَحْوَ العاصِمَةِ بَغْدادَ.

عَلَى الجَبْهَةِ المَدَنِيَّةِ، أَدَّتِ العَمَلِيّاتُ الجَوِّيَّةُ إلى حالاتِ طَوارِئَ جَوِّيَّةٍ في عِدَّةِ مَناطِقَ، مِمّا أَدَّى إلى نُزوحِ الآلافِ مِنَ المَدَنِيّينَ خَوْفًا مِنَ الغاراتِ الجَوِّيَّةِ. وَقَدْ أَقامَتِ القُوّاتُ الأَمْرِيكِيَّةُ مِنْطَقَةَ حَظْرٍ جَوِّيٍّ لِمَنْعِ أَيِّ هَجَماتٍ مُحْتَمَلَةٍ مِنْ قِبَلِ الطَّيَرانِ العِراقِيِّ أَوِ المِظَلِّيّينَ.

عَقِبَ الغَزْوِ، قامَتْ مُنَظَّمَةُ الطَّيَرانِ المَدَنِيِّ الدَّوْلِيِّ بِتَقْييمِ الأَضْرارِ الَّتي لَحِقَتْ بِالمَدَنِيّينَ وَالبِنْيَةِ التَّحْتِيَّةِ، وَتَمَّ العَمَلُ عَلَى إعادَةِ بِناءِ مَرافِقِ مُراقَبَةِ الحَرَكَةِ الجَوِّيَّةِ وَالمَدارِجِ الَّتي تَضَرَّرَتْ بِشَكْلٍ كَبيرٍ.

يُعْتَبَرُ الغَزْوُ الأَمْرِيكِيُّ لِلْعِراقِ في 2003 واحِدًا مِنْ أَبْرَزِ الأَحْداثِ الَّتي اسْتُخْدِمَتْ فيها القُوَّةُ الجَوِّيَّةُ بِشَكْلٍ كَبيرٍ، وَأَظْهَرَتِ القُدْرَةَ التَّكْتيكِيَّةَ وَالاسْتِراتيجِيَّةَ لِلْقُوّاتِ الجَوِّيَّةِ الأَمْرِيكِيَّةِ في تَنْفيذِ مَهامِّها.

The American Invasion of Iraq 2003: An Analysis of Aerial Operations

In 2003, Iraq experienced a major military intervention led by the United States. This invasion was part of the "War on Terror" launched by the US following the 9/11 attacks. The American Air Force played a pivotal role in the assault on Iraq.

At the onset of the invasion, US forces initiated a massive aerial bombardment targeting Iraq's infrastructure, especially radar sites and air defense systems. Advanced fighter jets capable of supersonic speeds and drones for reconnaissance and intelligence-gathering were deployed.

US bombers dominated the skies, releasing a slew of precision-guided air-to-ground missiles at strategic targets. The air force neutralized many Iraqi aircraft that attempted to counter the invasion. Swift aerial supremacy was achieved by the US, paving the way for ground forces to easily advance toward the capital, Baghdad.

On the civilian front, aerial operations triggered air emergencies in several areas, leading to the displacement of thousands of civilians in fear of air raids. US forces established a no-fly zone to prevent potential attacks by Iraqi aircraft or paratroopers.

Following the invasion, the International Civil Aviation Organization assessed the damage to civilians and infrastructure, leading to efforts to rebuild the heavily damaged air traffic control facilities and runways.

The 2003 US invasion of Iraq stands as one of the most prominent events showcasing extensive use of air power, and it highlighted the tactical and strategic prowess of the American Air Force in executing its missions.

7.2 Modern and Asymmetrical Warfare

7.2.1 Terrorism

Track **13**

to terrorize   • إرْهابٌ   أرْهَبَ

أرْهَبَ الإِرْهابِيّونَ القَرْيَةَ بِأعْمالِهِمِ العَنيفَةِ.

The terrorists terrorized the village with their violent acts.

to eliminate (as in taking out a threat)   • إزالَةٌ   أزالَ

أزالَتِ القُوّاتُ الخاصَّةُ التَّهْديدَ بِنَجاحٍ.

The special forces successfully neutralized the threat.

terrorism

إرْهابٌ

أَصْبَحَ إرْهابُ العَصْرِ الحَديثِ أَكْثَرَ تَعْقيدًا.

Modern terrorism has become more complicated.

terrorist

إرْهابيٌّ

اِعْتَقَلَتِ الشُّرْطَةُ إرْهابيًّا كانَ يُخَطِّطُ لِهُجومٍ عَلى مَطارِ العاصِمَةِ.

The police arrested a terrorist who was planning an attack on the capital's airport.

to kidnap

اِخْتَطَفَ • اِخْتِطافٌ

اِخْتَطَفَ الإرْهابيّونَ عِدَّةَ رَهائِنَ.

The terrorists kidnapped several hostages.

to target

اِسْتَهْدَفَ • اِسْتِهْدافٌ

اِسْتَهْدَفَ التَّفْجيرُ مَرْكَزًا تِجاريًّا مُزْدَحِمًا.

The bombing targeted a busy shopping center.

the war on terror

الحَرْبُ عَلى الإرْهاب • حُروبٌ

الحَرْبُ عَلى الإرْهابِ مُسْتَمِرَّةٌ عَلى مُسْتَوىً عالَميٍّ.

The war on terrorism continues globally.

suicide bomber

اِنْتِحاريٌّ

فَجَّرَ اِنْتِحاريٌّ نَفْسَهُ في سوقٍ مُكْتَظَّةٍ.

A suicide bomber detonated himself in a crowded market.

to track (as in tracking a terrorist)

تَتَبَّعَ • تَتَبُّعٌ

تَتَبَّعَ جِهازُ مُكافَحَةِ الإرْهابِ الخَلِيَّةَ الإرْهابيَّةَ لِشُهورٍ.

The counter-terrorism agency had been tracking the terrorist cell for months.

counter-terrorism coalition

تَحالُفُ مُكافَحَةِ الإرهاب

تَحالُفُ مُكافَحَةِ الإرهابِ يَشْمَلُ عِدَّةَ دُوَلٍ.

The counter-terrorism alliance includes several countries.

counter-terrorism investigation

تَحْقيقُ مُكافَحَةِ الإرهاب

أَسْفَرَ تَحْقيقُ مُكافَحَةِ الإرهابِ عَنِ القَبْضِ عَلى عَناصِرَ خَطيرَةٍ.

The counter-terrorism investigation led to the arrest of dangerous elements.

extremism, radicalization

تَطَرُّفٌ

جَرى اتِّخاذُ إجراءاتٍ لِمُكافَحَةِ التَّطَرُّفِ داخِلَ القُوّاتِ المُسَلَّحَةِ.

Measures were taken to combat extremism within the armed forces.

explosion, bombing

تَفْجيرٌ

أَسْفَرَ تَفْجيرُ القُنْبُلَةِ عَنِ الكَثيرِ مِنَ القَتْلى وَالجَرْحى.

The bomb explosion resulted in multiple deaths and injuries.

terrorist financing

تَمْويلُ الأرْهاب

تَمْويلُ الأرْهابِ يَجِبُ أَنْ يُقْطَعَ.

Funding for terrorism must be cut off.

terrorist organization

تَنْظيمٌ إرْهابِيٌّ

ظَهَرَ تَنْظيمٌ إرْهابِيٌّ جَديدٌ في المِنْطَقَةِ.

A new terrorist organization emerged in the region.

threat

تَهْديدٌ

تَهْديداتُ الإرهابِ تَأْتي في أَشْكالٍ مُتَعَدِّدَةٍ.

Terrorism threats come in various forms.

hate crime

جَرِيمَةُ كَرَاهِيَةٍ • جَرائِمُ

شَهِدَتْ جَرائِمُ الكَرَاهِيَةِ ارْتِفاعًا مُؤَخَّرًا.

Hate crimes have recently been on the rise.

executioner

جَلّادٌ

تَمَّ القَبْضُ عَلى جَلّادِ الخَلِيَّةِ الإرْهابِيَّةِ.

The executioner of the terrorist cell was captured.

to recruit

جَنَّدَ • تَجْنِيدٌ

جَنَّدَ التَّنْظِيمِ الإرْهابِيُّ أَعْضاءً جُدُدَ عَبْرَ الإنْتَرْنِتْ.

The terrorist organization recruited new members via the Internet.

counter-terrorism agency

جِهازُ مُكافَحَةِ الإرْهابِ • أَجْهِزَةٌ

نَجَحَ جِهازُ مُكافَحَةِ الإرْهابِ في تَفْكِيكِ خَلِيَّةٍ كانَتْ تَعْتَزِمُ شَنَّ هَجَماتٍ في البِلادِ.

The counter-terrorism agency succeeded in dismantling a cell that was planning to carry out attacks in the country.

to plot, plan

خَطَّطَ • تَخْطِيطٌ

خَطَّطَ الإرْهابِيّونَ لِهُجومٍ كَبيرٍ لَكِنَّهُ فَشِلَ.

The terrorists planned a major attack, but it failed.

dangerous

خَطِيرٌ

إنَّ الوَضْعَ خَطِيرٌ في المَناطِقِ المُتَأَثِّرَةِ بِالإرْهابِ.

The situation is dangerous in areas affected by terrorism.

terrorist cell

خَلِيَّةٌ إرْهابِيَّةٌ • خَلايا

تَمَّ تَفْكِيكُ خَلِيَّةٍ إرْهابِيَّةٍ بِنَجاحٍ.

A terrorist cell was successfully dismantled.

hostage رَهائِنُ • رَهينَةٌ

تَمَّ إِطْلاقُ سَراحِ رَهينَةٍ بَعْدَ عَمَلِيَّةٍ ناجِحَةٍ.

A hostage was released after a successful operation.

biological weapon أَسْلِحَةٌ • سِلاحٌ بَيولوجِيٌّ

تُشَكِّلُ الأَسْلِحَةُ البَيولوجِيَّةُ تَهْديدًا عالَمِيًّا.

Biological weapons pose a global threat.

chemical weapon سِلاحٌ كيمْيائِيٌّ

تَمَّ ضَبْطُ سِلاحٍ كيمْيائِيٍّ في مَخْزَنٍ سِرِّيٍّ.

A chemical weapon was seized in a secret storage facility.

anti-terrorism policy سِياسَةُ مُكافَحَةِ الإِرْهابِ

تَمَّ تَحْديثُ سِياسَةِ مُكافَحَةِ الإِرْهابِ لِتَشْمَلَ تِقْنِيّاتٍ جَديدَةً.

The anti-terrorism policy was updated to include new techniques.

counter-terrorism sanctions pl. عُقوباتُ مُكافَحَةِ الإِرْهابِ

أَصْبَحَتْ عُقوباتُ مُكافَحَةِ الإِرْهابِ أَشَدَّ صَرامَةً.

Counter-terrorism sanctions have become more stringent.

violent عُنْفٌ • عَنيفٌ

شَهِدَتِ المِنْطَقَةُ الحُدودِيَّةُ اشْتِباكاتٍ عَنيفَةً بَيْنَ القُوّاتِ المُعادِيَةِ وَالقُوّاتِ الوَطَنِيَّةِ.

The border area witnessed violent clashes between hostile forces and national troops.

unlawful غَيْرُ مَشْروعٍ

إِنَّ اسْتِخْدامَ القُوَّةِ ضِدَّ المَدَنِيّينَ غَيْرُ مَشْروعٍ.

The use of force against civilians is unlawful.

to detonate

فَجَّرَ • تَفْجيرٌ

فَجَّرَ الإرْهابِيّونَ عُبُوَّةً ناسِفَةً بِالْقُرْبِ مِنَ الْمَدْرَسَةِ.

The terrorists detonated an explosive device near the school.

anti-terrorism law

قانونُ مُكافَحَةِ الإرْهابِ • قَوانينُ

قانونُ مُكافَحَةِ الإرْهابِ يَحْتاجُ لِتَعْديلاتٍ.

The counter-terrorism law needs amendments.

extremist

مُتَطَرِّفٌ

يُشَكِّلُ الْمُتَطَرِّفونَ تَهْديدًا لِلْأَمْنِ الْقَوْمِيِّ.

Extremists pose a threat to national security.

deradicalization

مُكافَحَةُ التَّطَرُّفِ

تُعْتَبَرُ مُكافَحَةُ التَّطَرُّفِ جُزْءًا مُهِمًّا مِنَ اسْتِراتيجِيَّةِ الْأَمْنِ.

Countering extremism is an important part of the security strategy.

to attack

هاجَمَ • مُهاجَمَةٌ

هاجَمَ مُسَلَّحونَ قاعِدَةً عَسْكَرِيَّةً فِي اللَّيْلِ.

Armed men attacked a military base at night.

terrorist attack

هُجومٌ إرْهابِيٌّ

أَثارَ هُجومٌ إرْهابِيٌّ فِي الْمِتْرو الذُّعْرَ بَيْنَ الرُّكّابِ.

A terrorist attack on the subway caused panic among passengers.

to threaten

هَدَّدَ • تَهْديدٌ

هَدَّدَ الإرْهابِيّونَ بِشَنِّ هَجَماتٍ جَديدَةٍ.

The terrorists threatened to launch new attacks.

نَفَّذَتْ وَحْدَةُ مُكافَحَةِ الإِرْهابِ عَمَلِيَّةً ناجِحَةً لإِلْقاءِ القَبْضِ عَلَى الجُناةِ.

The counter-terrorism unit successfully executed an operation to apprehend the culprits.

7.2.1.1 Mini-Articles

Track **14**

اِسْتَهْدَفَ تَنْظيمٌ إِرْهابِيٌّ مَعْروفٌ السّوقَ المَرْكَزِيَّ بِواسِطَةِ انْتِحارِيٍّ اليَوْمَ، مِمّا أَدّى إلى سُقوطِ عَدَدٍ مِنَ الضَّحايا. قامَتْ وَحْدَةُ مُكافَحَةِ الإِرْهابِ بِتَتَبُّعِ خَلِيَّةٍ إِرْهابِيَّةٍ يُعْتَقَدُ أَنَّها وَراءَ الهُجومِ. تَعَهَّدَتِ الحُكومَةُ بِتَكْثيفِ جُهودِ مُكافَحَةِ التَّطَرُّفِ وَمُواصَلَةِ الحَرْبِ عَلى الإِرْهابِ بِكُلِّ قُوَّةٍ.

A well-known terrorist organization targeted the central market with a suicide bomber today, resulting in several casualties. The counter-terrorism unit tracked down a terrorist cell believed to be behind the attack. The government vowed to intensify efforts to combat extremism and continue the war on terror with full force.

أَرْهَبَتْ جَماعَةٌ مُتَطَرِّفَةٌ السُّكّانَ المَحَلِّيّينَ بَعْدَ أَنِ اخْتَطَفَتْ عَدَدًا مِنَ المَدَنِيّينَ كَرَهائِنَ. أَكَّدَتِ المَصادِرُ أَنَّ التَّنْظيمَ الإِرْهابِيَّ هَدَّدَ بِتَنْفيذِ تَفْجيراتٍ إذا لَمْ تُنَفَّذْ مَطالِبُهُمْ. قامَ جِهازُ مُكافَحَةِ الإِرْهابِ بِإِطْلاقِ عُقوباتٍ جَديدَةٍ ضِدَّ الأَفْرادِ المُرْتَبِطينَ بِالْجَماعَةِ.

An extremist group terrorized local residents after kidnapping several civilians as hostages. Sources confirmed that the terrorist organization threatened to carry out bombings if their demands were not met. The counter-terrorism agency introduced new sanctions against individuals linked to the group.

تَمَكَّنَ جِهازُ مُكافَحَةِ الإِرْهابِ مِنَ القَبْضِ عَلى خَلِيَّةٍ إِرْهابِيَّةٍ كانَتْ تُخَطِّطُ لِهُجومٍ بِاسْتِخْدامِ سِلاحٍ كيميائِيٍّ. تَمَّ التَّوَصُّلُ إلى الخَلِيَّةِ بِفَضْلِ تَحْقيقِ مُكافَحَةِ الإِرْهابِ المُسْتَمِرِّ وَجُهودِ التَّتَبُّعِ المُكَثَّفَةِ. وَقَدْ أُزيلَتْ جَميعُ المَوادِّ الخَطيرَةِ وَتَمَّ مَنْعُ هُجومٍ كَبيرٍ عَلى المَدينَةِ.

The counter-terrorism agency managed to capture a terrorist cell planning an attack using a chemical weapon. The cell was identified thanks to the ongoing counter-terrorism investigation and intensive tracking efforts. All hazardous materials were removed, preventing a major attack on the city.

الاِخْتِطافُ وَالفِدْيَةُ في مِنْطَقَةِ السّاحِلِ وَالمَغْرِبِ

في السَّنَواتِ الأَخيرَةِ، شَهِدَتْ مَناطِقُ السّاحِلِ وَالمَغْرِبِ ارْتِفاعًا في حَوادِثِ الاِخْتِطافِ الَّتي يُنَفِّذُها مُتَطَرِّفونَ. تُعْتَبَرُ هَذِهِ الحَوادِثُ وَسيلَةً لِلْمُتَطَرِّفينَ لِتَمْويلِ الإِرْهابِ وَتَعْزيزِ وُجودِهِمْ في المِنْطَقَةِ.

التَّهْديدُ بِأَخْذِ الرَّهائِنِ مِنْ قِبَلِ الإِرْهابِيّينَ يُعَمِّقُ القَلَقَ بَيْنَ السُّكّانِ المَحَلِّيّينَ وَالمُجْتَمَعِ الدَّوْلِيِّ عَلى حَدٍّ سَواءٍ. إِذْ يُعْتَبَرُ السُّيّاحُ، في كَثيرٍ مِنَ الأَحْيانِ، هَدَفًا لِهَذِهِ الجَماعاتِ لِأَنَّ الدُّوَلَ الأَصْلِيَّةَ لِهَؤُلاءِ السُّيّاحِ غالِبًا ما تَكونُ عُرْضَةً لِدَفْعِ فِدْياتٍ ضَخْمَةٍ.

وَبِالإِضافَةِ إلى ذَلِكَ، تَقومُ جَماعاتُ الإِرْهابِ بِتَحْقيقِ أَهْدافِها مِنْ خِلالِ اسْتِخْدامِ الرَّهائِنِ كَوَسيلَةٍ لِلضَّغْطِ. فَبَيْنَما تَسْعى الدُّوَلُ المَعْنِيَّةُ إلى حِمايَةِ مُواطِنيها، تَجِدُ نَفْسَها أَمامَ تَحَدِّياتٍ جَمَّةٍ في التَّعامُلِ مَعَ هَذِهِ الأَزَماتِ، وَخاصَّةً في ظِلِّ سِياساتِ مُكافَحَةِ الإِرْهابِ الَّتي تَحْظُرُ دَفْعَ الفِدْيَةِ.

يُؤَدّي هَذا النَّوْعُ مِنَ الإِرْهابِ، الَّذي يَشْمَلُ الاِخْتِطافَ وَالفِدْيَةَ، إلى تَقْويضِ الاِقْتِصاداتِ المَحَلِّيَّةِ. حَيْثُ يُؤَثِّرُ سَلْبًا عَلى قِطاعِ السِّياحَةِ، الَّذي يُعَدُّ العَمودَ الفَقْرِيَّ لِاقْتِصاداتِ العَديدِ مِنَ الدُّوَلِ في المِنْطَقَةِ.

تَعْمَلُ الحُكوماتُ المَحَلِّيَّةُ بِشَكْلٍ وَثيقٍ مَعَ تَحالُفِ مُكافَحَةِ الإِرْهابِ لِمُكافَحَةِ هَذا التَّهْديدِ النّاشِئِ وَضَمانِ سَلامَةِ المُواطِنينَ وَالزُّوّارِ في مِنْطَقَةِ السّاحِلِ وَالمَغْرِبِ.

Kidnapping and Ransom in the Sahel and Maghreb Region

In recent years, the Sahel and Maghreb regions have seen a rise in kidnappings carried out by extremists. These incidents serve as a means for extremists to finance terrorism and strengthen their presence in the area.

The threat of terrorists taking hostages deepens the concerns among local residents and the international community alike. Tourists are often targets for these groups because their home countries are frequently susceptible to paying hefty ransoms.

Furthermore, terrorist groups achieve their objectives by using hostages as a means of pressure. While the concerned nations strive to protect their citizens, they face numerous challenges in dealing with these crises, especially given counter-terrorism policies that prohibit ransom payments.

This form of terrorism, involving kidnapping and ransom, undermines local economies. It adversely impacts the tourism sector, which is the backbone of many countries' economies in the region.

Local governments work closely with the counter-terrorism coalition to combat this emerging threat and ensure the safety of citizens and visitors in the Sahel and Maghreb regions.

7.2.1.3 Informative Article: The War on Terror

Track **16**

الحَرْبُ عَلى الإِرْهابِ: الصُّعودُ وَالسُّقوطُ لِتَنْظيمِ "داعِشْ" في العِراقِ وَسوريا

في عام 2014، أرْهَبَ العالَمَ الصُّعودُ السَّريعُ لِتَنْظيمِ "داعِشْ" في العِراقِ وَسوريا. اسْتَهْدَفَ التَّنْظيمُ المُدُنَ الكُبْرى مِثْلَ المَوْصِلِ في العِراقِ وَالرَّقَّةِ في سوريا، مُحَوِّلًا المَناطِقَ إلى مَعاقِلَ إِرْهابيَّةٍ.

يَتَمَيَّزُ "داعِشْ" بِتِقْنِياتِهِ الإِرْهابيَّةِ المُتَطَرِّفَةِ، وَالَّتي تَشْمَلُ الهَجَماتِ الانْتِحاريَّةَ وَالاخْتِطافَ الجَماعيَّ لِلرَّهائِنِ. كَما يُمَوِّلونَ الإِرْهابَ عَبْرَ أنْشِطَةٍ غَيْرَ مَشْروعَةٍ، مِثْلِ تِجارَةِ النَّفْطِ في السّوقِ السَّوْداءِ وَالنَّهْبِ الثَّقافيِّ. كانَتْ تَهْديداتُ التَّنْظيمِ خَطيرَةً وَمُتَزايِدَةً، مِمّا أدّى إلى تَكْوينِ تَحالُفِ مُكافَحَةِ الإِرْهابِ الدَّوْليِّ لِمُواجَهَةِ هذا الكِيانِ الشَّنيعِ.

قامَ هذا التَّحالُفُ بِتَكْثيفِ جُهودِهِ ضِدَّ "داعِشْ"، وَبَدَأ في تَنْفيذِ سِياسَةٍ شامِلَةٍ لِمُكافَحَةِ الإِرْهابِ. خِلالَ سَنَواتٍ قَليلَةٍ، أدَّتِ العَمَلِياتُ العَسْكَريَّةُ إلى خَسارَةِ "داعِشْ" لِلْأراضي الَّتي احْتَلَّها. بِحُلولِ عام 2019، تَمَّتْ هَزيمَةُ التَّنْظيمِ الإِرْهابيِّ بِشَكْلٍ كَبيرٍ في المِنْطَقَةِ.

رَغْمَ النَّجاحِ في مُكافَحَةِ "داعِشْ"، تَظَلُّ المِنْطَقَةُ تُواجِهُ تَحَدِّياتٍ مُسْتَمِرَّةً لِمُكافَحَةِ التَّطَرُّفِ. فَالْهَجَماتُ الإِرْهابيَّةُ المُنْفَرِدَةُ وَخَلايا الإِرْهابِ المُتَفَرِّقَةُ ما زالَتْ تُهَدِّدُ الأمْنَ في بَعْضِ المَناطِقِ.

في الخِتامِ، تُجَسِّدُ الحَرْبُ عَلى "داعِشْ" في العِراقِ وَسوريا النِّضالَ المُسْتَمِرَّ ضِدَّ الإِرْهابِ. وَعَلى الرَّغْمِ مِنَ الانْتِصاراتِ العَسْكَريَّةِ، يَظَلُّ البَحْثُ عَنْ حُلولٍ دائِمَةٍ لِلتَّحَدِّياتِ الأمْنيَّةِ وَالاجْتِماعيَّةِ قائِمًا.

The War on Terror: The Rise and Fall of ISIS in Iraq and Syria

In 2014, the world was terrified by the swift rise of the ISIS organization in Iraq and Syria. The group targeted major cities such as Mosul in Iraq and Raqqa in Syria, turning these areas into terrorist strongholds.

ISIS distinguished itself with its extreme terrorist tactics, including suicide attacks and mass kidnappings of hostages. They also financed their terror through illicit activities, such as black-market oil trading and cultural looting. The threats posed by the organization were grave and escalating, leading to the formation of an international anti-terrorism coalition to combat this heinous entity.

This coalition intensified its efforts against ISIS and began implementing a comprehensive counter-terrorism policy. Within a few years, military operations led to ISIS losing the territories it had occupied. By 2019, the terrorist organization was significantly defeated in the region.

Despite the success against ISIS, the region still faces ongoing challenges in combating extremism. Lone-wolf terrorist attacks and isolated terrorist cells still threaten security in some areas.

In conclusion, the war against ISIS in Iraq and Syria epitomizes the ongoing struggle against terrorism. Despite military victories, the search for lasting solutions to security and social challenges remains.

7.2.2 Cyber-Terrorism

Track **17**

secure, safe

آمِنٌ

وَضَعَتِ الحُكُومَةُ خُطَطًا جَديدَةً لِجَعْلِ الشَّبَكاتِ الحُكُومِيَّةِ آمِنَةً مِنَ التَّهْديداتِ السَّيْبَرانِيَّةِ.

The government has put in place new plans to make government networks secure from cyber threats.

cyber-security

أَمْنٌ سَيْبَرانِيٌّ

الأَمْنُ السَّيْبَرانِيُّ أَصْبَحَ قَضِيَّةً وَطَنِيَّةً في العَديدِ مِنَ الدُّوَلِ.

Cyber-security has become a national issue in many countries.

to defraud

اِحْتالَ • اِحْتِيالٌ

اِحْتالَ المُجْرِمونَ عَلى النّاسِ عَبْرَ رَسائِلِ بَريدٍ إِلِكْترونِيٍّ مُزَيَّفَةٍ.

Criminals defrauded people through fake email messages.

online fraud

اِحْتيالٌ إِلِكْترونِيٌّ

تَعَرَّضَ البَنْكُ لِعَمَلِيَّةِ احْتِيالٍ إِلِكْترونِيٍّ مُعَقَّدَةٍ.

The bank was targeted in a sophisticated electronic fraud operation.

hacking

اِخْتِراقٌ

تَعَرَّضَتِ البِنْيَةُ التَّحْتِيَّةُ لِعَمَلِيّاتِ اخْتِراقٍ مُتَعَدِّدَةٍ.

The infrastructure was subjected to multiple hacking operations.

computer hacking

اِخْتِراقُ الحَواسيب

شَهِدْنا ازْديادًا في حالاتِ اخْتِراقِ الحَواسيبِ هَذا العامَ.

We've seen an increase in computer hacking cases this year.

to hack, infiltrate   اِخْتِراقٌ •   اِخْتَرَقَ

اِخْتَرَقَ المُخْتَرِقونَ نِظامَ الأَمْنِ في الشَّرِكَةِ.

Hackers breached the company's security system.

to hack   اِخْتِراقٌ •   اِخْتَرَقَ

اِخْتَرَقَتْ جِهاتٌ مَجْهولَةٌ الأَنْظِمَةَ الحُكوميَّةَ لِلْحُصولِ عَلى مَعْلوماتٍ مَحْظورَةٍ سِرِّيَّةٍ.

Unknown entities hacked government systems to obtain classified information.

intelligence   اِسْتِخْباراتٌ

تَعاوَنَتِ اسْتِخْباراتُ الدَّوْلَةِ مَعَ شُرَكاءَ دَوْلِيّينَ لِمُواجَهَةِ التَّهْديداتِ السَّيْبَرانيَّةِ.

State intelligence collaborated with international partners to counter cyber threats.

information strategy   اِسْتِراتيجيَّةُ مَعْلوماتٍ

يَعْمَلُ المُحَلِّلونَ عَلى تَطْويرِ اسْتِراتيجيَّةِ مَعْلوماتٍ لِمُكافَحَةِ التَّجَسُّسِ الإِلِكْترونِيِّ.

Analysts are working on developing an information strategy to counter digital espionage.

malware   بَرامِجُ •   بَرْنامَجٌ خَبيثٌ

اِنْتَشَرَتِ البَرامِجُ الخَبيثَةُ عَلى الشَّبَكَةِ وَأَصابَتِ العَديدَ مِنَ الأَجْهِزَةِ.

Malicious software spread across the network and infected numerous devices.

spam   بَريدٌ مُزْعِجٌ

تُعْتَبَرُ فَلاتِرُ البَريدِ المُزْعِجِ واحِدَةً مِنْ أَدَواتِ الحِمايَةِ الأَساسيَّةِ.

Spam filters are considered one of the basic protection tools.

to spy   تَجَسُّسٌ •   تَجَسَّسَ

قامَتْ وَحْداتُ الاسْتِخْباراتِ العَسْكَريَّةِ بِالتَّجَسُّسِ عَلى تَحَرُّكاتِ جَيْشِ العَدُوِّ.

The military intelligence units spied on the movements of the enemy army.

cyber-espionage

تَجَسُّسٌ إِلِكْتِرونِيٌّ = تَجَسُّسٌ سَيْبَرانِيٌّ

يُعْتَبَرُ التَّجَسُّسُ الإِلِكْتِرونِيُّ مِنْ أَخْطَرِ الأَشْكالِ الجَديدَةِ لِلتَّهْديدِ السَّيْبَرانِيِّ.

Digital espionage is considered one of the most dangerous new forms of cyber threat.

identity verification

تَحَقُّقٌ مِنَ الهُوِيَّةِ

يُعْتَبَرُ التَّحَقُّقُ مِنَ الهُوِيَّةِ خُطْوَةً مُهِمَّةً لِلْحِفاظِ عَلى الأَمْنِ السَّيْبَرانِيِّ.

Identity verification is an important step in maintaining cybersecurity.

encryption

تَشْفيرٌ

اِسْتَخْدَمَ المُخْتَرِقونَ تَشْفيرًا مُعَقَّدًا لِإِخْفاءِ هُوِيّاتِهِمْ.

The hackers used complex encryption to hide their identities.

phishing

تَصَيُّدٌ

عَمَلِيّاتُ التَّصَيُّدِ تَسْتَهْدِفُ الأَفْرادَ بِرَسائِلَ مُضَلِّلَةٍ.

Phishing operations target individuals with misleading messages.

adware phishing

تَصَيُّدٌ إِعْلانِيٌّ

العَديدُ مِنَ المَواقِعِ تَعَرَّضَتْ لِهَجَماتِ تَصَيُّدٍ إِعْلانِيٍّ.

Many websites have been subject to ad phishing attacks.

intrusion

تَطَفُّلٌ

اِشْتَبَهَتِ الحُكومَةُ في تَطَفُّلِ دَوْلَةٍ مُعادِيَةٍ عَلى شَبَكاتِها الأَمْنِيَّةِ.

The government suspected foreign state intrusion into its security networks.

to trace

تَعَقَّبَ • تَعَقُّبٌ

اِسْتَخْدَمَتِ الأَجْهِزَةُ الأَمْنِيَّةُ تِقْنِيّاتِ تَعَقُّبٍ لِتَحْديدِ مَوْقِعِ المُخْتَرِقينَ.

Security agencies used tracking techniques to locate the hackers.

to eavesdrop

تَنَصَّتَ • تَنَصُّتٌ

قامَتِ الأَجْهِزَةُ الأَمْنِيَّةُ بِالتَّنَصُّتِ عَلى مُكالَماتِ المُشْتَبَهِ بِهِمْ لِلْحِفاظِ عَلَى الأَمْنِ الوَطَنِيِّ.

Security agencies wiretapped the calls of suspects to maintain national security.

wiretapping, eavesdropping

تَنَصُّتٌ

قامَتْ أَجْهِزَةُ الأَمْنِ الوَطَنِيِّ بِعَمَلِيّاتِ تَنَصُّتٍ لِرَصْدِ الأَنْشِطَةِ الإِرْهابِيَّةِ.

National security agencies conducted eavesdropping to monitor terrorist activities.

espionage

جاسوسِيَّةٌ

كَشَفَتِ الحُكومَةُ عَنْ عَمَلِيّاتٍ جاسوسِيَّةٍ تَسْتَهْدِفُ الأَنْظِمَةَ العَسْكَرِيَّةَ.

The government revealed espionage operations targeting military systems.

firewall

جِدارُ حِمايَةٍ • جُدْرانٌ / جُدُرٌ

أَعْلَنَ الجَيْشُ عَنْ تَطْويرِ جِدارِ حِمايَةٍ مُتَقَدِّمٍ لِحِمايَةِ البَياناتِ.

The military announced the development of an advanced firewall to protect data.

cybercrime

جَريمَةٌ إِلِكْترونِيَّةٌ • جَرائِمُ

تَعاوَنَتِ الأَجْهِزَةُ الأَمْنِيَّةُ لِمُحارَبَةِ الجَرائِمِ الإِلِكْترونِيَّةِ الَّتي تُهَدِّدُ الأَمْنَ الوَطَنِيَّ.

Security agencies collaborated to combat cybercrime threatening national security.

to gather intelligence

جَمَعَ مَعْلوماتٍ اسْتِخْباراتِيَّةً • جَمْعٌ

تَمَّ جَمْعُ مَعْلوماتٍ اسْتِخْباراتِيَّةٍ حاسِمَةٍ لِإِفْشالِ مُخَطَّطاتِ هُجومٍ.

Crucial intelligence information was gathered to thwart attack plans.

to block

حَجَبَ • حَجْبٌ

قامَتِ الحُكومَةُ بِحَجْبِ مَواقِعَ إِلِكْترونِيَّةٍ تَنْشُرُ مَعْلوماتٍ مُضَلِّلَةً.

The government blocked websites disseminating misleading information.

cyber-warfare حُرُوبٌ • حَرْبٌ إِلِكْتِرُونِيَّةٌ = حَرْبٌ سِيبِرَانِيَّةٌ

يَعْتَبِرُ الخُبَرَاءُ أَنَّ الحَرْبَ الإِلِكْتِرُونِيَّةَ قَدْ تَكُونُ أَخْطَرَ مِنَ الحُرُوبِ التَّقْلِيدِيَّةِ.

Experts believe that cyber-warfare could be more dangerous than conventional warfare.

to protect حِمَايَةٌ • حَمَى

تَمَكَّنَتِ الوَحْدَاتُ العَسْكَرِيَّةُ مِنْ حِمَايَةِ الشَّبَكَةِ مِنْ هَجَمَاتِ القَرَاصِنَةِ.

Military units managed to safeguard the network from hacker attacks.

cyber-defense دِفَاعٌ إِلِكْتِرُونِيٌّ

وَضَعَتِ الدَّوْلَةُ اسْتِرَاتِيجِيَّةً لِلدِّفَاعِ الإِلِكْتِرُونِيِّ ضِدَّ التَّهْدِيدَاتِ.

The state developed a cyber-defense strategy against threats.

worm دُودٌ • دُودَةٌ إِلِكْتِرُونِيَّةٌ

اِكْتَشَفَتِ الاِسْتِخْبَارَاتُ عَمَلِيَّةً لِإِطْلَاقِ دُودَةٍ إِلِكْتِرُونِيَّةٍ تَسْتَهْدِفُ البِنْيَةَ التَّحْتِيَّةَ.

Intelligence discovered an operation to launch a worm targeting the infrastructure.

to monitor مُرَاقَبَةٌ • رَاقَبَ

رَاقَبَتِ الأَجْهِزَةُ الحُكُومِيَّةُ الأَنْشِطَةَ المَشْبُوهَةَ عَلَى الشَّبَكَاتِ الاِجْتِمَاعِيَّةِ.

Government agencies monitored suspicious activities on social networks.

to monitor رَصْدٌ • رَصَدَ

تَمَّ رَصْدُ هَجَمَاتٍ إِلِكْتِرُونِيَّةٍ مُوَجَّهَةٍ نَحْوَ المُنْشَآتِ العَسْكَرِيَّةِ.

Electronic attacks aimed at military facilities were detected.

digital رَقْمِيٌّ

تَمَّ تَطْوِيرُ أَنْظِمَةٍ رَقْمِيَّةٍ جَدِيدَةٍ لِتَأْمِينِ البَيَانَاتِ الحَسَّاسَةِ.

New digital systems were developed to secure sensitive data.

password

رُمُوزٌ • رَمْزُ مُرورٍ

تَمَّ تَحْديثُ رُموزِ المُرورِ لِجَميعِ الأَنْظِمَةِ الحُكوميَّةِ.

Passwords were updated for all government systems.

cyber weapon

أَسْلِحَةٌ • سِلاحٌ إِلِكْترونيٌّ

أَعْلَنَ الجَيْشُ عَنْ تَطْويرِ سِلاحٍ إِلِكْترونيٍّ جَديدٍ لِلدِّفاعِ عَنِ الشَّبَكاتِ.

The army announced the development of a new cyber weapon for network defense.

network security policy

سِياسَةُ أَمانِ الشَّبَكَةِ

تَبَنَّتِ الحُكومَةُ سِياسَةَ أَمانِ شَبَكَةٍ مُحْكَمَةً لِحِمايَةِ المَعْلوماتِ.

The government adopted a robust network security policy to protect information.

cyber

سَيْبَرانيٌّ

تَمَّ تَأْسيسُ وَحْدَةٍ سَيْبَرانيَّةٍ جَديدَةٍ لِلرَّصْدِ وَالتَّحْليلِ.

A new cyber unit was established for monitoring and analysis.

network

شَبَكَةٌ

شَدَّدَتِ الحُكومَةُ الأَمْنَ عَلى شَبَكَةِ الاِتِّصالاتِ العَسْكَريَّةِ.

The government tightened security on the military communications network.

to encrypt

تَشْفيرٌ • شَفَّرَ

تَقومُ الوَحْداتُ العَسْكَريَّةُ بِتَشْفيرِالمَعْلوماتِ الحَسّاسَةِ.

Military units encrypt sensitive information.

to distribute denial-of-service attacks (DDoS)

تَوْزيعٌ • شَنَّ هَجَماتِ حَجْبِ الخِدْمَةِ

شَنَّتْ جِهاتٌ مَجْهولَةٌ هَجَماتِ حَجْبِ الخِدْمَةِ عَلى مَواقِعَ حُكوميَّةٍ.

Unknown entities launched denial-of-service attacks on government websites.

unsecured

غَيْرُ مُؤَمَّنٍ

أُكْتُشِفَتْ نِقاطٌ غَيْرُ مُؤَمَّنَةٍ في الشَّبَكَةِ الحُكوميَّةِ.

Unsecured points were discovered in the government network.

> غَيْرُ functions similarly to the English prefixes 'un-' and 'non-,' negating the meaning of the adjective it precedes. Notice that this is a compound construction (idaafa), and as such, the adjective is always in the genitive case.

unencrypted

غَيْرُ مُشَفَّرٍ

صَدَرَ تَحْذيرٌ مِنْ نَقْلِ مَعْلوماتٍ غَيْرِ مُشَفَّرَةٍ عَبْرَ الشَّبَكَةِ.

A warning was issued about transferring unencrypted information across the network.

to decrypt

فَكَّ تَشْفيرًا

• فَكَّ

تَمَكَّنَتِ الأَجْهِزَةُ الأَمْنِيَّةُ مِنْ فَكِّ تَشْفيرِ الرَّسائِلِ المَشْبوهَةِ.

Security agencies managed to decrypt suspicious messages.

virus

فَيْروسٌ

اِنْتَشَرَ فَيْروسٌ جَديدٌ يَهْدُفُ لِتَعْطيلِ أَنْظِمَةِ الأَمْنِ الوَطَنِيِّ.

A new virus spread aiming to disable national security systems.

Trojan (malware)

فَيْروسُ حِصانِ طِرْوادَةَ

تَمَّ اكْتِشافُ فَيْروسِ حِصانِ طِرْوادَةَ جَديدٍ يَسْتَهْدِفُ البُنوكَ.

A new Trojan targeting banks has been discovered.

internet law

قانونُ الإِنْتَرْنِتْ

• قَوانينُ

سَنَّتِ الحُكومَةُ قانونًا جَديدًا لِلإِنْتَرْنِتْ لِتَجْريمِ الاِخْتِراقِ الإِلِكْترونِيِّ.

The government drafted a new internet law to criminalize hacking.

surveillance camera

كامِيرا مُراقَبةٍ

تَمَّ تَحْديثُ كامِيراتِ المُراقَبةِ لِتَوْفيرِ أمانٍ أكْبَرَ.

Surveillance cameras were updated to provide greater security.

secure

مُؤَمَّنٌ

كانَتِ الشَّبَكَةُ الحُكومِيَّةُ مُؤَمَّنَةً بِتِقْنِيّاتٍ مُتَطَوِّرَةٍ.

The government network was secured with advanced technologies.

eavesdropper

مُتَنَصِّتٌ

راقَبَ المُتَنَصِّتُ بِعِنايَةٍ نَشاطَ الشَّبَكَةِ وَقَنَواتِ الاتِّصالِ في المُؤَسَّسَةِ المُسْتَهْدَفَةِ لِجَمْعِ المَعْلوماتِ الحَسّاسَةِ.

The eavesdropper carefully monitored the network activity and communication channels of the targeted organization to collect sensitive information.

hacker

مُخْتَرِقٌ

تَمَّ القَبْضُ عَلى مُخْتَرِقٍ كانَ يُخَطِّطُ لِاخْتِراقِ الشَّبَكَةِ العَسْكَرِيَّةِ.

A hacker who was planning to infiltrate the military network was arrested.

hacker

مُخْتَرِقٌ

تَمَّ التَّعَرُّفُ عَلى المُخْتَرِقِ الَّذي حاوَلَ انْتِهاكَ أمْنِ الشَّبَكَةِ.

The hacker who tried to breach network security was identified.

security monitoring

مُراقَبةٌ أمْنِيَّةٌ

تَمَّ تَفْعيلُ المُراقَبةِ الأمْنِيَّةِ المُشَدَّدَةِ عَلى شَبَكاتِ القُوّاتِ المُسَلَّحَةِ.

Enhanced security monitoring was activated on the armed forces' networks.

internet surveillance

مُراقَبةُ الإنْتَرْنِتْ

يُراقِبُ الجَيْشُ الإنْتَرْنِتْ لِلتَّنَبُّؤِ بِأيِّ هَجَماتٍ مُحْتَمَلَةٍ.

The army is monitoring the internet to anticipate any potential attacks.

data center

مَرْكَزُ بَياناتٍ • مَراكِزُ

تَمَّ تَحْديثُ مَرْكَزِ البَياناتِ لِتَحْسينِ الأَمْنِ السَّيْبَرانِيِّ.

The data center was updated to improve cybersecurity.

fake

مُزَيَّفٌ

تَمَّ التَّحْذيرُ مِنْ مَواقِعِ إِنْتَرْنِتْ مُزَيَّفَةٍ تَسْتَهْدِفُ جَمْعَ المَعْلوماتِ الحَسّاسَةِ.

Warnings were issued about fake websites targeting the collection of sensitive information.

encrypted

مُشَفَّرٌ

تَأَكَّدْ مِنْ أَنَّ جَميعَ البَياناتِ مُشَفَّرَةً قَبْلَ الإِرْسالِ.

Make sure all data is encrypted before sending.

vulnerable, at risk

مُعَرَّضٌ لِلْخَطَرِ

إِنَّ الشَّبَكَةَ الحُكومِيَّةَ مُعَرَّضَةٌ لِلْخَطَرِ بِسَبَبِ ثَغَراتٍ أَمْنِيَّةٍ.

The government network is at risk due to security vulnerabilities.

classified information

مَعْلوماتٌ سِرِّيَّةٌ   *pl.*

تَمَّ تَسْريبُ مَعْلوماتٍ سِرِّيَّةٍ تَتَعَلَّقُ بِالأَمْنِ الوَطَنِيِّ.

Classified information related to national security was leaked.

counter-espionage

مُكافَحَةُ التَّجَسُّسِ

أَعْلَنَتِ الحُكومَةُ عَنْ إِجْراءاتٍ جَديدَةٍ لِمُكافَحَةِ التَّجَسُّسِ الإِلِكْترونِيِّ.

The government announced new measures for counter-espionage.

exposed

مَكْشوفٌ

لا تَتْرُكْ أَيَّ نِقاطٍ مَكْشوفَةٍ في النِّظامِ الأَمْنِيِّ.

Do not leave any exposed points in the security system.

security system

نِظامُ أَمانٍ • نُظُمٌ / أَنْظِمَةٌ

تَمَّ تَطْوِيرُ نِظامِ أَمانٍ جَدِيدٍ لِحِمايَةِ البِنْيَةِ التَّحْتِيَّةِ.

A new security system was developed to protect the infrastructure.

operating system

نِظامُ تَشْغِيلٍ

تَمَّ اكْتِشافُ ثَغْرَةٍ أَمْنِيَّةٍ في نِظامِ التَّشْغِيلِ المُسْتَخْدَمِ في الوِزاراتِ.

A security vulnerability was discovered in the operating system used in ministries.

information system

نِظامُ مَعْلوماتٍ

يَتَعَيَّنُ تَحْدِيثُ نِظامِ المَعْلوماتِ لِتَحْسِينِ الأَمانِ.

The information system needs to be updated to improve security.

cyber-attack

هُجومٌ إِلِكْتِرونِيٌّ = هُجومٌ سَيْبَرانِيٌّ

تَعَرَّضَتِ الشَّبَكَةُ العَسْكَرِيَّةُ لِهُجومٍ سَيْبَرانِيٍّ مُعَقَّدٍ.

The military network was subjected to a sophisticated cyber-attack.

technological attack

هُجومٌ تِكْنولوجِيٌّ

نَجَحَتِ الأَجْهِزَةُ الأَمْنِيَّةُ في التَّصَدِّي لِهُجومٍ تِكْنولوجِيٍّ مُحْتَمَلٍ.

Security agencies succeeded in thwarting a potential technological attack.

digital identity

هُوِيَّةٌ رَقْمِيَّةٌ

تَمَّ اسْتِخْدامُ هُوِيّاتٍ رَقْمِيَّةٍ مُزَيَّفَةٍ لِاخْتِراقِ النِّظامِ.

Fake digital identities were used to breach the system.

fake identity

هُوِيَّةٌ مُزَيَّفَةٌ

تَمَّ القَبْضُ عَلَى شَخْصٍ يَسْتَخْدِمُ هُوِيَّةً مُزَيَّفَةً لِلدُّخولِ إِلَى المَعْلوماتِ الحُكومِيَّةِ.

A person using a fake identity to access government information was arrested.

تَعَرَّضَ البَنْكُ الوَطَنِيُّ لِهُجومٍ سَيْبَرانِيٍّ ضَخْمٍ أَسْفَرَ عَنِ اخْتِراقِ الحَواسِيبِ وَتَسْرِيبِ مَعْلوماتٍ سِرِّيَّةٍ. اِسْتَخْدَمَ المُخْتَرِقونَ بَرْنامَجًا خَبِيثًا مُتَطَوِّرًا، مِمّا عَرَّضَ نِظامَ أَمانِ البَنْكِ لِلخَطَرِ. وَقَدْ قامَتْ فِرَقُ الأَمْنِ السَّيْبَرانِيِّ بِتَفْعيلِ جِدارِ الحِمايَةِ وَبَدْءِ التَّحَقُّقِ مِنَ الهُوِيَّةِ لِجَميعِ المُسْتَخْدِمينَ.

The National Bank was subjected to a massive cyber-attack resulting in a computer breach and the leak of confidential information. The hackers used an advanced malicious software, compromising the bank's security system. Cybersecurity teams activated firewalls and began verifying the identity of all users.

كَشَفَتِ اسْتِخْباراتُ الدَّوْلَةِ عَنْ حَمْلَةِ تَجَسُّسٍ إِلِكْترونِيٍّ واسِعَةٍ تَسْتَهْدِفُ عِدَّةَ شَرِكاتٍ رَئيسِيَّةٍ في البِلادِ. يُشْتَبَهُ أَنَّ جِهَةً أَجْنَبِيَّةً وَراءَ هَذِهِ الحَمْلَةِ حَيْثُ تَمَّ اسْتِخْدامُ فَيْروسِ حِصانِ طَرْوادَةَ لِجَمْعِ مَعْلوماتٍ اسْتِخْباراتِيَّةٍ. تُعْتَبَرُ هَذِهِ الحَمْلَةُ جُزْءًا مِنِ اسْتِراتيجِيَّةِ مَعْلوماتٍ دَوْلِيَّةٍ لِرَصْدِ الشَّرِكاتِ وَسَرِقَةِ بَياناتِها.

State intelligence revealed a widespread electronic espionage campaign targeting several major companies in the country. A foreign entity is suspected behind this campaign, having used a Trojan horse virus to gather intelligence. This campaign is considered part of an international information strategy to monitor companies and steal their data.

أَطْلَقَتْ شَرِكَةُ تِكْنولوجيا رائِدَةٌ نِظامَ أَمانٍ جَديدٍ صُمِّمَ خِصِّيصًا لِمُكافَحَةِ التَّجَسُّسِ الإِلِكْترونِيِّ. يَتَمَيَّزُ هَذا النِّظامُ بِقُدْرَتِهِ عَلى فَكِّ التَّشْفيرِ وَكَشْفِ الهُوِيّاتِ المُزَيَّفَةِ الَّتي تُحاوِلُ الوُصولَ إِلى الشَّبَكاتِ. كَما يَحْتَوي عَلى سِياسَةٍ مُتَقَدِّمَةٍ لِأَمانِ الشَّبَكَةِ لِكَيْ يَضْمَنَ حِمايَةَ البَياناتِ مِنْ أَيِّ هُجومٍ تِكْنولوجِيٍّ.

A leading technology company launched a new security system specifically designed to combat electronic espionage. This system is known for its ability to decrypt and detect fake identities attempting to access networks. It also features an advanced network security policy to protect data from any technological attack.

تَعَرَّضَتِ البِنْيَةُ التَّحْتِيَّةُ لِلدَّوْلَةِ لِهُجومٍ إِلِكْترونِيٍّ واسِعِ النِّطاقِ مِنْ جِهَةٍ مَجْهولَةٍ، يُعْتَقَدُ أَنَّها دَوْلَةٌ مُعادِيَةٌ. اِسْتَهْدَفَ الهُجومُ النِّظامَ المَعْلوماتِيَّ لِشَبَكَةِ الكَهْرَباءِ وَالمِياهِ، مِمّا أَثَّرَ عَلى تَوْفيرِ الخِدْماتِ لِلمُواطِنينَ. أَشارَ خُبَراءُ الأَمْنِ السَّيْبَرانِيِّ إِلى اسْتِخْدامِ أَسْلِحَةٍ إِلِكْترونِيَّةٍ مُتَطَوِّرَةٍ في الهُجومِ، وَقَدْ بَدَأَتِ الأَجْهِزَةُ المَعْنِيَّةُ بِرَصْدِ المُخْتَرِقينَ.

The state's infrastructure was subjected to a widespread cyber-attack by an unknown entity, believed to be a hostile country. The attack targeted the information system of the electricity and water network, affecting the provision of services to citizens. Cybersecurity experts pointed to the use of advanced electronic weapons in the attack, and relevant agencies began tracking the infiltrators.

أَفادَتْ مَصادِرُ اسْتِخْباراتِيَّةٌ بِأَنَّ وَكالاتٍ أَجْنَبِيَّةً قامَتْ بِشَنِّ حَمَلاتِ تَصَيُّدٍ إِلِكْترونيٍّ لِلْحُصولِ عَلى مَعْلوماتٍ اسْتِخْباراتِيَّةٍ حَسّاسَةٍ خِلالَ فَتْرَةِ النِّزاعِ. دَعَتِ الحُكومَةُ المُواطِنينَ وَالمُؤَسَّساتِ إلى تَوَخّي الحَذَرِ، وَعَدَمِ فَتْحِ أَيِّ رَسائِلَ بَريدِيَّةٍ مَشْبوهَةٍ، وَالتَّحَقُّقِ مِنَ الهُوِيَّةِ قَبْلَ مُشارَكَةِ أَيِّ مَعْلوماتٍ.

Intelligence sources reported that foreign agencies launched electronic phishing campaigns to obtain sensitive intelligence information during the conflict period. The government urged citizens and institutions to exercise caution, avoid opening any suspicious emails, and verify identity before sharing any information.

في ظِلِّ التَّصاعُدِ الحادِّ في الهَجَماتِ السّيبَرانِيَّةِ مِنْ قِبَلِ دُوَلٍ مُعادِيَةٍ، أَعْلَنَتْ وَزارَةُ الدِّفاعِ عَنْ إِطْلاقِ جِدارِ حِمايَةٍ جَديدٍ مُصَمَّمٍ خِصّيصًا لِصَدِّها. يَتَمَيَّزُ هَذا الجِدارُ بِقُدْرَتِهِ عَلى رَصْدِ وَمُكافَحَةِ أَيِّ تَجَسُّسٍ إِلِكْترونيٍّ أَوْ هَجَماتٍ مِنْ قُوىً خارِجِيَّةٍ تَسْتَهْدِفُ البِلادَ خِلالَ الحَرْبِ.

Amid the sharp escalation in cyber-attacks by hostile countries, the Defense Ministry announced the launch of a new firewall specifically designed to counteract them. This firewall is known for its ability to detect and combat any electronic espionage or attacks from external forces targeting the country during the war.

7.2.2.2 Historical Account: Russian Cyber Attack on US Elections

Track **19**

الهُجومُ السّيبَرانِيُّ الرّوسيُّ عَلى الاِنْتِخاباتِ الأَمْريكِيَّةِ

في السَّنَواتِ الأَخيرَةِ، كَشَفَتْ تَقاريرُ اسْتِخْباراتِيَّةٌ أَمْريكِيَّةٌ عَنْ تَدَخُّلٍ روسيٍّ مُحْتَمَلٍ في الاِنْتِخاباتِ الرِّئاسِيَّةِ الأَمْريكِيَّةِ عَبْرَ هَجَماتٍ سيبَرانِيَّةٍ. زَعَمَتْ هَذِهِ التَّقاريرُ أَنَّ مَجْموعاتٍ مِنَ المُخْتَرِقينَ الرّوسِ قَدِ اسْتَهْدَفَتْ نُظُمَ المَعْلوماتِ لِعِدَّةِ وِلاياتٍ أَمْريكِيَّةٍ.

اِسْتَخْدَمَ المُخْتَرِقونَ تِقْنِيّاتٍ مُتَقَدِّمَةً لِلتَّجَسُّسِ الإِلِكْترونيِّ، تَشْمَلُ بَرامِجَ خَبيثَةً وَهَجَماتِ تَصَيُّدٍ إِلِكْترونيٍّ لِلْحُصولِ عَلى مَعْلوماتٍ سِرِّيَّةٍ. كانَ هَدَفُهُمُ الرَّئيسيُّ هُوَ التَّأْثيرُ عَلى نَتائِجِ الاِنْتِخاباتِ وَزَعْزَعَةُ الثِّقَةِ في النِّظامِ الدّيمُقْراطِيِّ الأَمْريكيِّ.

رَدًّا عَلى ذَلِكَ، قامَتِ الوِلاياتُ المُتَّحِدَةُ بِتَعْزيزِ أَمْنِها السّيبَرانيِّ، مَعَ تَطْبيقِ سِياسَةٍ أَكْثَرَ صَرامَةً لِأَمانِ الشَّبَكَةِ وَتَأْسيسِ وَحَداتٍ خاصَّةٍ لِمُكافَحَةِ التَّجَسُّسِ الإِلِكْترونيِّ. أَثارَتْ هَذِهِ الأَحْداثُ تَوَتُّرًا دِبلوماسِيًّا بَيْنَ الوِلاياتِ المُتَّحِدَةِ وَروسْيا، مَعَ مُطالَباتٍ بِفَرْضِ عُقوباتٍ عَلى موسْكو.

يُظْهِرُ هَذا الحادِثُ تَزايُدَ التَّهْديداتِ السّيبَرانِيَّةِ وَالحاجَةَ المُلِحَّةَ لِنِظامِ أَمانٍ قَوِيٍّ يُمْكِنُهُ مُواجَهَةُ التَّحَدِّياتِ الرَّقْمِيَّةِ في العَصْرِ الحَديثِ.

Russian Cyber Attack on US Elections

In recent years, US intelligence reports have revealed potential Russian interference in the US presidential elections through cyber attacks. These reports alleged that groups of Russian hackers targeted the information systems of several US states.

The hackers employed advanced techniques for electronic espionage, including malicious software and phishing attacks to obtain confidential information. Their primary goal was to influence election outcomes and undermine trust in the American democratic system.

In response, the United States bolstered its cybersecurity, implementing a stricter network security policy and establishing special units to counter electronic espionage. These events sparked diplomatic tensions between the US and Russia, with calls to impose sanctions on Moscow.

This incident highlights the growing cyber threats and the urgent need for a robust security system capable of addressing digital challenges in the modern era.

7.2.3 Special Operations

Track **20**

to hide (as in concealment of activities)

إِخْفَاءٌ • أَخْفَى

أَخْفَتِ القُوّاتُ الخاصَّةُ مُعَدّاتِها فِي مَكانٍ سِرّيٍّ قَبْلَ العَمَلِيَّةِ.

The special forces hid their equipment in a secret location before the operation.

to use propaganda

اِسْتِخْدامٌ • اِسْتَخْدَمَ دِعايَةً

اِسْتَخْدَمَتِ الجَماعَةُ المُتَطَرِّفَةُ الدِّعايَةَ لِاكْتِسابِ مَزيدٍ مِنَ الدَّعْمِ.

The extremist group used propaganda to gain more support.

strategic

اِسْتِراتيجِيٌّ

تَمَّ وَضْعُ خُطَّةٍ اِسْتِراتيجِيَّةٍ لِمُكافَحَةِ الإِرْهابِ.

A strategic plan was developed to combat terrorism.

to spy

تَجَسُّسٌ • تَجَسَّسَ

تَجَسَّسَ العَميلُ عَلَى اِجْتِماعاتِ القادَةِ لِجَمْعِ مَعْلوماتٍ حَسّاسَةٍ.

The agent spied on the leaders' meetings to gather sensitive information.

espionage تَجَسُّس

كانَتْ مُهِمَّةُ التَّجَسُّسِ ناجِحَةً وَأَفْضَتْ إلى جَمْعِ مَعْلوماتٍ قَيِّمَةٍ.

The espionage mission was successful and led to the gathering of valuable information.

sabotage تَخْريب

قامَتِ القُوَّاتُ الخاصَّةُ بِتَخْريبِ مَرافِقِ العَدُوِّ.

The special forces sabotaged enemy facilities.

mobilization تَعْبِئَة

أَعْلَنَتِ الحُكومَةُ تَعْبِئَةَ القُوَّاتِ اسْتِعْدادًا لِلْأَزْمَةِ القادِمَةِ.

The government announced the mobilization of forces in preparation for the upcoming crisis.

terror tactics تَكْتيكاتُ الإرْهاب

دَرَسَ الجَيْشُ تَكْتيكاتِ الإرْهابِ لِمُواجَهَتِها بِفَعاليَّةٍ.

The army studied terrorist tactics to effectively counter them.

tactical تَكْتيكِيّ

كانَتِ المُناوَرَةُ التَّكْتيكيَّةُ مِفْتاحًا لِنَجاحِ العَمَليَّةِ.

The tactical maneuver was key to the success of the operation.

to rebel تَمَرَّدَ • تَمَرُّد

تَمَرَّدَتِ الوَحْداتُ المَحَلّيَّةُ ضِدَّ القُوَّاتِ المُحْتَلَّةِ.

The local units rebelled against the occupying forces.

insurgency, rebellion تَمَرُّد

اِنْدَلَعَ تَمَرُّدٌ في المِنْطَقَةِ الجَنوبيَّةِ، مِمّا اسْتَدْعى تَدَخُّلَ القُوَّاتِ الخاصَّةِ.

A rebellion broke out in the southern region, prompting the intervention of special forces.

spy   جَوَاسِيسُ •   جَاسُوسٌ

تَمَّ القَبْضُ عَلَى جَاسُوسٍ يُحَاوِلُ اخْتِرَاقَ الشَّبَكَةِ الأَمْنِيَّةِ.

A spy was caught trying to infiltrate the security network.

war crime   جَرَائِمُ •   جَرِيمَةُ حَرْبٍ

وُجِّهَتِ اتِّهَامَاتٌ بِجَرَائِمِ حَرْبٍ ضِدَّ قَادَةِ العَمَلِيَّاتِ.

War crime charges were leveled against the operation leaders.

civilian warfare   حُرُوبٌ •   حَرْبُ المَدَنِيِّينَ

أَسْفَرَتْ حَرْبُ المَدَنِيِّينَ عَنْ تَحَدِّيَاتٍ كَبِيرَةٍ لِلْقُوَّاتِ الخَاصَّةِ.

Civilian warfare posed significant challenges for special forces.

shadow war   حَرْبُ ظِلٍّ

تُعْتَبَرُ حَرْبُ الظِّلِّ مِنْ أَصْعَبِ أَنْوَاعِ النِّزَاعَاتِ الَّتِي تُوَاجِهُ القُوَّاتِ الخَاصَّةَ.

Shadow warfare is considered one of the most difficult types of conflicts that special forces face.

guerrilla warfare   حَرْبُ عِصَابَاتٍ

أَجْبَرَتْ حَرْبُ العِصَابَاتِ القُوَّاتِ عَلَى تَغْيِيرِ تَكْتِيكَاتِها.

Guerrilla warfare forced the forces to change their tactics.

unconventional warfare   حَرْبٌ غَيْرُ تَقْلِيدِيَّةٍ

اسْتَخْدَمَتِ القُوَّاتُ الخَاصَّةُ وَسَائِلَ حَرْبٍ غَيْرَ تَقْلِيدِيَّةٍ لِمُكَافَحَةِ المُتَمَرِّدِينَ.

The special forces used unconventional warfare methods to fight the rebels.

psychological warfare   حَرْبٌ نَفْسِيَّةٌ

اسْتَخْدَمَ العَدُوُّ الحَرْبَ النَّفْسِيَّةَ لِإِضْعَافِ مَعْنَوِيَّاتِ الجُنُودِ.

The enemy used psychological warfare to weaken the soldiers' morale.

to sabotage

خَرَّب • تَخْرِيب

خَرَّبَ المُتَمَرِّدونَ البِنْيَةَ التَّحْتِيَّةَ لِلْمَدِينَةِ.

The rebels sabotaged the city's infrastructure.

propaganda

دِعايَةٌ

اُسْتُخْدِمَتِ الدِّعايَةُ لِنَشْرِ أَخْبارٍ مُضَلِّلَةٍ حَوْلَ العَمَلِيَّةِ الخاصَّةِ.

Propaganda was used to spread misleading news about the special operation.

secret

سِرِّيٌّ

تَمَّتِ العَمَلِيَّةُ بِطَرِيقَةٍ سِرِّيَّةٍ لِضَمانِ نَجاحِها.

The operation was conducted secretly to ensure its success.

economic sanctions

عُقوباتٌ اقْتِصادِيَّةٌ   *pl.*

فَرَضَتِ الدَّوْلَةُ عُقوباتٍ اقْتِصادِيَّةً عَلى الجَماعاتِ المُتَطَرِّفَةِ.

The state imposed economic sanctions on extremist groups.

covert operation

عَمَلِيَّةٌ تَخْرِيبِيَّةٌ

نَفَّذَتِ القُوّاتُ عَمَلِيَّةً تَخْرِيبِيَّةً ضِدَّ مُعَسْكَرِ العَدُوِّ.

The forces carried out a sabotage operation against the enemy camp.

special operation

عَمَلِيَّةٌ خاصَّةٌ

تَمَّ تَنْفِيذُ عَمَلِيَّةٍ خاصَّةٍ لِإنْقاذِ الرَّهائِنِ.

A special operation was executed to rescue the hostages.

black ops

عَمَلِيَّةٌ في الخَفاءِ

تَمَّتْ عَمَلِيَّةٌ في الخَفاءِ لاعْتِقالِ الجاسوسِ.

An undercover operation was carried out to arrest the spy.

psyop (psychological operation)

عَمَلِيَّةٌ نَفْسِيَّةٌ

أُسْتُخْدِمَتِ العَمَلِيَّاتُ النَّفْسِيَّةُ لِزِيادَةِ الضَّغْطِ عَلَى العَدُوِّ.

Psychological operations were used to increase pressure on the enemy.

agent

عُمَلاءُ •

عَمِيلٌ

تَمَّ القَبْضُ عَلَى عَمِيلٍ كانَ يَجْمَعُ مَعْلوماتٍ اسْتِخْباراتِيَّةً.

An agent who was gathering intelligence information was caught.

illegal

غَيْرُ قانونيٍّ

كانَ التَّجْنيدُ في الميليشيا غَيْرَ قانونيٍّ.

Recruitment into the militia was illegal.

rule of engagement

قَواعِدُ •

قاعِدَةُ اشْتِباكٍ

تَمَّ تَحْديدُ قَواعِدِ الاشْتِباكِ قَبْلَ بَدْءِ العَمَلِيَّةِ.

The rules of engagement were set before the operation started.

special forces

pl.

قُوّاتٌ خاصَّةٌ

شارَكَتْ قُوّاتٌ خاصَّةٌ في عَمَلِيَّةِ مُكافَحَةِ التَّمَرُّدِ.

Special forces participated in a counter-insurgency operation.

insurgent, rebel

مُتَمَرِّدٌ

تَمَّ القَبْضُ عَلَى المُتَمَرِّدِ الَّذي خَطَّطَ لِلْهُجومِ.

The rebel who planned the attack was captured.

hidden

مَخْفِيٌّ

كانَتِ الأَسْلِحَةُ مَخْفِيَّةً داخِلَ المَخْزَنِ.

The weapons were hidden inside the warehouse.

civilian

مَدَنِيٌّ

أُصِيبَ مَدَنِيّونَ خِلالَ العَمَلِيَّةِ العَسْكَرِيَّةِ.

Civilians were injured during the military operation.

battle of minds

مَعارِكُ • مَعْرَكَةُ عُقولٍ

كانَتْ مَعْرَكَةُ العُقولِ جُزْءًا كَبيرًا مِنَ الحَرْبِ النَّفْسِيَّةِ.

The battle of minds was a major part of psychological warfare.

guerrilla fighter

مُقاتِلُ عِصاباتٍ

تَمَّ تَدْريبُ مُقاتِلي العِصاباتِ في مُعَسْكَراتٍ سِرِّيَّةٍ.

Guerrilla fighters were trained in secret camps.

counter-insurgency

مُكافَحَةُ التَّمَرُّدِ

بَدَأَتْ عَمَلِيّاتُ مُكافَحَةِ التَّمَرُّدِ لِاسْتِعادَةِ الأَمْنِ.

Counter-insurgency operations began to restore security.

militia

ميليشيا

قامَتِ الميليشْيا بِالْهُجومِ عَلى القُرى المَحَلِّيَّةِ.

The militia attacked local villages.

to escape

هُروبٌ • هَرَبَ

هَرَبَ الجاسوسُ عِنْدَما اكْتُشِفَتْ هُوِيَّتُهُ.

The spy escaped when his identity was discovered.

to smuggle

تَهْريبٌ • هَرَّبَ

هَرَّبَ المُتَمَرِّدونَ الأَسْلِحَةَ عَبْرَ الحُدودِ بِطَريقَةٍ سِرِّيَّةٍ.

The rebels smuggled weapons across the border covertly.

بِتَمْوِيلٍ سِرِّيٍّ، نَفَّذَتِ القُوَّاتُ الخَاصَّةُ لَيْلَةَ أَمْسِ عَمَلِيَّةً في الخَفَاءِ بِالعَاصِمَةِ لاسْتِهْدَافِ مُتَمَرِّدٍ كَانَ يُخَطِّطُ لِتَنْفِيذِ هَجَمَاتٍ تَخْرِيبِيَّةٍ. اسْتَخْدَمَتِ الوَحْدَةُ تَكْتِيكَاتٍ مُبْتَكَرَةً لِضَمَانِ نَجَاحِ العَمَلِيَّةِ دُونَ التَّأْثِيرِ عَلَى المَدَنِيِّينَ. تَمَّ تَأْكِيدُ النَّجَاحِ بِشَكْلٍ سِرِّيٍّ، مَعَ تَجَنُّبِ اسْتِخْدَامِ أَيِّ دِعَايَةٍ حَوْلَ الحَادِثِ.

Funded secretly, the special forces executed a covert operation last night in the capital to target a rebel planning sabotage attacks. The unit employed innovative tactics to ensure the operation's success without affecting civilians. The success was confirmed discreetly, avoiding any publicity about the incident.

كَشَفَتِ المُخَابَرَاتُ الوَطَنِيَّةُ عَنْ جَاسُوسٍ كَانَ يَعْمَلُ دَاخِلَ وَزَارَةِ الدِّفَاعِ، وَكَانَ قَدْ أَخْفَى هُوِيَّتَهُ لِسَنَوَاتٍ. كَانَ الجَاسُوسُ يَجْمَعُ المَعْلُومَاتِ وَيُهَرِّبُهَا إلى دَوْلَةٍ مُجَاوِرَةٍ. تَمَّ اتِّخَاذُ العُقُوبَاتِ القَانُونِيَّةِ ضِدَّهُ، وَأُعْلِنَتْ تَعْبِئَةُ جَمِيعِ الأَجْهِزَةِ الأَمْنِيَّةِ لِضَمَانِ أَلَّا يَتِمَّ تَكْرَارُ مِثْلِ هَذِهِ الحَوَادِثِ في المُسْتَقْبَلِ.

National intelligence uncovered a spy working within the Defense Ministry, who had concealed his identity for years. The spy was collecting information and smuggling it to a neighboring country. Legal sanctions were taken against him, and all security agencies were mobilized to ensure such incidents don't recur in the future.

في مِنْطَقَةِ الحُدُودِ، انْدَلَعَتْ مُوَاجَهَاتٌ بَيْنَ مِيلِيشِيَا مَحَلِّيَّةٍ وَقُوَّاتٍ خَاصَّةٍ مِنَ الجَيْشِ الوَطَنِيِّ. كَانَتِ المِيلِيشِيَا تَسْتَخْدِمُ تَكْتِيكَاتِ الإِرْهَابِ وَالحَرْبَ النَّفْسِيَّةَ لِزَعْزَعَةِ اسْتِقْرَارِ المِنْطَقَةِ. تَمَرْكَزَتِ القُوَّاتُ الخَاصَّةُ اسْتِرَاتِيجِيًّا وَاسْتَخْدَمَتْ تَكْتِيكَاتِ مُكَافَحَةِ التَّمَرُّدِ لِدَحْرِ المُتَمَرِّدِينَ وَاسْتِعَادَةِ السَّيْطَرَةِ.

In the border area, clashes erupted between a local militia and special forces of the national army. The militia employed terrorist tactics and psychological warfare to destabilize the region. The special forces strategically positioned themselves and used counter-insurgency tactics to repel the rebels and regain control.

أَكَّدَتْ مَصَادِرُ حُكُومِيَّةٌ أَنَّ هُنَاكَ عَمَلِيَّةً تَخْرِيبِيَّةً تَمَّتْ ضِدَّ مَرْكَزِ المَعْلُومَاتِ الاسْتِخْبَارِيَّةِ الرَّئِيسِيِّ. وَقَدْ خَرَّبَ المُتَمَرِّدُونَ أَجْهِزَةَ الاتِّصَالِ وَاسْتَخْدَمُوا الدِّعَايَةَ لِزَعْزَعَةِ الثِّقَةِ في الأَجْهِزَةِ الأَمْنِيَّةِ. وَمَعَ ذَلِكَ، تَمَكَّنَتِ القُوَّاتُ الخَاصَّةُ مِنَ التَّدَخُّلِ بِسُرْعَةٍ وَإِحْبَاطِ الهُجُومِ، وَتَمَّ القَبْضُ عَلَى المُشْتَبَهِ بِهِمْ.

Government sources confirmed that a sabotage operation was carried out against the main intelligence information center. Rebels damaged communication devices and used propaganda to undermine trust in the security agencies. However, special forces were able to intervene quickly and thwart the attack, arresting the suspects.

في عَمَلِيَّةٍ نَفْسِيَّةٍ مَدْروسَةٍ، أُلْقِيَ القَبْضُ عَلى جاسوسٍ كانَ يَعْمَلُ ضِمْنَ تَجَمُّعٍ اسْتِراتيجِيٍّ لِلدَّوْلَةِ. اُسْتُخْدِمَ عَميلٌ سِرِّيٌّ لِكَشْفِ هُوِيَّتِهِ وَجَمْعِ المَعْلوماتِ. بِفَضْلِ مَعْرَكَةِ العُقولِ الَّتي خاضَتْها وَحَداتُ الاسْتِخْباراتِ، تَمَكَّنَتْ مِنْ فَكِّ شَفَراتِ الاتِّصالِ المُسْتَخْدَمَةِ مِنْ قِبَلِ الجاسوسِ وَكَشْفِ نَواياهُ.

In a calculated psychological operation, a spy working within a strategic state assembly was apprehended. A covert agent was used to reveal his identity and gather information. Thanks to the intellectual battle waged by intelligence units, they managed to decipher the communication codes used by the spy and expose his intentions.

أَطْلَقَتْ وَزارَةُ الدِّفاعِ بَرْنامَجَ تَدْريبٍ جَديدٍ مُخَصَّصٍ لِقُوّاتِ العَمَلِيّاتِ الخاصَّةِ لِلتَّعامُلِ مَعَ حُروبِ العِصاباتِ وَالحُروبِ غَيْرِ التَّقْليدِيَّةِ. يَهْدُفُ هَذا التَّدْريبُ إلى تَحْسينِ الاسْتِجابَةِ لِلتَّهْديداتِ الحَديثَةِ وَتَطْويرِ تَكْتيكاتٍ جَديدَةٍ لِمُواجَهَةِ الأَعْداءِ الَّذينَ يَعْتَمِدونَ عَلى تَكْتيكاتِ الإرْهابِ وَالتَّمَرُّدِ.

The Defense Ministry launched a new training program dedicated to special operations forces to deal with guerrilla warfare and unconventional warfare. This training aims to improve responses to modern threats and develop new tactics to confront enemies who rely on terrorist and insurgent tactics.

7.3 Defense and Security

7.3.1 Military Strategies

Track **22**

to occupy — إِحْتَلَّ • اِحْتِلالٌ

اِحْتَلَّ الجَيْشُ المَدينَةَ بَعْدَ مَعْرَكَةٍ طَويلَةٍ.

The army occupied the city after a long battle.

strategic — اِسْتِراتيجِيٌّ

وَضَعَ القائِدُ الاسْتِراتيجِيُّ خُطَّةً لِلهُجومِ.

The strategic commander devised a plan for the attack.

strategy — اِسْتِراتيجِيَّةٌ

تَمَّ تَطْويرُ اسْتِراتيجِيَّةٍ جَديدَةٍ لِمُواجَهَةِ العَدُوِّ.

A new strategy was developed to confront the enemy.

attrition strategy

اِسْتِراتيجِيَّةُ الاسْتِنْزافِ

أُسْتُخْدِمَتِ اسْتِراتيجِيَّةُ الاسْتِنْزافِ لإضعافِ العَدُوِّ عَلى المَدى الطَّويلِ.

The strategy of attrition was used to weaken the enemy over the long term.

deterrence strategy

اِسْتِراتيجِيَّةُ الرَّدْعِ

تَمَّ تَنْفيذُ اسْتِراتيجِيَّةِ الرَّدْعِ لِمَنْعِ هَجَماتٍ مُحْتَمَلَةٍ.

The deterrence strategy was executed to prevent potential attacks.

military strategy

اِسْتِراتيجِيَّةٌ عَسْكَرِيَّةٌ

الاِسْتِراتيجِيَّةُ العَسْكَرِيَّةُ تَتَضَمَّنُ مَجموعَةً مِنَ التَّكْتيكاتِ المُتَقَدِّمَةِ.

The military strategy includes a set of advanced tactics.

to rest

اِسْتِراحَةٌ •

اِسْتَراحَ

اِسْتَراحَ الجُنودُ بَعْدَ العَمَلِيَّةِ النّاجِحَةِ.

The soldiers rested after the successful operation.

to surrender

اِسْتِسْلامٌ •

اِسْتَسْلَمَ

اِسْتَسْلَمَتِ المَدينَةُ المُحاصَرَةُ دونَ قِتالٍ.

The besieged city surrendered without fighting.

to scout, reconnoiter

اِسْتِطْلاعٌ •

اِسْتَطْلَعَ

اِسْتَطْلَعَ الجُنودُ المِنْطَقَةَ قَبْلَ الهُجومِ.

The soldiers reconnoitered the area before the attack.

to recapture

اِسْتِعادَةٌ •

اِسْتَعادَ

اِسْتَعادَ الجَيْشُ السَّيْطَرَةَ عَلى القاعِدَةِ المَفْقودَةِ.

The army regained control over the lost base.

to attrit • اِسْتِنْزاف اِسْتَنْزَفَ

اِسْتَنْزَفَ العَدُوُّ مَوارِدَنا عَبْرَ هَجَماتٍ مُتَكَرِّرَةٍ.

The enemy drained our resources through repeated attacks.

to invade • اِقْتِحامٌ اِقْتَحَمَ

اِقْتَحَمَ الجَيْشُ الغازي الحُدودَ وَسَيْطَرَ عَلى عِدَّةِ مُدُنٍ.

The invading army breached the borders and took control of several cities.

withdrawal اِنْسِحابٌ

أَمَرَ القائِدُ بِانْسِحابِ القُوّاتِ لِتَجَنُّبِ مَزيدٍ مِنَ الخَسائِرِ.

The commander ordered a withdrawal of the troops to avoid further losses.

to withdraw • اِنْسِحابٌ اِنْسَحَبَ

اِنْسَحَبَ الجَيْشُ مِنَ المَدينَةِ بَعْدَ عَمَلِيَّةٍ دِفاعِيَّةٍ فاشِلَةٍ.

The army withdrew from the city after a failed defensive operation.

to ally • تَحالُفٌ تَحالَفَ

تَحالَفَتِ الدَّوْلَتانِ لِمُواجَهَةِ التَّهْديداتِ الإِقْليمِيَّةِ.

The two countries formed an alliance to face regional threats.

military alliance تَحالُفٌ عَسْكَرِيٌّ

دَخَلَتِ الدَّوْلَتانِ في تَحالُفٍ عَسْكَرِيٍّ لِتَعْزيزِ الأَمْنِ الإِقْليمِيِّ.

The two countries entered into a military alliance to bolster regional security.

to control (as in controlling an area) • تَحَكُّمٌ تَحَكَّمَ

تَحَكَّمَ الجَيْشُ في المِنْطَقَةِ بَعْدَ أَيّامٍ مِنَ القِتالِ الشَّرِسِ.

The army gained control of the area after days of intense fighting.

strategic analysis

تَحْليلٌ اسْتِراتيجِيٌّ

أَجْرى الخُبَراءُ تَحْليلًا اسْتِراتيجِيًّا لِلْوَضْعِ الحالِيِّ.

The experts conducted a strategic analysis of the current situation.

to train

تَدَرَّبَ • تَدَرَّبُ

تَدَرَّبَ الجُنودُ عَلى عَمَليّاتِ الهُجومِ وَالدِّفاعِ.

The soldiers trained in both offensive and defensive operations.

training

تَدْريبٌ

يُعْتَبَرُ التَّدْريبُ العَسْكَرِيُّ جُزْءًا أساسِيًّا مِنَ الاسْتِعْدادِ لِلْحُروبِ.

Military training is considered a fundamental part of war preparedness.

to advance

تَقَدَّمَ • تَقَدَّمُ

تَقَدَّمَ الجَيْشُ بِبُطْءٍ لِاسْتِعادَةِ الأراضي.

The army slowly advanced to reclaim the land.

risk assessment

تَقْييمٌ مَخاطِرَ

تَمَّ إجْراءُ تَقْييمِ مَخاطِرَ لِتَحْديدِ الأماكِنِ المُحْتَمَلِ اسْتِهْدافُها.

A risk assessment was conducted to identify potential target locations.

tactic

تَكْتيكٌ

اُسْتُخْدِمَتْ تَكْتيكاتٌ مُبْتَكَرَةٌ لِلتَّغَلُّبِ عَلى العَدُوِّ.

Innovative tactics were used to overcome the enemy.

tactical

تَكْتيكِيٌّ

تَمَّ تَنْفيذُ عَمَليّةٍ تَكْتيكِيّةٍ لِضَرْبِ مُعَسْكَرِ العَدُوِّ.

A tactical operation was executed to strike the enemy camp.

front (as in a battlefront)

جَبْهَةٌ

تَمَّ تَأْمِينُ الجَبْهَةِ الشَّمالِيَّةِ مِنْ قِبَلِ القُوّاتِ المُسَلَّحَةِ.

The northern front was secured by the armed forces.

siege

حِصارٌ

فَرَضَ الجَيْشُ حِصارًا عَلى المَدينَةِ لِقَطْعِ الإمْداداتِ عَنِ العَدُوِّ.

The army laid siege to the city to cut off enemy supplies.

campaign

حَمْلَةٌ

شَنَّتِ القُوّاتُ حَمْلَةً لِاسْتِعادَةِ المَدينَةِ مِنَ العَدُوِّ.

The forces launched a campaign to retake the city from the enemy.

defense line

خُطوطٌ • خَطُّ دِفاعٍ

تَمَّ تَحْصينُ خَطِّ الدِّفاعِ لِمَنْعِ تَقَدُّمِ العَدُوِّ.

The defense line was fortified to prevent enemy advancement.

to defend

دِفاعٌ / مُدافَعَةٌ • دافَعَ

دافَعَ الجُنودُ بِبَسالَةٍ ضِدَّ الهُجومِ العَدائِيِّ.

The soldiers bravely defended against the hostile attack.

defense

دِفاعٌ

الدِّفاعُ عَنِ الوَطَنِ هُوَ واجِبُ كُلِّ مُواطِنٍ.

Defending the homeland is the duty of every citizen.

defensive

دِفاعِيٌّ

تَمَّ تَنْفيذُ خُطَّةٍ دِفاعِيَّةٍ لِحِمايَةِ المُنْشَآتِ الحَيَوِيَّةِ.

A defensive plan was executed to protect vital facilities.

operation

عَمَلِيَّةٌ

نَجَحَتِ العَمَلِيَّةُ العَسْكَرِيَّةُ في تَحْرِيرِ الرَّهائِنِ.

The military operation succeeded in freeing the hostages.

effective

فَعّالٌ

ثَبَتَ أَنَّ الِاسْتِراتِيجِيَّةَ فَعّالَةٌ في تَقْلِيلِ الخَسائِرِ.

The strategy proved effective in minimizing losses.

military base

• قَواعِدُ   قاعِدَةٌ عَسْكَرِيَّةٌ

تَمَّ بِناءُ قاعِدَةٍ عَسْكَرِيَّةٍ جَدِيدَةٍ لِتَحْسِينِ الأَمْنِ الإِقْلِيمِيِّ.

A new military base was established to improve regional security.

operations base

قاعِدَةُ عَمَلِيَّاتٍ

تَمَّ اخْتِيارُ قاعِدَةِ العَمَلِيَّاتِ بِعِنايَةٍ لِتَنْفِيذِ الهُجومِ.

The operations base was carefully chosen to execute the attack.

occupation forces

قُوّاتُ احْتِلالٍ

اِنْسَحَبَتْ قُوّاتُ الِاحْتِلالِ بَعْدَ اتِّفاقٍ دِبْلوماسِيٍّ.

The occupying forces withdrew after a diplomatic agreement.

coalition force

• قُوّاتٌ / قُوىً / قِوىً   قُوَّةُ تَحالُفٍ

شُكِّلَتْ قُوَّةُ التَّحالُفِ الدَّوْلِيِّ لِلتَّصَدِّي لِلتَّهْدِيداتِ.

The international coalition force was formed to address threats.

joint air power

قُوَّةٌ جَوِّيَّةٌ مُشْتَرَكَةٌ

شارَكَتِ القُوَّةُ الجَوِّيَّةُ المُشْتَرَكَةُ في عَمَلِيّاتِ القَصْفِ.

The joint air force participated in bombing operations.

defense force
قُوَّةُ دِفاعٍ

تَمَّ تَعْزِيزُ قُوَّةِ الدِّفاعِ لِحِمايَةِ الحُدودِ.

The defense force was bolstered to protect the borders.

principle of deterrence
مَبْدَأُ الرَّدْعِ

تَمَّ اسْتِخْدامُ مَبْدَأِ الرَّدْعِ لِمَنْعِ الهَجَماتِ العَدائِيَّةِ.

The principle of deterrence was used to prevent hostile attacks.

superior
مُتَفَوِّقٌ

أَظْهَرَتِ القُوّاتُ أَنَّها مُتَفَوِّقَةٌ عَسْكَرِيًّا عَلى العَدُوِّ.

The forces demonstrated military superiority over the enemy.

axis (as in a military alliance)
مَحاوِرُ •
مِحْوَرٌ

في الحَرْبِ العالَمِيَّةِ الثانِيَةِ، شَكَّلَتْ أَلْمانْيا وَإيطالْيا مِحْوَرًا عَسْكَرِيًّا لِمُواجَهَةِ الحُلَفاءِ.

In World War II, Germany and Italy formed an Axis to confront the Allies.

battle
مَعارِكُ •
مَعْرَكَةٌ

انْدَلَعَتْ مَعْرَكَةٌ شَرِسَةٌ عِنْدَ الحُدودِ الشَّمالِيَّةِ.

A fierce battle broke out at the northern border.

game theory (as in strategizing)
نَظَرِيَّةُ الأَلْعابِ

اُسْتُخْدِمَتْ نَظَرِيَّةُ الأَلْعابِ في التَّخْطيطِ الاِسْتِراتيجِيِّ.

Game theory was used in strategic planning.

to attack
مُهاجَمَةٌ •
هاجَمَ

هاجَمَتِ القُوّاتُ المَواقِعَ المُعادِيَةَ بِنَجاحٍ.

The forces successfully attacked the hostile positions.

attack

هُجومٌ

شَنَّ العَدُوُّ هُجومًا مُفاجِئًا عَلى القاعِدَةِ.

The enemy launched a surprise attack on the base.

offensive

هُجوميٌّ

تَمَّ اعْتِمادُ اسْتِراتيجِيَّةٍ هُجوميَّةٍ لِتَحْقيقِ التَّفَوُّقِ.

An offensive strategy was adopted to achieve superiority.

to strategize

وَضَعَ اسْتِراتيجِيَّة • وَضَعَ

وَضَعَ القادَةُ اسْتِراتيجِيَّةً جَديدَةً لِمُواجَهَةِ الأَزَماتِ.

The leaders devised a new strategy to deal with the crises.

7.3.1.1 Mini-Articles

Track **23**

بِناءً عَلى تَقْييمِ المَخاطِرِ الأَخيرِ، قَرَّرَتْ قُوّاتُ الدِّفاعِ تَبَنّي اسْتِراتيجِيَّةِ الرَّدْعِ لِحِمايَةِ الحُدودِ. دُرِّبَتِ القُوّاتُ عَلى أَحْدَثِ التَّكْتيكاتِ الدِّفاعيَّةِ وَقامَتْ بِتَقْوِيَةِ خَطِّ الدِّفاعِ. تَقومُ القاعِدَةُ العَسْكَرِيَّةُ بِتَنْظيمِ حَمَلاتِ اسْتِطْلاعٍ لِرَصْدِ أَيِّ تَحَرُّكاتٍ عَلى الجَبْهَةِ وَالاسْتِعْدادِ لِأَيِّ هُجومٍ مُحْتَمَلٍ.

Based on the recent risk assessment, the defense forces decided to adopt a deterrence strategy to protect the borders. The forces were trained in the latest defensive tactics and strengthened the defense line. The military base organizes reconnaissance campaigns to monitor any movements on the front and prepare for any potential attack.

بَعْدَ مَعْرَكَةٍ طَويلَةٍ، تَمَكَّنَ التَّحالُفُ العَسْكَرِيُّ مِنَ اسْتِعادَةِ المَدينَةِ مِنْ قُوّاتِ الاحْتِلالِ. تَمَّ تَطْبيقُ اسْتِراتيجِيَّةٍ عَسْكَرِيَّةٍ فَعّالَةٍ تُرَكِّزُ عَلى الهَجَماتِ العُدْوانيَّةِ وَالانْسِحاباتِ السَّريعَةِ، مِمّا أَدّى إلى إرْهاقِ وَاسْتِنْزافِ العَدُوِّ. القُوَّةُ الجَوِّيَّةُ المُشْتَرَكَةُ لَعِبَتْ دَوْرًا حاسِمًا في تَأْمينِ الانْتِصارِ.

After a prolonged battle, the military coalition managed to retake the city from the occupying forces. An effective military strategy focused on offensive attacks and rapid withdrawals was implemented, leading to the fatigue and exhaustion of the enemy. The joint air force played a decisive role in securing the victory.

قامَ خُبَراءُ اسْتِراتيجِيّونَ بِتَقْييمِ وَضْعِ قاعِدَةِ العَمَلِيّاتِ الرَّئيسيَّةِ وَوَضْعِ اسْتِراتيجِيَّةٍ جَديدَةٍ لِتَحْسينِ كَفاءَتِها. بِناءً عَلى نَظَرِيَّةِ الأَلْعابِ، تَمَّ تَحْليلُ مُخْتَلِفِ السّيناريوهاتِ المُحْتَمَلَةِ واقْتِراحُ تَكْتيكاتٍ جَديدَةٍ لِتَحْسينِ الدِّفاعِ والرَّدْعِ.

Strategic experts evaluated the situation of the main operations base and devised a new strategy to enhance its efficiency. Based on game theory, various potential scenarios were analyzed, and new tactics were proposed to improve defense and deterrence.

7.3.1.2 Interview: Military Strategies

Track **24**

مُقابَلَةٌ حَوْلَ اسْتِراتيجِيّاتِ الدِّفاعِ والأَمانِ العَسْكَرِيَّةِ

مُقَدِّمُ البَرْنامَج: مَرْحَبًا بِكُمْ في بَرْنامَجِنا الخاصِّ اليَوْمَ، حَيْثُ نَسْتَضيفُ اللِّواءَ مَحْمود العَزْبِ، الخَبيرَ الاسْتِراتيجِيَّ العَسْكَرِيَّ، لِمُناقَشَةِ التَّحَدِّياتِ والاسْتِراتيجِيّاتِ الحَديثَةِ في مَجالِ الدِّفاعِ والأَمانِ. مَرْحَبًا بِكَ يا سِيادَةَ اللِّواءِ.

اللِّواءُ مَحْمود: شُكْرًا لَكَ. تَشَرَّفْتُ بِالْحُضورِ.

مُقَدِّمُ البَرْنامَج: لِنَبْدَأْ بِالسُّؤالِ الأَوَّلِ: كَيْفَ تَرى أَهَمِّيَّةَ تَطْويرِ اسْتِراتيجِيَّةِ الرَّدْعِ في الوَقْتِ الحالِيِّ؟

اللِّواءُ مَحْمود: إِنَّ اسْتِراتيجِيَّةَ الرَّدْعِ عُنْصُرٌ أَساسِيٌّ في أَيِّ خَطٍّ دِفاعِيٍّ. في زَمَنِ الحُروبِ الحَديثَةِ، يَجِبُ أَنْ نَكونَ مُتَفَوِّقينَ، لَيْسَ فَقَطْ في القُوَّةِ الهُجوميَّةِ، وَلَكِنْ أَيْضًا في قُدْرَتِنا عَلى رَدْعِ أَيِّ هُجومٍ مُحْتَمَلٍ مِنَ العَدُوِّ.

مُقَدِّمُ البَرْنامَج: وَهَلْ تَعْتَقِدُ أَنَّ التَّحالُفاتِ العَسْكَرِيَّةَ تَلْعَبُ دَوْرًا مُهِمًّا في تَحْقيقِ التَّوازُنِ الاسْتِراتيجِيِّ؟

اللِّواءُ مَحْمود: بِالطَّبْعِ، يُمْكِنُ لِتَحالُفٍ عَسْكَرِيٍّ أَنْ يَزيدَ مِنْ قُوَّةِ الرَّدْعِ. عِنْدَما تَتَحالَفُ قُوّاتٌ جَوِّيَّةٌ مُشْتَرَكَةٌ مِنْ عِدَّةِ دُوَلٍ، يُصْبِحُ لَدَيْنا دِفاعٌ أَقْوى، وَيَصْعُبُ عَلى العَدُوِّ اسْتِنْزافُ مَوارِدِنا.

مُقَدِّمُ البَرْنامَج: في ضَوْءِ التَّطَوُّراتِ الحَديثَةِ، كَيْفَ يُمْكِنُ اسْتِخْدامُ التَّحْليلِ الاسْتِراتيجِيِّ لِتَقْوِيَةِ قُوّاتِنا؟

اللِّواءُ مَحْمود: التَّحْليلُ الاسْتِراتيجِيُّ يَمْنَحُنا نَظْرَةً عَميقَةً عَنْ قُوّاتِ العَدُوِّ، واسْتِراتيجِيَّتِهِمْ، وَنِقاطِ ضَعْفِهِمْ. بِالاعْتِمادِ عَلى تَقْييمِ المَخاطِرِ، يُمْكِنُنا وَضْعُ اسْتِراتيجِيَّةٍ عَسْكَرِيَّةٍ فَعّالَةٍ لِحِمايَةِ جَبْهَتِنا وَحِصارِ العَدُوِّ عِنْدَ الحاجَةِ.

مُقَدِّمُ البَرْنامَج: في الخِتامِ، ما هِيَ أَهَمُّ التَّكْتيكاتِ الَّتي يَجِبُ أَنْ نُرَكِّزَ عَلَيْها في المُسْتَقْبَلِ القَريبِ؟

اللِّواءُ مَحْمود: يَجِبُ التَّرْكيزُ عَلى تَدْريبِ قُوّاتِنا عَلى تَكْتيكاتٍ حَديثَةٍ، خاصَّةً في مَجالِ الاِسْتِطْلاعِ وَاسْتِعادَةِ المَواقِعِ المُحْتَلَّةِ. كَما يَجِبُ زِيادَةُ تَدْريباتِ الدِّفاعِ وَتَطْويرُ قُوَّةِ تَحالُفٍ أَكْثَرَ فَعاليَّةً.

مُقَدِّمُ البَرْنامَج: شُكْرًا لَكَ، سِيادَةَ اللِّواءِ مَحْمود، عَلى هَذا الحِوارِ المُفيدِ وَالمَعْلوماتِ القَيِّمَةِ.

اللِّواءُ مَحْمود: شُكْرًا لَكُمْ، وَأَتَمَنّى دَوامَ الأَمانِ وَالازْدِهارِ لِوَطَنِنا.

Interview on Military Defense and Security Strategies

Host: Welcome to our special program today where we host Major General Mahmoud Al-Azb, a military strategic expert, to discuss the challenges and modern strategies in the field of defense and security. Welcome, General.

Major General Mahmoud: Thank you. I am honored to be here.

Host: Let's start with the first question: How do you see the importance of developing a deterrence strategy at this time?

M.G.M.: Deterrence strategy is a fundamental element in any defense line. In the era of modern warfare, we must be superior not only in offensive power but also in our ability to deter any potential attack from the enemy.

Host: Do you think military alliances play a significant role in achieving strategic balance?

M.G.M.: Certainly, a military alliance can enhance deterrent power. When joint air forces from several countries ally, we have a stronger defense, making it hard for the enemy to exhaust our resources.

Host: In light of recent developments, how can strategic analysis be used to strengthen our forces?

M.G.M.:	Strategic analysis gives us a deep insight into enemy forces, their strategy, and their vulnerabilities. Based on risk assessment, we can devise an effective military strategy to protect our front and besiege the enemy when needed.
Host:	Finally, what are the key tactics we should focus on in the near future?
M.G.M.:	We should focus on training our forces on modern tactics, especially in reconnaissance and recapturing occupied sites. Also, there's a need to increase defensive drills and develop a more effective alliance force.
Host:	Thank you, General Mahmoud, for this enlightening conversation and valuable information.
M.G.M.:	Thank you, and I wish our homeland continued safety and prosperity.

7.3.2 Equipment and Technology

Track **25**

أَطْلَقَ النَّار • إِطْلَاقٌ

to shoot

أَطْلَقَ الجُنْدِيُّ النَّارَ عَلَى الهَدَفِ مِنْ بُنْدُقِيَّتِهِ.

The soldier fired at the target with his rifle.

أَمَّدَ • إِمْدَادٌ

to supply

أَمَّدَتِ القَاعِدَةُ العَسْكَرِيَّةُ القُوَّاتِ بِالإِمْدَادَاتِ والمُعَدَّاتِ الأَسَاسِيَّةِ قَبْلَ المُهِمَّةِ.

The military base supplied the troops with essential equipment and supplies before the mission.

أَمْنٌ وَطَنِيٌّ = أَمْنٌ قَوْمِيٌّ

national security

تُعْتَبَرُ تِكْنُولُوجْيا الطَّائِرَاتِ بِدُونِ طَيَّارٍ مُهِمَّةً لِلْأَمْنِ الوَطَنِيِّ.

Drone technology is considered important for national security.

اِسْتَهْدَفَ • اِسْتِهْدَافٌ

to target

اِسْتَهْدَفَتِ الصَّوَارِيخُ المَوَاقِعَ العَسْكَرِيَّةَ لِلْعَدُوِّ.

The missiles targeted the enemy's military sites.

القُوّاتُ الجَوِّيَّةُ الخاصَّةُ

special air forces

شارَكَتِ القُوّاتُ الجَوِّيَّةُ الخاصَّةُ في عَمَلِيّاتِ اسْتِطْلاعٍ عالِيَةِ الخُطورَةِ.

The special air forces participated in high-risk reconnaissance operations.

اِنْفَجَرَ • اِنْفِجارٌ

to detonate, explode

اِنْفَجَرَتِ القُنْبَلَةُ بِالْقُرْبِ مِنَ المُعَسْكَرِ دونَ إيقاعِ ضَحايا.

The bomb exploded near the camp without causing casualties.

> This verb is intransitive; it does not take an object. Compare to its transitive counterpart on page 80.

بُنْدُقِيَّةٌ • بَنادِقُ

rifle

اِسْتَخْدَمَ الجُنودُ بَنادِقَ عالِيَةَ الدِّقَّةِ في المَعْرَكَةِ.

The soldiers used high-precision rifles in the battle.

بُنْدُقِيَّةُ قَنْصٍ

sniper rifle

اِسْتَخْدَمَ القَنّاصُ بُنْدُقِيَّةَ قَنْصٍ لِإصابَةِ الهَدَفِ مِنْ مَسافَةٍ بَعيدَةٍ.

The sniper used a sniper rifle to hit the target from a long distance.

بَيولوجِيٌّ

biological

أُكْتُشِفَتْ مُحاوَلَةٌ لِاسْتِخْدامِ سِلاحٍ بَيولوجِيٍّ ضِدَّ المَدَنِيّينَ.

An attempt to use a biological weapon against civilians was discovered.

تِرْسانَةٌ = تَرْسانَةٌ

arsenal

تَمَّ تَحْديثُ التِّرْسانَةِ العَسْكَرِيَّةِ لِضَمانِ الجاهِزِيَّةِ.

The military arsenal was updated to ensure readiness.

ثَقيلٌ

heavy (as in heavy artillery)

تَمَّ نَشْرُ الأَسْلِحَةِ الثَّقيلَةِ عَلَى الجَبْهَةِ لِتَعْزيزِ الدِّفاعاتِ.

Heavy weapons were deployed at the front to bolster defenses.

logistical support wing

جَناحُ الدَّعْمِ اللّوجِسْتِيِّ

جَناحُ الدَّعْمِ اللّوجِسْتِيِّ ضَمِنَ تَوْفيرَ المُعَدّاتِ وَالإمْداداتِ بِفَعاليَّةٍ.

The logistical support wing ensured the efficient provision of equipment and supplies.

paratrooper

جُنْدِيٌّ مَظَلّاتٍ = جُنْدِيٌّ مَظَلّاتٍ • جُنودٌ

تَمَّ إنْزالُ جُنودِ المِظَلّاتِ خَلْفَ خُطوطِ العَدُوِّ لِتَنْفيذِ مُهِمّاتٍ خاصَّةٍ.

Paratroopers were dropped behind enemy lines to carry out special missions.

to equip

جَهَّزَ • تَجْهيزٌ

جُهِّزَ الجَيْشُ بِأَحْدَثِ الأَسْلِحَةِ وَالمُعَدّاتِ.

The army was equipped with the latest weapons and equipment.

> Notice that the verb is used in the passive mood in the example above.

information warfare

حَرْبٌ مَعْلوماتِيَّةٌ • حُروبٌ

جَرى شَنُّ حَرْبٍ مَعْلوماتِيَّةٍ ضِدَّ الدَّوْلَةِ لِتَضْليلِ الرَّأْيِ العامِّ.

An information war was waged against the country to mislead public opinion.

fifth-generation warfare

حُروبُ الجيلِ الخامِس

يُناقِشُ القادَةُ العَسْكَريّونَ تَأْثيرَ حُروبِ الجيلِ الخامِسِ عَلى الاسْتِراتيجيّاتِ الدِّفاعِيَّةِ.

Military leaders are discussing the impact of fifth-generation warfare on defensive strategies.

explosive belt

حِزامٌ ناسِفٌ • أَحْزِمَةٌ

أَحْبَطَتِ الأَجْهِزَةُ الأَمْنِيَّةُ مُحاوَلَةً لِتَفْجيرِ حِزامٍ ناسِفٍ في مَحَطَّةِ القِطارِ.

Security forces thwarted an attempt to detonate a suicide belt at the train station.

to mobilize

حَشَدَ • حَشْدٌ

تَمَّ حَشْدُ قُوّاتٍ كَبيرَةٍ عَلى الحُدودِ اسْتِعْدادًا لِأَيِّ تَصْعيدٍ.

A large force was mobilized at the border in preparation for any escalation.

armor

دِرْعٌ • دُروعٌ

اِسْتَخْدَمَ الجُنودُ دُروعًا لِحِمايَةِ أَنْفُسِهِمْ مِنَ الرَّصاصِ.

The soldiers used armor to protect themselves from bullets.

support

دَعْمٌ

جَرى تَقْديمُ الدَّعْمِ اللّوجِسْتِيِّ لِلْقُوّاتِ المُتَقَدِّمَةِ.

Logistical support was provided to the advancing forces.

civil defense

دِفاعٌ مَدَنِيٌّ

نَفَّذَتْ وَحْداتُ الدِّفاعِ المَدَنِيِّ تَمارينَ لِلتَّعامُلِ مَعَ الهَجَماتِ الكيمْيائِيَّةِ.

Civil defense units conducted exercises to handle chemical attacks.

nuclear deterrence

رَدْعٌ نَوَوِيٌّ

تَعْتَبِرُ الدَّوْلَةُ الرَّدْعَ النَّوَوِيَّ جُزْءًا مِنَ اسْتِراتيجِيَّتِها الدِّفاعِيَّةِ.

The country considers nuclear deterrence a part of its defensive strategy.

warship

سَفينَةٌ حَرْبِيَّةٌ • سُفُنٌ

تَمَّ إِطْلاقُ سَفينَةٍ حَرْبِيَّةٍ جَديدَةٍ لِتَعْزيزِ الأُسْطولِ البَحْرِيِّ.

A new warship was launched to strengthen the naval fleet.

logistics support ship

سَفينَةُ دَعْمٍ لوجِسْتِيٍّ

قامَتْ سَفينَةُ الدَّعْمِ اللّوجِسْتِيِّ بِإِمْدادِ القُوّاتِ بِالوَقودِ وَالمُؤَنِ.

The logistics support ship supplied the forces with fuel and provisions.

combat knife

سِكّينُ قِتالٍ • سَكاكينُ

عُثِرَ عَلى سِكّينِ قِتالٍ في حَقيبَةِ الجُنْدِيِّ المُشْتَبَهِ بِهِ.

A combat knife was found in the bag of the suspected soldier.

missile	صَواريخُ •	صاروخٌ

أَطْلَقَتِ الدِّفاعاتُ الجَوِّيَّةُ صاروخًا لِاعْتِراضِ الطّائِرَةِ المُعادِيَةِ.

The air defenses launched a missile to intercept the hostile aircraft.

to aim	تَصويبٌ •	صَوَّبَ

صَوَّبَ الجُنْدِيُّ المِدْفَعَ نَحْوَ الهَدَفِ.

The soldier aimed the artillery at the target.

torpedo		طورْبيدٌ

أَطْلَقَتِ الغَوّاصَةُ طورْبيدًا نَحْوَ سَفينَةِ العَدُوِّ.

The submarine launched a torpedo at the enemy ship.

to detonate	تَفْجيرٌ •	فَجَّرَ

فَجَّرَ الجُنْدِيُّ الجِسْرَ لِمَنْعِ تَقَدُّمِ قُوّاتِ العَدُوِّ.

The soldier blew up the bridge to prevent the advance of enemy forces.

detectable		قابِلٌ لِلْكَشْفِ

كانَتِ الطّائِرَةُ غَيْرَ قابِلَةٍ لِلْكَشْفِ بِواسِطَةِ الرّادارِ.

The aircraft was undetectable by radar.

rocket launcher	قَواذِفُ •	قاذِفُ صَواريخَ

اِسْتَخْدَمَ الجَيْشُ قاذِفَ صَواريخَ لِتَدْميرِ الأَهْدافِ الأَرْضِيَّةِ.

The army used a rocket launcher to destroy ground targets.

missile base	قَواعِدُ •	قاعِدَةُ صَواريخَ

تَمَّ تَدْميرُ قاعِدَةِ الصَّواريخِ بِواسِطَةِ ضَرْبَةٍ جَوِّيَّةٍ.

The missile base was destroyed by an airstrike.

قَمَرٌ صِناعِيٌّ • أَقْمارٌ

satellite

أَطْلَقَتِ الدَّوْلَةُ قَمَرًا صِناعِيًّا لِأَغْراضِ الِاسْتِطْلاعِ.

The country launched a satellite for reconnaissance purposes.

قُنْبُلَةٌ • قَنابِلُ

bomb

أَلْقَتِ الطّائِرَةُ قُنْبُلَةً عَلى مَوْقِعِ العَدُوِّ.

The plane dropped a bomb on the enemy position.

قُنْبُلَةُ دُخانٍ

smoke grenade

اِسْتَخْدَمَ الجُنودُ قَنابِلَ الدُّخانِ لِلتَّمْويهِ أَثْناءَ الِانْسِحابِ.

The soldiers used smoke bombs for concealment during the withdrawal.

قُنْبُلَةٌ مَوْقوتَةٌ = قُنْبُلَةٌ زَمنِيَّةٌ

time bomb

عُثِرَ عَلى قُنْبُلَةٍ مَوْقوتَةٍ في المِترو وَتَمَّ تَفْكيكُها.

A time bomb was found in the subway and defused.

قُنْبُلَةٌ يَدَوِيَّةٌ

grenade

رَمى الجُنديُّ قُنْبُلَةً يَدَوِيَّةً داخِلَ خَنْدَقِ الأَعْداءِ.

The soldier threw a hand grenade into the enemy trench.

قَنَصَ • قَنْصٌ

to snipe

رَصَدَ القَنّاصُ العَدُوَّ مِن مَوْقِعٍ سِرِّيٍّ وَقَنَصَ هَدَفًا مُهِمًّا.

The sniper observed the enemy from a hidden position and successfully sniped an important target.

قُوَّةٌ جَوِّيَّةٌ اسْتِراتيجِيَّةٌ

strategic air power

تَمَّ نَشْرُ قُوَّةٍ جَوِّيَّةٍ اسْتِراتيجِيَّةٍ لِتَعْزيزِ الرَّدْعِ العَسْكَرِيِّ.

A strategic air force was deployed to enhance military deterrence.

nuclear power

قُوَّةٌ نَوَوِيَّةٌ

تُعْتَبَرُ الدَّوْلَةُ قُوَّةً نَوَوِيَّةً، وَلَها تِرْسانَةٌ مِنَ الرُّؤُوسِ النَّوَوِيَّةِ.

The country is a nuclear power and has an arsenal of nuclear warheads.

chemical

كِيمْيائِيٌّ

أُسْتُخْدِمَتِ الأَسْلِحَةُ الكِيمْيائِيَّةُ في الحُروبِ بِطَريقَةٍ غَيْرِ إِنْسانِيَّةٍ.

Chemical weapons were used in wars in an inhumane manner.

landmine

لَغَمٌ (أَرْضِيّ) • أَلْغامٌ

اِنْفَجَرَ لَغَمٌ أَرْضِيٌّ عِنْدَ مُرورِ الدَّبّابَةِ فَوْقَهُ.

A landmine exploded as the tank passed over it.

weapon stockpile

مَخْزونُ أَسْلِحَةٍ

أُكْتُشِفَ مَخْزونُ أَسْلِحَةٍ ضَخْمٌ في مِنْطَقَةِ النِّزاعِ.

A large weapon stockpile was discovered in the conflict zone.

destructive

مُدَمِّرٌ

السِّلاحُ المُدَمِّرُ الجَديدُ يُمْكِنُهُ تَدْميرُ الهَدَفِ بِدِقَّةٍ عالِيَةٍ.

The new destructive weapon can destroy the target with high precision.

armored vehicle

مَرْكَبَةٌ مُدَرَّعَةٌ

أُسْتُخْدِمَتِ المَرْكَبَةُ المُدَرَّعَةُ لِنَقْلِ الجُنودِ بِأَمانٍ عَبْرَ المَناطِقِ الخَطِرَةِ.

The armored vehicle was used to safely transport soldiers through dangerous areas.

ammunition depot

مُسْتَوْدَعُ ذَخيرَةٍ

تَمَّ تَدْميرُ مُسْتَوْدَعِ الذَّخيرَةِ في عَمَلِيَّةٍ جَوِّيَّةٍ.

The ammunition depot was destroyed in an aerial operation.

pistol, handgun

مُسَدَّسٌ

حَمَلَ الجُنْدِيُّ مُسَدَّسًا كَسِلاحٍ ثانَوِيٍّ.

The soldier carried a pistol as a secondary weapon.

anti-tank

مُضادٌّ لِلدَّبابات

اُسْتُخْدِمَتِ الأَسْلِحَةُ المُضادَّةُ لِلدَّباباتِ لِوَقْفِ تَقَدُّمِ العَدُوِّ.

Anti-tank weapons were used to halt enemy advancement.

anti-ship

مُضادٌّ لِلسُّفُن

أَطْلَقَتِ البَطّارِيّاتُ المُضادَّةُ لِلسُّفُنِ الصَّواريخَ ضِدَّ الفَرْقاطَةِ المُعادِيَةِ.

The anti-ship batteries fired missiles against the enemy frigate.

anti-aircraft

مُضادٌّ لِلطّائِرات

اُسْتُخْدِمَتِ الأَسْلِحَةُ المُضادَّةُ لِلطّائِراتِ لِحِمايَةِ المِنْطَقَةِ مِنَ الهَجَماتِ الجَوِّيَةِ.

Anti-aircraft weapons were used to protect the area from aerial attacks.

military equipment

مُعَدَّةٌ عَسْكَرِيَّةٌ

المُعَدّاتُ العَسْكَرِيَّةُ مُهِمَّةٌ لِنَجاحِ العَمَلِيّاتِ.

Military equipment is important for the success of operations.

barracks, camp

مُعَسْكَرٌ

تَمَّ نَشْرُ الجُنودِ في مُعَسْكَرٍ قُرْبَ الحُدودِ.

Soldiers were deployed in a camp near the border.

air defense system

مَنْظومَةُ دِفاعٍ جَوِّيٍّ

تَمَّ تَحْديثُ مَنْظومَةِ الدِّفاعِ الجَوِّيِّ لِزيادَةِ الأَمانِ.

The air defense system was upgraded for increased security.

guided (as in guided missiles)

مُوَجَّهٌ

أُسْتُخْدِمَتِ الصَّوارِيخُ المُوَجَّهَةُ لِزِيادَةِ دِقَّةِ الهُجومِ.

Guided missiles were used for increased attack accuracy.

military port

مَوانٍ / مَوانِئُ •

ميناءٌ عَسْكَرِيٌّ

أُغْلِقَ المِيناءُ العَسْكَرِيُّ لِأَعْمالِ الصِّيانَةِ.

The military port was closed for maintenance.

nuclear disarmament

نَزْعُ الأَسْلِحَةِ النَّوَوِيَّةِ

جَرَتْ مُحادَثاتٌ لِنَزْعِ الأَسْلِحَةِ النَّوَوِيَّةِ وَالحَدِّ مِنَ التَّسَلُّحِ.

Talks were held for nuclear disarmament and arms reduction.

to ambush

نَصْبٌ •

نَصَبَ كَمينًا

نَصَبَ الجُنودُ كَمينًا لِاعْتِقالِ المُتَمَرِّدينَ.

The soldiers set up an ambush to capture the rebels.

weapons system

أَنْظِمَةٌ •

نِظامُ أَسْلِحَةٍ

نِظامُ الأَسْلِحَةِ المُتَطَوِّرُ يُعَزِّزُ قُدُراتِ الجَيْشِ.

The advanced weapons system enhances the army's capabilities.

missile defense system

أَنْظِمَةٌ •

نِظامُ دِفاعٍ صاروخِيٍّ

تَمَّ تَفْعيلُ نِظامِ الدِّفاعِ الصّاروخِيِّ لِمُواجَهَةِ التَّهْديداتِ الجَوِّيَّةِ.

The missile defense system was activated to counter aerial threats.

checkpoint

نِقاطٌ •

نُقْطَةُ تَفْتيشٍ

تَمَّ تَأْسيسُ نُقْطَةِ تَفْتيشٍ لِفَحْصِ السَّيّاراتِ المارَّةِ.

A checkpoint was established to inspect passing cars.

نَوَوِيٌّ

يُعْتَبَرُ الرَّدْعُ النَّوَوِيُّ وَسِيلَةً لِحِفْظِ الِاسْتِقْرَارِ الإِقْلِيمِيِّ.

Nuclear deterrence is considered a means to preserve regional stability.

7.3.2.1 Mini-Articles

Track **26**

أَطْلَقَتِ القُوَّاتِ الجَوِّيَّةِ الخَاصَّةُ صَارُوخًا جَدِيدًا مِنْ قَاعِدَةِ صَوَارِيخَ مَوْجُودَةٍ في المِنْطَقَةِ الشَّمَالِيَّةِ. تَمَّ تَجْهِيزُ هَذَا الصَّارُوخِ بِتِقْنِيَّاتٍ حَدِيثَةٍ تَجْعَلُ اكْتِشَافَهُ صَعْبًا. صَرَّحَ مَصْدَرٌ عَسْكَرِيٌّ أَنَّ هَذَا الصَّارُوخَ يُمْكِنُهُ اسْتِهْدَافُ سَفِينَةٍ حَرْبِيَّةٍ أَوْ مَرْكَبَةٍ مُدَرَّعَةٍ بِدِقَّةٍ.

The Special Air Forces launched a new missile from a missile base located in the northern region. This missile is equipped with modern technologies that make it hard to detect. A military source stated that this missile can precisely target a warship or armored vehicle.

بَدَأَتِ القُوَّةُ الجَوِّيَّةُ اسْتِرَاتِيجِيَّةً لِتَطْوِيرِ مَنْظُومَةِ دِفَاعٍ جَوِّيٍّ جَدِيدَةٍ تَهْدُفُ إلى الدِّفَاعِ ضِدَّ الهَجَمَاتِ الجَوِّيَّةِ وَالصَّوَارِيخِ بَعِيدَةِ المَدَى. تُعْتَبَرُ هَذِهِ المَنْظُومَةُ جُزْءًا مِنَ اسْتِرَاتِيجِيَّةِ الدِّفَاعِ المَدَنِيِّ لِحِمَايَةِ المُوَاطِنِينَ وَالبِنْيَةِ التَّحْتِيَّةِ. كَمَا تَمَّ تَزْوِيدُ المَنْظُومَةِ بِقَنَابِلِ دُخَانٍ لِإِعَاقَةِ رُؤْيَةِ العَدُوِّ.

The air force began a strategy to develop a new air defense system aimed at defending against aerial attacks and long-range missiles. This system is part of the civil defense strategy to protect citizens and infrastructure. The system is also equipped with smoke bombs to obstruct enemy visibility.

وَقَعَ انْفِجَارٌ ضَخْمٌ في مُسْتَوْدَعِ ذَخِيرَةٍ بِأَحَدِ المُعَسْكَرَاتِ العَسْكَرِيَّةِ، مِمَّا أَسْفَرَ عَنْ تَدْمِيرِ مَخْزُونٍ كَبِيرٍ مِنَ الأَسْلِحَةِ وَالمُعَدَّاتِ العَسْكَرِيَّةِ. بَيْنَمَا تَمَّ فَتْحُ تَحْقِيقٍ لِمَعْرِفَةِ أَسْبَابِ الِانْفِجَارِ، يُعْتَقَدُ أَنَّ قُنْبُلَةً مَوْقُوتَةً قَدْ تَكُونُ السَّبَبَ. القُوَّاتُ المُسَلَّحَةُ تَتَّخِذُ جَمِيعَ التَّدَابِيرِ اللَّازِمَةِ لِضَمَانِ أَمَانِ المُنْشَآتِ العَسْكَرِيَّةِ.

A massive explosion occurred in an ammunition warehouse in one of the military camps, resulting in the destruction of a large stock of weapons and military equipment. While an investigation was launched to determine the causes of the explosion, it is believed that a timed bomb might be the reason. The armed forces are taking all necessary measures to ensure the safety of military facilities.

أَعْلَنَ الأَمْنُ الوَطَنِيُّ عَنْ إِطْلَاقِ قَمَرٍ صِنَاعِيٍّ جَدِيدٍ مُخَصَّصٍ لِأَغْرَاضِ المُرَاقَبَةِ وَالِاسْتِطْلَاعِ. هَذَا القَمَرُ سَيُمَكِّنُ القُوَّاتِ المُسَلَّحَةَ مِنْ رَصْدِ أَيِّ تَحَرُّكَاتٍ عَسْكَرِيَّةٍ أَوْ نَشَاطَاتٍ مَشْبُوهَةٍ. سَيَكُونُ لَهُ القُدْرَةُ عَلى تَحْدِيدِ مَوَاقِعِ الصَّوَارِيخِ وَقَوَاعِدِ الأَعْدَاءِ بِدِقَّةٍ فَائِقَةٍ.

The national security announced the launch of a new satellite dedicated to surveillance and reconnaissance purposes. This satellite will enable the armed forces to monitor any military movements or suspicious activities. It will have the capability to pinpoint missile locations and enemy bases with utmost precision.

تَمَّ تَثْبِيتُ نِظامِ دِفاعٍ صاروخِيٍّ مُتَقَدِّمٍ عَلى الحُدودِ الجَنوبِيَّةِ لِلدَّوْلَةِ. يَتَمَيَّزُ هَذا النِّظامُ بِقُدْرَتِهِ عَلى التَّعامُلِ مَعَ الصَّواريخِ وَالطّائِراتِ بِدونِ طَيّارٍ. بِالإِضافَةِ إِلى ذَلِكَ، تَمَّ تَزْويدُهُ بِدِفاعاتٍ مُضادَّةٍ لِلطّائِراتِ وَسُفُنِ الدَّعْمِ اللّوجِسْتِيِّ، لِضَمانِ حِمايَةِ الحُدودِ مِنْ أَيِّ تَهْديداتٍ مُحْتَمَلَةٍ.

An advanced missile defense system has been installed on the southern borders of the state. This system is capable of handling missiles and drones. Furthermore, it has been equipped with anti-aircraft defenses and logistic support vessels to ensure the protection of the borders from any potential threats.

في خُطْوَةٍ اسْتِراتيجِيَّةٍ لِتَعْزيزِ وُجودِها عَلى الجَبْهَةِ، أَرْسَلَتِ القُوّاتُ المُسَلَّحَةُ حَشْدًا كَبيرًا مِنْ جَناحِ الدَّعْمِ اللّوجِسْتِيِّ. تَتَضَمَّنُ هَذِهِ القُوَّةُ مَجموعَةً مِنْ مَرْكَباتِ الدَّعْمِ وَمُسْتَوْدَعاتِ الذَّخيرَةِ. تُمَثِّلُ هَذِهِ الخُطْوَةُ جُزْءًا مِنْ اسْتِراتيجِيَّةِ الحَرْبِ لِلتَّأَكُّدِ مِنْ أَنَّ القُوّاتِ كامِلَةُ التَّجْهيزِ.

In a strategic move to bolster its presence on the front, the armed forces dispatched a large contingent from the logistics support wing. This force includes support vehicles and ammunition depots. This step is part of the information warfare strategy to ensure the forces are fully equipped.

7.3.2.2 Informative Article: The Yemeni Civil War

Track **27**

الأَسْلِحَةُ وَالتِّقْنِيّاتُ المُسْتَخْدَمَةُ في الحَرْبِ الأَهْلِيَّةِ اليَمَنِيَّةِ

مُنْذُ بِدايَةِ الحَرْبِ الأَهْلِيَّةِ اليَمَنِيَّةِ في عامِ 2015، شَهِدَتِ المِنْطَقَةُ اسْتِخْدامًا واسِعًا لِلْعَتادِ وَالتِّكْنولوجْيا الحَرْبِيَّةِ المُتَقَدِّمَةِ. الصِّراعُ، الَّذي يَدورُ بَيْنَ حُكومَةِ اليَمَنِ وَحَرَكَةِ الحوثِيِّ، وَالتَّحالُفِ بِقِيادَةِ المَمْلَكَةِ العَرَبِيَّةِ السُّعودِيَّةِ، أَظْهَرَ مَدى تَقَدُّمِ الأَسْلِحَةِ المُسْتَخْدَمَةِ في الحُروبِ الحَديثَةِ.

1. الصَّواريخُ: ظَهَرَتْ قَواعِدُ الصَّواريخِ كَواحِدَةٍ مِنْ أَبْرَزِ الأَدَواتِ المُسْتَخْدَمَةِ في الصِّراعِ. اِسْتَهْدَفَ الحوثِيّونَ عِدَّةَ مَواقِعَ داخِلَ السُّعودِيَّةِ بِاسْتِخْدامِ الصَّواريخِ بَعيدَةِ المَدى. بِالمُقابِلِ، اِسْتَخْدَمَ التَّحالُفُ العَرَبِيُّ القُوَّةَ الجَوِّيَّةَ الاِسْتِراتيجِيَّةَ لِشَنِّ غاراتٍ عَلى مَواقِعِ الحوثِيّينَ.

2. الطّائِراتُ بِدونِ طَيّارٍ: أَصْبَحَتْ طائِراتُ الاِسْتِطْلاعِ وَالهُجومِ بِدونِ طَيّارٍ جُزْءًا أَساسِيًّا مِنَ المَشْهَدِ. حَيْثُ اسْتُخْدِمَتْ لِجَمْعِ المَعْلوماتِ وَاسْتِهْدافِ المَواقِعِ الحَيَوِيَّةِ.

٣. أَنْظِمَةُ الدِّفاعِ الجَوِّيُّ: لِمُواجَهَةِ التَّهْديداتِ الجَوِّيَّةِ، اِسْتَخْدَمَ الحوثِيّونَ مَنْظوماتِ الدِّفاعِ الجَوِّيِّ لِرَصْدِ وَإِسْقاطِ الطَّائِراتِ المُعادِيَةِ.

٤. المُعَدّاتُ البَرِّيَّةُ: مِنْ بَيْنِ الأَسْلِحَةِ المُسْتَخْدَمَةِ، كانَتْ هُناكَ بَنادِقُ قَنْصٍ، قاذِفاتُ صَواريخَ مُضادَّةٍ لِلدَّبّاباتِ، وَمَرْكَباتٌ مُدَرَّعَةٌ. وَقَدْ تَمَّ اسْتِخْدامُ نِقاطِ التَّفْتيشِ وَالمُعَسْكَراتِ كَمَواقِعَ اسْتِراتيجِيَّةٍ لِلتَّحَكُّمِ في المَناطِقِ الحَيَوِيَّةِ.

٥. أَسْلِحَةُ الدَّمارِ الشّامِلِ: رَغْمَ أَنَّ الأَمْنَ الوَطَنِيَّ لَمْ يُؤَكِّدِ اسْتِخْدامَ أَسْلِحَةٍ نَوَوِيَّةٍ أَوْ بَيولوجِيَّةٍ أَوْ كيميائِيَّةٍ، فَقَدْ كانَتْ هُناكَ تَقاريرُ عَنِ اسْتِخْدامِ أَسْلِحَةٍ مُحَرَّمَةٍ دَوْلِيًّا.

يَظَلُّ الحَلُّ السِّياسِيُّ هُوَ السَّبيلَ الأَمْثَلَ لِإِنْهاءِ هَذا الصِّراعِ الدَّمَوِيِّ. وَلَكِنْ حَتّى ذَلِكَ الحينِ، سَتَسْتَمِرُّ الأَسْلِحَةُ وَالتَّكْنولوجْيا في لَعِبِ دَوْرٍ رَئيسِيٍّ في تَحْديدِ مَسارِ الحَرْبِ.

Weapons and Technologies Used in the Yemeni Civil War

Since the onset of the Yemeni civil war in 2015, the region has seen widespread use of advanced military equipment and technology. The conflict, between the Yemeni government and the Houthi movement, and the coalition led by Saudi Arabia, has showcased the advancement of weapons used in modern wars.

1. Missiles: Missile bases emerged as one of the most prominent tools used in the conflict. The Houthis targeted several sites within Saudi Arabia using long-range missiles. Conversely, the Arab coalition used strategic airpower to launch raids on Houthi positions.

2. Drones: Reconnaissance and attack drones have become an integral part of the battlefield. They were used for gathering information and targeting vital locations.

3. Air Defense Systems: To counter aerial threats, the Houthis employed air defense systems to monitor and shoot down hostile aircraft.

4. Ground Equipment: Among the weapons used were sniper rifles, anti-tank missile launchers, and armored vehicles. Checkpoints and camps were used as strategic locations to control vital areas.

5. Weapons of Mass Destruction: While national security hasn't confirmed the use of nuclear, biological, or chemical weapons, there were reports of internationally prohibited weapons being used.

A political solution remains the ideal way to end this bloody conflict. However, until then, weapons and technology will continue to play a pivotal role in determining the course of the war.

7.3.3 Military Training, Technology, and Economics

to supervise

إِشْرَافٌ • أَشْرَفَ

أَشْرَفَ الجِنْرالُ عَلى تَدْريباتِ القُوّاتِ الخاصَّةِ.

The general supervised the training of the special forces.

military academy

أَكاديمِيَّةٌ عَسْكَرِيَّةٌ

تَخَرَّجَ أَحْمَدُ مِنَ الأَكاديمِيَّةِ العَسْكَرِيَّةِ بِتَفَوُّقٍ.

Ahmed graduated with honors from the military academy.

cyber-security

أَمْنٌ سَيبَرانِيٌّ

يَلْعَبُ الأَمْنُ السَّيبَرانِيُّ دَوْرًا مُهِمًّا في حِمايَةِ المَعْلوماتِ العَسْكَرِيَّةِ.

Cyber-security plays an important role in protecting military information.

national security

أَمْنٌ وَطَنِيٌّ = أَمْنٌ قَوْمِيٌّ

اِسْتَعْرَضَ الرَّئيسُ التَّحَدِّياتِ الَّتي تُواجِهُ الأَمْنَ الوَطَنِيَّ.

The president reviewed the challenges facing national security.

logistics management

إِدارَةٌ لوجِسْتِيَّةٌ

قامَتْ وَحْدَةُ الإِدارَةِ اللّوجِسْتِيَّةِ بِتَنْظيمِ الإِمْدادِ وَالتَّموينِ.

The logistics management unit organized supply and provisioning.

supply and logistics

إِمْدادٌ وَتَمْوينٌ

الإِمْدادُ وَالتَّمْوينُ مُهِمّانِ لِنَجاحِ العَمَلِيّاتِ العَسْكَرِيَّةِ.

Supply and provisioning are essential for the success of military operations.

military spending

إِنْفاقٌ عَسْكَرِيٌّ

اِرْتَفَعَ الإِنْفاقُ العَسْكَرِيُّ في البِلادِ خِلالَ السَّنَواتِ الأَخيرَةِ.

Military spending in the country has increased in recent years.

to innovate, invent

اِبْتَكَرَ • اِبْتِكارٌ

اِبْتَكَرَ العُلَماءُ تِقْنِيَّةً جَديدَةً لِتَحْسينِ الأَسْلِحَةِ.

Scientists invented a new technology to improve weapons.

to invest

اِسْتَثْمَرَ • اِسْتِثْمارٌ

اِسْتَثْمَرَتِ الحُكومَةُ في تَطْويرِ الصِّناعَةِ العَسْكَرِيَّةِ.

The government invested in the development of the military industry.

strategic

اِسْتِراتيجِيٌّ

القَواعِدُ العَسْكَرِيَّةُ الاِسْتِراتيجِيَّةُ مُهِمَّةٌ لِلدِّفاعِ الوَطَنِيِّ.

Strategic military bases are important for national defense.

economic strategies

اِسْتِراتيجِيّاتٌ اقْتِصادِيَّةٌ

تَمَّتْ مُناقَشَةُ الاِسْتِراتيجِيّاتِ الاِقْتِصادِيَّةِ لِزيادَةِ كَفاءَةِ الدِّفاعِ.

Economic strategies were discussed to increase defense efficiency.

defense strategy

اِسْتِراتيجِيَّةُ دِفاعٍ

تَمَّ تَطْويرُ اِسْتِراتيجِيَّةِ دِفاعٍ جَديدَةٍ لِمُواجَهَةِ التَّهْديداتِ الحَديثَةِ.

A new defense strategy was developed to confront modern threats.

to review

اِسْتَعْرَضَ • اِسْتِعْراضٌ

اِسْتَعْرَضَتِ القُوّاتُ العَسْكَرِيَّةُ أَحْدَثَ الأَسْلِحَةِ في المَعْرِضِ.

The military forces showcased the latest weapons at the exhibition.

to clash, engage with

اِشْتَبَكَ مَعَ • اِشْتِباكٌ

اِشْتَبَكَتِ القُوّاتُ العَرَبِيَّةُ مَعَ العَناصِرِ الإِرْهابِيَّةِ في المِنْطَقَةِ الحُدودِيَّةِ.

Arab forces engaged with terrorist elements in the border region.

to purchase — شِرَاءٌ • اِشْتَرَى

اِشْتَرَتِ القُوّاتُ المُسَلَّحَةُ طائِراتٍ حَرْبِيَّةً جَدِيدَةً مِنْ فَرَنْسا.

The armed forces purchased new fighter jets from France.

> شِرَاءٌ is commonly used as the masdar (verbal noun) for اِشْتَرَى, even though it is technically the masdar for a different but related verb (شَرَى). This usage is more common than the actual masdar اِشْتِرَاءٌ for اِشْتَرَى, illustrating a case where a masdar from one verb is more frequently used with another verb.

economic — اِقْتِصادِيٌّ

يُعْتَبَرُ الدِّفاعُ عامِلًا مُهِمًّا في التَّطَوُّرِ الاِقْتِصادِيِّ.

Defense is considered an important factor in economic development.

economic impact of defense — التَّأْثِيرُ الاِقْتِصادِيُّ لِلدِّفاعِ

تَمَّتْ دِراسَةُ التَّأْثِيرِ الاِقْتِصادِيِّ لِلدِّفاعِ عَلَى الاِقْتِصادِ الوَطَنِيِّ.

The economic impact of military spending on the national economy was studied.

military industry — الصِّناعَةُ العَسْكَرِيَّةُ

تَوَسَّعَتِ الصِّناعَةُ العَسْكَرِيَّةُ لِتَشْمَلَ تِقْنِياتٍ حَدِيثَةً.

The military industry expanded to include modern technologies.

to participate in, engage in (training) — اِنْخَراطٌ • اِنْخَرَطَ في

اِنْخَرَطَ الجُنُودُ في تَدْرِيباتٍ شاقَّةٍ لِتَحْسِينِ مَهاراتِهِمْ.

The soldiers engaged in rigorous training to improve their skills.

research and development — بَحْثٌ وَتَطْوِيرٌ

تَعاوَنَ قِسْمُ البَحْثِ وَالتَّطْوِيرِ مَعَ الجامِعاتِ لِإِنْتاجِ أَسْلِحَةٍ ذَكِيَّةٍ.

The research and development department collaborated with universities to produce smart weapons.

strategic planning

تَخْطِيطٌ اسْتِراتِيجِيٌّ

أَدْرَجَ الجِنِرالُ الأَهْدافَ الرَّئِيسِيَّةَ في التَّخْطِيطِ الاسْتِراتِيجِيِّ لِلْعامِ القادِمِ.

The general included the main objectives in the strategic planning for the coming year.

military training

تَدْرِيبٌ عَسْكَرِيٌّ

يُعْتَبَرُ التَّدْرِيبُ العَسْكَرِيُّ شَرْطًا أَساسِيًّا لِلاِنْضِمامِ إلى الجَيْشِ.

Military training is a fundamental requirement for joining the army.

operational

تَّشْغِيلِيٌّ

تَمَّ تَنْفِيذُ العَمَلِيّاتِ العَسْكَرِيَّةِ وَفْقًا لِلْخُطَّةِ التَّشْغِيلِيَّةِ.

The military operations were carried out according to the operational plan.

inspection

تَفْتِيشٌ

قامَتِ الوَحْداتُ العَسْكَرِيَّةُ بِتَفْتِيشِ المِنْطَقَةِ بَحْثًا عَنْ أَسْلِحَةٍ مُهَرَّبَةٍ.

The military units inspected the area, looking for smuggled weapons.

report

تَقارِيرُ • تَقْرِيرٌ

قُدِّمَ تَقْرِيرٌ مُفَصَّلٌ عَنِ التَّكْتِيكاتِ المُسْتَخْدَمَةِ في الهُجومِ الأَخِيرِ.

A detailed report was submitted on the tactics used in the recent attack.

technical

تِقْنِيٌّ

يَعْتَمِدُ الجَيْشُ عَلَى مُعَدّاتٍ تِقْنِيَّةٍ مُتَطَوِّرَةٍ لِلتَّجَسُّسِ.

The army relies on advanced technical equipment for espionage.

civil-military integration

تَكامُلٌ مَدَنِيٌّ عَسْكَرِيٌّ

يَسْعَى التَّكامُلُ المَدَنِيُّ العَسْكَرِيُّ لِتَعْزِيزِ العَلاقاتِ بَيْنَ المَدَنِيِّينَ والقُوّاتِ المُسَلَّحَةِ.

Civil-military integration seeks to enhance relations between civilians and the armed forces.

tactic(s)

تَكْتيكٌ

اِسْتَخْدَمَ الجِنرالُ تَكْتيكَ الخِداعِ لِلتَّغَلُّبِ عَلى العَدُوِّ.

The general used the tactic of deception to overcome the enemy.

tactical

تَكْتيكِيٌّ

القَراراتُ التَّكْتيكِيَّةُ تُؤَثِّرُ عَلى نَتائِجِ المَعْرَكَةِ.

Tactical decisions affect the outcomes of the battle.

future warfare technologies

تِكْنولوجْيا الحُروبِ المُسْتَقْبَلِيَّةِ

تَشْمَلُ تِكْنولوجْيا الحُروبِ المُسْتَقْبَلِيَّةُ اسْتِخْدامَ الطَّائِراتِ بِدونِ طَيّارٍ.

Future warfare technology includes the use of drones.

cutting-edge technology

تِكْنولوجْيا حَديثَةٌ

تَمَّ تَجْهيزُ الجَيْشِ بِالتِّكْنولوجْيا الحَديثَةِ لِضَمانِ الفَعالِيَّةِ.

The army was equipped with cutting-edge technology to ensure effectiveness.

funding

تَمْويلٌ

زادَتِ الحُكومَةُ تَمْويلَ القُوّاتِ العَسْكَرِيَّةِ لِتَحْديثِ المُعَدّاتِ.

The government increased military funding to update the equipment.

leadership development

تَنْمِيَةُ القُدُراتِ القِياديَّة

تَمَّ تَصْميمُ بَرْنامَجٍ لِتَنْمِيَةِ القُدُراتِ القِياديَّةِ لِلْجُنودِ.

A program was designed for the development of leadership skills in soldiers.

قُدْرات can also be pronounced قُدُرات.

quality

جَوْدَةٌ

يَجْري التَّأْكيدُ عَلى جَوْدَةِ المُعَدّاتِ العَسْكَرِيَّةِ لِتَحْقيقِ النَّجاحِ.

The quality of military equipment is emphasized to achieve success.

حَسَّاسٌ

sensitive (as in information)

المَعْلوماتُ العَسْكَرِيَّةُ حَسَّاسَةٌ وَتَحْتاجُ لِحِمايَةٍ قَوِيَّةٍ.

Military information is sensitive and needs strong protection.

خَصَّصَ • تَخْصيصٌ

to allocate

خَصَّصَتِ الحُكومَةُ ميزانِيَّةً كَبيرَةً لِلدِّفاعِ عَنِ الوَطَنِ.

The government allocated a large budget for national defense.

خَطَّطَ • تَخْطيطٌ

to plan

خَطَّطَ القائِدُ العَسْكَرِيُّ لِلْعَمَلِيَّةِ بِعِنايَةٍ فائِقَةٍ لِتَجَنُّبِ الخَسائِرِ مِنَ المَدَنِيِّينَ.

The military commander carefully planned the operation to avoid civilian casualties.

دَرَّبَ • تَدْريبٌ

to train

دُرِّبَ الجُنودُ عَلى اسْتِخْدامِ الأَسْلِحَةِ الجَديدَةِ في المُناوَراتِ.

Soldiers were trained to use new weapons in maneuvers.

دَقيقٌ

precise

تَتَطَلَّبُ العَمَلِيّاتُ العَسْكَرِيَّةُ تَوْجيهًا دَقيقًا لِلضَّرَباتِ الجَوِّيَّةِ.

Military operations require precise guidance for airstrikes.

دَوْرَةٌ تَدْريبِيَّةٌ

training course

اِنْتَهَتِ الدَّوْرَةُ التَّدْريبِيَّةُ العَسْكَرِيَّةُ وَوُزِّعَتِ الشَّهاداتُ عَلى المُشارِكينَ.

The military training course ended, and certificates were distributed to the participants.

طالِبٌ عَسْكَرِيٌّ • طُلّابٌ / طَلَبَةٌ

cadet

يُعْتَبَرُ الطَّلَبَةُ العَسْكَرِيّونَ نُخْبَةً مِنَ الشَّبابِ يَتَلَقَّوْنَ تَدْريبًا مُكَثَّفًا.

Military cadets are considered an elite group of young men who receive intensive training.

to develop

طَوَّرَ • تَطْويرٌ

طُوِّرَ نِظامُ التَّواصُلِ العَسْكَرِيِّ لِيَكونَ أَكْثَرَ أَمانًا وَفَعالِيَّةً.

The military communication system was developed to be more secure and effective.

contract

عَقْدٌ • عُقودٌ

أَدارَ القِسْمُ اللّوجِسْتِيُّ في الجَيْشِ عَقْدَ نَقْلِ الإِمْداداتِ الأَساسِيَّةِ.

The army's logistics department managed the contract for the transportation of essential supplies.

to inspect

فَحَصَ • فَحْصٌ

فَحَصَتِ القُوّاتُ العَسْكَرِيَّةُ الشِّحْناتِ قَبْلَ إِرْسالِها لِلْجَبْهَةِ.

The military forces inspected the shipments before sending them to the front.

combat capability

قُدْرَةٌ قِتالِيَّةٌ

تَمَّ تَقْييمُ القُدْرَةِ القِتالِيَّةِ لِلْوَحْدَةِ قَبْلَ الاِنْتِشارِ في المِنْطَقَةِ المَعْنِيَّةِ.

The unit's combat capability was assessed before deployment in the concerned area.

to bid

قَدَّمَ عَرْضًا • تَقْديمٌ

قَدَّمَتِ الشَّرِكَةُ عَرْضًا لِبَيْعِ مُعَدّاتٍ عَسْكَرِيَّةٍ مُتَطَوِّرَةٍ لِلْحُكومَةِ.

The company submitted a proposal to sell advanced military equipment to the government.

armed forces

قُوّاتٌ مُسَلَّحَةٌ

pl.

اِنْتَشَرَتِ القُوّاتُ المُسَلَّحَةُ عَلى طولِ الحُدودِ لِتَعْزيزِ الأَمْنِ.

The armed forces were deployed along the border to enhance security.

armed force

قُوَّةٌ مُسَلَّحَةٌ

أُرْسِلَتْ قُوَّةٌ مُسَلَّحَةٌ صَغيرَةٌ لِتَنْفيذِ مُهِمَّةٍ اسْتِخْباراتِيَّةٍ خَطيرَةٍ.

A small armed force was sent to execute a high-risk intelligence mission.

The term قُوَّةٌ مُسَلَّحَةٌ in the singular refers to a small armed group or unit, typically dispatched to perform a specific mission or task. In contrast, the plural form قُوَّاتٌ مُسَلَّحَةٌ refers to the armed forces or the military in general, encompassing the entire army or defense establishment.

قَوَّى • تَقْوِيَةٌ

to enhance

تَمَّتْ تَقْوِيَةُ الجَيْشِ الوَطَنِيِّ بِإِضَافَةِ وَحْداتٍ جَديدَةٍ مُتَخَصِّصَةٍ في الأَمْنِ السَّيْبَرانِيِّ.

The national army was enhanced by adding new units specialized in cybersecurity.

قَيَّمَ • تَقْيِيمٌ

to evaluate

قَيَّمَ الجِنْرالُ أَداءَ القُوَّاتِ خِلالَ التَّمارينِ التَّدْريبِيَّةِ الشَّاقَّةِ.

The general evaluated the performance of the troops during the rigorous training exercises.

مالِيٌّ

financial

تُواجِهُ الحُكومَةُ تَحَدِّياتٍ مالِيَّةً في تَمْويلِ العَمَلِيّاتِ العَسْكَرِيَّةِ.

The government faces financial challenges in funding military operations.

مُبْتَكَرٌ

innovative

تَمَّ تَطْويرُ أَسْلِحَةٍ مُبْتَكَرَةٍ لِزِيادَةِ فَعالِيَّةِ القُوَّاتِ.

Innovative weapons were developed to increase the effectiveness of the forces.

مُتَعَدِّدُ الجِنْسِيّاتِ

multinational

شارَكَتْ في التَّحالُفِ العَسْكَرِيِّ قُوّاتٌ مُتَعَدِّدَةُ الجِنْسِيّاتِ.

Multinational forces participated in the military alliance.

مُتَقَدِّمٌ

advanced

أُسْتُخْدِمَتْ تِكْنولوجْيا عَسْكَرِيَّةٌ مُتَقَدِّمَةٌ في الحَمْلَةِ.

Advanced military technology was used in the campaign.

military-industrial complex   مَجْمَعٌ عَسْكَرِيٌّ صِناعِيٌّ

تَزايَدَ تَأْثيرُ المَجْمَعِ العَسْكَرِيِّ الصِّناعِيِّ عَلَى السِّياسَةِ الخارِجِيَّةِ.

The influence of the military-industrial complex on foreign policy increased.

laboratory   مُخْتَبَرٌ

يَجْري في المُخْتَبَراتِ العَسْكَرِيَّةِ اخْتِبارُ مَوادَّ جَديدَةٍ لِلأَسْلِحَةِ.

New materials for weapons are tested in military laboratories.

instructor, trainer   مُدَرِّبٌ

تَمَّ تَوْظيفُ مُدَرِّبينَ عَسْكَرِيّينَ مِنَ الخارِجِ لِتَحْسينِ المُسْتَوى.

Foreign military trainers were employed to improve standards.

high-cost   مُرْتَفِعُ التَّكْلِفَةِ

تَمَّ شِراءُ طائِراتٍ حَرْبِيَّةٍ مُرْتَفِعَةِ التَّكْلِفَةِ لِتَعْزيزِ القُوَّةِ الجَوِّيَّةِ.

High-cost fighter jets were purchased to bolster the air force.

research center   مَراكِزُ •   مَرْكَزُ أَبْحاثٍ

تَمَّ افْتِتاحُ مَرْكَزِ أَبْحاثٍ عَسْكَرِيٍّ جَديدٍ لِتَطْويرِ تِكْنولوجيا الدِّفاعِ.

A new military research center was opened to develop defense technology.

dual-use (as in technology)   مُزْدَوَجُ الِاسْتِخْدامِ

تَمَّ تَطْويرُ تِكْنُولوجْيا مُزْدَوَجَةِ الِاسْتِخْدامِ يُمْكِنُ اسْتِغْلالُها في الأَغْراضِ المَدَنِيَّةِ والعَسْكَرِيَّةِ.

Dual-use technology that can be utilized for both civilian and military purposes was developed.

procurement   *pl.*   مُشْتَرَياتٌ عَسْكَرِيَّةٌ

تَمَّ تَحْديثُ المُشْتَرَياتِ العَسْكَرِيَّةِ لِتَأْمينِ الجَبَهاتِ.

Military gear purchases were updated to secure the fronts.

project

مَشْروعٌ • مَشاريعُ / مَشْروعاتٌ

بَدَأَ مَشْروعٌ لِتَطْويرِ نِظامِ دِفاعٍ صاروخِيٍّ جَديدٍ.

A project to develop a new missile defense system began.

equipment, gear

مُعَدَّةٌ

تَمَّ تَجْهيزُ القُوّاتِ بِمُعَدّاتٍ عَسْكَرِيَّةٍ حَديثَةٍ.

The forces were equipped with modern military gear.

While this word can be found in the singular, it is most commonly used in its plural form.

tender (as in a bid)

مُناقَصَةٌ

تَمَّ الإعْلانُ عَنْ مُناقَصَةٍ لِشِراءِ مِرْوَحِيّاتٍ عَسْكَرِيَّةٍ.

A tender was announced for the purchase of military helicopters.

military exercise/maneuver

مُناوَرَةٌ عَسْكَرِيَّةٌ

نَفَّذَتِ القُوّاتُ العَسْكَرِيَّةُ مُناوَرَةً عَسْكَرِيَّةً مُكَثَّفَةً لِتَعْزيزِ التَّدْريبِ والجاهِزِيَّةِ.

The military forces conducted an intensive military maneuver to enhance training and preparedness.

low-cost

مُنْخَفِضُ التَّكْلِفَةِ

جَرى البَحْثُ عَنْ حُلولٍ عَسْكَرِيَّةٍ مُنْخَفِضَةِ التَّكْلِفَةِ لِتَقْليلِ الإنْفاقِ.

Low-cost military solutions were sought to reduce spending.

specialized skills   pl.

مَهاراتٌ مُتَخَصِّصَةٌ

يَتَطَلَّبُ العَمَلُ في الأمْنِ السِّيْبَرانِيِّ مَهاراتٍ مُتَخَصِّصَةً.

Working in cybersecurity requires specialized skills.

budget

ميزانِيَّةٌ

تَمَّتِ المُوافَقَةُ عَلى ميزانِيَّةِ الدِّفاعِ بَعْدَ جَلَساتٍ طَويلَةٍ في البَرْلَمانِ.

The defense budget was approved after lengthy sessions in the parliament.

to regulate   • تَنْظِيمٌ   نَظَّمَ

نَظَّمَتِ الحُكُومَةُ اسْتِخْدَامَ الطَّائِرَاتِ بِدُونِ طَيَّارٍ فِي المَنَاطِقِ الحَرْبِيَّةِ لِتَقْلِيلِ المَخَاطِرِ المَدَنِيَّةِ.

The government regulated the use of drones in war zones to minimize civilian risks.

to implement, execute   • تَنْفِيذٌ   نَفَّذَ

نَفَّذَ الجَيْشُ عَمَلِيَّةً نَاجِحَةً لِتَحْرِيرِ الرَّهَائِنِ.

The army executed a successful operation to free the hostages.

military expenditure   pl.   نَفَقَاتٌ عَسْكَرِيَّةٌ

شَهِدَتِ النَّفَقَاتُ العَسْكَرِيَّةُ ارْتِفَاعًا كَبِيرًا هَذَا العَامَ.

Military expenditures saw a significant increase this year.

7.3.3.1 Mini-Articles

Track **29**

أَشْرَفَ الجِنرَالُ مَحْمُود العِزِّي عَلَى حَفْلِ تَخْرِيجِ دُفْعَةٍ جَدِيدَةٍ مِنْ طُلَّابِ الأَكَادِيمِيَّةِ العَسْكَرِيَّةِ. خِلَالَ الحَفْلِ، اسْتَعْرَضَ الطُّلَّابُ المَهَارَاتِ المُتَخَصِّصَةَ الَّتِي اكْتَسَبُوها خِلَالَ الدَّوْرَاتِ التَّدْرِيبِيَّةِ. وَقَدْ أَعْلَنَتِ الإِدَارَةُ اللُّوجِسْتِيَّةُ عَنْ شِرَاءِ تِقْنِيَّاتٍ حَدِيثَةٍ لِتَطْوِيرِ التَّدْرِيبِ العَسْكَرِيِّ وَتَنْمِيَةِ القُدُرَاتِ القِيَادِيَّةِ.

General Mahmoud Al-Azbi presided over the graduation ceremony of a new batch of students from the Military Academy. During the event, the students showcased specialized skills they acquired during training courses. The logistics administration announced the purchase of modern technology to enhance military training and develop leadership abilities.

كَشَفَ تَقْرِيرٌ مَالِيٌّ حَدِيثٌ عَنْ نِيَّةِ وَزَارَةِ الدِّفَاعِ لِزِيَادَةِ النَّفَقَاتِ العَسْكَرِيَّةِ خِلَالَ العَامِ المُقْبِلِ. تُرَكِّزُ هَذِهِ الزِّيَادَةُ عَلَى دَعْمِ بَحْثِ وَتَطْوِيرِ تِكْنُولُوجْيا الحُرُوبِ المُسْتَقْبَلِيَّةِ. وَقَدِ ابْتَكَرَ مَرْكَزُ الأَبْحَاثِ العَسْكَرِيَّةِ أَنْظِمَةً مُتَقَدِّمَةً تَعْمَلُ بِتِكْنُولُوجْيا مُزْدَوَجَةِ الاسْتِخْدَامِ لِتَحْسِينِ القُدْرَةِ القِتَالِيَّةِ لِلْقُوَّاتِ المُسَلَّحَةِ.

A recent financial report revealed the Ministry of Defense's intention to increase military expenditures in the coming year. This increase focuses on supporting the research and development of future warfare technology. The military research center has developed advanced systems using dual-use technology to enhance the armed forces' combat capability.

دَعَتْ وَزَارَةُ الدِّفاعِ الشَّرِكاتِ الصِّناعِيَّةَ لِتَقْديمِ عُروضِها في مُناقَصَةٍ تَهْدُفُ إلى تَطْويرِ وَشِراءِ مُعَدّاتٍ عَسْكَرِيَّةٍ جَديدَةٍ. يَأْتي ذَلِكَ في إطارِ الاسْتِراتيجِيَّةِ الدِّفاعِيَّةِ الَّتي خَطَّطَتْ لَها الوَزارَةُ لِزِيادَةِ فَعالِيَّةِ القُوّاتِ البَرِّيَّةِ وَالجَوِّيَّةِ. وَقَدْ تَمَّ تَخْصيصُ مِيزانِيَّةٍ خاصَّةٍ لِهَذا المَشْروعِ، مَعَ التَّرْكيزِ عَلى جَوْدَةِ المُعَدّاتِ وَدِقَّتِها.

The Ministry of Defense has invited industrial companies to submit their bids in a tender aimed at developing and purchasing new military equipment. This comes within the framework of the defense strategy outlined by the ministry to enhance the efficiency of land and air forces. A special budget has been allocated for this project, emphasizing equipment quality and accuracy.

7.3.3.2 Editorial: Future Defense Technology

Track **30**

تِكْنولوجيا الدِّفاعِ المُسْتَقْبَلِيَّةُ: اسْتِثْمارٌ في أَمْنِ الوَطَنِ

يَمُرُّ الأَمْنُ الوَطَنِيُّ بِثَوْرَةٍ تِكْنولوجِيَّةٍ، حَيْثُ يَتِمُّ ابْتِكارُ تِقْنِياتٍ حَديثَةٍ مُتَعَدِّدَةٍ مِنَ الأَمْنِ السَّيْبَرانِيِّ إلى القُوَّةِ الجَوِّيَّةِ. في هَذا السِّياقِ، تُعْتَبَرُ الأَكاديمِياتُ العَسْكَرِيَّةُ المَرْكَزَ الرَّئيسِيَّ لِتَدْريبِ الجيلِ الجَديدِ عَلى هَذِهِ التِّكْنولوجْيا. لَكِنْ، هَلْ نُدْرِكُ التَّأْثيرَ الاقْتِصادِيَّ لِهَذا الاتِّجاهِ الجَديدِ؟

مَعَ ارْتِفاعِ الإنْفاقِ العَسْكَرِيِّ، نَجِدُ أَنَّ اسْتِثْماراتِ الدِّفاعِ تَنْخَرِطُ بِشَكْلٍ مُتَزايِدٍ في مَجالاتِ البَحْثِ وَالتَّطْويرِ. هَذِهِ الاسْتِراتيجِيّاتُ الاقْتِصادِيَّةُ، وَإنْ كانَتْ مُرْتَفِعَةَ التَّكْلِفَةِ في الوَقْتِ الحالِيِّ، تَهْدُفُ إلى تَحْقيقِ أمانٍ طَويلِ المَدى وَمُسْتَدامٍ. مِنَ المُهِمِّ أَنْ نُدْرِكَ أَنَّ الاسْتِثْمارَ في التَّخْطيطِ الاسْتِراتيجِيِّ وَالتَّدْريبِ العَسْكَرِيِّ يُحَقِّقُ التَّوازُنَ بَيْنَ الأَمْنِ وَالاقْتِصادِ.

يَبْدو أَنَّ الحاجَةَ الماسَّةَ لِلتَّكامُلِ المَدَنِيِّ العَسْكَرِيِّ قَدْ أَصْبَحَتْ أَكْثَرَ أَهَمِّيَّةً مِنْ أَيِّ وَقْتٍ مَضى. فَالتَّوازُنُ بَيْنَ القُوَّةِ العَسْكَرِيَّةِ، وَالتِّكْنولوجْيا المُتَقَدِّمَةِ، وَالاسْتِراتيجِيّاتِ الاقْتِصادِيَّةِ سَيُحَدِّدُ الدَّوْرَ المُسْتَقْبَلِيَّ لِلدَّوْلَةِ في حِمايَةِ أَمْنِها وَاقْتِصادِها.

Future Defense Technology: Investing in National Security

National security is undergoing a technological revolution, with the creation of new technologies ranging from cybersecurity to air power. In this context, military academies are the main hub for training the new generation in this technology. But do we recognize the economic impact of this new trend?

With rising military spending, we find that defense investments are increasingly engaged in research and development areas. While these economic strategies might be costly at present, they aim for long-term sustainable security. It's essential to understand that investing in strategic planning and military training strikes a balance between security and the economy.

The pressing need for civilian-military integration seems more critical than ever. The balance between military power, advanced technology, and economic strategies will determine the future role of the state in protecting its security and economy.

Unit 8
Religion and Society

In this unit, we delve into the multifaceted dimensions of religion, focusing on Islam and its broader implications in society, all within the context of media Arabic. Through this lens, we aim to equip you with the language and contextual understanding necessary to engage effectively with religious topics as they appear in academic contexts, news articles, and broadcasts.

We begin with an exploration of Islam and Islamic culture, encompassing its rich history, philosophical underpinnings, legal and theological frameworks, and contributions to arts and literature. We will explore the intricacies of Islamic thought, its evolution over time and its contemporary relevance.

Moving forward, we will examine interfaith relations and the importance of understanding and respecting religious diversity. This section will explore comparative religion, the rights of religious minorities, and the imperative of fostering dialogue and cooperation among different faith communities.

Furthermore, we will delve into social issues related to religion, including discussions on women's rights in Islamic societies, religious symbols and dress codes, the role of religious education and scholarship, and the challenges posed by religious extremism and sectarianism.

Finally, we will explore customs and practices in Islam, offering an introductory overview of Islamic rituals and traditions. From the Five Pillars of Islam to the significance of Ramadan, the Mosque, and the pilgrimage of Hajj, we will explore the depth and diversity of Islamic practices.

Throughout this unit, you will encounter a wealth of vocabulary, example sentences, and short articles designed to enhance your understanding of religious concepts and their expression in Arabic. By engaging with this material, you will not only expand your language skills but also deepen your appreciation for the role of religion in shaping societies and cultures.

8.1 Islam and Islamic Culture

Track **31**

religion
دينٌ • أَديانٌ

يُؤَكِّدُ الدِّينُ الإِسْلامِيُّ عَلى التَّوْحيدِ وَيَتْبَعُ تَعاليمَ القُرْآنِ.

Islamic religion emphasizes monotheism and follows the teachings of the Quran.

religious
دينِيٌّ

ظَهَرَتِ التَّوَتُّراتُ الدِّينِيَّةُ في مَدينَةِ البَصْرَةِ بَعْدَ حادِثِ اسْتِهْدافِ كَنيسَةٍ.

Religious tensions appeared in the city of Basra after an incident targeting a church.

Islam
إِسْلامٌ

أُفْتُتِحَ مَتْحَفٌ جَديدٌ في القاهِرَةِ يَهْدُفُ إلى تَسْليطِ الضَّوْءِ عَلى تاريخِ الإِسْلامِ.

A new museum was opened in Cairo, aiming to highlight the history of Islam.

Islamic
إِسْلامِيٌّ

في تونِسَ، انْدَلَعَتِ احْتِجاجاتٌ بَعْدَ قَرارِ الحُكومَةِ بِإِغْلاقِ مَدْرَسَةٍ إِسْلامِيَّةٍ شَهيرَةٍ.

In Tunisia, protests erupted after the government decided to close a well-known Islamic school.

Muslim
مُسْلِمٌ

في لُبْنانَ، أَظْهَرَ اسْتِطْلاعٌ لِلرَّأْيِ تَزايُدَ نِسْبَةِ الشَّبابِ المُسْلِمِ الَّذينَ يَرْغَبونَ في الهِجْرَةِ.

In Lebanon, a public opinion poll showed an increasing percentage of Muslim youth who wish to emigrate.

8.1.1 Islamic History and Philosophy

Track **32**

to date, to chronicle
أَرَّخَ • تَأْريخٌ

أَرَّخَ الكاتِبُ عَبْدُ اللهِ التَّطَوُّراتِ الأَخيرَةَ في الإِسْلامِ السِّياسِيِّ بِالْعِراقِ.

The writer Abdullah chronicled the recent developments in political Islam in Iraq.

to establish, to found

تَأْسِيسٌ • أَسَّسَ

أَسَّسَ الشَّيْخُ مَحْمُودٌ مَدْرَسَةً لِلْفِكْرِ الْإِسْلَامِيِّ فِي الْخُرْطُومِ.

Sheikh Mahmoud founded a school for Islamic thought in Khartoum.

political Islam

إِسْلَامٌ سِيَاسِيٌّ

تَزَايَدَ تَأْثِيرُ الْإِسْلَامِ السِّيَاسِيِّ فِي تُونِسَ.

The influence of political Islam has increased in Tunisia.

the Islamic State

دُوَلٌ • الدَّوْلَةُ الْإِسْلَامِيَّةُ

تَأَسَّسَتِ الدَّوْلَةُ الْإِسْلَامِيَّةُ الْجَدِيدَةُ بَعْدَ انْتِهَاءِ الثَّوْرَةِ لِتَحْقِيقِ الْعَدَالَةِ وَالْمُسَاوَاةِ بَيْنَ الْمُوَاطِنِينَ.

The new Islamic state was established after the revolution to achieve justice and equality among the citizens.

Salafism

السَّلَفِيَّةُ

شَهِدَتِ السَّلَفِيَّةُ تَزَايُدًا فِي الشَّعْبِيَّةِ بَيْنَ الشُّبَّانِ فِي مِصْرَ.

Salafism has seen an increase in its popularity among young people in Egypt.

Sunnis; Sunnism

السُّنَّةُ

حَاوَلَتِ الْمُنَظَّمَاتُ الدِّينِيَّةُ فِي بَغْدَادَ تَعْزِيزَ الْحِوَارِ بَيْنَ السُّنَّةِ وَالشِّيعَةِ.

Religious organizations in Baghdad tried to promote dialogue between Sunnis and Shiites.

the biography of the Prophet Muhammad

سِيَرٌ • السِّيرَةُ النَّبَوِيَّةُ

قَامَتْ دَارُ النَّشْرِ بِإِصْدَارِ كِتَابٍ جَدِيدٍ عَنِ السِّيرَةِ النَّبَوِيَّةِ.

The publishing house released a new book on the biography of the Prophet Muhammad.

the Holy Quran

الْقُرْآنُ الْكَرِيمُ

قَرَأَ الطُّلَّابُ الْقُرْآنَ الْكَرِيمَ فِي الْمَدْرَسَةِ.

The students read the Holy Quran in school.

the Sacred Mosque

مَساجِدُ • المَسْجِدُ الحَرامُ

شَهِدَ المَسْجِدُ الحَرامُ زِيادَةً في عَدَدِ الزُّوّارِ هَذا العامَ.

The Sacred Mosque saw an increase in the number of visitors this year.

the Prophet's Mosque

المَسْجِدُ النَّبَوِيُّ

تَمَّ تَوْسيعُ المَسْجِدِ النَّبَوِيِّ لِاسْتِيعابِ عَدَدٍ أَكْبَرَ مِنَ المُصَلّينَ وَالزّوّارِ القادِمينَ مِنْ جَميعِ أَنْحاءِ العالَمِ.

The Prophet's Mosque was expanded to accommodate a larger number of worshippers and visitors coming from all around the world.

to belong to

انْتِماءٌ • انْتَمى إلى

في مُقابَلَةٍ تِلِفِزْيونِيَّةٍ حَصْرِيَّةٍ، كَشَفَتِ الشَّيْخَةُ لَيْلى عَنْ كَيْفِيَّةِ انْتِمائِها إلى جَماعَةٍ دينِيَّةٍ تَعْمَلُ عَلى تَعْزيزِ التَّسامُحِ وَالتَّعايُشِ السِّلْمِيِّ في المِنْطَقَةِ.

In an exclusive television interview, Sheikhah Layla revealed her affiliation with a religious group working to promote tolerance and peaceful coexistence in the region.

history

تَواريخُ • تاريخٌ

تُدْرَسُ رُؤًى تاريخِيَّةٌ مُتَعَدِّدَةٌ في الجامِعاتِ العَرَبِيَّةِ.

Multiple historical perspectives are studied in Arab universities.

historical

تاريخِيٌّ

يَرْوي الكِتابُ التاريخِيُّ الجَديدُ قِصَّةَ الحُروبِ الإِسْلامِيَّةِ الكُبْرى بِأُسْلوبٍ شَيِّقٍ وَمُفَصَّلٍ.

The new historical book narrates the story of the major Islamic wars in an engaging and detailed manner.

Salafi

سَلَفِيٌّ

انْضَمَّ الشّابُّ إلى جَماعَةٍ سَلَفِيَّةٍ في اليَمَنِ.

The young man joined a Salafi group in Yemen.

Sunnah

سُنَّةٌ

يُحاوِلُ اَلْعُلَماءُ فَهْمَ السُّنَّةِ في سِياقِها التّاريخيِّ.

Scholars try to understand the Sunnah in its historical context.

The term سُنَّةٌ has two meanings: 1) The teachings and practices of the Prophet Muhammad, typically discussed in conjunction with the Qur'an and serving as guidance for Islamic behavior. This meaning is demonstrated in the previous example. 2) سُنَّةٌ is also a principal division of Islam, Sunnism, contrasted with Shi'ism (شيعَةٌ). This usage pertains to the followers of the traditional majority branch, as shown on page 103 and is also expressed using the nibsa adjective form, which denotes affiliation or relation, below.

Sunni

سُنِّيٌّ

تُعْتَبَرُ السُّعوديَّةُ بَوّابَةً لِلْعالَمِ السُّنِّيِّ.

Saudi Arabia is considered a gateway to the Sunni world.

biography

سيرَةٌ • سِيَرٌ

نَشَرَ الكاتِبُ سيرَةً ذاتِيَّةً لِلْفَيْلَسوفِ الإسْلاميِّ ابْنِ رُشْدٍ.

The writer published a biography of the Islamic philosopher Ibn Rushd.

Shia, Shiites; Shi'ism

شيعَةٌ

يَعيشُ الشّيعَةُ كَأَغْلَبِيَّةٍ في البَحْرَيْنِ.

The Shia live as a majority in Bahrain.

Shiite

شيعيٌّ

دَعا القائِدُ الشّيعيُّ إلى الوَحْدَةِ بَيْنَ جَميعِ المُسْلِمينَ.

The Shiite leader called for unity among all Muslims.

Sufi

صوفيٌّ

تُعْتَبَرُ الموسيقى الصّوفيَّةُ وَسيلَةً روحيَّةً لِلتَّعْبيرِ وَالتَّأَمُّلِ في العَلاقَةِ بَيْنَ الإنْسانِ وَاللهِ.

Sufi music is considered a spiritual means of expression and contemplation in the relationship between humans and God.

Sufism

صوفِيَّةٌ

تَتَجَذَّرُ الصّوفِيَّةُ في بَعْضِ المَناطِقِ الرّيفِيَّةِ بِالْمَغْرِبِ كَوَسيلَةٍ لِلتَّواصُلِ الرّوحِيِّ.

Sufism is deeply rooted in some rural areas of Morocco as a means of spiritual connection.

The term الصّوفِيَّةُ refers to Sufism, a mystical Islamic belief and practice. It is also known as التَّصَوُّفُ.

Islamic thought

فِكْرٌ إِسْلامِيٌّ

تَسْعى الجامِعاتُ العَرَبِيَّةُ لِإِضافَةِ مُقَرَّراتٍ تَتَناوَلُ الفِكْرَ الإِسْلامِيَّ بِشَكْلٍ عِلْمِيٍّ.

Arab universities are striving to add courses that scientifically address Islamic thought.

Salafist thought

فِكْرٌ سَلَفِيٌّ

يَتَناوَلُ الكِتابُ الفِكْرَ السَّلَفِيَّ وَتَأْثيرَهُ عَلى المُجْتَمَعِ.

The book addresses Salafist thought and its impact on society.

Sufi thought

فِكْرٌ صوفِيٌّ

أَقامَتْ جَمْعِيَّةٌ طُلّابِيَّةٌ نَدْوَةً حَوْلَ الفِكْرِ الصّوفِيِّ.

A student association held a seminar on Sufi thought.

philosophy

فَلْسَفَةٌ

يَجْري البَحْثُ في الفَلْسَفَةِ الإِسْلامِيَّةِ في الجامِعَةِ.

Research in Islamic philosophy is being conducted at the university.

philosophical

فَلْسَفِيٌّ

تُعَدُّ الإِشاراتُ الفَلْسَفِيَّةُ مُهِمَّةً في الأَعْمالِ الأَدَبِيَّةِ لِجَلالِ الدّينِ الرّومِيِّ.

Philosophical references are important in the literary work of Jalaluddin Rumi.

نَظَرَ في • نَظَرٌ

to look at, to consider

نَظَرَ العُلَماءُ في العَلاقَةِ بَيْنَ الإسْلامِ وَالدّيمُقْراطِيَّةِ.

Scholars looked at the relationship between Islam and democracy.

نَظَرَ إلى means 'to [physically] look at,' while نَظَرَ في means 'to consider or examine.'

8.1.1.1 Mini-Articles

في سِلْسِلَةِ نَدَواتٍ حَديثَةٍ، نَظَرَ مُفَكِّرونَ مِنْ مُخْتَلِفِ المَذاهِبِ الإسْلامِيَّةِ في أُسُسِ الفَلْسَفَةِ الإسْلامِيَّةِ وَسُبُلِ تَجْديدِها لِمُواكَبَةِ العَصْرِ. شَمَلَ الحِوارُ مَواضيعَ مُتَنَوِّعَةً مِثلَ الفِكْرِ السَّلَفِيِّ وَالصّوفِيِّ وَتاريخِ مَراحِلِ تَطَوُّرِ الدّينِ الإسْلامِيِّ، مَعَ تَسْليطِ الضَّوْءِ عَلى السّيرَةِ النَّبَوِيَّةِ كَمَصْدَرِ إلْهامٍ.

In a recent series of seminars, thinkers from various Islamic schools of thought examined the foundations of Islamic philosophy and ways to renew it to keep pace with the times. The dialogue included diverse topics such as Salafi and Sufi thought and a history of the stages of the development of Islam, with an emphasis on the prophetic biography as a source of inspiration.

أَعْلَنَتْ دارُ الوَثائِقِ القَوْمِيَّةِ عَنِ اكْتِشافِ مَخْطوطاتٍ تاريخِيَّةٍ تَنْتَمي إلى عَصْرِ السَّلَفِ وَتَحْتَوي عَلى نُصوصٍ فَلْسَفِيَّةٍ تَعودُ إلى القَرْنِ الثّالِثِ الهِجْرِيِّ. هَذِهِ النُّصوصُ تُشيرُ إلى انْتِماءِ أَصْحابِها إلى مَدْرَسَةٍ فِكْرِيَّةٍ غَنِيَّةٍ بِالنَّظَرِ في مَسائِلَ دينِيَّةٍ وَاجْتِماعِيَّةٍ مُعَقَّدَةٍ.

The National Archives announced the discovery of historical manuscripts belonging to the Salafi era containing philosophical texts dating back to the third Hijri century. These texts indicate that their owners belonged to a school of thought rich in considering complex religious and social issues.

اِفْتَتَحَتِ الجامِعَةُ الكُبْرى مَرْكَزًا لِلدِّراساتِ الإسْلامِيَّةِ يُرَكِّزُ عَلى تاريخِ الدُّوَلِ الإسْلامِيَّةِ وَالفِكْرِ الإسْلامِيِّ، بِما في ذَلِكَ الفَلْسَفَةِ الصّوفِيَّةِ وَالسُّنِّيَّةِ وَالشّيعِيَّةِ. يَهْدُفُ المَرْكَزُ إلى تَعْزيزِ الحِوارِ بَيْنَ مُخْتَلِفِ الأَدْيانِ وَالمَذاهِبِ.

The grand university opened a center for Islamic studies focusing on the history of Islamic states and Islamic thought, including Sufi, Sunni, and Shiite philosophy. The center aims to promote dialogue between different religions and schools of thought.

شَهِدَتِ العاصِمَةُ مُؤْتَمَرًا دَوْلِيًّا حَوْلَ الإسْلامِ السّياسِيِّ وَتَأْثيرِهِ عَلى تَأْسيسِ الدُّوَلِ في التّاريخِ الإسْلامِيِّ. ناقَشَ الخُبَراءُ الدَّوْرَ الَّذي لَعِبَتْهُ السّيرَةُ النَّبَوِيَّةُ في تَشْكيلِ الأَنْظِمَةِ السّياسِيَّةِ وَالاجْتِماعِيَّةِ، وَكَيْفَ تَطَوَّرَتْ مَفاهيمُ الحُكْمِ في الإسْلامِ.

The capital hosted an international conference on political Islam and its impact on the founding of states in Islamic history. Experts discussed the role that the prophetic biography played in shaping political and social systems and how concepts of governance in Islam have evolved.

أَعْلَنَتِ الهَيْئَةُ الدِّينِيَّةُ عَنْ خُطَطٍ لِتَرْمِيمِ المَسْجِدِ النَّبَوِيِّ، مَعَ الحِرْصِ عَلَى المُحَافَظَةِ عَلَى الطِّرَازِ التَّارِيخِيِّ لِلْمَسْجِدِ. سَيَشْمَلُ المَشْرُوعُ أَعْمَالَ تَرْمِيمٍ لِلْأَقْسَامِ الأَثَرِيَّةِ القَدِيمَةِ وَتَحْسِينَاتٍ لِلْمَرَافِقِ الحَدِيثَةِ لِاسْتِيعَابِ عَدَدٍ أَكْبَرَ مِنَ المُسْلِمِينَ خِلَالَ مَوْسِمِ الحَجِّ.

The religious authority announced plans for the restoration of the Prophet's Mosque, with care to preserve the historical style of the mosque. The project will include restoration work on the old archaeological sections and improvements to the modern facilities to accommodate more Muslims during the Hajj season.

8.1.1.2 Essay: Islamic Thought

Track 34

الفِكْرُ الإِسْلامِيُّ في مُوَاجَهَةِ تَحَدِّيَاتِ العَصْرِ

في زَمَانِنَا هَذَا، يَبْدُو أَنَّ الفِكْرَ الإِسْلامِيَّ، بِمَا في ذَلِكَ الفَلْسَفَةَ الصُّوفِيَّةَ وَالسَّلَفِيَّةَ، يُوَاجِهُ تَحَدِّيَاتٍ جَمَّةً. فَكَيْفَ يُمْكِنُ لِهَذَا الفِكْرِ أَنْ يَنْتَمِيَ إلى سِيَاقِهِ التَّارِيخِيِّ وَفي الوَقْتِ نَفْسِهِ يَتَأَقْلَمَ مَعَ المُعْطَيَاتِ المُعَاصِرَةِ؟

لا يُمْكِنُنَا النَّظَرُ إلى الدِّينِ الإِسْلامِيِّ دُونَ أَخْذِ تَارِيخِهِ الغَنِيِّ بِعَيْنِ الاعْتِبَارِ. فَتَارِيخُ الإِسْلامِ يَشْمَلُ حِقَبًا زَمَنِيَّةً مُخْتَلِفَةً وَأَحْدَاثًا جِسَامًا أَسَّسَتْ لِلْأُمَمِ وَالدُّوَلِ الإِسْلامِيَّةِ. وَلَعَلَّ مِنْ أَبْرَزِ هَذِهِ الدُّوَلِ مَا كَانَ يُعْرَفُ بِالدَّوْلَةِ الإِسْلامِيَّةِ في العُصُورِ الوُسْطَى، حَيْثُ كَانَتِ السُّنَّةُ وَالشِّيعَةُ تَتَشَارَكَانِ في بِنَاءِ حَضَارَةٍ مَا تَزَالُ آثَارُهَا بَاقِيَةً إلى اليَوْمِ.

يَتَبَايَنُ الفِكْرُ الإِسْلامِيُّ بَيْنَ التَّيَّارَاتِ المُخْتَلِفَةِ كَالسَّلَفِيَّةِ الَّتِي تُنَادِي بِالْعَوْدَةِ إلى أُسْلُوبِ حَيَاةِ السَّلَفِ الصَّالِحِ، وَالصُّوفِيَّةِ الَّتِي تُرَكِّزُ عَلَى البُعْدِ الرُّوحِيِّ وَالشَّخْصِيِّ في العِبَادَةِ. هَذِهِ التَّنَوُّعَاتُ في الفِكْرِ الدِّينِيِّ لا تَعْكِسُ الانْقِسَامَ فَحَسْبُ، بَلْ تُظْهِرُ غِنَى الإِسْلامِ وَتَعَدُّدَ أَبْعَادِهِ.

وَمِنَ الجَدِيرِ بِالذِّكْرِ أَيْضًا أَنَّ القُرْآنَ الكَرِيمَ وَالسِّيرَةَ النَّبَوِيَّةَ قَدْ قَدَّمَا مُسَاهَمَاتٍ فِكْرِيَّةً وَتَارِيخِيَّةً لا تُقَدَّرُ بِثَمَنٍ. وَعَلَى وَجْهِ التَّحْدِيدِ، يَظْهَرُ تَأْثِيرُ القُرْآنِ الكَرِيمِ وَالسِّيرَةِ النَّبَوِيَّةِ في تَوْجِيهِ الفِكْرِ الإِسْلامِيِّ نَحْوَ مَفَاهِيمِ التَّعَايُشِ وَالعَدَالَةِ الاجْتِمَاعِيَّةِ، مُكَرِّسَيْنِ بِذَلِكَ مَبَادِئَ السَّلامِ وَالتَّسَامُحِ كَأَسَاسٍ لِلتَّفَاعُلِ مَعَ التَّحَدِّيَاتِ.

في خِضَمِّ هَذِهِ التَّحَدِّيَاتِ، يَبْقَى السُّؤَالُ مَفْتُوحًا: كَيْفَ يُمْكِنُ لِلْفِكْرِ الإِسْلامِيِّ أَنْ يُحَافِظَ عَلَى جُذُورِهِ التَّارِيخِيَّةِ وَفي الوَقْتِ نَفْسِهِ يُسْهِمُ في إِثْرَاءِ الحِوَارِ الثَّقَافِيِّ وَالفَلْسَفِيِّ المُعَاصِرِ؟ إِنَّ الإِجَابَةَ عَلَى هَذَا السُّؤَالِ تَتَطَلَّبُ مِنَّا جَمِيعًا، مُسْلِمِينَ وَغَيْرَ مُسْلِمِينَ، أَنْ نَنْظُرَ في التَّارِيخِ وَنَسْتَلْهِمَ مِنْهُ الدُّرُوسَ وَنُطَبِّقَهَا عَلَى وَاقِعِنَا اليَوْمَ.

Islamic Thought Facing the Challenges of the Era

In our time, Islamic thought, including Sufi and Salafi philosophy, seems to face numerous challenges. How can this thought belong to its historical context while at the same time adapting to contemporary realities?

We cannot look at Islam without taking into account its rich history. The history of Islam includes different eras and significant events that established nations and Islamic states. One of the most prominent of these states was known as the Islamic state in the medieval period, where Sunnis and Shiites collaborated in building a civilization whose effects remain to this day.

Islamic thought varies among different currents such as Salafism, which advocates returning to the lifestyle of the righteous ancestors, and Sufism, which focuses on the spiritual and personal dimensions of worship. These variations in religious thought reflect not only division but also the richness of Islam and its multiple dimensions.

It is also worth mentioning that the Holy Quran and the Prophetic biography have provided invaluable intellectual and historical contributions. And it is worth mentioning that the Quran and the Prophetic biography have provided invaluable intellectual and historical contributions. Specifically, their influence is evident in directing Islamic thought toward concepts of coexistence and social justice, establishing principles of peace and tolerance as the foundation for addressing contemporary challenges.

Amidst these challenges, the question remains open: How can Islamic thought maintain its historical roots while at the same time contributing to the enrichment of contemporary cultural and philosophical dialogue? Answering this question requires all of us, Muslims and non-Muslims alike, to look into history, draw lessons from it, and apply them to our reality today.

8.1.2 Islamic Law and Theology

Track **35**

أَصْدَرَ فَتْوى • إِصْدارٌ

to issue a legal opinion or ruling

أَصْدَرَ المُفْتي فَتْوى تُحَرِّمُ اسْتِهْلاكَ الكُحولِ.

The Mufti issued a fatwa prohibiting the consumption of alcohol.

أُصولُ الفِقْهِ الإِسْلامِيِّ

principles of Islamic jurisprudence   *pl.*

أَلْقى الدُّكْتورُ حُسَيْنٌ مُحاضَرَةً عَنْ أُصولِ الفِقْهِ الإِسْلامِيِّ في جامِعَةِ الأَزْهَرِ.

Dr. Hussein gave a lecture on the principles of Islamic jurisprudence at Al-Azhar University.

أَفْتَى   to issue a legal opinion or ruling

في خِلالِ النَّدْوَةِ الدّينِيَّةِ، أَفْتَى الشَّيْخُ بِجَوازِ تَقْديمِ المُساعَداتِ لِلْفُقَراءِ وَالمُحْتاجينَ في الشَّهْرِ الكَريمِ.

During the religious seminar, the Sheikh ruled on the permissibility of providing assistance to the needy and the poor during the holy month.

اِجْتَهَدَ   • اِجْتِهادٌ   to strive or exert oneself (in Islamic scholarship or jurisprudence)

اِجْتَهَدَ العُلَماءُ في تَفْسيرِ نُصوصِ القُرْآنِ الكَريمِ.

Scholars have endeavored to interpret the texts of the Holy Quran.

In Islamic contexts, اِجْتِهادٌ refers to the scholarly effort to interpret texts and formulate rulings for contemporary situations, involving intellectual innovation and acknowledging the possibility of error due to its human origin.

اِسْتَنْتَجَ   • اِسْتِنْتاجٌ   to deduce/infer (in Islamic legal rulings)

اِسْتَنْتَجَ الفُقَهاءُ قَواعِدَ جَديدَةً مِنَ الحَديثِ الشَّريفِ.

Jurists deduced new rules from the sacred Hadith.

الخِلافَةُ   Caliphate (the Islamic political system)

أَعْلَنَتْ جَماعَةٌ مُسَلَّحَةٌ في سوريا عَنْ إقامَةِ الخِلافَةِ.

An armed group in Syria announced the establishment of a Caliphate.

تَفْسيرُ (القُرْآن)   • تَفْسيراتٌ / تَفاسيرُ   Quranic exegesis/interpretation

يُقَدِّمُ الدُّكْتورُ عادِل سِلْسِلَةَ مُحاضَراتٍ عَنْ تَفْسيرِ القُرْآنِ في جامِعَةِ بَغْدادَ.

Dr. Adel is offering a lecture series on Quranic exegesis at the University of Baghdad.

حَدَّدَ   • تَحْديدٌ   to determine/specify (in Islamic legal rulings)

حَدَّدَ العُلَماءُ الأُمورَ الحَلالَ وَالحَرامَ في المُعامَلاتِ المالِيَّةِ.

Scholars determined the permissible and forbidden matters in financial transactions.

Hadith (sayings of Prophet Muhammad)

أَحاديثُ • حَديثٌ

رَكَّزَ الباحِثونَ عَلى دِراسَةِ حَديثٍ عَنِ الصَّلاةِ.

Researchers focused on studying a Hadith about prayer.

forbidden (in Islamic law)

حَرامٌ

تُعْتَبَرُ الموسيقى حَرامًا وَفْقًا لِبَعْضِ الفُقَهاءِ.

Music is considered forbidden according to some jurists.

permissible (in Islamic law)

حَلالٌ

في السّوقِ الشَّعْبِيَّةِ، توجَدُ مَحَلّاتٌ تَبيعُ اللَّحْمَ الحَلالَ المُعْتَمَدَ وَالمُنْتَجاتِ الغِذائِيَّةَ الَّتي تُلَبّي احْتِياجاتِ المُسْلِمينَ.

In the local market, there are shops selling certified halal meat and food products that meet the needs of Muslims.

Prophetic example or practice

سُنَنْ • سُنَّةٌ

يَعْتَبِرُ العُلَماءُ السُّنَّةَ مَصْدَرًا ثانِيًا لِلتَّشْريعِ بَعْدَ القُرْآنِ.

Scholars consider the Sunnah a second source of legislation after the Quran.

relating to the Prophetic example or practice

سُنِّيٌّ

تَبَنّى الكِتابُ المَنْهَجَ السُّنِّيَّ في تَفْسيرِ النُّصوصِ.

The book adopted the Sunni approach in interpreting the texts.

pertaining/according to Islamic law

شَرْعِيٌّ

طَبَّقَ القاضي الحُكْمَ الشَّرْعِيَّ في القَضِيَّةِ.

The judge applied the Sharia-based ruling in the case.

Sharia, Islamic law

شَرائِعُ • شَريعَةٌ

يَعْمَلُ النُّوّابُ عَلى تَعْديلاتٍ لِتَطْبيقِ الشَّريعَةِ في القَوانينِ المَحَلِّيَّةِ.

Lawmakers are working on amendments to implement Islamic law in local legislation.

theological or pertaining to beliefs

عَقائِدِيٌّ

يُغَطّي الكِتابُ مَوْضوعاتٍ عَقائِدِيَّةً مُتَعَدِّدَةً.

The book covers multiple theological topics.

creed or belief system

عَقائِدُ •

عَقيدَةٌ

أَظْهَرَ اسْتِطْلاعُ الرَّأْيِ تَنَوُّعًا في العَقائِدِ الإِسْلامِيَّةِ بَيْنَ المُسْلِمينَ.

A public opinion poll showed diversity in Islamic beliefs among Muslims.

legal opinion or ruling

فَتاوى •

فَتْوى

أَثارَتِ الفَتْوى الَّتي أَصْدَرَها الشَّيْخُ عَبْدُ اللهِ جَدَلًا واسِعًا.

The fatwa issued by Sheikh Abdullah sparked widespread controversy.

to interpret/explain (especially Quranic verses)

تَفْسيرٌ •

فَسَّرَ

فَسَّرَ العُلَماءُ الآيَةَ بِاسْتِخْدامِ مُخْتَلِفِ المَناهِجِ.

Scholars interpreted the verse using various approaches.

fiqh, Islamic jurisprudence

فِقْهٌ (إِسْلامِيٌّ)

قامَ القاضي بِتَطْبيقِ الفِقْهِ الإِسْلامِيِّ في الحُكْمِ.

The judge applied Islamic jurisprudence in the ruling.

In Islamic terms, الشَّريعَةُ is the divine law covering all aspects of life, while الفِقْهُ is the interpretation and application of Sharia in practical legal matters.

Islamic judge

قُضاةٌ •

قاضٍ

أَصْدَرَ القاضي مُحَمَّد حُكْمًا في القَضِيَّةِ يَعْتَمِدُ عَلى المَبادِئِ الإِسْلامِيَّةِ.

Judge Mohammed issued a ruling in the case based on Islamic principles.

Islamic law

قَوانينُ •

قانونٌ إسْلاميٌّ

أعادَ البَرْلَمانُ العِراقيُّ النَّظَرَ في القَوانينِ الإسْلاميَّةِ المُتَعَلِّقَةِ بِالزَّواجِ.

The Iraqi parliament revisited Islamic laws related to marriage.

Islamic legal theory

pl.

مَبادئُ الفِقْهِ الإسْلاميِّ

قَرَّرَ القاضي الحُكْمَ بِناءً عَلى الفِقْهِ الإسْلاميِّ.

The judge decided the ruling based on Islamic jurisprudence.

gathering or council of Islamic scholars

مَجالِسُ •

مَجْلِسُ عُلَماءَ

اِنْعَقَدَ مَجْلِسُ عُلَماءَ في الرِّياضِ لِمُناقَشَةِ قَضايا مُعاصِرَةٍ.

A council of Islamic scholars convened in Riyadh to discuss contemporary issues.

Islamic court

مَحاكِمُ •

مَحْكَمَةٌ شَرْعيَّةٌ

أصْدَرَتِ المَحْكَمَةُ الشَّرْعيَّةُ حُكْمًا بِالطَّلاقِ.

The Sharia court issued a divorce ruling.

Islamic school of thought

مَذاهِبُ •

مَذْهَبٌ إسْلاميٌّ

أثارَ النِّقاشُ العامُّ حَوْلَ المَذْهَبِ الإسْلاميِّ في السّودانِ الجَدَلَ بِشَكْلٍ كَبيرٍ، حَيْثُ تَتَّجِهُ البِلادُ نَحْوَ تَحْقيقِ تَوازُنٍ بَيْنَ الأمورِ الدّينيَّةِ والسّياسيَّةِ.

The public debate about the Islamic sect in Sudan has sparked significant controversy as the country moves toward balancing religious and political matters.

Islamic legal school or tradition

مَذاهِبُ •

مَذْهَبٌ فِقْهيٌّ

يُمْكِنُ لِلْمُؤْمِنينَ اخْتِيارُ مَذْهَبٍ فِقْهيٍّ يَتَوافَقُ مَعَ تَفْسيرِهِمْ لِلشَّريعةِ الإسْلاميَّةِ وَمُعْتَقَداتِهِمِ الدّينيَّةِ.

Believers can choose a jurisprudential school of thought that aligns with their interpretation of Islamic Sharia and their religious beliefs.

أَصْدَرَ مَجْلِسُ عُلَماءَ بارِزٌ في الجامِعِ الكَبيرِ فَتْوَى جَديدَةً تُحَدِّدُ مَعاييرَ الحَلالِ والحَرامِ في المُعامَلاتِ الماليَّةِ الحَديثَةِ. اسْتَنْتَجَ العُلَماءُ، بَعْدَ اجْتِهادٍ واسِعٍ وَبَعْدَ مُراجَعَةِ أُصولِ الفِقْهِ الإِسْلامِيِّ، ما يَتَوافَقُ مَعَ الشَّريعَةِ الإِسْلامِيَّةِ.

A prominent council of scholars at the Grand Mosque has issued a new fatwa defining the criteria of halal and haram in modern financial transactions. The scholars concluded, after extensive effort and after reviewing the principles of Islamic jurisprudence, what is in accordance with Islamic Sharia.

في الجامِعَةِ الإِسْلامِيَّةِ، نُظِّمَتْ نَدْوَةٌ لِتَفْسيرِ بَعْضِ الأَحاديثِ النَّبَويَّةِ وَمُناقَشَةِ تَأْثيرِها عَلى مَبادِئِ الفِقْهِ الإِسْلامِيِّ. شارَكَ في النَّدْوَةِ عَدَدٌ مِنَ القُضاةِ والفُقَهاءِ الَّذينَ أَصْدَروا فَتاوى في كَيْفِيَّةِ تَطْبيقِ هَذِهِ السُّنَنِ في القانونِ الإِسْلامِيِّ المُعاصِرِ.

At the Islamic University, a seminar was organized to interpret some prophetic hadiths and discuss their impact on the principles of Islamic jurisprudence. A number of judges and jurists who have issued fatwas on how to apply these traditions in contemporary Islamic law participated in the seminar.

تَمَّ تَحْديدُ مَوْضوعِ الخِلافَةِ كَمِحْوَرٍ رَئيسِيٍّ لِمُؤْتَمَرٍ عَقيدِيٍّ يَسْتَضيفُهُ مَذْهَبٌ فِقْهِيٌّ مَعْروفٌ. سَيَتِمُّ اسْتِنْتاجُ كَيْفِيَّةِ تَأَقْلُمِ مَفاهيمِ الخِلافَةِ مَعَ القَوانينِ الإِسْلامِيَّةِ والمَذاهِبِ الفِقْهِيَّةِ الحَديثَةِ.

The subject of the caliphate was identified as a central theme for a creedal conference hosted by a well-known school of jurisprudence. It will be deduced how concepts of the caliphate can adapt to Islamic laws and modern jurisprudential schools.

أُفْتُتِحَتْ مَحْكَمَةٌ شَرْعِيَّةٌ جَديدَةٌ في المَدينَةِ لِلنَّظَرِ في القَضايا وَفْقًا لِأُصولِ الفِقْهِ الإِسْلامِيِّ. تَسْعى المَحْكَمَةُ إلى تَحْقيقِ العَدالَةِ بِناءً عَلى الشَّريعَةِ وَتَوْجيهاتِ العُلَماءِ مِنْ مُخْتَلِفِ المَذاهِبِ الإِسْلامِيَّةِ.

A new Sharia court has been opened in the city to consider cases according to the principles of Islamic jurisprudence. The court seeks to achieve justice based on Sharia and the guidance of scholars from various Islamic schools.

أُقيمَ مُؤْتَمَرٌ دَوْلِيٌّ حَوْلَ تَفاسيرِ القُرْآنِ الكَريمِ وَتَأْثيرِها عَلى تَشْكيلِ الشَّريعَةِ الإِسْلامِيَّةِ. ناقَشَ العُلَماءُ والمُفَسِّرونَ مُخْتَلِفَ التَّفْسيراتِ وَكَيْفِيَّةَ تَطْبيقِها في فِقْهِ العَصْرِ، مَعَ التَّرْكيزِ عَلى التَّفاسيرِ العَقائِدِيَّةِ والشَّرْعِيَّةِ.

An international conference on the interpretations of the Holy Quran and their impact on the formation of Islamic Sharia was held. Scholars and interpreters discussed various interpretations and how to apply them in the jurisprudence of the age, with a focus on doctrinal and legal interpretations.

فَتْوى جَديدَةٌ: الشَّريعَةُ وَالعُمْلاتُ الرَّقْمِيَّةُ

المُذيعُ: مَرْحَبًا بِكُمْ في بَرْنامَجِنا الحِوارِيِّ الخاصِّ. نَسْتَضيفُ اليَوْمَ فَضيلَةَ المُفْتي جَمالِ الدّينِ الَّذي أَصْدَرَ فَتْوى جَديدَةً تَتَناوَلُ العُمْلاتِ الرَّقْمِيَّةَ وَفْقًا لِأُصولِ الفِقْهِ الإِسْلامِيِّ. مَرْحَبًا بِكَ يا فَضيلَةَ المُفْتي.

المُفْتي: السَّلامُ عَلَيْكُمْ وَرَحْمَةُ اللهِ، شُكْرًا لِدَعْوَتِكُمْ.

المُذيعُ: فَضيلَةَ المُفْتي، فَضْلًا، أَخْبِرْنا عَنْ كَيْفِيَّةِ إِصْداركُمْ لِهَذِهِ الفَتْوى، وَالتَّحَدِّياتِ الَّتي واجَهْتُموها.

المُفْتي: بِالطَّبْعِ، لَقَدْ اسْتَنْتَجْنا بَعْدَ اجْتِهادٍ وَدِراسَةٍ مُعَمَّقَةٍ لِأَحْكامِ الشَّريعَةِ وَمَبادِئِ الفِقْهِ الإِسْلامِيِّ أَنَّ العُمْلاتِ الرَّقْمِيَّةَ يُمْكِنُ أَنْ تَكونَ حَلالًا طالَما اسْتُخْدِمَتْ ضِمْنَ ضَوابِطَ مُعَيَّنَةٍ تَحْفَظُ حُقوقَ النّاسِ وَتَمْنَعُ الغِشَّ وَالاحْتِيالَ.

المُذيعُ: هَلْ يُمْكِنُكَ تَفْسيرُ كَيْفَ تَوَصَّلْتُمْ إلى هَذا الاسْتِنْتاجِ؟

المُفْتي: نَعَمْ، لَقَدْ حَدَّدْنا أَنَّ العُمْلاتِ الرَّقْمِيَّةَ يَجِبُ أَنْ تَكونَ مَبْنِيَّةً عَلى مَبادِئَ مالِيَّةٍ تَتَّسِمُ بِالشَّفافِيَّةِ وَأَنْ تَكونَ مُتَوافِقَةً مَعَ مَقاصِدِ الشَّريعَةِ الإِسْلامِيَّةِ. وَقَدْ فَسَّرْنا النُّصوصَ الدّينِيَّةَ بِما يَتَماشى مَعَ الحَياةِ المُعاصِرَةِ وَتِقْنِيّاتِها.

المُذيعُ: وَما هِيَ الشُّروطُ الشَّرْعِيَّةُ الَّتي وَضَعْتُموها لِتَداوُلِ هَذِهِ العُمْلاتِ؟

المُفْتي: لَقَدْ أَفْتَيْنا أَنَّهُ يَجِبُ أَنْ تَكونَ هَذِهِ العُمْلاتُ خالِيَةً مِنَ المُقامَرَةِ وَالمُضارَباتِ غَيْرِ المَضْمونَةِ، وَأَنْ لا تُسْتَخْدَمَ في مُعامَلاتٍ حَرامٍ كالتِّجارَةِ في المَوادِّ المَحْظورَةِ شَرْعًا.

المُذيعُ: كَيْفَ اسْتَقْبَلَتِ الأُمَّةُ الإِسْلامِيَّةُ وَمَجالِسُ العُلَماءِ فَتْواكُمْ؟

المُفْتي: كانَ هُناكَ بَعْضُ الجَدَلِ وَالخِلافِ، وَلَكِنَّ مَجْلِسَ العُلَماءِ قَدَّرَ جُهودَنا في الاجْتِهادِ وَالتَّفْسيرِ المُسْتَقِلَّيْنِ، وَنَحْنُ نَعْمَلُ مَعَ المَحاكِمِ الشَّرْعِيَّةِ لِتَطْويرِ إِطارٍ قانونِيٍّ يَحْمي المُشاركينَ.

المُذيعُ: شُكْرًا جَزيلًا لَكُمْ يا فَضيلَةَ المُفْتي عَلى هَذا الحِوارِ الشَّيِّقِ.

المُفْتي: شُكْرًا لَكُمْ، وَأَسْأَلُ اللهَ أَنْ يَنْفَعَ بِما نَقولُ وَنَفْعَلُ.

New Fatwa: Sharia and Cryptocurrencies

Anchor: Welcome to our special talk show. Today, we host the esteemed Mufti Jamal Al-Din who has issued a new fatwa addressing cryptocurrencies according to the principles of Islamic jurisprudence. Welcome, Mufti.

Mufti: May the peace and blessings of God be upon you; thank you for your invitation.

Anchor: Esteemed Mufti, please tell us about how you issued this fatwa and the challenges you faced.

Mufti: Certainly. After thorough research and study of Sharia laws and the principles of Islamic jurisprudence, we concluded that cryptocurrencies could be halal as long as they are used within certain parameters that protect people's rights and prevent fraud and deception.

Anchor: Can you explain how you reached this conclusion?

Mufti: Yes, we determined that cryptocurrencies must be based on transparent financial principles and be in accordance with the objectives of Islamic Sharia. We interpreted religious texts in a way that aligns with contemporary life and its technologies.

Anchor: What are the Sharia conditions you have set for the trading of these currencies?

Mufti: We have issued that these currencies must be free from gambling and uncertain speculation and must not be used in haram transactions, such as trading in substances prohibited by Sharia.

Anchor: How has the Muslim community and the councils of scholars received your fatwa?

Mufti: There was some controversy and disagreement, but the council of scholars appreciated our efforts in independent reasoning and interpretation, and we are working with Sharia courts to develop a legal framework that protects the participants.

Anchor: Thank you very much, Mufti, for this fascinating discussion.

Mufti: Thank you, and I ask God to make what we say and do beneficial.

8.1.3 Islamic Arts and Literature

Islamic literature • آدابٌ أَدَبٌ إِسْلامِيٌّ

يَتَمَيَّزُ الأَدَبُ الإِسْلامِيُّ بِمَجموعَةٍ مِنَ الأَعْمالِ الأَدَبِيَّةِ الَّتي تَرْوي القِصَصَ الدِّينِيَّ وَتُسَلِّطُ الضَّوْءَ عَلى القِيَمِ وَالأَخْلاقِ الإِسْلامِيَّةِ.

Islamic literature is characterized by a range of literary works that narrate religious stories and highlight Islamic values and ethics.

to inspire • إِلْهامٌ أَلْهَمَ

أَلْهَمَتِ الطَّبيعَةُ الفَنّانَةَ ريم لِإِنْشاءِ لَوْحاتٍ روحانِيَّةٍ.

Nature inspired the artist Reem to create spiritual paintings.

Islamic heritage تُراثٌ إِسْلامِيٌّ

يُرَكِّزُ مَتْحَفُ الدَّوْحَةِ عَلى التُّراثِ الإِسْلامِيِّ مِنْ مُخْتَلِفِ العُصورِ.

The Doha Museum focuses on Islamic heritage from various eras.

to recite (the Quran) • تِلاوَةٌ تَلا (القُرآنَ)

بَيْنَما كانَ القارِئُ يَتْلو القُرآنَ في المَسْجِدِ القَديمِ، انْتابَتِ الحُضورَ أَجْواءٌ مِنَ الرّوحانِيَّةِ وَالتَّأَمُّلِ.

As the reciter was reciting the Quran in the ancient mosque, a sense of spirituality and contemplation enveloped the congregation.

Thuluth calligraphy • خُطوطٌ خَطُّ الثُّلُثِ

تَسْتَضيفُ الرِّياضُ مَعْرَضًا فَنِّيًّا يُرَكِّزُ عَلى خَطِّ الثُّلُثِ، أَحَدِ أَرْقى أَنْواعِ الخَطِّ العَرَبِيِّ.

Riyadh is hosting an art exhibition focusing on Thuluth calligraphy, one of the finest types of Arabic script.

Naskh calligraphy خَطُّ النَّسْخِ

يَتَمَيَّزُ خَطُّ النَّسْخِ بِقابِلِيَّتِهِ لِلْقِراءَةِ وَيُسْتَخْدَمُ في كِتابَةِ القُرآنِ.

Naskh calligraphy is characterized by its readability and is used in writing the Quran.

spiritual

روحانِيٌّ

تَتَناوَلُ الرِّوايَةُ مَوْضوعاتٍ روحانِيَّةً.

The novel addressed spiritual topics.

to narrate

رَوى • رِوايَةٌ

رَوى الكاتِبُ قِصَّةَ حَياةِ النَّبِيِّ مُحَمَّدٍ.

The writer narrated the life story of Prophet Muhammad.

poetry

شِعْرٌ • أَشْعارٌ

قامَتْ جامِعَةُ الأَزْهَرِ بِتَنْظيمِ نَدْوَةٍ حَوْلَ شِعْرِ العَصْرِ الأُمَوِيِّ، كَجُزْءٍ مِنْ تُراثِها الأَدَبِيِّ.

Al-Azhar University organized a seminar on Umayyad-era poetry as part of its literary heritage.

classical Arabic poetry

شِعْرٌ عَرَبِيٌّ كِلاسيكِيٌّ

في حَفْلٍ أَدَبِيٍّ مُمَيَّزٍ، تَمَّتْ قِراءَةُ قَصائِدَ مِنَ الشِّعْرِ العَرَبِيِّ الكِلاسيكِيِّ الشَّهيرِ لِإِبْرازِ إِرْثِ الأَدَبِ العَرَبِيِّ.

At a special literary event, verses from the famous classical Arab poetry were recited to highlight the heritage of Arabic literature.

Nabati poetry

شِعْرٌ نَبَطِيٌّ • أَشْعارٌ

تَأَلَّقَ الشّاعِرُ الإِماراتِيُّ فارِس العَزْمي في إِلْقاءِ قَصائِدِهِ مِنَ الشِّعْرِ النَّبَطِيِّ في مَهْرَجانِ الشِّعْرِ العَرَبِيِّ.

Emirati poet Fares Al-Azmi shined in reciting his Nabati poetry at the Arabic Poetry Festival.

to portray

صَوَّرَ • تَصْويرٌ

صَوَّرَ الفيلْمُ قِصَّةَ حَياةِ الشّاعِرِ العَظيمِ.

The film portrayed the life story of the great poet.

to express

عَبَّرَ • تَعْبيرٌ

يُعَبِّرُ الشِّعْرُ عَنْ مَشاعِرِ وَأَحاسيسِ النّاسِ.

Poetry expresses the feelings and sensations of people.

عَرِيقٌ

ancient

يُعَدُّ الجامِعُ الأَمَوِيُّ في دِمَشْقَ مِنَ المِعْمارِ العَرِيقِ.

The Umayyad Mosque in Damascus is considered ancient architecture.

عَزَفَ •

to play (an instrument)

عَزَفَ الموسيقيُّ يونُسُ عَلى العودِ في الحَفْلَةِ.

The musician Younes played the oud at the party.

عُظَماءُ / عِظامٌ •

عَظِيمٌ

great

تُعَدُّ العِمارَةُ الإِسْلامِيَّةُ في قُرْطُبَةَ مِثالًا عَظِيمًا عَلى الاِبْتِكارِ الفَنِّيِّ.

Islamic architecture in Cordoba is a great example of artistic innovation.

عَكَسَ •

عَكَسَ

to reflect

عَكَسَتِ اللَّوْحَةُ البَساطَةَ والرّوحانِيَّةَ.

The painting reflected simplicity and spirituality.

عِمارَةٌ إِسْلامِيَّةٌ

Islamic architecture

يُظْهِرُ الجامِعُ الأَمَوِيُّ في دِمَشْقَ رَوْعَةَ العِمارَةِ الإِسْلامِيَّةِ.

The Umayyad Mosque in Damascus shows the splendor of Islamic architecture.

فَنٌّ إِسْلامِيٌّ

فُنونٌ •

Islamic art

نُشِرَتْ دِراسَةٌ جَدِيدَةٌ تُناقِشُ تَأْثِيرَ الفَنِّ الإِسْلامِيِّ عَلى الثَّقافَةِ الغَرْبِيَّةِ.

A new study was published discussing the impact of Islamic art on Western culture.

فَنُّ الخَطِّ العَرَبِيِّ

Arabic calligraphy

أُقِيمَ في مَكَّةَ مَعْرِضٌ لِفَنِّ الخَطِّ العَرَبِيِّ، يُظْهِرُ مَدى تَأْثِيرِهِ عَلى الفَنِّ الإِسْلامِيِّ.

An exhibition for the art of Arabic calligraphy was held in Mecca, showing its impact on Islamic art.

artistic

فَنِّيٌّ

يُظْهِرُ فَنُّ الخَطِّ العَرَبِيِّ مَهاراتٍ فَنِّيَّةً عالِيَةً.

Arabic calligraphy shows high artistic skills.

classical

كِلاسيكِيٌّ

أُطْلِقَتْ مُبادَرَةٌ جَديدَةٌ لِحِفْظِ وَتَوْثيقِ الشِّعْرِ العَرَبِيِّ الكِلاسيكِيِّ.

A new initiative was launched to preserve and document classical Arabic poetry.

to attribute (as in, attributing a quote to a specific poet or writer)

نَسَبَ • نَسَبَ

نُسِبَتِ القَصيدَةُ الكِلاسيكِيَّةُ إلى شاعِرٍ مَشْهورٍ مِنَ العُصورِ القَديمَةِ.

The classical poem was attributed to a famous poet from ancient times.

8.1.3.1 Mini-Articles

Track **39**

أُفْتُتِحَ في المَتْحَفِ الإسْلامِيِّ العَريقِ مَعْرِضٌ جَديدٌ يَحْتَفي بِفَنِّ الخَطِّ العَرَبِيِّ، عُرِضَتْ فيه أَمْثِلَةٌ مُبْهِرَةٌ مِنْ خَطِّ الثُّلُثِ وَخَطِّ النَّسْخِ. تَمَّتْ دَعْوَةُ الزُّوّارِ لِتَجْرِبَةِ هذا الفَنِّ العَظيمِ بِإشْرافِ خَطّاطينَ عُظَماءَ.

A new exhibition celebrating the art of Arabic calligraphy was inaugurated at the prestigious Islamic Museum, where stunning examples of Thuluth and Naskh scripts were displayed. Visitors were invited to experience this magnificent art under the supervision of great calligraphers.

أُقيمَتْ أُمْسِيَّةٌ شِعْرِيَّةٌ تَناوَلَتْ أَشْعارًا مِنَ الشِّعْرِ العَرَبِيِّ الكِلاسيكِيِّ وَالشِّعْرِ النَّبَطِيِّ. أَلْهَمَ الشُّعَراءُ الحُضورَ بِقَصائِدَ تُعَبِّرُ عَنِ التُّراثِ الإسْلامِيِّ العَريقِ وَروحانِيَّتِه.

A poetic evening was held that featured poems from classical Arabic and Nabati poetry. The poets inspired the audience with verses that reflect the rich Islamic heritage and its spirituality.

في الجامِعِ الكَبيرِ، نُظِّمَتْ مُسابَقَةٌ لِتِلاوَةِ القُرْآنِ جَذَبَتْ مُشارِكينَ مِنْ مُخْتَلِفِ الأَعْمارِ. عَكَسَتِ التِّلاواتُ العُمْقَ الفَنِّيَّ وَالرّوحِيَّ لِلتُّراثِ الإسْلامِيِّ.

At the Grand Mosque, a Quran recitation competition was organized, attracting participants of various ages. The recitations reflected the artistic depth and spirituality of the Islamic heritage.

اِسْتَضَافَتِ الجامِعَةُ مُؤْتَمَرًا دَوْلِيًّا عَنِ العِمارَةِ الإِسْلامِيَّةِ، حَيْثُ ناقَشَ الخُبَراءُ كَيْفَ تُنْسَبُ التَّصامِيمُ العُمْرانِيَّةُ الإِسْلامِيَّةُ إلى التُّراثِ الفَنِّيِّ وَالثَّقافِيِّ العَظيمِ.

The university hosted an international conference on Islamic architecture, where experts discussed how Islamic urban designs are attributed to the great artistic and cultural heritage.

اِفْتَتَحَ مَعْرِضٌ فَنِّيٌّ عَرْضًا مُؤَقَّتًا يُبْرِزُ فُنونًا إِسْلامِيَّةً مِنْ مُخْتَلِفِ العُصورِ. تَنَوَّعَتِ الأَعْمالُ بَيْنَ التَّصْويرِ الفَنِّيِّ وَالأَدَبِ الإِسْلامِيِّ، وَقَدَّمَتْ لَمَحاتٍ مِنَ الإِلْهامِ التَّارِيخِيِّ وَالرّوحِيِّ.

An art gallery opened a temporary exhibition highlighting Islamic arts from various eras. The works varied between visual art and Islamic literature, offering glimpses of historical and spiritual inspiration.

8.1.3.2 Informative Article: Arabic Calligraphy

Track **40**

الخَطُّ العَرَبِيُّ: فَنٌّ تَتَوارَثُهُ الأَجْيالُ وَيُعَبِّرُ عَنِ الهُوِيَّةِ الإِسْلامِيَّةِ

في قَلْبِ العالَمِ العَرَبِيِّ وَالإِسْلامِيِّ، يَقْبَعُ فَنٌّ عَرِيقٌ يُعَبِّرُ عَنِ الهُوِيَّةِ الثَّقافِيَّةِ وَالرّوحِيَّةِ لِلْأُمَّةِ: إِنَّهُ فَنُّ الخَطِّ العَرَبِيِّ. يُعَدُّ هَذا الفَنُّ مِنَ الفُنونِ الإِسْلامِيَّةِ الَّتي تَلازَمَتْ مَعَ تَطَوُّرِ الحَضارَةِ العَرَبِيَّةِ الإِسْلامِيَّةِ، وارْتَبَطَتْ ارْتِباطًا وَثيقًا بِتُراثِها الغَنِيِّ وَعَظَمَتِها الثَّقافِيَّةِ.

تُعْرَفُ الخُطوطُ العَرَبِيَّةُ بِتَنَوُّعِها وَجَمالِها، حَيْثُ يَبْرُزُ خَطُّ الثُّلُثِ وَخَطُّ النَّسْخِ كَأَمْثِلَةٍ حَيَّةٍ عَلَى الإِتْقانِ وَالجَمالِيَّةِ في هَذا الفَنِّ. وَقَدِ انْتَقَلَ هَذا الفَنُّ عَبْرَ الأَجْيالِ، مُحْتَفِظًا بِروحِهِ الكلاسيكِيَّةِ وَمُواكِبًا لِلْعَصْرِ بِأَشْكالِهِ المُعاصِرَةِ.

وَيُمْكِنُ رُؤْيَةُ تَأْثيرِ هَذا الفَنِّ في جَميعِ أَنْحاءِ العالَمِ الإِسْلامِيِّ، مِنَ المَساجِدِ ذاتِ العِمارَةِ الإِسْلامِيَّةِ المُعَقَّدَةِ إلى الأَدَبِ الإِسْلامِيِّ وَالمَخْطوطاتِ الَّتي تَزَيَّنَتْ بِزَخارِفِهِ. وَلَعَلَّ مِنْ أَرْوَعِ الأَمْثِلَةِ عَلى ذَلِكَ، الآياتِ القُرْآنِيَّةِ الَّتي خُطَّتْ بِدِقَّةٍ وَعِنايَةٍ لِتُزَيِّنَ جُدْرانَ المَسْجِدِ الحَرامِ وَالمَسْجِدِ النَّبَوِيِّ، وَتُضْفِيَ جَوًّا مِنَ الرّوحانِيَّةِ وَالخُشوعِ.

في السَّنَواتِ الأَخيرَةِ، عادَ فَنُّ الخَطِّ العَرَبِيِّ كَمَوْضِعِ اهْتِمامٍ، حَيْثُ يُعَبِّرُ الفَنّانونَ الشَّبابُ عَنْ مَواهِبِهِمْ مِنْ خِلالِ دَمْجِ الخَطِّ العَرَبِيِّ بِأَساليبَ فَنِّيَّةٍ حَديثَةٍ، ما يَعْكِسُ الطَّابَعَ الفَنِّيَّ وَالإِبْداعِيَّ لِهَذا التُّراثِ. وَقَدْ أَدّى ذَلِكَ إلى اسْتِحْداثِ أَشْكالٍ وَتَصاميمَ تَجْمَعُ بَيْنَ الأَصالَةِ وَالحَداثَةِ، مِمّا يُعَزِّزُ مِنْ مَكانَةِ هَذا الفَنِّ كَرَمْزٍ لِلْهُوِيَّةِ العَرَبِيَّةِ الإِسْلامِيَّةِ.

وَمِنَ الجَديرِ بِالذِّكْرِ أَنَّ الأُمَمَ المُتَّحِدَةَ قَدْ أَدْرَجَتِ الخَطَّ العَرَبِيَّ في قائِمَةِ التُّراثِ الثَّقافِيِّ غَيْرِ المادِّيِّ، تَقْديرًا لِقيمَتِهِ الفَنِّيَّةِ وَالثَّقافِيَّةِ. وَيُواصِلُ الخَطّاطونَ في العالَمِ العَرَبِيِّ تَعْليمَ هَذا الفَنِّ الفَريدِ لِلْأَجْيالِ القادِمَةِ، مُؤَكِّدينَ عَلى أَهَمِّيَّةِ حِفْظِ هَذا الإِرْثِ الثَّقافِيِّ العَظيمِ.

إِنَّ فَنَّ الخَطِّ العَرَبِيِّ، بِجَمَالِيَّتِهِ وَعُمْقِهِ الرّوحِيِّ، يَظَلُّ شَاهِدًا عَلَى عَرَاقَةِ وَعَظَمَةِ الثَّقَافَةِ الإِسْلَامِيَّةِ، وَيُعَدُّ عُنْصُرًا أَسَاسِيًّا مُتَكَامِلًا مِنَ الهُوِيَّةِ الثَّقَافِيَّةِ.

Arabic Calligraphy: An Art Passed Down Through Generations, Expressing Islamic Identity

At the heart of the Arab and Islamic world lies an ancient art form that expresses the cultural and spiritual identity of the nation: Arabic calligraphy. This art is one of the Islamic arts that accompanied the development of the Arab-Islamic civilization and is closely linked to its rich heritage and cultural greatness.

Arabic scripts are known for their diversity and beauty, with Thuluth and Naskh scripts standing out as living examples of mastery and aesthetics in this art form. This art has been passed down through generations, maintaining its classical spirit while keeping pace with the times in its contemporary forms.

The influence of this art can be seen throughout the Islamic world, from mosques with intricate Islamic architecture to Islamic literature and manuscripts adorned with its decorations. One of the most magnificent examples is the Quranic verses meticulously scripted to embellish the walls of the Holy Mosque and the Prophet's Mosque, creating an atmosphere of spirituality and reverence.

In recent years, Arabic calligraphy has experienced a resurgence of interest, with young artists expressing their talents by integrating Arabic script with modern artistic styles. This reflects the artistic and creative character of this heritage and has led to the creation of forms and designs that combine authenticity with modernity, enhancing the status of this art as a symbol of Arab-Islamic identity.

It is noteworthy that the United Nations has included Arabic calligraphy in the list of Intangible Cultural Heritage in recognition of its artistic and cultural value. Calligraphers in the Arab world continue to teach this unique art to the coming generations, emphasizing the importance of preserving this great cultural legacy.

Indeed, Arabic calligraphy, with its beauty and spiritual depth, remains a testament to the richness and grandeur of Islamic culture and is an integral part of cultural identity.

دَليلُ الخَطِّ العَرَبِيِّ: التِّقْنِيَاتُ وَالأَساليبُ

1. **خَطُّ النَّسْخِ:** خَطٌّ عَمَلِيٌّ وَواضِحٌ يُسْتَخْدَمُ عادَةً في الكُتُبِ وَالمَطبوعاتِ. يَتَمَيَّزُ بِالتَّجانُسِ وَالوُضوحِ، مِمَّا يَجعَلُهُ سَهْلَ القِراءَةِ، وَبِالتَّالي فَإِنَّهُ مِثاليٌّ لِلنُّصوصِ الطَّويلَةِ.

2. **خَطُّ الثُّلُثِ:** أَحَدُ أَجْمَلِ وَأَكْثَرِ أَنْواعِ الخُطوطِ إِجْلالًا في العالَمِ الإِسْلامِيِّ. يَتَمَيَّزُ بِأَشْكالِهِ المُعَقَّدَةِ وَالمُزَخْرَفَةِ، وَغالِبًا ما يُسْتَخْدَمُ في كِتابَةِ الآياتِ القُرْآنِيَّةِ وَاللَّوْحاتِ الفَنِّيَّةِ.

3. **الخَطُّ الدّيوانِيُّ:** خَطٌّ انْسِيابِيٌّ يَتَمَيَّزُ بِكَثافَةِ الزَّخارِفِ وَتَداخُلِ الحُروفِ، وَغالِبًا ما كانَ يُسْتَخْدَمُ في البَلاطِ العُثْمانِيِّ، وَيَحْظى بِشَعْبِيَّةٍ في كِتابَةِ الشَّهاداتِ وَالدَّعَواتِ.

4. **خَطُّ الرُّقْعَةِ:** خَطٌّ بَسيطٌ يَشيعُ اسْتِخْدامُهُ لِلْكِتابَةِ اليَوْمِيَّةِ وَالمُراسَلاتِ. يَتَمَيَّزُ بِسُهولَةِ كِتابَتِهِ وَقِراءَتِهِ، وَهُوَ مُناسِبٌ لِلْمُبْتَدِئينَ في تَعَلُّمِ الخَطِّ العَرَبِيِّ.

5. **الخَطُّ الفارِسِيُّ:** يُعْرَفُ أَيْضًا بِخَطِّ النَّسْتَعْليقِ، يَتَمَيَّزُ بِالحُروفِ وَالأَشْكالِ الهَوائِيَّةِ المُعَقَّدَةِ، وَهُوَ شائِعٌ في الأَعْمالِ الفَنِّيَّةِ وَالشِّعْرِيَّةِ.

6. **الخَطُّ الكوفِيُّ:** واحِدٌ مِنْ أَقْدَمِ أَنْواعِ الخَطِّ العَرَبِيِّ، يَتَمَيَّزُ بِخُطوطِهِ المُسْتَقيمَةِ وَزَواياهُ الحادَّةِ، وَقَدِ اسْتُخْدِمَ بِشَكْلٍ واسِعٍ في كِتابَةِ المَصاحِفِ القُرْآنِيَّةِ الأولى.

7. **خَطُّ الطُّغْراءِ:** خَطٌّ فَنِّيٌّ يَتَمَيَّزُ بِالتَّعْقيدِ وَالتَّفَرُّدِ، وَكانَ يُسْتَخْدَمُ في العَهْدِ العُثْمانِيِّ لِكِتابَةِ الأَخْتامِ وَالمَراسيمِ السُّلْطانِيَّةِ.

8. **الخَطُّ المَغْرِبِيُّ:** يَتَمَيَّزُ بِدَوَرانِ حُروفِهِ وَتَصاميمِهِ المُعَقَّدَةِ، وَهُوَ شائِعٌ في مِنْطَقَةِ المَغْرِبِ. يُسْتَخْدَمُ بِشَكْلٍ خاصٍّ في الزَّخْرَفَةِ وَالمَخْطوطاتِ الدّينِيَّةِ.

كُلُّ نَوْعٍ مِنْ هَذِهِ الخُطوطِ يَحْمِلُ تاريخًا غَنِيًّا وَيُعَبِّرُ عَنْ جُزْءٍ مِنَ الهُوِيَّةِ الثَّقافِيَّةِ في العالَمِ العَرَبِيِّ وَالإِسْلامِيِّ.

1. **Naskh Script:** A practical and clear script commonly used in books and publications. It is characterized by its consistency and clarity, which makes it easy to read and thus ideal for lengthy texts.

2. **Thuluth Script:** One of the most beautiful and revered script types in the Islamic world. It is known for its complex and ornate shapes and is often used in writing Quranic verses and artistic panels.

3. **Diwani Script:** A flowing script characterized by the density of decorations and the interweaving of letters, often used in the Ottoman courts and popular in writing certificates and invitations.

4. **Ruq'ah Script:** A simple script commonly used for everyday writing and correspondence. It is easy to write and read and is suitable for beginners learning Arabic calligraphy.

5. **Persian Script:** Also known as Nasta'liq, this script is characterized by curved letters and complex aerial shapes and is popular in artistic and poetic works.

6. **Kufic Script:** One of the oldest Arabic script types, distinguished by its straight lines and sharp angles, it was widely used in writing the earliest Quranic manuscripts.

7. **Tughra Script:** An artistic script characterized by complexity and uniqueness, used in the Ottoman era for writing seals and sultanic logos.

8. **Maghrebi Script:** Known for the curvature of its letters and complex designs, it is common in the Maghreb region. It is especially used in decoration and religious manuscripts.

Each of these script types carries a rich history and expresses a part of the cultural identity in the Arab and Islamic world.

8.2 Interfaith Relations and Religious Diversity

Track **42**

religious tolerance

تَسامُحٌ دِينِيٌّ

تُظْهِرُ المُؤْتَمَراتُ الدَّوْلِيَّةُ أَهَمِّيَّةَ التَّسامُحِ الدِّينِيِّ في العالَمِ المُعاصِرِ.

International conferences highlight the importance of religious tolerance in the modern world.

peaceful coexistence

تَعايُشٌ سِلْمِيٌّ

تُنَظِّمُ الجَمْعِيّاتُ الخَيْرِيَّةُ فَعالِيّاتٍ تَهْدِفُ إلى تَعْزيزِ التَّعايُشِ السِّلْمِيِّ وَالتَّفاهُمِ بَيْنَ مُخْتَلِفِ الأَدْيانِ.

Charitable organizations organize events aimed at promoting peaceful coexistence and understanding among different religions.

freedom of belief

حُرِّيَّةُ اعْتِقادٍ

ضَمِنَ الدُّسْتُورُ الجَديدُ حُرِّيَّةَ الِاعْتِقادِ لِجَميعِ المُواطِنينَ.

The new constitution guaranteed freedom of belief for all citizens.

religious freedom

حُرِّيَّةٌ دينيَّةٌ

نادِرًا ما يُناقَشُ مَوْضوعُ الحُرِّيَّةِ الدّينِيَّةِ في البَرْلَمانِ.

The topic of religious freedom is rarely discussed in the parliament.

religious dialogue

حِوارٌ دينيٌّ

أُقيمَ حِوارٌ دينيٌّ بَيْنَ العُلَماءِ المُسْلِمينَ وَالمَسيحيّينَ في القاهِرَةِ.

A religious dialogue was held between Muslim and Christian scholars in Cairo.

8.2.1 Comparative Religion and Theology

Track **43**

to lead to understanding

تَأْديَةٌ •

أَدَّى إلى تَفاهُمٍ

أَدَّى الحِوارُ الدّينِيُّ إلى التَّفاهُمِ بَيْنَ المُسْلِمينَ وَاليَهودِ في بَغْدادَ.

Religious dialogue led to understanding between Muslims and Jews in Baghdad.

to lead to conflict

تَأْديَةٌ •

أَدَّى إلى صِراعٍ

أَدَّى الجَهْلُ الدّينِيُّ إلى صِراعاتٍ طائِفِيَّةٍ في بَعْضِ المَناطِقِ.

Religious ignorance led to sectarian conflicts in some areas.

Islam

إِسْلامٌ

يُشَكِّلُ الحَجُّ نُقْطَةً مُهِمَّةً في الإِسْلامِ وَيَعْرِفُهُ أَيْضًا أَتْباعُ الدّياناتِ الأُخْرى.

The Hajj pilgrimage is an important point in Islam and is also known to followers of other religions.

to agree	اِتَّفَقَ • اِتِّفَاقٌ	اِتَّفَقَ

اِتَّفَقَ العُلَماءُ المُسْلِمونَ وَالنَّصارى عَلى أَهَمِّيَّةِ العَمَلِ الخَيْرِيِّ.

Muslim and Christian scholars agreed on the importance of charitable work.

> وافَقَ and اِتَّفَقَ both translate as 'agree,' but they are not interchangeable:
>
> وافَقَ typically means to agree with someone or something, suggesting an alignment or consent to a particular opinion, idea, or proposal by an individual.
>
> اِتَّفَقَ is used to denote a mutual agreement or consensus among parties, implying that all involved have come to a common understanding or decision.

mutual respect	اِحْتِرامٌ مُتَبادَلٌ

إِنَّ الاِحْتِرامَ المُتَبادَلَ بَيْنَ الدِّياناتِ مِفْتاحُ التَّعايُشِ السِّلْمِيِّ.

Mutual respect between religions is the key to peaceful coexistence.

to respect	اِحْتَرَمَ • اِحْتِرامٌ	اِحْتَرَمَ

اِحْتَرَمَ المُفَكِّرُ الإِسْلامِيُّ المَذاهِبَ الأُخْرى في كِتاباتِه.

The Islamic thinker respected other doctrines in his writings.

to respect the other	اِحْتَرَمَ الآخَرَ

"اِحْتَرِمِ الآخَرَ" هُوَ شِعارُ نادي الحِوارِ بَيْنَ الأَدْيانِ.

"Respect the other" is the slogan of the interfaith dialogue club.

religious difference	اِخْتِلافٌ دينيٌّ

خَلَقَ الاِخْتِلافُ الدِّينيُّ بَيْنَ الطُّلَّابِ تَحَدِّياتٍ وَفُرَصًا لِلتَّعْليمِ.

Religious difference among students created challenges and opportunities for education.

to differ	اِخْتَلَفَ • اِخْتِلافٌ	اِخْتَلَفَ

اِخْتَلَفَ الباحِثونَ في تَفْسيراتِهِمْ لِلنُّصوصِ الدِّينيَّةِ.

Researchers differed in their interpretations of religious texts.

الوَحدَةُ في التَّنَوُّعِ الدّينِيِّ

unity in religious diversity

أَثْبَتَتِ المُناظَراتُ العامَّةُ أَهَمِّيَّةَ الوَحدَةِ في التَّنَوُّعِ الدّينِيِّ.

Public debates have demonstrated the importance of unity in religious diversity.

بوذِيَّةٌ

Buddhism

تَأْتي البوذِيَّةُ في المَرْكَزِ الثّالِثِ مِنْ حَيْثُ عَدَدِ المُعْتَنِقينَ في العالَمِ.

Buddhism comes third in terms of the number of adherents globally.

تَعَدُّدِيَّةٌ دينِيَّةٌ

religious pluralism

تُعَزِّزُ التَّعَدُّدِيَّةُ الدّينِيَّةُ الفَهْمَ المُتَبادَلَ بَيْنَ مُخْتَلِفِ الثَّقافاتِ.

Religious pluralism enhances mutual understanding among different cultures.

تَفاهُمٌ

understanding

تَسْعى المُنَظَّماتُ الدّينِيَّةُ لِتَحْقيقِ التَّفاهُمِ بَيْنَ مُخْتَلِفِ الدّياناتِ.

Religious organizations strive for understanding between different faiths.

تَنَوُّعٌ دينِيٌّ

religious diversity

يُعَزِّزُ التَّنَوُّعُ الدّينِيُّ في المُجْتَمَعِ الحِوارَ وَالتَّفاهُمَ.

Religious diversity in society promotes dialogue and understanding.

دِراسَةٌ دينِيَّةٌ مُقارَنَةٌ

comparative religious study

تُقَدِّمُ جامِعَةُ الأَزْهَرِ الدِّراساتِ الدّينِيَّةَ المُقارَنَةَ كَجُزْءٍ مِنْ مَناهِجِها.

Al-Azhar University offers comparative religious studies as part of its curriculum.

دِيانَةٌ سَماوِيَّةٌ

Abrahamic religion

يَنْتَمي الإسْلامُ وَالمَسيحِيَّةُ وَاليَهودِيَّةُ إلى الدّياناتِ السَّماوِيَّةِ.

Islam, Christianity, and Judaism belong to the Abrahamic religions.

| Eastern religion | • أَدْيانٌ | دِيانَةٌ شَرْقِيَّةٌ |

الهِنْدوسِيَّةُ وَالبوذِيَّةُ هُما مِنَ الأَدْيانِ الشَّرْقِيَّةِ الرَّئيسِيَّةِ.

Hinduism and Buddhism are among the major Eastern religions.

| comparative law | • شَرائِعُ | شَريعَةٌ مُقارَنَةٌ |

يَعْتَمِدُ القَضاءُ في الإمارات عَلَى الشَّريعَةِ المُقارَنَةِ في بَعْضِ القَضايا.

The judiciary in the UAE relies on comparative law in some cases.

| creed | • عَقائِدُ | عَقيدَةٌ |

تُعْتَبَرُ العَقيدَةُ الإسْلامِيَّةُ مَوْضوعًا هامًّا في الدِّراساتِ الدّينِيَّةِ.

The Islamic creed is considered an important subject in religious studies.

| to compare | • مُقارَنَةً | قارَنَ |

قارَنَ الباحِثُ بَيْنَ المَفاهيمِ الإسْلامِيَّةِ وَالمَسيحِيَّةِ لِلْعَدْلِ.

The researcher compared the Islamic and Christian concepts of justice.

| to sanctify | • تَقْديسٌ | قَدَّسَ |

تَقْديسُ الأماكِنِ مَوْجودٌ في الدِّياناتِ السَّماوِيَةِ وَبَعْضِ الدِّياناتِ الشَّرْقِيَّةِ.

The sanctification of places exists in Abrahamic religions and some Eastern religions.

| multicultural | | مُتَعَدِّدُ الثَّقافاتِ |

يُعْتَبَرُ لُبْنانُ مِثالًا جَيِّدًا لِلْمُجْتَمَعِ مُتَعَدِّدِ الثَّقافاتِ.

Lebanon is considered a good example of a multicultural society.

| multi-denominational | | مُتَعَدِّدُ المَذاهِبِ |

المَدينَةُ الكَبيرَةُ تُعْتَبَرُ مُجْتَمَعًا مُتَعَدِّدَ المَذاهِبِ حَيْثُ يَعيشُ النّاسُ مِنْ خَلْفِيّاتٍ دينِيَّةٍ وَثَقافِيَّةٍ مُخْتَلِفَةٍ.

The large city is considered a multi-denominational community where people from diverse religious and cultural backgrounds coexist.

diverse

مُتَنَوِّعٌ

لَدَيْنا مُجْتَمَعٌ مُتَنَوِّعٌ يَضُمُّ مُعْتَنِقِي دِياناتٍ مُخْتَلِفَةٍ.

We have a diverse community that includes followers of different religions.

school of thought

مَدَارِسُ • مَدْرَسَةُ فِكْرٍ

المَدْرَسَةُ الأَشْعَرِيَّةُ وَمَدْرَسَةُ المُعْتَزَلَةِ هُما مَدْرَسَتا فِكْرٍ إِسْلامِيٍّ.

The Ash'ari school and the Mu'tazili school are two Islamic schools of thought.

sect, denomination

مَذاهِبُ • مَذْهَبٌ

الشِّيعَةُ وَالسُّنَّةُ هُما مَذْهَبانِ رَئِيسِيّانِ في الإِسْلامِ.

Shia and Sunni are two major sects in Islam.

Christianity

مَسِيحِيَّةٌ

لَفَتَتْ مَسِيحِيَّةُ الشَّرْقِ الأَوْسَطِ انْتِباهَ العُلَماءِ لأَوْجُهِ التَّفَرُّدِ فيها.

Middle Eastern Christianity has attracted scholars' attention for its unique aspects.

comparative religion

مُقَارَنَةُ أَدْيانٍ

نَظَّمَتِ الجامِعَةُ وَرْشَةَ عَمَلٍ حَوْلَ مُقَارَنَةِ الأَدْيانِ لِتَعْزِيزِ التَّفاهُمِ المُتَبادَلِ.

The university organized a workshop on comparative religion to promote mutual understanding.

sanctified, holy

مُقَدَّسٌ

تُعْتَبَرُ الكَعْبَةُ مُقَدَّسَةً في الإِسْلامِ وَتَجْتَذِبُ مَلايِينَ الحُجّاجِ كُلَّ عامٍ.

The Kaaba is considered sanctified in Islam and attracts millions of pilgrims every year.

to discuss

نِقاشٌ / مُناقَشَةٌ • ناقَشَ

ناقَشَ العُلَماءُ آثارَ الدِّينِ عَلى الفُنُونِ الإِسْلامِيَّةِ في المُؤْتَمَرِ.

Scholars discussed the effects of religion on Islamic arts at the conference.

نَشَرَ • نَشَرَ وَعْيًا دِينِيًّا

يُنَظِّمُ مَرْكَزُ الثَّقَافَةِ الإِسْلَامِيَّةِ فَعَالِيَّاتٍ لِنَشْرِ الوَعْيِ الدِّينِيِّ بَيْنَ الشَّبَابِ.

The Islamic Culture Center organizes events to spread religious awareness among the youth.

Christianity نَصْرَانِيَّةٌ

تُعْتَبَرُ النَّصْرَانِيَّةُ دِيَانَةً رَئِيسِيَّةً فِي العَالَمِ ذَاتَ تَأْثِيرٍ كَبِيرٍ عَلَى الثَّقَافَاتِ المُخْتَلِفَةِ.

Christianity is a major religion in the world with a significant impact on various cultures.

> In Arabic, there are two terms used to refer to Christianity: النَّصْرَانِيَّةُ and المَسِيحِيَّةُ. The former is the term generally preferred by Arab Christians as it directly relates to المَسِيحُ (the Messiah). On the other hand, نَصْرَانِيَّةٌ is derived from نَصَارَى, an early term for Christians, but it is often associated with extremist discourse and thus not favored by the Christian community in Arab regions.

religious discussion نِقَاشٌ دِينِيٌّ

يُشَجِّعُ الحِوَارُ الدِّينِيُّ عَلَى النِّقَاشِ الدِّينِيِّ المُنْفَتِحِ وَالهَادِفِ بَيْنَ مُخْتَلِفِ الدِّيَانَاتِ.

Religious dialogue encourages open and purposeful religious discussion among different faiths.

Hinduism هِنْدُوسِيَّةٌ

الهِنْدُوسِيَّةُ لَهَا تَأْثِيرٌ كَبِيرٌ عَلَى الفَلْسَفَةِ وَالفَنِّ فِي الهِنْدِ وَمَا وَرَاءَهَا.

Hinduism has a significant impact on philosophy and art in India and beyond.

Judaism يَهُودِيَّةٌ

تُظْهِرُ اليَهُودِيَّةُ تَنَوُّعًا كَبِيرًا فِي المُعْتَقَدَاتِ وَالطُّقُوسِ وَالتَّارِيخِ.

Judaism shows great diversity in beliefs, rituals, and history.

أُخْتُتِمَتْ فَعالِيّاتُ مُؤْتَمَرِ التَّنَوُّعِ الدِّينِيِّ الَّذي ناقَشَ مَواضيعَ مِثْلَ الوَحْدَةِ في التَّنَوُّعِ الدِّينِيِّ وَأَهَمِّيّةِ الاِحْتِرامِ المُتَبادَلِ. اِسْتَعْرَضَ العُلَماءُ دِراساتٍ مُقارَنَةً بَيْنَ الدِّياناتِ السَّماوِيّةِ وَالدِّياناتِ الشَّرْقِيّةِ كَالبوذِيّةِ وَالهِنْدوسِيّةِ، مُؤَكِّدينَ عَلى أَنَّ التَّعَدُّدِيّةَ الدِّينِيّةَ يُمْكِنُ أَنْ تُؤَدِّيَ إلى تَفاهُمٍ أَعْمَقَ بَيْنَ الثَّقافاتِ المُخْتَلِفَةِ.

The events of the Religious Diversity Conference, which discussed topics such as unity in religious diversity and the importance of mutual respect, have concluded. Scholars presented comparative studies between Abrahamic religions and Eastern religions like Buddhism and Hinduism, emphasizing that religious pluralism can lead to a deeper understanding among different cultures.

تَمَّ تَنْظيمُ حِوارٍ بَيْنَ الأَدْيانِ في المَرْكَزِ الثَّقافِيِّ مُتَعَدِّدِ الثَّقافاتِ حَيْثُ الْتَقى مُمَثِّلونَ مِنَ الإسْلامِ وَالمَسيحِيّةِ وَاليَهودِيّةِ لِنَشْرِ الوَعْيِ الدِّينِيِّ وَتَعْزيزِ احْتِرامِ الآخَرِ. تَمَّتْ مُناقَشَةُ مَواضيعَ مِثْلِ الشَّريعَةِ وَالعَقيدَةِ المُقارَنَةِ، وَكَيْفَ يُمْكِنُ لِلْمَذاهِبِ المُخْتَلِفَةِ أَنْ تَتَعايَشَ بِسَلامٍ.

An interfaith dialogue was organized at the multicultural cultural center, where representatives from Islam, Christianity, and Judaism met to spread religious awareness and promote respect for others. Topics such as comparative jurisprudence and doctrine were discussed, and how different denominations can coexist peacefully.

عَقَدَتِ الجامِعَةُ نَدْوَةً تَعْليمِيّةً حَوْلَ الدِّياناتِ الشَّرْقِيّةِ، بِما في ذَلِكَ البوذِيّةِ وَالهِنْدوسِيّةِ، لِتَوْضيحِ مَدى تَأْثيرِها عَلى التَّنَوُّعِ الدِّينِيِّ في المُجْتَمَعاتِ مُتَعَدِّدَةِ المَذاهِبِ. تَمَّتِ المُقارَنَةُ بَيْنَ مَفاهيمَ مِثْلِ المُقَدَّسِ في هَذِهِ الدِّياناتِ مَعَ تِلْكَ المَوْجودَةِ في الدِّياناتِ الإبْراهيمِيّةِ.

The university held an educational seminar on Eastern religions, including Buddhism and Hinduism, to illustrate their impact on religious diversity in multi-denominational societies. Concepts like the sacred in these religions were compared to those in the Abrahamic religions.

أُقيمَتْ وَرْشَةُ عَمَلٍ لِطُلّابِ المَدارِسِ حَوْلَ التَّعَدُّدِيّةِ الدِّينِيّةِ لِتَعْزيزِ الوَعْيِ بِالتَّنَوُّعِ الدِّينِيِّ وَأَهَمِّيّةِ احْتِرامِ الآخَرِ. اِسْتَخْدَمَ الطُّلّابُ مَفاهيمَ مِثْلَ الاِخْتِلافِ الدِّينِيِّ وَمَدارِسِ الفِكْرِ لِتَطْويرِ مَشاريعَ تَعْليمِيّةٍ تَهْدُفُ إلى تَحْقيقِ الوَحْدَةِ في التَّنَوُّعِ الدِّينِيِّ.

A workshop for school students on religious pluralism was held to promote awareness of religious diversity and the importance of respecting others. Students used concepts like religious differences and schools of thought to develop educational projects aimed at achieving unity in religious diversity.

أُفْتُتِحَ مَعْرِضٌ فَنِّيٌّ يَضُمُّ أَعْمالًا تُعَبِّرُ عَنِ الدِّياناتِ المُخْتَلِفَةِ وَتُقَدِّمُ نَظْرَةً مُقارَنَةً بَيْنَها. تَناوَلَ الفَنّانونَ مَواضيعَ مِثْلَ المَذْهَبِ وَالعَقيدَةِ، مُسْتَخْدِمينَ الفَنَّ كَوَسيلَةٍ لِلتَّعْبيرِ عَنِ التَّفاهُمِ المُتَبادَلِ وَالاِحْتِرامِ بَيْنَ الأَدْيانِ المُتَنَوِّعَةِ.

An art exhibition was inaugurated featuring works that express different religions and offer a comparative view between them. The artists addressed topics like sect and creed, using art as a means to express mutual understanding and respect among diverse religions.

8.2.1.2 Informative Article: Abrahamic Religions

لَمْحَةٌ عامَّةٌ عَنِ الأَدْيانِ الإِبْراهيمِيَّةِ

في دِراسَةِ الأَدْيانِ المُقارَنَةِ، تَبْرُزُ الأَدْيانُ الإِبْراهيمِيَّةُ كَفِئَةٍ تَضُمُّ الدِّياناتِ التَّوْحيدِيَّةَ الثَّلاثَ: المَسيحِيَّةَ وَالإِسْلامَ وَاليَهودِيَّةَ. تَشْتَرِكُ هَذِهِ الدِّياناتُ في نَسَبِها الرّوحِيِّ لِلنَّبِيِّ إِبْراهيمَ، الَّذي يَعْتَبِرونَهُ جُزْءًا مِنْ تاريخِهِم المُقَدَّسِ. تَشْمَلُ هَذِهِ الفِئَةُ أَيْضًا أَحْيانًا بَعْضَ الدِّياناتِ الصَّغيرَةِ كَالدِّيانَةِ البَهائِيَّةِ.

تَطَوَّرَ الإِيمانُ الأَصْلِيُّ بِإِلَهِ إِبْراهيمَ لِيُصْبِحَ التَّوْحيدَ الصّارِمَ الَّذي تُمَثِّلُهُ اليَهودِيَّةُ الرَّبّانِيَّةُ المُعاصِرَةُ. يَعْتَقِدُ اليَهودُ المُتَدَيِّنونَ أَنَّ اليَهودِيَّةَ هِيَ تَعْبيرٌ عَنِ العَهْدِ الَّذي أَقامَهُ اللهُ مَعَ بَني إِسْرائيلَ، وَيَرَوْنَ أَنَّ التَّوْراةَ جُزْءٌ مِنْ نَصٍّ أَوْسَعَ يُعْرَفُ بِالتَّناخِ أَوِ الكِتابِ المُقَدَّسِ العِبْرِيِّ، وَيُؤْمِنونَ كَذَلِكَ بِتَقاليدَ شَفَهِيَّةٍ مُكَمِّلَةٍ مُمَثَّلَةٍ في نُصوصٍ لاحِقَةٍ مِثْلِ المِدْراشِ وَالتَّلْمودِ.

يَعْتَقِدُ المَسيحِيّونَ أَنَّ المَسيحِيَّةَ هِيَ اسْتِمْرارٌ وَتَحْقيقٌ لِلْعَهْدِ القَديمِ اليَهودِيِّ. يُؤْمِنونَ أَنَّ يَسوعَ هُوَ المَسيحُ المُنْتَظَرُ المُتَنَبَّأُ بِهِ في نُبوءاتِ العَهْدِ القَديمِ، وَيَتَّبِعونَ كِتاباتِ العَهْدِ الجَديدِ اللاحِقَةِ. يَعْتَقِدُ المَسيحِيّونَ عُمومًا أَنَّ يَسوعَ هُوَ تَجْسيدٌ أَوِ ابْنُ اللهِ، وَتَتَّفِقُ عَقائِدُهُمْ عَلى أَنَّ تَجَسُّدَهُ وَآلامَهُ وَمَوْتَهُ عَلى الصَّليبِ وَقِيامَتَهُ كانَتْ مِنْ أَجْلِ خَلاصِ البَشَرِيَّةِ.

يُؤْمِنُ المُسْلِمونَ بِأَنَّ الكُتُبَ المَسيحِيَّةَ وَاليَهودِيَّةَ الحالِيَّةَ قَدْ تَمَّ تَحْريفُها عَبْرَ الزَّمَنِ وَلَمْ تَعُدِ الوَحْيَ الإِلَهِيَّ الأَصْلِيَّ الَّذي أُعْطِيَ لِلشَّعْبِ اليَهودِيِّ وَلِموسى وَيَسوعَ وَغَيْرِهِمْ مِنَ الأَنْبِياءِ. بِالنِّسْبَةِ لِلْمُسْلِمينَ، القُرْآنُ هُوَ الوَحْيُ النِّهائِيُّ وَالكامِلُ مِنَ اللهِ، الَّذي يَعْتَقِدونَ أَنَّهُ أُنْزِلَ عَلى مُحَمَّدٍ وَحْدَهُ، الَّذي يَعْتَبِرُهُ المُسْلِمونَ نَبِيَّ الإِسْلامِ وَخاتَمَ الأَنْبِياءِ.

تَتَقاطَعُ هَذِهِ الأَدْيانُ في الكَثيرِ مِنَ المُعْتَقَداتِ الأَساسِيَّةِ وَالتّاريخِ، لَكِنَّ كُلًّا مِنْها يَحْتَفِظُ بِخَصائِصِهِ الفَريدَةِ الَّتي تُشَكِّلُ هُوِيَّتَهُ. يَسْتَمِرُّ الحِوارُ بَيْنَ هَذِهِ الدِّياناتِ، مِمّا يُساعِدُ عَلى تَعْزيزِ التَّفاهُمِ المُتَبادَلِ وَالاحْتِرامِ بَيْنَ أَتْباعِها.

An Overview of the Abrahamic Religions

In the study of comparative religion, the Abrahamic religions stand out as a category that includes the three monotheistic faiths: Christianity, Islam, and Judaism. These religions share a spiritual lineage to the prophet Abraham, whom they consider part of their sacred history. This category also occasionally includes some smaller religions, such as the Bahá'í Faith.

The original faith in the Abrahamic God evolved into the strict monotheism represented by contemporary Rabbinic Judaism. Religious Jews believe that Judaism is an expression of the covenant that God established with the Children of Israel, and they see the Torah as part of a broader text known as the Tanakh or the Hebrew Bible; they also believe in complementary oral traditions represented in subsequent texts like the Midrash and the Talmud.

Christians believe that Christianity is the continuation and fulfillment of the Old Testament covenant of Judaism. They believe that Jesus is the awaited Messiah prophesied in the Old Testament prophecies, and they follow the subsequent writings of the New Testament. Christians generally believe that Jesus is the incarnation or the Son of God, and their doctrines agree that His incarnation, sufferings, death on the cross, and resurrection were for the salvation of humanity.

Muslims believe that the current Christian and Jewish scriptures have been distorted over time and are no longer the original divine revelation that was given to the Jewish people and to Moses, Jesus, and other prophets. For Muslims, the Quran is the final and complete revelation from God, which they believe was revealed solely to Muhammad, whom Muslims consider the prophet of Islam and the last prophet.

These religions intersect in many of their fundamental beliefs and history, yet each retains unique characteristics that shape its identity. Dialogue continues between these faiths, which helps to foster mutual understanding and respect among their followers.

8.2.2 Religious Minorities and Their Rights

Track **46**

other religions   *pl.*   أَديانٌ أُخْرى

نَظَّمَ مَرْكَزُ الثَّقافَةِ الإِسْلامِيَّةِ في بَيْروتَ نَدْوَةً لِتَعْزيزِ التَّفاهُمِ المُتَبادَلِ بَيْنَ الإِسْلامِ وَأَدْيانٍ أُخْرى.

The Islamic Culture Center in Beirut organized a seminar to promote mutual understanding between Islam and other religions.

religious minority   أَقَلِّيَّةٌ دينِيَّةٌ

أَقامَتْ جَمْعِيَّةُ حُقوقِ الإِنْسانِ نَدْوَةً لِدَعْمِ حُقوقِ الأَقَلِّيَّةِ الدّينِيَّةِ في لُبْنانَ.

The Human Rights Association held a seminar to support the rights of the religious minority in Lebanon.

Christian minority   أَقَلِّيَّةٌ مَسيحِيَّةٌ

تُواجِهُ الأَقَلِّيّاتُ المَسيحِيَّةُ في العالَمِ العَرَبِيِّ تَحَدِّياتٍ عِدَّةً مِنْها الإِنْدِماجُ الإِجْتِماعِيُّ.

Christian minorities in the Arab world face several challenges, including social integration.

Jewish minority

أَقَلِّيَّةٌ يَهُودِيَّةٌ

تَعْمَلُ المُنَظَّماتُ الحُقوقِيَّةُ عَلَى حِمايَةِ الأَقَلِّيّاتِ اليَهودِيَّةِ في المِنْطَقَةِ.

Human rights organizations work to protect Jewish minorities in the region.

Islamophobia

إِسْلاموفوبْيا

يَرْتَفِعُ مُسْتَوى الإِسْلاموفوبْيا في بَعْضِ البُلْدانِ، مِمّا يُثيرُ قَلَقَ المُجْتَمَعاتِ المُسْلِمَةِ.

The level of Islamophobia is rising in some countries, causing concern among Muslim communities.

Gospel

إِنْجيلٌ • أَناجيلُ

تُقَدِّمُ الكَنيسَةُ مُساعَداتٍ لِلْفُقَراءِ وَفْقًا لِتَعاليمِ الإِنْجيلِ.

The church offers aid to the poor in accordance with the teachings of the Gospel.

Orthodoxy

الأُرْثوذُكْسِيَّةُ

تُظْهِرُ الأُرْثوذُكْسِيَّةُ تَأْثيرًا كَبيرًا عَلَى الحَياةِ الدّينِيَّةِ في روسْيا.

Orthodoxy has a significant impact on religious life in Russia.

Old/New Testament

العَهْدُ القَديمُ / العَهْدُ الجَديدُ

اقْتَصَرَتْ دِراساتُ بَعْضِ الطُّلّابِ عَلَى العَهْدِ القَديمِ دونَ العَهْدِ الجَديدِ.

Some students' studies focused only on the Old Testament, not the New Testament.

Russian Orthodox Church

الكَنيسَةُ الأُرْثوذُكْسِيَّةُ الرّوسِيَّةُ • كَنائِسُ

تُعْتَبَرُ الكَنيسَةُ الأُرْثوذُكْسِيَّةُ الرّوسِيَّةُ نَشِطَةً في الشَّرْقِ الأَوْسَطِ، وَتُحاوِلُ بِناءَ عَلاقاتٍ مَعَ المُسْلِمينَ.

The Russian Orthodox Church is active in the Middle East and is attempting to build relations with Muslims.

Armenian Orthodox Church

الكَنيسَةُ الأَرْمَنِيَّةُ الأُرْثوذُكْسِيَّةُ

تُعْتَبَرُ الكَنيسَةُ الأَرْمَنِيَّةُ الأُرْثوذُكْسِيَّةُ واحِدَةً مِنْ أَقْدَمِ الكَنائِسِ المَسيحِيَّةِ.

The Armenian Orthodox Church is considered one of the oldest Christian churches.

Anglican Church

الكَنيسَةُ الأَنْغليكانِيَّةُ

تَأَسَّسَتِ الكَنيسَةُ الأَنْجِليكانِيَّةُ في إِنْجلْترا، وَلَها جُذورٌ تاريخِيَّةٌ عَميقَةٌ.

The Anglican Church was founded in England and has deep historical roots.

Evangelical Church in Egypt

الكَنيسَةُ الإِنْجيليَّةُ في مِصرَ

تَلْعَبُ الكَنيسَةُ الإِنْجيليَّةُ في مِصرَ دَوْرًا مُهِمًّا في الحَياةِ الدّينِيَّةِ لِلْأَقَلِّيّاتِ المَسيحِيَّةِ هُناكَ.

The Evangelical Church in Egypt plays a significant role in the religious life of Christian minorities there.

Syriac Orthodox Church

الكَنيسَةُ السُّرْيانِيَّةُ الأُرْثوذُكْسِيَّةُ

تُعتَبَرُ الكَنيسَةُ السُّرْيانِيَّةُ الأُرْثوذُكْسِيَّةُ مِنْ أَقْدَمِ الكَنائِسِ المَسيحِيَّةِ في الشَّرْقِ الأَوْسَطِ.

The Syriac Orthodox Church is considered among the oldest Christian churches in the Middle East.

Coptic Orthodox Church

الكَنيسَةُ القِبْطِيَّةُ الأُرْثوذُكْسِيَّةُ

يَعيشُ الأَقْباطُ في مِصرَ، وَهُمْ يَتْبَعونَ الكَنيسَةَ القِبْطِيَّةَ الأُرْثوذُكْسِيَّةَ.

The Copts live in Egypt and follow the Coptic Orthodox Church.

Coptic Catholic Church

الكَنيسَةُ الكاثوليكِيَّةُ القِبْطِيَّةُ

تُمَثِّلُ الكَنيسَةُ الكاثوليكِيَّةُ القِبْطِيَّةُ جُزْءًا مِنَ التَّنَوُّعِ المَسيحِيِّ في مِصرَ.

The Coptic Catholic Church represents a part of the Christian diversity in Egypt.

Chaldean Church

الكَنيسَةُ الكِلْدانِيَّةُ

تُعتَبَرُ الكَنيسَةُ الكِلْدانِيَّةُ مُهِمَّةً في الحَياةِ الدّينِيَّةِ لِلْمَسيحِيّينَ في العِراقِ.

The Chaldean Church is important in the religious life of Christians in Iraq.

Maronite Church

الكَنيسَةُ المارونِيَّةُ

تَأَسَّسَتِ الكَنيسَةُ المارونِيَّةُ في لُبْنانَ، وَلَها تَأْثيرٌ كَبيرٌ عَلى الحَياةِ الثَّقافِيَّةِ والدّينِيَّةِ هُناكَ.

The Maronite Church was founded in Lebanon and has a significant impact on cultural and religious life there.

Christianity

مَسيحيَّةٌ

المَسيحيَّةُ هِيَ واحِدَةٌ مِنَ الدِّياناتِ السَّماويَّةِ الثَّلاثَةِ.

Christianity is one of the three Abrahamic religions.

Protestant Christianity

المَسيحيَّةُ البُروتِستانْتيَّةُ

تُعْتَبَرُ المَسيحيَّةُ البُروتِستانْتيَّةُ في لُبْنانَ نَشِطَةً، لَكِنَّها تُمَثِّلُ أَقَلِّيَّةً دينيَّةً.

Protestant Christianity in Lebanon is active but represents a religious minority.

Judaism

يَهوديَّةٌ

تُمَثِّلُ اليَهوديَّةُ إِحْدى الدِّياناتِ الرَّئيسيَّةِ في العالَمِ، وَلَها تاريخٌ وَتُراثٌ ثَقافِيٌّ عَريقٌ.

Judaism represents one of the major religions in the world and has a long and rich cultural history and heritage.

to violate the rights of religious minorities

اِنْتَهَكَ حُقوقَ أَقَلِّيَّاتٍ دينيَّةٍ • اِنْتِهاكٌ

اِنْتِهاكُ حُقوقِ الأَقَلِّيَّاتِ الدِّينيَّةِ يُعَدُّ مُشْكِلَةً عالَميَّةً تَتَطَلَّبُ اهْتِمامًا دَوْليًّا.

Violating the rights of religious minorities is a global issue that requires international attention.

Patriarch

بَطْرِيَرْكٌ • بَطارِكَةٌ / بَطاريك / بَطارُك

يُعْتَبَرُ البَطْرِيَرْكُ رَئيسًا روحيًّا لِلْكَنيسَةِ في بَعْضِ التَّقاليدِ المَسيحيَّةِ.

The Patriarch is considered the spiritual head of the church in some Christian traditions.

Religious Coexistence

تَعايُشٌ دينيٌّ

أَطْلَقَتْ مُؤَسَّساتٌ دينيَّةٌ مَشْروعًا لِتَعْزيزِ التَّعايُشِ الدِّينيِّ في الأُرْدُنِّ.

Religious institutions launched a project to promote religious coexistence in Jordan.

تَعَصُّبٌ دِينِيٌّ

religious bigotry

يُظْهِرُ التَّعَصُّبُ الدِّينِيُّ نَقْصًا فِي التَّسامُحِ وَالاحْتِرامِ المُتَبادَلِ بَيْنَ مُخْتَلِفِ الدِّياناتِ.

Religious bigotry shows a lack of tolerance and mutual respect among different religions.

تَعَصُّبٌ ضِدَّ أَقَلِّيّاتٍ دِينِيَّةٍ

bigotry against religious minorities

التَّعَصُّبُ ضِدَّ الأَقَلِّيّاتِ الدِّينِيَّةِ يُعَرِّضُ النّاسَ لِلْخَطَرِ وَيُؤَجِّجُ النِّزاعاتِ.

Bigotry against religious minorities puts people at risk and fuels conflicts.

تَمَتَّعَ بِحُرِّيَّةٍ دِينِيَّةٍ • تَمَتَّعَ

to enjoy religious freedom

إِنَّ التَّمَتُّعَ بِالْحُرِّيَّةِ الدِّينِيَّةِ يُعَدُّ حَقًّا أَساسِيًّا فِي الدِّيمُقْراطِيّاتِ الحَدِيثَةِ.

Enjoying religious freedom is considered a fundamental right in modern democracies.

تَوْراةٌ

Torah

تُعْتَبَرُ التَّوْراةُ الكِتابَ المُقَدَّسَ فِي الدِّيانَةِ اليَهودِيَّةِ.

The Torah is considered the holy book in Judaism.

حاخامٌ

Rabbi

الحاخامُ هُوَ القائِدُ الدِّينِيُّ فِي المُجْتَمَعِ اليَهودِيِّ.

The Rabbi is the religious leader in the Jewish community.

حانوكا = عيدُ الأَنْوارِ

Hanukkah

يَحْتَفِلُ اليَهودُ بِحانوكا، وَالَّذي يُعْرَفُ أَيْضًا بِعيدِ الأَنْوارِ.

Jews celebrate Hanukkah, which is also known as the Festival of Lights.

حُرِّيَّةُ مُمارَسَةِ العَقيدَةِ

freedom to practice religion

حُرِّيَّةُ مُمارَسَةِ العَقيدَةِ تُعْتَبَرُ مِنَ الحُقوقِ الأَساسِيَّةِ الَّتي يَجِبُ أَنْ تُحْفَظَ.

Freedom to practice religion is considered one of the fundamental rights that should be preserved.

حُقوقُ أَقَلِّيّاتٍ دينِيّةٍ *pl.*   rights of religious minorities

حُقوقُ الأَقَلِّيّاتِ الدّينِيّةِ تُعْتَبَرُ مَوْضوعًا مُهِمًّا في حِواراتِ حُقوقِ الإِنْسانِ.

The rights of religious minorities are considered an important subject in human rights dialogues.

دافَعَ عَنْ حُقوقِ أَقَلِّيّاتٍ دينِيّةٍ • دِفاعٌ / مُدافَعَةٌ   to defend the rights of religious minorities

يُعْتَبَرُ الدِّفاعُ عَنْ حُقوقِ الأَقَلِّيّاتِ الدّينِيّةِ مِنْ مَسْؤولِيّاتِ الحُكوماتِ وَالمُنَظَّماتِ الدَّوْلِيّةِ.

Defending the rights of religious minorities is considered a responsibility of governments and international organizations.

صَدَقَةٌ لِلْفُقَراءِ   Charity to the Poor

تُعْتَبَرُ الصَّدَقَةُ لِلْفُقَراءِ جُزْءًا مُهِمًّا مِنَ التَّقاليدِ الدّينِيّةِ في الإِسْلامِ وَالمَسيحِيّةِ.

Charity to the poor is considered an important part of religious traditions in both Islam and Christianity.

In Islam, زَكاةٌ (see page 191) and صَدَقَةٌ (above) refer to two different concepts of charitable giving:

زَكاةٌ is one of the Five Pillars of Islam, an obligatory tax on the wealth of every eligible Muslim, intended to purify wealth and support the needy.

صَدَقَةٌ, on the other hand, is voluntary charity given beyond the obligatory zakat, reflecting personal generosity and is not limited by specific requirements or amounts.

عُنْصُرِيٌّ   racist

العُنْصُرِيُّ هُوَ شَخْصٌ يُمَيِّزُ بَيْنَ النّاسِ عَلى أَساسِ العِرْقِ أَوِ الدّيانَةِ، وَهُوَ مَوْضوعٌ يُثيرُ الجَدَلَ في العَلاقاتِ بَيْنَ المَذاهِبِ الدّينِيّةِ.

A racist is someone who discriminates between people on the basis of race or religion, which is a contentious issue in interfaith relations.

عَهْدٌ = ميثاقٌ • عُهودٌ / مَواثيقُ   covenant

العَهْدُ أَوِ الميثاقُ يُعْتَبَرُ وَثيقَةً مُقَدَّسَةً في العَديدِ مِنَ الدّياناتِ، مِثْلِ اليَهودِيّةِ وَالمَسيحِيّةِ.

A covenant is considered a sacred document in many religions, such as Judaism and Christianity.

Feast of Tabernacles

عيدُ العَرْشِ = عيدُ المِظَلَّةِ = عيدُ المِظَلَّةِ • أَعْيادٌ

عيدُ العَرْشِ أَوْ عيدُ المِظَلَّةِ هُوَ أَحَدُ الأَعْيادِ المُهِمَّةِ في التَّقْويمِ اليَهوديِّ.

The Feast of Tabernacles, also known as Sukkot, is an important holiday in the Jewish calendar.

Easter

عيدُ الفِصْحِ = عيدُ القيامَة

يَحْتَفِلُ المَسيحيّونَ بعيدِ الفِصْحِ لإِحْياءِ ذِكْرى قيامَةِ المَسيحِ.

Christians celebrate Easter to commemorate the resurrection of Christ.

Christmas

عيدُ الميلاد

عيدُ الميلاد هُوَ اليَوْمُ الَّذي يَحْتَفِلُ فيه المَسيحيّونَ بِميلادِ يَسوعَ المَسيحِ.

Christmas is the day when Christians celebrate the birth of Jesus Christ.

Copt, Coptic

قِبْطيٌّ • أَقْباطٌ

يَعيشُ الأَقْباطُ في مِصْرَ كَأَقَلِّيَّةٍ دينيَّةٍ تاريخيَّةٍ.

The Copts live in Egypt as a historical religious minority.

Eastern Catholics in Iraq

كاثوليك الشَّرْقِ في العِراقِ

يَعيشُ كاثوليك الشَّرْقِ في العِراقِ تَحْتَ ظُروفٍ صَعْبَةٍ وَيُواجِهونَ تَمْييزًا عَلى أَساسٍ دينيٍّ.

Eastern Catholics in Iraq live under difficult conditions and face religious discrimination.

synagogue

كَنيسٌ = مَعْبَدٌ يَهوديٌّ • كُنُسٌ

الكَنيسُ هُوَ مَكانُ العِبادَةِ في الدِّيانَةِ اليَهوديَّةِ، وَيُعْتَبَرُ مَرْكَزًا لِلْحَياةِ الاِجْتِماعِيَّةِ والدِّينِيَّةِ.

The synagogue is a place of worship in Judaism and serves as a center for social and religious life.

church

كَنيسَةٌ • كَنائِسُ

في الكَنيسَةِ، يَجْتَمِعُ المَسيحيّونَ لِلصَّلاةِ والتَّرْنيمِ وَسَماعِ العِظاتِ.

In the church, Christians gather for prayer, hymn singing, and listening to sermons.

Melkite Church

كَنِيسَةُ المَلَكِيِّينَ

كَنِيسَةُ المَلَكِيِّينَ هِيَ جُزْءٌ مِنَ الكَنائِسِ الشَّرْقِيَّةِ، وَلَها أَتْباعٌ فِي الشَّرْقِ الأَوْسَطِ.

The Melkite Church is part of the Eastern churches and has followers in the Middle East.

to exercise religious rights

مارَسَ حُقوقًا دينِيَّةً • مُمارَسَةٌ

تُعْتَبَرُ مُمارَسَةُ الحُقوقِ الدِّينِيَّةِ حَقًّا أَساسِيًّا فِي مُعْظَمِ الدُّوَلِ الدِّيمُقْراطِيَّةِ.

Exercising religious rights is considered a fundamental right in most democratic countries.

bigoted

مُتَعَصِّبٌ

الشَّخْصُ المُتَعَصِّبُ لا يُقَدِّرُ التَّنَوُّعَ الدِّينِيَّ، وَغالِبًا ما يَكونُ لَدَيْهِ آراءٌ سَلْبِيَّةٌ تُجاهَ الدِّياناتِ الأُخْرى.

A bigoted person does not appreciate religious diversity and often holds negative views toward other religions.

Christian

نَصْرانِيٌّ • نَصارى

النَّصْرانِيُّ هُوَ مُتَّبِعُ الدِّيانَةِ المَسيحِيَّةِ، وَيُمْكِنُ أَنْ يَكونَ مِنْ أَيِّ مَذْهَبٍ مَسيحِيٍّ.

A Christian is a follower of Christianity and can be from any Christian denomination.

religious convergence

نُقْطَةُ تَلاقٍ دينِيٍّ • نِقاطٌ

تَعْكِسُ نُقْطَةُ التَّلاقي الدِّينِيِّ التَّفاعُلاتِ وَالتَّشابُهاتِ بَيْنَ مُخْتَلِفِ الدِّياناتِ.

A point of religious convergence reflects the interactions and similarities between different religions.

Jew

يَهودِيٌّ • يَهودٌ

اليَهودِيُّ هُوَ شَخْصٌ يَتَّبِعُ الدِّيانَةَ اليَهودِيَّةَ أَوْ يَنْتَمي لِلشَّعْبِ اليَهودِيِّ.

A Jew is a person who follows the Jewish religion or belongs to the Jewish people.

Sabbath

يَوْمُ السَّبْتِ • أَيّامٌ

يَوْمُ السَّبْتِ هُوَ يَوْمُ الرّاحَةِ وَالعِبادَةِ فِي الدِّيانَةِ اليَهودِيَّةِ.

The Sabbath is a day of rest and worship in the Jewish religion.

Yom Kippur

يَوْمُ كِيبورَ = يَوْمُ الغُفْرانِ

يَوْمُ كِيبورَ، المَعْروفُ أَيْضًا بِيَوْمِ الغُفْرانِ، هُوَ أَحَدُ أَهَمِّ الأَعْيادِ الدّينِيَّةِ في اليَهودِيَّةِ.

Yom Kippur, also known as the Day of Atonement, is one of the most important religious holidays in Judaism.

8.2.2.1 Mini-Articles

Track **47**

في إطارِ الجُهودِ المَبْذولَةِ لِتَعْزيزِ حُقوقِ الأَقَلِّيّاتِ الدّينِيَّةِ، أَعْلَنَتْ حُكومَةُ لُبْنانَ عَنْ مُبادَرَةٍ جَديدَةٍ تَسْمَحُ لِلْكَنيسَةِ المارونِيَّةِ بِإِنْشاءِ مَراكِزَ تَعْليمِيَّةٍ تَهْدُفُ إلى تَعْليمِ الشَّبابِ قِيَمَ التَّعايُشِ الدّينِيِّ وَاحْتِرامَ التَّنَوُّعِ الثَّقافِيِّ.

In an effort to enhance the rights of religious minorities, the Lebanese government announced a new initiative allowing the Maronite Church to establish educational centers aimed at teaching youth the values of religious coexistence and respect for cultural diversity.

في صَنْعاءَ، اليَمَنِ، دَعا حاخامُ الأَقَلِّيَّةِ اليَهودِيَّةِ إلى تَعْزيزِ الحِوارِ بَيْنَ الأَدْيانِ مِنْ خِلالِ سِلْسِلَةٍ مِنَ اللِّقاءاتِ الَّتي تَجْمَعُ القادَةَ الدّينِيّينَ وَالمُفَكِّرينَ. جاءَتْ هَذِهِ الدَّعْوَةُ بَعْدَ احْتِفالٍ مُجْتَمَعِيٍّ بِحانوكا نَظَّمَتْهُ الأَقَلِّيَّةُ اليَهودِيَّةُ، حَيْثُ يَعْكِسُ رَغْبَةَ الأَقَلِّيّاتِ في تَأْكيدِ حَقِّهِمْ في مُمارَسَةِ شَعائِرِهِمِ الدّينِيَّةِ وَالعَيْشِ بِسَلامٍ في ظِلِّ التَّحَدِّياتِ الرّاهِنَةِ.

In Sanaa, Yemen, the rabbi of the Jewish minority called for enhancing interfaith dialogue through a series of meetings that bring together religious leaders and thinkers. This call came after a community Hanukkah celebration organized by the Jewish minority, reflecting the minorities' desire to affirm their right to practice their religious rituals and live in peace amid current challenges.

أَصْدَرَتِ الأَقَلِّيَّةُ المَسيحِيَّةُ في الأُرْدُنِّ بَيانًا يُثَمِّنُ جُهودَ المَمْلَكَةِ في حِمايَةِ حُقوقِ الأَقَلِّيّاتِ الدّينِيَّةِ، وَذَلِكَ بَعْدَ اعْتِمادِ قانونٍ جَديدٍ يَضْمَنُ حُرِّيَّةَ مُمارَسَةِ العَقيدَةِ لِجَميعِ الطَّوائِفِ. أَشادَ البَيانُ بِالتَّقَدُّمِ الَّذي أَحْرَزَتْهُ البِلادُ في مَجالِ الحُرِّيّاتِ الدّينِيَّةِ.

The Christian minority in Jordan issued a statement appreciating the Kingdom's efforts in protecting the rights of religious minorities, following the adoption of a new law that ensures the freedom of creed practice for all denominations. The statement praised the progress the country has made in the field of religious freedoms.

في مِصْرَ، نَظَّمَتِ الكَنيسَةُ القِبْطِيَّةُ الكاثوليكِيَّةُ مُؤْتَمَرًا دَوْلِيًّا لِمُناقَشَةِ تَحَدِّياتِ الأَقَلِّياتِ الدِّينِيَّةِ في الشَّرْقِ الأَوْسَطِ. شَهِدَ المُؤْتَمَرُ حُضورَ شَخْصِيّاتٍ دينِيَّةٍ عالَمِيَّةٍ، وناقَشَ سُبُلَ دَعْمِ حُقوقِ الأَقَلِّياتِ وَضَمانِ مُمارَسَةِ شَعائِرِهِمُ الدِّينِيَّةِ بِحُرِّيَّةٍ.

In Egypt, the Coptic Catholic Church organized an international conference to discuss the challenges faced by religious minorities in the Middle East. The conference saw the attendance of global religious figures and discussed ways to support the rights of minorities and ensure the freedom to practice their religious rituals.

أَطْلَقَتِ الكَنيسَةُ السُّرْيانِيَّةُ الأُرْثوذُكْسِيَّةُ في العِراقِ مُبادَرَةً لِلتَّوْعِيَةِ بِأَهَمِّيَّةِ التَّعايُشِ الدِّينِيِّ، مُشيرَةً إلى دَوْرِ الأَدْيانِ المُخْتَلِفَةِ في تَعْزيزِ السَّلامِ. تَضَمَّنَتِ المُبادَرَةُ سِلْسِلَةً مِنَ اللِّقاءاتِ بَيْنَ القادَةِ الدِّينِيِّينَ لِتَعْزيزِ الحِوارِ وَالتَّفاهُمِ.

The Syriac Orthodox Church in Iraq launched an initiative to raise awareness of the importance of religious coexistence, highlighting the role of different religions in promoting peace. The initiative included a series of meetings between religious leaders to enhance dialogue and understanding.

8.2.2.2 Analysis: Religious Freedom in Arab Countries

Track **48**

الحُرِّيَّةُ الدّينِيَّةُ في الدُّوَلِ العَرَبِيَّةِ: تَحْليلٌ وَتَقْييمٌ

مَشْهَدُ الحُرِّيَّةِ الدّينِيَّةِ في الدُّوَلِ العَرَبِيَّةِ مُتَنَوِّعٌ وَمُعَقَّدٌ، يَتَشَكَّلُ مِنْ خِلالِ الإِعْلاناتِ الدُّسْتورِيَّةِ وَسِياساتِ الحُكومَةِ وَتَوَجُّهاتِ المُجْتَمَعِ. تُقَدِّمُ كُلُّ دَوْلَةٍ حالَةً فَريدَةً في مُمارَسَةِ وَحُدودِ الحُرِّيَّةِ الدّينِيَّةِ، تَتَأَثَّرُ بِالسِّياقِ التّاريخِيِّ وَالطّائِفَةِ الدّينِيَّةِ السّائِدَةِ وَالدّينامِيّاتِ السِّياسِيَّةِ. يَهْدُفُ هَذا التَّقْريرُ إلى تَقْديمِ لَمْحَةٍ عَنِ الوَضْعِ الحالِيِّ لِلْحُرِّيَّةِ الدّينِيَّةِ في مَجْموعَةٍ مُخْتارَةٍ مِنَ الدُّوَلِ العَرَبِيَّةِ، مُسَلِّطًا الضَّوْءَ عَلى التَّفاصيلِ وَالاتِّجاهاتِ الَّتي تُحَدِّدُ العَلاقَةَ بَيْنَ الدَّوْلَةِ وَالدّينِ وَحُرِّيّاتِ الأَفْرادِ.

الأُرْدُنُّ: يُوَفِّرُ الأُرْدُنُّ الحُرِّيَّةَ الدّينِيَّةَ مَعَ بَعْضِ القُيودِ، وَعادَةً ما تَحْتَرِمُ الحُكومَةُ هَذِهِ الحُقوقَ. وَمَعَ ذَلِكَ، تُواجِهُ الجَماعاتُ الدّينِيَّةُ غَيْرُ المُعْتَرَفِ بِها تَمْييزًا، وَيَتِمُّ مُراقَبَةُ الأَنْشِطَةِ بِعِنايَةٍ مِنْ قِبَلِ أَجْهِزَةِ الأَمْنِ.

الإِماراتُ العَرَبِيَّةُ المُتَّحِدَةُ: في الإِماراتِ العَرَبِيَّةِ المُتَّحِدَةِ، يَسْمَحُ الدُّسْتورُ بِالحُرِّيَّةِ الدّينِيَّةِ وَفْقًا لِلْعُرْفِ، طالَما أَنَّها لا تَتَعارَضُ مَعَ السِّياسَةِ العامَّةِ أَوِ الأَخْلاقِ، مَعَ كَوْنِ الإِسْلامِ ديانَةَ الدَّوْلَةِ. عادَةً ماتَكونُ الحُكومَةُ مُتَسامِحَةً مَعَ الجَماعاتِ غَيْرِ المُسْلِمَةِ.

البَحْرَيْن: لا يَحْمي دُستورُ البَحْرَيْنِ بِشَكْلٍ صَريحٍ الحُرِّيَّةَ الدِّينِيَّةَ، وَلَكِنَّهُ يَسْمَحُ بِحُرِّيَّةِ العِبادَةِ، مَعَ مَنْحِ الأَفْضَلِيَّةِ عادَةً لِلْمُسْلِمينَ السُّنِّيِّينَ. السُّكّانُ الشِّيعَةُ، الذينَ تَعَرَّضوا لِلرِّقابَةِ والعُنْفِ مِنْ قِبَلِ الحُكومَةِ، ما زالوا يَحْتَجّونَ مِنْ أَجْلِ الإِصْلاحِ السِّياسِيِّ.

الجَزائِرُ: يَضْمَنُ دُستورُ الجَزائِرِ الحُرِّيَّةَ الدِّينِيَّةَ، وَلَكِنْ أَحيانًا يَتِمُّ تَقْييدُ ذَلِكَ في الواقِعِ. يَميلُ غَيْرُ المُسْلِمينَ، خاصَّةً المُرْتَدّينَ عَنِ الإِسْلامِ، والجالياتِ اليَهودِيَّةَ، إلى الانْزِواءِ بِسَبَبِ المَخاوِفِ المُتَعَلِّقَةِ بِالسَّلامَةِ والعَواقِبِ القانونِيَّةِ والاجْتِماعِيَّةِ المُحْتَمَلَةِ.

العِراقُ: يَكْفُلُ دُستورُ العِراقِ الحُرِّيَّةَ الدِّينِيَّةَ، وَبَيْنَما تَحْتَرِمُ الحُكومَةُ هَذا الحَقَّ بِشَكْلٍ نَظَرِيٍّ، لَكِنَّها تَفْرِضُ أَيْضًا الإِسْلامَ كَمَصْدَرٍ لِلتَّشْريعِ. هُناكَ حالاتٌ مِنَ العُنْفِ ضِدَّ مُمارَساتٍ دينِيَّةٍ مِنْ قِبَلِ مَجْموعاتٍ مِثْلَ القاعِدَةِ في العِراقِ.

الكُوَيْتُ: دُستورُ الكُوَيْتِ يَسْمَحُ بِالحُرِّيَّةِ الدِّينِيَّةِ، هُناكَ قَوانينُ وَسِياساتٌ أُخْرى تَفْرِضُ قُيودًا. تَفْرِضُ الحُكومَةُ هَذِهِ القُيودَ، مِمّا يُؤَدّي إلى التَّمْييزِ ضِدَّ الأَقَلِّيّاتِ الدِّينِيَّةِ وَفَرْضِ العُقوباتِ عَلى التَّجْديفِ وَتَحْقيرِ الطَّوائِفِ الدِّينِيَّةِ.

المَغْرِبُ: تَحْتَرِمُ الحُكومَةُ حَقَّ مُمارَسَةِ الدِّينِ لِمُعْظَمِ المُواطِنينَ، وَلَكِنَّها تُثْني عَنِ الارْتِدادِ عَنِ الإِسْلامِ وَتُرَوِّجُ لَهُ. تُحْظَرُ المَوادُّ الدِّينِيَّةُ غَيْرُ الإِسْلامِيَّةِ، وَتُواجِهُ الجَماعاتُ الدِّينِيَّةُ الصَّغيرَةُ قُيودًا رَسْمِيَّةً.

المَمْلَكَةُ العَرَبِيَّةُ السُّعودِيَّةُ: يُعامَلُ مَوضوعُ الحُرِّيَّةِ الدِّينِيَّةِ وَفْقَ إِطارِ الشَّريعَةِ الإِسْلامِيَّةِ، وَتَشْتَهِرُ البِلادُ بِالتِزامِها بِالحِفاظِ عَلى التُّراثِ الإِسْلامِيِّ. يُسْمَحُ لِغَيْرِ المُسْلِمينَ بِمُمارَسَةِ دِيانَتِهِمْ بِشَكْلٍ خاصٍّ، وَتوجَدُ أَماكِنُ مُخَصَّصَةٌ لِلْعِبادَةِ لِلْمُجْتَمَعاتِ الوافِدَةِ. قامَتِ البِلادُ بِاتِّخاذِ خُطُواتٍ لِتَعْزيزِ حِوارِ التَّعايُشِ الدِّينِيِّ والتَّفاهُمِ، مَعَ التَّأْكيدِ عَلى تَرْسيخِ مَبادِئِ الإِسْلامِ.

اليَمَنُ: في اليَمَنِ، لا يَحْمي الدُّستورُ الحُرِّيَّةَ الدِّينِيَّةَ بِشَكْلٍ كامِلٍ، حَيْثُ يَميلُ إلى تَفْضيلِ الإِسْلامِ كَدِيانَةِ الدَّوْلَةِ وَأَساسٍ لِلْقانونِ، وَيُقَيِّدُ أَفْعالًا مِثْلَ الرِّدَّةِ عَنِ الإِسْلامِ. فَقَدْ فَرَضَتِ الجَماعاتُ المُتَطَرِّفَةُ تَفْسيراتٍ قاسِيَةً لِلْقَوانينِ الدِّينِيَّةِ في بَعْضِ المَناطِقِ.

تونِس: تُوَفِّرُ الحُكومَةُ الحُرِّيَّةَ الدِّينِيَّةَ مَعَ وُجودِ بَعْضِ القُيودِ، واتَّخَذَتْ خُطُواتٍ لِتَعْزيزِ التَّسامُحِ بَيْنَ الأَدْيانِ. وَمَعَ ذَلِكَ، تَقومُ الأَقَلِّيّاتُ الدِّينِيَّةُ بِالإِبْلاغِ عَنْ عَدَمِ حِمايَتِها الكافِيَةِ مِنَ التَّحَرُّشِ والهَجَماتِ مِنْ قِبَلِ الجَماعاتِ المُتَطَرِّفَةِ.

سوريا: انْخَفَضَ احْتِرامُ الحُكومَةِ لِلْحُرِّيَّةِ الدِّينِيَّةِ، مَعَ زِيادَةِ اسْتِهْدافِ الجَماعاتِ الّتي تُعْتَبَرُ تَهْديدًا، خاصَّةً خِلالَ النِّزاعِ الأَهْلِيِّ. تَمَّ الإِبْلاغُ عَنْ تَمْييزٍ اجْتِماعِيٍّ وانْتِهاكاتٍ، غالِبًا ما تَكونُ مَصْحوبَةً بِنَعَراتٍ طائِفِيَّةٍ.

قَطَرُ: الإِسْلَامُ دِيانَةُ الدَّوْلَةِ، حَيْثُ يُمَارِسُهُ المُسْلِمُونَ السُّنَّةُ وَالشِّيعَةُ بِحُرِّيَّةٍ، بَيْنَما يَتَعَبَّدُ مُتَّبِعُو الأَدْيانِ الأُخْرَى فِي مَناطِقَ مُخَصَّصَةٍ. يَتِمُّ تَقْيِيدُ العِبادَةِ العَلَنِيَّةِ لِغَيْرِ المُسْلِمِينَ، الَّذِينَ يُواجِهُونَ أَيْضًا القُيُودَ عَلَى التَّبْشِيرِ وَمُراقَبَةِ وَسائِلِ الإِعْلامِ.

لُبْنانُ: تَحْتَرِمُ الحُكُومَةُ عُمُومًا حُرِّيَّةَ الدِّيانَةِ، مُوازِنَةً لِلْقُوَى بَيْنَ الجَماعاتِ الدِّينِيَّةِ الرَّئِيسِيَّةِ. تَسْتَمِرُّ التَّوَتُّراتُ الاِجْتِماعِيَّةُ وَالتَّمْيِيزُ، وَغالِبًا ما تَكُونُ مُرْتَبِطَةً بِالمُنافَسَةِ السِّياسِيَّةِ وَإِرْثِ الصِّراعِ الأَهْلِيِّ، مَعَ تَسَبُّبِ قَضايا إِقْلِيمِيَّةٍ حَدِيثَةٍ أَيْضًا فِي زِيادَةِ هَذِهِ التَّوَتُّراتِ.

لِيبِيا: تَحْتَرِمُ الحُرِّيَّةَ الدِّينِيَّةَ عُمُومًا بَعْدَ الثَّوْرَةِ عامَ 2011، مَعَ تَقْلِيلِ التَّحَكُّمِ فِي الحَياةِ الدِّينِيَّةِ. وَمَعَ ذَلِكَ، تُعانِي الحُكُومَةُ مِنَ الصُّعُوبَةِ فِي السَّيْطَرَةِ عَلَى جَماعاتٍ مُتَطَرِّفَةٍ عَنِيفَةٍ، مِمّا يُؤَدِّي إِلَى هَجَماتٍ عَلَى الأَقَلِّيّاتِ الدِّينِيَّةِ.

مِصْرُ: يُظْهِرُ السِّياقُ الثَّقافِيُّ المُتَنَوِّعُ فِي مِصْرَ التَّسامُحَ وَاحْتِرامَ حُقُوقِ الإِنْسانِ، حَيْثُ يُتِيحُ النِّظامُ القانُونِيُّ الدِّيمُقْراطِيُّ فُرَصًا مُتَساوِيَةً لِلْمُواطِنِينَ مِنْ مُخْتَلِفِ الأَدْيانِ لِمُمارَسَةِ عَقائِدِهِمْ بِدُونِ تَمْيِيزٍ. يَزْدادُ تَعْزِيزُ قِيَمِ التَّعايُشِ السِّلْمِيِّ فِي مِصْرَ مِنْ خِلالِ الاِحْتِرامِ المُتَبادَلِ لِحُرِّيَّةِ مُمارَسَةِ الدِّيانَةِ، وَتَبْرُزُ التَّدابِيرُ القانُونِيَّةُ وَالاِجْتِماعِيَّةُ الَّتِي تُعَزِّزُ هَذا الحَقَّ كَجُزْءٍ أَساسِيٍّ مِنَ الهُوِيَّةِ الوَطَنِيَّةِ.

تَتَراوَحُ الحُرِّيَّةُ الدِّينِيَّةُ فِي الدُّوَلِ العَرَبِيَّةِ بَيْنَ الاِنْفِتاحِ النِّسْبِيِّ وَالقُيُودِ الصّارِمَةِ، ما يَعْكِسُ التَّنَوُّعَ فِي الأَسالِيبِ المُسْتَخْدَمَةِ فِي الحُكْمِ وَإِنْفاذِ القانُونِ فِي المِنْطَقَةِ. بَيْنَما تُظْهِرُ بَعْضُ الدُّوَلِ مُسْتَوًى مِنَ التَّسامُحِ وَالحِمايَةِ لِمُمارَساتِ الأَدْيانِ المُخْتَلِفَةِ، يَفْرِضُ البَعْضُ الآخَرُ تَدابِيرَ مُقَيِّدَةً يُمْكِنُ أَنْ تُؤَدِّيَ إِلَى التَّمْيِيزِ وَالعُنْفِ ضِدَّ الأَقَلِّيّاتِ. تَزِيدُ المَشاهِدُ السِّياسِيَّةُ المُتَقَلِّبَةُ وَالنِّزاعاتُ المُسْتَمِرَّةُ مِنْ تَعْقِيداتِ السَّعْيِ نَحْوَ الحُرِّيَّةِ الدِّينِيَّةِ الحَقِيقِيَّةِ. يُبْرِزُ هَذا التَّقْرِيرُ الحاجَةَ إِلَى المُتابَعَةِ وَالحِوارِ المُسْتَمِرَّيْنِ لِتَعْزِيزِ بِيئَةٍ يُمْكِنُ لِجَمِيعِ الأَفْرادِ مُمارَسَةُ دِيانَتِهِمْ فِيها دُونَ خَوْفٍ مِنَ الاِضْطِهادِ أَوِ الإِكْراهِ.

Religious Freedom in Arab Countries: Analysis and Assessment

The landscape of religious freedom in Arab countries is varied and complex, shaped by constitutional declarations, government policies, and societal attitudes. Each nation presents a unique case in the exercise and limitation of religious freedom, influenced by historical context, the dominant religious sect, and political dynamics. This report aims to offer a snapshot of the current state of religious freedom across a selection of Arab countries, highlighting the nuances and trends that define the relationship between state, religion, and individual liberties.

Jordan: Jordan provides for religious freedom with some limitations, and the government typically respects these rights. However, unrecognized religious groups face discrimination, and activities are closely monitored by security services.

The UAE: In the UAE, the constitution allows religious freedom according to customary practice, as long as it doesn't clash with public policy or morals, with Islam as the state religion. The government is generally tolerant of non-Muslim groups.

Bahrain: Bahrain's constitution does not explicitly protect religious freedom but allows for the freedom of worship, with Sunni Muslims generally holding favored status. The Shia population, which has faced government scrutiny and violence, continues to protest for political reform.

Algeria: Algeria's constitution guarantees religious freedom, but this is sometimes restricted in practice. Non-Muslims, especially converts from Islam, and Jewish communities tend to keep a low profile due to safety concerns and potential legal and social repercussions.

Iraq: Iraq's constitution guarantees religious freedom, and while the government respects this in theory, it also enforces Islam as a source of legislation. There are instances of violence against religious practices by groups like Al-Qaeda in Iraq.

Kuwait: Kuwait's constitution allows for religious freedom, but other laws and policies impose restrictions. The government enforces these, leading to discrimination against religious minorities and punishments for blasphemy and denigrating religious sects.

Morocco: The government respects the right to practice religion for most citizens but discourages conversion from Islam and proselytizes it. Non-Islamic religious materials are restricted, and small religious groups face official limitations.

Saudi Arabia: The issue of religious freedom is addressed within the framework of Islamic law, and the country is known for its commitment to preserving Islamic heritage. Non-Muslims are allowed to practice their faith privately, and there are designated places of worship for expatriate communities. The country has taken steps to promote interfaith dialogue and understanding, emphasizing coexistence while adhering to the principles of Islam.

Yemen: In Yemen, the constitution doesn't protect religious freedom fully, favoring Islam as the state religion and basis for law, and restricting actions like conversion from Islam. Extremist groups have enforced harsh interpretations of religious law in some regions.

Tunisia: The government provides for religious freedom with some restrictions and has taken steps to promote interfaith tolerance. However, religious minorities report inadequate protection from harassment and attacks by fundamentalist groups.

Syria: The government's respect for religious freedom has declined, with increased targeting of groups deemed threats, particularly during the civil conflict. Societal discrimination and abuses have been reported, often with sectarian overtones.

Qatar: Islam is the state religion, with Sunni and Shia Muslims practicing freely, while other religions worship in designated areas. Public worship is restricted for non-Muslims, who also face proselytizing prohibitions and media monitoring.

Lebanon: The government generally respects religious freedom, balancing power among major religious groups. Societal tensions and discrimination persist, often linked to political competition and the legacy of civil conflict, with recent regional issues also contributing to frictions.

Libya: Religious freedom is generally respected following the 2011 revolution, with less regulation of religious life. However, the government struggles to control violent extremist groups, leading to attacks on religious minorities.

Egypt: Egypt's diverse cultural context demonstrates tolerance and respect for human rights, with a democratic legal system providing equal opportunities for citizens of various religions to practice their beliefs without discrimination. The promotion of peaceful coexistence in Egypt is enhanced through mutual respect for the freedom of religion, highlighting legal and social measures that reinforce this right as an essential part of the national identity.

Religious freedom in Arab countries ranges from relative openness to strict limitations, reflecting the diverse approaches to governance and law enforcement in the region. While some countries exhibit a level of tolerance and protection for various religious practices, others enforce restrictive measures that can lead to discrimination and violence against minority groups. The fluctuating political landscapes and ongoing conflicts further complicate the pursuit of true religious liberty. This report underscores the need for continued observation and dialogue to foster an environment where all individuals can practice their faith without fear of persecution or coercion.

8.2.3 Religious Dialogue and Cooperation

Track **49**

respect for religions

اِحْتِرامُ أَدْيانٍ

اِحْتَفَلَتْ مَدينَةُ القاهِرَةِ بِمَهْرَجانٍ لِتَعْزيزِ احْتِرامِ الأَدْيانِ، وَشارَكَ فيه رِجالُ دينٍ مِنْ مُخْتَلِفِ الدِّياناتِ.

Cairo celebrated a festival to promote respect for religions, with clergy from various faiths participating.

integration

اِنْدِماجٌ = دَمْجٌ

وَفْقًا لِآخِرِ التَّقاريرِ، نَجَحَ بَرْنامَجُ الإِنْدِماجِ في دُبَيَّ في دَمْجِ الجالِياتِ الدّينِيَّةِ المُخْتَلِفَةِ.

According to the latest reports, Dubai's integration program has successfully merged various religious communities.

exchanging opinions

تَبادُلُ آراءٍ

أقامَتْ جامِعَةُ بَيْروتَ جَلْسَةً لِتَبادُلِ الآراءِ حَوْلَ القِيَمِ المُشْتَرَكَةِ بَيْنَ الإِسْلامِ وَالمَسيحِيَّةِ.

Beirut University hosted a session for exchanging opinions on common values between Islam and Christianity.

tolerance

تَسامُحٌ

أَطْلَقَتِ السُّعوديَّةُ مُبادَرَةً جَديدَةً لِتَعْزيزِ التَّسامُحِ الدّينيِّ بَيْنَ جَميعِ طَوائِفِ المُجْتَمَعِ.

Saudi Arabia launched a new initiative to promote religious tolerance among all segments of society.

coexistence

تَعايُشٌ

تَقَدَّمَتْ مَدينَةُ مَراكِشَ بِمَشْروعٍ لِتَعْزيزِ التَّعايُشِ بَيْنَ المُسْلِمينَ والمَسيحيّينَ في المَدينَةِ.

The city of Marrakech has put forth a project to enhance coexistence between Muslims and Christians in the city.

peaceful coexistence

تَعايُشٌ سِلْميٌّ

أَصْدَرَتْ جَمْعيَّةُ التَّعايُشِ السِّلْميِّ في عَمّانَ بَيانًا يُشيدُ بِالْجُهودِ المَبْذولَةِ لِتَعْزيزِ العَلاقاتِ بَيْنَ مُخْتَلِفِ الأَدْيانِ.

The Association for Peaceful Coexistence in Amman issued a statement praising efforts to enhance relations between different religions.

religious pluralism

تَعَدُّديَّةٌ دينيَّةٌ

أَبْرَزَتِ القِمَّةُ الإِسْلاميَّةُ السَّنَويَّةُ الأَخيرَةُ أَهَمّيَّةَ التَّعَدُّديَّةِ الدّينيَّةِ كَجُزْءٍ مِنَ التَّفاهُمِ الدَّوْليِّ.

The recent annual Islamic Summit highlighted the importance of religious pluralism as part of international understanding.

religious understanding

تَفاهُمٌ دينيٌّ

تُشيرُ التَّقاريرُ إلى ازْديادِ التَّفاهُمِ الدّينيِّ بَيْنَ المُجْتَمَعاتِ المُسْلِمَةِ واليَهوديَّةِ في مَدينَةِ نيويورْكَ.

Reports indicate an increase in religious understanding between Muslim and Jewish communities in New York City.

religious and cultural diversity

تَنَوُّعٌ ثَقافيٌّ وَدينيٌّ

قامَتْ مُنَظَّماتٌ مَحَلّيَّةٌ في الجَزائِرِ بِتَنْظيمِ مَعارِضَ تَعْليميَّةٍ لِزيادَةِ الوَعْي بِالتَّنَوُّعِ الثَّقافيِّ والدّينيِّ.

Local organizations in Algeria organized educational exhibitions to raise awareness about religious and cultural diversity.

freedom of belief
حُرِّيَّةُ مُعْتَقَدٍ

وَقَّعَتْ مُنَظَّماتُ حُقوقِ الإنْسانِ بَيانًا مُشْتَرَكًا يَدْعو لِحُرِّيَّةِ المُعْتَقَدِ في جَميعِ أنْحاءِ العالَمِ.

Human rights organizations signed a common statement calling for freedom of belief worldwide.

interfaith dialogue
حِوارٌ بَيْنَ أَدْيانٍ

اِسْتَضافَتْ دُبَيٌّ مُنْتَدًى حِوارِيًّا لِتَعْزيزِ الحِوارِ بَيْنَ الأَدْيانِ شارَكَ فيهِ مُمَثِّلونَ مِنَ الدِّياناتِ الرَّئيسِيَّةِ.

Dubai hosted a dialogue forum to enhance interfaith dialogue with representatives from major religions participating.

supportive
داعِمٌ

أَبْرَزَتِ المُنَظَّماتُ النِّسائِيَّةُ دَوْرَها الدّاعِمَ في تَعْزيزِ الحِوارِ الدّينِيِّ بَيْنَ النِّساءِ مِنْ مُخْتَلِفِ الخَلْفِيّاتِ الدّينِيَّةِ.

Women's organizations highlighted their supportive role in enhancing religious dialogue among women from various religious backgrounds.

tolerant
مُتَسامِحٌ

يُظْهِرُ اسْتِطْلاعٌ جَديدٌ أَنَّ الجيلَ الصّاعِدَ في الشَّرْقِ الأَوْسَطِ يَعْتَبِرُ نَفْسَهُ مُتَسامِحًا تِجاهَ الأَدْيانِ الأُخْرى.

A new survey shows that the rising generation in the Middle East considers itself tolerant toward other religions.

peaceful
مُسالِمٌ

في مَجالِ الدّينِ، يَسْعَى النّاسُ جَميعًا إلى أنْ تَكونَ شُعوبُهُمْ شُعوبًا مُسالِمَةً، مُسْتَلْهِمينَ مِنْ قِيَمِ التَّسامُحِ وَالسَّلامِ الَّتي يُعَلِّمُها دينُهُمْ.

In the field of religion, people all strive for their nations to be peaceful nations, drawing inspiration from the values of tolerance and peace that their religion teaches.

Notice the difference in usage between مُسالِمٌ, which is typically used to describe individuals or human behavior, indicating peacefulness or non-aggression, while سِلْمِيٌّ (see page 124) is used with inanimate nouns or concepts, suggesting a peaceful nature or approach.

common

مُشْتَرَك

أَظْهَرَتِ المُؤْتَمَراتُ الدِّينِيَّةُ الأَخِيرَةُ أَنَّ المَسْؤُولِينَ الدِّينِيِّينَ في الهِنْدِ وَباكِسْتانَ يَبْحَثُونَ عَنْ قَواسِمَ مُشْتَرَكَةٍ لِلتَّعايُشِ السِّلْمِيِّ.

Recent religious conferences have shown that religious officials in India and Pakistan are seeking common ground for peaceful coexistence.

dialogue forum

مُنْتَدَىً حِوارِيٌّ

نَظَّمَتِ الجامِعَةُ الأَمْرِيكِيَّةُ مُنْتَدَى حِوارِيًّا لِطُلّابِها لِتَبادُلِ الآراءِ حَوْلَ الفَهْمِ المُتَبادَلِ وَالتَّعايُشِ بَيْنَ مُخْتَلِفِ الدِّياناتِ.

The American University organized a dialogue forum for its students to exchange opinions on mutual understanding and coexistence among various religions.

spreading awareness

نَشْرُ الوَعْي

أَطْلَقَتِ الأُمَمُ المُتَّحِدَةُ حَمْلَةً جَدِيدَةً لِنَشْرِ الوَعْي حَوْلَ أَهَمِّيَّةِ التَّعايُشِ السِّلْمِيِّ وَالتَّسامُحِ بَيْنَ الأَدْيانِ.

The United Nations launched a new campaign to spread awareness about the importance of peaceful coexistence and tolerance among religions.

8.2.3.1 Mini-Articles

Track **50**

في القاهِرَةِ، انْعَقَدَ مُنْتَدَى حِوارِيٌّ حَوْلَ تَعايُشِ الأَدْيانِ، حَيْثُ تَجَمَّعَ مُتَّبِعو الأَدْيانِ المُخْتَلِفَةِ لِتَبادُلِ الآراءِ وَالخِبْراتِ. وَقَدْ أَكَّدَ المُشارِكونَ عَلى أَهَمِّيَّةِ التَّسامُحِ وَحُرِّيَّةِ المُعْتَقَدِ في إِرْساءِ قَواعِدِ مُجْتَمَعٍ مُسالِمٍ وَمُتَنَوِّعٍ ثَقافِيًّا وَدِينِيًّا.

In Cairo, a dialogue forum on religious coexistence was held, bringing together followers of different religions to exchange views and experiences. Participants emphasized the importance of tolerance and freedom of belief in establishing a culturally and religiously diverse and peaceful society.

أَطْلَقَتْ مَجْموعَةٌ مِنَ الدّاعِمينَ لِلتَّعَدُّدِيَّةِ الدِّينِيَّةِ مُبادَرَةً جَدِيدَةً تَهْدُفُ إلى نَشْرِ الوَعْي بِأَهَمِّيَّةِ التَّفاهُمِ الدِّينِيِّ بَيْنَ الشَّبابِ. يَسْعى المَشْروعُ إلى خَلْقِ جِيلٍ جَدِيدٍ مُتَسامِحٍ وَقادِرٍ عَلى احْتِرامِ أَدْيانِ الآخَرينَ.

A group of supporters of religious pluralism launched a new initiative aimed at raising awareness of the importance of religious understanding among young people. The project aims to create a new generation that is tolerant and capable of respecting the religions of others.

شَهِدَتِ العاصِمَةُ افْتِتاحَ مَرْكَزٍ جَديدٍ لِلْحِوارِ بَيْنَ الأَدْيانِ، يُسَمّى "دارَ التَّعايُشِ السِّلْمِيِّ". يَقومُ المَرْكَزُ بِتَنْظيمِ وَرَشِ عَمَلٍ وَمُؤْتَمَراتٍ تَدْعو لِلتَّعايُشِ وَالِانْدِماجِ بَيْنَ أَتْباعِ الدِّياناتِ المُخْتَلِفَةِ، وَتَدْعَمُ تَبادُلَ الآراءِ بِشَكْلٍ بَنّاءٍ.

The capital witnessed the opening of a new center for interfaith dialogue called "House of Peaceful Coexistence." The center organizes workshops and conferences that promote coexistence and integration among followers of different faiths and support constructive exchange of ideas.

في إطارِ دَعْمِ التَّنَوُّعِ الثَّقافِيِّ وَالدِّينِيِّ، أَعْلَنَتْ مُؤَسَّسَةٌ مَحَلِّيَّةٌ عَنْ مِنْحَةٍ دِراسِيَّةٍ لِلطُّلّابِ الَّذينَ يُسْهِمونَ في أَنْشِطَةٍ تُعَزِّزُ التَّفاهُمَ بَيْنَ أَتْباعِ الدِّياناتِ المُتَعَدِّدَةِ. تُعْتَبَرُ هَذِهِ المِنْحَةُ خُطْوَةً هامَّةً نَحْوَ تَشْجيعِ الشَّبابِ عَلى الِانْخِراطِ في أَنْشِطَةٍ تَحْتَرِمُ أَدْيانَ وَمُعْتَقَداتِ بَعْضِهِمِ البَعْضِ.

As part of supporting cultural and religious diversity, a local foundation announced a scholarship for students who contribute to activities that enhance understanding among followers of multiple religions. This scholarship is considered an important step in encouraging young people to engage in activities that respect the religions and beliefs of others.

في خُطْوَةٍ لافِتَةٍ نَحْوَ السَّلامِ، الْتَقى قادَةٌ دينِيّونَ مِنْ مُخْتَلِفِ الأَدْيانِ في حَديقَةِ الأُخُوَّةِ لِزَرْعِ شَجَرَةِ السَّلامِ. هَذا الحَدَثُ الَّذي يَدْعَمُهُ مُشْتَرِكونَ مِنْ مُخْتَلِفِ الخَلْفِيّاتِ، يَرْمُزُ إلى النُّمُوِّ المُشْتَرَكِ وَالتَّسامُحِ الَّذي يُمْكِنُ أَنْ يَجْمَعَ بَيْنَ النّاسِ مِنْ كُلِّ الخَلْفِيّاتِ الدِّينِيَّةِ.

In a remarkable step toward peace, religious leaders from various faiths gathered at the Brotherhood Park to plant the Tree of Peace. This event, supported by participants from different backgrounds, symbolizes the common growth and tolerance that can bring people of all religious backgrounds together.

8.2.3.2 Street Interviews: Religion in Lebanon

Track **51**

التَّنَوُّعُ الدِّينِيُّ وَالتَّعايُشُ السِّلْمِيُّ في لُبْنانَ: لِقاءاتٌ في الشّارِعِ

المُراسِل: أَهْلاً بِكُمْ مِنْ قَلْبِ بَيْروتَ، حَيْثُ نَلْتَقي اليَوْمَ بِالْمُواطِنينَ لِنَقيسَ آراءَهُمْ حَوْلَ دَوْرِ الدّينِ في لُبْنانَ. سَيِّدَتي، ما هُوَ شُعورُكِ تُجاهَ التَّنَوُّعِ الدِّينِيِّ في لُبْنانَ؟

امْرَأَةٌ مُتَقاعِدَةٌ: التَّنَوُّعُ الدِّينِيُّ يَعْكِسُ تَنَوُّعَنا الثَّقافِيَّ وَتاريخَنا الغَنِيَّ. لَكِنْ لا يُمْكِنُنا إنْكارُ أَنَّ هَذا التَّنَوُّعَ كانَ مَصْدَرَ تَوَتُّرٍ في أَوْقاتٍ مِنْ تاريخِنا الحَديثِ.

المُراسِل: وَماذا عَنْ حُرِّيَّةِ المُعْتَقَدِ؟ هَلْ تَرى أَنَّها مُحْتَرَمَةٌ في مُجْتَمَعِنا؟

رَجُلُ أَعْمالٍ: في الظّاهِرِ، نَعَم. لَكِنْ في الواقِعِ، ما زالَتْ هُناكَ تَحَدِّياتٌ. بَعْضُ النّاسِ مُتَسامِحونَ، لَكِنْ آخَرونَ يَرَوْنَ أَنَّ حُرِّيَّةَ المُعْتَقَدِ يَجِبُ أَنْ تَنْتَهِيَ حَيْثُ تَبْدَأُ مُعْتَقَداتُهُمْ.

المُراسِلُ: سَمِعْنا عَنِ المُنْتَدَياتِ الحِوارِيَّةِ وَجُهودِها في تَعْزيزِ الحِوارِ وَالتَّعايُشِ السِّلْمِيِّ. هَلْ تَشْعُرُ أَنَّ هَذِهِ الجُهودَ كافِيَةٌ؟

طالِبٌ جامِعِيٌّ: هَذِهِ المُنْتَدَياتُ خُطْوَةٌ في الاتِّجاهِ الصَّحيحِ، لَكِنَّنا نَحْتاجُ إِلى المَزيدِ. الحِوارُ بَيْنَ الأَدْيانِ مُهِمٌّ، وَلَكِنَّ التَّحَدِّيَ الحَقيقِيَّ هُوَ تَحْويلُ هَذِهِ المُحادَثاتِ إِلى تَغْييرٍ مَلْموسٍ.

المُراسِلُ: وَبِالنِّسْبَةِ لِلدّاعِمينَ لِهَذِهِ المُبادَراتِ، هَلْ تَعْتَقِدُ أَنَّ جُهودَهُمْ فَعّالَةٌ في نَشْرِ الوَعْيِ؟

أُمٌّ شابَّةٌ: بَعْضُ الدّاعِمينَ يَعْمَلونَ بِصِدْقٍ لِنَشْرِ الوَعْيِ وَالمَحَبَّةِ بَيْنَ الأَدْيانِ، لَكِنَّ البَعْضَ يَسْتَغِلّونَ هَذِهِ المُبادَراتِ لِأَغْراضٍ سِياسِيَّةٍ، مِمّا يُعَقِّدُ الأُمورَ أَكْثَرَ.

المُراسِلُ: بِالنَّظَرِ إِلى تاريخِ لُبْنانَ مَعَ الانْقِساماتِ الدّينِيَّةِ، هَلْ تَرَوْنَ أَنَّ هُناكَ تَقَدُّمًا حَقيقِيًّا نَحْوَ التَّعايُشِ السِّلْمِيِّ؟

رَجُلٌ مُتَقاعِدٌ: لَقَدْ عانى لُبْنانُ كَثيرًا مِنَ الصِّراعاتِ الدّينِيَّةِ. وَبَيْنَما نَشْهَدُ بَعْضَ التَّقَدُّمِ، الطَّريقُ لا يَزالُ طَويلًا. نَحْتاجُ إِلى تَجاوُزِ شِعاراتِ التَّعايُشِ وَالتَّسامُحِ وَجَعْلِها واقِعًا يَعيشُهُ الجَميعُ.

المُراسِلُ: في الخِتامِ، هَلْ تَعْتَقِدُ أَنَّ مَفْهومَ التَّعايُشِ السِّلْمِيِّ قابِلٌ لِلتَّحْقيقِ في مُجْتَمَعِنا؟

شابٌّ مُهَنْدِسٌ: أَمَلي كَبيرٌ، لَكِنَّ التَّحَدِّياتِ جَمَّةٌ. نَحْتاجُ لِلْعَمَلِ عَلى احْتِرامِ أَدْيانِ الآخَرينَ بِشَكْلٍ عَمَلِيٍّ وَيَوْمِيٍّ، وَلَيْسَ فَقَطْ في المُناسَباتِ العامَّةِ.

المُراسِلُ: شُكْرًا لِآرائِكُمُ المُتَنَوِّعَةِ. إِنَّ بَيْروتَ لَيْسَتْ فَقَطْ شاهِدَةً عَلى تاريخِ لُبْنانَ العَريقِ، بَلْ هِيَ أَيْضًا مَسْرَحٌ لِتَفاعُلاتِهِ الثَّقافِيَّةِ وَالدّينِيَّةِ الغَنِيَّةِ. مِنْ بَيْروتَ، كانَ مَعَكُمْ مُراسِلُكُمْ، إِلى اللِّقاءِ.

Religious Diversity and Peaceful Coexistence in Lebanon: Street Interviews

Correspondent: Hello from the heart of Beirut, where we meet citizens today to gauge their opinions on the role of religion in Lebanon. Madam, how do you feel about religious pluralism in Lebanon?

Retired Woman: Religious pluralism reflects our cultural diversity and rich history. However, we cannot deny that this diversity has been a source of tension at times in our recent history.

Correspondent: What about freedom of belief? Do you find it respected in our society?

Businessman: On the surface, yes. But in reality, there are still challenges. Some people are tolerant, but others believe that freedom of belief should end where their beliefs begin.

Correspondent: We've heard about dialogue forums and their efforts to promote dialogue and peaceful coexistence. Do you feel these efforts are sufficient?

University Student: These forums are a step in the right direction, but we need more. Interfaith dialogue is important, but the real challenge is to turn these conversations into tangible change.

Correspondent: Regarding the supporters of these initiatives, do you think their efforts are effective in raising awareness?

Young Mother: Some supporters sincerely work to spread awareness and love between religions, but some exploit these initiatives for political purposes, which complicates matters further.

Correspondent: Looking at Lebanon's history with religious divisions, do you see real progress toward peaceful coexistence?

Retired Man: Lebanon has suffered a lot from religious conflicts. While we witness some progress, the road is still long. We need to go beyond slogans of coexistence and tolerance and make them a reality for everyone.

Correspondent: In conclusion, do you believe that the concept of peaceful coexistence is achievable in our society?

Young Engineer:	I am very hopeful, but the challenges are numerous. We need to work on respecting the religions of others in a practical and daily manner, not just on public occasions.
Correspondent:	Thank you for your diverse opinions. Beirut is not only a witness to Lebanon's venerable history but also a stage for its rich cultural and religious interactions. From Beirut, this is your correspondent signing off.

8.3 Social Issues Related to Religion

Track **52**

the Quran

القُرْآنُ

اِنْطَلَقَتْ مُبادَرَةٌ جَديدَةٌ في الأُرْدُنِّ تَسْتَهْدِفُ تَعْزيزَ المُساواةِ الدِّينِيَّةِ عَبْرَ تَوْزيعِ نُسَخٍ مِنَ القُرْآنِ وَالإِنْجيلِ في المَدارِسِ.

A new initiative has been launched in Jordan aimed at promoting religious equality by distributing copies of the Quran and the Bible in schools.

Quranic (relating to the Quran)

قُرْآنِيٌّ

أَصْدَرَتْ لَجْنَةٌ دينِيَّةٌ في مِصْرَ فَتْوى قُرْآنِيَّةً تَحُثُّ عَلى التَّسامُحِ وَالتَّفاهُمِ بَيْنَ مُخْتَلِفِ طَوائِفِ المُجْتَمَعِ.

A religious committee in Egypt issued a Quranic fatwa urging tolerance and understanding among different communities.

tolerant

مُتَسامِحٌ

في لُبْنانَ، تَعاوَنَتْ مُؤَسَّساتٌ مُتَعَدِّدَةُ الأَدْيانِ لإِطْلاقِ حَمْلَةٍ تَوْعِيَةٍ تَسْتَهْدِفُ الشَّبابَ لِتَعْزيزِ قِيَمِ التَّعايُشِ السِّلْمِيِّ.

In Lebanon, multi-religious institutions collaborated to launch an awareness campaign targeting youth to promote the values of peaceful coexistence.

multi-religious

مُتَعَدِّدُ الأَدْيانِ

في البَلْدَةِ مُتَعَدِّدَةِ الأَدْيانِ، يَحْتَفِلُ النّاسُ مِنْ جَميعِ الأَدْيانِ بِالأَعْيادِ مَعًا بِروحِ التَّعايُشِ.

In the multi-religious town, people from all faiths celebrate holidays together in a spirit of coexistence.

مُساواةٌ دينِيَّةٌ
religious equality

نَشَرَتْ مُنَظَّمَةٌ لِحُقوقِ الإِنْسانِ تَقْريرًا يُؤَكِّدُ عَلى أَهَمِّيَّةِ تَعْزيزِ المُساواةِ الدّينِيَّةِ في العالَمِ.

A human rights organization published a report emphasizing the importance of promoting religious equality worldwide.

8.3.1 Women's Rights in Islamic Societies

Track 53

اِعْتِداءٌ عَلى المَرْأَةِ
assault against women

شَهِدَتْ تونِسُ تَزايُدًا في الدَّعَواتِ لِمُكافَحَةِ الاِعْتِداءِ عَلى المَرْأَةِ، مَعَ الضَّغْطِ لِتَعْديلِ القَوانينِ الَّتي تُقَيِّدُ العُقوباتِ.

Tunisia has seen a rise in calls to combat assault against women, with pressure to amend laws that limit penalties.

> Notice that, in the term above, المَرْأَة is grammatically singular but refers to women in general, while النِّساءُ is the actual plural form for specific, multiple women.

تَحَرُّرٌ مِنَ القُيودِ الاِجْتِماعِيَّةِ
liberation from social constraints

تُرَكِّزُ الجَمْعِيّاتُ النِّسائِيَّةُ في العِراقِ عَلى تَحَرُّرِ النِّساءِ مِنَ القُيودِ الاِجْتِماعِيَّةِ مِنْ خِلالِ بَرامِجِ التَّمْكينِ الاِقْتِصادِيِّ.

Women's associations in Iraq are focusing on the liberation of women from social constraints through economic empowerment programs.

تَحَرُّشٌ جِنْسِيٌّ
sexual harassment

أَثارَتْ حالاتُ التَّحَرُّشِ الجِنْسِيِّ في إيرانَ جَدَلًا واسِعًا وَدَعَواتٍ لِتَشْديدِ العُقوباتِ.

Cases of sexual harassment in Iran have sparked widespread controversy and calls for stricter penalties.

تَحْريرُ المَرْأَةِ
women's liberation

أَصْدَرَتْ مَجَلَّةٌ نِسائِيَّةٌ في تُرْكِيا سِلْسِلَةَ مَقالاتٍ تَتَناوَلُ قَضايا تَحْريرِ المَرْأَةِ وَتَمْكينِها في المُجْتَمَعِ.

A women's magazine in Turkey has issued a series of articles addressing issues of women's liberation and empowerment in society.

تَعْليمُ المَرْأةِ
women's education

نَظَّمَتْ جامِعَةُ الأزْهَرِ دَوْراتٍ تَعْليمِيَّةً مُخَصَّصَةً لِتَعْليمِ المَرْأةِ حُقوقَها الشَّرْعِيَّةَ وَالاجْتِماعِيَّةَ.

Al-Azhar University organized educational courses dedicated to women's education about their legal and social rights.

تَقْليدِيٌّ
traditional

يُنْظَرُ إلى التَّقاليدِ الَّتي تُقَيِّدُ حُرِّيَّةَ المَرْأةِ في بَعْضِ المُجْتَمَعاتِ الإسْلامِيَّةِ كَعَقَباتٍ أمامَ التَّقَدُّمِ الاقْتِصادِيِّ وَالاجْتِماعِيِّ.

Traditional practices that restrict women's freedom in some Islamic societies are seen as obstacles to economic and social progress.

تَمْكينُ المَرْأةِ
women's empowerment

تُظْهِرُ الإحْصائِيّاتُ في الهِنْدِ تَحَسُّنًا مَلْحوظًا في تَمْكينِ المَرْأةِ بِفَضْلِ البَرامِجِ التَّعْليمِيَّةِ وَالقَوانينِ الجَديدَةِ.

Statistics in India show notable improvement in women's empowerment thanks to educational programs and new laws.

تَمْييزٌ جِنْسِيٌّ
gender discrimination

في مِصْرَ، لا تَزالُ قَضايا التَّمْييزِ الجِنْسِيِّ تُواجِهُ مُعارَضَةً شَديدَةً مِنْ جَماعاتِ حُقوقِ المَرْأةِ.

In Egypt, issues of gender discrimination still face strong opposition from women's rights groups.

تَمْييزٌ ضِدَّ المَرْأةِ
discrimination against women

أثارَ تَقْريرٌ حَديثٌ عَنِ التَّمْييزِ ضِدَّ المَرْأةِ في القِطاعِ التِّكْنولوجِيِّ العَرَبِيِّ جَدَلًا واسِعًا.

A recent report on discrimination against women in the Arab tech sector has sparked widespread controversy.

تَوْعِيَةٌ بِحُقوقِ المَرْأةِ
raising awareness about women's rights

في لُبْنانَ، انْتَشَرَتْ حَمَلاتٌ عَبْرَ الإنْتَرْنِتْ لِلتَّوْعِيَةِ بِحُقوقِ المَرْأةِ وَالمُطالَبَةِ بِإصْلاحاتٍ قانونِيَّةٍ.

In Lebanon, online campaigns for raising awareness about women's rights and calling for legal reforms have proliferated.

to fight against sexual harassment • مُحارَبَةٌ   حارَبَ التَّحَرُّشَ الجِنْسيَّ

تَعَهَّدَتِ الحُكومَةُ الأُرْدُنِّيَّةُ بِمُحارَبَةِ التَّحَرُّشِ الجِنْسيِّ مِنْ خِلالِ تَشْديدِ العُقوباتِ.

The Jordanian government has committed to fight against sexual harassment by strengthening penalties.

modernity   حَداثَةٌ

عَلى الرَّغْمِ مِنَ التَّقاليدِ الصّارِمَةِ في أَفْغانِسْتانَ، يُظْهِرُ بَعْضُ النَّشاطِ الاجْتِماعِيِّ وَالثَّقافِيِّ تَوَجُّهًا نَحْوَ الحَداثَةِ في مَجالِ حُقوقِ المَرْأَةِ.

Despite strict traditions in Afghanistan, some social and cultural activity shows a trend toward modernity in the field of women's rights.

personal freedom   حُرِّيَّةٌ شَخْصِيَّةٌ

تَظَلُّ الحُرِّيَّةُ الشَّخْصِيَّةُ لِلْمَرْأَةِ مَوْضوعًا يُثيرُ الجَدَلَ في المُجْتَمَعاتِ العَرَبِيَّةِ، حَيْثُ يَتَطَلَّبُ التَّوازُنَ بَيْنَ الحُرِّيَّةِ وَالمَسْؤوليَّةِ.

Personal freedom for women remains a controversial issue in Arab societies, requiring a balance between freedom and responsibility.

travel ban   حَظْرُ سَفَرٍ

أَثارَ حَظْرُ السَّفَرِ دونَ مُوافَقَةِ وَلِيِّ الأَمْرِ، المَفْروضُ عَلى النِّساءِ السُّعودِيّاتِ، جَدَلًا عالَمِيًّا حَوْلَ حُقوقِ المَرْأَةِ في الإِسْلامِ.

A travel ban imposed on Saudi women without the consent of their guardian has sparked global controversy about women's rights in Islam.

women's rights   *pl.*   حُقوقُ المَرْأَةِ

تَمَّ إِصْدارُ قانونٍ جَديدٍ يَحْمي حُقوقَ المَرْأَةِ في مَجالاتٍ مِثْلِ العَمَلِ وَالتَّعْليمِ.

A new law has been enacted to protect women's rights in areas such as employment and education.

women's rights in Islam   *pl.*   حُقوقُ المَرْأَةِ في الإِسْلامِ

يَجْري حِوارٌ دينيٌّ لِمُناقَشَةِ التَّفْسيراتِ المُخْتَلِفَةِ لِحُقوقِ المَرْأَةِ في الإِسْلامِ وَكَيْفَ يُمْكِنُ تَعْزيزُها.

A religious dialogue is taking place to discuss various interpretations of women's rights in Islam and how to enhance them.

حِمايَةٌ •   حَمى حُقوقَ المَرأَةِ

to protect women's rights

شَهِدَتِ المَمْلَكَةُ المُتَّحِدَةُ نُمُوًّا في الجَمْعِيّاتِ الَّتي تَعْمَلُ عَلى حِمايَةِ حُقوقِ المَرأَةِ مِنَ التَّمْييزِ وَالعُنْفِ.

The United Kingdom has seen growth in organizations working to protect women's rights from discrimination and violence.

دَعْمٌ •   دَعَمَ

to support

في إِندونيسيا، تُحْرِزُ البَرامِجُ الحُكومِيَّةُ تَقَدُّمًا في دَعْمِ المَرأَةِ في المُجْتَمَعِ مِنْ خِلالِ التَّدْريبِ المِهْنِيِّ وَالقُروضِ الصَّغيرَةِ.

In Indonesia, government programs are making strides in supporting women in society through vocational training and micro-lending.

زِيادَةٌ •   زادَ الوَعْيَ بِـ

to raise awareness about

أَطْلَقَتْ جَمْعِيَّةٌ خَيْرِيَّةٌ في تُرْكيا حَمْلَةً لِزِيادَةِ الوَعْي بِحُقوقِ المَرأَةِ، تَسْتَهْدِفُ بِشَكْلٍ خاصٍّ الأُمورَ المُتَعَلِّقَةَ بِالعُنْفِ الأُسَرِيِّ.

A charitable organization in Turkey has launched a campaign to raise awareness about women's rights, specifically targeting issues related to domestic violence.

زَواجٌ مُبَكِّرٌ

early marriage

في اليَمَنِ، يُعْتَبَرُ الزَّواجُ المُبَكِّرُ لِلفَتَياتِ مُشْكِلَةً اجْتِماعِيَّةً تَحْتاجُ إلى حُلولٍ عاجِلَةٍ.

In Yemen, early marriage for girls is considered a social issue that requires urgent solutions.

عَصْرِيٌّ = مُعاصِرٌ

modern

عَلى الرَّغْمِ مِنَ التَّقاليدِ القَديمَةِ، تُعْتَبَرُ مَدينَةُ دُبَيِّ مِثالًا عَلى التَّفْكيرِ العَصْرِيِّ في مَجالِ حُقوقِ المَرأَةِ.

Despite age-old traditions, the city of Dubai serves as an example of modern thinking in the area of women's rights.

عُنْفٌ أُسَرِيٌّ

domestic violence

تُكافِحُ العَديدُ مِنَ الدُّوَلِ الأوروبِّيَّةِ لِلْحَدِّ مِنْ حالاتِ العُنْفِ الأُسَرِيِّ ضِدَّ المَرأَةِ، مَعَ تَنامي الأَعْدادِ سَنَوِيًّا.

Many European countries are struggling to curb incidents of domestic violence against women, as the numbers increase annually.

equality issues   *pl.*   قَضايا المُساواة

تَأْتي قَضايا المُساواةِ بَيْنَ الجِنْسَيْنِ في مَرْكَزِ الاهْتِمامِ لِلْعَديدِ مِنَ المُنَظَّماتِ النِّسْوِيَّةِ العالَمِيَّةِ.

Gender equality issues are at the center of attention for many global feminist organizations.

liberated   مُتَحَرِّرٌ

رَغْمَ الضُّغوطِ الثَّقافِيَّةِ، يُعْتَبَرُ عَدَدٌ مُتَزايِدٌ مِنَ النِّساءِ في الشَّرْقِ الأَوْسَطِ مُتَحَرِّراتٍ في مَجالِ التَّعْليمِ وَالعَمَلِ.

Despite cultural pressures, an increasing number of women in the Middle East are considered liberated in the fields of education and employment.

extremist   مُتَطَرِّفٌ

يُدينُ المُجْتَمَعُ الدَّوْلِيُّ المَواقِفَ المُتَطَرِّفَةَ الَّتي تُقَيِّدُ حُرِّيَّةَ وَحُقوقَ المَرْأَةِ في بَعْضِ الدُّوَلِ.

The international community condemns extremist stances that restrict the freedom and rights of women in certain countries.

educated   مُتَعَلِّمٌ

تُظْهِرُ الأَبْحاثُ الأَخيرَةُ أَنَّ المَرْأَةَ المُتَعَلِّمَةَ تُسْهِمُ بِفَعالِيَّةٍ أَكْبَرَ في تَطْويرِ المُجْتَمَعِ.

Recent research shows that educated women contribute more effectively to societal development.

conservative   مُحافِظٌ

يُعْتَبَرُ النِّظامُ المُحافِظُ في بَعْضِ البُلْدانِ عائِقًا أَمامَ تَقَدُّمِ حُقوقِ المَرْأَةِ.

The conservative system in some countries is considered an obstacle to the advancement of women's rights.

deprived   مَحْرومٌ

تُواجِهُ النِّساءُ المَحْروماتُ في الأَحْياءِ الفَقيرَةِ صُعوباتٍ عِدَّةً، مِنْها الوُصولُ إلى التَّعْليمِ وَالرِّعايَةِ الصِّحِّيَّةِ.

Deprived women in poor neighborhoods face multiple challenges, including access to education and healthcare.

equality between genders

مُساواةٌ بَيْنَ الجِنْسَيْنِ

حَقَّقَتِ المَمْلَكَةُ العَرَبِيَّةُ السُّعودِيَّةُ تَقَدُّمًا في مَجالِ المُساواةِ بَيْنَ الجِنْسَيْنِ مِنْ خِلالِ السَّماحِ لِلنِّساءِ بِالقِيادَةِ.

Saudi Arabia has made progress in the field of equality between genders by allowing women to drive.

gender equality

مُساواةٌ جِنْسانِيَّةٌ

في المَغْرِبِ، أُطْلِقَتْ مُبادَراتٌ لِتَعْزِيزِ المُساواةِ الجِنْسانِيَّةِ في الوَظائِفِ العامَّةِ وَالتَّعْليمِ.

In Morocco, initiatives have been launched to promote gender equality in public jobs and education.

independent

مُسْتَقِلٌّ

أَصْبَحَتِ العَديدُ مِنَ النِّساءِ مُسْتَقِلّاتٍ مالِيًّا بِفَضْلِ فَتْحِ الفُرَصِ في سوقِ العَمَلِ.

Many women have become financially independent thanks to the opening of opportunities in the job market.

oppressed

مُضْطَهَدٌ

المَرْأَةُ المُضْطَهَدَةُ في بَعْضِ النُّظُمِ السِّياسِيَّةِ تَحْتاجُ إلى حِمايَةٍ دَوْلِيَّةٍ.

Women who are oppressed in certain political systems require international protection.

neglected

مُهْمَلٌ

تُعْتَبَرُ الأُمورُ المُتَعَلِّقَةُ بِالمَرْأَةِ المُهْمَلَةِ غَيْرَ مَحَلِّ اهْتِمامٍ في العَديدِ مِنَ النِّقاشاتِ العامَّةِ.

Issues concerning neglected women are often overlooked in many public discussions.

8.3.1.1 Mini-Articles

Track **54**

أَطْلَقَتْ جَمْعِيَّةُ حُقوقِ المَرْأَةِ حَمْلَةً تَوْعَوِيَّةً واسِعَةَ النِّطاقِ حَوْلَ أَهَمِّيَّةِ تَحْرِيرِ المَرْأَةِ وَتَمْكِينِها في المُجْتَمَعاتِ العَرَبِيَّةِ. تُسَلِّطُ الحَمْلَةُ الضَّوْءَ عَلى الأَضْرارِ النَّفْسِيَّةِ وَالاجْتِماعِيَّةِ النّاجِمَةِ عَنِ التَّمْييزِ ضِدَّ المَرْأَةِ، وَتُشَجِّعُ عَلى تَحَرُّرِ المَرْأَةِ مِنَ القُيودِ الاجْتِماعِيَّةِ المُتَرَسِّخَةِ.

The Women's Rights Association launched a widespread awareness campaign on the importance of women's liberation and empowerment in Arab societies. The campaign highlights the psychological and social harm caused by discrimination against women and encourages the liberation of women from entrenched social constraints.

في خُطْوَةٍ نَحْوَ الحَداثَةِ وَالتَّقَدُّمِ، قامَتْ وِزارَةُ التَّعْليمِ بِإِطْلاقِ بَرامِجَ تَعْليمِيَّةٍ مُكَثَّفَةٍ تَهْدُفُ إِلى تَحْسينِ مُسْتَوى تَعْليمِ المَرْأَةِ في المَناطِقِ الرِّيفِيَّةِ. تَسْعى هَذِهِ البَرامِجُ إِلى مُحارَبَةِ الزَّواجِ المُبَكِّرِ وَتَعْزيزِ مَفْهومِ المُساواةِ الجِنْسانِيَّةِ.

In a step toward modernity and progress, the Ministry of Education launched intensive educational programs aimed at improving the level of education for women in rural areas. These programs strive to combat early marriage and promote the concept of gender equality.

اِلتَقَتْ مَجْموعَةٌ مِنَ النِّساءِ المُتَعَلِّماتِ وَالمُسْتَقِلّاتِ في مُؤْتَمَرٍ يُناقِشُ قَضايا المُساواةِ وَيُحارِبُ التَّحَرُّشَ الجِنْسِيَّ في الأَماكِنِ العامَّةِ. يُعَدُّ المُؤْتَمَرُ خُطْوَةً مُهِمَّةً في زِيادَةِ الوَعْيِ بِحُقوقِ المَرْأَةِ في الإِسْلامِ وَتَحْقيقِ التَّقَدُّمِ الاِجْتِماعِيِّ.

A group of educated and independent women gathered at a conference to discuss issues of equality and combat sexual harassment in public places. The conference is an important step in raising awareness of women's rights in Islam and achieving social progress.

في رَدِّ فِعْلٍ ضِدَّ الاِعْتِداءِ عَلى المَرْأَةِ وَالعُنْفِ الأُسَرِيِّ، شَكَّلَتْ مَجْموعَةٌ مِنَ النِّساءِ المُتَحَرِّراتِ مُنَظَّمَةً غَيْرَ حُكومِيَّةٍ تَهْدُفُ إِلى حِمايَةِ وَتَعْزيزِ حُرِّيَّةِ المَرْأَةِ الشَّخْصِيَّةِ. تَعْمَلُ المُنَظَّمَةُ عَلى دَعْمِ الضَّحايا وَتَقْديمِ الإِرْشادِ القانونِيِّ وَالنَّفْسِيِّ لَهُنَّ.

In response to assaults on women and domestic violence, a group of liberated women formed a non-governmental organization aimed at protecting and promoting women's personal freedom. The organization works to support victims and provide legal and psychological counseling.

نَظَّمَتْ جَمْعِيَّةٌ مَحَلِّيَّةٌ مَعْرِضًا يَحْتَفي بِالنِّساءِ المُتَحَرِّراتِ وَالرّائِداتِ في مَجالاتِهِنَّ، كَالعِلْمِ وَالفَنِّ وَالأَعْمالِ، لِإِظْهارِ إِمْكاناتِ المَرْأَةِ العَرَبِيَّةِ المُتَحَرِّرَةِ. يَهْدُفُ المَعْرِضُ إِلى دَعْمِ المُساواةِ بَيْنَ الجِنْسَيْنِ وَتَحْفيزِ النِّساءِ الشّابّاتِ عَلى تَحْقيقِ الاِسْتِقْلالِيَّةِ وَالنَّجاحِ.

A local association organized an exhibition celebrating liberated and pioneering women in their fields, such as science, art, and business, to showcase the potential of the liberated Arab woman. The exhibition aims to support gender equality and inspire young women to achieve independence and success.

8.3.1.2 Informative Article: Early Marriage in Yemen

Track **55**

الزَّواجُ المُبَكِّرُ في اليَمَنِ

إِنَّ الزَّواجَ المُبَكِّرَ قَضِيَّةٌ تُؤَرِّقُ العَديدَ مِنَ البُلْدانِ، وَلَكِنَّها تَبْرُزُ بِشَكْلٍ خاصٍّ في اليَمَنِ، حَيْثُ يَتَزَوَّجُ 32% مِنَ الفَتَياتِ قَبْلَ سِنِّ الـ18، وَ 9% قَبْلَ الـ15. الفَقْرُ المُدْقِعُ والنِّزاعُ المُسْتَمِرُّ يَحُثَّانِ الأُسَرَ عَلى تَزْويجِ الفَتَياتِ صَغيراتِ السِّنِّ. "زَواجُ السِّياحَةِ" يَتَّخِذُ شَكْلَ اسْتِغْلالٍ جِنْسِيٍّ لِلقاصِراتِ عَلى يَدِ رِجالٍ مِنَ الخَليجِ. يُفاقِمُ التَّعْليمُ المَحْدودُ المُشْكِلَةَ، إِذْ أَنَّ مِلْيونَيْ طِفْلَةٍ خارِجَ المَدارِسِ. مَسْأَلَةُ الشَّرَفِ تُجْبِرُ بَعْضَ العائِلاتِ عَلى تَزْويجِ بَناتِها لِتَفادي "السُّلوكِ المُشينِ". تَفَشّي كوفيد - 19 والنِّزاعُ المُسَلَّحُ يَزيدانِ مِنْ نِسَبِ الزَّواجِ المُبَكِّرِ كَآلِيَّةٍ لِلتَّأَقْلُمِ مَعَ الظُّروفِ القاهِرَةِ. رَغْمَ الالْتِزاماتِ الدَّوْلِيَّةِ لِإِنْهاءِ هَذِهِ المُمارَسَةِ بِحُلولِ 2030، إِلّا أَنَّ اليَمَنَ لَمْ يُحْرِزْ تَقَدُّمًا مَلْحوظًا بِسَبَبِ النِّزاعِ وَغَيْرِهِ مِنَ التَّحَدِّياتِ، وَتُواجِهُ المُنَظَّماتُ صُعوباتٍ بِسَبَبِ المُقاوَمَةِ الثَّقافِيَّةِ.

Early Marriage in Yemen

Early marriage is an issue that troubles many countries, but it is particularly prominent in Yemen, where 32% of girls marry before the age of 18, and 9% before 15. Extreme poverty and ongoing conflict prompt families to marry off young girls. "Tourist marriages" take the form of sexual exploitation of minors by men from the Gulf. Limited education exacerbates the problem, with two million girls out of school. Honor issues force some families to marry off their daughters to avoid "shameful behavior." The spread of COVID-19 and the armed conflict increase the rates of early marriage as a coping mechanism with the overwhelming circumstances. Despite international commitments to end this practice by 2030, Yemen has not made significant progress due to the conflict and other challenges, and organizations face difficulties due to cultural resistance.

8.3.1.3 Article: Gender Equality in Arab Society

Track **56**

الجُهودُ المُتَزايِدَةُ نَحْوَ تَحْقيقِ المُساواةِ الجِنْسانِيَّةِ في المُجْتَمَعاتِ العَرَبِيَّةِ

في ظِلِّ مَوْجاتِ التَّغَيُّرِ الاجْتِماعِيِّ الَّتي تَجْتاحُ المِنْطَقَةَ العَرَبِيَّةَ، تَبْرُزُ قَضايا حُقوقِ المَرْأَةِ كَنُقْطَةٍ مِحْوَرِيَّةٍ في الخِطابِ العامِّ. تَعْمَلُ مُنَظَّماتُ المُجْتَمَعِ المَدَنِيِّ، بِالتَّعاوُنِ مَعَ المُؤَسَّساتِ الحُكومِيَّةِ، عَلى تَنْظيمِ حَمَلاتِ تَوْعِيَةٍ بِحُقوقِ المَرْأَةِ، مَعَ التَّرْكيزِ عَلى أَهَمِّيَّةِ تَمْكينِ المَرْأَةِ وَتَحْريرِها مِنَ القُيودِ الاجْتِماعِيَّةِ التَّقْليدِيَّةِ.

مُؤَخَّرًا، شَهِدَتْ دَوْلَةٌ عَرَبِيَّةٌ رائِدَةٌ انْعِقادَ مُنْتَدًى حِوارِيٍّ وَطَنِيٍّ حَوْلَ تَحْريرِ المَرْأَةِ وَتَعْليمِها. وَقَدْ جاءَ المُنْتَدى كَفُرْصَةٍ لِتَبادُلِ الآراءِ وَنَشْرِ الوَعْيِ حَوْلَ أَهَمِّيَّةِ تَحْقيقِ المُساواةِ الجِنْسانِيَّةِ الحَقيقِيَّةِ في جَميعِ جَوانِبِ الحَياةِ العامَّةِ والخاصَّةِ.

خِلالَ المُنْتَدى، تَمَّ تَسْلِيطُ الضَّوْءِ عَلَى قَضَايَا مِثْلِ العُنْفِ الأُسَرِيِّ وَالتَّحَرُّشِ الجِنْسِيِّ، وَقَدْ أَشَادَ الحُضُورُ بِالتَّدَابِيرِ الحُكُومِيَّةِ الأَخِيرَةِ كَفَرْضِ حَظْرِ السَّفَرِ عَلَى الجُنَاةِ وَتَشْدِيدِ العُقُوبَاتِ عَلَى الاعْتِدَاءِ عَلَى المَرْأَةِ. وَقَدْ أَكَّدَ المُشَارِكُونَ عَلَى ضَرُورَةِ دَعْمِ النِّسَاءِ المَحْرُومَاتِ وَالمُضْطَهَدَاتِ، وَتَقْدِيمِ المَوَارِدِ اللَّازِمَةِ لَهُنَّ لِيُصْبِحْنَ مُتَعَلِّمَاتٍ وَمُسْتَقِلَّاتٍ.

تُشِيرُ الإِحْصَائِيَّاتُ الأَخِيرَةُ إِلَى ارْتِفَاعِ مُسْتَوَى الوَعْيِ بِأَهَمِّيَّةِ تَعْلِيمِ المَرْأَةِ وَحُقُوقِهَا فِي الإِسْلَامِ، مِمَّا يَعْكِسُ تَحَوُّلًا اجْتِمَاعِيًّا نَحْوَ الحَدَاثَةِ وَالتَّقَدُّمِ. وَقَدْ تَمَّ الإِعْلَانُ عَنْ عِدَّةِ مُبَادَرَاتٍ لِمُحَارَبَةِ التَّمْيِيزِ الجِنْسِيِّ وَتَشْجِيعِ النِّسَاءِ عَلَى الانْخِرَاطِ فِي الأَعْمَالِ السِّيَاسِيَّةِ وَالاقْتِصَادِيَّةِ.

مَعَ هَذِهِ الجُهُودِ المُتَجَدِّدَةِ، يَبْدُو أَنَّ المُجْتَمَعَاتِ العَرَبِيَّةَ تَسِيرُ بِخُطًى ثَابِتَةٍ نَحْوَ تَحْقِيقِ مُجْتَمَعٍ مُتَحَرِّرٍ وَمُتَسَامِحٍ، يَحْتَرِمُ حُقُوقَ المَرْأَةِ وَيُعَزِّزُ مَفْهُومَ الحُرِّيَّةِ الشَّخْصِيَّةِ. وَيَظَلُّ السُّؤَالُ مَطْرُوحًا: هَلْ سَتُوَاصِلُ هَذِهِ الجُهُودُ زَخْمَهَا نَحْوَ تَحْقِيقِ التَّحَرُّرِ الكَامِلِ لِلْمَرْأَةِ فِي العَالَمِ العَرَبِيِّ؟ الأَيَّامُ القَادِمَةُ وَحْدَهَا كَفِيلَةٌ بِالإِجَابَةِ.

The Increasing Efforts Toward Achieving Gender Equality in Arab Societies

Amidst the waves of social change sweeping the Arab region, women's rights issues emerge as a pivotal point in the public discourse. Civil society organizations, in collaboration with governmental institutions, are organizing awareness campaigns on women's rights, focusing on the importance of empowering women and liberating them from traditional social constraints.

Recently, a leading Arab country held a national dialogue forum on women's liberation and education. The forum served as an opportunity to exchange views and raise awareness about the importance of achieving true gender equality in all aspects of public and private life.

During the forum, issues such as domestic violence and sexual harassment were highlighted, and attendees praised recent government measures such as travel bans on offenders and stricter penalties for assaults on women. Participants emphasized the need to support deprived and oppressed women, providing them with the necessary resources to become educated and independent.

Recent statistics indicate an increased level of awareness of the importance of women's education and rights in Islam, reflecting a societal shift toward modernity and progress. Several initiatives have been announced to combat gender discrimination and encourage women's participation in political and economic activities.

With these renewed efforts, it appears that Arab societies are making steady strides toward achieving a liberated and tolerant society that respects women's rights and promotes the concept of personal freedom. The question remains: Will these efforts continue their momentum toward achieving full liberation for women in the Arab world? Only the coming days will tell.

8.3.2 Religious Symbols and Dress Codes

covering, isdal

إِسْدالٌ

النِّساءُ في هَذا البَلَدِ يَتْبَعْنَ تَقْليدَ ارْتِداءِ الْإِسْدالِ في المُناسَباتِ الدّينِيَّةِ.

Women in this country adhere to the tradition of wearing "الإسدال" during religious ceremonies.

respect for modesty and religion

اِحْتِرامُ الاِحْتِشامِ وَالدّينِ

أَظْهَرَتِ الدِّراساتُ ارْتِفاعَ مُسْتَوى احْتِرامِ الاِحْتِشامِ وَالدّينِ في المُجْتَمَعاتِ مُتَعَدِّدَةِ الثَّقافاتِ.

Studies have shown an increased level of respect for modesty and religion in multicultural societies.

to be modest, to dress modestly

اِحْتَشَمَ • اِحْتِشامٌ

العَديدُ مِنَ النِّساءِ يَخْتَرْنَ الاِحْتِشامَ بِارْتِداءِ الحِجابِ كَجُزْءٍ مِنْ عَقيدَتِهِنَّ.

Many women choose to be modest by wearing the hijab as part of their faith.

to wear

اِرْتَدى • اِرْتِداءٌ

يَرْتَدي الرِّجالُ الثَّوْبَ في الجُمْعَةِ كَتَقْليدٍ قَديمٍ.

Men wear the thawb on Fridays as an ancient tradition.

to adorn oneself, to dress up

تَزَيَّنَ • تَزَيُّنٌ

تَتَزَيَّنُ النِّساءُ بِالْأَكْسِسْواراتِ الدّينِيَّةِ في المُناسَباتِ الخاصَّةِ.

Women adorn themselves with religious accessories on special occasions.

traditions of religious attire

تَقاليدُ الزِّيِّ الدّينِيِّ

تَقاليدُ الزِّيِّ الدّينِيِّ تَعْكِسُ التّاريخَ وَالثَّقافَةَ العَميقَةَ لِلْمُجْتَمَعِ.

Traditions of religious attire reflect the deep history and culture of the community.

thawb (traditional long white garment worn by some Muslim men)

ثَوْبٌ • ثِيابٌ

اِرْتَدى الشَّيْخُ الثَّوْبَ الأَبْيَضَ في الصَّلاةِ.

The Sheikh wore a white thawb during the prayer.

jilbab (long loose-fitting outer garment
　　worn by some Muslim women)
　　　　　　　　　　　　　　　　جَلابيبُ •　　　　جِلْبابٌ

يُعْتَبَرُ الجِلْبابُ رَمْزًا لِلْحِشْمَةِ في بَعْضِ الثَّقافاتِ الإِسْلامِيَّةِ.

The jilbab is considered a symbol of modesty in some Islamic cultures.

veil, hijab
　　　　　　　　　　　حُجُبٌ / أَحْجِبَةٌ •　　　　حِجابٌ

لِلْحِجابِ أَبْعادٌ مُتَعَدِّدَةٌ، مِنْها الدِّينِيُّ وَالثَّقافِيُّ وَالاِجْتِماعِيُّ.

The hijab has multiple dimensions, including religious, cultural, and social.

to veil, to cover
　　　　　　　　　　　　　　　　تَحْجيبٌ •　　　　حَجَّبَ

في المُجْتَمَعاتِ المُسْلِمَةِ، يُعْتَبَرُ تَحْجيبُ النِّساءِ خِلالَ الصَّلاةِ واجِبًا دينِيًّا.

In Muslim communities, veiling women during prayer is considered a religious duty.

religious attire
　　　　　　　　　　　　　　　　أَزْياءٌ •　　　　زِيٌّ دينِيٌّ

الزِّيُّ الدِّينِيُّ يُعَبِّرُ عَنِ الهُوِيَّةِ وَالاِنْتِماءِ لِمُجْتَمَعٍ مُعَيَّنٍ.

Religious attire expresses identity and belonging to a particular community.

religious dress
　　　　　　　　　　　　　　　　أَزْياءٌ •　　　　زِيٌّ شَرْعِيٌّ

في العَديدِ مِنَ المُدُنِ الإِسْلامِيَّةِ، يُفَضَّلُ ارْتِداءُ الزِّيِّ الشَّرْعِيِّ في المَساجِدِ.

In many Islamic cities, wearing religious dress is preferred in mosques.

shemagh (traditional headdress worn
　　in the Arab world)
　　　　　　　　　　　　　　　　أَشْمِغَةٌ •　　　　شِماغٌ

يَرْتَدي الرِّجالُ الشِّماغَ كَجُزْءٍ مِنَ التُّراثِ الثَّقافِيِّ في بَعْضِ الدُّوَلِ العَرَبِيَّةِ.

Men wear the keffiyeh as part of the cultural heritage in some Arab countries.

taqiyah (cap worn by some Muslim
　　men in Islamic cultures)
　　　　　　　　　　　طاقِيّاتٌ / طَواقٍ •　　　　طاقِيَّةٌ

تُعْتَبَرُ الطّاقِيَّةُ رَمْزًا لِلدِّينِ وَالتَّقْوى في بَعْضِ الثَّقافاتِ الإِسْلامِيَّةِ.

The taqiyah is considered a symbol of religion and piety in some Islamic cultures.

عَباءَةٌ

abaya (loose black robe worn by some Muslim women)

تَرْتَدي النِّساءُ العَباءَةَ في الأَماكِنِ العامَّةِ كَعَلامَةٍ عَلى الحِشْمَةِ وَالِاحْتِرامِ.

Women wear the abaya in public places as a sign of modesty and respect.

عَفيفٌ

chaste, modest

يُعْتَبَرُ العَفافُ مِنَ القِيَمِ المُهِمَّةِ في الإِسْلامِ، وَيَتَجَلّى في السُّلوكِ وَالمَلْبَسِ.

Chastity is considered an important value in Islam and is reflected in behavior and attire.

عِمامَةٌ • عَمائِمُ / عِماماتٌ / عِمامٌ

imamah (turban worn by some Muslim men)

يَرْتَدي بَعْضُ الرِّجالِ العِمامَةَ كَعَلامَةٍ عَلى العِلْمِ وَالتَّقْوى في الإِسْلامِ.

Some men wear the imamah as a sign of knowledge and piety in Islam.

كَشَفَ • كَشْفٌ

to uncover, to unveil

في بَعْضِ الحالاتِ، يُعْتَبَرُ الكَشْفُ عَنِ الشَّعْرِ عَمَلًا مُحَرَّمًا شَرْعًا.

In some cases, uncovering the hair is considered religiously prohibited.

كوفِيَّةٌ

keffiyeh (traditional Palestinian headgear)

الكوفِيَّةُ تُعْتَبَرُ جُزْءًا مِنَ التُّراثِ الفِلَسْطينِيِّ، وَتُرْتَدى كَرَمْزٍ لِلهُوِيَّةِ.

The keffiyeh is considered a part of Palestinian heritage and is worn as a symbol of identity.

لِباسٌ تَقْليدِيٌّ • أَلْبِسَةٌ / لُبُسٌ

traditional dress

يَعْكِسُ اللِّباسُ التَّقْليدِيُّ الثَّقافَةَ وَالعاداتِ السّائِدَةَ في مُجْتَمَعٍ مُعَيَّنٍ.

Traditional dress reflects the culture and prevailing customs of a particular society.

لِباسٌ دينِيٌّ

religious dress

يُرْتَدى اللِّباسُ الدّينِيُّ في المُناسَباتِ الدّينِيَّةِ لِلتَّعْبيرِ عَنِ التَّدَيُّنِ.

Religious dress is worn on religious occasions to express piety.

to put on
لَبِسَ = ارْتَدى • لُبْسٌ / ارْتِداءٌ

يَلْبِسُ النَّاسُ المَلابِسَ الدِّينِيَّةَ كَجُزْءٍ مِنْ عِباداتِهِمْ وَإِيمانِهِمْ.

People put on religious clothes as part of their worship and faith.

veiled, covered
مُتَحَجِّبٌ = مُحَجَّبٌ

النِّساءُ المُتَحَجِّباتُ يَعْتَبِرْنَ الحِجابَ جُزْءًا مِنْ هُوِيَّتِهِنَّ الدِّينِيَّةِ.

Veiled women consider the hijab a part of their religious identity.

pious, devout
مُتَدَيِّنٌ

الشَّخْصُ المُتَدَيِّنُ يُظْهِرُ التَّقْوى مِنْ خِلالِ أَفْعالِهِ وَكَلامِهِ.

The devout person exhibits piety through his actions and speech.

modest, having modesty
مُحْتَشِمٌ

الأَشْخاصُ المُحْتَشِمونَ يُفَضِّلونَ ارْتِداءَ مَلابِسَ تُظْهِرُ احْتِرامَهُمْ لِأَنْفُسِهِمْ وَلِلْآخَرينَ.

Modest individuals prefer to wear clothes that show respect for themselves and others.

niqab (full-face veil worn by some Muslim women)
نِقابٌ • نُقُبٌ

بَعْضُ النِّساءِ يَرْتَدينَ النِّقابَ كَخِيارٍ شَخْصِيٍّ لِلْحِفاظِ عَلى الحِشْمَةِ وَالخُصوصِيَّةِ.

Some women wear niqab as a personal choice to maintain modesty and privacy.

8.3.2.1 Mini-Articles

يُعْتَبَرُ الاحْتِشامُ قِيمَةً ثَقافِيَّةً تُعَزِّزُ التَّقاليدَ وَتَعْكِسُ روحَ المُجْتَمَعِ السُّعودِيِّ. فَالعَباءَةُ وَالحِجابُ يُشَكِّلانِ جُزْءًا لا يَتَجَزَّأُ مِنَ التُّراثِ الثَّقافِيِّ. يَتَجَلّى الحِجابُ كَرَمْزٍ لِلتَّواضُعِ وَاحْتِرامِ الذّاتِ، مَعَ تَأْكيدِ دَوْرِهِ كَتَعْبيرٍ عَنِ الهُوِيَّةِ الثَّقافِيَّةِ وَالدِّينِيَّةِ.

Modesty is considered a cultural value that enhances traditions and reflects the spirit of Saudi society. The abaya and hijab form an integral part of cultural heritage. The hijab manifests as a symbol of humility and self-respect, reaffirming its role as an expression of cultural and religious identity.

في مِصْرَ، يُعْتَبَرُ الإِسْدالُ زِيًّا إِسْلامِيًّا تَرْتَدِيهِ السَّيِّداتُ أَثْناءَ الصَّلاةِ فَوْقَ المَلابِسِ لِسَتْرِ الجَسَدِ كَما تَنُصُّ تَعالِيمُ الدِّينِ. هَذا وَيَتَوَفَّرُ الإِسْدالُ بِالْعَدِيدِ مِنَ الألْوانِ وَالأَشْكالِ الَّتِي تَتَّفِقُ مَعَ مُخْتَلِفِ الأَذْواقِ.

In Egypt, the Isdal is considered an Islamic attire that women wear during prayers over their clothing, covering their bodies in adherence to the teachings of the religion. The Isdal is available in various colors and styles to cater to different tastes and preferences.

في مُبادَرَةٍ لِتَعْزِيزِ الهُوِيَّةِ الثَّقافِيَّةِ، دَعَتْ حُكومَةُ الرِّباطِ المُواطِنِينَ لِارْتِداءِ الزِّيِّ التَّقْلِيدِيِّ في المُناسَباتِ الوَطَنِيَّةِ. تَشْمَلُ هَذِهِ الدَّعْوَةُ الشِّماغَ وَالعِمامَةَ لِلرِّجالِ، وَالجِلْبابَ وَالنِّقابَ لِلنِّساءِ، في مُحاوَلَةٍ لِلْحِفاظِ عَلَى الثَّقافَةِ المَغْرِبِيَّةِ الغَنِيَّةِ وَتَقْدِيرِها.

In an initiative to promote cultural identity, the government of Rabat has invited citizens to wear traditional attire during national occasions. This invitation includes the shemagh and turban for men, and the jalabiya and niqab for women, in an effort to preserve and appreciate the rich Moroccan culture.

أُفْتُتِحَ في دُبَيَّ أَوَّلُ بوتِيكٍ فاخِرٍ مُخَصَّصٍ لِبَيْعِ العَباءاتِ وَالحِجاباتِ المُصَمَّمَةِ خِصِّيصًا لِلنِّساءِ المُتَحَجِّباتِ. يُقَدِّمُ البوتِيكُ تَشْكِيلَةً واسِعَةً مِنَ الأَزْياءِ الَّتِي تَتَناسَبُ مَعَ النِّساءِ المُتَدَيِّناتِ اللّواتي يَرْغَبْنَ في تَزْيِينِ مَلابِسِهِنَّ مَعَ الحِفاظِ عَلَى الاِحْتِشامِ.

Dubai has opened its first luxury boutique dedicated to selling abayas and hijabs specifically designed for veiled women. The boutique offers a wide range of outfits that cater to religious women who wish to adorn their clothing while maintaining modesty.

شَهِدَتِ العاصِمَةُ السّورِيَّةُ دِمَشْقُ مُظاهَراتٍ سِلْمِيَّةً تُطالِبُ بِحُرِّيَّةِ اللِّباسِ الدِّينِيِّ في الجامِعاتِ. يَأْتِي ذَلِكَ بَعْدَ سِلْسِلَةٍ مِنَ الإِجْراءاتِ الحُكومِيَّةِ الَّتِي تُحاوِلُ حَجْبَ الرُّموزِ الدِّينِيَّةِ مِنَ الحَياةِ العامَّةِ، حَيْثُ يَسْعَى المُتَظاهِرونَ لِلدِّفاعِ عَنْ حَقِّهِمْ في ارْتِداءِ الثَّوْبِ وَالطّاقِيَّةِ وَالكوفِيَّةِ كَتَعْبِيرٍ عَنْ هُوِيَّتِهِمِ الدِّينِيَّةِ وَالثَّقافِيَّةِ.

The Syrian capital, Damascus, witnessed peaceful demonstrations demanding the freedom of religious clothing in universities. This comes after a series of governmental measures trying to conceal religious symbols from public life, with demonstrators defending their right to wear the thobe, taqiyah, and keffiyeh as an expression of their religious and cultural identity.

الزِّيُّ الشَّرْعِيُّ وَالهُوِيَّةُ الثَّقافِيَّةُ في المَمْلَكَةِ العَرَبِيَّةِ السُّعودِيَّةِ

في المَمْلَكَةِ العَرَبِيَّةِ السُّعودِيَّةِ، يَتِمُّ إيلاءُ احْتِرامٍ كَبيرٍ لِلتَّقاليدِ وَالأَعْرافِ الدِّينِيَّةِ، وَهذا يَنْعَكِسُ بِوُضوحٍ في القَوانينِ وَالمُتَطَلَّباتِ الاجْتِماعِيَّةِ المُتَعَلِّقَةِ بِاللِّباسِ. لِلرِّجالِ، يُعَدُّ الشِّماغُ وَالثَّوْبُ جُزْءًا لا يَتَجَزَّأُ مِنَ الزِّيِّ اليَوْمِيِّ، خاصَّةً في الأَماكِنِ العامَّةِ وَالمُناسَباتِ الرَّسْمِيَّةِ، مِمّا يَعْكِسُ العِفَّةَ وَالذَّوْقَ المُتَوَقَّعَيْنِ في المُجْتَمَعِ.

بِالنِّسْبَةِ لِلنِّساءِ، يُنْظَرُ إلى العَباءَةِ وَالحِجابِ عَلى أَنَّهُما مُكَوِّنانِ أَساسِيّانِ لِلِّباسِ الشَّرْعِيِّ وَالدِّينِيِّ، وَهُما يُعَبِّرانِ عَنِ التِزامِهِنَّ بِالاحْتِشامِ وَفْقًا لِلتَّعاليمِ الإسْلامِيَّةِ. النِّقابُ، وَهُوَ غِطاءٌ يَكْشِفُ فَقَطِ العَيْنَيْنِ، كانَ مَوْضوعًا لِلنِّقاشِ في السَّنَواتِ الأَخيرَةِ، مَعَ تَعاظُمِ الاخْتِيارِ الشَّخْصِيِّ وَالتَّنَوُّعِ في التَّفْسيراتِ الدِّينِيَّةِ.

تُشَجِّعُ السُّلُطاتُ عَلى ارْتِداءِ اللِّباسِ التَّقْليدِيِّ وَالدِّينِيِّ لِكِلا الجِنْسَيْنِ، وَهُناكَ قَوانينُ تُطَبَّقُ لِضَمانِ الالْتِزامِ بِهَذِهِ المَعايِيرِ. عَلى الرَّغْمِ مِنَ التَّحْديثاتِ وَالإصْلاحاتِ الاجْتِماعِيَّةِ الأَخيرَةِ، الَّتي أَدَّتْ إلى مَزيدٍ مِنَ الحُرِّيَّةِ الشَّخْصِيَّةِ، إلّا أَنَّ الاحْتِشامَ لا يَزالُ يُعْتَبَرُ قيمَةً مَرْكَزِيَّةً في المَمْلَكَةِ.

مَعَ تَحْريرِ المَرْأَةِ وَزِيادَةِ الوَعْيِ بِحُقوقِها، بَدَأَ المُجْتَمَعُ يَتَقَبَّلُ بِشَكْلٍ مُتَزايِدٍ تَنَوُّعَ الأَزْياءِ الدِّينِيَّةِ وَالدُّنْيَوِيَّةِ. تَحْرِصُ الحُكومَةُ عَلى المُوازَنَةِ بَيْنَ تَمْكينِ المَرْأَةِ وَالحِفاظِ عَلى القِيَمِ التَّقْليدِيَّةِ، مِمّا يَجْعَلُ الزِّيَّ السُّعودِيَّ مِثالًا عَلى الهُوِيَّةِ الثَّقافِيَّةِ وَالدِّينِيَّةِ المُعاصِرَةِ.

Religious Attire and Cultural Identity in Saudi Arabia

In Saudi Arabia, great respect is paid to religious traditions and customs, which is clearly reflected in the laws and social requirements related to dress. For men, the shemagh and thobe are integral parts of daily attire, especially in public places and official events, reflecting the modesty and decorum expected in society.

For women, the abaya and hijab are seen as fundamental components of religious and legal dress, expressing their commitment to modesty in accordance with Islamic teachings. The niqab, a veil revealing only the eyes, has been the subject of debate in recent years, with increasing personal choice and diversity in religious interpretations.

Authorities encourage the wearing of traditional and religious attire for both genders, and there are laws implemented to ensure adherence to these standards. Despite recent social updates and reforms leading to more personal freedom, modesty is still considered a central value in the kingdom.

With the empowerment of women and increased awareness of their rights, society is increasingly accepting a diversity of religious and secular attire. The government strives to balance between empowering women and maintaining traditional values, making Saudi dress an example of contemporary cultural and religious identity.

8.3.3 Religious Education and Scholarship

to believe

آمَنَ • إِيمانٌ

الإِيمانُ بِاللهِ وَرَسُولِهِ جُزْءٌ أَساسِيٌّ مِنَ التَّعْلِيمِ الدِّينِيِّ.

Believing in God and His Messenger is a fundamental part of religious education.

to issue a religious verdict

أَفْتى • إِفْتاءٌ

العُلَماءُ يُفْتونَ لِتَوْجِيهِ المُسْلِمِينَ في مَسائِلِ الحَياةِ اليَوْمِيَّةِ.

Scholars issue religious verdicts to guide Muslims in matters of daily life.

the biography of the Prophet Muhammad

السِّيرَةُ النَّبَوِيَّةُ • سِيَرٌ

السِّيرَةُ النَّبَوِيَّةُ تُعْتَبَرُ مَصْدَرًا هامًّا لِفَهْمِ تَعالِيمِ الإِسْلامِ وَحَياةِ النَّبِيِّ.

The biography of Prophet Muhammad is an important source for understanding the teachings of Islam and the life of the Prophet.

to be affiliated with

اِنْتَسَبَ • اِنْتِسابٌ

الاِنْتِسابُ إلى مَدْرَسَةٍ دِينِيَّةٍ يُعْتَبَرُ خُطْوَةً نَحْوَ الاِرْتِقاءِ الرّوحِيِّ.

Being affiliated with a religious school is considered a step toward spiritual advancement.

to learn

تَعَلَّمَ • تَعَلُّمٌ

التَّعَلُّمُ هُوَ جُزْءٌ لا يَتَجَزَّأُ مِنَ التَّطْوِيرِ الرّوحِيِّ وَالفِكْرِيِّ في الإِسْلامِ.

Learning is an integral part of spiritual and intellectual development in Islam.

religious education

تَعْلِيمٌ دِينِيٌّ

إِنَّ التَّعْلِيمَ الدِّينِيَّ القَوِيَّ يُسْهِمُ في بِناءِ شَخْصِيَّةٍ مُتَوازِنَةٍ.

Strong religious education contributes to building a balanced personality.

Quranic exegesis, interpretation, tafseer — تَفْسيرُ (القُرآن)

يُعْتَبَرُ تَفْسيرُ القُرآنِ مِنْ أَهَمِّ المَوْضوعاتِ الَّتي تُدَرَّسُ في المُؤَسَّساتِ الدّينيَّةِ.

Quranic exegesis is considered one of the most important subjects taught in religious institutions.

to recite — تَلا • تِلاوَةٌ

تُعْتَبَرُ تِلاوَةُ القُرآنِ عِبادَةً وَوَسيلَةً لِلتَّقَرُّبِ مِنَ اللهِ.

Reciting the Quran is considered an act of worship and a means to draw closer to God.

Hadith (sayings of Prophet Muhammad) — حَديثٌ • أَحاديثُ

الأَحاديثُ النَّبَوِيَّةُ تُسْتَخْدَمُ كَمَرْجِعٍ لِفَهْمِ الإِسْلامِ وَتَطْبيقِ تَعاليمِهِ.

Prophetic sayings are used as a reference for understanding Islam and applying its teachings.

sayings and actions of the Prophet Muhammad — حَديثٌ شَريفٌ

يُعْتَبَرُ الحَديثُ الشَّريفُ مِنْ أَهَمِّ المَصادِرِ لِفَهْمِ تَعاليمِ الإِسْلامِ وَتَطْبيقِها.

The sayings and actions of the Prophet Muhammad are considered among the most important sources for understanding and applying the teachings of Islam.

to memorize — حَفِظَ • حِفْظٌ

يُعْتَبَرُ حِفْظُ القُرآنِ والأَحاديثِ الشَّريفَةِ جُزْءًا مِنَ التَّرْبِيَةِ الإِسْلامِيَّةِ.

Memorizing the Quran and the sayings of the Prophet is considered a part of Islamic upbringing.

Islamic studies — *pl.* — دِراساتٌ إِسْلامِيَّةٌ

تُقَدِّمُ الدِّراساتُ الإِسْلامِيَّةُ فَهْمًا شامِلًا لِلدّينِ وَتاريخِهِ.

Islamic studies offer a comprehensive understanding of the religion and its history.

to teach — دَرَّسَ • تَدْريسٌ

يُعْتَبَرُ التَّدْريسُ وَسيلَةً لِنَقْلِ المَعْرِفَةِ الدّينِيَّةِ وَالثَّقافِيَّةِ إِلى الأَجْيالِ الجَديدَةِ.

Teaching is considered a means of transferring religious and cultural knowledge to new generations.

دَرَسَ الدّينَ

to study religion

• دِراسَةُ الدّينِ

دِراسَةُ الدّينِ تُساعِدُ في تَكْوينِ وُجْهَةِ نَظَرٍ مُتَّزِنَةٍ تِجاهَ الحَياةِ.

Studying religion helps in forming a balanced perspective toward life.

شَرْعِيٌّ

pertaining/according to Islamic law

أَصْدَرَ القاضي حُكْمًا شَرْعِيًّا بِناءً عَلى القُرْآنِ وَالسُّنَّةِ النَّبَوِيَّةِ في قَضِيَّةِ الإِرْثِ المُعَقَّدَةِ.

The judge issued a Sharia-compliant ruling based on the Quran and the Sunnah in the complex inheritance case.

شَريعَةٌ إِسْلامِيَّةٌ

Islamic law

• شَرائِعُ

تُعْتَبَرُ الشَّريعَةُ الإِسْلامِيَّةُ نِظامًا شامِلًا لِلْحَياةِ في المُجْتَمَعاتِ المُسْلِمَةِ.

Islamic law is considered a comprehensive system for life in Muslim societies.

عالِمُ دينٍ = شَيْخٌ

religious scholar

• عُلَماءُ / شُيوخٌ

عُلَماءُ الدّينِ يَلْعَبونَ دَوْرًا مُهِمًّا في تَوْجيهِ المُجْتَمَعِ وَفْقًا لِمَبادِئِ الإِسْلامِ.

Religious scholars play an important role in guiding society according to Islamic principles.

عَقيدَةٌ

creed

• عَقائِدُ

تُعْتَبَرُ العَقيدَةُ الإِسْلامِيَّةُ الأَساسَ لِفَهْمِ الدّينِ وَمُمارَسَتِه.

The Islamic creed is considered the foundation for understanding and practicing the religion.

عَلَّمَ الدّينَ

to teach religion

• تَعْليمٌ

يُعْتَبَرُ تَعْليمُ الدّينِ مِنَ الأَوْلَوِيّاتِ في التَّرْبِيَةِ الإِسْلامِيَّةِ.

Teaching religion is considered a priority in Islamic upbringing.

عِلْمٌ دينِيٌّ

religious scholarship or knowledge

• عِلومٌ

تُمَثِّلُ العُلومُ الدّينِيَّةُ أساسًا حَيَوِيًّا في فَهْمِ القِيَمِ وَالمَبادِئِ الرّوحِيَّةِ الَّتي تُوَجِّهُ تَصَرُّفاتِ الأَفْرادِ وَالمُجْتَمَعاتِ.

Religious knowledge constitutes a vital foundation for understanding the spiritual values and principles that guide the actions of individuals and communities.

Islamic science — عِلْمٌ شَرْعِيٌّ

يُعْتَبَرُ العِلْمُ الشَّرْعِيُّ جُزْءًا مُهِمًّا مِنَ الفِقْهِ الإِسْلامِيِّ، وَيَتَناوَلُ الأَحْكامَ وَالمَبادِئَ.

Islamic science is considered an important part of Islamic jurisprudence and deals with rulings and principles.

scholarly — عِلْمِيٌّ

البَحْثُ العِلْمِيُّ في الدّينِ يَتَطَلَّبُ نَقْدًا عِلْمِيًّا وَمَنْهَجِيَّةً مَدْروسَةً.

Scholarly research in religion requires scientific critique and a well-thought-out methodology.

religious verdict — فَتَوى • فَتاوى — فَتْوى دينِيَّةٌ

الفَتْوى الدّينِيَّةُ تُعْتَبَرُ إجابَةً شَرْعِيَّةً عَلى سُؤالٍ مُحَدَّدٍ في الإِسْلامِ.

A religious verdict is considered a lawful answer to a specific question in Islam.

to interpret — تَفْسيرٌ • فَسَّرَ

يُعْتَبَرُ التَّفْسيرُ وَسيلَةً لِفَهْمِ النُّصوصِ الدّينِيَّةِ بِشَكْلٍ أَعْمَقَ.

Interpretation is considered a means to understand religious texts more deeply.

Islamic jurisprudence — فِقْهٌ (إِسْلامِيٌّ)

الفِقْهُ الإِسْلامِيُّ يَدْرُسُ الشَّريعَةَ، وَيُعْنى بِالتَّطْبيقِ العَمَلِيِّ لِلْإِسْلامِ.

Islamic jurisprudence studies Sharia and is concerned with the practical application of Islam.

religious book — كُتُبٌ • كِتابٌ دينِيٌّ

تُعْتَبَرُ الكُتُبُ الدّينِيَّةُ مَصْدَرًا لِلتَّوْجيهِ وَالإِرْشادِ الرّوحِيِّ.

Religious books are considered a source of guidance and spiritual direction.

religious institution

مُؤَسَّسَةٌ دينِيَّةٌ

تَلْعَبُ المُؤَسَّساتُ الدّينِيَّةُ دَوْرًا كَبيرًا في تَوْجيهِ وَتَعْليمِ المُجْتَمَعِ.

Religious institutions play a significant role in guiding and educating the community.

conservative

مُحافِظٌ

التَّوَجُّهُ المُحافِظُ يُفَضِّلُ الالْتِزامَ بِالتَّقاليدِ وَالشَّريعَةِ الإِسْلامِيَّةِ.

A conservative approach favors adherence to traditions and Islamic law.

religious school

مَدْرَسَةٌ دينِيَّةٌ

تُعْنى المَدارِسُ الدّينِيَّةُ بِتَعْليمِ مَبادِئِ الدّينِ وَالأَخْلاقِ الإِسْلامِيَّةِ.

Religious schools focus on teaching the principles of the religion and Islamic ethics.

Islamic denomination or school of thought

• مَذاهِبُ   مَذْهَبٌ إِسْلامِيٌّ

كُلُّ مَذْهَبٍ إِسْلامِيٍّ لَهُ فَهْمُهُ وَتَفْسيرُهُ الخاصُّ لِلشَّريعَةِ وَالعَقيدَةِ.

Each Islamic denomination has its own understanding and interpretation of Sharia and creed.

denominational

مَذْهَبِيٌّ

تَعْكِسُ المَسائِلُ المَذْهَبِيَّةُ التَّنَوُّعَ الفِكْرِيَّ داخِلَ الإِسْلامِ.

Denominational issues reflect intellectual diversity within Islam.

religious authority

مَرْجِعِيَّةٌ دينِيَّةٌ

تُعْتَبَرُ المَرْجِعِيّاتُ الدّينِيَّةُ مَصْدَرًا لِلْفَتاوى وَالإِرْشادِ الدّينِيِّ.

Religious authorities are considered a source for religious verdicts and guidance.

Islamic institute

• مَعاهِدُ   مَعْهَدٌ إِسْلامِيٌّ

تُقَدِّمُ المَعاهِدُ الإِسْلامِيَّةُ بَرامِجَ مُتَخَصِّصَةً في الدِّراساتِ الإِسْلامِيَّةِ.

Islamic institutes offer specialized programs in Islamic studies.

يُسْهِمُ نَشْرُ المَعْرِفَةِ الدِّينِيَّةِ في تَوْسِيعِ الفَهْمِ وَالوَعْيِ حَوْلَ مَبادِئِ الإِسْلامِ.

Disseminating religious knowledge contributes to expanding understanding and awareness about the principles of Islam.

8.3.3.1 Mini-Articles

Track **61**

أَعْلَنَ مَعْهَدُ النَّهْضَةِ في القاهِرَةِ عَنْ بَدْءِ دَوْراتٍ تَعْلِيمِيَّةٍ مُكَثَّفَةٍ في تَفْسِيرِ القُرْآنِ وَالسِّيرَةِ النَّبَوِيَّةِ، وَذَلِكَ لِنَشْرِ المَعْرِفَةِ الدِّينِيَّةِ بَيْنَ الشَّبابِ. تَهْدُفُ هَذِهِ الدَّوْراتُ إلى تَعْمِيقِ الفَهْمِ الدِّينِيِّ وَحِفْظِ الحَدِيثِ الشَّرِيفِ.

Al-Nahdah Institute in Cairo has announced the commencement of intensive educational courses in the interpretation of the Quran and Prophetic biography to spread religious knowledge among the youth. These courses aim to deepen religious understanding and preserve the noble Hadith.

في الرِّياضِ، أَصْدَرَ عالِمُ دِينٍ بارِزٌ فَتْوى دِينِيَّةً تَتَعَلَّقُ بِأَحْدَثِ القَضايا المُعاصِرَةِ، مُسْتَنِدَةً إلى الفِقْهِ الإِسْلامِيِّ وَالشَّرِيعَةِ الإِسْلامِيَّةِ، مِمّا أَثارَ نِقاشًا واسِعًا في أَوْساطِ الدِّراساتِ الإِسْلامِيَّةِ.

In Riyadh, a prominent religious scholar issued a religious edict related to the latest contemporary issues, based on Islamic jurisprudence and Sharia law, which sparked a wide debate in Islamic studies circles.

أُفْتُتِحَتْ في دُبَيَّ مُؤَسَّسَةٌ دِينِيَّةٌ جَدِيدَةٌ تُرَكِّزُ عَلى الدِّراساتِ الإِسْلامِيَّةِ المُتَقَدِّمَةِ، وَتَشْمَلُ عِلْمَ الفِقْهِ وَالعَقِيدَةِ. تَهْدُفُ المُؤَسَّسَةُ إلى تَرْسِيخِ القِيَمِ الدِّينِيَّةِ وَتَأْمِينِ مِنَصَّةٍ لِلنِّقاشِ المَذْهَبِيِّ البَنّاءِ.

A new religious institution focusing on advanced Islamic studies, including the science of jurisprudence and creed, was inaugurated in Dubai. The institution aims to establish religious values and provide a platform for constructive sectarian debate.

في الدَّوْحَةِ، أَطْلَقَتْ مَدْرَسَةٌ دِينِيَّةٌ حَمْلَةً لِحِفْظِ القُرْآنِ الكَرِيمِ، مُوَجَّهَةً لِجَمِيعِ الأَعْمارِ. تَتَضَمَّنُ الحَمْلَةُ تِلاوَةَ القُرْآنِ وَتَعْلِيمَ الحَدِيثِ، مَعَ التَّأْكِيدِ عَلى الأَسالِيبِ التَّعْلِيمِيَّةِ الَّتِي تَحْتَرِمُ التَّقالِيدَ الشَّرْعِيَّةَ.

In Doha, a religious school launched a campaign to memorize the Holy Quran, aimed at all ages. The campaign includes Quran recitation and Hadith teaching, with an emphasis on educational methods that respect legitimate traditions.

في مَدِينَةِ الدّارِ البَيْضاءِ، نَظَّمَتْ مُؤَسَّسَةٌ دِينِيَّةٌ سِلْسِلَةَ مُحاضَراتٍ حَوْلَ أَهَمِّيَّةِ العِلْمِ الدِّينِيِّ في المُجْتَمَعِ المُعاصِرِ. تَشْمَلُ المُحاضَراتُ مَواضِيعَ مُتَنَوِّعَةً مِثْلَ فِقْهِ الأُسْرَةِ وَالتَّعامُلِ مَعَ الآخَرِينَ ضِمْنَ إِطارِ الشَّرِيعَةِ الإِسْلامِيَّةِ.

In Casablanca, a religious institution organized a series of lectures on the importance of religious knowledge in contemporary society. The lectures cover diverse topics such as family jurisprudence and dealing with others within the framework of Islamic Sharia.

8.3.3.2 Article: Religious Education

Track **62**

ثَوْرَةٌ في التَّعْليمِ الدِّينيِّ: المَنْهَجُ الإِبْتِكاريُّ لِمَعْهَدِ المَدينَة

في قَلْبِ مَدينَةِ فاس التَّاريخيَّةِ بِالمَغْرِب، يَجْري تَنْفيذُ مُبادَرَةٍ رائِدَةٍ في مَعْهَدِ المَدينَة، المَرْكَزِ المَعْروفِ لِلدِّراساتِ الإِسْلاميَّة. لَقَدْ شَرَعَ المَعْهَدُ في بَرْنامَجٍ تَعْليميٍّ رائِدٍ يَهْدُفُ إلى تَناغُمِ التَّعْليمِ الإِسْلاميِّ التَّقْليديِّ مَعَ الدِّراساتِ المُعاصِرَة.

أَعْلَنَ مُديرُ مَعْهَدِ المَدينَة، الشَّيْخُ عبدُالله الفَيَّاض، وَهُوَ شَخْصيَّةٌ بارِزَةٌ في مَجالِ العِلْمِ الدِّينيِّ، عَنْ إِدْخالِ مَنْهَجٍ شامِلٍ يَدْمُجُ دِراسَةَ القُرْآنِ والحَديثِ بِتِقْنيّاتٍ تَعْليميَّةٍ حَديثَة. قالَ الشَّيْخُ الفَيَّاض: "هَدَفُنا هُوَ المُحافَظَةُ عَلى إرْثِ التَّعَلُّمِ الإِسْلاميِّ الغَنيِّ مَعَ ضَمانِ تَجْهيزِ عُلَمائِنا لِمُواجَهَةِ احْتِياجاتِ مُجْتَمَعِنا الدّينامِيكيِّ".

تَتَمَحْوَرُ هَذِهِ المُبادَرَةُ حَوْلَ الإهْتِمامِ بِتَفْسيرِ القُرْآنِ، حَيْثُ يَتَعَمَّقُ الطُّلّابُ في شَرْحِ النَّصِّ المُقَدَّسِ، وَيَتَعَلَّمونَ تَفْسيرَ مَعانيهِ وَتَطْبيقِ حِكْمَتِهِ في سِياقاتٍ اجْتِماعيَّةٍ مُخْتَلِفَة. كَما أَنْشَأَ المَعْهَدُ فُصولًا خاصَّةً مُكَرَّسَةً لِدِراساتِ الحَديثِ، حَيْثُ يُشَجَّعُ الطُّلّابُ عَلى حِفْظِ أَقْوالِ النَّبيِّ مُحَمَّدٍ (صَلّى اللهُ عَلَيْهِ وَسَلَّمَ) والمَعْروفَةِ بِالحَديثِ الشَّريفِ.

في مُحاوَلَةٍ لِتَوْسيعِ نِطاقِ التَّعْليمِ الدِّينيِّ، أَدْخَلَ المَعْهَدُ دَوْراتٍ في الـ "فِقْه" (القانون الإِسْلاميِّ)، الَّتي تَبْحَثُ في القَضايا المُعاصِرَةِ مِنْ خِلالِ عَدَسَةِ الشَّريعَةِ الإِسْلاميَّةِ. عِلاوَةً عَلى ذَلِكَ، تَهْدُفُ جَلَساتُ "العَقيدَةِ الإِسْلاميَّةِ" إلى تَعْميقِ فَهْمِ الطُّلّابِ لِمَبادِئِ مُعْتَقَدِهِمْ، وَمُعالَجَةِ المَفاهيمِ الخاطِئَةِ وَتَعْزيزِ رُؤْيَةٍ عالَميَّةٍ مُتَوازِنَةٍ.

تَمَّ تَوْسيعُ مَكْتَبَةِ المَعْهَدِ لِتَشْمَلَ مَجْموعَةً واسِعَةً مِنَ النُّصوصِ الدِّينيَّةِ، مِنَ السّيرَةِ النَّبَويَّةِ الشَّريفَةِ إلى مُخْتَلِفِ كُتُبِ الفِقْهِ الإِسْلاميِّ. هَذا المَخْزونُ مِنَ المَعْرِفَةِ يُعْتَبَرُ تَقْديرًا لِلتُّراثِ العِلْميِّ الإِسْلاميِّ وَمَصْدَرًا لِلتَّعَلُّمِ المُسْتَمِرِّ.

رُبَّما يَكونُ الأَمْرُ الأَبْرَزُ هُوَ أَنَّ المَدينَةَ قَدِ افْتَتَحَتْ مِنَصَّةً عَلى الإِنْتِرْنِتَ، مِمّا جَعَلَ مَعارِفَها الدِّينيَّةَ مُتاحَةً لِجُمْهورٍ عالَميٍّ. لَقَدْ سَهَّلَ هَذا التَّقَدُّمُ الرَّقْميُّ نَشْرَ الفَتاوى مِنْ قِبَلِ عُلَماءِ المَعْهَدِ، مِمّا سَمَحَ بِتَأْثيرٍ أَوْسَعَ وَتَفاعُلٍ مَعَ الأُمَّةِ الإِسْلاميَّةِ بِأَسْرِها.

لَمْ يَنْجَحِ المَعْهَدُ في تَنْشِئَةِ جيلٍ جَديدٍ مِنَ العُلَماءِ فَحَسْبُ، بَلِ احْتَضَنَ الحَداثَةَ أَيْضًا مِنْ خِلالِ إِنْشاءِ "مَجْلِسٍ فِقْهيٍّ" يُصْدِرُ تَوْجيهاتٍ بِشَأْنِ المُعْضِلاتِ المُعاصِرَة. لَقَدْ وَضَعَ هَذا المَنْهَجُ المَدينَةَ كَحِصْنٍ لِدِراساتِ الشَّريعَةِ، يَرْبِطُ بَيْنَ القَديمِ والحَديثِ، والعِلْميِّ والعَمَليِّ.

نَجاحُ مَعْهَدِ المَدينَةِ هُوَ شَهادَةٌ عَلَى الجَدْوى الدّائِمَةِ لِلْعِلْمِ الدّينِيِّ في القَرْنِ الحادي وَالعِشرينَ. فَهُوَ يُظْهِرُ مَزيجًا مُتَناغِمًا مِنَ الاحْتِرامِ لِلْماضي المُقَدَّسِ مَعَ تَوَقُّعاتٍ مُتَبَصِّرَةٍ لِلْمُسْتَقْبَلِ، مِمّا يَضْمَنُ اسْتِمْرارَ ضَوْءِ المَعْرِفَةِ في إنارَةِ الطَّريقِ لِلْمُؤْمِنينَ في جَميعِ أَنْحاءِ العالَمِ.

Revolution in Religious Education: The Innovative Curriculum of Al-Madina Institute

In the heart of the historic city of Fez, Morocco, a pioneering initiative is being implemented at Al-Madina Institute, a well-known center for Islamic studies. The institute has embarked on a groundbreaking educational program aimed at harmonizing traditional Islamic education with contemporary studies.

The director of Al-Madina Institute, Sheikh Abdullah Al-Fayyad, a prominent figure in religious scholarship, announced the introduction of a comprehensive curriculum that integrates the study of the Quran and Hadith with modern teaching techniques. Sheikh Al-Fayyad said, "Our goal is to preserve the rich legacy of Islamic learning while ensuring our scholars are equipped to meet the needs of our dynamic society."

The initiative centers around the focus on "Tafsir of the Quran," where students delve into the explanation of the holy text, learning to interpret its meanings and apply its wisdom in various social contexts. The institute has also established dedicated classes for "Hadith studies," encouraging students to memorize the sayings of Prophet Muhammad (peace be upon him), known as "Al-Hadith Al-Sharif."

In an effort to broaden the scope of religious education, the institute introduced courses in "Fiqh" (Islamic law), which examine contemporary issues through the lens of Islamic Sharia. Moreover, the "Islamic Aqeedah" sessions aim to deepen students' understanding of the principles of their faith, address misconceptions, and promote a balanced global vision.

The institute's library has been expanded to include a wide array of religious texts, from the respected Prophetic biography to various books of Islamic jurisprudence. This repository of knowledge serves as a tribute to the Islamic scholarly tradition and a source of continuous learning.

Perhaps most notably, Al-Madina has launched an online platform, making its religious knowledge accessible to a global audience. This digital advancement has facilitated the dissemination of fatwas by the institute's scholars, allowing for broader influence and engagement with the entire Islamic nation.

The institute has not only succeeded in nurturing a new generation of scholars but has also embraced modernity by establishing a "Fiqh Council" that issues guidelines on contemporary conundrums. This approach has positioned the city as a bastion for Sharia studies, bridging the old and the new, the scholarly and the practical.

The success of Al-Madina Institute is a testament to the enduring relevance of religious knowledge in the 21st century. It demonstrates a harmonious blend of respect for the sacred past with visionary expectations for the future, ensuring the light of knowledge continues to illuminate the path for believers worldwide.

8.3.4 Religious Extremism and Sectarianism

إرْهابٌ

terrorism

تَفْجِيرٌ إِرْهابِيٌّ يَسْتَهْدِفُ كَنِيسَةً فِي الإِسْكَنْدَرِيَّةِ وَيُخَلِّفُ العَدِيدَ مِنَ القَتْلى.

A terrorist bombing targets a church in Alexandria and leaves many dead.

إرْهابٌ دِينِيٌّ

religious terrorism

أَلْقَتِ الشُّرْطَةُ القَبْضَ عَلَى شَخْصٍ يُشْتَبَهُ فِي ارْتِكابِهِ إِرْهابًا دِينِيًّا فِي الرِّياضِ.

Police have arrested an individual suspected of committing religious terrorism in Riyadh.

إرْهابٌ طائِفِيٌّ

sectarian terrorism

تَمَّ القَبْضُ عَلَى مَجْموعَةٍ مُتَوَرِّطَةٍ فِي إِرْهابٍ طائِفِيٍّ فِي بَغْدادَ.

A group involved in sectarian terrorism was arrested in Baghdad.

إرْهابِيٌّ

terrorist

اِعْتَقَلَتِ السُّلْطاتُ رَجُلًا يُعْتَقَدُ أَنَّهُ إِرْهابِيٌّ فِي مَطارِ بَيْروتَ.

Authorities arrested a man believed to be a terrorist at Beirut Airport.

اِنْتَمى إلى • اِنْتِماءٌ

to belong to

يَنْتَمِي الجانِي المُتَّهَمُ بِالهُجومِ إلى جَماعَةٍ مُتَطَرِّفَةٍ.

The perpetrator accused of the attack belongs to an extremist group.

اِنْحِرافٌ دِينِيٌّ

religious deviance

أدانَتِ السُّلْطاتُ الاِنْحِرافَ الدِّينِيَّ واتَّخَذَتْ إِجْراءاتٍ ضِدَّ مُعْتَنِقِيهِ.

The authorities condemned religious deviance and took measures against its adherents.

to adopt, embrace	تَبَنَّ •	تَبَنَّى

أَعْلَنَ تَنْظِيمُ الدَّوْلَةِ الإِسْلَامِيَّةِ مَسْؤُولِيَّتَهُ عَنِ الهُجُومِ الَّذِي وَقَعَ فِي عَمَّانَ.

ISIS claimed responsibility for the attack that occurred in Amman.

incitement	تَحْرِيضٌ

وُجِّهَتْ لِلنَّاشِطِ تُهْمَةُ التَّحْرِيضِ ضِدَّ الأَقَلِّيَّاتِ الدِّينِيَّةِ.

The activist was charged with incitement against religious minorities.

religious incitement	تَحْرِيضٌ دِينِيٌّ

أُدِينَ مُدَوِّنٌ فِي الكُوَيْتِ بِتُهْمَةِ التَّحْرِيضِ الدِّينِيِّ.

A blogger was convicted of religious incitement in Kuwait.

to lead	تَزَعُّمْ •	تَزَعَّمَ

تَزَعَّمَ حُسَيْنٌ المَجْمُوعَةَ الَّتِي تُعْتَبَرُ مُتَطَرِّفَةً مِنْ قِبَلِ الحُكُومَةِ.

Hussein led the group considered extremist by the government.

to become radicalized	تَشَدَّدَ •	تَشَدَّدَ

تَشَدَّدَ الشَّابُّ بَعْدَ سَفَرِهِ لِلْخَارِجِ وَانْضَمَّ لِتَنْظِيمٍ مُتَطَرِّفٍ.

The young man became radicalized after traveling abroad and joining an extremist organization.

radicalization	تَشَدُّدٌ

شَهِدَتِ المِنْطَقَةُ ازْدِيَادًا فِي حَالَاتِ التَّشَدُّدِ بَيْنَ الشَّبَابِ.

The region has seen an increase in cases of radicalization among the youth.

to become extremist	تَطَرَّفَ •	تَطَرَّفَ

تَطَرَّفَ الجِهَادِيُّ بَعْدَ تَعَرُّضِهِ لِأَفْكَارٍ مُتَطَرِّفَةٍ عَلَى الإِنْتَرْنِتِ.

The jihadist became extremist after being exposed to extremist ideas on the Internet.

تَطَرُّفٌ

extremism

مُكافَحَةُ التَّطَرُّفِ تَتَطَلَّبُ جُهودًا مُشْتَرَكَةً مِنَ المُجْتَمَعِ الدَّوْلِيِّ.

Combatting extremism requires joint efforts from the international community.

تَطَرُّفٌ إِسْلامِيٌّ

Islamic extremism

حَذَّرَتِ المُنَظَّماتُ الحُقوقِيَّةُ مِنَ انْتِشارِ التَّطَرُّفِ الإِسْلامِيِّ في شَمالِ إِفْريقْيا.

Human rights organizations warned of the spread of Islamic extremism in North Africa.

تَطَرُّفٌ دينِيٌّ

religious extremism

أُثيرَ جَدَلٌ كَبيرٌ حَوْلَ انْتِشارِ التَّطَرُّفِ الدّينِيِّ في مَدارِسِ البَحْرَيْنِ.

A significant debate arose about religious extremism spreading in Bahraini schools.

تَطَرُّفٌ طائِفِيٌّ

sectarian extremism

تُعاني العِراقُ مِنْ مُشْكِلَةِ التَّطَرُّفِ الطّائِفِيِّ بَيْنَ السُّنَّةِ والشّيعَةِ.

Iraq suffers from the problem of sectarian extremism between Sunnis and Shiites.

تَفْرِقَةٌ طائِفِيَّةٌ

sectarianism

تَصاعَدَتْ حالاتُ التَّفْرِقَةِ الطّائِفِيَّةِ في مَدينَةِ النَّجَفِ مُؤَخَّرًا.

Cases of sectarianism have escalated recently in the city of Najaf.

تَيّارٌ دينِيٌّ

religious current

يَنْتَشِرُ تَيّارٌ دينِيٌّ مُتَشَدِّدٌ في مُحافَظَةِ صَلاحِ الدّينِ.

A radical religious current is spreading in Salah al-Din province.

جَماعَةٌ إِرْهابِيَّةٌ

terrorist group

تَمَّ تَفْكيكُ جَماعَةٍ إِرْهابِيَّةٍ كانَتْ تُخَطِّطُ لِهَجَماتٍ في الدَّمّامِ.

A terrorist group planning attacks in Dammam was dismantled.

jihad

جِهادٌ

تَناقَلَتِ الشَّبَكاتُ الاِجْتِماعِيَّةُ فيديو يَظْهَرُ فيهِ رَجُلٌ يَدْعو لِلْجِهادِ في سوريا.

Social networks circulated a video showing a man calling for jihad in Syria.

to urge, encourage

حَثَّ عَلى • حَثَّ

حَثَّ الإمامُ في خُطْبَتِهِ عَلى التَّعايُشِ السِّلْمِيِّ بَيْنَ مُخْتَلِفِ الفِئاتِ الدِّينِيَّةِ.

The Imam urged peaceful coexistence among different religious groups in his sermon.

religious propaganda

دِعايَةٌ دينِيَّةٌ

نَشَرَتِ الجَماعَةُ المُتَطَرِّفَةُ دِعايَةً دينِيَّةً تُحَرِّضُ عَلى العُنْفِ.

The extremist group published religious propaganda that incites violence.

Sunni

سُنِّيٌّ

تَأجَّجَتِ العَلاقاتُ بَيْنَ السُّنَّةِ والشّيعَةِ بَعْدَ التَّفْجيرِ في بَغْدادَ.

Relations between Sunnis and Shiites flared up after the bombing in Baghdad.

Shiites and Sunnis

شيعَةٌ وَسُنَّةٌ

أسْفَرَ الصِّراعُ بَيْنَ الشّيعَةِ والسُّنَّةِ عَنْ فُقْدانِ العَديدِ مِنَ الأرْواحِ.

The conflict between Shiites and Sunnis resulted in the loss of many lives.

Shiite

شيعِيٌّ

حَقَّقَتْ قُوّاتُ الأمْنِ العِراقِيَّةُ مَكاسِبَ ضِدَّ المَيليشْياتِ الشّيعِيَّةِ في البَصْرَةِ.

Iraqi security forces made gains against Shiite militias in Basra.

sectarian

طائِفِيٌّ

أُعْتُبِرَتِ التَّصْريحاتُ السِّياسِيَّةُ لِلزَّعيمِ مُحاوَلَةً لِإثارَةِ التَّوَتُّرِ الطّائِفِيِّ.

The leader's political statements were considered an attempt to stir up sectarian tension.

عُنْفٌ دينِيٌّ

religious violence

اِزْدَادَتْ حَوادِثُ العُنْفِ الدّينِيِّ في اليَمَنِ خِلالَ السَّنَواتِ الأخيرَةِ.

Incidents of religious violence in Yemen have increased in recent years.

عُنْفٌ طائِفِيٌّ

sectarian violence

أَسْفَرَ تَفْجيرٌ في العِراقِ عَنْ عُنْفٍ طائِفِيٍّ، ما عَقَّدَ الوَضْعَ الأَمْنِيَّ.

A bombing in Iraq has led to sectarian violence, thus complicating the security situation.

عَنيفٌ • عُنُفٌ

violent

أُعْتُبِرَ الشَّخْصُ المُتَوَرِّطُ في الحادِثِ عَنيفًا وَتَمَّ تَوْقيفُهُ.

The person involved in the incident was considered violent and was arrested.

فِتْنَةٌ طائِفِيَّةٌ • فِتَنٌ

sectarian strife

شَهِدَتِ المَناطِقُ الجَنوبِيَّةُ لِليبيا فِتْنَةً طائِفِيَّةً عَنيفَةً.

The southern regions of Libya witnessed violent sectarian strife.

فِكْرٌ تَكْفيرِيٌّ

Takfiri ideology

نَشَرَتِ القاعِدَةُ فيدْيو يُرَوِّجُ لِلفِكْرِ التَّكْفيرِيِّ.

Al-Qaeda published a video promoting Takfiri ideology.

فِكْرٌ مُتَطَرِّفٌ

extremist ideology

ظَهَرَ الفِكْرُ المُتَطَرِّفُ في بَعْضِ المُنْتَدَياتِ الإلِكْترونِيَّةِ.

Extremist ideology appeared in some online forums.

قَتْلٌ جَماعِيٌّ

mass killing

أَوْدى هُجومٌ في سوريا بِحَياةِ العَديدِ في حادِثِ قَتْلٍ جَماعِيٍّ.

An attack in Syria resulted in a mass killing.

to undermine   تَقْوِيضٌ •   قَوَّضَ

تَعْمَلُ الجَماعاتُ المُتَطَرِّفَةُ عَلَى تَقْوِيضِ النِّظامِ الحاكِمِ في مِصْرَ.

Extremist groups are working to undermine the governing system in Egypt.

extremist   مُتَشَدِّدٌ

تَمَّ القَبْضُ عَلَى المُتَشَدِّدِ الَّذي كانَ يُخَطِّطُ لِهُجومٍ في عَدَنَ.

The extremist planning an attack in Aden was arrested.

extremist, radical   مُتَطَرِّفٌ

تُلاحِقُ الأَجْهِزَةُ الأَمْنِيَّةُ مُتَطَرِّفًا يُشْتَبَهُ في تَوَرُّطِهِ بِأَعْمالِ عُنْفٍ.

Security forces are pursuing an extremist suspected of being involved in violent acts.

religious sect   مَذاهِبُ •   مَذْهَبٌ دينِيٌّ

تَسَبَّبَ الخِلافُ بَيْنَ المَذاهِبِ الدينِيَّةِ المُخْتَلِفَةِ في تَوَتُّراتٍ اجْتِماعِيَّةٍ.

The disagreement between different religious sects led to social tensions.

to spread   نَشْرٌ •   نَشَرَ

مُكافَحَةُ نَشْرِ التَّطَرُّفِ الدّينِيِّ تُعْتَبَرُ مُهِمَّةً ضَرورِيَّةً لِضَمانِ الأَمْنِ وَالاسْتِقْرارِ العامِّ.

Fighting the spread of religious extremism is a crucial task to maintain public security and stability.

terrorist attack   هُجومٌ إِرْهابِيٌّ

تَمَّ تَنْفيذُ هُجومٍ إِرْهابِيٍّ في القاهِرَةِ، وَأَسْفَرَ عَنْ مَقْتَلِ عَشَراتِ الأَشْخاصِ.

A terrorist attack was carried out in Cairo, resulting in the deaths of dozens of people.

Wahhabism   وَهّابِيَّةٌ

نَشَرَتِ الصُّحُفُ تَقْريرًا يُحَذِّرُ مِنْ تَزايُدِ الوَهّابِيَّةِ في الأُرْدُنِّ.

Newspapers published a report warning of the rise of Wahhabism in Jordan.

في عَمَلِيَّةٍ أمْنِيَّةٍ نَوْعِيَّةٍ، تَمَكَّنَتِ القُوَّاتُ الخاصَّةُ مِنَ اعْتِقال خَلِيَّةٍ إرْهابِيَّةٍ كانَتْ تُخَطِّطُ لِتَنْفيذِ هُجومٍ إرْهابِيٍّ في قَلْبِ العاصِمَة. وَقَدْ أشارَ المُتَحَدِّثُ باسْمِ الأمْنِ إلى أنَّ الخَلِيَّةَ انْحَرَفَتْ عَنْ تَعاليمِ الدّينِ الحَنيفِ، وَانْتَمَتْ إلى تَيّارٍ دينِيٍّ مُتَطَرِّفٍ. وَأكَّدَ أنَّ التَّحْريضَ الدّينِيَّ الَّذي مارَسَتْهُ هَذِهِ الجَماعَةُ عَبْرَ الدِّعايَةِ الدّينِيَّةِ المُتَشَدِّدَةِ كانَ يَهْدُفُ إلى نَشْرِ الفِتْنَةِ الطّائِفِيَّةِ.

In a special security operation, the special forces managed to arrest a terrorist cell that was planning to carry out a terrorist attack in the heart of the capital. The security spokesperson indicated that the cell deviated from the teachings of the true religion and belonged to an extremist religious stream. He confirmed that the religious incitement practiced by this group through militant religious propaganda aimed to spread sectarian strife.

فَجَّرَ إرْهابِيٌّ مُتَطَرِّفٌ نَفْسَهُ في سوقٍ شَعْبِيٍّ مُزْدَحِمٍ، ما أسْفَرَ عَنْ سُقوطِ عَشَراتِ الضَّحايا. الإرْهابِيُّ، الَّذي يُعْتَقَدُ بِانْتِمائِهِ لِجَماعَةٍ إرْهابِيَّةٍ مَعْروفَةٍ بِآرائِها الطّائِفِيَّةِ، قامَ بِتَحْريضِ أتْباعِهِ عَلى العُنْفِ الدّينِيِّ مِنْ خِلالِ رَسائِلَ مُتَشَدِّدَةٍ، مِمّا أثارَ مَوْجَةً مِنَ القَلَقِ في أوْساطِ المُجْتَمَعِ المَدَنِيِّ.

A terrorist extremist detonated himself in a crowded popular market, resulting in dozens of victims. The terrorist, who claimed affiliation with a terrorist group known for its sectarian views, incited his followers to religious violence through extremist messages, sparking a wave of concern among civil society.

أعْلَنَتِ السُّلُطاتُ اليَوْمَ عَنْ إحْباطِ مُخَطَّطٍ إرْهابِيٍّ طائِفِيٍّ كانَ يَسْتَهْدِفُ أحْياءً سَكَنِيَّةً مُحَدَّدَةً في المَدينَةِ. وَأوْضَحَتْ أنَّ الجَماعَةَ الإرْهابِيَّةَ، الَّتي تَبَنَّتِ الفِكْرَ التَّكْفيرِيَّ، كانَتْ تَسْعى لِزَعْزَعَةِ الاسْتِقْرارِ وَنَشْرِ التَّفْرِقَةِ بَيْنَ أبْناءِ الوَطَنِ. وَأشادَ المَسْؤولونَ بِيَقَظَةِ الأجْهِزَةِ الأمْنِيَّةِ الَّتي أحْبَطَتْ مُحاوَلاتِ التَّحْريضِ وَالعُنْفِ الطّائِفِيِّ.

The authorities announced today the thwarting of a sectarian terrorist plot that targeted specific residential areas in the city. It was clarified that the terrorist group, which adopted Takfiri ideology, was seeking to destabilize and spread division among the nation's people. Officials praised the vigilance of the security agencies that foiled attempts at incitement and sectarian violence.

اِنْدَلَعَتِ اشْتِباكاتٌ عَنيفَةٌ بَيْنَ جَماعَتَيْنِ مُتَطَرِّفَتَيْنِ مِنْ مَذاهِبَ دينِيَّةٍ مُخْتَلِفَةٍ، ما أدّى إلى حَوادِثِ قَتْلٍ جَماعِيٍّ. التَّحْريضُ الدّينِيُّ وَالتَّفْرِقَةُ الطّائِفِيَّةُ كانا وَراءَ هَذِهِ الفِتْنَةِ الطّائِفِيَّةِ الَّتي طالَتْ حَتّى المَدَنِيّينَ الأبْرِياءَ، مُخَلِّفَةً وَراءَها أزْمَةً إنْسانِيَّةً وَدَعَواتٍ عاجِلَةً لِلسَّلامِ.

Violent clashes erupted between two extremist groups from different religious sects, leading to mass killings. Religious incitement and sectarian division were behind this sectarian strife that affected even innocent civilians, leaving behind a humanitarian crisis and urgent calls for peace.

في ظِلِّ تَزايُدِ التَّحَدِّياتِ الَّتي يَفرِضُها الإرهابُ الدِّينِيُّ، دَعَتِ الأُمَمُ المُتَّحِدَةُ إلى تَعزيزِ التَّعاوُنِ الدَّوْلِيِّ لِمُواجَهَةِ هَذِهِ الظّاهِرَةِ. وَتَمَّ التَّأكيدُ عَلى أَهَمِّيَّةِ مُكافَحَةِ الفِكرِ المُتَطَرِّفِ وَمَنْعِ انْتِشارِهِ بَيْنَ الشَّبابِ. وَأَشارَتِ التَّقاريرُ إلى أَنَّ مَذاهِبَ دينِيَّةً مُتَعَدِّدَةً قَدْ تَأَثَّرَتْ بِتَيّاراتٍ مُتَطَرِّفَةٍ كالوَهّابِيَّةِ، مِمّا يَتَطَلَّبُ جُهودًا مُشتَرَكَةً لِمُكافَحَةِ التَّطَرُّفِ الإسلامِيِّ وَالتَّطَرُّفِ الدِّينِيِّ بِشَكلٍ عامٍّ.

In light of the increasing challenges posed by religious terrorism, the United Nations called for strengthening international cooperation to combat this phenomenon. The importance of fighting extremist thought and preventing its spread among the youth was emphasized. Reports indicated that multiple religious sects have been affected by extremist currents such as Wahhabism, which requires joint efforts to combat Islamic extremism and religious extremism in general.

نَفَّذَ مُتَشَدِّدونَ مُتَطَرِّفونَ هُجومًا إرهابِيًّا عَلى عِدَّةِ دورِ عِبادَةٍ، مِمّا أَدّى إلى اسْتِنكارٍ عالَمِيٍّ. الهَجَماتُ، الَّتي اتُّهِمَتْ فيها جَماعَةٌ إرهابِيَّةٌ تَنْتَمي إلى تَيّارٍ دينِيٍّ مُعَيَّنٍ، حَثَّتْ عَلى الانْتِقامِ وَالتَّطَرُّفِ الدِّينِيِّ، مِمّا يُنذِرُ بِتَصاعُدِ العُنْفِ الطّائِفِيِّ.

Extremist militants carried out a terrorist attack on several houses of worship, leading to global condemnation. The attacks, which a terrorist group belonging to a certain religious stream was accused of, encouraged revenge and religious extremism, warning of an escalation of sectarian violence.

كَشَفَتِ القُوّاتُ الأَمْنِيَّةُ عَنْ نَجاحِها في تَفكيكِ شَبَكاتِ تَحْريضٍ دينِيٍّ كانَتْ تَنْشَطُ عَبْرَ وَسائِلِ التَّواصُلِ الاجْتِماعِيِّ. وَأَكَّدَ المُحَقِّقونَ أَنَّ هَذِهِ الشَّبَكاتِ كانَتْ تَسْتَغِلُّ الخِلافاتِ بَيْنَ الشّيعَةِ وَالسُّنَّةِ لِنَشْرِ رَسائِلَ تَشَدُّدٍ وَعُنْفٍ دينِيٍّ. وَقَدْ أَدّى التَّدَخُّلُ الأَمْنِيُّ السَّريعُ إلى تَقْويضِ هَذِهِ الجُهودِ وَحِمايَةِ النَّسيجِ الاجْتِماعِيِّ مِنَ الانْقِسامِ.

The security forces revealed their success in dismantling religious incitement networks that were active on social media. Investigators confirmed that these networks were exploiting the differences between Shia and Sunni to spread messages of religious strictness and violence. The swift security intervention undermined these efforts and protected the social fabric from division.

أَعْلَنَتِ السُّلُطاتُ الأَمْنِيَّةُ عَنْ كَشْفِ مَخْبَأٍ كَبيرٍ لِلأَسْلِحَةِ تابِعٍ لِجَماعَةٍ إرهابِيَّةٍ تَتَبَنّى فِكرًا مُتَطَرِّفًا. الجَماعَةُ، الَّتي كانَتْ تَنْشُرُ أَفْكارَها التَّكفيرِيَّةَ وَتُحَرِّضُ عَلى العُنْفِ الدِّينِيِّ، كانَتْ تُخَطِّطُ لِسِلسِلَةٍ مِنَ الهَجَماتِ الطّائِفِيَّةِ واسِعَةِ النِّطاقِ.

The security authorities announced the discovery of a large arms cache belonging to a terrorist group adopting extremist ideology. The group, which was spreading its takfiri ideas and inciting religious violence, was planning a series of wide-scale sectarian attacks.

أَطْلَقَتِ الحُكومَةُ حَمْلَةً وَطَنِيَّةً واسِعَةَ النِّطاقِ لِمُحارَبَةِ التَّشَدُّدِ الدِّينِيِّ والفِكْرِ المُتَطَرِّفِ. وَتَهْدُفُ الحَمْلَةُ إلى تَوْعِيَةِ المُواطِنينَ بِأَهَمِّيَّةِ التَّمَسُّكِ بِقِيَمِ التَّسامُحِ والاعْتِدالِ، وَتَحْصينِ المُجْتَمَعِ ضِدَّ أَيِّ أَفْكارٍ تَدْعو إلى العُنْفِ أو التَّفْرِقَةِ الطّائِفِيَّةِ. وَتَتَضَمَّنُ الحَمْلَةُ بَرامِجَ تَعْليمِيَّةً وَوَرَشَ عَمَلٍ تُناقِشُ مَخاطِرَ الإرْهابِ الدِّينِيِّ والطّائِفِيِّ.

The government launched a widespread national campaign to combat religious extremism and radical ideology. The campaign aims to educate citizens about the importance of adhering to the values of tolerance and moderation and to immunize society against any ideas that advocate violence or sectarian division. The campaign includes educational programs and workshops that discuss the dangers of religious and sectarian terrorism.

تَحَوَّلَتْ مُظاهَراتٌ سِلْمِيَّةٌ إلى أَعْمالِ شَغَبٍ عِنْدَما اسْتَغَلَّ مُتَطَرِّفونَ الحَدَثَ لِبَثِّ دِعايَةٍ دينِيَّةٍ تَحْريضِيَّةٍ. الاِشْتِباكاتُ الَّتي تَلَتْ ذَلِكَ بَيْنَ السُّنَّةِ والشّيعَةِ قَوَّضَتْ جُهودَ الوَحْدَةِ الوَطَنِيَّةِ، وَأَظْهَرَتِ الحاجَةَ الماسَّةَ لِمُعالَجَةِ التَّشَدُّدِ والتَّطَرُّفِ الدِّينِيِّ في المُجْتَمَعِ.

Peaceful demonstrations turned into riots when extremists exploited the event to spread provocative religious propaganda. The subsequent clashes between Sunnis and Shiites undermined national unity efforts and highlighted the urgent need to address religious radicalism and extremism in society.

8.4 Customs and Practices in Islam

8.4.1 Introduction to Islamic Practices

Track **65**

آمَنَ
• إيمانٌ

to believe

المَلايينُ يُؤْمِنونَ بِالقِيَمِ والتَّعاليمِ الإسْلامِيَّةِ في جَميعِ أَنْحاءِ العالَمِ.

Millions believe in Islamic values and teachings worldwide.

(الحَياةُ) الآخِرَةُ

afterlife

يُرَكِّزُ الإسْلامُ عَلى أَهَمِّيَّةِ الحَياةِ الآخِرَةِ بِالمُقارَنَةِ مَعَ الحَياةِ الدُّنْيا.

Islam emphasizes the importance of the afterlife compared to worldly life.

(الحَياةُ) الدُّنْيا (as opposed to the afterlife)

the life of this world

تَحْكُمُ القِيَمُ الإسْلامِيَّةُ حَياةَ المُسْلِمينَ في الحَياةِ الدُّنْيا والآخِرَةِ.

Islamic values govern the lives of Muslims in this world and the hereafter.

الدُّنْيا literally means 'lowest,' referring to the earthly life in contrast to the higher spiritual life expected in heaven.

تابَ • تَوْبَةٌ   **to repent**

التَّوْبَةُ هِيَ عَمَلِيَّةٌ هامَّةٌ في الإِسْلامِ، حَيْثُ يَتوبُ المُؤْمِنونَ عَنِ الأَخْطاءِ وَيَسْعَوْنَ لِلْغُفْرانِ.

Repentance is a crucial process in Islam, where believers repent for their mistakes and seek forgiveness.

تَوْبَةٌ   **repentance**

يُؤْمِنُ المُسْلِمونَ أَنَّ التَّوْبَةَ الصّادِقَةَ تُساعِدُ الإِنْسانَ عَلى تَصْحيحِ مَسارِ حَياتِهِ.

Muslims believe that sincere repentance helps a person correct the course of their life.

تَوْحيدٌ   **asserting oneness** (that there's only one God)

يُعْتَبَرُ التَّوْحيدُ مِنْ أَهَمِّ مَبادِئِ الإِسْلامِ.

Asserting oneness is one of the most important principles of Islam.

ثَوابٌ   **reward**

يُؤْمِنُ المُسْلِمونَ بِأَنَّ الثَّوابَ يَنْتَظِرُهُمْ في الجَنَّةِ.

Muslims believe that reward awaits them in heaven.

جَنَّةٌ • جِنانٌ / جَنّاتٌ   **heaven**

يُؤْمِنُ المُسْلِمونَ أَنَّ الجَنَّةَ هِيَ الجَزاءُ الأَعْلى الَّذي يَنْتَظِرُ المُؤْمِنينَ في الحَياةِ الآخِرَةِ.

Muslims believe that heaven is the ultimate reward awaiting the believers in the hereafter.

حَسَنَةٌ   **good deed, credit for good deeds**

الحَسَنَةُ هِيَ عَمَلٌ صالِحٌ يُحْتَسَبُ لِلْمُؤْمِنينَ كَرَصيدٍ لِأَعْمالِهِمِ الصّالِحَةِ في الآخِرَةِ.

A good deed is a righteous act credited to the believers for their good deeds in the hereafter.

سَيِّئَة

bad deed, credit for bad deeds

تُمَثِّلُ السَّيِّئَةُ عَمَلًا سَيِّئًا يُسَجَّلُ لِلْأَشْخَاصِ كَرَصِيدٍ لِأَعْمَالِهِمِ السَّيِّئَةِ فِي الآخِرَةِ.

A bad deed represents a wrongful act recorded for individuals as credit for their bad deeds in the hereafter.

صَبْرٌ

perseverance

يُعْتَبَرُ الصَّبْرُ مِنْ أَعْظَمِ الفَضَائِلِ فِي الإِسْلَامِ.

Perseverance is considered one of the greatest virtues in Islam.

عَبَدَ • عِبَادَةٌ

to worship

المُسْلِمُونَ يَعْبُدُونَ اللهَ بِإِخْلَاصٍ وَتَفَانٍ فِي أَعْمَالِ العِبَادَةِ اليَوْمِيَّةِ.

Muslims worship God with sincerity and dedication in their daily acts of worship.

عَبْدٌ • عِبَادٌ

servant, slave

فِي الإِسْلَامِ، يُعْتَبَرُ المُؤْمِنُونَ عِبَادًا لله، وَهُمْ يُقَدِّمُونَ لَهُ العِبَادَةَ وَالِامْتِثَالَ لِوَصَايَاهُ.

In Islam, believers are considered servants of God, and they offer worship and obedience to His commandments.

فِرْدَوْسٌ

paradise

يَصِفُ القُرْآنُ الفِرْدَوْسَ كَأَعْلَى مُسْتَوَيَاتِ الجَنَّةِ.

The Quran describes Paradise as the highest levels of heaven.

كَافِرٌ • كَافِرُونَ / كُفَّارٌ

infidel, disbeliever

لَا يَعْتَبِرُ الإِسْلَامُ كُلَّ غَيْرِ المُسْلِمِينَ كُفَّارًا.

Islam does not consider all non-Muslims as infidels.

مُؤْمِنٌ

believer

المُؤْمِنُ هُوَ مَنْ يُؤْمِنُ بِاللهِ وَرُسُلِهِ وَالكُتُبِ السَّمَاوِيَّةِ.

A believer is someone who believes in God, His messengers, and the divine scriptures.

نارٌ   **hell**

يُحَذِّرُ الإِسْلامُ مِنْ نارِ جَهَنَّمَ لِلْكُفّارِ وَالظّالِمينَ.

Islam warns of the Hellfire for disbelievers and wrongdoers.

8.4.1.1 Mini-Articles

أَطْلَقَتْ مُؤَسَّسَةٌ دينيّةٌ مُبادَرَةً تَهْدِفُ إلى تَعْزيزِ الإيمانِ بَيْنَ الشَّبابِ، مُؤَكِّدَةً عَلى أَهَمِّيَّةِ الحَياةِ الآخِرَةِ وَمُقارَنَتِها بِزَوالِ الحَياةِ الدُّنْيا. وَتَشْمَلُ المُبادَرَةُ وَرَشَ عَمَلٍ تَعْليميَّةٍ تَسْتَعْرِضُ مَفاهيمَ التَّوْبَةِ وَالصَّبْرِ وَتَشْجيعِ العَمَلِ الصّالِحِ.

A religious foundation has launched an initiative aimed at promoting faith among young people, emphasizing the importance of the afterlife and comparing it to the transience of this worldly life. The initiative includes educational workshops that discuss concepts of repentance, patience, and encouraging the doing of good deeds.

بادَرَتْ جَمْعيّةٌ إِسْلاميّةٌ بِحَمْلَةٍ تَوْعَويّةٍ لِتَذْكيرِ المُؤْمِنينَ بِأَهَمِّيَّةِ التَّوْحيدِ وَالابْتِعادِ عَنِ الشِّرْكِ. تَسْتَهْدِفُ الحَمْلَةُ تَقْوِيَةَ الصِّلَةِ بَيْنَ العَبْدِ وَخالِقِهِ، وَتُنَظِّمُ سِلْسِلَةً مِنَ المُحاضَراتِ حَوْلَ الثَّوابِ المُرْتَبِطِ بِالعِبادَةِ الصّادِقَةِ وَالاعْتِقادِ الرّاسِخِ.

An Islamic association initiated an awareness campaign to remind believers of the importance of monotheism and avoiding polytheism. The campaign aims to strengthen the connection between the servant and their Creator and organizes a series of lectures on the rewards associated with sincere worship and steadfast belief.

يُشَدِّدُ الدّينُ الإِسْلاميُّ عَلى ضَرورَةِ تَجَنُّبِ السَّيِّئاتِ وَالمُسارَعَةِ نَحْوَ الحَسَناتِ، لِتَحْقيقِ التَّقْوى وَالتَّطْهيرِ الرّوحيِّ. كَما يَحُثُّ عَلى البَحْثِ عَنْ فُرَصٍ لِلتَّكْفيرِ عَنِ السَّيِّئاتِ وَزِيادَةِ الأَعْمالِ الصّالِحَةِ لِلارْتِقاءِ بِالرّوحانيّةِ وَالقُرْبِ مِنَ اللهِ.

The Islamic faith emphasizes the importance of avoiding sins and hastening toward good deeds, aiming to achieve piety and spiritual purification. It also encourages seeking opportunities for atonement for sins and increasing righteous actions to enhance spirituality and draw closer to God.

اِسْتَضافَتِ العاصِمَةُ مُؤْتَمَرًا دَوْليًّا حَوْلَ دَوْرِ العِبادَةِ في تَحْقيقِ السَّكينَةِ وَالسَّلامِ النَّفْسيِّ. وَقَدْ شارَكَ في المُؤْتَمَرِ عَدَدٌ مِنَ المُتَعَبِّدينَ مِنْ مُخْتَلِفِ أَنْحاءِ العالَمِ، مُسْتَعْرِضينَ تَجارِبَهُمْ في كَيْفِيَّةِ أَنَّ الإيمانَ وَالتَّقَرُّبَ إلى اللهِ يُمْكِنُ أَنْ يُؤَدِّيا إلى حَياةٍ مِلؤُها الرِّضا وَالاطْمِئْنانُ.

The capital hosted an international conference on the role of worship in achieving tranquility and psychological peace. A number of worshippers from various parts of the world participated in the conference, presenting their experiences on how faith and drawing closer to God can lead to a life filled with contentment and reassurance.

188 | Religion and Society

The capital hosted an international conference on the role of worship in achieving tranquility and mental peace. Several worshippers from different parts of the world participated in the conference, sharing their experiences on how faith and drawing closer to God can lead to a life filled with contentment and serenity.

8.4.2 The Five Pillars of Islam

Track **67**

آيَةٌ

verse, ayah

جَرى تَداوُلُ آيَةٍ قُرآنِيَّةٍ عَلى نِطاقٍ واسِعٍ عَبْرَ وَسائِلِ التَّواصُلِ الاجْتِماعِيِّ بَعْدَ الزِّلْزالِ الَّذي ضَرَبَ بَيْروتَ مُؤَخَّرًا.

A Quranic verse was widely circulated on social media after the recent earthquake that hit Beirut.

أَذانٌ

call to prayer

يُرْفَعُ الأَذانُ يَوْمِيًّا لِدَعْوَةِ المُسْلِمينَ لِأَداءِ الصَّلَواتِ الخَمْسِ في الوَقْتِ المُحَدَّدِ.

The call to prayer is raised daily to invite Muslims to perform the five daily prayers at their designated times.

إقامَةٌ

second call to prayer

أَعْلَنَ المُؤَذِّنُ إقامَةَ الصَّلاةِ، داعِيًا المُؤْمِنينَ لِأَداءِ عِبادَتِهِمْ.

The muezzin announced the commencement of the prayer, calling the faithful to their worship.

> In a religious context, إقامَةٌ has two meanings: 1) the second call to prayer, signaling the start of the prayer service, and 2) the act of performing the prayer itself. Thus, the second pillar of Islam, إقامَةُ الصَّلاةِ.

الحَمْدُ لله

praise be to God

أَعْرَبَ الرَّئيسُ عَنْ شُكْرِهِ لِلْجُهودِ المَبْذولَةِ في مُكافَحَةِ الجائِحَةِ وقالَ: الْحَمْدُ لله.

The President expressed his gratitude for efforts made in combating the pandemic and said: "Praise be to God."

الشَّهادَةُ

profession of faith

يُعْتَبَرُ نُطْقُ الشَّهادَةِ أَوَّلَ أَرْكانِ الْإِسلامِ.

Reciting the Shahada is considered one of the fundamental pillars of Islam.

The term الشَّهَادَةُ refers to the declaration of faith in Islam, confessing that there is no god but God and that Muhammad is God's messenger. The Arabic wording with tashkeel is: أَشْهَدُ أَنْ لَا إِلَهَ إِلَّا اللَّهُ، وَأَنَّ مُحَمَّدًا رَسُولُ اللَّهِ.

God is the greatest
اللهُ أَكْبَرُ

يَهْتِفُ الحُجَّاجُ "اَللَّهُ أَكْبَرُ" أَثْنَاءَ طَوَافِهِمْ بِالْكَعْبَةِ.

Pilgrims chant "Allahu Akbar" while circumambulating the Kaaba.

takbir
تَكْبِيرٌ

يَبْدَأُ المُسْلِمونَ صَلَواتِهِم الخَمْسَ بِالتَّكْبِيرِ.

Muslims start their five daily prayers with the Takbir.

تَكْبِيرٌ refers to the act of saying اللَّهُ أَكْبَرُ, a phrase is used in various Islamic rituals and practices, symbolizing the greatness and supremacy of God over all things.

dry ablution
تَيَمُّمٌ

تَوَجَّهَتْ وِزَارَةُ الشُّؤُونِ الدِّينِيَّةِ بِنَصَائِحَ لِلْمُسْلِمِينَ حَوْلَ القِيامِ بِالتَّيَمُّمِ فِي حَالاتِ الجَفَافِ.

The Ministry of Religious Affairs issued guidelines for Muslims on performing dry ablution during drought conditions.

impurity
جَنَابَةٌ

عِنْدَما يَكُونُ المُسْلِمُ عَلَى جَنَابَةٍ، يَجِبُ عَلَيْهِ الغُسْلُ قَبْلَ أَنْ يَكُونَ مُؤَهَّلًا لِأَداءِ الصَّلاةِ.

When a Muslim is in a state of janabah, they must perform a ritual purification (ghusl) before they are eligible to perform the prayer.

Hajji, pilgrim
حُجَّاجٌ • حَاجٌّ

أَفادَتِ التَّقارِيرُ الأَخِيرَةُ بِأَنَّ عَدَدَ الحُجَّاجِ هَذا العامَ تَجاوَزَ المِلْيونَ شَخْصٍ.

Recent reports indicate that the number of pilgrims this year has exceeded one million people.

Hajj, pilgrimage
حَجٌّ

تَشْهَدُ مَكَّةُ المُكَرَّمَةُ إِقْبَالًا كَبِيرًا مِنَ المُسْلِمِينَ مِنْ جَمِيعِ أَنْحَاءِ العَالَمِ لِأَداءِ الحَجِّ هَذا العَامَ.

Mecca is witnessing a high turnout of Muslims from around the world for the pilgrimage this year.

دُعَاءٌ • أَدْعِيَةٌ

supplication, prayer, dua

طَالَبَ الشَّيْخُ الأُمَّةَ بِالدُّعاءِ لِضَحايا الإِعْصارِ.

The Sheikh asked the people to pray for the victims of the cyclone.

دعاء refers to supplication or personal prayer, where individuals directly communicate with God to ask for help, guidance, forgiveness, or anything they wish, outside the formal structure of Salah (see page 193).

ذِكْرٌ • أَذْكَارٌ

remembrance, dhikr

أَطْلَقَتِ الحُكُومَةُ حَمْلَةً جَدِيدَةً لِتَعْزِيزِ الذِّكْرِ وَالصَّلاةِ في المُجْتَمَعِ.

The government has launched a new campaign to promote remembrance and prayer in the community.

رَكْعَةٌ

bow, rak'ah

وَثَّقَتِ الكاميراتُ لَحْظَةَ قِيامِ المُصَلِّينَ بِالرَّكْعَةِ الأَخِيرَةِ في المَسْجِدِ الأَقْصى.

Cameras captured the moment worshippers performed the last rak'ah at the Al-Aqsa Mosque.

رُكْنُ الإِسْلام • أَرْكانٌ

pillar of Islam

رُكْنُ الإِسْلامِ الخامِسُ هوَ أَداءُ الحَجِّ إِذا اسْتَطاعَ المُسْلِمُ أَداءَهُ.

The fifth pillar of Islam is performing the Hajj if a Muslim is able to do so.

زَكاةٌ

almsgiving, zakat

أَكَّدَتِ الجِهاتُ الدِّينِيَّةُ عَلى أَهَمِّيَّةِ الزَّكاةِ كَرُكْنٍ مِنْ أَرْكانِ الإِسْلامِ في المُؤْتَمَرِ السَّنَوِيِّ.

Religious authorities emphasized the importance of almsgiving as a pillar of Islam at the annual conference.

زَكّى • تَزْكِيَةٌ

purify

أَعْلَنَتْ وِزارَةُ الشُّؤونِ الإِسْلامِيَّةِ عَنْ مُبادَرَةٍ لِتَزْكِيَةِ الأَمْوالِ لِدَعْمِ الأَيْتامِ.

The Ministry of Islamic Affairs announced an initiative to purify wealth to support orphans.

glory be to God

سُبْحانَ اللهِ

تَجَمَّعَ السُّيّاحُ لِمُشاهَدَةِ الشَّلّالاتِ بِانْبِهارٍ مُرَدِّدينَ "سُبْحانَ اللهِ".

Tourists gather to watch the waterfalls in awe, chanting "Subhanallah" (Glory be to God).

prayer mat

سَجّادَةُ صَلاةٍ • سَجّاداتٌ / سَجاجيدُ / سَجّادٌ

أَصْبَحَتْ سَجاجيدُ الصَّلاةِ المَصْنوعَةُ مِنَ المَوادِّ الصَّديقَةِ لِلْبيئَةِ رائِجَةً في الأَسْواقِ.

Eco-friendly prayer mats have become popular in markets.

to prostrate

سَجَدَ • سُجودٌ

سَجَدَ اللّاعِبُ شُكْرًا للهِ بَعْدَ تَسْجيلِهِ الهَدَفَ.

The player prostrated in gratitude to God after scoring the goal.

prostration, sujood

سَجْدَةٌ

تَفاعَلَ الجُمْهورُ مَعَ مَشْهَدِ السَّجْدَةِ في الفيلْمِ الجَديدِ الَّذي يَتَناوَلُ قَضايا اجْتِماعِيَّةً مُهِمَّةً.

The audience reacted to the scene of prostration in the new film that addresses important social issues.

tradition, sunnah

سُنَّةٌ • سُنَنْ

شَهِدَتْ مَدارِسُ الرِّياضِ تَعْزيزًا لِتَعْليمِ السُّنَّةِ والتَّقاليدِ الإِسْلامِيَّةِ في المَناهِجِ الدِّراسِيَّةِ.

Schools in Riyadh have seen an enhancement in teaching the Sunnah and Islamic traditions in the curriculum.

In Islam, prayers (Salah) are categorized into two main types: فَرْضٌ and سُنَّةٌ:

فَرْضٌ refers to the mandatory prayers, the five daily prayers that are obligatory for every Muslim to perform (see page 195).

سُنَّةٌ refers to the additional, voluntary prayers that are recommended but not obligatory. These are performed in addition to the Fard prayers and are considered meritorious, offering extra opportunities for worship and spiritual growth. It is common for Muslims to refer to these extra prayers as having prayed 'the Sunnah.'

سُوَرٌ •

سُورَةٌ

chapter, surah

تُعْتَبَرُ سُورَةُ الفَاتِحَةِ مِنْ أَهَمِّ سُوَرِ القُرْآنِ الكَرِيمِ وَهِيَ السُّورَةُ الِافْتِتَاحِيَّةُ فِيهِ.

Surat Al-Fatiha is considered one of the most important chapters of the Holy Quran and is its opening chapter.

صَدَقَةٌ

charity, sadaqah

نَظَّمَتِ الجَمْعِيَّاتُ الخَيْرِيَّةُ حَمْلَةً لِجَمْعِ الصَّدَقَاتِ لِدَعْمِ مَشْرُوعَاتِ التَّنْمِيَةِ فِي غَزَّةَ.

Charitable associations organized a campaign to collect sadaqah to support development projects in Gaza.

صَلَوَاتٌ •

صَلَاةٌ

ritual prayer, Salah

خُطْبَةُ الجُمْعَةِ الَّتِي أَلْقَاهَا الشَّيْخُ فِي مَسْجِدِ الإِمَامِ الأَكْبَرِ بِبَغْدَادَ رَكَّزَتْ عَلَى فَضْلِ الصَّلَاةِ وَأَهَمِّيَتِهَا.

The Friday sermon delivered by the Sheikh at the Grand Imam Mosque in Baghdad focused on the virtues of prayer and its importance.

صَلَاةٌ refers to the Islamic ritual prayer, a structured form of worship performed five times a day at specified times, involving specific physical and verbal actions. Compare to دُعَاءٌ on page 191.

صَلَاةٌ •

صَلَّى

to pray

تُشَجِّعُ المُنَظَّمَاتُ الإِسْلَامِيَّةُ النَّاسَ عَلَى التَّرْبِيَةِ الإِيمَانِيَّةِ مِنْ خِلَالِ التَّأْكِيدِ عَلَى فَضْلِ الصَّلَاةِ وَالتَّسْبِيحِ.

Islamic organizations are encouraging people toward spiritual upbringing by emphasizing the virtues of prayer and glorification (Tasbeeh).

صَوْمٌ = صِيَامٌ

fasting

أَعْلَنَتْ جَمْعِيَّةُ الصِّحَّةِ العَامَّةِ عَنْ بَرْنَامَجٍ جَدِيدٍ يُعْنَى بِصِحَّةِ الأَفْرَادِ أَثْنَاءَ الصَّوْمِ.

The Public Health Association announced a new program concerned with individual health during fasting.

While صَوْمٌ and صِيَامٌ are often used interchangeably to refer to fasting, there is a distinction according to some interpretations. صِيَامٌ specifically refers to the Islamic pillar of fasting during Ramadan, which involves abstaining from food, drink, and other physical needs from dawn until sunset. صَوْمٌ, on the other hand, is used more generally to denote abstention, not only from food and

---

drink but also from things like speaking offensive language, and can be practiced at any time, not just during Ramadan.

forenoon, duha

ضُحًى

أَصْبَحَتْ صَلاةُ الضُّحى جُزْءًا مِنَ الرّوتينِ اليَوْمِيِّ لِلْعَديدِ مِنَ المُوَظَّفينَ في دُبَيّ.

Duha prayer has become part of the daily routine for many employees in Dubai.

noon, dhuhr

ظُهْر

أَشارَتِ التَّقاريرُ إلى زِيادَةٍ في أَعْدادِ النّاسِ الَّذينَ يُؤَدّونَ صَلاةَ الظُّهْرِ في المَساجِدِ بَعْدَ تَخْفيفِ القُيودِ.

Reports indicate an increase in the number of people performing Dhuhr prayer in mosques after the easing of restrictions.

evening, isha

عِشاءٌ

أَكَّدَتِ اللَّجْنَةُ الدّينِيَّةُ أَنَّ صَلاةَ العِشاءِ تُعْتَبَرُ جُزْءًا مُهِمًّا مِنَ الفَعالِيّاتِ الدّينِيَّةِ خِلالَ رَمَضانَ.

The religious committee confirmed that the Isha prayer is an important part of religious activities during Ramadan.

afternoon, asr

عَصْرٌ

أَعْلَنَتِ الحُكومَةُ عَنْ تَغْييرِ مَواقيتِ صَلاةِ العَصْرِ في الفَتْرَةِ الصَّيْفِيّةِ لِلْمُحافَظَةِ عَلى الطّاقَةِ.

The government announced a change in the timing of Asr prayers in the summer to conserve energy.

major ablution, ghusl

غُسْلٌ

أَصْدَرَتِ اللَّجْنَةُ الدّينِيَّةُ تَوْجيهاتٍ جَديدَةً حَوْلَ غُسْلِ الجَنابَةِ لِلْحُجّاجِ القادِمينَ هَذا العامَ.

The religious committee issued new guidelines on major ablution (ghusl) for pilgrims arriving this year.

dawn, fajr

فَجْر

شَهِدَتِ المَساجِدُ حُضورًا مُكَثَّفًا لِأَداءِ صَلاةِ الفَجْرِ خِلالَ العَشْرِ الأَواخِرِ مِنْ رَمَضانَ.

Mosques have witnessed a high attendance for the Fajr prayer during the last ten days of Ramadan.

obligation, fard

فَرْضٌ • فُرُوضٌ

أَكَّدَتِ المُنَظَّماتُ الدِّينِيَّةُ عَلَى أَهَمِّيَّةِ الفُرُوضِ الإِسْلامِيَّةِ في بِناءِ شَخْصِيَّةِ المُسْلِمِ.

Religious organizations emphasized the importance of Islamic obligations (fard) in building a Muslim's character.

> فَرْضٌ often specifically denotes the five obligatory daily prayers but can apply to any compulsory act of worship or conduct in Islam.

direction, qibla

قِبْلَةٌ

في الوَقْتِ الَّذي يُؤَدّي فيه المُسْلِمونَ الصَّلاةَ في أَيِّ مَكانٍ حَوْلَ العالَمِ، يَتَّجِهونَ نَحْوَ القِبْلَةِ، وَهيَ الكَعْبَةُ في مَكَّةَ.

While Muslims are performing their prayers anywhere in the world, they face the Qibla, which is the Kaaba in Mecca.

there is no god but God

لا إِلَهَ إِلّا اللهُ

أُطْلِقَتْ حَمْلَةٌ تَوْعِيَةٍ جَديدَةٌ تَحْتَ شِعارِ لا إِلَهَ إِلّا اللهُ لِتَعْزيزِ الوَحْدَةِ الإِسْلامِيَّةِ.

A new awareness campaign was launched under the slogan "There is no god but God" to promote Islamic unity.

as God wills, God willing

ما شاءَ اللهُ

زَرَعَ مَشْروعُ ما شاءَ اللهُ أَلْفَ شَجَرَةٍ في المَناطِقِ الصَّحْراوِيَّةِ لِمُكافَحَةِ التَّصَحُّرِ.

The "As God Wills" project planted a thousand trees in desert areas to combat desertification.

> The phrase ما شاءَ اللهُ is commonly used when admiring something beautiful or impressive, to acknowledge that all things occur by the will of God and to ward off envy or the 'evil eye.' In Muslim culture, saying ما شاءَ اللهُ when giving compliments is a practice to prevent harm caused by jealousy, as it is believed that envy can lead to misfortune.

prayer beads

مِسْبَحَةٌ • مَسابِحُ

تَزايَدَ اسْتِخْدامُ المِسْبَحَةِ في أَوْساطِ الشَّبابِ كَوَسيلَةٍ لِلتَّأَمُّلِ وَالذِّكْرِ.

The use of prayer beads is increasing among young people as a means of meditation and remembrance.

مَغْرِبٌ

sunset, maghrib

في رَمَضانَ، يُفْطِرُ المُسْلِمونَ عِنْدَ أَذانِ المَغْرِبِ.

In Ramadan, Muslims break their fast at the call to prayer for Maghrib.

نافِلَةٌ • نَوافِلُ

supererogatory, nafilah

أَطْلَقَتِ الجَمْعِيّاتُ الدّينِيَّةُ بَرْنامَجًا لِتَعْليمِ النَّوافِلِ وَأَهَمِّيَّتِها في الحَياةِ اليَوْمِيَّةِ.

Religious associations launched a program to teach supererogatory prayers (nafilah) and their importance in daily life.

نِيَّةٌ • نَوايا / نِيّاتٌ

intention, niyyah

قَبْلَ الصَّوْمِ في شَهْرِ رَمَضانَ، يَجِبُ عَلى المُسْلِمينَ أَنْ يَجْعَلوا نِيَّتَهُمْ لِلصَّوْمِ في قُلوبِهِمْ.

Before fasting in the month of Ramadan, Muslims must make their intention to fast in their hearts.

وِرْدٌ • أَوْرادٌ

set portion of dhikr, wird

تَمَّ تَوْزيعُ وِرْدٍ لِلذِّكْرِ عَلى المُشاركينَ في المُؤْتَمَرِ الإِسْلامِيِّ السَّنَوِيِّ.

A set portion of dhikr (wird) was distributed to participants in the annual Islamic conference.

وُضوءٌ

(partial) ablution

دَعَتِ الوِزارَةُ المَعْنِيَّةُ بِالشُّؤونِ الدّينِيَّةِ المُواطِنينَ إِلى أَداءِ الوُضوءِ بِطَريقَةٍ صَحيحَةٍ لِضَمانِ صَلاةٍ مَقْبولَةٍ.

The ministry responsible for religious affairs urged citizens to perform ablution correctly to ensure an acceptable prayer.

8.4.2.1 Mini-Articles

Track **68**

في احْتِفالِيَّةٍ بَهيجَةٍ، كُرِّمَ حاجٌّ مُسِنٌّ لِأَدائِهِ فَريضَةَ الحَجِّ لِلْمَرَّةِ العاشِرَةِ. بَدَأَ الحَفْلُ بِأَذانِ الظُّهْرِ وَتِلاوَةِ آياتٍ مِنْ سورَةِ الحَجِّ. بَعْدَ الصَّلاةِ، أَلْقى الحاجُّ دُعاءً مُؤَثِّرًا شَكَرَ فيهِ اللهَ وَتَحَدَّثَ عَنْ أَهَمِّيَّةِ الرُّكْنِ الخامِسِ مِنْ أَرْكانِ الإِسْلامِ وَالنِّيَّةِ الخالِصَةِ لِلْعِبادَةِ.

In a joyful celebration, an elderly pilgrim was honored for performing the Hajj for the tenth time. The ceremony began with the Dhuhr call to prayer and the recitation of verses from Surah Al-Hajj. After the prayer, the pilgrim made a heartfelt supplication, thanking God and speaking about the importance of the fifth pillar of Islam and the pure intention for worship.

أَعْلَنَتْ مُؤَسَّسَةٌ خَيْرِيَّةٌ عَنْ إِطْلاقِ مُبَادَرَةٍ لِجَمْعِ الزَّكاةِ وَالصَّدَقاتِ مِنْ أَهْلِ الحَيِّ لِمُساعَدَةِ الفُقَراءِ وَالمُحْتاجِينَ. أُقِيمَ الحَدَثُ بَعْدَ صَلاةِ العِشاءِ، حَيْثُ رُفِعَ التَّكْبِيرُ وَتَمَّ تَوْزِيعُ سَجّاداتِ الصَّلاةِ في المَيْدانِ العامِّ لِيُشارِكَ المُؤْمِنُونَ في الصَّلاةِ، مُجَسِّدِينَ مَعانِيَ التَّكافُلِ الاِجْتِماعِيِّ.

A charitable organization announced the launch of an initiative to collect Zakat and Sadaqat from the local community to help the poor and needy. The event was held after the Isha prayer, where Takbir was raised and prayer mats were distributed in the public square for believers to participate in the prayer, embodying the meanings of social solidarity.

خِلالَ شَهْرِ رَمَضانَ المُبارَكِ، اسْتَضافَتْ إِحْدى الجامِعاتِ الكُبْرى مُسابَقَةً لِحِفْظِ القُرْآنِ. شَهِدَتِ المُسابَقَةُ مُشارَكَةً واسِعَةً مِنَ الطُّلّابِ الَّذِينَ تَنافَسُوا في تِلاوَةِ السُّوَرِ وَالآياتِ بَعْدَ صَلاةِ المَغْرِبِ. أُخْتُتِمَ الحَدَثُ بِتَوْزِيعِ المَسابِحِ وَسَجّاداتِ الصَّلاةِ عَلى المُشارِكِينَ، وَأُعْلِنَ عَنِ الفائِزِينَ بَعْدَ أَداءِ صَلاةِ العِشاءِ، في احْتِفالٍ بِرُوحانِيَّةِ الشَّهْرِ الكَرِيمِ.

During the blessed month of Ramadan, one of the major universities hosted a Quran memorization competition. The contest saw wide participation from students who competed in the recitation of Surahs and verses after the Maghrib prayer. The event concluded with the distribution of prayer beads and mats to the participants, and the winners were announced after the Isha prayer, celebrating the spirituality of the holy month.

8.4.2.2 Reference: The Five Pillars of Islam

Track **69**

أَرْكانُ الإِسْلامِ الخَمْسَةُ: أَساسُ الحَياةِ الإِيمانِيَّةِ لِكُلِّ مُسْلِمٍ

الإِسْلامُ دِينٌ يَقُومُ عَلى خَمْسَةِ أَرْكانٍ أَساسِيَّةٍ تُشَكِّلُ الأَساسَ لِحَياةِ كُلِّ مُسْلِمٍ، وَهِيَ مُعْتَقَداتٌ وَأَفْعالٌ يَجِبُ أَنْ يَعْمَلَ بِها المُسْلِمُونَ في حَياتِهِمِ اليَوْمِيَّةِ لِيَحْيَوْا حَياةً يَمْلَؤُها الإِيمانُ وَالعَمَلُ الصّالِحُ.

الرُّكْنُ الأَوَّلُ: الشَّهادَةُ

أَوَّلُ أَرْكانِ الإِسْلامِ هُوَ شَهادَةٌ أَنْ لا إِلَهَ إِلّا اللهُ وَأَنَّ مُحَمَّدًا رَسُولُ اللهِ. هَذِهِ الشَّهادَةُ هِيَ المَدْخَلُ إِلى الإِسْلامِ وَالَّتِي يَنْطِقُ بِها المُسْلِمُ في أَذانِ كُلِّ صَلاةٍ، وَهِيَ تَعْبِيرٌ عَنِ التَّوْحِيدِ وَالإِيمانِ الخالِصِ بِاللهِ وَرَسُولِهِ.

الرُّكْنُ الثّانِي: الصَّلاةُ

الصَّلاةُ عَمودُ الدِّينِ، وَهِيَ فَرْضٌ عَلى كُلِّ مُسْلِمٍ مُكَلَّفٍ. تُؤَدّى الصَّلاةُ خَمْسَ مَرّاتٍ فِي اليَوْمِ وَاللَّيْلَةِ، وَتَبْدَأُ بِتَكْبيرَةِ الإِحْرامِ وَتَنْتَهي بِالتَّسْليمِ. الصَّلَواتُ الخَمْسُ هِيَ: الفَجْرُ، الظُّهْرُ، العَصْرُ، المَغْرِبُ وَالعِشاءُ، وَكُلُّ صَلاةٍ تَحْتَوي عَلى رَكَعاتٍ مُحَدَّدَةٍ وَتُتْلى فيها آياتٌ مِنَ القُرْآنِ الكَريمِ.

الرُّكْنُ الثّالِثُ: الزَّكاةُ

الزَّكاةُ هِيَ الرُّكْنُ الثّالِثُ وَهِيَ حَقٌّ لِلْفُقَراءِ وَالمَساكينِ، وَواجِبَةٌ عَلى كُلِّ مُسْلِمٍ قادِرٍ، وَهِيَ تَعْبيرٌ عَنِ التَّكافُلِ الاِجْتِماعِيِّ وَالتَّطْهيرِ لِلْمالِ. تُؤْخَذُ مِنَ الأَمْوالِ بِنِسْبَةٍ مُحَدَّدَةٍ وَتُوَزَّعُ عَلى الفِئاتِ المُسْتَحِقَّةِ كَما وَرَدَ فِي القُرْآنِ.

الرُّكْنُ الرّابِعُ: الصَّوْمُ

صَوْمُ شَهْرِ رَمَضانَ هُوَ الرُّكْنُ الرّابِعُ، حَيْثُ يُمْسِكُ المُسْلِمونَ عَنِ الطَّعامِ وَالشَّرابِ وَالشَّهَواتِ مِنَ الفَجْرِ وَحَتّى غُروبِ الشَّمْسِ. الصَّوْمُ تَزْكِيَةٌ لِلنَّفْسِ وَتَعْويدٌ عَلى الصَّبْرِ وَالطّاعَةِ، وَفيهِ تَتَضاعَفُ الحَسَناتُ وَتُفْتَحُ أَبْوابُ الجَنَّةِ.

الرُّكْنُ الخامِسُ: الحَجُّ

وَأَخيرًا، الحَجُّ إِلى بَيْتِ اللهِ الحَرامِ فِي مَكَّةَ المُكَرَّمَةِ، وَهُوَ فَرْضٌ عَلى كُلِّ مُسْلِمٍ قادِرٍ مَرَّةً واحِدَةً فِي العُمْرِ. يُؤَدّي الحُجّاجُ مَناسِكَ الحَجِّ الَّتي تَبْدَأُ بِالإِحْرامِ وَتَنْتَهي بِالطَّوافِ وَالسَّعْيِ وَرَمْيِ الجَمَراتِ، وَهُوَ تَجْسيدٌ لِلْوَحْدَةِ الإِسْلامِيَّةِ وَتَذْكيرٌ بِالحَياةِ الآخِرَةِ.

هَذِهِ الأَرْكانُ الخَمْسَةُ تَجْمَعُ المُسْلِمينَ حَوْلَ أَعْمالِ العِبادَةِ وَتُعَمِّقُ شُعورَ الاِنْتِماءِ لِلْأُمَّةِ الإِسْلامِيَّةِ، وَتُذَكِّرُ بِأَهَمِّيَّةِ السَّعْيِ لِلْفَلاحِ فِي الدُّنْيا وَالآخِرَةِ.

The Five Pillars of Islam: The Foundation of Spiritual Life for Every Muslim

Islam is a religion based on five fundamental pillars that form the basis of every Muslim's life, consisting of beliefs and actions that Muslims must practice in their daily lives to lead a life filled with faith and righteous deeds.

First Pillar: The Testimony

The first pillar of Islam is the testimony that there is no god but God and that Muhammad is the messenger of God. This testimony is the entry into Islam and is pronounced by a Muslim in the call to prayer for each Salah; it is an expression of monotheism and sincere faith in God and His messenger.

Second Pillar: The Prayer

Prayer is the pillar of the religion, and it is obligatory for every accountable Muslim. The prayers are performed five times a day and night, starting with the Takbirat al-Ihram and ending with Taslim. The five daily prayers are: Fajr, Dhuhr, Asr, Maghrib, and Isha, each containing a specific number of units and in which verses from the Holy Quran are recited.

Third Pillar: Almsgiving (Zakat)

Zakat is the third pillar and is a right for the poor and needy, obligatory for every capable Muslim, expressing social solidarity and purification of wealth. It is taken from the wealth at a specified rate and distributed to the deserving categories as stated in the Quran.

Fourth Pillar: Fasting

Fasting the month of Ramadan is the fourth pillar, where Muslims abstain from food, drink, and desires from dawn until sunset. Fasting is a purification for the soul, accustoming to patience and obedience, where rewards are multiplied, and the gates of paradise are opened.

Fifth Pillar: The Pilgrimage (Hajj)

Lastly, the Hajj to the Sacred House of God in Mecca is obligatory for every capable Muslim once in a lifetime. The pilgrims perform the rituals of Hajj that start with Ihram and end with Tawaf, Sa'i, and the stoning of the Jamarat, embodying Islamic unity and a reminder of the hereafter.

These five pillars bring Muslims together around acts of worship, deepen the sense of belonging to the Islamic nation, and remind of the importance of striving for success in this world and the hereafter.

8.4.3 The Mosque and Its Components

Track **70**

imam   أَئِمَّةٌ •   إِمامٌ

أَعْلَنَ الإمامُ الشَّيْخُ مُحَمَّد عَبْد الكَريم عَنْ سِلْسِلَةٍ مِنَ الخُطَبِ التَّعْليميَّةِ حَوْلَ البيئَةِ.

Imam Sheikh Mohammed Abd Al-Karim announced a series of educational sermons about the environment.

(large) mosque   جَوامِعُ •   جامِعٌ

انْخَرَطَتْ جَوامِعُ المَدينَةِ في حَمَلاتٍ تَوْعِيَةٍ لِمُكافَحَةِ الفَقْرِ والجَهْلِ.

The mosques in the city have engaged in awareness campaigns to combat poverty and ignorance.

جامِعٌ (also commonlly known as مَسْجِدٌ جامِعٌ) refers to a type of mosque that is larger and often used for community gatherings, especially for Friday prayers. The word جامِعٌ stems from the root for 'gathering' or 'collecting.' This type of mosque is often the site for major religious gatherings, educational activities, and community events, distinguishing it from smaller, neighborhood mosques.

		خُطْبَةٌ
sermon	خُطَبٌ •	

تَنَاوَلَتْ خُطْبَةُ الجُمُعَةِ الأَخِيرَةِ مَوْضُوعَ العُنْفِ المُجْتَمَعِيِّ وَأَهَمِّيَّةَ السَّلَامِ.

Last Friday's sermon addressed the issue of social violence and the importance of peace.

		خَطِيبٌ
preacher	خُطَبَاءُ •	

أَثَارَ خَطِيبٌ مَعْرُوفٌ تَسَاؤُلَاتٍ حَوْلَ الدَّوْرِ الِاجْتِمَاعِيِّ لِلْمَسْجِدِ فِي خُطْبَةِ الجُمُعَةِ.

A well-known preacher raised questions about the social role of the mosque in his Friday sermon.

		صَلَاةُ جَمَاعَةٍ
congregational prayer	صَلَوَاتٌ •	

أُقِيمَتْ فِي الجَامِعِ الكَبِيرِ بِالْقَاهِرَةِ صَلَاةُ جَمَاعَةٍ لِلتَّضَامُنِ مَعَ ضَحَايا الكَوَارِثِ الطَّبِيعِيَّةِ.

A congregational prayer was held at the Grand Mosque in Cairo to show solidarity with the victims of natural disasters.

	مُؤَذِّنٌ
prayer caller, muazzin	

تَمَّ تَعْيِينُ مُؤَذِّنٍ جَدِيدٍ فِي المَسْجِدِ النَّبَوِيِّ بِالمَدِينَةِ المُنَوَّرَةِ، وَهُوَ يَتَمَتَّعُ بِصَوْتٍ رَائِعٍ.

A new muazzin with a wonderful voice has been appointed at the Prophet's Mosque in Medina.

		مِئْذَنَةٌ
minaret	مَآذِنُ •	

اِنْتَهَتْ أَعْمَالُ البِنَاءِ لِمِئْذَنَةٍ جَدِيدَةٍ تُضَافُ إلى مَعَالِمِ مَدِينَةِ جَدَّةَ الدِّينِيَّةِ.

Construction was completed on a new minaret that adds to the religious landmarks of the city of Jeddah.

		مِحْرَابٌ
prayer niche, mihrab	مَحَارِيبُ •	

وَقَعَ الِاخْتِيَارُ عَلَى مِحْرَابِ مَسْجِدِ السُّلْطَانِ أَحْمَد فِي إِسْطَنْبُولَ ضِمْنَ أَجْمَلِ المَحَارِيبِ الإِسْلَامِيَّةِ عَالَمِيًّا.

The mihrab of the Sultan Ahmed Mosque in Istanbul was selected among the most beautiful Islamic mihrabs worldwide.

		مَسْجِدٌ
mosque, masjid	مَسَاجِدُ •	

تَمَّ افْتِتَاحُ مَسْجِدٍ جَدِيدٍ فِي عَمَّانَ يَتَّسِعُ لِأَكْثَرَ مِنْ خَمْسَةِ آلَافِ مُصَلٍّ.

A new mosque that can accommodate more than five thousand worshippers was inaugurated in Amman.

The difference between مَسْجِدٌ and جامِعٌ is primarily in their functions and size. Every جامِعٌ, which is a larger mosque designed for community gatherings, qualifies as a مَسْجِدٌ, but not every مَسْجِدٌ qualifies as a جامِعٌ. A مَسْجِدٌ is generally smaller and is used for the daily five prayers. However, the Friday prayer, which requires a larger gathering, is specifically held in a جامِعٌ.

pulpit, minbar   مَنابِرُ •   مِنْبَرٌ

تَجَدَّدَتِ الدَّعَواتُ لِتَرْميمِ المَنابِرِ القَديمَةِ في مَساجِدِ العِراقِ لِلْحِفاظِ عَلى التُّراثِ الإِسْلاميِّ.

Calls have been renewed to restore the old pulpits (minbars) in the mosques of Iraq to preserve Islamic heritage.

8.4.3.1 Mini-Articles

Track 71

في قَلْبِ مَدينَةِ مَراكِشَ المَغْرِبِيَّةِ، شَهِدَ جامِعُ الكُتُبِيَّةِ تَجْديداتٍ مُبْهِرَةً أَعادَتْ إِلَيْهِ رَوْنَقَهُ التّاريخِيَّ. تَمَّ تَرْميمُ المِحْرابِ بِحِرَفِيَّةٍ عالِيَةٍ، مَعَ المُحافَظَةِ عَلى الزَّخارِفِ الإِسْلامِيَّةِ الأَصيلَةِ. كَما تَمَّ تَحْديثُ المِنْبَرِ لِيَتَواكَبَ مَعَ العَصْرِ، مَعَ الاِحْتِفاظِ بِروحِهِ التَّقْليدِيَّةِ. يَشْتَهِرُ الجامِعُ بِخُطَبِهِ المُؤَثِّرَةِ الَّتي يُلْقيها خُطَباؤُهُ البارِزونَ، وَيُعْتَبَرُ مَكانًا روحِيًّا مُهِمًّا في المَدينَةِ.

In the heart of Marrakech, Morocco, the Koutoubia Mosque has witnessed stunning renovations that have restored its historical charm. The mihrab has been expertly restored, maintaining the authentic Islamic decorations. Additionally, the pulpit has been updated to keep pace with the times while retaining its traditional spirit. The mosque is famous for its impactful sermons delivered by prominent preachers and is considered an important spiritual place in the city.

يَقَعُ مَسْجِدُ الفِرْدَوْسِ في مَدينَةِ الدَّمّامِ، وَهُوَ مَعْروفٌ بِالتَّنَوُّعِ الثَّقافِيِّ لِمُصَلّيهِ. يَأْتي المُصَلّونَ مِنْ مُخْتَلِفِ الجِنْسِيّاتِ لِأَداءِ صَلاةِ الجَماعَةِ، مِمّا يَجْعَلُهُ مِثالًا رائِعًا لِلْوَحْدَةِ وَالتَّناغُمِ في الإِسْلامِ. الإِمامُ، المَعْروفُ بِحِكْمَتِهِ وَفَهْمِهِ العَميقِ لِلدّينِ، يَقودُ الصَّلاةَ بِصَوْتِهِ العَذْبِ، مِمّا يُعَزِّزُ الشُّعورَ بِالسَّكينَةِ وَالإِخاءِ بَيْنَ المُصَلّينَ. كَما يَضُمُّ المَسْجِدُ مِئْذَنَةً عالِيَةً تُمَثِّلُ مَعْلَمًا بارِزًا في المَدينَةِ، حَيْثُ يَرْتَفِعُ الأَذانُ مِنْها خَمْسَ مَرّاتٍ يَوْمِيًّا.

The Firdaws Mosque, located in Dammam, is known for its culturally diverse congregation. Worshippers of different nationalities come to perform the congregational prayer, making it a wonderful example of unity and harmony in Islam. The Imam, known for his wisdom and deep understanding of the religion, leads the prayers with his melodious voice, enhancing the sense of tranquility and brotherhood among the worshippers. The mosque also has a tall minaret that stands as a prominent landmark in the city, from where the call to prayer resonates five times a day.

مَسْجِدُ الحُسَيْنِ في قَلْبِ القاهِرَةِ، مِصْرَ، يُعْتَبَرُ مِنَ المَعالِمِ الدّينِيَّةِ المُهِمَّةِ في المَدينَةِ. بَعْدَ التَّجْديداتِ الأَخيرَةِ، أَصْبَحَ المَسْجِدُ يَجْمَعُ بَيْنَ الجَمالِ الكلاسيكيِّ وَالحَداثَةِ، مَعَ مِحْرابٍ مُزَخْرَفٍ بِدِقَّةٍ وَمِنْبَرٍ حَديثٍ. يَشْهَدُ المَسْجِدُ حُضورًا كَبيرًا في صَلاةِ الجُمُعَةِ، حَيْثُ يَجْذِبُ خُطَباؤُهُ المَعْروفونَ بِخُطَبِهِمِ القَوِيَّةِ الجَماهيرَ مِنْ مُخْتَلِفِ أَنْحاءِ المَدينَةِ.

The Al-Hussein Mosque in the heart of Cairo, Egypt, is considered one of the important religious landmarks in the city. Following recent renovations, the mosque now combines classic beauty with modernity, featuring a precisely decorated mihrab and a modern pulpit. The mosque witnesses a large attendance for Friday prayers, attracting crowds from all over the city with its well-known preachers and their powerful sermons.

8.4.4 Ramadan and Fasting

Track **72**

to break fast — إِفْطار • أَفْطَرَ

يُفْطِرُ النّاسُ في مَساجِدِ المَدينَةِ عَلَى التُّمورِ وَالماءِ عِنْدَ الغُروبِ.

People break their fast in the city's mosques with dates and water at sunset.

breaking fast, iftar — إِفْطارٌ

أَعْلَنَتْ وِزارَةُ الشُّؤونِ الدّينِيَّةِ أَنَّ الإِفْطارَ سَيَكونُ في تَمامِ السّاعَةِ 7:00 مَساءً بِالتَّوْقيتِ المَحَلِّيِّ.

The Ministry of Religious Affairs announced that breaking the fast will be exactly at 7:00 PM local time.

abstaining — إِمْساكٌ

في شَهْرِ رَمَضانَ، يَجِبُ عَلَى المُسْلِمينَ الإِمْساكُ عَنِ الطَّعامِ وَالشَّرابِ مِنْ طُلوعِ الفَجْرِ حَتَّى غُروبِ الشَّمْسِ.

In the month of Ramadan, Muslims must abstain from food and drink from dawn until sunset.

religious retreat, i'tikaf — اِعْتِكافٌ

أَعْلَنَ الجامِعُ الكَبيرُ بِالرِّياضِ عَنْ مَواعيدِ الاِعْتِكافِ لِلْعَشْرِ الأَواخِرِ مِنْ رَمَضانَ.

The Grand Mosque in Riyadh announced the schedule for i'tikaf during the last ten days of Ramadan.

تَّراويحُ
pl.

tarawih prayers

تَجْري اسْتِعْداداتٌ كَبيرَةٌ في المَسْجِدِ النَّبَويِّ لِصَلاةِ التَّراويحِ المُرْتَقَبَةِ هَذا العامَ.

Extensive preparations are underway at the Prophet's Mosque for the anticipated Tarawih prayers this year.

تَّهَجُّدٌ

night prayer, tahajjud

يُشَجِّعُ عُلَماءُ الدّينِ عَلى أَداءِ صَلاةِ التَّهَجُّدِ في اللَّيالي الأَخيرَةِ مِنْ رَمَضانَ.

Religious scholars are encouraging the performance of Tahajjud prayers on the last nights of Ramadan.

رَمَضانُ

Ramadan

شَهِدَتِ القاهِرَةُ ظُهورَ هِلالِ رَمَضانَ وَسَطَ احْتِفالاتٍ شَعْبِيَّةٍ.

Cairo witnessed the sighting of the Ramadan crescent amid public celebrations.

سُحورٌ

pre-dawn meal, suhoor

تُواصِلُ الأُسَرُ السُّعودِيَّةُ تَقْديمَ السُّحورِ في جَوٍّ مِنَ الأُلْفَةِ والإيمانِ.

Saudi families continue to serve Suhoor in an atmosphere of affection and faith.

صامَ
• صِيامٌ / صَوْمٌ

to fast

نَشَرَتْ وِزارَةُ الصِّحَّةِ تَوْجيهاتٍ لِلَّذينَ يَصومونَ في رَمَضانَ لِلْحِفاظِ عَلى صِحَّتِهِمْ.

The Ministry of Health published guidelines for those who fast during Ramadan to maintain their health.

فِدْيَةٌ
• فِدْياتٌ / فِدًى

expiation, fidya

تَذْكيرٌ لِلْمُسْلِمينَ بِإِمْكانِيَّةِ دَفْعِ الفِدْيَةِ في حالَةِ عَدَمِ القُدْرَةِ عَلى الصِّيامِ.

A reminder to Muslims about the possibility of paying fidya in case they are unable to fast.

لَيْلَةُ القَدْرِ

Night of Power

اِحْتَفَلَ النّاسُ في مَكَّةَ المُكَرَّمَةِ بِلَيْلَةِ القَدْرِ بِأَداءِ الصَّلَواتِ والدُّعاءِ.

People in Mecca celebrated the Night of Decree by performing prayers and supplications.

> In English, لَيْلَةُ القَدْرِ may also be known as Night of Destiny, Precious Night, Night Of Decree, or Night of Determination.

لَيْلَةُ رُؤْيَةٍ
night of sighting

أَشَارَ المَرْصَدُ الفَلَكِيُّ إلى أَنَّ لَيْلَةَ رُؤْيَةِ الهِلالِ سَتَكونُ في الثَّلاثينَ مِنْ شَعْبَانَ.

The astronomical observatory indicated that the night of the moon sighting would be on the thirtieth of Sha'ban.

مِدْفَعُ إِفْطارٍ • مَدافِعُ
iftar cannon

أُطْلِقَ مِدْفَعُ الإِفْطارِ في مَدينَةِ دُبَيّ عِنْدَ الغُروبِ، مُعْلِنًا بَدْءَ وَقْتِ الإِفْطارِ.

The iftar cannon was fired in Dubai at sunset, announcing the start of the iftar time.

هِلالُ رَمَضانَ • أَهِلَّةٌ
Ramadan crescent

تَمَّ رَصْدُ هِلالِ رَمَضانَ في الرِّياضِ، وَأَعْلَنَتِ السُّلُطاتُ أَنَّ الشَّهْرَ الفَضيلَ سَيَبْدَأُ غَدًا.

The Ramadan crescent was sighted in Riyadh, and authorities announced that the holy month will begin tomorrow.

8.4.4.1 Mini-Articles

Track **73**

في رَمَضانَ هَذا العَامِ، شَهِدَ مَسْجِدَ الشَّيْخِ زايِد في الإماراتِ تَجْرِبَةً روحانِيَّةً عَميقَةً، حَيْثُ اعْتَكَفَ العَديدُ مِنَ المُصَلّينَ طيلَةَ الشَّهْرِ الكَريمِ. كانَتْ لَيْلَةُ القَدْرِ أَبْرَزَ اللَّيالي، حَيْثُ قَضى المُعْتَكِفونَ الوَقْتَ في التَّهَجُّدِ وَالدُّعاءِ. بَدَأَتِ الأَيّامُ بالسُّحورِ الجَماعِيِّ قَبْلَ الإِمْساكِ، وَاخْتُتِمَتْ بِصَلاةِ التَّراويحِ الَّتي أَضْفَتْ جَوًّا مِنَ الخُشوعِ وَالسَّكينَةِ.

In Ramadan this year, Sheikh Zayed Mosque in the UAE witnessed a profound spiritual experience, as many worshippers spent the entire holy month in seclusion. The Night of Decree was the highlight, with those in seclusion spending time in night prayer and supplication. The days began with communal pre-dawn meals before fasting and ended with Tarawih prayers, adding an atmosphere of devotion and tranquility.

في مِصْرَ، أَطْلَقَتْ مَجْموعَةٌ مِنَ المُتَطَوِّعينَ مُبادَرَةً لِتَوْزيعِ وَجَباتِ الإِفْطارِ خِلالَ شَهْرِ رَمَضانَ عَلى الأُسَرِ المُحْتاجَةِ. وَشارَكَ في المُبادَرَةِ الأَشْخاصُ الَّذينَ لا يَسْتَطيعونَ الصِّيامَ وَيَرْغَبونَ في دَفْعِ فِدْيَةِ الإِفْطارِ. تُعَدُّ هَذِهِ المُبادَرَةُ تَجْسيدًا لِروحِ التَّكافُلِ وَالتَّعاطُفِ في شَهْرِ الصِّيامِ.

In Egypt, a group of volunteers launched an initiative to distribute iftar meals during Ramadan to needy families. Individuals unable to observe fasting actively and who wish to pay the fasting ransom participated in the initiative. This initiative embodies the spirit of solidarity and compassion in the fasting month.

في الأُرْدُنِّ، يَحْتَفِلُ المُسْلِمُونَ بِشَكْلٍ خاصٍّ بِلَيْلَةِ رُؤْيَةِ هِلالِ رَمَضانَ. تَتَزَيَّنُ الشَّوارِعُ وَالمَساجِدُ اسْتِعْدادًا لِاسْتِقْبالِ الشَّهْرِ الفَضيلِ. يُطْلَقُ مِدْفَعُ الإِفْطارِ إيذانًا بِبِدايَةِ الشَّهْرِ، وَتَتَلَأْلَأُ الأَسْواقُ بِالزِّينَةِ وَالفَوانيسِ. يَشْتَهِرُ الأُرْدُنِّيُّونَ بِتَنْظيمِ مَوائِدِ الرَّحْمَنِ، حَيْثُ يَجْتَمِعُ النّاسُ لِتَناوُلِ الإِفْطارِ جَماعِيًّا، مُعَبِّرينَ عَنِ الأُخُوَّةِ وَالوَحْدَةِ في هَذا الشَّهْرِ المُبارَكِ.

In Jordan, Muslims celebrate the sighting of the Ramadan crescent in a special way. Streets and mosques are adorned in preparation for the holy month. The iftar cannon is fired to mark the start of the month, and markets glitter with decorations and lanterns. Jordanians are known for organizing 'Ma'idat Al-Rahman,' where people gather to break their fast collectively, expressing brotherhood and unity in this blessed month.

في تونُسَ، أَطْلَقَتْ وِزارَةُ الصِّحَّةِ حَمْلَةً تَوْعَوِيَّةً حَوْلَ أَهَمِّيَّةِ الصِّيامِ الصِّحّيِّ خِلالَ شَهْرِ رَمَضانَ. تُرَكِّزُ الحَمْلَةُ عَلى تَثْقيفِ الصّائِمينَ حَوْلَ أَهَمِّيَّةِ تَجَنُّبِ الأَطْعِمَةِ غَيْرِ الصِّحِّيَّةِ، وَأَهَمِّيَّةِ تَناوُلِ الإِفْطارِ المُتَوازِنِ. أُقيمَتْ فَعالِيّاتٌ في مُخْتَلِفِ المُدُنِ، مَعَ التَّأْكيدِ عَلى أَهَمِّيَّةِ السُّحورِ كَوَجْبَةٍ أَساسِيَّةٍ لِلْحِفاظِ عَلى النَّشاطِ وَالحَيَوِيَّةِ طَوالَ يَوْمِ الصِّيامِ.

In Tunisia, the Ministry of Health launched an awareness campaign about the importance of healthy fasting during Ramadan. The campaign focuses on educating fasters about avoiding unhealthy foods and the importance of a balanced iftar. Events were held in various cities, emphasizing the importance of the pre-dawn meal as a vital part of maintaining energy and vitality throughout the fasting day.

في مَدينَةِ الرِّباطِ المَغْرِبِيَّةِ، يُحْتَفَلُ بِلَيْلَةِ القَدْرِ بِتَقْديرٍ وَاحْتِفاءٍ خاصٍّ. يَتِمُّ تَزْيينُ المَساجِدِ وَالشَّوارِعِ بِالفَوانيسِ وَالزَّخارِفِ الإِسْلامِيَّةِ. يَقومُ المُؤَذِّنونَ بِالتَّكْبيرِ وَالتَّهْليلِ في الأَذانِ وَالإِقامَةِ، مُعْلِنينَ دُخولَ وَقْتِ الصَّلاةِ. تُصَلّى صَلاةُ التَّراويحِ بِحُضورٍ كَبيرٍ، وَتُقامُ حَلَقاتُ الذِّكْرِ وَالدُّعاءِ. يُشارِكُ النّاسُ في أَداءِ الصَّدَقاتِ وَالأَعْمالِ الخَيْرِيَّةِ، مُتَّخِذينَ مِنْ هَذِهِ اللَّيْلَةِ فُرْصَةً لِلتَّقَرُّبِ إِلى اللهِ وَكَسْبِ الثَّوابِ.

In the Moroccan city of Rabat, the Night of Decree is celebrated with special appreciation and festivity. Mosques and streets are adorned with lanterns and Islamic decorations. Muezzins perform takbeer and tahleel in the call to prayer and the iqamah, announcing the time for prayer. Tarawih prayer is performed with large attendance, and circles of remembrance and supplication are held. People participate in giving alms and charitable acts, using this night as an opportunity to draw closer to God and earn rewards.

التَّعامُلُ مَعَ تَحَدِّياتِ الصِّيامِ الصِّحِّيِّ في حَرارَةِ الصَّيْفِ القَطَرِيِّ

في قَطَرَ، حَيْثُ تَرْتَفِعُ دَرَجاتُ الحَرارَةِ بِشَكْلٍ مَلْحوظٍ خِلالَ شَهْرِ رَمَضانَ، تُطْلِقُ وِزارَةُ الصِّحَّةِ القَطَرِيَّةُ حَمْلَةً تَوْعَوِيَّةً حَوْلَ أَهَمِّيَّةِ الحِفاظِ عَلى الصِّحَّةِ وَالتَّغْذِيَةِ السَّليمَةِ خِلالَ الصِّيامِ. يُواجِهُ الصّائِمونَ تَحَدِّياتٍ خاصَّةً في ظِلِّ الحَرارَةِ الشَّديدَةِ، خاصَّةً عِنْدَما يَمْتَنِعونَ عَنِ الأَكْلِ وَالشُّرْبِ مِنَ الفَجْرِ حَتّى المَغْرِبِ.

تُرَكِّزُ الحَمْلَةُ عَلى التَّوْعِيَةِ بِأَهَمِّيَّةِ التَّغْذِيَةِ السَّليمَةِ خِلالَ وَجْبَتَي الإِفْطارِ وَالسُّحورِ. كَما تُشَدِّدُ عَلى أَهَمِّيَّةِ تَناوُلِ وَجْبَةِ سُحورٍ مُتَوازِنَةٍ تَشْمَلُ الأَطْعِمَةَ الغَنِيَّةَ بِالماءِ وَالأَلْيافِ لِمُساعَدَةِ الجِسْمِ عَلى البَقاءِ رَطْبًا خِلالَ ساعاتِ الصِّيامِ.

تُنْصَحُ العائِلاتُ بِتَجَنُّبِ الأَطْعِمَةِ الثَّقيلَةِ وَالدُّهْنِيَّةِ وَتَشْجيعِ تَناوُلِ الإِفْطارِ الَّذي يَحْتَوي عَلى الفَواكِهِ وَالخَضْراواتِ. يُمْنَحُ تَوْجيهٌ خاصٌّ حَوْلَ تَناوُلِ كَمِّيّاتٍ كافِيَةٍ مِنَ الماءِ خِلالَ اللَّيْلِ لِضَمانِ البَقاءِ رَطْبًا خِلالَ النَّهارِ.

في المَساجِدِ، يُقامُ بَرْنامَجٌ تَوْعَوِيٌّ بَعْدَ صَلاةِ التَّراويحِ يُسَمّى "الصِّحَّةَ في رَمَضانَ"، يَتِمُّ فيهِ اسْتِضافَةُ أَطِبّاءَ وَخُبَراءِ تَغْذِيَةٍ لِتَقْديمِ نَصائِحَ حَوْلَ الصِّيامِ الصِّحِّيِّ وَكَيْفِيَّةِ التَّعامُلِ مَعَ حَرارَةِ الصَّيْفِ. يُشَجِّعُ البَرْنامَجُ أَيْضًا عَلى المُشارَكَةِ في الأَنْشِطَةِ البَدَنِيَّةِ الخَفيفَةِ بَعْدَ الإِفْطارِ.

تُسَلِّطُ هَذِهِ الحَمْلَةُ الضَّوْءَ عَلى الجُهودِ المَبْذولَةِ لِتَوْعِيَةِ الصّائِمينَ في قَطَرَ بِأَهَمِّيَّةِ الاعْتِناءِ بِصِحَّتِهِمْ خِلالَ رَمَضانَ، مَعَ التَّرْكيزِ عَلى التَّحَدِّياتِ الخاصَّةِ الَّتي يَفْرِضُها الطَّقْسُ الحارُّ. تَعْكِسُ الحَمْلَةُ الْتِزامَ الدَّوْلَةِ بِالتَّوْعِيَةِ بِالرِّعايَةِ الصِّحِّيَّةِ لِكُلٍّ مِنَ السُّكّانِ المَحَلِّيِّينَ وَالمُقيمينَ.

Dealing with the Challenges of Healthy Fasting in the Qatari Summer Heat

In Qatar, where temperatures are soaring significantly during the month of Ramadan, the Qatari Ministry of Health is launching an awareness campaign about the importance of maintaining health and proper nutrition during fasting. Fasters face special challenges in the intense heat, especially when abstaining from food and drink from dawn to dusk.

The campaign focuses on raising awareness of the importance of proper nutrition during the meals of Iftar and Suhoor. It emphasizes the importance of having a balanced Suhoor meal that includes foods rich in water and fiber to help the body stay hydrated during fasting hours.

Families are advised to avoid heavy, fatty foods and to encourage the consumption of Iftar that includes fruits and vegetables. Special guidance is given on drinking sufficient amounts of water at night to ensure staying hydrated during the day.

In mosques, an awareness program called 'Health in Ramadan' is held after the Tarawih prayers. It hosts doctors and nutrition experts to provide tips on healthy fasting and how to deal with summer heat. The program also encourages participation in light physical activities after Iftar.

This campaign highlights the efforts made to educate fasters in Qatar about the importance of taking care of their health during Ramadan, focusing on the special challenges posed by the hot weather. The campaign reflects the state's commitment to raising awareness about healthcare for both local residents and expatriates.

8.4.5 Islamic Holidays

Track **75**

أُضْحِيَّةٌ • أَضَاحٍ

sacrifice

قَامَتْ جَمْعِيَّاتٌ خَيْرِيَّةٌ بِتَوْزِيعِ لُحومِ الأَضَاحِي عَلَى الفُقَرَاءِ في عِيدِ الأَضْحَى.

Charitable associations distributed the meat of the sacrifices to the poor on Eid al-Adha.

إِسْرَاءٌ وَمِعْرَاجٌ

Israa and Mi'raj

اِحْتَفَلَ المُسْلِمونَ في الأُرْدُنِّ بِذِكْرى الإِسْرَاءِ وَالمِعْرَاجِ بِالصَّلاةِ وَالدُّعاءِ.

Muslims in Jordan celebrated the anniversary of the Israa and Mi'raj with prayers and supplications.

المَوْلِدُ النَّبَوِيُّ الشَّرِيفُ • مَوالِدُ

prophet's birthday

سَيَكونُ هُناكَ فَعالِيّاتٌ مُتَعَدِّدَةٌ لِلاِحْتِفالِ بِالمَوْلِدِ النَّبَوِيِّ الشَّرِيفِ في مِصْرَ.

There will be multiple events to celebrate the Prophet's Birthday in Egypt.

النِّصْفُ مِنْ شَعْبانَ

mid-Sha'ban

تَجْري التَّحْضِيراتُ في المَمْلَكَةِ العَرَبِيَّةِ السُّعودِيَّةِ لِاسْتِقْبالِ النِّصْفِ مِنْ شَعْبانَ وَالاِحْتِفالِ بِهِ.

Preparations are underway in Saudi Arabia to welcome and celebrate mid-Sha'ban.

ذَبَحَ • ذَبْحٌ

to sacrifice, slaughter

يَقومُ النّاسُ بِذَبْحِ الأَضاحِي في صَباحِ عيدِ الأَضْحى بَعْدَ صَلاةِ العيدِ.

People slaughter the sacrifices on the morning of Eid al-Adha after the Eid prayer.

رَأْسُ السَّنةِ الهِجْرِيَّةِ

Islamic new year

تَسْتَعِدُّ الأُمَّةُ الإِسْلامِيَّةُ لِلاحْتِفالِ بِرَأْسِ السَّنةِ الهِجْرِيَّةِ بِالدُّعاءِ والصَّدَقاتِ.

The Islamic nation is preparing to celebrate the Islamic New Year with prayers and alms.

صَلاةُ عيدٍ • صَلَواتٌ

eid prayer

يَحْرِصُ المُسْلِمونَ عَلى أَداءِ صَلاةِ عيدِ الفِطْرِ في المَساجِدِ والسّاحاتِ العامَّةِ.

Muslims make sure to perform Eid al-Fitr prayers in mosques and public squares.

ضَحّى • تَضْحِيَةٌ

to sacrifice

يُضَحّي المُسْلِمونَ في عيدِ الأَضْحى لِلاحْتِفالِ بِذِكْرى النَّبِيِّ إِبْراهيمَ.

Muslims sacrifice during Eid al-Adha to celebrate the memory of the Prophet Ibrahim (Abraham).

عاشوراءُ

Ashura

يُحْيي الشّيعَةُ عاشوراءَ بِالصَّوْمِ وَإِقامَةِ مَجالِسِ العَزاءِ.

Shia Muslims observe Ashura by fasting and holding mourning assemblies.

عيدُ أَضْحىً • أَعْيادٌ

Eid al-Adha

قامَتْ جَمْعِيّاتٌ خَيْرِيَّةٌ بِتَوْزيعِ لُحومِ الأَضاحي عَلى الفُقَراءِ في عيدِ الأَضْحى.

Charitable associations distributed the meat of the sacrifices to the poor on Eid al-Adha.

عيدُ فِطْرٍ

Eid al-Fitr

أَعْلَنَتْ وِزارَةُ الأَوْقافِ عَنْ جَدْوَلِ النَّشاطاتِ لِعيدِ الفِطْرِ المُبارَكِ.

The Ministry of Endowments announced the schedule of activities for Eid al-Fitr.

مِعْراجٌ • مَعاريجُ

ascension, Mi'raj

أَثارَتْ قِصَّةُ المِعْراجِ إِعْجابَ الجُمْهورِ في مَهْرَجانِ الثَّقافَةِ الإِسْلامِيَّةِ.

The story of the Mi'raj captivated the audience at the Islamic Culture Festival.

‏تُناقِشُ وَرْشَةُ عَمَلٍ حَوْلَ الهِجْرَةِ النَّبَوِيَّةِ تَأْثيرَها عَلى التّاريخِ الإِسْلامِيِّ.‏

A workshop discussing the prophetic Hijrah and its impact on Islamic history is taking place.

8.4.5.1 Mini-Articles

Track **76**

‏في القاهِرَةِ، اِحْتَفَلَتِ المَدينَةُ بِالمَوْلِدِ النَّبَوِيِّ الشَّريفِ بِطَريقَةٍ فَريدَةٍ، حَيْثُ نَظَّمَتِ الحُكومَةُ المِصْرِيَّةُ مَعْرِضًا لِلْفَنِّ الإِسْلامِيِّ في قَلْبِ المَدينَةِ. شَمَلَ المَعْرِضُ لَوْحاتٍ وَمَنْحوتاتٍ تَحْكي قِصَّةَ ميلادِ النَّبِيِّ، بِالإِضافَةِ إلى فَعالِياتٍ تُراثِيَّةٍ وَثَقافِيَّةٍ تُعَرِّفُ الزُّوّارَ بِتاريخِ وَأَهَمِّيَّةِ هذا اليَوْمِ العَظيمِ.‏

In Cairo, the city celebrated the Prophet's Birthday in a unique way, with the Egyptian government organizing an exhibition of Islamic art in the heart of the city. The exhibition included paintings and sculptures depicting the story of the Prophet's Birthday, in addition to cultural and heritage activities that introduced visitors to the history and significance of this great day.

‏في الجَزائِرِ، اِعْتَمَدَتِ الحُكومَةُ هذا العامَ نَهْجًا جَديدًا في الاِحْتِفالِ بِعيدِ الأَضْحى، حَيْثُ قامَتْ بِتَنْظيمِ حَمْلَةٍ وَطَنِيَّةٍ لِذَبْحِ الأَضاحي بِطُرُقٍ صَديقَةٍ لِلْبيئَةِ. كَما شَجَّعَتِ الحَمْلَةُ عَلى تَوْزيعِ لُحومِ الأُضْحِيَّةِ عَلى الفُقَراءِ وَالمُحْتاجينَ، مُؤَكِّدَةً عَلى روحِ العَطاءِ وَالمُشارَكَةِ الَّتي يُمَثِّلُها العيدُ.‏

In Algeria, the government adopted a new approach to celebrating Eid al-Adha this year, organizing a national campaign for environmentally friendly slaughtering of sacrificial animals. The campaign also encouraged distributing the meat to the poor and needy, emphasizing the spirit of giving and sharing that the feast represents.

‏في العاصِمَةِ الأُرْدُنِّيَّةِ عَمّانَ، اِحْتَفَلَتِ الجالِياتُ المُسْلِمَةُ بِرَأْسِ السَّنَةِ الهِجْرِيَّةِ بِفَعالِياتٍ مُتَنَوِّعَةٍ تَحْتَفي بِذِكْرى الهِجْرَةِ النَّبَوِيَّةِ. نَظَّمَتِ الحُكومَةُ الأُرْدُنِّيَّةُ مَسيراتٍ وَمُحاضَراتٍ تَعْليمِيَّةً في المَساجِدِ، وَأُقيمَتْ أُمْسِياتٌ شِعْرِيَّةٌ وَموسيقِيَّةٌ تُحاكي روحَ هذِهِ المُناسَبَةِ العَظيمَةِ، مُعَبِّرَةً عَنِ الأَمَلِ وَالتَّجْديدِ الَّذي يَرْمُزُ لَهُ العامُ الهِجْرِيُّ الجَديدُ.‏

In the Jordanian capital, Amman, Muslim communities celebrated the Islamic New Year with a variety of events commemorating the Hijra. The Jordanian government organized marches and educational lectures in mosques, and evenings of poetry and music reflecting the spirit of this great occasion, expressing hope and renewal symbolized by the new Hijri year.

‏في تونُسَ، اِحْتَفَلَتِ البِلادُ بِعيدِ الفِطْرِ المُبارَكِ بِفَعالِياتٍ تُراثِيَّةٍ مُتَمَيِّزَةٍ. أُقيمَ في العاصِمَةِ تونُسَ مَهْرَجانٌ لِلْفُنونِ وَالحِرَفِ اليَدَوِيَّةِ، يَعْكِسُ التُّراثَ الثَّقافِيَّ الغَنِيَّ لِلْبِلادِ. اِمْتَلَأَتِ الشَّوارِعُ بِالزّينَةِ وَالأَنْوارِ، وَتَجَمَّعَ النّاسُ لِلصَّلاةِ وَتَبادُلِ التَّهاني، مُعَبِّرينَ عَنْ فَرْحَتِهِمْ بِانْتِهاءِ شَهْرِ رَمَضانَ المُعَظَّمِ وَبِدايَةِ شَهْرِ شَوّالٍ.‏

In Tunisia, the country celebrated the blessed Eid al-Fitr with distinctive heritage events. A festival for arts and handicrafts was held in the capital, Tunis, reflecting the rich cultural heritage of the country. The streets were filled with decorations and lights, and people gathered for prayer and exchanged greetings, expressing their joy at the end of the holy month of Ramadan and the beginning of the month of Shawwal.

In Tunisia, the country celebrated Eid al-Fitr with distinctive heritage activities. A festival of arts and crafts, reflecting the rich cultural heritage of the country, was held in the capital, Tunis. The streets were filled with decorations and lights, and people gathered for prayer and to exchange greetings, expressing their joy at the end of the holy month of Ramadan and the beginning of Shawwal.

في بَيْروتَ، لُبْنانَ، شَهِدَتِ المَدينةُ احْتِفالاتٍ مُتَنَوِّعَةً بِمُناسَبةِ يَوْمِ عاشوراءَ. اخْتَلَطَتِ الطُّقوسُ الدِّينيَّةُ بِالْفَعاليّاتِ الثَّقافيّةِ، حَيْثُ نَظَّمَتِ الجَمْعيّاتُ الخَيْريَّةُ وَالمُؤسَّساتُ الثَّقافيَّةُ سِلْسِلَةً مِنَ النَّدَواتِ وَالوَرَشِ الَّتي سَلَّطَتِ الضَّوْءَ عَلى تاريخِ هَذا اليَوْمِ وَأَهَمِّيَّتِه. كَما شَهِدَتِ المَدينَةُ تَجَمُّعاتٍ لِمُشارَكَةِ القِصَصِ وَالتَّأَمُّلِ في مَعاني التَّضْحيةِ وَالتَّقْوى الَّتي يُمَثِّلُها هَذا اليَوْمُ.

In Beirut, Lebanon, the city witnessed diverse celebrations for Ashura. Religious rituals mixed with cultural activities, with charities and cultural institutions organizing a series of seminars and workshops highlighting the history and significance of this day. The city also saw gatherings for sharing stories and reflecting on the meanings of sacrifice and piety that this day represents.

8.4.6 Hajj and Umrah

Track **77**

to perform Umrah   • اِعْتِمارٌ   اِعْتَمَرَ

أَكَّدَتْ وِزارَةُ الحَجِّ وَالعُمْرَةِ أَنَّهُ تَمَّ اسْتِقْبالُ آلافِ الحُجّاجِ الَّذينَ اعْتَمَروا هَذا العامَ.

The Ministry of Hajj and Umrah confirmed that thousands of pilgrims who performed Umrah this year have been received.

The Makkan Sanctuary   الحَرَمُ المَكِّيُّ

تَمَّ الإعْلانُ عَنْ تَجْديداتٍ جَديدَةٍ في الحَرَمِ المَكِّيِّ لِتَحْسينِ تَجْرِبَةِ الحُجّاجِ.

New renovations have been announced in the Makkan Sanctuary to improve the pilgrims' experience.

Safa and Marwah   الصَّفا وَالمَرْوَةُ

يَقومُ الحُجّاجُ بِالسَّعْيِ بَيْنَ الصَّفا وَالمَرْوَةِ كَجُزْءٍ مِنْ مَناسِكِ الحَجِّ.

Pilgrims perform the ritual walk between Safa and Marwah as part of the Hajj rites.

Ka'bah   الكَعْبَةُ

شَهِدَتِ الكَعْبَةُ تَوافُدَ حُشودٍ كَبيرَةٍ مِنَ الحُجّاجِ خِلالَ مَوْسِمِ الحَجِّ هَذا العامَ.

The Ka'bah witnessed a large influx of pilgrims during this year's Hajj season.

Medina المَدينَةُ المُنَوَّرَةُ

أَعْلَنَتِ السُّلُطاتُ السُّعوديَّةُ عَنْ إِجْراءاتٍ صِحِّيَّةٍ جَديدَةٍ لِزُوّارِ المَدينَةِ المُنَوَّرَةِ.

The Saudi authorities have announced new health measures for visitors to Medina.

Prophet's Mosque المَسجِدُ النَّبَوِيُّ • مَساجِدُ

زارَ الرَّئيسُ الجَديدُ المَدينَةَ المُنَوَّرَةَ وَأَدّى الصَّلاةَ في المَسجِدِ النَّبَوِيِّ.

The new president visited Medina and performed prayers in the Prophet's Mosque.

Mount Arafat جَبَلُ عَرَفاتٍ • جِبالٌ

تَجَمَّعَ الحُجّاجُ عَلى جَبَلِ عَرَفاتٍ في يَوْمِ عَرَفَةَ خِلالَ مَوْسِمِ الحَجِّ.

Pilgrims gather on Mount Arafat on the Day of Arafah during the Hajj season.

pilgrimage, Hajj حَجٌّ

بَدَأَتِ الطّائِراتُ في نَقْلِ الحُجّاجِ إِلى مَكَّةَ المُكَرَّمَةِ لِأَداءِ فَريضَةِ الحَجِّ.

Planes have started to transport pilgrims to Mecca to perform the Hajj pilgrimage.

to perform Hajj حَجَّ • حَجَّ

تَحَدَّثَ المُفتي العامُّ عَنْ أَهَمِّيَّةِ الإِعْدادِ الجَيِّدِ قَبْلَ أَنْ يَحُجَّ المُسْلِمونَ.

The Grand Mufti spoke about the importance of good preparation before Muslims perform the Hajj pilgrimage.

stoning of the devil رَمْيُ الجَمَراتِ

يَقومُ الحُجّاجُ بِرَمْيِ الجَمَراتِ في مِنّى كَجُزْءٍ مِنْ مَناسِكِ الحَجِّ.

Pilgrims carry out the stoning of the devil in Mina as part of the Hajj rituals.

ihram garment زِيُّ إِحْرامٍ • أَزْياءٌ

وُجِّهَتِ الدَّعَواتُ لِلْحُجّاجِ بِأَهَمِّيَّةِ ارْتِداءِ زِيِّ الإِحْرامِ بِشَكْلٍ صَحيحٍ.

Calls have been directed to pilgrims about the importance of wearing the ihram garment correctly.

Calls were directed to the pilgrims on the importance of properly wearing the ihram garment.

to walk, take steps   سَعَى • سَعْيٌ

اِخْتَتَمَ الرَّئِيسُ زِيَارَتَهُ لِلْمَمْلَكَةِ بِأَداءِ السَّعْيِ بَيْنَ الصَّفا وَالْمَرْوَةِ.

The president concluded his visit to the Kingdom by performing the ritual of walking between Safa and Marwah.

to circumambulate the Ka'bah   طَافَ • طَوافٌ

حَظَرَتِ السُّلُطاتُ السُّعوديَّةُ اسْتِخْدامَ الهَواتِفِ المَحْمولَةِ أَثْناءَ الطَّوافِ حَوْلَ الكَعْبَةِ.

Saudi authorities have banned the use of mobile phones while circumambulating the Ka'bah.

lesser pilgrimage, umrah   عُمْرَةٌ

تَجاوَزَ عَدَدُ الزُّوّارِ القادِمينَ لِأَداءِ العُمْرَةِ هَذا الشَّهْرَ المِلْيونَ شَخْصٍ.

The number of visitors coming to perform Umrah this month has exceeded one million.

Mecca   مَكَّةُ

تُعْتَبَرُ مَكَّةُ المُكَرَّمَةُ مَرْكَزًا دينيًّا عالَميًّا يَسْتَقْطِبُ مَلايينَ الحُجّاجِ سَنَويًّا.

Mecca is considered a global religious center that attracts millions of pilgrims annually.

Day of Standing at Arafat   وَقْفَةُ عَرَفاتٍ

شَهِدَتْ وَقْفَةُ عَرَفاتٍ مُشارَكَةً كَبيرَةً مِنَ الحُجّاجِ هَذا العامَ، رَغْمَ الظُّروفِ الصِّحِّيَّةِ الصَّعْبَةِ.

The Day of Standing at Arafat witnessed large participation from pilgrims this year despite challenging health conditions.

في خُطْوَةٍ تَهْدُفُ إلى تَيْسيرِ تَجْرِبَةِ الحُجّاجِ، افْتَتَحَتِ السُّلُطاتُ السُّعودِيَّةُ مَرْكَزًا تَوْجيهيًّا جَديدًا بالقُرْبِ مِنَ الحَرَمِ المَكِّيِّ في مَكَّةَ. يُقَدِّمُ المَرْكَزُ خَدَماتٍ مَعْلوماتِيَّةً وَتَوْجيهيَّةً للحُجّاجِ حَوْلَ مَناسِكِ الحَجِّ والعُمْرَةِ، يَشْمَلُ ذَلِكَ الطَّوافَ حَوْلَ الكَعْبَةِ والسَّعْيَ بَيْنَ الصَّفا والمَرْوَةِ. كَما يُوَفِّرُ المَرْكَزُ تَسْهيلاتٍ لِأَداءِ رَمْي الجَمَراتِ بأمانٍ وَيُسْرٍ.

In a step aimed at facilitating the experience of pilgrims, the Saudi authorities have opened a new guidance center near the Holy Mosque in Mecca. The center provides informational and guidance services for pilgrims on Hajj and Umrah rituals, including Tawaf around the Kaaba and Sa'i between Safa and Marwah. The center also offers facilities for performing the stoning of the Jamarat safely and easily.

أَطْلَقَتِ الحُكومَةُ السُّعودِيَّةُ مُبادَرَةً بيئيَّةً في المَدينَةِ المُنَوَّرَةِ تُرَكِّزُ عَلى حِمايَةِ جَبَلِ عَرَفاتٍ، المَوْقِعِ الرَّئيسِيِّ لِأَداءِ وَقْفَةِ عَرَفاتٍ خِلالَ الحَجِّ. تَهْدُفُ المُبادَرَةُ إلى الحِفاظِ عَلى البيئَةِ الطَّبيعيَّةِ للجَبَلِ وَضَمانِ تَجْرِبَةٍ روحانيَّةٍ نَقيَّةٍ لِلحُجّاجِ. تَتَضَمَّنُ المُبادَرَةُ بَرامِجَ للتَّوْعِيَةِ البيئيَّةِ وَتَرْكيبَ أَنْظِمَةٍ فَعّالَةٍ لِإدارَةِ النُّفاياتِ خِلالَ مَوْسِمِ الحَجِّ.

The Saudi government has launched an environmental initiative in Medina focused on protecting Mount Arafat, the main site for the Arafat standing during Hajj. The initiative aims to preserve the natural environment of the mountain and ensure a pure spiritual experience for pilgrims. The initiative includes environmental awareness programs and the installation of effective waste management systems during the Hajj season.

الحَجُّ: رِحْلَةُ الإيمانِ والرّوحانيَّةِ في الإسْلامِ

الحَجُّ هُوَ أَحَدُ أَرْكانِ الإسْلامِ الخَمْسَةِ، وَيُعْتَبَرُ رِحْلَةً دينيَّةً يَقومُ بها المُسْلِمونَ إلى مَكَّةَ، المَدينَةِ المُقَدَّسَةِ في الإسْلامِ. يَتِمُّ تَنْفيذُ هَذِهِ الشَّعيرَةِ مَرَّةً واحِدَةً في العامِ خِلالَ الشَّهْرِ الإسْلامِيِّ ذي الحِجَّةِ.

1. **الإحْرامُ:** يَبْدَأُ الحُجّاجُ رِحْلَتَهُمْ بِارْتِداءِ زِيِّ الإحْرامِ، وَهُوَ عِبارَةٌ عَنْ قِطْعَتَيْنِ مِنَ القُماشِ الأَبْيَضِ غَيْرِ المَخيطِ. يُظْهِرُ هَذا الزِّيُّ المُساواةَ والتَّواضُعَ بَيْنَ جَميعِ المُسْلِمينَ.

2. **طَوافُ القُدومِ حَوْلَ الكَعْبَةِ:** بَعْدَ الوُصولِ إلى الحَرَمِ المَكِّيِّ، يُؤَدّي الحُجّاجُ الطَّوافَ، بالدَّوَرانِ حَوْلَ الكَعْبَةِ سَبْعَ مَرّاتٍ، والكَعْبَةُ هِيَ البِناءُ المَرْكَزِيُّ داخِلَ المَسْجِدِ الحَرامِ.

3. **السَّعْيُ بَيْنَ الصَّفا والمَرْوَةِ (السَّعْيُ):** يُعَدُّ السَّعْيُ جُزْءًا أَساسِيًّا مِنْ مَناسِكِ الحَجِّ، حَيْثُ يَسيرُ الحُجّاجُ سَبْعَ مَرّاتٍ بَيْنَ تَلَّيْنِ صَغيرَيْنِ يَقَعانِ بالقُرْبِ مِنَ الكَعْبَةِ، يُعْرَفانِ بالصَّفا والمَرْوَةِ. يُحاكي هَذا الطَّقْسُ رِحْلَةَ

هاجَرَ، زَوجَةِ النَّبِيِّ إِبْراهِيمَ، الَّتِي بَحَثَتْ عَنِ الماءِ لِابْنِها إِسْماعِيلَ. يُظْهِرُ السَّعْيُ تَصْمِيمَ هاجَرَ وَثِقَتَها بِاللَّهِ، وَيُعْتَبَرُ رَمْزًا لِلصَّبْرِ وَالثِّقَةِ وَالتَّوَكُّلِ فِي الإِسْلامِ.

4. **وَقْفَةُ عَرَفاتٍ:** تُعْتَبَرُ أَهَمَّ رُكْنٍ فِي الحَجِّ. يَقِفُ الحُجّاجُ عَلى جَبَلِ عَرَفاتٍ، يُصَلُّونَ وَيَدْعونَ، وَهِيَ لَحْظَةُ تَأَمُّلٍ وَتَقَرُّبٍ إِلى اللَّهِ.

5. **رَمْيُ الجَمَراتِ:** بَعْدَ يَوْمِ عَرَفاتٍ، يَقومُ الحُجّاجُ بِرَمْيِ الجَمَراتِ، وَهُوَ طَقْسٌ يَرْمُزُ لِرَفْضِ إِغْراءاتِ الشَّيْطانِ، كَما فَعَلَ إِبْراهِيمُ عَلَيْهِ السَّلامُ.

6. **الأُضْحِيَّةُ:** يَقومُ الحُجّاجُ بِذَبْحِ الأَضاحِي تَقَرُّبًا إِلى اللَّهِ، تَذْكِيرًا بِفِداءِ إِبْراهِيمَ لِابْنِهِ إِسْماعِيلَ بِأَمْرٍ مِنَ اللَّهِ.

7. **طَوافُ الوَداعِ:** قَبْلَ مُغادَرَةِ مَكَّةَ، يَقومُ الحُجّاجُ بِطَوافِ الوَداعِ حَوْلَ الكَعْبَةِ، كَتَوْدِيعٍ رَمْزِيٍّ لِلْمَدِينَةِ المُقَدَّسَةِ.

يُعَدُّ الحَجُّ تَجْرِبَةً روحانِيَّةً عَمِيقَةً، حَيْثُ يَجْتَمِعُ المُسْلِمونَ مِنْ جَمِيعِ أَنْحاءِ العالَمِ فِي وَحْدَةٍ وَإِخاءٍ، مُتَخَلِّينَ عَنِ الفُروقِ الاِجْتِماعِيَّةِ وَالعِرْقِيَّةِ وَمَظاهِرِ الثَّرْوَةِ، وَهُوَ يُمَثِّلُ التَّجْسِيدَ الحَقِيقِيَّ لِمَبادِئِ الإِسْلامِ مِنَ التَّسامُحِ وَالتَّعاضُدِ وَالتَّقَرُّبِ إِلى اللَّهِ.

Hajj: A Journey of Faith and Spirituality in Islam

Hajj is one of the five pillars of Islam and is a religious journey undertaken by Muslims to Mecca, the holy city in Islam. This ritual is performed once a year during the Islamic month of Dhu al-Hijjah.

1. **Ihram:** Pilgrims begin their journey by wearing Ihram, consisting of two pieces of unstitched white cloth. This attire symbolizes equality and humility among all Muslims.

2. **Tawaf of Arrival around the Kaaba:** Upon reaching the Masjid al-Haram, pilgrims perform Tawaf, circling the Kaaba, which is the central structure inside the mosque, seven times.

3. **Sa'i between Safa and Marwah (Sa'i):** Sa'i is a fundamental part of the Hajj rituals, where pilgrims walk seven times between two small hills near the Kaaba, known as Safa and Marwah. This ritual emulates the journey of Hagar, wife of the Prophet Ibrahim, who searched for water for her son Ishmael. The Sa'i demonstrates Hagar's determination and her trust in God and is considered a symbol of patience, trust, and reliance in Islam.

4. **Standing at Arafat:** Considered the most important pillar of Hajj. Pilgrims stand on Mount Arafat, praying and supplicating, a moment for reflection and drawing closer to God.

5. **Stoning of the Jamarat:** After the day of Arafat, pilgrims perform the ritual of stoning the Jamarat, symbolizing the rejection of Satan's temptations, as Abraham did.

6. **Sacrifice:** Pilgrims perform the sacrifice of animals to draw closer to God, commemorating Abraham's sacrifice of his son Ishmael by God's command.

7. **Farewell Tawaf:** Before leaving Mecca, pilgrims perform the Farewell Tawaf around the Kaaba, symbolically bidding farewell to the holy city.

Hajj is a profound spiritual experience where Muslims from around the world gather in unity and brotherhood, shedding social and racial differences and signs of wealth, representing the true embodiment of Islamic principles of tolerance, solidarity, and drawing closer to God.

8.4.7 Other Rituals and Practices

Track **80**

إيجابٌ وَقَبُولٌ

consent and acceptance

شَدَّدَ الخَطيبُ في خُطْبَةِ الجُمُعَةِ عَلى ضَرورَةِ تَوَفُّرِ شَرْطِ الإيجابِ وَالقَبولِ لِإِتْمامِ الزَّواجِ.

The Friday sermon's speaker emphasized the importance of having the conditions of consent and acceptance for a marriage to be valid.

تَعَدُّدٌ

polygamy

أَكَّدَ المُفْتي أَنَّ التَّعَدُّدَ لَهُ شُروطٌ مُحَدَّدَةٌ يَنْبَغي مُراعاتُها.

The Mufti affirmed that polygamy has specific conditions that should be taken into consideration.

حَرامٌ

forbidden, haram

نَفى النّاطِقُ الرَّسْمِيُّ لِلْوِزارَةٍ شائِعاتٍ حَوْلَ تَقْنينِ الأَغْذِيَةِ الحَرامِ في الأَسْواقِ.

The ministry's official spokesperson denied rumors about the legalization of haram foods in markets.

حَلالٌ

permissible, halal

أَصْدَرَتِ الحُكومَةُ قائِمَةً جَديدَةً تُوَضِّحُ المُنْتَجاتِ الحَلالَ المُعْتَرَفَ بِها رَسْمِيًّا.

The government issued a new list clarifying the officially recognized halal products.

خِطْبَةٌ

engagement

تَمَّ الإِعْلانُ عَنْ خِطْبَةِ الأَميرَةِ في حَفْلٍ ضَخْمٍ حَضَرَهُ العَديدُ مِنَ الشَّخْصِيّاتِ البارِزَةِ.

The princess's engagement was announced in a grand ceremony attended by many prominent figures.

The words خِطْبَة (engagement) and خُطْبَة (sermon; see page 200) share the same spelling in an unvoweled text but have different meanings and pronunciations. Context will help you determine which meaning and pronunciation is intended.

---

burial

دَفْنٌ

أَشادَ مُفْتي المِنْطَقَةِ بِالْتِزامِ المُجْتَمَعِ في دَفْنِ المُتَوَفّيْنَ بِطَريقَةٍ شَرْعِيَّةٍ.

The regional Mufti praised the community's commitment to burying the deceased in a Sharia-compliant manner.

wedding

زِفافٌ

يُعْتَبَرُ حَفْلُ الزِّفافِ وَسيلَةً لِإِشْهارِ الزَّواجِ في الإِسْلامِ.

A wedding ceremony is considered a means of officially announcing the marriage in Islam.

marriage

زَواجٌ

نَظَّمَتْ جَمْعِيَّةُ الزَّواجِ الإِسْلامِيِّ وَرْشَةَ عَمَلٍ حَوْلَ فَضائِلِ الزَّواجِ في الإِسْلامِ.

The Islamic Marriage Association organized a workshop on the virtues of marriage in Islam.

tent for mourning

سُرادِقٌ

أَقامَتِ العائِلَةُ سُرادِقًا لِلْعَزاءِ بَعْدَ وَفاةِ الأَبِ، وَحَضَرَهُ العَديدُ مِنَ المَشايِخِ وَالعُلَماءِ.

The family set up a mourning tent after the father's death, attended by many sheikhs and scholars.

witness

شُهودٌ • شاهِدٌ

في حَفْلِ الزَّواجِ الإِسْلامِيِّ، يَلْعَبُ الشُّهودُ دَوْرًا حَيَوِيًّا، حَيْثُ يَشْهَدونَ عَلى جِدِّيَّةِ وَصِحَّةِ عَقْدِ الزَّواجِ.

In an Islamic marriage ceremony, witnesses play a vital role as they testify to the seriousness and validity of the marriage contract.

funeral prayer

صَلَواتٌ • صَلاةُ جَنازَةٍ

أُقيمَتْ صَلاةُ الجَنازَةِ في مَسْجِدِ الفِرْدَوْسِ وَسَطَ حُضورٍ كَبيرٍ مِنَ المُعَزّينَ.

The funeral prayer was held in Al-Firdous Mosque with a large attendance of mourners.

shrine

ضَرِيحٌ • أَضْرِحَةٌ

تَجَمَّعَ النَّاسُ حَوْلَ ضَرِيحِ الوَلِيِّ الصَّالِحِ لِأَداءِ الصَّلَواتِ وَالدُّعاءِ.

People gathered around the shrine of the pious saint to perform prayers and supplications.

mourning, aza

عَزاءٌ

أُقِيمَ العَزاءُ في مَسْجِدِ الإمامِ الشَّافِعِيِّ وَحَضَرَهُ عَدَدٌ مِنَ الشَّخْصِيّاتِ الدِّينِيَّةِ.

The mourning ceremony was held in Imam Al-Shafi'i Mosque and was attended by a number of religious figures.

marriage contract

عَقْدُ قِرانٍ

أُعْلِنَ عَنْ قِيمَةِ المَهْرِ في عَقْدِ القِرانِ وَفْقَ الشَّرِيعَةِ الإسْلامِيَّةِ.

The value of the dowry was announced in the marriage contract in accordance with Islamic law.

grave

قَبْرٌ • قُبورٌ

دُفِنَ الفَقِيدُ في قَبْرٍ يَقَعُ بِالقُرْبِ مِنَ المَسْجِدِ الكَبِيرِ في القاهِرَةِ.

The deceased was buried in a grave located near the Great Mosque in Cairo.

marriage official

مَأْذونٌ

حَصَلَ المَأْذونُ عَلى تَرْخِيصٍ رَسْمِيٍّ لِإتْمامِ عُقودِ الزَّواجِ في المَدِينَةِ.

The marriage official received an official license to complete marriage contracts in the city.

dowry, mahr

مَهْرٌ • مُهورٌ

تَحَدَّثَتِ الجَمْعِيّاتُ النِّسائِيَّةُ عَنْ ضَرورَةِ وَضْعِ قَوانِينَ تَقْيِيدِيَّةٍ لِلمَهْرِ في عُقودِ الزَّواجِ.

Women's associations discussed the necessity of enacting restrictive laws for dowry in marriage contracts.

نِكَاحٌ

أَكَّدَ العُلَماءُ عَلَى أَهَمِّيَّةِ النِّكاحِ في الإِسلامِ وَدَوْرِهِ في بِناءِ المُجْتَمَعِ.

Scholars emphasized the importance of matrimony in Islam and its role in building society.

8.4.7.1 Mini Articles

Track **81**

في قَلْبِ القاهِرَةِ، شَهِدَ مَأْذونٌ احْتِفاليَّةَ عَقْدِ قِرانٍ مُمَيَّزَةٍ. تَمَيَّزَ الحَفْلُ بِخُطْبَةٍ تَقْليديَّةٍ تَضَمَّنَتْ كَلِماتِ الإيجابِ وَالقُبولِ، مِمّا يَعْكِسُ أَهَمِّيَّةَ الرِّضا المُتَبادَلِ في الزَّواجِ الإِسلاميِّ. وَقَدْ تَمَّ تَحْديدُ المَهْرِ بِما يَتَناسَبُ مَعَ القُدْراتِ الماليَّةِ لِلْعَريسِ، مَعَ التَّأْكيدِ عَلَى أَهَمِّيَّةِ العَلاقاتِ الأُسَريَّةِ وَالرَّوابِطِ الاِجْتِماعيَّةِ في هَذِهِ المُناسَبَةِ.

In the heart of Cairo, a marriage officer witnessed a unique marriage contract ceremony. The ceremony featured a traditional sermon, including the words of proposal and acceptance, reflecting the importance of mutual consent in Islamic marriage. The dowry was set according to the groom's financial ability, emphasizing the importance of family relationships and social ties on this occasion.

اِحْتَفَلَتِ العاصِمَةُ السُّعوديَّةُ بِزِفافٍ تَقْليديٍّ حَيْثُ تَمَّتِ الاِحْتِفالاتُ بِروحِ الإِسلامِ. تَمَّتْ مَراسِمُ الزَّواجِ وَفْقَ الشَّريعَةِ الإِسلاميَّةِ، حَيْثُ تُلِيَتِ الخُطْبَةُ وَأُعْلِنَ النِّكاحُ بِحُضورِ شاهِدَيْنِ. الزِّفافُ، الَّذي أُقيمَ في سُرادِقٍ كَبيرٍ، كانَ يُمَثِّلُ مَزيجًا مِنَ الفَخامَةِ وَالتَّقاليدِ، مَعَ احْتِرامِ الحُدودِ بَيْنَ الحَلالِ وَالحَرامِ.

The Saudi capital celebrated a traditional wedding where the festivities were conducted in the spirit of Islam. The marriage ceremony was performed according to Islamic law, with the sermon recited and the marriage announced in the presence of two witnesses. The wedding, held in a large tent, represented a blend of luxury and tradition, respecting the boundaries between halal and haram.

في الدّارِ البَيْضاءِ، جَرى دَفْنُ رَجُلٍ مُحْتَرَمٍ وَفْقًا لِلطُّقوسِ الإِسلاميَّةِ. أُقيمَتْ صَلاةُ الجِنازَةِ في المَسْجِدِ المَحَلِّيِّ، حَيْثُ حَضَرَ المُجْتَمَعُ لِتَقْديمِ العَزاءِ وَالدُّعاءِ لِلْمُتَوَفّى. تَمَّ دَفْنُ الجَسَدِ بِسُرْعَةٍ وَفْقَ الشَّريعَةِ الإِسلاميَّةِ، مَعَ وَضْعِ الجَسَدِ في القَبْرِ بِطَريقَةٍ تُواجِهُ مَكَّةَ.

In Casablanca, a respected man was buried according to Islamic rituals. The funeral prayer was held at the local mosque, where the community gathered to offer condolences and prayers for the deceased. The body was buried quickly according to Islamic law, with the body placed in the grave facing Mecca.

في عَمّانَ، تَجَمَّعَ المُجْتَمَعُ لِتَقْديمِ العَزاءِ لِأُسْرَةٍ فَقَدَتْ عَزيزًا. في روحٍ مِنَ التَّعاطُفِ وَالتَّضامُنِ، أُقيمَ السُّرادِقُ لِاسْتِقْبالِ المُعَزّينَ. أَظْهَرَتْ هَذِهِ المُناسَبَةُ كَيْفَ يَجْتَمِعُ المُسْلِمونَ لِدَعْمِ بَعْضِهِمْ بَعْضًا في أَوْقاتِ الحُزْنِ، مَعَ الحِفاظِ عَلَى كَرامَةِ العائِلَةِ وَتَقْديرِها.

In Amman, the community gathered to offer condolences to a family that lost a loved one. In the spirit of compassion and solidarity, a tent was set up to receive mourners. This occasion showed how Muslims come together to support each other in times of sorrow, maintaining the dignity and respect of the family.

في الخُرْطوم، شَهِدَتِ السّاحَةُ الِاجْتِماعِيَّةُ احْتِفالًا بِزَواجِ رَجُلٍ بِزَوْجَتِهِ الثّانِيَةِ. أَثارَ هَذا الحَدَثُ النِّقاشَ حَوْلَ تَقْليدِ تَعَدُّدِ الزَّوْجاتِ في الإِسْلامِ. تَمَّ الزَّواجُ بِمُوافَقَةِ الزَّوْجَةِ الأُولى وَوَفْقًا لِلشُّروطِ الشَّرْعِيَّةِ، مِمّا يُبْرِزُ التَّعْقيداتِ الثَّقافِيَّةَ وَالدّينِيَّةَ المُتَعَلِّقَةَ بِهَذِهِ المُمارَسَةِ.

In Khartoum, the social scene witnessed a celebration of a man marrying his second wife. This event sparked discussion about the tradition of polygamy in Islam. The marriage was done with the first wife's consent and according to religious conditions, highlighting the cultural and religious complexities associated with this practice.

Unit 9
Weather and Natural Disasters

In this unit, we focus on language surrounding meteorological phenomena and the devastating impact of natural calamities. The unit is divided into two sections, each shedding light on different aspects of nature's influence on our lives.

The first section centers on Weather, offering a nuanced exploration of weather reporting, forecasting, and the ever-relevant issue of climate change. Here, you'll encounter examples of current or recent weather news alongside forecasts, providing insight into how temperatures and weather conditions are expressed in Arabic. Additionally, we delve into the pressing topic of climate change, a subject frequently making headlines in today's news landscape.

Moving on to the second section, Natural Disasters, we begin with a general vocabulary list encompassing terms applicable to various natural calamities. This serves as a foundation for the subsequent subsections, each dedicated to exploring a specific type of natural disaster. From earthquakes and tsunamis to cyclones, floods, wildfires, volcanic eruptions, droughts, and landslides, each subsection provides insights into the language and terminology associated with these catastrophic events.

By immersing yourself in this unit, you'll not only expand your Arabic language proficiency but also deepen your understanding of the forces of nature that shape our world. Whether grappling with the unpredictability of weather or the aftermath of natural disasters, the vocabulary and language presented here will equip you to navigate and comprehend these phenomena as they are discussed in the media.

9.1 Weather

9.1.1 Weather Reporting and Forecasting

Track **82**

أَثْلَجَ • إِثْلاجٌ

to snow

أَثْلَجَ الجَوُّ في جِبالِ لُبْنانَ اللَّيْلَةَ الماضِيَةَ، مُزَيِّنًا القِمَمَ بِالثُّلوجِ البَيْضاءِ.

It snowed in the mountains of Lebanon last night, adorning the peaks with white snow.

أَرْصادٌ

forecast

pl.

تَتَوَقَّعُ الأَرْصادُ أَنْ يَكونَ الطَّقْسُ بارِدًا خِلالَ الأُسْبوعِ المُقْبِلِ.

The weather forecast predicts cold weather for the coming week.

أَصْدَرَ تَحْذيرًا • إِصْدارٌ

to issue a warning

أَصْدَرَتِ السُّلُطاتُ في شيكاغو تَحْذيرًا بِسَبَبِ العاصِفَةِ الشِّتْوِيَّةِ المُتَوَقَّعَةِ.

The authorities in Chicago issued a warning due to the expected winter storm.

اِتِّجاهُ رِياحٍ

wind direction

يُؤَثِّرُ تَغَيُّرُ اتِّجاهِ الرِّياحِ عَلى دَرَجاتِ الحَرارَةِ المُنْخَفِضَةِ في سْتوكْهولْمْ.

The change in wind direction is affecting the low temperatures in the Stockholm.

اِنْقِطاعُ تَيّارٍ كَهْرَبائِيٍّ

power outage

تَسَبَّبَتِ العاصِفَةُ في انْقِطاعِ التَّيّارِ الكَهْرَبائِيِّ في عِدَّةِ أَحْياءٍ.

The storm caused power outages in several neighborhoods.

بارِدٌ

cold

يُتَوَقَّعُ أَنْ يَكونَ الطَّقْسُ بارِدًا جِدًّا في فارَيا خِلالَ عُطْلَةِ نِهايَةِ الأُسْبوعِ.

The weather in Faraya is expected to be very cold during the weekend.

weather observation tower

بُرْجُ رَصْدٍ جَوِّيٌّ • أَبْراجٌ

اِسْتَخْدَمَ الخُبَراءُ في بُرْجِ الرَّصْدِ الجَوِّيِّ أَحْدَثَ التِّقْنِيّاتِ لِتَحْليلِ الظُّروفِ الجَوِّيَّةِ.

Experts in the weather observation tower used the latest technologies to analyze weather conditions.

hail

بَرَدٌ

شَهِدَتِ المَدينَةُ تَساقُطَ بَرَدٍ مُفاجِئٍ اليَوْمَ مِمّا تَسَبَّبَ في بَعْضِ الأَضْرارِ.

The city experienced sudden hail today, causing some damage.

lightning

بَرْقٌ • بُروقٌ

لوحِظَ بَرْقٌ شَديدٌ خِلالَ العاصِفَةِ اللَّيْلَةَ الماضِيَةَ.

Intense lightning was observed during last night's storm.

weather update

تَحْديثُ طَقْسٍ

يَجْري تَحْديثُ طَقْسِ المِنْطَقَةِ كُلَّ ساعَةٍ لِضَمانِ تَوْفيرِ مَعْلوماتٍ دَقيقَةٍ.

The region's weather is updated every hour to ensure accurate information.

light snowfall

تَساقُطُ ثَلْجٍ خَفيفٍ

خِلالَ اللَّيْلِ، كانَ هُناكَ تَساقُطُ ثَلْجٍ خَفيفٍ مِمّا جَمَّلَ الشَّوارِعَ بِمَنْظَرِهِ الشِّتْوِيِّ.

During the night, there was light snowfall, which beautified the streets with its winter scenery.

heavy snowfall

تَساقُطُ ثَلْجٍ كَثيفٍ

حَذَّرَتِ الأَرْصادُ الجَوِّيَّةُ مِنْ تَساقُطِ ثَلْجٍ كَثيفٍ في المَناطِقِ الجَبَلِيَّةِ غَدًا.

The meteorological department warned of heavy snowfall in the mountainous areas tomorrow.

drastic weather change

تَغَيُّرٌ جَذْرِيٌّ في طَقْسٍ

شَهِدَتِ القاهِرَةُ تَغَيُّرًا جَذْرِيًّا في الطَّقْسِ، حَيْثُ انْخَفَضَتْ دَرَجاتُ الحَرارَةِ بِشَكْلٍ مُفاجِئٍ.

Cairo experienced a drastic change in weather, with temperatures dropping suddenly.

weather change تَغَيُّرُ طَقْسٍ

تَغَيَّرَ طَقْسُ بَيْروتَ بِسُرْعَةٍ مِنْ مُشْمِسٍ إِلى غائِمٍ.

Beirut's weather changed quickly from sunny to cloudy.

weather report • تَقاريرُ تَقْريرُ حالَةِ طَقْسٍ

أَصْدَرَتْ هَيْئَةُ الأَرْصادِ في الإِماراتِ تَقْريرَ حالَةِ الطَّقْسِ الأُسْبوعِيِّ.

The UAE meteorological authority issued a weekly weather report.

to predict, forecast • تَنَبُّؤٌ تَنَبَّأَ

تَنَبَّأَتِ الأَرْصادُ الجَوِّيَّةُ بِأَمْطارٍ غَزيرَةٍ في جِدَّةَ خِلالَ اليَوْمَيْنِ المُقْبِلَيْنِ.

The meteorological forecast predicted heavy rain in Jeddah in the next two days.

weather forecasting تَنَبُّؤٌ بِطَقْسٍ

يَعْتَمِدُ التَّنَبُّؤُ بِطَقْسِ الرِّياضِ عَلى بَياناتٍ دَقيقَةٍ مِنْ مَحَطّاتِ الرَّصْدِ.

The weather forecast for Riyadh relies on accurate data from observation stations.

long-term forecast تَنَبُّؤٌ طَويلُ الأَجَلِ

يُشيرُ التَّنَبُّؤُ طَويلُ الأَجَلِ إِلى مَوْجَةٍ حارَّةٍ شَديدَةٍ في الخُرْطومِ خِلالَ الصَّيْفِ.

The long-term forecast indicates a severe heatwave in Khartoum during the summer.

weather alert تَنْبيهُ طَقْسٍ

أَرْسَلَتِ الأَرْصادُ في المَغْرِبِ تَنْبيهَ طَقْسٍ بِشَأْنِ الرِّياحِ القَوِيَّةِ المُتَوَقَّعَةِ.

The Moroccan meteorological service sent a weather alert about the expected strong winds.

to predict, forecast • تَوَقَّعَ تَوَقَّعَ

تَتَوَقَّعُ الأَرْصادُ الجَوِّيَّةُ زِيادَةً تَدْريجِيَّةً في دَرَجاتِ الحَرارَةِ عَلى مَدى الأُسْبوعِ، وَتَصِلُ إِلى مُسْتَوَياتٍ أَعْلى مِنَ المُتَوَسِّطِ.

Meteorologists predict a gradual temperature increase throughout the week, reaching above-average highs.

ocean currents

تَيّارٌ بَحرِيٌّ

تُؤَثِّرُ التَّيّاراتُ البَحرِيَّةُ في البَحرِ الأَحْمَرِ عَلى الطَّقْسِ عَلى طولِ السّاحِلِ.

The marine currents in the Red Sea affect the weather along the coast.

jet stream

تَيّارٌ نَفّاثٌ

يُؤَدّي التَّيّارُ النَّفّاثُ فَوْقَ الأُرْدُنِّ إلى تَغْييراتٍ سَريعَةٍ في أَنْماطِ الطَّقْسِ.

The jet stream over Jordan leads to rapid changes in weather patterns.

air current

تَيّارٌ هَوائِيٌّ

تَسَبَّبَ التَّيّارُ الهَوائِيُّ القادِمُ مِنَ الصَّحْراءِ في ارْتِفاعِ دَرَجاتِ الحَرارَةِ في القاهِرَةِ.

The air current coming from the desert caused a rise in temperatures in Cairo.

snow

ثَلْجٌ • ثُلوجٌ

الثَّلْجُ يُغَطّي شَوارِعَ هِلْسِنْكي الآنَ، مِمّا يَجْعَلُ القِيادَةَ صَعْبَةً.

Snow currently covers the streets of Helsinki, making driving difficult.

snowy

ثَلْجِيٌّ

الطَّقْسُ الثَّلْجِيُّ في أوسْلو يَمْنَحُ المَدينَةَ جَمالًا خاصًّا.

The snowy weather in Oslo brings a special beauty to the city.

dry

جافٌّ

يَتَمَيَّزُ الطَّقْسُ في القاهِرَةِ بِأَنَّهُ جافٌّ وَمُشْمِسٌ في مُعْظَمِ السَّنَةِ.

The weather in Cairo is mostly dry and sunny throughout the year.

drought

جَفافٌ

يُعاني الشَّرْقُ الأَوْسَطُ مِنْ جَفافٍ مُتَزايِدٍ بِسَبَبِ التَّغَيُّراتِ المُناخِيَّةِ.

The Middle East is experiencing increasing drought due to climate changes.

ice
جَليدٌ

تُغَطّي طَبَقَةٌ مِنَ الجَليدِ الطُّرُقَ في لُبْنانَ، مِمّا يَتَطَلَّبُ القِيادَةَ بِحَذَرٍ.

A layer of ice covers the roads in Lebanon, requiring cautious driving.

weather
جَوٌّ • أَجْواءٌ

الجَوُّ في دُبَيَّ حارٌّ جِدًّا اليَوْمَ، مَعَ دَرَجاتِ حَرارَةٍ تَتَجاوَزُ الأَرْبَعينَ.

The weather in Dubai is very hot today, with temperatures exceeding forty degrees.

weather(-related)
جَوِّيٌّ

رِحْلاتُ الطَّيَرانِ قَدْ تَتَأَثَّرُ بِالظُّروفِ الجَوِّيَّةِ المُتَغَيِّرَةِ.

Flights may be affected by changing weather conditions.

hot
حارٌّ

تَشْتَهِرُ دُبَيَّ بِطَقْسِها الحارِّ وَالمُشْمِسِ طَوالَ العامِ.

Dubai is known for its hot and sunny weather throughout the year.

weather condition
حالَةُ طَقْسٍ

حالَةُ الطَّقْسِ في طوكيو مُتَقَلِّبَةٌ اليَوْمَ، مَعَ فُرَصٍ لِسُقوطِ أَمْطارٍ خَفيفَةٍ.

The weather in Tokyo is variable today, with chances of light rain.

to determine
حَدَّدَ • تَحْديدٌ

حَدَّدَتِ الأَرْصادُ الجَوِّيَّةُ في بِرْلينَ احْتِماليَّةَ هُطولِ الأَمْطارِ بِنِسْبَةِ 60 غَدًا.

The meteorological department in Berlin has determined a 60% chance of rain tomorrow.

to analyze
حَلَّلَ • تَحْليلٌ

حَلَّلَ خُبَراءُ الطَّقْسِ في لَنْدَنَ بَياناتِ الرّادارِ لِتَوَقُّعِ حالَةِ الطَّقْسِ لِلْأُسْبوعِ المُقْبِلِ.

Weather experts in London analyzed radar data to predict the weather for the coming week.

temperature

درَجَةُ حَرارَةٍ

درَجَةُ حَرارَةِ القاهِرَةِ اليَوْمَ سَتَصِلُ إلى 35 دَرَجَةً مِئَوِيَّةً، مِمّا يَجْعَلُ الجَوَّ حارًّا.

The temperature in Cairo today will reach 35 degrees Celsius, making the weather hot.

low temperature

درَجَةُ حَرارَةٍ صُغْرى

سَجَّلَتِ الدَّوْحَةُ دَرَجَةَ حَرارَةٍ صُغْرى بَلَغَتْ 25 دَرَجَةً مِئَوِيَّةً هَذا الصَّباحَ.

Doha recorded a low of 25 degrees Celsius this morning.

high temperature

درَجَةُ حَرارَةٍ عُظْمى

درَجَةُ الحَرارَةِ العُظْمى في دُبَيِّ اليَوْمَ تُقارِبُ الـ40 دَرَجَةً مِئَوِيَّةً، مِمّا يَتَطَلَّبُ الحَذَرَ.

The maximum temperature in Dubai today is close to 40 degrees Celsius, requiring caution.

weather radar

رادارُ طَقْسٍ

يُسْتَخْدَمُ رادارُ الطَّقْسِ في جِدَّةَ لِتَتَبُّعِ السُّحُبِ والأَمْطارِ المُحْتَمَلَةِ.

The weather radar in Jeddah is used to track clouds and potential rain.

to monitor

رَصَدَ • رَصْدٌ

رَصَدَتْ مَحَطّاتُ الأَرْصادِ في عَمّانَ ارْتِفاعًا في الرُّطوبَةِ اليَوْمَ.

Meteorological stations in Amman observed an increase in humidity today.

humid

رَطْبٌ

الجَوُّ رَطْبٌ في بَيْروتَ اليَوْمَ، مِمّا يَجْعَلُ الشُّعورَ بِالْحَرارَةِ أَكْثَرَ.

The weather is humid in Beirut today, making it feel hotter.

humidity

رُطوبَةٌ

تُتَوَقَّعُ رُطوبَةٌ عالِيَةٌ في الإِسْكَنْدَرِيَّةِ غَدًا، مِمّا قَدْ يُؤَدّي إلى صُعوبَةٍ في التَّنَفُّسِ لَدى البَعْضِ.

High humidity is expected in Alexandria tomorrow, which may lead to breathing difficulties for some.

thunder رَعْدٌ • رُعودٌ

سُمِعَ صَوْتُ الرَّعْدِ في الرِّياضِ اللَّيْلَةَ الماضِيَةَ، مِمّا يُشيرُ إلى احْتِمالِ هُطولِ أَمْطارٍ.

Thunder was heard in Riyadh last night, indicating the possibility of rain.

wind pl. رِياحٌ

الرِّياحُ القَوِيَّةُ في الكُوَيْتِ أَدَّتْ إلى تَحْذيراتٍ مِنَ السُّلُطاتِ لِلْمِلاحَةِ البَحْرِيَّةِ.

Strong winds in Kuwait have led to warnings from authorities for maritime navigation.

south wind رِياحٌ جَنوبِيَّةٌ

الرِّياحُ الجَنوبِيَّةُ في الخُرْطومِ تَزيدُ مِنَ الشُّعورِ بِالحَرارَةِ.

The south winds in Khartoum are making it feel hotter.

east wind رِياحٌ شَرْقِيَّةٌ

الرِّياحُ الشَّرْقِيَّةُ في دِمَشْقَ تُقَلِّلُ مِنْ مُسْتَوَياتِ التَّلَوُّثِ اليَوْمَ.

The east winds in Damascus are reducing pollution levels today.

north wind رِياحٌ شَمالِيَّةٌ

تَهُبُّ رِياحٌ شَمالِيَّةٌ في الإسْكَنْدَرِيَّةِ اليَوْمَ، مِمّا يَجْلِبُ البُرودَةَ إلى المَدينَةِ.

North winds are blowing in Alexandria today, bringing coolness to the city.

west wind رِياحٌ غَرْبِيَّةٌ

تُؤَثِّرُ الرِّياحُ الغَرْبِيَّةُ عَلى طَقْسِ بَيْروتَ، حَيْثُ تَجْلِبُ الرُّطوبَةَ مِنَ البَحْرِ.

The west winds are affecting Beirut's weather, bringing humidity from the sea.

hot ساخِنٌ

الطَّقْسُ ساخِنٌ جِدًّا في العَيْنِ، حَيْثُ تَتَجاوَزُ دَرَجاتُ الحَرارَةِ 45 دَرَجَةً مِئَوِيَّةً.

The weather is very hot in Al Ain, with temperatures exceeding 45 degrees Celsius.

to record

سَجَّلَ • تَسْجيلٌ

سَجَّلَت مَكَّةُ أَعْلى دَرَجَةِ حَرارَةٍ هَذا الصَّيفَ في المِنْطَقَةِ.

Mecca recorded the highest temperature this summer in the region.

flash flood

سَيْلٌ • سُيولٌ

يَتَشَكَّلُ سَيْلٌ قَوِيٌّ في وادي رَم بَعْدَ الأَمْطارِ الغَزيرَةِ.

A strong flood is forming in Wadi Rum after heavy rains.

fog

ضَبابٌ

يُغَطّي الضَّبابُ مَدينَةَ الرِّباطِ صَباحَ اليَوْمِ، مِمّا يُقَلِّلُ الرُّؤْيَةَ عَلى الطُّرُقِ.

Fog covers Rabat this morning, reducing visibility on the roads.

foggy

ضَبابِيٌّ

الطَّقْسُ ضَبابِيٌّ في صَنْعاءَ، مِمّا يَتَطَلَّبُ القِيادَةَ بِحَذَرٍ.

The weather is foggy in Sana'a, requiring cautious driving.

barometric pressure, air pressure

ضَغْطٌ جَوِّيٌّ

الضَّغْطُ الجَوِّيُّ المُرْتَفِعُ في مَسْقَطَ يُؤَدّي إلى اسْتِقْرارِ الطَّقْسِ.

The high atmospheric pressure in Muscat leads to stable weather.

weather

طَقْسٌ

الطَّقْسُ في القاهِرَةِ اليَوْمَ مُشْمِسٌ وَمُسْتَقِرٌّ.

The weather in Cairo today is sunny and stable.

weather phenomenon

ظاهِرَةٌ جَوِّيَّةٌ • ظَواهِرُ

هُناكَ ظاهِرَةٌ جَوِّيَّةٌ نادِرَةٌ تَحْدُثُ في البَحْرِ المَيِّتِ، حَيْثُ تَظْهَرُ السُّحُبُ بِأَشْكالٍ مُمَيَّزَةٍ.

A rare meteorological phenomenon occurs in the Dead Sea, where clouds appear in unique shapes.

stormy

عاصِفٌ

يُتَوَقَّعُ أَنْ تَكونَ الأَجْواءُ عاصِفَةً في جِدَّةَ غَدًا.

It is expected to be stormy in Jeddah tomorrow.

storm

عاصِفَةٌ • عَواصِفُ

تَضْرِبُ عاصِفَةٌ قَوِيَّةٌ مِنْطَقَةَ الرِّياضِ، مِمّا يُؤَدّي إلى انْخِفاضٍ في دَرَجاتِ الحَرارَةِ.

A strong storm hits Riyadh, leading to a drop in temperatures.

hailstorm

عاصِفَةُ بَرَدٍ • عَواصِفُ

تُواجِهُ الإِسْكَنْدَرِيَّةُ عاصِفَةَ بَرَدٍ، مِمّا يَتَطَلَّبُ تَوَخّي الحَذَرِ.

Alexandria is facing a hailstorm, requiring caution.

dust storm

عاصِفَةٌ تُرابِيَّةٌ • عَواصِفُ

تَشْهَدُ الكُوَيْتُ عاصِفَةً تُرابِيَّةً، مِمّا يُؤَثِّرُ عَلى الرُّؤْيَةِ الأُفُقِيَّةِ.

Kuwait is experiencing a dust storm, affecting horizontal visibility.

thunderstorm

عاصِفَةٌ رَعْدِيَّةٌ • عَواصِفُ

عاصِفَةٌ رَعْدِيَّةٌ تَضْرِبُ دِمَشْقَ، مَصْحوبَةٌ بِأَمْطارٍ غَزيرَةٍ.

A thunderstorm hits Damascus, accompanied by heavy rain.

meteorologist

عالِمُ أَرْصادٍ • عُلَماءُ

يُحَلِّلُ عالِمُ أَرْصادٍ في الأُرْدُنِّ بَياناتِ الطَّقْسِ لِتَوَقُّعِ التَّغَيُّراتِ المُناخِيَّةِ.

A meteorologist in Jordan analyzes weather data to predict climate changes.

cloudy

غائِمٌ

السَّماءُ غائِمَةٌ في بَيْروتَ اليَوْمَ، مَعَ احْتِمالِيَّةٍ لِسُقوطِ أَمْطارٍ خَفيفَةٍ.

The sky is cloudy in Beirut today, with a possibility of light rain.

unsettled

غَيْرُ مُسْتَقِرٍّ

الطَّقْسُ غَيْرُ مُسْتَقِرٍّ في المَغْرِبِ، مَعَ تَوَقُّعاتٍ بِتَقَلُّباتٍ جَوِّيَّةٍ.

The weather is unstable in Morocco, with expectations of atmospheric fluctuations.

clouds

• غُيومٌ

غَيْمٌ

تَظْهَرُ الغُيومُ فَوْقَ الجِبالِ في مَراكِشَ، مِمّا يُعْطي مَنْظَرًا خَلّابًا.

Clouds appear over the mountains in Marrakech, giving a picturesque view.

to measure temperature

• قِياسٌ

قاسَ دَرَجَةَ حَرارَةٍ

قاسَ العُلَماءُ دَرَجَةَ الحَرارَةِ في أَبو ظَبْي، وَوَجَدوا أَنَّها تَتَجاوَزُ الـ 40 دَرَجَةً مِئَوِيَّةً.

Scientists measured the temperature in Abu Dhabi and found it to exceed 40 degrees Celsius.

to estimate humidity levels

• تَقْديرٌ

قَدَّرَ نِسْبَةَ رُطوبَةٍ

في القُدْسِ، قَدَّرَتْ خِدْمَةُ الأَرْصادِ نِسْبَةَ الرُّطوبَةِ بِحَوالَيْ 60% اليَوْمَ.

In Jerusalem, the meteorological service estimated the humidity level at around 60% today.

strong, powerful

قَوِيٌّ

الرِّياحُ قَوِيَّةٌ عَلى ساحِلِ الإِسْكَنْدَرِيَّةِ، مِمّا يُؤَثِّرُ عَلى الأَنْشِطَةِ البَحْرِيَّةِ.

The winds are strong on the coast of Alexandria, affecting maritime activities.

wind indicator

مُؤَشِّرُ رِياحٍ

مُؤَشِّرُ الرِّياحِ في البَحْرَيْنِ يُشيرُ إلى رِياحٍ شَماليَّةٍ شَرْقِيَّةٍ.

The wind indicator in Bahrain shows north-eastern winds.

barometric pressure indicator

مُؤَشِّرُ ضَغْطٍ جَوِّيٍّ

مُؤَشِّرُ الضَّغْطِ الجَوِّيِّ في مَسْقَطَ يُنْذِرُ بِتَقَلُّباتٍ جَوِّيَّةٍ خِلالَ اليَوْمَيْنِ المُقْبِلَيْنِ.

The atmospheric pressure indicator in Muscat warns of weather fluctuations in the next two days.

variable مُتَغَيِّرٌ

في بَغْدادَ، الطَّقْسُ مُتَغَيِّرٌ بِشَكْلٍ مَلْحوظٍ، مَعَ تَبايُنٍ في دَرَجاتِ الحَرارَةِ خِلالَ اليَوْمِ.

In Baghdad, the weather is noticeably variable, with fluctuations in temperature throughout the day.

unstable مُتَقَلِّبٌ

الطَّقْسُ في بَيْروتَ مُتَقَلِّبٌ، مَعَ تَغَيُّراتٍ سَريعَةٍ مِنْ مُشْمِسٍ إلى مُمْطِرٍ.

The weather in Beirut is unstable, with quick changes from sunny to rainy.

contradictory مُتَناقِضٌ

التَّوَقُّعاتُ الجَوِّيَّةُ لِنِهايَةِ الأُسْبوعِ تَظَلُّ مُتَناقِضَةً، مَعَ تَوَقُّعِ فَتَراتٍ مُشْمِسَةٍ بَيْنَ هُطولِ أَمْطارٍ مُتَفَرِّقَةٍ.

The weather forecast for the weekend remains contradictory, with sunny intervals expected amidst scattered showers.

snowy مُثْلِجٌ

في الجَزائِرِ، تَتَوَقَّعُ الأَرْصادُ أَجْواءً مُثْلِجَةً في المَناطِقِ الجَبَلِيَّةِ.

In Algeria, meteorologists expect snowy conditions in the mountainous regions.

satellite monitoring مُراقَبَةُ أَقْمارٍ صِناعِيَّةٍ

تُسْتَخْدَمُ مُراقَبَةُ الأَقْمارِ الصِّناعِيَّةِ في دُبَيَّ لِتَتَبُّعِ حَرَكَةِ السُّحُبِ وَالتَّنَبُّؤِ بِالطَّقْسِ.

Satellite monitoring in Dubai is used to track cloud movements and predict the weather.

high-pressure area مُرْتَفَعٌ جَوِّيٌّ

يُؤَدّي المُرْتَفَعُ الجَوِّيُّ في الرِّياضِ إلى طَقْسٍ مُسْتَقِرٍّ وَجافٍّ.

The high-pressure area in Riyadh leads to stable and dry weather.

stable مُسْتَقِرٌّ

الطَّقْسُ مُسْتَقِرٌّ في مَسْقَطَ، مَعَ قَليلٍ مِنَ السُّحُبِ وَبِلا تَوَقُّعاتٍ لِهُطولِ الأَمْطارِ.

The weather in Muscat is stable, with few clouds and no expectation of rain.

مُسْتَوى سُقوطِ أَمْطارٍ

rainfall level

مُسْتَوى سُقوطِ الأَمْطارِ في الإِسْكَنْدَرِيَّةِ مُرْتَفِعٌ هَذا العامَ، مِمّا يُؤَثِّرُ عَلى الزِّراعَةِ.

The level of rainfall in Alexandria is high this year, affecting agriculture.

مُشْمِسٌ

sunny

الجَوُّ مُشْمِسٌ وَجَميلٌ في الغَرْدَقَةِ، مِمّا يَجْعَلُها مِثالِيَّةً لِلسِّياحَةِ الشّاطِئِيَّةِ.

The weather is sunny and beautiful in Hurghada, making it perfect for beach tourism.

مَطَرٌ • أَمْطارٌ

rain

يُتَوَقَّعُ هُطولُ مَطَرٍ في بَيْروتَ اليَوْمَ، مِمّا يَسْتَلْزِمُ اصْطِحابَ المِظَلّاتِ.

Rain is expected in Beirut today, necessitating the carrying of umbrellas.

مُمْطِرٌ

rainy

الأَجْواءُ مُمْطِرَةٌ في الدّارِ البَيْضاءِ، مِمّا يَجْلِبُ الانْتِعاشَ لِلْمَدينَةِ.

The weather is rainy in Casablanca, bringing refreshment to the city.

مُنْخَفَضٌ جَوِّيٌّ

low-pressure area

يُؤَثِّرُ المُنْخَفَضُ الجَوِّيُّ في عَمّانَ عَلى الطَّقْسِ، مِمّا يَزيدُ مِنْ فُرَصِ الأَمْطارِ.

The low-pressure system in Amman affects the weather, increasing the chances of rain.

مَوْجَةٌ بارِدَةٌ

cold spell

تَشْهَدُ تونُسُ مَوْجَةً بارِدَةً هَذا الأُسْبوعَ، مِمّا يَتَطَلَّبُ مَلابِسَ دافِئَةً.

Tunisia is experiencing a cold wave this week, requiring warm clothing.

مَوْجَةُ حَرٍّ

heat wave

مَوْجَةُ حَرٍّ شَديدَةٌ تَضْرِبُ القاهِرَةَ، حَيْثُ تَصِلُ دَرَجاتُ الحَرارَةِ إلى مُسْتَوى أَعْلى مِنَ المُعْتادِ.

A severe heatwave hits Cairo, with temperatures reaching higher than usual.

seasonal   مَوْسِمِيٌّ

الأَمْطارُ المَوْسِمِيَّةُ في جِدَّةَ تُساهِمُ في تَغْيِيرِ البِيئَةِ الطَّبيعِيَّةِ.

The seasonal rains in Jeddah contribute to changing the natural environment.

dew point   نُقْطَةُ تَكَثُّفٍ • نِقاطٌ

نُقْطَةُ التَّكَثُّفِ في الرِّياضِ تَصِلُ إلى مُسْتَوًى مُرْتَفِعٍ بِسَبَبِ الرُّطوبَةِ العالِيَةِ.

The dew point in Riyadh reaches a high level due to high humidity.

weather model   نَموذَجُ طَقْسٍ • نَماذِجُ

يُسْتَخْدَمُ نَموذَجُ الطَّقْسِ في الكُوَيْتِ لِتَوَقُّعِ الظُّروفِ المُناخِيَّةِ لِلْأَيَّامِ المُقْبِلَةِ.

The weather model in Kuwait is used to predict climatic conditions for the coming days.

to blow   هَبَّ • هُبوبٌ

هَبَّتْ رِياحٌ قَوِيَّةٌ في القاهِرَةِ، مِمَّا أَدَّى إلى اضْطِراباتٍ في حَرَكَةِ المُرورِ.

Strong winds blew in Cairo, leading to traffic disruptions.

air pressure drop   هُبوطُ ضَغْطٍ جَوِّيٍّ

شَهِدَتْ بَيْروتُ هُبوطًا في الضَّغْطِ الجَوِّيِّ، مِمَّا يُنْذِرُ بِتَغَيُّراتٍ جَوِّيَّةٍ.

Beirut experienced a drop in atmospheric pressure, indicating weather changes.

rainfall   هُطولُ أَمْطارٍ

هُطولُ الأَمْطارِ في الدّارِ البَيْضاءِ يُعَزِّزُ المَوارِدَ المائِيَّةَ لِلْمَدينَةِ.

Rainfall in Casablanca enhances the city's water resources.

air   هَواءٌ

الهَواءُ البارِدُ في دِمَشْقَ يَجْعَلُ الجَوَّ مِثالِيًّا لِلتَّنَزُّهِ.

The cold air in Damascus makes the weather ideal for walks.

وَجَّهَتِ السُّلُطَاتُ في مَرَاكِشَ إِرْشَادَاتٍ لِلسُّكَّانِ بِسَبَبِ تَوَقُّعَاتٍ بِمَوْجَةِ بَرْدٍ قَوِيَّةٍ.

The authorities in Marrakech issued guidelines to residents due to expectations of a strong cold wave.

9.1.1.1 Mini-Articles

أَصْدَرَتِ الأَرْصَادُ الجَوِّيَّةُ في إِسْطَنْبُولَ تَحْذِيرَاتٍ مُسْبَقَةً مِنْ تَسَاقُطِ ثَلْجٍ كَثِيفٍ مِنَ المُتَوَقَّعِ أَنْ يَضْرِبَ المَدِينَةَ هَذَا الأُسْبُوعَ. تَنَبَّأَتِ التَّقَارِيرُ بِانْخِفَاضِ دَرَجَاتِ الحَرَارَةِ إِلَى تَحْتِ الصِّفْرِ، مَعَ تَوَقُّعَاتٍ بِتَسَاقُطِ الثَّلْجِ الَّذِي قَدْ يُؤَدِّي إِلَى انْقِطَاعِ تَيَّارٍ كَهْرَبَائِيٍّ في بَعْضِ المَنَاطِقِ. حَثَّتِ السُّلُطَاتُ المُوَاطِنِينَ عَلَى أَخْذِ الحِيطَةِ وَالاسْتِعْدَادِ لِلظُّرُوفِ الشِّتَوِيَّةِ القَاسِيَةِ.

The meteorological department in Istanbul has issued early warnings of heavy snow expected to hit the city this week. Reports have predicted a drop in temperatures below zero, with expectations of snowfall that could lead to power outages in some areas. Authorities have urged citizens to be cautious and prepare for harsh winter conditions.

تَضْرِبُ مَوْجَةُ حَرٍّ غَيْرُ مَسْبُوقَةٍ القَاهِرَةَ، حَيْثُ تَتَنَبَّأُ الأَرْصَادُ الجَوِّيَّةُ بِارْتِفَاعِ دَرَجَاتِ الحَرَارَةِ لِتَصِلَ إِلَى دَرَجَاتِ حَرَارَةٍ عُظْمَى قِيَاسِيَّةٍ. تَأَثَّرَتِ الحَيَاةُ اليَوْمِيَّةُ بِشَكْلٍ كَبِيرٍ، وَسَطَ تَحْذِيرَاتٍ مِنْ تَزَايُدِ اسْتِهْلَاكِ الكَهْرَبَاءِ وَالحَاجَةِ لِتَرْشِيدِ اسْتِخْدَامِ المِيَاهِ. وَقَدْ أَصْدَرَتِ السُّلُطَاتُ تَنْبِيهَاتٍ لِلْمُوَاطِنِينَ بِضَرُورَةِ البَقَاءِ في أَمَاكِنَ مُظَلَّلَةٍ وَمُكَيَّفَةٍ خِلَالَ سَاعَاتِ الظَّهِيرَةِ.

An unprecedented heatwave is hitting Cairo, with weather forecasts predicting a rise in temperatures to record highs. Daily life has been significantly affected, amid warnings of increased electricity consumption and the need for water conservation. Authorities have issued alerts to citizens to stay in shaded and air-conditioned places during the afternoon hours.

تَعَرَّضَتْ لَنْدَنُ لِضَبَابٍ كَثِيفٍ هَذَا الصَّبَاحَ، مِمَّا أَدَّى إِلَى تَعْطِيلٍ في حَرَكَةِ المُرُورِ وَإِلْغَاءِ بَعْضِ الرِّحْلَاتِ الجَوِّيَّةِ. سَجَّلَتِ الأَرْصَادُ الجَوِّيَّةُ انْخِفَاضًا في مُسْتَوَيَاتِ الرُّؤْيَةِ إِلَى مَا يَقِلُّ عَنْ 50 مِتْرًا في بَعْضِ المَنَاطِقِ. وَجَّهَتِ السُّلُطَاتُ إِرْشَادَاتٍ لِلسَّائِقِينَ بِضَرُورَةِ تَوَخِّي الحَذَرِ وَاسْتِخْدَامِ مَصَابِيحِ الضَّبَابِ.

London experienced dense fog this morning, leading to traffic delays and the cancellation of some flights. The meteorological department recorded visibility levels dropping to less than 50 meters in some areas. Authorities have directed drivers to be cautious and use fog lights.

ضَرَبَتْ عاصِفَةٌ رَمْلِيَّةٌ مُفاجِئَةٌ الرِّياضَ، مِمّا أَدّى إلى تَغَيُّرٍ جَذْرِيٍّ في الطَّقْسِ وَتَقْلِيلِ الرُّؤْيَةِ الأُفُقِيَّةِ بِشَكْلٍ كَبِيرٍ. حَذَّرَتِ الأَرْصادُ الجَوِّيَّةُ مِنْ رِياحٍ قَوِيَّةٍ قَدْ تُؤَدّي إلى اِنْقِطاعاتٍ في الكَهْرَباءِ وَصُعُوباتٍ في الحَرَكَةِ بِالشَّوارِعِ. وَقَدْ تَلَقّى المُواطِنونَ وَالمُقِيمونَ تَوْصِياتٍ بِالبَقاءِ داخِلَ المَنازِلِ إلى أَنْ تَسْتَقِرَّ الأَحْوالُ الجَوِّيَّةُ.

A sudden sandstorm struck Riyadh, leading to a drastic change in weather and significantly reducing horizontal visibility. The meteorological department warned of strong winds that may lead to power outages and difficulties in street movement. Citizens and residents were advised to stay indoors until the weather stabilizes.

اِسْتَقْبَلَتْ بَيْروتُ أَمْطارًا غَزِيرَةً اِسْتَمَرَّتْ لِعِدَّةِ أَيّامٍ، مِمّا أَنْعَشَ المَدِينَةَ بَعْدَ فَتْرَةٍ طَوِيلَةٍ مِنَ الجَفافِ. سَجَّلَتِ الأَرْصادُ الجَوِّيَّةُ كَمِّيّاتِ هُطولِ أَمْطارٍ فاقَتِ التَّوَقُّعاتِ، ما أَدّى إلى اِمْتِلاءِ السُّدودِ وَتَحَسُّنِ مُسْتَوَياتِ المِياهِ الجَوْفِيَّةِ. حَثَّتِ السُّلُطاتُ المُواطِنِينَ عَلى اتِّخاذِ الاِحْتِياطاتِ اللازِمَةِ لِتَجَنُّبِ السُّيولِ المُحْتَمَلَةِ في المَناطِقِ المُنْخَفِضَةِ.

Beirut received heavy rainfall for several days, rejuvenating the city after a long period of drought. The meteorological department recorded rainfall amounts exceeding expectations, which led to the filling of dams and improved groundwater levels. Authorities urged citizens to take necessary precautions to avoid potential floods in low-lying areas.

9.1.1.2 Mini Weather Forecasts

Track **84**

القاهِرَةُ، مِصْرُ (الرَّبِيعُ): غَدًا تَتَوَقَّعُ الأَرْصادُ الجَوِّيَّةُ ارْتِفاعَ دَرَجاتِ الحَرارَةِ في القاهِرَةِ، مَعَ دَرَجَةِ حَرارَةٍ عُظْمى تَصِلُ إلى 33 دَرَجَةً مِئَوِيَّةً وَصُغْرى تَنْخَفِضُ إلى 17 دَرَجَةً مِئَوِيَّةً. تَشْهَدُ الأَيّامُ القادِمَةُ اسْتِقْرارًا في الطَّقْسِ مَعَ احْتِمالٍ طَفِيفٍ لِارْتِفاعِ الحَرارَةِ.

Cairo, Egypt (Spring): Tomorrow, the weather forecast anticipates a rise in temperatures in Cairo, with a high reaching 33 degrees Celsius and a low dropping to 17 degrees Celsius. The coming days will see stable weather with a slight chance of a temperature increase.

نيويورك، الوِلاياتُ المُتَّحِدَةُ (الخَرِيفُ): تُشِيرُ التَّوَقُّعاتُ إلى يَوْمٍ بارِدٍ نِسْبِيًّا في نيويورك، حَيْثُ تَصِلُ الحَرارَةُ العُظْمى إلى 15 دَرَجَةً مِئَوِيَّةً، وَتَهْبِطُ الصُّغْرى إلى 9 دَرَجاتٍ مِئَوِيَّةٍ. قَدْ نَشْهَدُ تَساقُطًا خَفِيفًا لِلأَمْطارِ في الأَيّامِ القَلِيلَةِ المُقْبِلَةِ.

New York, United States (Autumn): Forecasts indicate a relatively cold day in New York, with a high of 15 degrees Celsius and a low falling to 9 degrees Celsius. Light rain might occur in the next few days.

طوكْيو، اليابانُ (الصَّيْفُ): تَسْتَمِرُّ دَرَجاتُ الحَرارَةِ في طوكْيو في الاِرْتِفاعِ، مَعَ تَوَقُّعاتٍ بِحَرارَةٍ عُظْمى تَبْلُغُ 30 دَرَجَةً مِئَوِيَّةً وَصُغْرى لَيْلًا حَوْلَ 24 دَرَجَةً مِئَوِيَّةً. الرُّطوبَةُ العالِيَةُ قَدْ تَجْعَلُ الشُّعورَ بِالحَرارَةِ أَكْثَرَ حِدَّةً.

Tokyo, Japan (Summer): Temperatures in Tokyo continue to rise, with forecasts predicting a high of 30 degrees Celsius and a nightly low around 24 degrees Celsius. The high humidity may make the heat feel more intense.

سيدْني، أُسْتُراليا (الشِّتاءُ): تَسْتَقْبِلُ سيدْني أَيَّامًا بارِدَةً نِسْبِيًّا مَعَ دَرَجَةِ حَرارَةٍ عُظْمى تَصِلُ إلى 16 دَرَجَةً مِئَوِيَّةً وَصُغْرى تُقارِبُ 9 دَرَجاتٍ مِئَوِيَّةٍ. لا توجَدُ تَوَقُّعاتٌ بِسُقوطِ أَمْطارٍ، مِمّا يوَفِّرُ طَقْسًا مُسْتَقِرًّا لِلْأَيّامِ القادِمَةِ.

Sydney, Australia (Winter): Sydney welcomes relatively cold days with a high reaching 16 degrees Celsius and a low around 9 degrees Celsius. There are no forecasts for rain, providing stable weather for the coming days.

موسْكو، روسْيا (الشِّتاءُ): يُسَيْطِرُ البَرْدُ القارِسُ عَلى موسْكو، مَعَ تَوَقُّعاتٍ بِدَرَجَةِ حَرارَةٍ عُظْمى لا تَتَجاوَزُ -5 دَرَجاتٍ مِئَوِيَّةٍ وَصُغْرى تَصِلُ إلى -9 دَرَجاتٍ مِئَوِيَّةٍ. وَيُتَوَقَّعُ تَساقُطُ ثَلْجٍ كَثيفٌ خِلالَ الأُسْبوعِ.

Moscow, Russia (Winter): Bitter cold dominates Moscow, with forecasts predicting a maximum temperature of no more than -5 degrees Celsius and a low reaching -9 degrees Celsius. Heavy snowfall is expected throughout the week.[*]

دُبَيُّ، الإماراتُ العَرَبِيَّةُ المُتَّحِدَةُ (الصَّيْفُ): دَرَجاتُ الحَرارَةِ في دُبَيَّ تَظَلُّ مُرْتَفِعَةً، مَعَ حَرارَةٍ عُظْمى تَصِلُ إلى 40 دَرَجَةً مِئَوِيَّةً وَصُغْرى تَبْلُغُ 30 دَرَجَةً مِئَوِيَّةً. سَيَكونُ الطَّقْسُ جافًّا وَحارًّا في الأَيّامِ القَليلَةِ القادِمَةِ.

Dubai, United Arab Emirates (Summer): Temperatures in Dubai remain high, with a maximum temperature reaching 40 degrees Celsius and a minimum of 30 degrees Celsius. The weather will be dry and hot for the next few days.

بوينِس آيرِس، الأَرْجَنْتينُ (الرَّبيعُ): تَوَقُّعاتٌ بِطَقْسٍ مُعْتَدِلٍ في بوينِس آيرِس مَعَ دَرَجَةِ حَرارَةٍ عُظْمى تَبْلُغُ 22 دَرَجَةً مِئَوِيَّةً وَصُغْرى تَصِلُ إلى 13 دَرَجَةً مِئَوِيَّةً. قَدْ نَشْهَدُ زَخّاتٍ خَفيفَةً مِنَ المَطَرِ في مُنْتَصَفِ الأُسْبوعِ.

Buenos Aires, Argentina (Spring): The weather is expected to be mild in Buenos Aires with a high of 22 degrees Celsius and a low reaching 13 degrees Celsius. Light rain showers might occur mid-week.

كيبْ تاونْ، جَنوبُ أَفْريقْيا (الصَّيْفُ): تَرْتَفِعُ الحَرارَةُ في كيبْ تاونْ مَعَ تَوَقُّعاتٍ بِدَرَجَةِ حَرارَةٍ عُظْمى تَصِلُ إلى 27 دَرَجَةً مِئَوِيَّةً وَصُغْرى حَوْلَ 16 دَرَجَةً مِئَوِيَّةً. تَشْهَدُ الأَيّامُ المُقْبِلَةُ طَقْسًا مُشْمِسًا وَجافًّا.

---

[*] In Arabic, minus degrees are usually read as 'below zero' (تَحْتَ الصِّفْرِ), following the numeral, as you will hear in the audio. A less common variant is literally 'minus' (سالِبُ), as in 'minus five degrees' (سالِبُ خَمْسِ دَرَجاتٍ).

Cape Town, South Africa (Summer): Temperatures are rising in Cape Town with forecasts predicting a high of 27 degrees Celsius and a low around 16 degrees Celsius. The upcoming days will see sunny and dry weather.

بِرْلِينُ، أَلْمَانِيَا (الخَرِيفُ): يَجْلِبُ الخَرِيفُ بُرُودَةً مَلْحُوظَةً إِلَى بِرْلِينَ، حَيْثُ تَتَوَقَّعُ الأَرْصَادُ دَرَجَةَ حَرَارَةٍ عُظْمَى تَبْلُغُ 14 دَرَجَةً مِئَوِيَّةً وَصُغْرَى تَنْخَفِضُ إِلَى 6 دَرَجَاتٍ مِئَوِيَّةٍ. وَتَزْدَادُ احْتِمَالِيَّةُ تَسَاقُطِ الأَمْطَارِ فِي نِهَايَةِ الأُسْبُوعِ.

Berlin, Germany (Autumn): Autumn brings noticeable coolness to Berlin, with forecasts predicting a high of 14 degrees Celsius and a low dropping to 6 degrees Celsius. The chance of rain increases towards the end of the week.

رِيو دِي جَانِيرو، البَرَازِيلُ (الصَّيْفُ): تَسْتَعِدُّ رِيو لِأَيَّامٍ حَارَّةٍ مَعَ دَرَجَاتِ حَرَارَةٍ عُظْمَى تَصِلُ إِلَى 35 دَرَجَةً مِئَوِيَّةً وَصُغْرَى فِي حُدُودِ 25 دَرَجَةً مِئَوِيَّةً. سَتَكُونُ السَّمَاءُ صَافِيَةً مُعْظَمَ الأَيَّامِ، مِمَّا يُوَفِّرُ طَقْسًا مِثَالِيًّا لِلشَّاطِئِ.

Rio de Janeiro, Brazil (Summer): Rio is preparing for hot days with highs reaching 35 degrees Celsius and lows around 25 degrees Celsius. The sky will be clear most days, providing perfect beach weather.

9.1.1.3 TV Weather Forecast

Track 85

مَرْحَبًا بِكُمْ فِي نَشْرَةِ الطَّقْسِ عَلَى قَنَاتِنَا، حَيْثُ نَجْلِبُ لَكُمْ آخَرَ تَحْدِيثَاتِ الأَحْوَالِ الجَوِّيَّةِ مِنْ جَمِيعِ أَنْحَاءِ الشَّرْقِ الأَوْسَطِ. دَعُونَا نُلْقِي نَظْرَةً عَلَى خَرِيطَةِ المِنْطَقَةِ وَنَسْتَعْرِضُ دَرَجَاتِ الحَرَارَةِ وَالأَحْوَالَ الجَوِّيَّةَ فِي بَعْضِ المُدُنِ الرَّئِيسِيَّةِ.

نَبْدَأُ مِنَ القَاهِرَةِ، مِصْرَ، حَيْثُ تَشْهَدُ المَدِينَةُ طَقْسًا حَارًّا نَهَارًا مَعَ دَرَجَاتِ حَرَارَةٍ تَصِلُ إِلَى 35 دَرَجَةً مِئَوِيَّةً. فِي المَسَاءِ، تَنْخَفِضُ الحَرَارَةُ قَلِيلًا لِتَصِلَ إِلَى 25 دَرَجَةً مِئَوِيَّةً. يُنْصَحُ بِارْتِدَاءِ مَلَابِسَ خَفِيفَةٍ وَشُرْبِ كَمِّيَّاتٍ وَفِيرَةٍ مِنَ المَاءِ.

نَنْتَقِلُ إِلَى بَيْرُوتَ، لُبْنَانَ، نَجِدُ أَنَّ الطَّقْسَ مُعْتَدِلٌ بِشَكْلٍ عَامٍّ مَعَ دَرَجَاتِ حَرَارَةٍ تَتَرَاوَحُ بَيْنَ 27 دَرَجَةً مِئَوِيَّةً نَهَارًا وَ 20 دَرَجَةً مِئَوِيَّةً لَيْلًا. هُنَاكَ فُرْصَةٌ لِتَسَاقُطِ أَمْطَارٍ خَفِيفَةٍ، لِذَا قَدْ تَحْتَاجُ إِلَى اصْطِحَابِ مِظَلَّةٍ إِذَا كُنْتَ خَارِجَ المَنْزِلِ.

فِي الرِّيَاضِ، السُّعُودِيَّةِ، يَسْتَمِرُّ الطَّقْسُ الحَارُّ وَالجَافُّ، مَعَ دَرَجَاتِ حَرَارَةٍ تَصِلُ إِلَى 40 دَرَجَةً مِئَوِيَّةً خِلَالَ النَّهَارِ. وَتَكُونُ اللَّيَالِي أَكْثَرَ بُرُودَةً قَلِيلًا، مَعَ دَرَجَاتِ حَرَارَةٍ تُقَارِبُ 30 دَرَجَةً مِئَوِيَّةً. يُنْصَحُ السُّكَّانُ بِتَجَنُّبِ التَّعَرُّضِ المُبَاشِرِ لِأَشِعَّةِ الشَّمْسِ خِلَالَ سَاعَاتِ الظَّهِيرَةِ.

أَمَّا فِي عَمَّانَ، الأُرْدُنِّ، فَالطَّقْسُ مُسْتَقِرٌّ نِسْبِيًّا، مَعَ دَرَجَاتِ حَرَارَةٍ تَتَرَاوَحُ بَيْنَ 32 دَرَجَةً مِئَوِيَّةً نَهَارًا وَ 22 دَرَجَةً مِئَوِيَّةً لَيْلًا. السَّمَاءُ صَافِيَةٌ مَعَ رِيَاحٍ خَفِيفَةٍ تَجْعَلُ الطَّقْسَ مِثَالِيًّا لِلنَّشَاطَاتِ الخَارِجِيَّةِ.

وَأَخِيرًا، فِي بَغْدَادَ، العِراقِ، نَشْهَدُ تَغَيُّرًا جِذْرِيًّا فِي الطَّقْسِ، مَعَ دَرَجاتِ حَرارَةٍ عالِيَةٍ تَصِلُ إِلى 42 دَرَجَةً مِئَوِيَّةً نَهارًا. تَهُبُّ رِياحٌ شَمالِيَّةٌ تُساهِمُ فِي بَعْضِ الِانْخِفاضِ فِي الحَرارَةِ لَيْلًا، حَيْثُ تَصِلُ الدَّرَجاتُ إِلى حَوالَيْ 27 دَرَجَةً مِئَوِيَّةً.

كانَتْ هَذِهِ لَمْحَةً سَرِيعَةً عَنِ الأَحْوالِ الجَوِّيَّةِ فِي بَعْضِ مُدُنِ الشَّرْقِ الأَوْسَطِ. تَذَكَّروا دائِمًا التَّحَقُّقَ مِنَ التَّوَقُّعاتِ الجَوِّيَّةِ وَأَخْذَ الِاحْتِياطاتِ اللّازِمَةِ لِحِمايَةِ أَنْفُسِكُمْ مِنْ أَيِّ تَغَيُّراتِ طَقْسٍ مُفاجِئَةٍ. شُكْرًا لِمُتابَعَتِكُمْ، وَإِلى اللِّقاءِ فِي نَشْرَةِ الطَّقْسِ القادِمَةِ.

Welcome to our weather bulletin on our channel, where we bring you the latest weather updates from around the Middle East. Let's take a look at the regional map and review the temperatures and weather conditions in some of the major cities.

Starting with Cairo, Egypt, where the city is experiencing hot weather during the day with temperatures reaching up to 35 degrees Celsius. In the evening, temperatures cool down slightly to 25 degrees Celsius. It is advisable to wear light clothing and drink plenty of water.

Moving on to Beirut, Lebanon, we find that the weather is generally moderate with temperatures ranging from 27 degrees Celsius during the day to 20 degrees Celsius at night. There's a chance of light rain, so you might need to carry an umbrella if you're going out.

In Riyadh, Saudi Arabia, the hot and dry weather continues, with daytime temperatures reaching up to 40 degrees Celsius. Nights are slightly cooler with temperatures around 30 degrees Celsius. Residents are advised to avoid direct exposure to the sun during peak afternoon hours.

In Amman, Jordan, the weather is relatively stable with temperatures ranging from 32 degrees Celsius during the day to 22 degrees Celsius at night. The sky is clear with light winds making the weather ideal for outdoor activities.

Finally, in Baghdad, Iraq, we witness a radical change in the weather with high temperatures reaching up to 42 degrees Celsius during the day. North winds blow, contributing to a slight decrease in temperature at night, with temperatures reaching around 27 degrees Celsius.

This was a quick overview of the weather conditions in some cities of the Middle East. Always remember to check the weather forecast and take necessary precautions to protect yourselves from any sudden weather changes. Thank you for following, and see you in the next weather bulletin.

9.1.2 Climate Change

to impact

أَثَّرَ • تَأْثِيرٌ

أَثَّرَتِ التَّغَيُّراتُ المُناخِيَّةُ بِشَكْلٍ مَلْحوظٍ عَلى تَوْزيعِ الأَمْطارِ العالَمِيِّ.

Climate changes significantly affected the global rainfall distribution.

climate crisis

أَزْمَةٌ مُناخِيَّةٌ

تُواجِهُ البِلادُ أَزْمَةً مُناخِيَّةً تُهَدِّدُ بَقاءَ الأَنْظِمَةِ البيئِيَّةِ الهَشَّةِ.

The country is facing a climate crisis that threatens the survival of fragile ecosystems.

food security

أَمْنٌ غِذائِيٌّ

يُعْتَبَرُ الأَمْنُ الغِذائِيُّ تَحَدِّيًا مُتَزايِدًا بِسَبَبِ التَّقَلُّباتِ الشَّديدَةِ في الأَحْوالِ الجَوِّيَّةِ.

Food security is an increasingly challenging issue due to severe weather fluctuations.

climate security

أَمْنٌ مُناخِيٌّ

يَسْعى العُلَماءُ لِتَطْويرِ اسْتِراتيجِيّاتٍ فَعّالَةٍ لِضَمانِ أَمْنٍ مُناخِيٍّ مُسْتَدامٍ.

Scientists are striving to develop effective strategies to ensure sustainable climate security.

global warming

اِحْتِباسٌ حَرارِيٌّ عالَمِيٌّ

ساهَمَ الاِحْتِباسُ الحَرارِيُّ العالَمِيُّ في تَفاقُمِ الجَفافِ وَالفَيَضاناتِ في أَنْحاءٍ مُخْتَلِفَةٍ مِنَ العالَمِ.

Global warming has contributed to worsening droughts and floods in various parts of the world.

global temperature rise

اِرْتِفاعُ دَرَجَةِ الحَرارَةِ العالَمِيَّةِ

تُشيرُ الدِّراساتُ إلى ارْتِفاعِ دَرَجَةِ الحَرارَةِ العالَمِيَّةِ بِمُعَدَّلٍ غَيْرِ مَسْبوقٍ خِلالَ العُقودِ الأَخيرَةِ.

Studies indicate an unprecedented rise in global temperatures over recent decades.

sea level rise

اِرْتِفاعُ مُسْتَوى سَطْحِ البَحْرِ

يَتَسَبَّبُ ارْتِفاعُ مُسْتَوى سَطْحِ البَحْرِ في تَهْديدِ الجُزُرِ الصَّغيرَةِ وَالمَناطِقِ السّاحِلِيَّةِ.

Rising sea levels are threatening small islands and coastal regions.

to rise

ارْتَفَعَ • ارْتِفَاعٌ

ارْتَفَعَتْ نِسَبُ الِانْبِعَاثَاتِ الضَّارَّةِ نَتيجَةً لِلتَّوَسُّعِ الصِّناعِيِّ واسْتِهْلاكِ الوَقودِ الأُحْفورِيِّ.

Emission levels have risen due to industrial expansion and fossil fuel consumption.

resource optimization

اسْتِخْدامٌ أَمْثَلُ لِمَوْرِدٍ

يَدْعو الخُبَراءُ إلى اسْتِخْدامٍ أَمْثَلَ لِلْمَوارِدِ لِتَقْليلِ البَصْمَةِ الكَرْبونِيَّةِ وَحِمايَةِ البيئَةِ.

Experts are calling for the optimal use of resources to reduce the carbon footprint and protect the environment.

environmental sustainability

اسْتِدامَةٌ بيئِيَّةٌ

تُعْتَبَرُ الِاسْتِدامَةُ البيئِيَّةُ ضَرورِيَّةً لِلْحِفاظِ عَلى التَّوازُنِ الطَّبيعِيِّ لِلْكَوْكَبِ.

Environmental sustainability is essential for maintaining the planet's natural balance.

climate sustainability

اسْتِدامَةٌ مُناخٍ

تُعَدُّ اسْتِدامَةُ المُناخِ مِفْتاحًا لِمُسْتَقْبَلٍ أَكْثَرَ اخْضِرارًا وَنَظافَةً.

Climate sustainability is key to a greener, cleaner future.

sustainable energy consumption

اسْتِهْلاكُ طاقَةٍ مُسْتَدامٌ

يُعَزِّزُ اسْتِهْلاكُ الطَّاقَةِ المُسْتَدامُ تَقْليلَ التَّأْثيرِ السَّلْبِيِّ عَلى البيئَةِ.

Sustainable energy consumption enhances the reduction of negative environmental impact.

carbon dioxide emissions

انْبِعاثُ ثاني أُكْسيدِ الكَرْبونِ

يَرْتَبِطُ انْبِعاثُ ثاني أُكْسيدِ الكَرْبونِ ارْتِباطًا وَثيقًا بِتَغَيُّرِ المُناخِ العالَمِيِّ.

Carbon dioxide emissions are closely linked to global climate change.

greenhouse gas emissions

انْبِعاثُ غازاتٍ دَفيئَةٍ

تُسْهِمُ انْبِعاثاتُ الغازاتِ الدَّفيئَةِ في تَفاقُمِ ظاهِرَةِ الِاحْتِباسِ الحَرارِيِّ.

Greenhouse gas emissions contribute to the worsening of global warming.

انْبِعاثٌ كَرْبونِيٌّ

carbon emissions

أَثَّرَتِ الِانْبِعاثاتُ الكَرْبونِيَّةُ بِشَكْلٍ مَلْحوظٍ عَلى تَوْزيعِ الأَمْطارِ العالَمِيِّ.

Carbon emissions significantly affected the global rainfall distribution.

انْبَعَثَ • انْبِعاثٌ

to emit

انْبَعَثَتِ الغازاتُ الدَّفيئَةُ مِنَ المَصانِعِ بِمُعَدَّلاتٍ مُرْتَفِعَةٍ.

Greenhouse gases were emitted from factories at high rates.

انْخِفاضُ دَرَجاتِ حَرارَةٍ

temperature decrease

أَدّى انْفِجارٌ بُرْكانِيٌّ في إندونيسيا إلى انْخِفاضٍ مُؤَقَّتٍ في دَرَجاتِ الحَرارَةِ في المَناطِقِ المُحيطَةِ.

A volcanic eruption in Indonesia led to a temporary decrease in temperatures in the surrounding areas.

انْخِفاضٌ في مُسْتَوى الأُكْسِجينِ

oxygen level decrease

أَدّى انْخِفاضٌ في مُسْتَوى الأُكْسِجينِ في بُحَيْرَةِ طَبَرِيّا إلى تَغَيُّراتٍ بيئِيَّةٍ كَبيرَةٍ.

A decrease in oxygen levels in the Sea of Galilee has led to significant environmental changes.

انْخِفاضُ مُسْتَوى سَطْحِ البَحْرِ

sea level drop

أَفادَتِ التَّقاريرُ بِحُدوثِ انْخِفاضٍ طَفيفٍ في مُسْتَوى سَطْحِ البَحْرِ بِالْقُرْبِ مِنَ السّاحِلِ الشَّرْقِيِّ لِأُسْتُراليا نَتيجَةً لِلتَّغَيُّراتِ الجيولوجِيَّةِ.

Reports indicated a slight decrease in sea level near the east coast of Australia due to geological changes.

انْقِراضُ نَوْعٍ

species extinction

حَذَّرَتِ الأُمَمُ المُتَّحِدَةُ مِنْ أَنَّ تَغَيُّرَ المُناخِ يُهَدِّدُ بِانْقِراضِ أَنْواعٍ عَديدَةٍ حَوْلَ العالَمِ.

The United Nations warned that climate change threatens the extinction of numerous species worldwide.

environmental

بِيئِيٌّ

وَضَعَتِ الحُكومَةُ خُطَّةً لِتَحْسينِ الجَوْدَةِ البِيئِيَّةِ في المُدُنِ الكُبْرى لِمُكافَحَةِ التَّلَوُّثِ.

The government implemented a plan to improve environmental quality in major cities to combat pollution.

effect, impact on

تَأْثيرٌ عَلى

ناقَشَتِ القِمَّةُ البِيئِيَّةُ الدَّوْلِيَّةُ تَأْثيرَ التَّلَوُّثِ عَلى التَّنَوُّعِ البَيولوجِيِّ في الأَنْظِمَةِ البِيئِيَّةِ البَحْرِيَّةِ.

The international environmental summit discussed the impact of pollution on biodiversity in marine ecosystems.

to deteriorate

تَدَهْوَرَ • تَدَهْوُرٌ

تَدَهْوَرَتْ جَوْدَةُ الهَواءِ في المُدُنِ الكُبْرى بِسَبَبِ التَّلَوُّثِ.

Air quality in major cities deteriorated due to pollution.

to escalate

تَصاعَدَ • تَصاعُدٌ

سَتَتَصاعَدُ دَرَجاتُ الحَرارَةِ العالَمِيَّةُ إذا لَمْ نَتَّخِذْ تَدابيرَ فَوْرِيَّةً.

Global temperatures will escalate if immediate measures are not taken.

desertification

تَصَحُّرٌ

أَظْهَرَتِ الدِّراساتُ أَنَّ التَّصَحُّرَ يَتَسارَعُ في مِنْطَقَةِ السّاحِلِ الإِفْريقِيِّ، مِمّا يُؤَثِّرُ سَلْبًا عَلى الزِّراعَةِ وَالتَّنَوُّعِ البَيولوجِيِّ.

Studies have shown that desertification is accelerating in the African Sahel region, negatively affecting agriculture and biodiversity.

to be damaged

تَضَرَّرَ • تَضَرُّرٌ

تَضَرَّرَتِ الأَنْظِمَةُ البِيئِيَّةُ البَحْرِيَّةُ بِشَكْلٍ كَبيرٍ نَتيجَةً لِلتَّغَيُّراتِ المُناخِيَّةِ.

Marine ecosystems were greatly harmed due to climate changes.

تَغَيُّرُ مُناخٍ = تَغَيُّرٌ مُناخِيٌّ

climate change

يُعْتَبَرُ تَغَيُّرُ المُناخِ أَحَدَ أَكْبَرِ التَّحَدِّياتِ العالَمِيَّةِ الَّتي تُواجِهُ الإِنْسانِيَّةَ اليَوْمَ.

Climate change is considered one of the greatest global challenges facing humanity today.

تَغَيُّرُ مُناخٍ عالَمِيٌّ

global climate change

يُؤَدّي تَغَيُّرُ المُناخِ العالَمِيِّ إلى تَفاقُمِ الظَّواهِرِ الجَوِّيَّةِ القُصْوى كالْعَواصِفِ وَحَرائِقِ الغاباتِ.

Global climate change leads to the exacerbation of extreme weather phenomena like storms and wildfires.

تَغَيُّرٌ مُناخِيٌّ طارِئٌ

climate emergency

تَسَبَّبَ التَّغَيُّرُ المُناخِيُّ الطّارِئُ في زِيادَةِ التَّحَدِّياتِ الَّتي تُواجِهُ الجُهودَ الدَّوْلِيَّةَ لِمُكافَحَةِ الاِحْتِباسِ الحَرارِيِّ.

The climate emergency has increased the challenges facing international efforts to combat global warming.

تَغَيُّرُ نَمَطِ أَمْطارٍ

rain pattern changes

لوحِظَ تَغَيُّرُ نَمَطِ الأَمْطارِ في مَناطِقَ مُخْتَلِفَةٍ، مِمّا أَدّى إلى جَفافٍ في بَعْضِ المَناطِقِ وَفَيَضاناتٍ في مَناطِقَ أُخْرى.

A change in the pattern of rainfall has been observed in various regions, leading to drought in some areas and floods in others.

تَغَيُّرُ نَمَطٍ بيئيٍّ

environmental pattern change

أَثَّرَ تَغَيُّرُ النَّمَطِ البيئيِّ عَلى الأَنْواعِ الحَيَوانِيَّةِ وَالنَّباتِيَّةِ، مِمّا يُهَدِّدُ التَّوازُنَ البيئيَّ.

The change in the ecological pattern has affected animal and plant species, threatening the ecological balance.

تَقَلُّبُ مُناخٍ

climate variability

يُؤَدّي تَقَلُّبُ المُناخِ إلى صُعوبَةِ التَّنَبُّؤِ بِالأَحْوالِ الجَوِّيَّةِ، مِمّا يُؤَثِّرُ عَلى الزِّراعَةِ وَالأَمْنِ الغِذائِيِّ.

Climate variability leads to difficulties in predicting weather conditions, affecting agriculture and food security.

emission reduction
تَقْليلُ انْبِعاثٍ

تَعْمَلُ الدُّوَلُ عَلى تَقْليلِ انْبِعاثاتِ الغازاتِ الضّارَّةِ بِتَطْويرِ مَصادِرِ الطّاقَةِ المُتَجَدِّدَةِ.

Countries are working to reduce harmful gas emissions by developing renewable energy sources.

carbon reduction
تَقْليلُ كَرْبونٍ

تَعْمَلُ الشَّرِكاتُ عَلى تَقْليلِ آثارِ الكَرْبونِ في مُنْتَجاتِها لِلْمُساهَمَةِ في حِمايَةِ البيئَةِ.

Companies are working to reduce the carbon footprint of their products to contribute to environmental protection.

waste reduction
تَقْليلُ نُفاياتٍ

شَجَّعَتِ الحُكوماتُ عَلى تَقْليلِ النُّفاياتِ مِنْ خِلالِ إعادَةِ التَّدويرِ واسْتِخْدامِ مُنْتَجاتٍ صَديقَةٍ لِلْبيئَةِ.

Governments have encouraged waste reduction through recycling and the use of environmentally friendly products.

climate adaptation
تَكَيُّفٌ مَعَ تَغَيُّرٍ مُناخِيٍّ

تَتَبَنّى المُدُنُ سِياساتِ تَكَيُّفٍ مَعَ التَّغَيُّرِ المُناخِيِّ لِحِمايَةِ البِنْيَةِ التَّحْتِيَّةِ والمُجْتَمَعات.

Cities are adopting climate change adaptation policies to protect infrastructure and communities.

plastic pollution
تَلَوُّثٌ بِلاسْتيكِيٌّ

يُشَكِّلُ التَّلَوُّثُ البِلاسْتيكِيُّ تَحَدِّيًا كَبيرًا لِلْمُحيطاتِ، حَيْثُ يُؤَثِّرُ عَلى الحَياةِ البَحْرِيَّةِ.

Plastic pollution poses a significant challenge to the oceans, affecting marine life.

environmental pollution
تَلَوُّثٌ بيئِيٌّ

يُعَدُّ التَّلَوُّثُ البيئِيُّ مَسْؤولًا عَنِ العَديدِ مِنَ المُشْكِلاتِ الصِّحِّيَّةِ والتَّدَهْوُرِ البيئِيِّ.

Environmental pollution is responsible for many health issues and environmental degradation.

air pollution
تَلَوُّثٌ هَواءٍ

يُساهِمُ تَلَوُّثُ الهَواءِ في زِيادَةِ الأَمْراضِ التَّنَفُّسِيَّةِ ويُؤَثِّرُ عَلى جَوْدَةِ الحَياةِ.

Air pollution contributes to an increase in respiratory diseases and affects the quality of life.

sustainable development
تَنْمِيَةٌ مُسْتَدامَةٌ

تُرَكِّزُ التَّنْمِيَةُ المُسْتَدامَةُ عَلَى تَحْقيقِ النُّمُوِّ الاِقْتِصاديِّ مَعَ الحِفاظِ عَلَى البيئَةِ لِلْأَجْيالِ القادِمَةِ.

Sustainable development focuses on achieving economic growth while preserving the environment for future generations.

biodiversity
تَنَوُّعٌ بيئيٌّ = تَنَوُّعٌ بَيولوجيٌّ

يُعْتَبَرُ التَّنَوُّعُ البيئيُّ أساسيًّا لِلْحِفاظِ عَلَى الأَنْظِمَةِ البيئيَّةِ وَمُواجَهَةِ التَّحَدِّياتِ البيئيَّةِ.

Biodiversity is essential for maintaining ecosystems and facing environmental challenges.

environmental policy direction
تَوْجيهُ سِياسَةٍ بيئيَّةٍ

يَلْعَبُ تَوْجيهُ السِّياسَةِ البيئيَّةِ دَوْرًا حاسِمًا في التَّعامُلِ مَعَ التَّغَيُّرِ المُناخيِّ وَحِمايَةِ المَوارِدِ الطَّبيعيَّةِ.

Directing environmental policy plays a crucial role in dealing with climate change and protecting natural resources.

ozone hole
ثُقْبُ الأوزونِ

أفادَتْ تَقاريرُ جَديدَةٌ عَنْ تَوَسُّعِ ثُقْبِ الأوزونِ فَوْقَ القارَّةِ القُطْبِيَّةِ الجَنوبيَّةِ، مِمّا يُثيرُ المَخاوِفَ البيئيَّةِ.

New reports indicate the expansion of the ozone hole over Antarctica, raising environmental concerns.

extreme drought
جَفافٌ شَديدٌ

يُعاني القَرْنُ الإفْريقيُّ مِنْ جَفافٍ شَديدٍ لِلْعامِ الثّالِثِ عَلَى التَّوالي، مِمّا يُهَدِّدُ الأَمْنَ الغِذائيَّ في المِنْطَقَةِ.

The Horn of Africa is experiencing severe drought for the third consecutive year, threatening food security in the region.

melting ice
جَليدٌ ذائِبٌ

سَجَّلَتِ الأَقْمارُ الصِّناعيَّةُ ارْتِفاعًا مَلْحوظًا في الجَليدِ الذّائِبِ في القُطْبِ الشَّماليِّ، مِمّا يَعْكِسُ تَأْثيراتِ تَغَيُّرِ المُناخِ.

Satellites recorded a significant increase in melting ice in the Arctic, reflecting the impacts of climate change.

air quality

جَوْدَةُ هَوَاءٍ

أَطْلَقَتِ الحُكومَةُ حَمْلَةً لِتَحْسينِ جودَةِ الهَواءِ في المُدُنِ الكُبْرى مِنْ خِلالِ تَقْييدِ اسْتِخْدامِ السَّيّاراتِ.

The government launched a campaign to improve air quality in major cities by restricting car use.

severe

حادٌّ

يَشْهَدُ العالَمُ تَغَيُّراتٍ مُناخِيَّةً حادَّةً تَتَطَلَّبُ اسْتِجابَةً دَوْلِيَّةً عاجِلَةً.

The world is experiencing severe climate changes that require an immediate international response.

extreme weather event

حادِثَةٌ جَوِّيَّةٌ شَديدَةٌ   • حَوادِثُ

وَقَعَت حادِثَةٌ جَوِّيَّةٌ شَديدَةٌ في جَنوبِ آسيا نَتيجَةَ الأَعاصيرِ المُفاجِئَةِ، مِمّا أَدّى إلى خَسائِرَ بَشَرِيَّةٍ وَمادِّيَّةٍ كَبيرَةٍ.

A severe weather incident occurred in South Asia due to sudden cyclones, leading to significant human and material losses.

mitigation of temperature rise

حَدٌّ مِنَ ارْتِفاعِ الحَرارَةِ

اِعْتَمَدَت دَوْلَةُ الإماراتِ سياساتٍ جَديدَةً لِلْحَدِّ مِنَ ارْتِفاعِ الحَرارَةِ، وَيَشْمَلُ ذَلِكَ زيادَةَ المِساحاتِ الخَضْراءِ وَتَشْجيعَ الطّاقَةِ المُتَجَدِّدَةِ.

The UAE adopted new policies to limit temperature rise, including increasing green spaces and promoting renewable energy.

erratic temperature

حَرارَةٌ مُتَأَرْجِحَةٌ

شَهِدَت مِنْطَقَةُ البَحْرِ المُتَوَسِّطِ حَرارَةً مُتَأَرْجِحَةً خِلالَ الصَّيْفِ، مِمّا أَثَّرَ عَلى السِّياحَةِ وَالزِّراعَةِ.

The Mediterranean region experienced fluctuating temperatures during the summer, affecting tourism and agriculture.

thermal

حَرارِيٌّ

أَظْهَرَتِ الدِّراساتُ أَنَّ النَّشاطَ الحَرارِيَّ البُرْكانِيَّ تَحْتَ المُحيطاتِ يُمْكِنُ أَنْ يُؤَثِّرَ عَلى الأَنْظِمَةِ البيئِيَّةِ البَحْرِيَّةِ.

Studies have shown that volcanic thermal activity under the oceans can affect marine ecosystems.

environmental conservation
حِفاظٌ عَلَى البِيئَة

أَطْلَقَتِ الحُكومَةُ المِصْريَّةُ مَشْروعًا وَطَنِيًّا لِلْحِفاظِ عَلَى البِيئَةِ يُرَكِّزُ عَلَى اسْتِصْلاحِ الأَراضِي الصَّحْراوِيَّةِ.

The Egyptian government launched a national project for environmental conservation focusing on rehabilitating desert lands.

energy conservation
حِفاظٌ عَلَى طاقَة

تَبَنَّتْ دُبَيُّ مُبادَرَةً لِلْحِفاظِ عَلَى الطّاقَةِ تَشْمَلُ تَرْكيبَ أَنْظِمَةِ الإِضاءَةِ المُوَفِّرَةِ لِلطّاقَةِ في المَباني العامَّةِ.

Dubai adopted an energy conservation initiative that includes installing energy-efficient lighting systems in public buildings.

protecting migratory birds
حِمايَةُ طُيورٍ مُهاجِرَةٍ

نَفَّذَتِ السُّلُطاتُ في إِسْبانِيا بَرْنامَجًا لِحِمايَةِ الطُّيورِ المُهاجِرَةِ، وَذَلِكَ بِتَقْييدِ الصَّيْدِ في المَناطِقِ السّاحِلِيَّةِ.

Spanish authorities implemented a program to protect migratory birds by restricting hunting in coastal areas.

marine life
حَياةٌ بَحْرِيَّةٌ • حَيَواتٌ

أَعْلَنَتْ مُنَظَّمَةُ الحِفاظِ عَلَى الحَياةِ البَحْرِيَّةِ عَنْ إِنْشاءِ مَناطِقَ مَحْمِيَّةٍ جَديدَةٍ لِلْحِفاظِ عَلَى التَّنَوُّعِ البَيولوجِيِّ في البَحْرِ الأَحْمَرِ.

The Marine Life Conservation Organization announced the creation of new protected areas to preserve biodiversity in the Red Sea.

to melt
ذابَ • ذَوَبانٌ

ذابَتْ كُتَلُ الجَليدِ في القُطْبِ الشَّماليِّ بِسُرْعَةٍ غَيْرِ مَسْبوقَةٍ.

Ice masses in the Arctic melted at an unprecedented rate.

to increase
زادَ • زِيادَةٌ

زادَتْ مُسْتَوَياتُ المِياهِ في الأَنْهارِ نَتيجَةً لِذَوَبانِ الأَنْهارِ الجَليدِيَّةِ.

Water levels in rivers increased due to the melting of glaciers.

ocean warming

زِيادَةُ حَرارَةِ مُحيطٍ

سَجَّلَتْ مِنْطَقَةُ المُحيطِ الهادِئِ زِيادَةَ حَرارَةٍ مَلْحوظَةً، مِمّا أَثَّرَ عَلى الأَنْظِمَةِ البيئِيَّةِ البَحْرِيَّةِ.

The Pacific region recorded a notable increase in ocean temperature, affecting marine ecosystems.

extreme

شَديدٌ

تَعَرَّضَتِ الهِنْدُ لِظاهِرَةٍ جَوِّيَّةٍ شَديدَةٍ، تَمَثَّلَتْ في عَواصِفَ رَعْدِيَّةٍ مُتَتالِيَةٍ أَدَّتْ إلى خَسائِرَ فادِحَةٍ.

India experienced a severe weather phenomenon, consisting of consecutive thunderstorms, leading to significant losses.

harmful to health

ضارٌّ بالصِّحَّةِ

حَذَّرَتْ مُنَظَّمَةُ الصِّحَّةِ العالَمِيَّةُ مِنْ أَنَّ التَّلَوُّثَ الجَوِّيَّ في المُدُنِ الكُبْرى أَصْبَحَ ضارًّا بالصِّحَّةِ بِشَكْلٍ مُتَزايِدٍ.

The World Health Organization warned that air pollution in major cities has become increasingly harmful to health.

renewable energy

طاقَةٌ مُتَجَدِّدَةٌ

أَعْلَنَتْ أَلْمانِيا عَنْ خُطَّتِها لِلِاعْتِمادِ بِشَكْلٍ كامِلٍ عَلى الطّاقَةِ المُتَجَدِّدَةِ بِحُلولِ عامِ 2035.

Germany announced its plan to fully rely on renewable energy by 2035.

natural

طَبيعِيٌّ

يَتَطَلَّبُ تَغَيُّرُ المُناخِ اتِّخاذَ إجراءاتٍ عاجِلَةٍ لِلحِفاظِ على النُّظُمِ البيئِيَّةِ الطَّبيعِيَّةِ والتَّنَوُّعِ البَيولوجِيِّ.

Climate change necessitates urgent action to preserve natural ecosystems and biodiversity.

extreme weather event

ظَواهِرُ • ظاهِرَةٌ جَوِّيَّةٌ شَديدَةٌ

شَهِدَتِ اليابانُ ظاهِرَةً جَوِّيَّةً شَديدَةً، تَمَثَّلَتْ في إعْصارٍ قَوِيٍّ أَدّى إلى إجْلاءِ آلافِ السُّكّانِ.

Japan experienced a severe weather event, consisting of a powerful typhoon that led to the evacuation of thousands of residents.

global

عالَمِيٌّ

أَثارَتْ زِيادَةُ حِدَّةِ الظَّواهِرِ الجَوِّيَّةِ الشَّديدَةِ حَوْلَ العالَمِ القَلَقَ بِشَأْنِ تأثيراتِ تَغَيُّرِ المُناخِ العالَمِيِّ.

The increasing severity of extreme weather events globally has raised concerns about the impacts of global climate change.

carbon sequestration

عَزْلُ الكَرْبونِ

تَبَنَّتِ الصّينُ سِياسَةً عالَمِيَّةً جَديدَةً لِعَزْلِ الكَرْبونِ بِهَدَفِ تَقْليلِ انْبِعاثاتِ ثاني أُكْسيدِ الكَرْبونِ.

China adopted a new global policy for carbon sequestration aimed at reducing carbon dioxide emissions.

rainforest

غابَةٌ مَطيرَةٌ

تَسَبَّبَتِ الحَرائِقُ الشَّديدَةُ في الأمازون في تَدْميرِ مِساحاتٍ واسِعَةٍ مِنَ الغابَةِ المَطيرَةِ، مِمّا يُهَدِّدُ الحَياةَ البَرِّيَّةَ.

Severe fires in the Amazon resulted in the destruction of vast areas of the rainforest, threatening wildlife.

greenhouse gases   *pl.*

غازاتٌ دَفيئَةٌ

تَسَبَّبَ ارْتِفاعُ مُسْتَوَياتِ الغازاتِ الدَّفيئَةِ في تَغْييراتٍ مُقْلِقَةٍ في الغِلافِ الجَوِّيِّ.

The rise in greenhouse gas levels has caused concerning changes in the atmosphere.

atmosphere   • أغْلِفَةٌ

غِلافٌ جَوِّيٌّ

تَسَبَّبَ تَغَيُّرُ المُناخِ في تَغَيُّراتٍ مَلْحوظَةٍ في الغِلافِ الجَوِّيِّ، مِمّا يُؤَدّي إلى زِيادَةِ تَواتُرِ وَشِدَّةِ الكَوارِثِ الطَّبيعِيَّةِ.

Climate change has caused noticeable changes in the atmosphere, leading to an increase in the frequency and severity of natural disasters.

unpredictable

غَيْرُ مُتَوَقَّع

أَدَّتِ الظَّواهِرُ الجَوِّيَّةُ غَيْرُ المُتَوَقَّعَةِ إلى صُعوباتٍ في التَّخْطيطِ الزِّراعِيِّ وَإدارَةِ المَوارِدِ الطَّبيعِيَّةِ.

Unexpected weather phenomena have led to difficulties in agricultural planning and natural resource management.

غَيْر functions similarly to the English prefixes 'un-' and 'non-,' negating the meaning of the adjective it precedes. Notice that this is a compound construction (idaafa), and as such, the adjective is always in the genitive case.

غَيْرُ مُسْتَدامٍ

unsustainable

حَذَّرَ الخُبَراءُ مِنْ أَنَّ النُّمُوَّ الاقْتِصادِيَّ غَيْرَ المُسْتَدامِ يُمْكِنُ أَنْ يُؤَدِّيَ إلى مَشاكِلَ بيئِيَّةٍ خَطيرَةٍ.

Experts warned that unsustainable economic growth could lead to serious environmental problems.

غَيْرُ مُسْتَقِرٍّ

unstable

يُعاني الشَّرْقُ الأَوْسَطُ مِنْ مُناخٍ غَيْرِ مُسْتَقِرٍّ، مِمّا يُؤَدِّي إلى تَحَدِّياتٍ في تَأْمينِ المِياهِ وَالغِذاءِ.

The Middle East is experiencing unstable climate, leading to challenges in securing water and food.

فَيَضانٌ

flood

تَسَبَّبَ فَيَضانٌ شَديدٌ في تايلاند في تَدْميرِ المَنازِلِ وَالمَزارِعِ، مِمّا يُؤَثِّرُ عَلى الاقْتِصادِ المَحَلِّيِّ.

A severe flood in Thailand caused the destruction of homes and farms, affecting the local economy.

كارِثَةٌ طَبيعِيَّةٌ • كَوارِثُ

natural disaster

تُعْتَبَرُ الكَوارِثُ الطَّبيعِيَّةُ المُتَكَرِّرَةُ، كالأَعاصيرِ وَالفَيَضاناتِ، مُؤَشِّرًا عَلى تَأْثيراتِ تَغَيُّرِ المُناخِ.

Repeated natural disasters, such as cyclones and floods, are an indicator of the impacts of climate change.

مُؤَثِّرٌ عَلى بيئَةٍ

environmentally impactful

أَشارَتِ الدِّراساتُ إلى أَنَّ التَّلَوُّثَ الصِّناعِيَّ يُعْتَبَرُ مُؤَثِّرًا سَلْبِيًّا عَلى البيئَةِ وَصِحَّةِ الإنْسانِ.

Studies have indicated that industrial pollution is a negative factor affecting the environment and human health.

مُتَطَوِّرٌ

evolving

تَعْكِسُ سِياساتُ المُناخِ المُتَطَوِّرَةُ الجُهودَ المُسْتَمِرَّةَ لِمُواجَهَةِ التَّحَدِّياتِ الَّتي تَنْشَأُ نَتيجَةً لِلتَّغَيُّراتِ البيئِيَّةِ.

Evolving climate policies reflect the ongoing efforts to confront the challenges posed by environmental changes.

changing, variable   مُتَغَيِّرٌ

يَتَّسِمُ المُناخُ في هَذِهِ المِنْطَقَةِ بِأَنَّهُ مُتَغَيِّرٌ، مِمَّا يَجْعَلُ التَّنَبُّؤَ بِالطَّقْسِ أَكْثَرَ صُعوبَةً.

The climate in this region is variable, making weather prediction more challenging.

balanced   مُتَوازِنٌ

يُعْتَبَرُ النِّظامُ البِيئِيُّ في الغابَةِ المَطيرَةِ مُتَوازِنًا بِشَكْلٍ طَبيعِيٍّ، لَكِنَّهُ الآنَ مُهَدَّدٌ بِسَبَبِ القَطْعِ الجائِرِ لِلْأَشْجارِ.

The ecosystem in the rainforest is naturally balanced, but now it is threatened due to excessive logging.

improved   مُحَسَّنٌ

التِّقْنِياتُ المُحَسَّنَةُ ضَرورِيَّةٌ لِمُعالَجَةِ تَحَدِّياتِ التَّغَيُّرِ المُناخِيِّ بِفَعَّالِيَّةٍ.

Improved technologies are crucial for addressing climate change challenges effectively.

frightening, scary   مُخيفٌ

أَظْهَرَتْ إِحْصائِيَّةٌ مُخيفَةٌ أَنَّ نِسْبَةَ ارْتِفاعِ دَرَجَةِ حَرارَةِ الأَرْضِ قَدْ تَجاوَزَتِ التَّوَقُّعاتِ السَّابِقَةَ.

A frightening statistic showed that the rate of Earth's temperature rise has exceeded previous expectations.

polluted   مُلَوَّثٌ

أَصْبَحَتِ المِياهُ في خَليجِ البِنْغالِ مُلَوَّثَةً بِشَكْلٍ مُتَزايِدٍ، مِمَّا يُهَدِّدُ النِّظامَ البِيئِيَّ البَحْرِيَّ.

The waters in the Bay of Bengal have become increasingly polluted, threatening the marine ecosystem.

threatened   مُهَدَّدٌ

تُعْتَبَرُ الغاباتُ المَطيرَةُ مُهَدَّدَةً بِسَبَبِ القَطْعِ الجائِرِ وَتَغَيُّرِ المُناخِ.

Rainforests are threatened due to deforestation and climate change.

human activity   أَنْشِطَة •   نَشاطٌ بَشَرِيٌّ

أَدَّى النَّشاطُ البَشَرِيُّ المُكَثَّفُ، كَإِزالَةِ الغاباتِ وَالتَّلَوُّثِ الصِّناعِيِّ، إِلى تَدَهْوُرِ الأَنْظِمَةِ البِيئِيَّةِ في أَمْريكا الجَنوبِيَّةِ.

Intense human activity, such as deforestation and industrial pollution, has led to the degradation of ecosystems in South America.

ecosystem

نِظامٌ بِيئِيٌّ

يُؤَثِّرُ تَغَيُّرُ المُناخِ عَلى الأَنْظِمَةِ البِيئِيَّةِ، مِمّا يُعَرِّضُ التَنَوُّعَ البَيولوجِيَّ لِلْخَطَرِ في مَناطِقَ مِثْلِ حَوْضِ الأَمازون.

Climate change is affecting ecosystems, putting biodiversity at risk in areas like the Amazon Basin.

precipitation pattern

نَمَطُ هُطولٍ

لوحِظَ تَغَيُّرٌ في نَمَطِ هُطولِ الأَمْطارِ في مِنْطَقَةِ السّاحِلِ الأَفْريقِيِّ، مِمّا يُؤَدّي إلى مَشاكِلَ في الزِّراعَةِ وَإِمْداداتِ المِياهِ.

A change in the rainfall pattern has been observed in the African Sahel region, leading to challenges in agriculture and water supply.

climate awareness

وَعْيٌ مُناخِيٌّ

يَتَزايَدُ الوَعْيُ المُناخِيُّ بَيْنَ الشَّبابِ حَوْلَ العالَمِ، مِمّا يَدْفَعُهُمْ إلى المُطالَبَةِ بِسِياساتٍ بِيئِيَّةٍ فَعّالَةٍ.

Climate awareness is increasing among young people worldwide, prompting them to demand effective environmental policies.

9.1.2.1 Mini-Articles

Track **87**

مَعَ اسْتِمْرارِ تَغَيُّرِ المُناخِ، تُواجِهُ مِصْرُ أَزْمَةَ مِياهٍ مُتَفاقِمَةً تُؤَثِّرُ بِشَكْلٍ مُباشِرٍ عَلى الأَمْنِ الغِذائِيِّ لِلْبِلادِ. انْخِفاضُ أَنْماطِ هُطولِ الأَمْطارِ وارْتِفاعُ دَرَجاتِ الحَرارَةِ العالَمِيَّةِ يُقَلِّلانِ مِنْ تَوافُرِ المِياهِ العَذْبَةِ، مِمّا يَضَعُ ضُغوطًا كَبيرَةً عَلى الزِّراعَةِ. تَسْعى الحُكومَةُ الآنَ لِلتَّكَيُّفِ مَعَ هذا التَّغَيُّرِ المُناخِيِّ مِنْ خِلالِ تَطْويرِ أَساليبِ رَيٍّ مُسْتَدامَةٍ والاسْتِخْدامِ الأَمْثَلِ لِلْمَوارِدِ المائِيَّةِ.

As climate change continues, Egypt faces an escalating water crisis that directly affects the country's food security. The decrease in rainfall patterns and the rise in global temperatures reduce the availability of fresh water, putting significant pressure on agriculture. The government is now seeking to adapt to this climate change through the development of sustainable irrigation methods and the optimal use of water resources.

تَشْهَدُ دُوَلُ الخَليجِ العَرَبِيِّ زِيادَةً مُقْلِقَةً في حَرارَةِ المِياهِ المُحيطَةِ، مِمّا يُؤَدّي إلى تَبِعاتٍ بِيئِيَّةٍ وَاقْتِصادِيَّةٍ خَطيرَةٍ. يُهَدِّدُ ارْتِفاعُ دَرَجَةِ حَرارَةِ البَحْرِ الحَياةَ البَحْرِيَّةَ وَيَتَسَبَّبُ في انْبِعاثِ كَمِّيّاتٍ كَبيرَةٍ مِنْ غازاتِ الدَّفيئَةِ نَتيجَةَ تَحَلُّلِ

الكائِناتِ البَحرِيَّةِ المُتَأَثِّرَةِ بِالحَرارَةِ. تَعمَلُ الدُّوَلُ عَلَى تَعزِيزِ الاِستِدامَةِ البِيئِيَّةِ وَحِمايَةِ التَّنَوُّعِ البِيولوجِيِّ البَحرِيِّ مِنْ خِلالِ تَطبِيقِ سِياساتٍ بِيئِيَّةٍ مُحَسَّنَةٍ.

The Arab Gulf states are experiencing a worrying increase in the temperature of surrounding waters, leading to serious environmental and economic consequences. The rise in sea temperature threatens marine life and causes the emission of large amounts of greenhouse gases due to the decomposition of marine organisms affected by the heat. These states are working to enhance environmental sustainability and protect marine biodiversity through the implementation of improved environmental policies.

تُشِيرُ دِراسَةٌ حَدِيثَةٌ إِلَى أَنَّ تَغَيُّرَ المُناخِ العالَمِيِّ يُسرِعُ مِنْ وَتِيرَةِ ذَوَبانِ الجَلِيدِ فِي القُطبِ الشَّمالِيِّ، مِمّا يُؤَدِّي إِلَى اِرتِفاعِ مُستَوَياتِ سَطحِ البَحرِ عَلَى نِطاقٍ عالَمِيٍّ. يُهَدِّدُ هَذا التَّغَيُّرُ الجِذرِيُّ بِغَرقِ مَناطِقَ ساحِلِيَّةٍ وَيُؤَثِّرُ عَلَى الأَنظِمَةِ البِيئِيَّةِ. يَدعو العُلَماءُ إِلَى تَحَرُّكٍ دَولِيٍّ مُشتَرَكٍ لِلحَدِّ مِنَ اِنبِعاثاتِ ثانِي أُكسِيدِ الكَربونِ وَتَحقِيقِ الاِستِدامَةِ البِيئِيَّةِ.

A new study indicates that global climate change is accelerating the pace of ice melting in the Arctic, leading to a global rise in sea levels. This radical change threatens to submerge coastal areas and affect ecosystems. Scientists call for joint international action to reduce carbon dioxide emissions and achieve environmental sustainability.

يُواجِهُ جَنوبُ آسِيا فَيَضاناتٍ شَدِيدَةً وَغَيرَ مُتَوَقَّعَةٍ نَتِيجَةَ تَغَيُّرِ نَمَطِ الأَمطارِ، وَهُوَ تَأثِيرٌ مُباشِرٌ لِلتَّغَيُّرِ المُناخِيِّ العالَمِيِّ. أَدَّتِ الأَمطارُ الغَزِيرَةُ إِلَى فَيَضاناتٍ جارِفَةٍ تَسَبَّبَتْ فِي دَمارٍ واسِعِ النِّطاقِ وَتَهجِيرِ الآلافِ مِنَ النّاسِ. تُبرِزُ هَذِهِ الظّاهِرَةُ الجَوِّيَّةُ الشَّدِيدَةُ الحاجَةَ الماسَّةَ لِتَطوِيرِ اِستِراتيجِيّاتِ تَكَيُّفٍ مَعَ تَغَيُّرِ المُناخِ وَتَعزِيزِ الاِستِعدادِ لِلْكَوارِثِ.

South Asia faces severe and unexpected flooding as a result of changing rainfall patterns, a direct effect of global climate change. Heavy rains have led to devastating floods that have caused widespread destruction and displaced thousands of people. This extreme weather phenomenon highlights the urgent need for developing climate change adaptation strategies and enhancing disaster preparedness.

تُعَدُّ مَوجَةُ الحَرِّ الشَّدِيدِ الَّتي اِجتاحَتْ أُوروبا مُؤَخَّرًا مُؤَشِّرًا واضِحًا عَلَى تَأثِيراتِ الاِحتِباسِ الحَرارِيِّ العالَمِيِّ. أَدَّتْ دَرَجاتُ الحَرارَةِ القِياسِيَّةُ إِلَى جَفافٍ شَدِيدٍ، مِمّا يُؤَثِّرُ سَلبًا عَلَى الأَمنِ الغِذائِيِّ وَمَوارِدِ المِياهِ. تُسارِعُ الحُكوماتُ الأُوروبِيَّةُ إِلَى تَطبِيقِ تَدابِيرَ لِتَقلِيلِ الكَربونِ وَتَعزِيزِ الاِستِهلاكِ المُستَدامِ لِلطّاقَةِ لِمُواجَهَةِ هَذِهِ الأَزمَةِ المُناخِيَّةِ.

The recent extreme heatwave that swept across Europe is a clear indicator of the effects of global warming. Record temperatures have led to severe drought, negatively affecting food security and water resources. European governments are hastening to implement carbon reduction measures and promote sustainable energy consumption to address this climate crisis.

تَغَيُّرُ المُناخِ في الشَّرقِ الأَوْسَطِ وَشَمالِ إفْريقْيا: تَحَدِّياتٌ وَاسْتِجاباتٌ

الشَّرْقُ الأَوْسَطُ وَشَمالُ إفْريقْيا، المِنْطَقَةُ المَعْروفَةُ بِتَنَوُّعِها الثَّقافِيِّ وَالجُغْرافِيِّ الغَنِيِّ، تُواجِهُ اليَوْمَ تَحَدِّيًا مُتَزايِدًا بِسَبَبِ تَغَيُّرِ المُناخِ. هَذِهِ المِنْطَقَةُ، الَّتي تُعاني بِالفِعْلِ مِنْ شُحِّ المِياهِ وَالجَفافِ، تَشْهَدُ تَأْثيراتٍ مُتَسارِعَةً لِلتَّغَيُّراتِ المُناخِيَّةِ الَّتي تُهَدِّدُ الأَمْنَ الغِذائِيَّ وَالمائِيَّ وَتُؤَثِّرُ عَلى مَعيشَةِ مَلايينِ النّاسِ.

اِرْتِفاعُ دَرَجاتِ الحَرارَةِ: يُعَدُّ الشَّرْقُ الأَوْسَطُ وَشَمالُ إفْريقْيا مِنْ بَيْنِ المَناطِقِ الأَكْثَرِ تَأَثُّرًا بِارْتِفاعِ دَرَجاتِ الحَرارَةِ العالَمِيَّةِ. يَتَوَقَّعُ العُلَماءُ أَنْ تَشْهَدَ هَذِهِ المِنْطَقَةُ ارْتِفاعًا في دَرَجاتِ الحَرارَةِ أَكْبَرَ مِنَ المُتَوَسِّطِ العالَمِيِّ، مِمّا يُؤَدّي إلى زِيادَةٍ في مَوْجاتِ الحَرِّ وَالجَفافِ.

نُدْرَةُ المِياهِ: أَحَدُ أَبْرَزِ تَحَدِّياتِ التَّغَيُّرِ المُناخِيِّ في المِنْطَقَةِ هُوَ تَفاقُمُ أَزْمَةِ المِياهِ. تُؤَدّي الزِّيادَةُ في التَّبَخُّرِ بِسَبَبِ الحَرارَةِ المُرْتَفِعَةِ، إلى جانِبِ نَقْصِ الأَمْطارِ، إلى انْخِفاضٍ في مُسْتَوَياتِ المِياهِ الجَوْفِيَّةِ وَتَقْليلِ تَدَفُّقِ الأَنْهارِ، مِمّا يُؤَثِّرُ عَلى الزِّراعَةِ وَمَصادِرِ مِياهِ الشُّرْبِ.

التَّأْثيراتُ عَلى التَّنَوُّعِ البَيولوجِيِّ: يُهَدِّدُ التَّغَيُّرُ المُناخِيُّ التَّنَوُّعَ البَيولوجِيَّ في المِنْطَقَةِ، حَيْثُ يُؤَدّي التَّصَحُّرُ وَتَغَيُّرُ النُّظُمِ البيئِيَّةِ إلى خَطَرِ انْقِراضِ الأَنْواعِ وَفُقْدانِ المَواطِنِ الطَّبيعِيَّةِ.

الاسْتِجابَةُ لِلتَّغَيُّرِ المُناخِيِّ: تَتَّخِذُ دُوَلُ المِنْطَقَةِ خُطُواتٍ لِمُواجَهَةِ تَحَدِّياتِ التَّغَيُّرِ المُناخِيِّ مِنْ خِلالِ تَطْويرِ السِّياساتِ البيئِيَّةِ وَالاسْتِثْمارِ في الطّاقَةِ المُتَجَدِّدَةِ وَتَعْزيزِ كَفاءَةِ اسْتِخْدامِ المِياهِ. يُعَدُّ العَمَلُ عَلى تَحْقيقِ اسْتِدامَةٍ بيئِيَّةٍ وَمُناخِيَّةٍ أَوْلَوِيَّةً لِضَمانِ مُسْتَقْبَلٍ مُسْتَدامٍ لِلْأَجْيالِ القادِمَةِ.

الدَّعْوَةُ لِلْعَمَلِ الجَماعِيِّ: تَتَطَلَّبُ مُواجَهَةُ تَغَيُّرِ المُناخِ جُهودًا مُشْتَرَكَةً عَلى المُسْتَوى الإقْليمِيِّ وَالدَّوْلِيِّ. سَيَكونُ التَّعاوُنُ في مَجالِ البَحْثِ العِلْمِيِّ وَتَبادُلِ المَعْرِفَةِ وَالتِّكْنولوجْيا، بِالإضافَةِ إلى التَّمْويلِ المُسْتَدامِ، حاسِمَيْنِ في التَّخْفيفِ مِنْ تَأْثيراتِ التَّغَيُّرِ المُناخِيِّ وَتَعْزيزِ قُدْرَةِ المِنْطَقَةِ عَلى التَّكَيُّفِ مَعَ التَّحَدِّياتِ المُسْتَقْبَلِيَّةِ.

في ظِلِّ تَزايُدِ تَأْثيراتِ التَّغَيُّرِ المُناخِيِّ، يَظَلُّ العَمَلُ العاجِلُ وَالمُتَواصِلُ لِتَعْزيزِ الاسْتِدامَةِ وَالتَّكَيُّفِ مَعَ التَّغَيُّراتِ المُناخِيَّةِ أَمْرًا ضَرورِيًّا لِضَمانِ اسْتِمْرارِيَّةِ وَازْدِهارِ الشَّرْقِ الأَوْسَطِ وَشَمالِ إفْريقْيا.

Climate Change in the Middle East and North Africa: Challenges and Responses

The Middle East and North Africa, a region known for its rich cultural and geographical diversity, faces an increasing challenge due to climate change. This region, already suffering from water scarcity and drought, is experiencing accelerated effects of climate changes that threaten food and water security and affect the livelihoods of millions of people.

Rising Temperatures: The Middle East and North Africa are among the regions most affected by global temperature increases. Scientists expect this area to experience a higher-than-average rise in temperatures, leading to more frequent heatwaves and droughts.

Water Scarcity: One of the most significant challenges of climate change in the region is the exacerbation of the water crisis. Increased evaporation due to higher temperatures, coupled with a lack of rainfall, leads to a decrease in groundwater levels and reduced river flow, impacting agriculture and drinking water sources.

Impacts on Biodiversity: Climate change threatens the region's biodiversity, as desertification and changes in ecosystems lead to the risk of species extinction and loss of natural habitats.

Response to Climate Change: Countries in the region are taking steps to address the challenges of climate change through the development of environmental policies, investment in renewable energy, and enhancing water use efficiency. Working toward environmental and climate sustainability is a priority to ensure a sustainable future for coming generations.

Call for Collective Action: Addressing climate change requires joint efforts at both regional and international levels. Cooperation in scientific research, knowledge, and technology exchange, in addition to sustainable financing, will be crucial in mitigating the impacts of climate change and enhancing the region's ability to adapt to future challenges.

As the effects of climate change continue to intensify, urgent and ongoing action to enhance sustainability and adapt to climate changes remains essential to ensure the continuity and prosperity of the Middle East and North Africa.

9.1.2.3 Opinion Piece: Rising Sea Levels

Track **89**

التَّأْثِيراتُ المُتَوَقَّعَةُ لِارْتِفاعِ مُسْتَوَياتِ سَطْحِ البَحْرِ عَلَى المُدُنِ السّاحِلِيَّةِ: تَحَدِّياتٌ وَاسْتِراتيجِيّاتٌ

مَعَ اسْتِمْرارِيَّةِ النَّغَيُّرِ المُناخِيِّ العالَمِيِّ، تَبْرُزُ أَزْمَةُ ارْتِفاعِ مُسْتَوى سَطْحِ البَحْرِ كَواحِدَةٍ مِنْ أَكْبَرِ التَّحَدِّياتِ الَّتي تُواجِهُ المُدُنَ السّاحِلِيَّةَ حَوْلَ العالَمِ. يَعودُ هَذا التَّغَيُّرُ بِشَكْلٍ رَئيسِيٍّ إلى ظاهِرَةِ الاحْتِباسِ الحَرارِيِّ العالَمِيِّ، وَالَّتي تُؤَدّي إلى ذَوَبانِ الجَليدِ القُطْبِيِّ وَزِيادَةِ حَرارَةِ المُحيطاتِ، مِمّا يَنْتُجُ عَنْهُ انْبِعاثاتُ غازاتِ الدَّفيئَةِ المُسَبِّبَةِ لِتَغَيُّرِ المُناخِ.

الأَثَرُ البيئِيُّ وَالِاقْتِصادِيُّ: يُهَدِّدُ ارْتِفاعُ مُسْتَوَياتِ سَطْحِ البَحْرِ بِغَمْرِ مَناطِقَ سَكَنِيَّةٍ واسِعَةٍ، مِمّا يَتَسَبَّبُ في تَهْجيرِ السُّكّانِ وَفِقْدانِ الأَراضي الزِّراعِيَّةِ وَالتَّأْثيرِ سَلْبًا عَلَى الأَمْنِ الغِذائِيِّ. كَما يُعَرِّضُ البِنْيَةَ التَّحْتِيَّةَ لِلْخَطَرِ، بِما في ذَلِكَ الطُّرُقَ، وَالجُسورَ، وَشَبَكاتِ الصَّرْفِ الصَّحِّيِّ، مِمّا يَفْرِضُ عِبْئًا اقْتِصادِيًّا كَبيرًا عَلَى المُجْتَمَعاتِ المُتَأَثِّرَةِ.

التَّأْثيرُ عَلَى النُّظُمِ البيئِيَّةِ: تُعْتَبَرُ المَناطِقُ السّاحِلِيَّةُ مَناطِقَ غَنِيَّةً بالتَّنَوُّعِ البَيولوجِيِّ، وَيُهَدِّدُ ارْتِفاعُ مُسْتَوى سَطْحِ البَحْرِ هَذا التَّنَوُّعَ مِنْ خِلالِ تَدْميرِ المَواطِنِ الطَّبيعِيَّةِ مِثْلِ الشِّعابِ المَرْجانِيَّةِ وَغاباتِ المانْغروف، وَالَّتي تَلْعَبُ دَوْرًا حاسِمًا في حِمايَةِ السَّواحِلِ وَدَعْمِ الحَياةِ البَحْرِيَّةِ.

اسْتِراتيجِيّاتُ التَّكَيُّفِ وَالتَّخْفيفِ: لِمُواجَهَةِ هَذِهِ التَّحَدِّياتِ، تَتَّجِهُ المُدُنُ السّاحِلِيَّةُ نَحْوَ تَطْويرِ اسْتِراتيجِيّاتٍ للتَّكَيُّفِ مَعَ تَغَيُّرِ المُناخِ وَتَخْفيفِ آثارِهِ. مِنْ بَيْنِ هَذِهِ الاسْتِراتيجِيّاتِ بِناءُ السُّدودِ وَالجُدْرانِ البَحْرِيَّةِ لِحِمايَةِ السَّواحِلِ، وَتَعْزيزُ الاسْتِدامَةِ البيئِيَّةِ مِنْ خِلالِ الحِفاظِ عَلَى غاباتِ المانْغروفِ، وَتَطْويرُ مَشاريعِ الطّاقَةِ المُتَجَدِّدَةِ لِتَقْليلِ انْبِعاثاتِ ثاني أُكْسيدِ الكَرْبونِ.

الدَّوْرُ المُجْتَمَعِيُّ وَالعالَمِيُّ: يَتَطَلَّبُ تَحْقيقُ الاسْتِدامَةِ البيئِيَّةِ وَمُواجَهَةُ تَغَيُّرِ المُناخِ جُهودًا مُشْتَرَكَةً مِنْ جَميعِ الأَطْرافِ، بِما في ذَلِكَ الحُكوماتِ، وَالقِطاعِ الخاصِّ، وَالمُجْتَمَعاتِ المَحَلِّيَّةِ. يُعْتَبَرُ تَوْجيهُ سِياساتٍ بيئِيَّةٍ فَعّالَةٍ وَزيادَةُ الوَعْي بِأَهَمِّيَّةِ الحِفاظِ عَلَى البيئَةِ وَدَعْمُ التَّنْمِيَةِ المُسْتَدامَةِ أُمورًا ضَرورِيَّةً لِضَمانِ مُسْتَقْبَلٍ أَكْثَرَ أَمانًا وَاسْتِقْرارًا لِلْأَجْيالِ القادِمَةِ.

في ظِلِّ التَّحَدِّياتِ الجَسيمَةِ الَّتي يَفْرِضُها تَغَيُّرُ المُناخِ، تُصْبِحُ الحاجَةُ إلى اتِّخاذِ إجْراءاتٍ سَريعَةٍ وَمَحْسوبَةٍ أَمْرًا لا يَقْبَلُ التَّأْجيلَ لِحِمايَةِ مُدُنِنا السّاحِلِيَّةِ وَضَمانِ اسْتِدامَةِ بيئَتِنا. يَتَطَلَّبُ هَذا تَعاوُنًا دَوْلِيًّا غَيْرَ مَسْبوقٍ وَتَحالُفاتٍ بَيْنَ الحُكوماتِ، وَالقِطاعاتِ الخاصَّةِ، وَالمُنَظَّماتِ غَيْرِ الحُكومِيَّةِ، وَالمُواطِنينَ لِتَوْحيدِ الجُهودِ نَحْوَ هَدَفٍ مُشْتَرَكٍ. إنَّ التِزامَ الجَميعِ بِتَقْليلِ الانْبِعاثاتِ الكَرْبونِيَّةِ، وَتَعْزيزِ اسْتِخْدامِ الطّاقَةِ المُتَجَدِّدَةِ، وَتَطْبيقِ مَبادِئِ الاقْتِصادِ الأَخْضَرِ لَيْسَ فَقَط ضَرورِيًّا لِمُكافَحَةِ تَغَيُّرِ المُناخِ، بَلْ هُوَ أَيْضًا اسْتِثْمارٌ في مُسْتَقْبَلِ الأَجْيالِ القادِمَةِ.

مِنَ الضَّرورِيِّ أَيْضًا زيادَةُ الاسْتِثْمارِ في البَحْثِ وَالتَّطْويرِ لِابْتِكارِ تِقْنِيّاتٍ جَديدَةٍ تُساعِدُ في التَّكَيُّفِ مَعَ التَّغَيُّراتِ المُناخِيَّةِ وَتَخْفيفِ آثارِها. تَعْزيزُ الوَعْي المُناخِيِّ بَيْنَ المُواطِنينَ وَتَشْجيعُهُمْ عَلى اتِّباعِ نَمَطِ حَياةٍ مُسْتَدامٍ مِنْ خِلالِ الاسْتِهْلاكِ الواعي وَإعادَةِ التَّدْويرِ يُمْكِنُ أَنْ يُحْدِثا تَغْييرًا إيجابِيًّا كَبيرًا.

عِلاوَةً عَلى ذَلِكَ، فَإنَّ تَطْويرَ سِياساتٍ فَعّالَةٍ تَدْعَمُ الابْتِكارَ في مَجالِ الاسْتِدامَةِ وَتَوْفيرَ الحَوافِزِ لِلْمَشاريعِ الصَّديقَةِ لِلْبيئَةِ سَيَكونُ لَهُ دَوْرٌ حاسِمٌ في تَسْريعِ عَمَلِيَّةِ الانْتِقالِ إلى اقْتِصاداتٍ خَضْراءَ. تَحْتاجُ الحُكوماتُ إلى تَوْجيهِ الاسْتِثْماراتِ نَحْوَ مَشاريعِ البِنْيَةِ التَّحْتِيَّةِ المُسْتَدامَةِ الَّتي تَحْمي المُدُنَ السّاحِلِيَّةَ وَتُحافِظُ عَلى المَوارِدِ الطَّبيعِيَّةِ.

بِالإضافَةِ إلى ذَلِكَ، فَإنَّ دَعْمَ المُبادَراتِ العالَمِيَّةِ لِحِمايَةِ الغاباتِ المَطيرَةِ وَالمُحيطاتِ وَتَعْزيزِ التَّنَوُّعِ البَيولوجِيِّ يُعْتَبَرُ جُزْءًا لا يَتَجَزَّأُ مِنْ جُهودِ مُكافَحَةِ تَغَيُّرِ المُناخِ. فَهَذِهِ النُّظُمُ البيئِيَّةُ تَلْعَبُ دَوْرًا رَئيسِيًّا في تَنْظيمِ المُناخِ العالَمِيِّ وَتَوْفيرِ مَوْطِنٍ لِمَلايينِ الأَنْواعِ.

مَعًا، مِنْ خِلالِ التِزامِنا الجَماعِيِّ بِالعَمَلِ الفَوْرِيِّ وَالمُسْتَمِرِّ، يُمْكِنُنا مُواجَهَةُ تَحَدِّياتِ تَغَيُّرِ المُناخِ، وَحِمايَةُ كَوْكَبِنا، وَضَمانُ مُسْتَقْبَلٍ مُزْدَهِرٍ وَمُسْتَدامٍ لِلْأَجْيالِ القادِمَةِ. حانَ وَقْتُ العَمَلِ.

Expected Impacts of Rising Sea Levels on Coastal Cities: Challenges and Strategies

As global climate change continues, the crisis of rising sea levels emerges as one of the biggest challenges facing coastal cities around the world. This change is primarily due to global warming, which leads to the melting of polar ice and the warming of the oceans, resulting in the emissions of greenhouse gases that cause climate change.

Environmental and Economic Impact: Rising sea levels threaten to submerge extensive residential areas, causing displacement of populations, loss of agricultural land, and negatively affecting food security. It also puts infrastructure at risk, including roads, bridges, and sewage networks, imposing a significant economic burden on affected communities.

Impact on Ecosystems: Coastal areas are rich in biodiversity, and rising sea levels threaten this diversity by destroying natural habitats such as coral reefs and mangrove forests, which play a crucial role in protecting coastlines and supporting marine life.

Adaptation and Mitigation Strategies: To address these challenges, coastal cities are developing strategies to adapt to climate change and mitigate its effects. Among these strategies are building dams and sea walls to protect coastlines and enhancing environmental sustainability by preserving mangrove forests and developing renewable energy projects to reduce carbon dioxide emissions.

Community and Global Role: Achieving environmental sustainability and addressing climate change requires joint efforts from all parties, including governments, the private sector, and local communities. Implementing effective environmental policies and increasing awareness of the importance of environmental conservation and support for sustainable development are essential to ensure a safer and more stable future for future generations.

Given the significant challenges posed by climate change, the need for swift and calculated action is undeniable to protect our coastal cities and ensure the sustainability of our environment. This requires unprecedented international cooperation and alliances between governments, private sectors, non-governmental organizations, and citizens to unify efforts towards a common goal. Everyone's commitment to reducing carbon emissions, promoting the use of renewable energy, and applying green economy principles is not only necessary to combat climate change but is also an investment in the future of upcoming generations.

It is also essential to increase investment in research and development to innovate new technologies that help adapt to and mitigate the effects of climate change. Enhancing climate awareness among citizens and encouraging them to adopt a sustainable lifestyle through conscious consumption and recycling can make a significant positive change.

Furthermore, developing effective policies that support innovation in sustainability and provide incentives for environmentally friendly projects will play a crucial role in accelerating the transition to green economies. Governments need to direct investments towards sustainable infrastructure projects that protect coastal cities and conserve natural resources.

In addition, supporting global initiatives to protect rainforests and oceans and promote biodiversity is an integral part of efforts to combat climate change. These ecosystems play a key role in regulating the global climate and providing habitats for millions of species.

Together, through our collective commitment to immediate and ongoing action, we can face the challenges of climate change, protect our planet, and ensure a prosperous and sustainable future for future generations. The time to act is now.

9.2 Natural Disasters

Track **90**

to impact

أَثَّرَ • تَأْثِيرٌ

أَثَّرَ الجَفَافُ بِشَكْلٍ كَبِيرٍ عَلَى الزِّرَاعَةِ، مِمَّا أَدَّى إِلَى نَقْصٍ فِي المَحَاصِيلِ.

The drought significantly affected agriculture, leading to a crop shortage.

to evacuate

أَجْلَى • إِجْلَاءٌ

أَجْلَى السُّكَّانُ مَنَازِلَهُمْ بِسَبَبِ ارْتِفَاعِ مُسْتَوَيَاتِ الفَيَضَانَاتِ المُهَدِّدَةِ لِلْمِنْطَقَةِ.

Residents evacuated their homes due to rising flood levels threatening the area.

personal safety

أَمَانٌ شَخْصِيٌّ

أَكَّدَتِ السُّلُطَاتُ عَلَى أَهَمِّيَّةِ الأَمَانِ الشَّخْصِيِّ وَطَالَبَتِ السُّكَّانَ بِتَجَنُّبِ المَنَاطِقِ المَغْمُورَةِ بِالْمِيَاهِ.

Authorities emphasized the importance of personal safety and asked residents to avoid waterlogged areas.

mandatory evacuation

إِجْلَاءٌ إِلْزَامِيٌّ

فَرَضَتِ السُّلُطَاتُ إِجْلَاءً إِلْزَامِيًّا فِي المَنَاطِقِ الأَكْثَرِ تَأْثُّرًا بِالْفَيَضَانَاتِ.

Authorities imposed mandatory evacuation in areas most affected by the floods.

evacuation of residents

إِجْلَاءُ سُكَّانٍ

تَمَّ إِجْلَاءُ السُّكَّانِ مِنَ المَنَاطِقِ السَّاحِلِيَّةِ بَعْدَ تَحْذِيرَاتٍ مِنْ فَيَضَانٍ شَدِيدٍ.

Residents were evacuated from coastal areas following warnings of severe flooding.

إِشَارَةُ إِنْذَارٍ مُبَكِّرٍ

early warning signal

تَمَّ تَفْعِيلُ إِشَارَةِ الْإِنْذَارِ الْمُبَكِّرِ بَيْنَما اقْتَرَبَتِ الْعَاصِفَةُ الِاسْتِوائِيَّةُ مِنَ السَّاحِلِ.

The early warning signal was activated as the tropical storm approached the coast.

إِصَابَاتٌ وَضَحَايَا   *pl.*

injuries and casualties

أَسْفَرَتِ الزَّلَازِلُ عَنْ إِصَابَاتٍ وَضَحَايَا، مِمَّا اسْتَدْعَى تَدَخُّلَ فِرَقِ الْإِنْقَاذِ.

The earthquakes resulted in injuries and casualties, necessitating the intervention of rescue teams.

إِعْلَانُ حَالَةِ طَوارِئَ

emergency declaration

أَعْلَنَتِ الْحُكُومَةُ حَالَةَ طَوارِئَ اسْتِجَابَةً لِلتَّهْدِيدِ الْمُتَزايِدِ مِنَ الثَّوْرَةِ الْبُرْكَانِيَّةِ.

The government declared a state of emergency in response to the increasing threat of volcanic eruption.

إِمْدادَاتٌ غِذائِيَّةٌ   *pl.*

food provisions

نَظَّمَتِ السُّلُطاتُ تَوْزِيعَ إِمْدادَاتٍ غِذائِيَّةٍ لِلْمُتَضَرِّرِينَ مِنَ الْكَوارِثِ الطَّبِيعِيَّةِ.

Authorities organized the distribution of food supplies to those affected by natural disasters.

إِنْذَارٌ مُبَكِّرٌ

early warning

أَصْدَرَتِ السُّلُطاتُ إِنْذارًا مُبَكِّرًا لِسُكَّانِ الْمَناطِقِ الْمُعَرَّضَةِ لِخَطَرِ حَرائِقِ الْغاباتِ.

Authorities issued an early warning to residents in areas at risk of wildfires.

إِنْقاذٌ

rescue

شارَكَتْ فِرَقُ الْإِنْقاذِ فِي عَمَلِيَّاتٍ مُكَثَّفَةٍ لِلْبَحْثِ عَنْ ناجِينَ بَعْدَ الِانْهِيارَاتِ الْأَرْضِيَّةِ.

Rescue teams engaged in intensive operations to search for survivors after the landslides.

اِسْتِجابَةٌ سَرِيعَةٌ

rapid response

نَفَّذَتِ الْفِرَقُ اسْتِجابَةً سَرِيعَةً لِإِجْلاءِ السُّكَّانِ مِنَ الْمَناطِقِ الْخَطِرَةِ.

Teams executed a rapid response to evacuate residents from dangerous areas.

emergency response

اِسْتِجابَةُ طَوارِئَ

تَمَّ تَفْعِيلُ خُطَطِ الِاسْتِجابَةِ لِلطَّوارِئِ لِمُواجَهَةِ تَحَدِّياتِ الفَيَضاناتِ.

Emergency response plans were activated to address the challenges of the floods.

crisis response

اِسْتِجابَةٌ لِأَزْمَةٍ

تَمَّ تَنْفِيذُ اسْتِجابَةٍ لِأَزْمَةِ الجَفافِ، شَمِلَتْ تَوْزِيعَ المِياهِ وَالمُساعَداتِ الغِذائِيَّةِ.

A response to the drought crisis was implemented, including the distribution of water and food aid.

power outage

اِنْقِطاعُ كَهْرَباءَ

تَسَبَّبَ الفَيَضانُ في انْقِطاعِ الكَهْرَباءِ في العَدِيدِ مِنَ المَناطِقِ، مِمّا أَثَّرَ عَلى الحَياةِ اليَوْمِيَّةِ لِلسُّكّانِ.

The flood caused power outages in many areas, affecting the daily lives of residents.

preventive measures

تَدابِيرُ • تَدْبِيرٌ وِقائِيٌّ

اِتَّخَذَتِ الحُكومَةُ تَدابِيرَ وِقائِيَّةً، بِما في ذَلِكَ إِنْشاءَ حَواجِزَ لِلْحِمايَةِ مِنَ الفَيَضاناتِ.

The government took preventive measures, including the construction of barriers to protect against flooding.

destruction

تَدْمِيرٌ

تَدْمِيرُ الطُّرُقِ وَالجُسورِ جَعَلَ عَمَلِيّاتِ الإِنْقاذِ أَكْثَرَ صُعوبَةً بَعْدَ الفَيَضاناتِ.

The destruction of roads and bridges made rescue operations more difficult after the floods.

to result in, cause

تَسَبَّبَ • تَسَبَّبَ في

تَسَبَّبَ الزِّلْزالُ في انْهِيارِ عِدَّةِ مَبانٍ في المَدِينَةِ.

The earthquake caused several buildings in the city to collapse.

property damage

تَضَرُّرُ مُمْتَلَكاتٍ

تَضَرَّرَتِ العَدِيدُ مِنَ المُمْتَلَكاتِ جَرّاءَ فَيَضانٍ ضَرَبَ المِنْطَقَةَ، بِما في ذَلِكَ المَنازِلَ وَالمَحَلّاتِ التِّجارِيَّةَ.

Many properties were damaged due to a flood that hit the area, including homes and shops.

evacuation instructions *pl.* تَعْليماتُ إِجْلاءٍ

تَلَقَّى السُّكّانُ تَعْليماتِ الإِجْلاءِ بَعْدَ تَحْذيراتٍ مِنَ احْتِمالِ وُقوعِ تْسونامي.

Residents received evacuation instructions following warnings of a potential tsunami.

damage assessment تَقْديرُ ضَرَرٍ

قامَتِ السُّلُطاتُ بِتَقْديرِ الضَّرَرِ النّاجِمِ عَنِ الفَيَضانِ لِتَحْديدِ حَجْمِ المُساعَداتِ اللّازِمَةِ.

Authorities estimated the damage caused by the flood to determine the extent of necessary assistance.

preliminary report • تَقارير ← تَقْريرٌ أَوَّليٌّ

أَصْدَرَتِ السُّلُطاتُ تَقْريرًا أَوَّليًّا حَوْلَ حَجْمِ الضَّرَرِ النّاجِمِ عَنْ حَرائِقِ الغاباتِ.

Authorities issued a preliminary report on the extent of damage caused by the wildfires.

damage assessment تَقْييمُ أَضْرارٍ

بَدَأَتْ فِرَقُ الطَّوارِئِ في تَقْييمِ الأَضْرارِ بَعْدَ انْحِسارِ العاصِفَةِ.

Emergency teams began assessing the damage after the storm subsided.

to predict • تَوَقَّع ← تَوَقَّعَ

تَوَقَّعَ العُلَماءُ جَفافًا في المُسْتَقْبَلِ نَتيجَةً لِلتَّغَيُّراتِ المُناخِيَّةِ وانْخِفاضِ مُعَدَّلاتِ الأَمْطارِ.

Scientists predicted future droughts due to climate changes and decreasing rainfall rates.

state of emergency حالَةُ طَوارِئَ

أَعْلَنَتِ الحُكومَةُ حالَةَ طَوارِئَ بِسَبَبِ خُطورَةِ الفَيَضاناتِ الَّتي اجْتاحَتِ المِنْطَقَةَ.

The government declared a state of emergency due to the severity of the floods that swept through the region.

to warn • تَحْذيرٌ ← حَذَّر

حَذَّرَتْ وَكالاتُ الأَرْصادِ الجَوِّيَّةِ مِنَ احْتِماليَّةِ حُدوثِ فَيَضاناتٍ بِسَبَبِ الأَمْطارِ الغَزيرَةِ.

Meteorological agencies warned of the potential for flooding due to heavy rains.

breaking news • أَخْبارٌ خَبَرٌ عاجِلٌ

أُذيعَ خَبَرٌ عاجِلٌ عَنِ الإعْصارِ الَّذي يَقْتَرِبُ مِنَ السّاحِلِ.

A breaking news alert was broadcast about the cyclone approaching the coast.

relief service خِدْمَةُ إغاثَةٍ

تُوَفِّرُ خَدَماتُ الإغاثَةِ الدَّعْمَ لِلْمُتَضَرِّرينَ مِنَ الكَوارِثِ الطَّبيعيَّةِ، بِما في ذَلِكَ الطَّعامَ وَالمَأْوى.

Relief services provide support to those affected by natural disasters, including food and shelter.

medical service خِدْمَةٌ طِبِّيَّةٌ

تَمَّ تَوْفيرُ خِدْماتٍ طِبِّيَّةٍ لِلْمُتَضَرِّرينَ مِنَ البُرْكانِ وَالمُقيمينَ في المَلاجِئِ.

Medical services were provided to those affected by the volcano and residing in shelters.

human loss • خَسائِرُ خَسارَةٌ بَشَريَّةٌ

أَدَّتْ حَرائِقُ الغاباتِ إلى خَسارَةٍ بَشَريَّةٍ، بِما في ذَلِكَ إصاباتٍ وَوَفَياتٍ.

Wildfires led to human loss, including injuries and fatalities.

human and material loss خَسارَةٌ بَشَريَّةٌ وَمادِّيَّةٌ

أَدَّتِ العاصِفَةُ إلى خَسارَةٍ بَشَريَّةٍ وَمادِّيَّةٍ كَبيرَةٍ في المِنْطَقَةِ المُتَضَرِّرَةِ.

The storm led to significant human and material loss in the affected area.

danger • أَخْطارٌ خَطَرٌ

كانَتْ تَحْذيراتُ السُّلُطاتِ مِنْ خَطَرِ الفَيَضانِ حاسِمَةً في إنْقاذِ الأَرْواحِ.

Warnings from authorities about the danger of flooding were crucial in saving lives.

danger خُطورَةٌ

تَسَبَّبَ الطَّقْسُ الجافُّ وَالرِّياحُ القَوِيَّةُ في زِيادَةِ خُطورَةِ الحَرائِقِ في المِنْطَقَةِ.

Dry weather and strong winds increased the danger of fires in the region.

hazardous, dangerous   خَطِيرٌ

أَصْبَحَ البُرْكانُ خَطِيرًا بِشَكْلٍ مُتَزايِدٍ، مِمّا اسْتَدْعى تَحْذيراتٍ مُسْتَمِرَّةً.

The volcano became increasingly dangerous, necessitating ongoing warnings.

to destroy   تَدْمِيرٌ •   دَمَّرَ

دَمَّرَتِ الحَرائِقُ عِدَّةَ مَنازِلَ وَمِساحاتٍ واسِعَةً مِنَ الأَراضي، مِمّا أَدّى إلى خَسائِرَ كَبيرَةٍ.

The fires destroyed several homes and vast areas of land, resulting in significant losses.

resident   سُكّانٌ •   ساكِنٌ

بَقِيَ السُّكّانُ المُقيمونَ بِالْقُرْبِ مِنَ الشّاطِئِ في حالَةِ تَأَهُّبٍ قُصْوى خِلالَ الإِعْصارِ.

Residents living near the beach remained on high alert during the cyclone.

personal safety   سَلامَةٌ شَخْصِيَّةٌ

يَجِبُ عَلى السُّكّانِ اتِّخاذُ كافَّةِ الإِجْراءاتِ لِضَمانِ سَلامَتِهِم الشَّخْصِيَّةِ خِلالَ الكَوارِثِ الطَّبيعِيَّةِ.

Residents must take all necessary actions to ensure their personal safety during natural disasters.

severe   شَديدٌ

كانَ الزِّلْزالُ شَديدَ القُوَّةِ، مِمّا تَسَبَّبَ في تَدْميرٍ واسِعِ النِّطاقِ.

The earthquake was intense, causing widespread destruction.

victim   ضَحايا •   ضَحِيَّةٌ

كانَتْ هُناكَ عِدَّةُ ضَحايا نَتيجَةَ الإِعْصارِ، مِمّا أَثارَ الحُزْنَ في المُجْتَمَعِ المَحَلِّيِّ.

There were several victims of the cyclone, causing grief in the local community.

emergency   طَوارِئٌ •   طارِئٌ

نَشَرَتِ الوَكالاتُ تَقْريرًا طارِئًا حَوْلَ انْتِشارِ حَرائِقِ الغاباتِ والجُهودِ المَبْذولَةِ لِاحْتِوائِها.

Agencies released an emergency report on the spread of wildfires and efforts to contain them.

fierce

عاتٍ

وَصَلَتْ رِياحُ الإِعْصارِ إلى سُرْعاتٍ عاتِيَةٍ، مِمّا زادَ مِنْ خُطورَةِ الوَضْعِ.

The cyclone's winds reached fierce speeds, increasing the danger.

violent

عُنْفٌ •   عَنيفٌ

كانَ الثَّوَرانُ عَنيفًا، مِمّا أَدّى إلى إِطْلاقِ كَمِّياتٍ هائِلَةٍ مِنَ الرَّمادِ.

The eruption was violent, releasing massive amounts of ash.

rescue team

فَرَقٌ •   فَريقُ إِنْقاذٍ

تَدَخَّلَ فَريقُ الإِنْقاذِ بِسُرْعَةٍ لِمُساعَدَةِ الأَشْخاصِ العالِقينَ في المَناطِقِ المُتَضَرِّرَةِ مِنَ الانْهِيارِ الأَرْضِيِّ.

The rescue team quickly intervened to help people stranded in areas affected by the landslide.

deadly

قاتِلٌ

كانَ الحَريقُ قاتِلًا، مِمّا أَسْفَرَ عَنْ وَفَياتٍ وَإِصاباتٍ عَديدَةٍ.

The fire was deadly, resulting in numerous fatalities and injuries.

to provide assistance

تَقْديمٌ •   قَدَّمَ مُساعَدَةً

تُقَدِّمُ المُنَظَّماتُ الإِنْسانِيَّةُ المُساعَدَةَ لِضَحايا الفَيَضانِ، بِما في ذَلِكَ تَوْفيرَ الغِذاءِ وَالمَأْوى.

Humanitarian organizations provide assistance to flood victims, including food and shelter.

natural disaster

كَوارِثُ •   كارِثَةٌ طَبيعِيَّةٌ

ضَرَبَتْ كارِثَةٌ طَبيعِيَّةٌ المِنْطَقَةَ، مِمّا أَسْفَرَ عَنْ دَمارٍ هائِلٍ في البِنْيَةِ التَّحْتِيَّةِ وَالمَساكِنِ.

A natural disaster struck the area, resulting in massive destruction of infrastructure and homes.

tragedy

مَآسٍ •   مَأْساةٌ

تَحَوَّلَتِ الكارِثَةُ إلى مَأْساةٍ عِنْدَما فَقَدَتِ العَديدُ مِنَ الأُسَرِ مَنازِلَها وَأَحِبّاءَها.

The disaster turned into a tragedy as many families lost their homes and loved ones.

shelter

مَأْوًى • مَآوٍ

لَجَأَ السُّكَّانُ إلى مَأْوًى آمِنٍ اسْتِعْدادًا لِوُصولِ الإعْصارِ المُتَوَقَّعِ.

Residents sought safe shelter in preparation for the expected arrival of the cyclone.

frightening, terrifying

مُخيفٌ

كانَ المَشْهَدُ المُخيفُ للزِّلْزالِ يُثيرُ الذُّعْرَ بَيْنَ السُّكَّانِ.

The frightening scene of the earthquake caused panic among the residents.

destructive, devastating

مُدَمِّرٌ

وَصَلَ الإعْصارُ إلى مَرْحَلَةٍ مُدَمِّرَةٍ، مِمّا يَعْني احْتِمالَ وُقوعِ دَمارٍ شامِلٍ.

The cyclone reached a destructive stage, indicating the potential for widespread devastation.

terrifying

مُرْعِبٌ

وَصَفَ النّاجونَ مِنَ الإعْصارِ الوَضْعَ بِأَنَّهُ مُرْعِبٌ، حَيْثُ دَمَّرَ كُلَّ شَيْءٍ في طَريقِهِ.

Survivors of the cyclone described the situation as terrifying, as it destroyed everything in its path.

humanitarian aid

مُساعَدَةٌ إنْسانِيَّةٌ

تَمَّ تَوْفيرُ مُساعَدَةٍ إنْسانِيَّةٍ، بِما في ذلِكَ الغِذاءِ والماءِ، لِلمُتَضَرِّرينَ مِنَ الفَيَضاناتِ.

Humanitarian assistance, including food and water, was provided to those affected by the floods.

emergency equipment

مُعَدَّةُ طَوارِئَ

جُلِبَتْ مُعَدّاتُ الطَّوارِئِ إلى المَناطِقِ المُتَضَرِّرَةِ لِلمُساعَدَةِ في عَمَليّاتِ الإنْقاذِ.

Emergency equipment was brought to the affected areas to assist in rescue operations.

emergency shelter

مَلْجَأُ طَوارِئَ • مَلاجِئُ

فَتَحَتِ السُّلُطاتُ مَلاجِئَ الطَّوارِئِ لِإيواءِ الأشْخاصِ الَّذينَ تَمَّ إجْلاؤُهُمْ مِنْ مَنازِلِهِمْ بِسَبَبِ الحَرائِقِ.

Authorities opened emergency shelters to house people evacuated from their homes due to the fires.

deadly, lethal   مُميتٌ

كانَ الحَريقُ مُميتًا، مِمّا أَدّى إلى خَسائِرَ في الأَرْواحِ وَإصاباتٍ بالِغَةٍ.

The fire was deadly, leading to loss of lives and serious injuries.

disaster zone   مَناطِقُ •   مِنْطَقَةٌ مَنْكوبَةٌ

أَعْلَنَتِ السُّلُطاتُ المِنْطَقَةَ مَنْكوبَةً وَبَدَأَتْ في تَنْفيذِ خُطَطِ الإغاثَةِ والإنْقاذِ.

Authorities declared the area a disaster zone and began implementing relief and rescue plans.

to survive   نَجاةٌ •   نَجا

نَجا العَديدُ مِنَ الأَشْخاصِ بِأُعْجوبَةٍ مِنْ تَحْتِ الأَنْقاضِ بَعْدَ الإنْهِيارِ الأَرْضِيِّ.

Many people miraculously survived under the rubble after the landslide.

personal survival   نَجاةٌ شَخْصِيَّةٌ

كانَتِ النَّجاةُ الشَّخْصِيَّةُ مِنَ الكارِثَةِ الطَبيعِيَّةِ قِصَّةً مُلْهِمَةً لِلآخَرينَ.

Personal survival from the natural disaster was an inspiring story for others.

mass panic   هَلَعٌ جَماعِيٌّ

أَدّى الإعْلانُ عَنْ تْسونامي إلى هَلَعٍ جَماعِيٍّ في المَناطِقِ السّاحِلِيَّةِ.

The announcement of a tsunami led to mass panic in coastal areas.

9.2.1.1 Mini-Articles

Track **91**

في خَبَرٍ عاجِلٍ، أَعْلَنَتِ الحُكومَةُ الجَزائِرِيَّةُ حالَةَ طَوارِئَ بَعْدَ أَنْ ضَرَبَ زِلْزالٌ عَنيفٌ المَناطِقَ الشَّمالِيَّةَ مِنَ البِلادِ. تَسَبَّبَ الزِّلْزالُ في تَدْميرِ مُمْتَلَكاتٍ وَإصاباتٍ وَضَحايا عَديدَةٍ. تَعْمَلُ فِرَقُ الإنْقاذِ عَلى اسْتِجابَةٍ سَريعَةٍ لِلأَزْمَةِ، وَقَدْ تَمَّ إجْلاءُ سُكّانِ المَناطِقِ المُتَأَثِّرَةِ إلى مَلاجِئِ الطَّوارِئِ مَعَ تَقْديمِ المُساعَدَةِ الإنْسانِيَّةِ والإمْداداتِ الغِذائِيَّةِ لِلْمُتَضَرِّرينَ.

In breaking news, the Algerian government has declared a state of emergency after a violent earthquake struck the northern regions of the country. The earthquake caused destruction of property, injuries, and numerous casualties. Rescue teams are working on a rapid response to the crisis, and residents of the affected areas have been evacuated to emergency shelters, with humanitarian assistance and food supplies provided to those affected.

تُواجِهُ تايْلانْد كارِثَةً طَبيعيَّةً بَعْدَ هُطولِ أَمْطارٍ غَزيرَةٍ أَدَّتْ إلى فَيَضاناتٍ عاتِيَةٍ في الجَنوبِ. أَصْدَرَتِ الحُكومَةُ إنْذارًا مُبَكِّرًا وَأَعْلَنَتْ عَنْ إجْلاءٍ إلْزاميٍّ لِسُكَّانِ المَناطِقِ الأكْثَرِ خُطورَةً. دَمَّرَتِ الفَيَضاناتُ البِنْيَةَ التَّحْتِيَّةَ وَتَسَبَّبَتْ في خَسارَةٍ بَشَرِيَّةٍ وَمادِّيَّةٍ كَبيرَةٍ. تَعْمَلُ فِرَقُ الإنْقاذِ وَخَدَماتُ الإغاثَةِ جاهِدَةً لِتَوْفيرِ المَأْوى وَالدَّعْمِ لِلنّاجينَ.

Thailand is facing a natural disaster after heavy rains led to severe flooding in the south. The government issued an early warning and announced mandatory evacuation for residents of the most dangerous areas. The floods destroyed infrastructure and caused significant human and material loss. Rescue teams and relief services are working hard to provide shelter and support to the survivors.

تَسْتَعِدُّ الفِلِبّينُ لِوُصولِ إعْصارٍ مِنَ المُتَوَقَّعِ أَنْ يَكونَ شَديدَ الخُطورَةِ، حَيْثُ أَصْدَرَتِ السُّلُطاتُ تَعْليماتِ إجْلاءٍ وَإشاراتِ إنْذارٍ مُبَكِّرٍ لِلسُّكَّانِ في المَناطِقِ المُعَرَّضَةِ لِلْخَطَرِ. تَمَّ تَفْعيلُ اسْتِجابَةِ الطَّوارِئِ وَالتَّدابيرِ الوِقائِيَّةِ لِتَقْليلِ الأَضْرارِ المُحْتَمَلَةِ وَضَمانِ أَمانِ السُّكَّانِ. كَما جُهِّزَتْ مَراكِزُ الإغاثَةِ وَمَلاجِئُ الطَّوارِئِ لاسْتِقْبالِ المُتَضَرِّرينَ.

The Philippines is preparing for the arrival of a typhoon expected to be extremely dangerous, with authorities issuing evacuation instructions and early warning signals to residents in vulnerable areas. Emergency responses and preventive measures have been activated to minimize potential damage and ensure the safety of the population. Relief centers and emergency shelters have been prepared to receive those affected.

اِنْدَلَعَتْ حَرائِقُ غاباتٍ شَديدَةٌ في كاليفورْنيا، مِمّا أَجْبَرَ السُّلُطاتِ عَلى إصْدارِ أَوامِرِ إجْلاءٍ لآلافِ السُّكَّانِ. التَهَمَتِ النّيرانُ مِساحاتٍ واسِعَةً وَتَسَبَّبَتْ في تَدْميرِ المَنازِلِ وَانْقِطاعِ الكَهْرَباءِ. تَعْمَلُ فِرَقُ الإنْقاذِ وَالإطْفاءِ بِلا تَوَقُّفٍ لِلسَّيْطَرَةِ عَلى الحَرائِقِ وَتَقْديمِ المُساعَدَةِ لِلْمُتَضَرِّرينَ، فيما يَظَلُّ الوَضْعُ مُتَوَتِّرًا وَالمُجْتَمَعاتُ في حالَةِ هَلَعٍ.

Severe wildfires broke out in California, forcing authorities to issue evacuation orders for thousands of residents. The flames consumed vast areas and caused the destruction of homes and power outages. Rescue and firefighting teams are working non-stop to control the fires and provide assistance to those affected, as the situation remains tense and communities are in panic.

تُعاني تونِسُ مِنْ مَوْجَةِ حَرٍّ شَديدَةٍ وَغَيْرِ مَسْبوقَةٍ، حَيْثُ تَجاوَزَتْ دَرَجاتُ الحَرارَةِ العُظْمى المُعَدَّلاتِ الطَّبيعِيَّةَ، مِمّا أَثارَ مَخاوِفَ مِنْ خَطَرِ الجَفافِ. أَعْلَنَتِ الحُكومَةُ عَنْ تَدابيرَ اسْتِجابَةٍ لِلطَّوارِئِ، بِما في ذَلِكَ تَوْجيهاتٍ لِتَرْشيدِ اسْتِهْلاكِ المِياهِ وَتَقْديمِ الدَّعْمِ لِلْمُزارِعينَ المُتَضَرِّرينَ. المُواطِنونَ مَدْعُوّونَ لاتِّباعِ إرْشاداتِ السَّلامَةِ وَالحَذَرِ مِنَ التَّأْثيراتِ الصِّحِّيَّةِ لِلْحَرارَةِ الشَّديدَةِ.

Tunisia is suffering from an intense and unprecedented heatwave, with temperatures exceeding normal levels, raising concerns about the risk of drought. The government announced emergency response measures, including directives for rationalizing water consumption and providing support to affected farmers. Citizens are urged to follow safety guidelines and be cautious of the health impacts of the extreme heat.

9.2.1.2 Interview: Preparing for Natural Disasters

مُقَدِّمُ البَرْنَامَج: مَرْحَبًا بِكُمْ فِي بَرْنَامَجِنا اليَوْمَ حَيْثُ نُناقِشُ مَوْضوعًا حَيَوِيًّا يَتَعَلَّقُ بِكَيْفِيَّةِ الِاسْتِعْدادِ لِلْكَوارِثِ الطَّبيعِيَّةِ. مَعَنا اليَوْمَ فِي الِاسْتوديو الدُّكْتورَة أميرَة الزَّهْراني، خَبيرَةُ إِدارَةِ الطَّوارِئِ وَالكَوارِثِ الطَّبيعِيَّةِ. دُكْتورَة أميرَة، ما هِيَ الخُطُواتُ الأَساسِيَّةُ الَّتي يَنْبَغي عَلى الأَفْرادِ اتِّخاذُها لِلِاسْتِعْدادِ لِلْكَوارِثِ الطَّبيعِيَّةِ؟

الدُّكْتورَة أميرَة الزَّهْراني: شُكْرًا لِدَعْوَتي. الِاسْتِعْدادُ لِلْكَوارِثِ الطَّبيعِيَّةِ يَبْدَأُ بِالتَّخْطيطِ وَالتَّعْليمِ. أَوَّلًا، مِنَ المُهِمِّ جِدًّا أَنْ يَكونَ لَدى كُلِّ أُسْرَةٍ خُطَّةُ طَوارِئَ شَخْصِيَّةٌ تَتَضَمَّنُ مَعْلوماتِ الِاتِّصالِ، وَأَماكِنَ الإِجْلاءِ، وَمَساراتِ الهُروبِ.

مُقَدِّمُ البَرْنَامَج: هَلْ هُناكَ أَدَواتٌ أَوْ مُعَدّاتٌ مُحَدَّدَةٌ يَجِبُ أَنْ تَكونَ لَدى الأَشْخاصِ لِمُساعَدَتِهِمْ عَلى النَّجاةِ خِلالَ كارِثَةٍ؟

الدُّكْتورَة أميرَة الزَّهْراني: نَعَمْ، مِنَ المُهِمِّ تَجْهيزُ حَقيبَةِ طَوارِئَ تَحْتَوي عَلى مَوادٍّ غِذائِيَّةٍ غَيْرِ قابِلَةٍ لِلتَّلَفِ، وَماءٍ لِلشُّرْبِ، وَمِصْباحٍ يَدَوِيٍّ، وَبَطّارِيّاتٍ احْتِياطِيَّةٍ، وَمَجْموعَةِ إِسْعافٍ أَوَّلِيٍّ، وَأَدْوِيَةٍ ضَرورِيَّةٍ. كَما يَجِبُ أَنْ تَشْمَلَ الوَثائِقَ الهامَّةَ مِثْلَ بِطاقاتِ الهُوِيَّةِ وَالسِّجِلّاتِ الطِّبِّيَّةِ.

مُقَدِّمُ البَرْنَامَج: وَماذا عَنِ الِاسْتِجابَةِ خِلالَ الكارِثَةِ نَفْسِها؟

الدُّكْتورَة أميرَة الزَّهْراني: خِلالَ الكارِثَةِ، مِنَ الضَّروريِّ البَقاءُ هادِئًا وَاتِّباعُ خُطَّةِ الطَّوارِئِ. اِسْتَخْدِمِ الإِشاراتِ المُبَكِّرَةَ وَتَعْليماتِ الإِجْلاءِ الصّادِرَةِ عَنِ السُّلُطاتِ لِتَحْديدِ مَتى وَكَيْفَ تَتَحَرَّكُ. إِذا كُنْتَ في مَنْزِلِكَ، اِبْقَ في مَكانٍ آمِنٍ بَعيدًا عَنِ النَّوافِذِ وَالأَبْوابِ الزُّجاجِيَّةِ.

مُقَدِّمُ البَرْنَامَج: هَلْ هُناكَ أَيَّةُ نَصائِحَ خاصَّةٍ لِلْأَشْخاصِ الَّذينَ يَعيشونَ في مَناطِقَ عالِيَةِ الخُطورَةِ؟

الدُّكْتورَة أميرَة الزَّهْراني: الأَشْخاصُ الَّذينَ يَعيشونَ في مَناطِقَ عالِيَةِ الخُطورَةِ يَجِبُ أَنْ يَكونوا أَكْثَرَ وَعْيًا وَاسْتِعْدادًا. يَنْبَغي عَلَيْهِمْ مُراقَبَةُ أَنْماطِ الطَّقْسِ وَالتَّحْديثاتِ مِنَ الأَرْصادِ الجَوِّيَّةِ بِانْتِظامٍ، وَالمُشارَكَةُ في تَدْريباتِ الإِجْلاءِ المُجْتَمَعِيَّةِ. كَما يَجِبُ تَأْمينُ المَنازِلِ

وَالمُمْتَلَكَاتِ بِتَدَابِيرَ وِقَائِيَّةٍ لِلْحَدِّ مِنَ الضَّرَرِ، كَتَعْزِيزِ الأَسْقُفِ وَتَرْكِيبِ النَّوَافِذِ المُقَاوِمَةِ لِلْعَوَاصِفِ.

مُقَدِّمُ البَرْنَامَج: دُكْتُورَة أَمِيرَة، شُكْرًا جَزِيلًا لَكِ عَلَى هَذِهِ المَعْلُومَاتِ القَيِّمَةِ وَالنَّصَائِحِ العَمَلِيَّةِ. قَبْلَ أَنْ نَخْتَتِمَ، هَلْ مِنْ كَلِمَةٍ أَخِيرَةٍ تَوَدِّينَ تَوْجِيهَهَا لِلْمُشَاهِدِينَ حَوْلَ أَهَمِّيَّةِ الِاسْتِعْدَادِ لِلْكَوَارِثِ الطَّبِيعِيَّةِ؟

الدُّكْتُورَة أَمِيرَة الزَّهْرَانِي: بِالتَّأْكِيدِ. أَوَدُّ أَنْ أُؤَكِّدَ عَلَى أَنَّ الِاسْتِعْدَادَ لِلْكَوَارِثِ الطَّبِيعِيَّةِ لَيْسَ فَقَطْ مَسْؤُولِيَّةَ الحُكُومَاتِ وَالوِكَالَاتِ، بَلْ هُوَ مَسْؤُولِيَّةُ كُلِّ فَرْدٍ. الوَعْيُ وَالتَّحْضِيرُ المُسْبَقُ يُمْكِنُ أَنْ يُنْقِذَا حَيَاتَكَ وَحَيَاةَ مَنْ تُحِبُّ. لَا تَتَجَاهَلِ التَّحْذِيرَاتِ وَالإِرْشَادَاتِ، وَشَارِكْ فِي بِنَاءِ مُجْتَمَعٍ أَكْثَرَ أَمَانًا وَاسْتِعْدَادًا. الطَّبِيعَةُ قَوِيَّةٌ، لَكِنْ بِالمَعْرِفَةِ وَالتَّحْضِيرِ، يُمْكِنُنَا التَّخْفِيفُ مِنَ الأَضْرَارِ وَحِمَايَةُ أَنْفُسِنَا وَمُجْتَمَعَاتِنَا.

مُقَدِّمُ البَرْنَامَج: شُكْرًا لَكِ مَرَّةً أُخْرَى، دُكْتُورَة أَمِيرَة، عَلَى تَوْجِيهَاتِكِ القَيِّمَةِ وَوَقْتِكِ. وَشُكْرًا لَكُمْ، مُشَاهِدِينَا، عَلَى المُتَابَعَةِ. نَأْمُلُ أَنْ تَكُونَ هَذِهِ الحَلْقَةُ قَدْ قَدَّمَتْ لَكُمُ المَعْلُومَاتُ الضَّرُورِيَّةَ لِتَكُونُوا أَكْثَرَ اسْتِعْدَادًا لِمُوَاجَهَةِ الكَوَارِثِ الطَّبِيعِيَّةِ. تَذَكَّرُوا، الِاسْتِعْدَادُ هُوَ المِفْتَاحُ. إِلَى اللِّقَاءِ فِي حَلْقَةٍ جَدِيدَةٍ مِنْ بَرْنَامَجِنَا. ابْقَوْا بِأَمَانٍ.

Program Host: Welcome to our show today where we discuss a vital topic related to preparing for natural disasters. Joining us in the studio today is Dr. Amira Al-Zahrani, an expert in emergency and natural disaster management. Dr. Amira, what are the basic steps individuals should take to prepare for natural disasters?

Dr. Amira Al-Zahrani: Thank you for having me. Preparing for natural disasters starts with planning and education. First, it's very important for every family to have a personal emergency plan that includes contact information, evacuation places, and escape routes.

Program Host: Are there specific tools or equipment that people should have to help them survive during a disaster?

Dr. Amira Al-Zahrani: Yes, it's important to prepare an emergency bag containing non-perishable food items, drinking water, a flashlight, spare batteries, a first aid kit, and necessary medications. It should also include important documents such as identification cards and medical records.

Program Host:

What about responding during the disaster itself?

Dr. Amira Al-Zahrani:

During the disaster, it's crucial to stay calm and follow the emergency plan. Use early signals and evacuation instructions issued by authorities to determine when and how to move. If you're at home, stay in a safe place away from windows and glass doors.

Program Host:

Are there any special tips for people living in high-risk areas?

Dr. Amira Al-Zahrani:

People living in high-risk areas need to be more aware and prepared. They should regularly monitor weather patterns and updates from meteorological services and participate in community evacuation drills. It's also essential to secure homes and properties with preventative measures to minimize damage, such as reinforcing roofs and installing storm-resistant windows.

Program Host:

Dr. Amira, thank you very much for these valuable insights and practical tips. Before we conclude, any final words you'd like to share with the viewers about the importance of preparing for natural disasters?

Dr. Amira Al-Zahrani:

Certainly. I want to emphasize that preparing for natural disasters is not only the responsibility of governments and agencies but is the responsibility of every individual. Awareness and prior preparation can save your life and the lives of those you love. Do not ignore warnings and guidelines; participate in building a safer and more prepared community. Nature is powerful, but with knowledge and preparation, we can mitigate damages and protect ourselves and our communities.

Program Host:

Thank you once again, Dr. Amira, for your valuable guidance and your time. And thank you, our viewers, for tuning in. We hope this episode has provided you with the necessary information to be better prepared for facing natural disasters. Remember, preparation is key. Goodbye until the next episode of our program. Stay safe.

9.2.2 Earthquakes

debris   *pl.*   أَنْقاضٌ

بَعْدَ الزِّلْزالِ، امْتَلَأَتِ الشَّوارِعُ بِأَنْقاضِ المَباني المُنْهارَةِ، وَبَدَأَتْ فِرَقُ الإِنْقاذِ في البَحْثِ عَنِ النَّاجينَ.

After the earthquake, the streets were filled with debris from collapsed buildings, and rescue teams began searching for survivors.

to slip   • انْزِلاقٌ   انْزَلَقَ

انْزَلَقَتِ التُّرْبَةُ بِشَكْلٍ مُفاجِئٍ في مِنْطَقَةِ الزِّلْزالِ، مِمّا أَدّى إلى انْهياراتٍ أَرْضِيَّةٍ.

The soil slipped suddenly in the earthquake area, leading to landslides.

to collapse   • انْهِيارٌ   انْهارَ

انْهارَتِ العَديدُ مِنَ المَباني القَديمَةِ بِسَبَبِ الزِّلْزالِ، مِمّا تَسَبَّبَ في خَسائِرَ كَبيرَةٍ.

Many old buildings collapsed due to the earthquake, causing significant losses.

to shake   • اهْتِزازٌ   اهْتَزَّ

اهْتَزَّتِ العاصِمَةُ بِأَكْمَلِها بِفِعْلِ الزِّلْزالِ القَوِيِّ الَّذي بَلَغَتْ قُوَّتُهُ 7.8 دَرَجَةً عَلى مِقْياسِ ريخْتَرَ.

The entire capital shook due to the strong earthquake, which measured 7.8 on the Richter scale.

building at risk of collapse   بِناءٌ مُهَدَّدٌ بِانْهِيارٍ

تَمَّ إخْلاءُ بِناءٍ مُهَدَّدٍ بِالانْهِيارِ بَعْدَ الهَزَّةِ الأَرْضِيَّةِ كَإِجْراءٍ احْتِرازِيٍّ.

A building threatened with collapse was evacuated after the tremor as a precautionary measure.

aftershock   • تَوابِعُ   تابِعٌ

شَعَرَ السُّكّانُ بِتَوابِعِ الزِّلْزالِ الَّتي اسْتَمَرَّتْ لِعِدَّةِ أَيّامٍ بَعْدَ الهَزَّةِ الأولى.

Residents felt the aftershocks of the earthquake, which continued for several days after the initial tremor.

underground   تَحْتَ الأَرْضِ

رَصَدَ العُلَماءُ تَحَرُّكاتٍ تَحْتَ الأَرْضِ قَبْلَ الزِّلْزالِ، مِمّا ساعَدَ في تَوَقُّعِ حُدوثِهِ.

Scientists detected underground movements before the earthquake, helping to predict its occurrence.

earthquake warning
تَحْذيرٌ مِنْ زِلْزالٍ

أَصْدَرَتِ السُّلُطاتُ تَحْذيرًا مِنَ الزِّلْزالِ بَعْدَ رَصْدِ سِلْسِلَةِ هَزّاتٍ أَرْضِيّةٍ صَغيرَةٍ.

Authorities issued an earthquake warning after detecting a series of small tremors.

to cause building collapse
تَسَبَّبَ في تَحْطيمِ مَبانٍ • تَسَبَّبَ

تَسَبَّبَ الزِّلْزالُ في تَحْطيمِ مَبانٍ عَديدَةٍ في وَسَطِ المَدينَةِ، مِمّا أَدّى إلى خَسائِرَ فادِحَةٍ.

The earthquake caused the collapse of many buildings in the city center, resulting in significant losses.

tsunami
تْسونامي

أَدّى الزِّلْزالُ القَوِيُّ إلى حُدوثِ تْسونامي، مِمّا تَسَبَّبَ في دَمارٍ شامِلٍ عَلى طولِ السّاحِلِ.

The strong earthquake led to a tsunami, causing widespread destruction along the coast.

fissure, crack
تَصَدُّعٌ = شَقٌّ

شوهِدَتْ تَصَدُّعاتٌ واسِعَةٌ في الأَرْضِ بَعْدَ الهَزّةِ الأَرْضِيّةِ، مِمّا يُشيرُ إلى قُوَّتِها.

Wide cracks were observed in the ground after the earthquake, indicating its strength.

infrastructure damage
تَضَرُّرُ بِنْيَةٍ تَحْتِيّةٍ

أَدّى الزِّلْزالُ إلى تَضَرُّرِ البِنْيَةِ التَّحْتِيّةِ بِشَكْلٍ كَبيرٍ، حَيْثُ انْهارَتْ جُسورٌ وَتَصَدَّعَتْ طُرُقٌ رَئيسِيّةٌ.

The earthquake caused significant damage to the infrastructure, with bridges collapsing and main roads cracking.

structural inspection
تَفْتيشٌ هَيْكَلِيٌّ

بَدَأَتِ السُّلُطاتُ في تَفْتيشٍ هَيْكَلِيٍّ لِلْمَباني لِتَقْييمِ الأَضْرارِ وَضَمانِ سَلامَةِ المُواطِنينَ.

Authorities began structural inspections of buildings to assess damage and ensure citizen safety.

earthquake-resistant construction technique

تِقْنِيَّةُ بِناءٍ مُضادَّةٌ لِلزَّلازِلِ

تَبَنَّتِ الدَّوْلَةُ تِقْنِيَّةَ بِناءٍ مُضادَّةً لِلزَّلازِلِ في المَناطِقِ الجَديدَةِ لِتَقْليلِ الأَضْرارِ في المُسْتَقْبَلِ.

The country adopted earthquake-resistant building technology in new areas to minimize future damage.

to predict

تَبَنَّأَ • تَنَبُّؤٌ

يَأْمُلُ العُلَماءُ في أَنْ يَتَمَكَّنوا يَوْمًا ما مِنْ التَّنَبُّؤِ بِوُقوعِ الزَّلازِلِ بِفَضْلِ التَّقَدُّمِ المُسْتَمِرِّ في تِكْنولوجْيا الرَّصْدِ الزِّلْزاليِّ.

Scientists hope to someday be able to predict earthquakes thanks to ongoing advances in seismic monitoring technology.

earthquake-related incident

حادِثٌ مُتَعَلِّقٌ بِالزَّلازِلِ • حَوادِثُ

وَقَعَ حادِثٌ مُتَعَلِّقٌ بِالزَّلازِلِ في المَكْسيكِ، حَيْثُ انْهارَتْ عِدَّةُ بِناياتٍ وَقُطِعَتِ الطُّرُقُ.

An earthquake-related incident occurred in Mexico, where several buildings collapsed and roads were cut off.

to analyze an earthquake

حَلَّلَ زِلْزالًا • تَحْليلٌ

قامَ عُلَماءُ الجيولوجْيا بِتَحْليلِ الزِّلْزالِ الَّذي ضَرَبَ اليابانَ لِفَهْمِ آلِيّاتِهِ وَتَأْثيراتِهِ.

Geologists analyzed the earthquake that struck Japan to understand its mechanisms and impacts.

ground tremor

رَجْفَةٌ أَرْضِيَّةٌ

شَعَرَ السُّكّانُ بِرَجْفَةٍ أَرْضِيَّةٍ خَفيفَةٍ قَبْلَ الهَزَّةِ الرَّئيسِيَّةِ، مِمّا أَثارَ القَلَقَ بَيْنَهُمْ.

Residents felt a slight ground tremor before the main shake, causing concern among them.

earthquake

زِلْزالٌ • زَلازِلُ

ضَرَبَ زِلْزالٌ بِقُوَّةِ 6 دَرَجاتٍ مِنْطَقَةَ شَمالِ إيطالْيا، مِمّا أَدّى إلى إِجْلاءِ السُّكّانِ.

An earthquake with a magnitude of 6 struck the northern region of Italy, leading to the evacuation of residents.

massive earthquake زِلْزالٌ هائِلٌ

ضَرَبَ زِلْزالٌ هائِلٌ بِقُوَّةِ 7 دَرَجاتٍ سَواحِلَ تِشيلي، مِمّا تَسَبَّبَ في أَمْواجِ تِسونامي وَدَمارٍ واسِعِ النِّطاقِ.

A massive earthquake of magnitude 7 struck the coast of Chile, causing tsunami waves and widespread destruction.

seismic زِلْزالِيٌّ

تَعَرَّضَتْ مِنْطَقَةُ كاليفورْنيا لِنَشاطٍ زِلْزالِيٍّ مُتَزايِدٍ، مِمّا أَدّى إلى تَشْديدِ إجْراءاتِ السَّلامَةِ.

California experienced increased seismic activity, leading to heightened safety measures.

to record an earthquake سَجَّلَ زِلْزالًا • تَسْجيلٌ

سَجَّلَتِ المَحَطّاتُ الجيولوجِيَّةُ زِلْزالًا بِقُوَّةِ 7 دَرَجاتٍ في المُحيطِ الهادِئِ، مِمّا أثارَ المَخاوِفَ مِنْ حُدوثِ تسونامي.

Geological stations recorded a 7-magnitude earthquake in the Pacific Ocean, raising concerns about a potential tsunami.

shallow سَطْحِيٌّ

كانَ الزِّلْزالُ سَطْحِيًّا، حَيْثُ وَقَعَ على عُمْقٍ قَليلٍ، مِمّا زادَ مِنْ شُعورِ النّاسِ بِقُوَّتِهِ.

The earthquake was shallow, occurring at a small depth, which increased the intensity felt by people.

seismic fault صَدْعٌ زِلْزالِيٌّ • صُدوعٌ

تَسَبَّبَ الصَّدْعُ الزِّلْزالِيُّ الَّذي حَدَثَ بِالْقُرْبِ مِنْ سَواحِلِ اليابانِ في تَغَيُّراتٍ جيولوجِيَّةٍ مَلْحوظَةٍ.

The seismic fault that occurred near the coasts of Japan caused noticeable geological changes.

to strike ضَرَبَ • ضَرْبٌ

ضَرَبَ زِلْزالٌ قَوِيٌّ مِنْطَقَةَ آسْيا الوُسْطى، مِمّا أَدّى إلى تَضَرُّرِ العَديدِ مِنَ المَنازِلِ وَالْمُنْشَآتِ.

A strong earthquake struck Central Asia, causing damage to many homes and facilities.

damage ضَرَرٌ • أَضْرارٌ

تَعَرَّضَتِ المَدينَةُ لِضَرَرٍ كَبيرٍ بَعْدَ الزِّلْزالِ، شَمِلَ ذلِكَ انْقِطاعَ الكَهْرَباءِ وَتَصَدُّعَ الطُّرُقِ.

The city suffered significant damage following the earthquake, including power outages and cracked roads.

weak

ضَعِيفٌ

كانَ الزِّلْزالُ ضَعِيفًا وَلَمْ يَشْعُرْ بِهِ سِوى قَلِيلٍ مِنَ النّاسِ في المَناطِقِ النّائِيَةِ.

The earthquake was weak and only felt by a few people in remote areas.

seismograph

عَدّادُ زَلازِلَ

أَظْهَرَ عَدّادُ الزِّلازِلِ تَسْجِيلَ أَكْثَرَ مِنْ سَبْعِ هَزّاتٍ أَرْضِيَّةٍ خَفِيفَةٍ خِلالَ الأُسْبُوعِ الماضِي.

The seismograph recorded more than seven minor tremors over the past week.

deep

عَمِيقٌ

وَقَعَ الزِّلْزالُ عَلى عُمْقٍ كَبِيرٍ تَحْتَ سَطْحِ الأَرْضِ، مِمّا قَلَّلَ مِنْ تَأْثِيرِهِ عَلى السَّطْحِ.

The earthquake occurred at a great depth below the earth's surface, reducing its impact on the surface.

magnitude

قُوَّةُ زِلْزالِ

قُدِّرَتْ قُوَّةُ الزِّلْزالِ الَّذِي ضَرَبَ شَمالَ إِيطالْيا بِ 6 دَرَجاتٍ عَلى مِقْياسِ رِيخْتَرْ.

The strength of the earthquake that struck northern Italy was estimated at 6 on the Richter scale.

strong

قَوِيٌّ

كانَ الزِّلْزالُ قَوِيًّا بِما يَكْفِي لِإِحْداثِ تَصَدُّعاتٍ في العَدِيدِ مِنَ المَباني القَدِيمَةِ بِالمَدِينَةِ.

The earthquake was strong enough to cause cracks in many of the city's old buildings.

seismological monitoring center

مَرْكَزُ رَصْدِ زَلازِلَ   • مَراكِزُ

قامَ مَرْكَزُ رَصْدِ الزِّلازِلِ بِإِصْدارِ تَحْذِيراتٍ لِلْمَناطِقِ المُحِيطَةِ بَعْدَ رَصْدِ النَّشاطِ الزِّلْزالِيِّ.

The earthquake monitoring center issued warnings to the surrounding areas after detecting seismic activity.

epicenter

مَرْكَزُ زِلْزالٍ • مَراكِزُ

حَدَّدَتِ السُّلُطاتُ مَرْكَزَ الزِّلْزالِ في مِنْطَقَةٍ بَعيدَةٍ عَنِ السّاحِلِ، مِمّا ساعَدَ في تَقْليلِ الأَضْرارِ.

The authorities located the earthquake's epicenter in an area far from the coast, helping to minimize damage.

sudden

مُفاجِئٌ

وَقَعَ الزِّلْزالُ بِشَكْلٍ مُفاجِئٍ، مِمّا تَسَبَّبَ في حالَةٍ مِنَ الذُّعْرِ بَيْنَ سُكّانِ المَدينَةِ.

The earthquake occurred suddenly, causing panic among the city's residents.

Richter scale

مِقْياسُ ريخْتَرَ

بَلَغَتْ قُوَّةُ الزِّلْزالِ 7.5 عَلى مِقْياسِ ريخْتَرَ، مِمّا أَدّى إلى حالَةٍ مِنَ الهَلَعِ بَيْنَ السُّكّانِ.

The earthquake reached a magnitude of 7.5 on the Richter scale, causing panic among the residents.

seismic zone

مِنْطَقَةٌ زِلْزالِيَّةٌ • مَناطِقُ

تُعْتَبَرُ هَذِهِ المِنْطَقَةُ زِلْزالِيَّةً نَشِطَةً وَتَشْهَدُ هَزّاتٍ أَرْضِيَّةً بِشَكْلٍ مُتَكَرِّرٍ.

This region is an active seismic area and experiences frequent earthquakes.

نَشاطُ صَفائِحَ تِكْتونِيَّةٍ

يُتابِعُ العُلَماءُ نَشاطَ الصَّفائِحِ التِّكْتونِيَّةِ في المِنْطَقَةِ لِتَقْييمِ احْتِمالِ حُدوثِ زَلازِلَ مُسْتَقْبَلِيَّةٍ.

Scientists are monitoring tectonic plate activity in the region to assess the likelihood of future earthquakes.

seismic tremor

هَزَّةٌ أَرْضِيَّةٌ صَغيرَةٌ

سَجَّلَتِ المَحَطّاتُ الجيولوجِيَّةُ هَزَّةً أَرْضِيَّةً صَغيرَةً بِقُوَّةِ 3.4 عَلى مِقْياسِ ريخْتَرَ.

Geological stations recorded a minor seismic tremor with a magnitude of 3.4 on the Richter scale.

هَزَّةٌ ارْتِدادِيَّةٌ
aftershock

تَلَتِ الزِّلْزالَ الرَّئيسيَّ عِدَّةُ هَزّاتٍ ارْتِداديَّةٍ، مِمّا أَثارَ قَلَقَ السُّكّانِ الَّذينَ كانوا قَدْ بَدَأوا في اسْتِعادَةِ حَياتِهِمِ الطَّبيعيَّةِ.

Several aftershocks followed the main earthquake, causing concern among residents who were beginning to return to normal life.

هَزَّةٌ زِلْزاليَّةٌ
seismic shaking

شَعَرَ النّاسُ بِالهَزَّةِ الزِّلْزاليَّةِ بِقُوَّةٍ، وَهَرَعوا إِلى الشَّوارِعِ خَوْفًا مِنْ تَداعِياتِها.

The seismic tremor was strongly felt, and people rushed to the streets in fear of its consequences.

9.2.2.1 Mini-Articles

Track **94**

في ساعاتِ الفَجْرِ الأولى، ضَرَبَ زِلْزالٌ بِقُوَّةِ 6.5 دَرَجاتٍ عَلى مِقْياسِ ريخْتَر العاصِمَةَ المِصْريَّةَ، القاهِرَةَ. تَسَبَّبَتِ الهَزَّةُ الأَرْضِيَّةُ في تَحْطيمِ عِدَّةِ مَبانٍ وَأَدَّتْ إِلى تَضَرُّرِ البِنْيَةِ التَّحْتِيَّةِ في مَناطِقَ مُتَفَرِّقَةٍ مِنَ المَدينَةِ. تابَعَتْ فِرَقُ الإنْقاذِ عَمَلِيّاتِ البَحْثِ عَنْ ناجينَ تَحْتَ الأَنْقاضِ، بَيْنَما حَذَّرَتْ مَراكِزُ رَصْدِ الزَّلازِلِ مِنِ احْتِماليَّةِ وُقوعِ هَزّاتٍ ارْتِداديَّةٍ.

In the early dawn hours, a 6.5-magnitude earthquake on the Richter scale struck the Egyptian capital, Cairo. The earthquake caused several buildings to collapse and damaged infrastructure in various parts of the city. Rescue teams continued searching for survivors under the rubble, while earthquake monitoring centers warned of the possibility of aftershocks.

ضَرَبَ زِلْزالٌ هائِلٌ بِقُوَّةِ 9 دَرَجاتٍ سَواحِلَ إِنْدونيسْيا، مِمّا أَدّى إِلى تسونامي مُفاجِئٍ ضَرَبَ المَناطِقَ السّاحِليَّةَ بَعْدَ دَقائِقَ. كانَ الدَّمارُ الَّذي لَحِقَ بِالمَباني وَالبِنْيَةِ التَّحْتِيَّةِ هائِلًا، مَعَ تَقاريرَ أَوَّليَّةٍ تُشيرُ إِلى آلافِ الضَّحايا. أَعْلَنَتِ السُّلُطاتُ حالَةَ الطَّوارِئِ وَطَلَبَتْ مُساعَداتٍ دَوْليَّةً لِلتَّعامُلِ مَعَ الكارِثَةِ.

A massive 9-magnitude earthquake hit the coasts of Indonesia, leading to a sudden tsunami that struck the coastal areas minutes later. The destruction to buildings and infrastructure was enormous, with initial reports indicating thousands of victims. The authorities declared a state of emergency and requested international aid to deal with the disaster.

شَهِدَتْ مِنْطَقَةُ شَمالِ لُبْنانَ هَزَّةً أَرْضِيَّةً صَغيرَةً بِقُوَّةِ 4.2 دَرَجاتٍ، تَسَبَّبَتْ في قَلَقِ السُّكّانِ لَكِنْ دونَ وُقوعِ أَضْرارٍ كَبيرَةٍ. أَشارَ الخُبَراءُ في مَرْكَزِ رَصْدِ الزَّلازِلِ إِلى أَنَّ الهَزَّةَ كانَتْ نَتيجَةَ نَشاطِ الصَّفائِحِ التِّكْتونِيَّةِ في المِنْطَقَةِ، وَأَكَّدوا عَلى أَهَمِّيَّةِ تَطْويرِ تِقْنِيّاتِ البِناءِ المُضادَّةِ لِلزَّلازِلِ في المُسْتَقْبَلِ.

A massive 9-magnitude earthquake hit the coasts of Indonesia, leading to a sudden tsunami that struck the coastal areas minutes later. The destruction to buildings and infrastructure was enormous, with initial reports indicating thousands of victims. The authorities declared a state of emergency and requested international aid to deal with the disaster.

The northern region of Lebanon experienced a minor earthquake of 4.2 magnitude, causing concern among residents but without causing significant damage. Experts at the earthquake monitoring center indicated that the tremor was the result of tectonic plate activity in the area and emphasized the importance of developing anti-earthquake construction technologies in the future.

ضَرَبَ زِلْزالٌ بِقُوَّةِ 7 دَرَجاتٍ شَرْقَ اليابان، مُعيدًا ذِكْرَياتِ الدَّمارِ الَّذي خَلَّفَهُ زِلْزالُ 2011. أَصْدَرَتِ السُّلُطاتُ تَحْذيراتٍ مِنْ زِلْزالٍ مُحْتَمَلٍ وَنَبَّهَتِ المُواطِنينَ إلى ضَرورَةِ الِاسْتِعْدادِ. عَلى الرَّغْمِ مِنَ الخَسائِرِ المادِّيَّةِ، أَظْهَرَتِ البِلادُ قُدْرَتَها عَلى التَّعامُلِ مَعَ مِثْلِ هَذِهِ الحَوادِثِ بِفَضْلِ التَّقَدُّمِ في تِقْنِيّاتِ البِناءِ وَالتَّفْتيشِ الهَيْكَلِيِّ المُسْتَمِرِّ.

A 7-magnitude earthquake struck eastern Japan, reviving memories of the destruction caused by the 2011 earthquake. The authorities issued warnings of a possible earthquake and alerted citizens to the need for preparedness. Despite material losses, the country demonstrated its ability to handle such incidents thanks to advances in construction technologies and continuous structural inspections.

ضَرَبَ زِلْزالٌ بِقُوَّةِ 5.5 دَرَجاتٍ جَنوبَ المَغْرِبِ، مُتَسَبِّبًا في أَضْرارٍ مُتَفاوِتَةٍ لِلْمَباني وَالطُّرُقِ. الِاسْتِجابَةُ السَّريعَةُ مِنَ السُّلُطاتِ وَالمُواطِنينَ ساهَمَتْ في تَقْليلِ الخَسائِرِ البَشَرِيَّةِ وَالمادِّيَّةِ. وَقَدْ أَكَّدَتِ الحُكومَةُ عَلى أَهَمِّيَّةِ تَحْديثِ البِنْيَةِ التَّحْتِيَّةِ وَتَطْبيقِ مَعايِيرِ البِناءِ الحَديثَةِ لِمُواجَهَةِ مِثْلِ هَذِهِ الكَوارِثِ في المُسْتَقْبَلِ.

A 5.5-magnitude earthquake hit southern Morocco, causing varying degrees of damage to buildings and roads. The swift response from authorities and citizens contributed to reducing human and material losses. The government emphasized the importance of updating infrastructure and applying modern building standards to face such disasters in the future.

9.2.2.2 Historical Account: The 2023 Turkey-Syria Earthquakes

الزِّلْزالُ المُدَمِّرُ في سورْيا: تَأْثيراتٌ وَتَحَدِّياتٌ في مُواجَهَةِ الكارِثَةِ

في السّادِسِ مِنْ فَبْرايِرَ 2023، وَقَعَ زِلْزالٌ مُدَمِّرٌ بِقُوَّةِ 8 دَرَجاتٍ عَلى مِقْياسِ ريخْتَرْ، ضارِبًا جَنوبَ تُرْكيا وَشَمالَ غَرْبِ سورْيا. وَعَلى الرَّغْمِ مِنْ أَنَّ تُرْكيا شَهِدَتِ العَدَدَ الأَكْبَرَ مِنَ الوَفَياتِ وَالدَّمارِ، إلّا أَنَّ تَأْثيرَ الزِّلْزالِ عَلى سورْيا كانَ كارِثِيًّا أَيْضًا، خُصوصًا في ظِلِّ الصُّعوباتِ الَّتي يُواجِهُها البَلَدُ بِالفِعْلِ نَتيجَةَ سَنَواتٍ مِنَ النِّزاعِ. شَهِدَتْ مُحافَظَةُ إِدْلِب في شَمالِ غَرْبِ سورْيا، وَالَّتي تُعَدُّ مِنَ المَناطِقِ الأَكْثَرِ تَضَرُّرًا، دَمارًا هائِلًا لِلْمَنازِلِ وَالبِنْيَةِ التَّحْتِيَّةِ، مِمّا تَرَكَ العَديدَ مِنَ السُّكّانِ بِلا مَأْوًى وَفي ظُروفٍ قاسِيَةٍ وَبَرْدٍ شَديدٍ. في هَذا المَقالِ، سَنَسْتَكْشِفُ بِالتَّفْصيلِ تَأْثيرَ الزِّلْزالِ عَلى سورْيا وَالتَّحَدِّياتِ الَّتي تُواجِهُ البِلادَ في أَعْقابِ هَذِهِ الكارِثَةِ.

مُدَّةُ الزِّلْزالِ وَالهَزّاتِ الِارْتِداديَّةِ: اسْتَمَرَّ الزِّلْزالُ لِمُدَّةِ 85 ثانِيَةً، تَبِعَتْهُ أَكْثَرُ مِنْ 570 هَزَّةً ارْتِداديَّةً خِلالَ الـ 24 ساعَةً الأولى. إحْدى هَذِهِ الهَزّاتِ الِارْتِداديَّةِ بَلَغَتْ قُوَّتُها 7.5 دَرَجَةً وَحَدَثَتْ شَمالَ مَرْكَزِ الزِّلْزالِ الأَصْلِيِّ في مُحافَظَةِ كَهْرَمان مَرْعَش التُّرْكِيَّةِ.

التَّأْثِيرُ في سُورْيا: فاقَمَ الزَّلْزالُ الحاجاتِ الإنْسانِيَّةَ المَوْجودَةَ مُسْبَقًا في المِنْطَقَةِ، مُضيفًا تَحَدِّياتٍ كَبيرَةً أَمامَ اسْتِجابَةِ سوريا لِلْكارِثَةِ. أَدَّى الدَّمارُ إلى تَضَرُّرِ بِنْيَةٍ تَحْتِيَّةٍ حَيَوِيَّةٍ وَخَسائِرَ في الأَرْواحِ، حَيْثُ أَعْلَنَ المَسْؤولونَ المَدْعومونَ مِنْ تُرْكِيا عَنْ وَفاةِ أَكْثَرَ مِنْ 4 آلافِ شَخْصٍ في المَناطِقِ الخاضِعَةِ لِسَيْطَرَةِ المُعارَضَةِ، بَيْنَما قُتِلَ أَكْثَرُ مِنْ أَلْفٍ في المَناطِقِ الخاضِعَةِ لِلْحُكومَةِ.

الاسْتِجابَةُ الإنْسانِيَّةُ: أَدَّتِ الكارِثَةُ إلى عَمَلِيَّةِ إنْقاذٍ وَمُساعَداتٍ دَوْلِيَّةٍ ضَخْمَةٍ شَمِلَتْ عَشَراتِ الدُّوَلِ وَالمُنَظَّماتِ. وَمَعَ ذَلِكَ، واجَهَتْ جُهودُ الإغاثَةِ تَحَدِّياتٍ مُبَكِّرَةً بِسَبَبِ الطُّرُقِ وَالمَطاراتِ المُتَضَرِّرَةِ، وَالأَحْوالِ الجَوِّيَّةِ السَّيِّئَةِ، وَنَقْصٍ في العِمالَةِ وَالمُعَدّاتِ. وَواجَهَتِ المُساعَداتُ المُوَجَّهَةُ إلى إدْلِبَ تَأْخيراتٍ بِسَبَبِ تَقْييدِ عُبورِ الحُدودِ بَيْنَ تُرْكِيا وَسوريا.

جُهودُ إعادَةِ الإعْمارِ: عَلى الرَّغْمِ مِنَ التَّحَدِّياتِ الهائِلَةِ، تَسْتَمِرُّ جُهودُ إعادَةِ الإعْمارِ في كُلٍّ مِنْ تُرْكِيا وَسوريا. وَمَعَ ذَلِكَ، لا تَزالُ هُناكَ تَساؤُلاتٌ حَوْلَ مُسْتَقْبَلِ المَناطِقِ المُدَمَّرَةِ وَعَمَلِيَّةِ التَّعافي طَويلَةِ الأَمَدِ. يُقَدَّرُ أَنَّ أَكْثَرَ مِنْ 5 مَلايينِ شَخْصٍ في سوريا قَدْ أَصْبَحوا بِلا مَأْوًى، بَيْنَما تَأَثَّرَ قُرابَةُ 11 مِلْيونَ شَخْصٍ، ما يَقْرُبُ مِنْ نِصْفِ سُكّانِ سوريا، بِالزَّلْزالِ. وَقَدْ تَضَرَّرَتْ عَشَراتُ المَناطِقِ السَّكَنِيَّةِ، وَدُمِّرَتْ أَوْ تَضَرَّرَتِ العَديدُ مِنَ المُنْشَآتِ العامَّةِ، بِما في ذَلِكَ المَدارِسُ وَالوَحَداتُ السَّكَنِيَّةُ.

The Devastating Earthquake in Syria: Impacts and Challenges in Facing the Disaster

On February 6, 2023, a devastating earthquake with a magnitude of 8 on the Richter scale occurred, striking southern Turkey and northwestern Syria. Although Turkey experienced the highest number of deaths and destruction, the impact of the earthquake on Syria was also catastrophic, especially given the difficulties the country is already facing due to years of conflict. Idlib province in northwestern Syria, one of the most affected areas, witnessed massive destruction of homes and infrastructure, leaving many residents homeless and in harsh and cold conditions. In this article, we will explore in detail the impact of the earthquake on Syria and the challenges the country faces in the aftermath of this disaster.

Duration of the Earthquake and Aftershocks: The earthquake lasted for 85 seconds, followed by more than 570 aftershocks within the first 24 hours. One of these aftershocks reached a magnitude of 7.5 and occurred north of the original earthquake's center in Kahramanmaraş province, Turkey.

Impact in Syria: The earthquake exacerbated the pre-existing humanitarian needs in the region, adding significant challenges to Syria's disaster response. The destruction led to damaged vital infrastructure and loss of lives, with officials supported by Turkey announcing the death of more than 4,000 people in opposition-controlled areas, while more than a thousand were killed in government-controlled areas.

Humanitarian Response: The disaster triggered a massive international rescue and aid operation involving dozens of countries and organizations. However, early relief efforts faced challenges due to damaged roads and airports, adverse weather conditions, and a shortage of labor and equipment. Aid directed to Idlib experienced delays due to border crossing restrictions between Turkey and Syria.

Reconstruction Efforts: Despite the enormous challenges, reconstruction efforts continue in both Turkey and Syria. However, questions remain about the future of the devastated areas and the long-term recovery process. It is estimated that more than 5 million people in Syria have become homeless, while about 11 million people, nearly half of Syria's population, were affected by the earthquake. Dozens of residential areas were damaged, and many public facilities, including schools and housing units, were destroyed or damaged.

9.2.3 Tsunamis

Track **96**

أَغْرَقَ • إِغْراقٌ

to inundate, flood, drown

أَغْرَقَتْ مَوْجَةُ التْسونامي مَناطِقَ واسِعَةً مِنَ السّاحِلِ، مِمّا أَدّى إلى تَدْميرِ البِنْيَةِ التَّحْتِيَّةِ وَالمَنازِلِ.

The tsunami inundated vast coastal areas, leading to the destruction of infrastructure and homes.

إِجْلاءٌ ساحِلِيٌّ

coastal evacuation

نَفَّذَتِ السُّلُطاتُ إِجْلاءً ساحِلِيًّا عاجِلًا بَعْدَ تَحْذيراتٍ مِنَ احْتِمالِ حُدوثِ تْسونامي.

Authorities urgently evacuated the coast following warnings of a potential tsunami.

إِنْذارُ تْسونامي

tsunami warning

أَصْدَرَتِ المَراكِزُ الجيولوجِيَّةُ إِنْذارَ تْسونامي بَعْدَ رَصْدِ زِلْزالٍ قَوِيٍّ تَحْتَ البَحْرِ.

Geological centers issued a tsunami warning after detecting a strong underwater earthquake.

اِجْتاحَ • اِجْتِياحٌ

to strike

اِجْتاحَتْ مَوْجاتُ التْسونامي القُرى السّاحِلِيَّةِ، مِمّا أَسْفَرَ عَنْ خَسائِرَ فادِحَةٍ.

Tsunami waves swept through coastal villages, resulting in significant losses.

اِحْتِمالُ حُدوثِ تْسونامي

tsunami occurrence probability

تُشيرُ الدِّراساتُ إلى احْتِمالِ حُدوثِ تْسونامي في المُحيطِ الهادِئِ بِسَبَبِ النَّشاطِ الزِّلْزالِيِّ المُتَزايِدِ.

Studies indicate the possibility of a tsunami in the Pacific Ocean due to increased seismic activity.

state preparedness

اِسْتِعْدادُ دَوْلَةٍ

بَدَأَتِ الدَّوْلَةُ فِي تَعْزِيزِ اسْتِعْدادِها لِمُواجَهَةِ أَيِّ تْسونامي مُحْتَمَلٍ.

The country began strengthening its preparedness for any potential tsunami.

water surge

اِنْدِفاعُ مِياهٍ

شَهِدَتِ السَّواحِلُ انْدِفاعَ مِياهٍ قَوِيًّا نَتِيجَةَ التْسونامي، مِمّا أَلْحَقَ الضَّرَرَ بِالسُّفُنِ وَالمَرافِقِ البَحْرِيَّةِ.

The coasts experienced a strong surge of water due to the tsunami, damaging ships and marine facilities.

search and rescue

بَحْثٌ وَإِنْقاذٌ

شارَكَتْ فِرَقُ البَحْثِ وَالإِنْقاذِ فِي عَمَلِيّاتٍ مُكَثَّفَةٍ لِلْعُثورِ عَلى النّاجينَ وَتَقْديمِ الإغاثَةِ.

Search and rescue teams engaged in intensive operations to find survivors and provide relief.

tsunami impact

تَأْثيرُ تْسونامي

كانَ لِتَأْثيرِ التْسونامي عَلى الجَزيرَةِ تَداعِياتٌ كارِثِيَّةٌ، مِمّا أَسْفَرَ عَنْ دَمارٍ واسِعِ النِّطاقِ.

The impact of the tsunami on the island had catastrophic consequences, resulting in widespread destruction.

coastal impact

تَأْثيرٌ عَلى شاطِئٍ

شَهِدَ الشّاطِئُ تَأْثيرًا مُدَمِّرًا نَتيجَةَ التْسونامي، مَعَ ارْتِفاعِ مُسْتَوَياتِ المِياهِ وَغَمْرِ المَناطِقِ السّاحِلِيَّةِ.

The beach experienced devastating effects from the tsunami, with rising water levels and inundation of coastal areas.

tsunami warning

تَحْذيرٌ مِنْ تْسونامي

أَصْدَرَتِ السُّلُطاتُ تَحْذيرًا مِنْ تْسونامي عَقِبَ الزِّلْزالِ البَحْرِيِّ القَوِيِّ.

Authorities issued a tsunami warning following the strong marine earthquake.

tsunami analysis

تَحْليلُ تْسونامي

قامَ العُلَماءُ بِتَحْليلِ بَياناتِ التْسونامي لِفَهْمِ ديناميكِيّاتِهِ وَالتَّنَبُّؤِ بِالْمَوْجاتِ المُسْتَقْبَلِيَّةِ.

Scientists analyzed tsunami data to understand its dynamics and predict future waves.

disaster planning

تَخْطِيطٌ لِلْكَوَارِثِ

بَدَأَتِ الْحُكُومَةُ فِي تَخْطِيطٍ لِلْكَوَارِثِ لِتَعْزِيزِ الِاسْتِعْدَادِ لِمُوَاجَهَةِ الْأَحْدَاثِ الطَّبِيعِيَّةِ مِثْلِ التّْسُونَامِي.

The government began disaster planning to enhance preparedness for natural events like tsunamis.

infrastructure damage

تَدْمِيرُ بِنْيَةٍ تَحْتِيَّةٍ

تَسَبَّبَ التّْسُونَامِي فِي تَدْمِيرِ الْبِنْيَةِ التَّحْتِيَّةِ، بِمَا فِي ذَلِكَ الطُّرُقِ وَالْجُسُورِ.

The tsunami caused the destruction of infrastructure, including roads and bridges.

tsunami

تْسُونَامِي

ضَرَبَتْ مَوْجَةُ التّْسُونَامِي السَّوَاحِلَ بِقُوَّةٍ، مِمَّا تَسَبَّبَ فِي إِجْلَاءٍ عَاجِلٍ وَإِنْقَاذٍ لِلْمُتَضَرِّرِينَ.

The tsunami hit the coasts forcefully, causing urgent evacuations and rescue of those affected.

environmental damage assessment

تَقْيِيمُ ضَرَرٍ بِيئِيٍّ

قَامَ خُبَرَاءُ الْبِيئَةِ بِتَقْيِيمِ الضَّرَرِ الْبِيئِيِّ النَّاتِجِ عَنِ التّْسُونَامِي، خَاصَّةً فِي الْمَنَاطِقِ الْبَحْرِيَّةِ وَالشَّوَاطِئِ.

Environmental experts assessed the environmental damage caused by the tsunami, especially in marine areas and beaches.

early warning

تَنْبِيهٌ مُبَكِّرٌ

أُرْسِلَ تَنْبِيهٌ مُبَكِّرٌ لِلسُّكَّانِ عَقِبَ رَصْدِ نَشَاطٍ زِلْزَالِيٍّ قَدْ يُؤَدِّي إِلَى تْسُونَامِي.

An early warning was sent to residents following the detection of seismic activity that could lead to a tsunami.

tsunami forecast

تَوَقُّعُ تْسُونَامِي

تَوَقُّعُ التّْسُونَامِي يَعْتَمِدُ عَلَى تَحْلِيلِ الْبَيَانَاتِ الزِّلْزَالِيَّةِ وَأَنْمَاطِ حَرَكَةِ الْمُحِيطَاتِ.

The prediction of a tsunami relies on analyzing seismic data and ocean movement patterns.

زِلْزَالٌ بَحْرِيٌّ

seafloor earthquake

• زَلازِلُ

أَدّى الزِّلْزَالُ البَحْرِيُّ إلى إثارَةِ مَخاوِفَ مِنْ حُدوثِ تْسونامي في المَناطِقِ المُحيطَةِ.

The marine earthquake raised concerns about a tsunami in the surrounding areas.

سِلْسِلَةُ مَوْجاتٍ

series of waves

• سَلاسِلُ

تَسَبَّبَ الزِّلْزَالُ في تَوْليدِ سِلْسِلَةٍ مِنْ مَوْجاتِ التْسونامي الَّتي اجْتاحَتِ السَّواحِلَ.

The earthquake generated a series of tsunami waves that swept across the coasts.

ضَرَبَ

to hit, strike

• ضَرْبٌ

ضَرَبَ التْسونامي المِنْطَقَةَ بِقُوَّةٍ، مِمّا تَسَبَّبَ في دَمارٍ واسِعٍ.

The tsunami struck the area forcefully, causing widespread destruction.

غَمَرَ

to flood, inundate, engulf

• غَمْرٌ

غَمَرَتْ مَوْجاتُ التْسونامي المَدينَةَ بِأَكْمَلِها، مِمّا أَدّى إلى إجْلاءٍ طارِئٍ لِلسُّكّانِ.

The tsunami waves inundated the entire city, leading to an emergency evacuation of residents.

مُجْتَمَعٌ سّاحِلِيٌّ

coastal community

تَأَثَّرَ المُجْتَمَعُ السّاحِلِيُّ بِشَكْلٍ كَبيرٍ بِالتْسونامي، مِمّا اسْتَدْعى جُهودَ إعادَةِ بِناءٍ واسِعَةَ النِّطاقِ.

The coastal community was greatly affected by the tsunami, necessitating extensive rebuilding efforts.

مَحَطَّةُ رَصْدِ تْسونامي

tsunami monitoring station

سَجَّلَتْ مَحَطَّةُ رَصْدِ التْسونامي الزِّلْزَالَ وأَصْدَرَتْ تَحْذيراتٍ فَوْرِيَّةً لِلْمَناطِقِ المُعَرَّضَةِ لِلْخَطَرِ.

The tsunami monitoring station recorded the earthquake and issued immediate warnings to the at-risk areas.

مُراقَبَةُ مَدٍّ وَجَزْرٍ

tide monitoring

تُعْتَبَرُ مُراقَبَةُ المَدِّ والجَزْرِ ضَرورِيَّةً لِلتَّنَبُّؤِ بِحُدوثِ التْسونامي.

Monitoring the tides is essential for predicting a tsunami.

distance مَسافَةٌ

قَطَعَتِ المَوْجَةُ العِمْلاقَةُ مَسافَةً كَبيرَةً في البَحْرِ قَبْلَ أَنْ تَصِلَ إلى الشّاطِئِ.

The giant wave traveled a great distance in the ocean before reaching the shore.

coastal area مِنْطَقَةٌ ساحِلِيَّةٌ • مَناطِقُ

غَمَرَتْ مَوْجاتُ التْسونامي مِنْطَقَةً ساحِلِيَّةً بِكامِلِها، مِمّا تَسَبَّبَ في خَسائِرَ كَبيرَةٍ.

Tsunami waves engulfed an entire coastal area, resulting in significant losses.

giant wave مَوْجَةٌ عِمْلاقَةٌ = مَوْجَةٌ عاتِيَةٌ • مَوْجاتٌ

اِجْتاحَتْ مَوْجَةٌ عِمْلاقَةٌ السّاحِلَ، مُدَمِّرَةً كُلَّ شَيْءٍ في طَريقِها.

A giant wave swept the coast, destroying everything in its path.

damaged port ميناءٌ مُحَطَّمٌ • مَوانِئُ

تَحَوَّلَ الميناءُ إلى ميناءٍ مُحَطَّمٍ بَعْدَ أَنْ ضَرَبَتْهُ مَوْجاتُ التْسونامي العَنيفَةُ.

The port turned into a shattered harbor after being hit by the violent tsunami waves.

to issue a warning نَشَرَ تَحْذيرًا • نَشْرٌ

نَشَرَتِ السُّلُطاتُ تَحْذيرًا فَوْرِيًّا بَعْدَ رَصْدِ مَوْجاتِ التْسونامي.

Authorities issued an immediate warning after detecting tsunami waves.

to rush, hurry هَرَعَ • هَرَعٌ

هَرَعَ النّاسُ إلى الأماكِنِ المُرْتَفِعَةِ بَحْثًا عَنِ الأمانِ بَعْدَ سَماعِهِمْ تَحْذيراتِ التْسونامي.

People rushed to higher ground in search of safety after hearing tsunami warnings.

ضَرَبَ زِلْزَالٌ بَحْرِيٌّ بِقُوَّةِ 7 دَرَجاتٍ سَواحِلَ اليابان، مِمّا أَدّى إلى إِطْلاقِ إِنْذارِ تسونامي في المِنْطَقَة. أَجْرَتِ السُّلُطاتُ اليابانِيَّةُ عَمَلِيَّةَ إِجْلاءٍ ساحِلِيٍّ واسِعَةَ النِّطاقِ اسْتِعْدادًا لِاحْتِمالِ حُدوثِ تسونامي. عَمِلَتْ مَحَطّاتُ رَصْدِ تسونامي وَمَراكِزُ مُراقَبَةِ المَدِّ وَالجَزْرِ عَلى تَقْييمِ الوَضْعِ وَصَدَرَتْ تَحْذيراتٌ لِلْمُجْتَمَعاتِ السّاحِلِيَّةِ.

A 7-magnitude undersea earthquake struck off the coasts of Japan, triggering a tsunami warning in the area. The Japanese authorities conducted a wide-scale coastal evacuation in preparation for the potential tsunami. Tsunami monitoring stations and tide observation centers assessed the situation and issued warnings to coastal communities.

اِجْتاحَ تسونامي سَواحِلَ تْشيلي بَعْدَ زِلْزالٍ عَنيفٍ بَلَغَتْ قُوَّتُهُ 8 دَرَجاتٍ. تَسَبَّبَتِ المَوْجاتُ العاتِيَةُ في تَدْميرِ البِنْيَةِ التَّحْتِيَّةِ وَغَمَرَتْ مَناطِقَ ساحِلِيَّةً بِالْكامِلِ. هُرِعَتْ فِرَقُ البَحْثِ وَالإِنْقاذِ لِلْمِنْطَقَةِ لِتَقْديمِ المُساعَدَةِ وَإِجْراءِ عَمَلِيّاتِ إِنْقاذٍ لِلْمُتَضَرِّرينَ. تَمَّ تَحْليلُ تَأْثيرِ التسونامي وَبَدَأَتْ عَمَلِيّاتُ تَقْييمِ الضَّرَرِ البِيئِيِّ.

A tsunami swept the coasts of Chile after a powerful earthquake of 8-magnitude. The fierce waves caused infrastructure destruction and completely submerged coastal areas. Search and rescue teams rushed to the area to provide assistance and conduct rescue operations for those affected. The impact of the tsunami was analyzed, and environmental damage assessment operations began.

اِسْتِجابَةً لِتَحْذيراتٍ عِلْمِيَّةٍ بِزِيادَةِ احْتِمالِ حُدوثِ تسونامي، عَزَّزَتْ إندونيسْيا اسْتِعْداداتِها عَبْرَ تَحْديثِ نِظامِ التَّنْبيهِ المُبَكِّرِ وَالتَّخْطيطِ لِلْكَوارِثِ. تَمَّ تَنْظيمُ تَدْريباتِ إِجْلاءٍ في المَناطِقِ السّاحِلِيَّةِ لِتَعْزيزِ الوَعْيِ وَالجاهِزِيَّةِ لَدى المُجْتَمَعاتِ السّاحِلِيَّةِ.

In response to scientific warnings of an increased probability of a tsunami, Indonesia enhanced its preparedness by updating its early warning system and disaster planning. Evacuation drills were organized in coastal areas to raise awareness and readiness among coastal communities.

ضَرَبَ تسونامي ميناءً رَئيسِيًّا في الفِلِبّين، مُتَسَبِّبًا في دَمارٍ واسِعِ النِّطاقِ. اِنْدَفَعَتِ المِياهُ بِقُوَّةٍ نَحْوَ اليابِسَةِ، مِمّا أَغْرَقَ المِنْطَقَةَ وَدَمَّرَ البِنْيَةَ التَّحْتِيَّةَ الحَيَوِيَّةَ. تَجْري عَمَلِيّاتُ بَحْثٍ وَإِنْقاذٍ مُكَثَّفَةٌ لِمُساعَدَةِ المُتَضَرِّرينَ وَتَقْديمِ الإِغاثَةِ العاجِلَةِ.

A tsunami hit a major port in the Philippines, causing widespread destruction. The waters rushed towards the land, flooding the area and destroying vital infrastructure. Intensive search and rescue operations are underway to assist the affected and provide urgent relief.

بَعْدَ تَلَقِّي تَوَقُّعاتٍ بِحُدوثِ تسونامي قَدْ يُؤَثِّرُ عَلَى السَّواحِلِ، اِتَّخَذَتْ سَلْطَنَةُ عُمانَ تَدابيرَ وِقائِيَّةً شَمِلَتْ إِجْلاءَ المَناطِقِ السّاحِلِيَّةِ الأَكْثَرِ عُرْضَةً وَتَفْعيلَ نِظامِ التَّنْبيهِ المُبَكِّرِ. أَكَّدَتِ الحُكومَةُ عَلَى أَهَمِّيَّةِ اسْتِعْدادِ الدَّوْلَةِ وَالتَّخْطيطِ الفَعّالِ لِلْكَوارِثِ لِحِمايَةِ الأَرْواحِ وَالمُمْتَلَكاتِ.

After receiving forecasts of a tsunami that could affect the coasts, the Sultanate of Oman took preventive measures, including evacuating the most vulnerable coastal areas and activating the early warning system. The government emphasized the importance of the country's preparedness and effective disaster planning to protect lives and properties.

9.2.4 Cyclones and Tornadoes

Track 98

heavy rainfall | أَمْطارٌ غَزيرَةٌ

ضَرَبَ إِعْصارٌ اسْتِوائِيٌّ قَوِيٌّ سَواحِلَ عُمانَ، مِمّا أَدّى إلى هُطولِ أَمْطارٍ غَزيرَةٍ وَحُدوثِ فَيَضاناتٍ في المَناطِقِ السّاحِلِيَّةِ.

A strong tropical cyclone hit the coasts of Oman, causing heavy rainfall and floods in coastal areas.

cyclone, typhoon, hurricane | • أَعاصيرُ | إِعْصارٌ

تَتَعَرَّضُ المِنْطَقَةُ كُلَّ عامٍ لِأَعاصيرَ مُتَعَدِّدَةٍ، مِمّا يَسْتَدْعي اسْتِعْداداتٍ مُكَثَّفَةٍ.

The region faces multiple cyclones each year, necessitating extensive preparations.

In English, the terms 'hurricane,' 'typhoon,' and 'cyclone' refer to the same meteorological phenomenon but differ based on geographic location (hurricanes in the Atlantic and Northeast Pacific, typhoons in the Northwest Pacific, and cyclones in the South Pacific and Indian Ocean). However, in Arabic, all three are generally referred to by a single term: إِعْصارٌ.

Atlantic hurricane | إِعْصارٌ أَطْلَسِيٌّ

أَصابَ إِعْصارٌ أَطْلَسِيٌّ السّاحِلَ الشَّرْقِيَّ لِلْوِلاياتِ المُتَّحِدَةِ الأَمْريكِيَّةِ، مِمّا تَسَبَّبَ في إِجْلاءٍ واسِعِ النِّطاقِ وَأَضْرارٍ جَسيمَةٍ.

An Atlantic hurricane struck the east coast of the United States, resulting in widespread evacuation and significant damage.

tropical cyclone | إِعْصارٌ اسْتِوائِيٌّ = إِعْصارٌ مَدارِيٌّ

تَحَوَّلَ الإِعْصارُ الاسْتِوائِيُّ إلى إِعْصارٍ مَدارِيٍّ شَديدٍ، مُهَدِّدًا الجُزُرَ وَالمَناطِقَ السّاحِلِيَّةَ.

The tropical storm escalated into a severe cyclone, threatening islands and coastal areas.

tornado

إعْصارٌ قُمْعِيٌّ

شوهِدَ إعْصارٌ قُمْعِيٌّ مُفاجِئٌ في الرّيفِ، مِمّا أَدّى إلى تَدْميرِ المَنازِلِ والبِنْيَةِ التَّحْتِيَّةِ.

A sudden tornado was observed in the countryside, leading to the destruction of homes and infrastructure.

to strike

اِجْتاحَ • اِجْتِياحٌ

اِجْتاحَ الإعْصارُ المَناطِقَ السّاحِلِيَّةَ، مِمّا أَدّى إلى دَمارٍ كَبيرٍ في البِنْيَةِ التَّحْتِيَّةِ والمَساكِنِ.

The cyclone swept through coastal areas, causing significant destruction to infrastructure and homes.

wave height

اِرْتِفاعُ مَوْجَةٍ

شَهِدَتِ المِنْطَقَةُ اِرْتِفاعًا كَبيرًا لِأَمْواجِ البَحْرِ خِلالَ الإعْصارِ، مِمّا أَثارَ قَلَقَ السُّكّانِ.

The region experienced a significant rise in sea wave height during the cyclone, raising concerns among residents.

wind surge

اِنْدِفاعُ رِياحٍ

كانَ اِنْدِفاعُ الرّياحِ خِلالَ الإعْصارِ شَديدًا، مِمّا تَسَبَّبَ في سُقوطِ الأَشْجارِ وانْقِطاعِ الكَهْرَباءِ.

The wind surge during the cyclone was intense, causing trees to fall and power outages.

water surge

اِنْدِفاعُ مِياهٍ

تَسَبَّبَ اِنْدِفاعُ المِياهِ النّاجِمُ عَنِ الإعْصارِ في فَيَضاناتٍ في المَناطِقِ المُنْخَفِضَةِ.

The water surge caused by the cyclone resulted in flooding in low-lying areas.

storm impact

تَأْثيرُ عاصِفَةٍ

كانَ تَأْثيرُ العاصِفَةِ واضِحًا في الأَضْرارِ الواسِعَةِ الَّتي لَحِقَتْ بِالمُمْتَلَكاتِ والمَزْروعاتِ.

The impact of the storm was evident in the extensive damage to properties and crops.

storm resurgence

تَجَدُّدُ عاصِفَةٍ

شَهِدَتِ المِنْطَقَةُ تَجَدُّدَ عَوَاصِفَ عِدَّةَ مَرَّاتٍ خِلالَ مَوْسِمِ الأَعَاصِيرِ، مِمَّا زَادَ مِنْ تَعْقِيدِ عَمَلِيَّاتِ الإِنْقَاذِ وَالإِغَاثَةِ.

The region experienced the resurgence of storms several times during the cyclone season, complicating rescue and relief operations.

evacuation preparations
pl. تَجْهِيزَاتُ إِجْلَاءٍ

بَدَأَتِ السُّلُطَاتُ فِي تَجْهِيزَاتِ إِجْلَاءِ السُّكَّانِ مِنَ المَنَاطِقِ الأَكْثَرِ خُطورَةً اسْتِعْدَادًا لِوُصُولِ الإِعْصَارِ.

Authorities began evacuation preparations for residents in the most dangerous areas in anticipation of the cyclone's arrival.

cyclone warning
تَحْذِيرٌ مِنْ إِعْصَارٍ

أَصْدَرَتِ الأَرْصَادُ الجَوِّيَّةُ تَحْذِيرًا مِنْ إِعْصَارٍ مِنَ المُتَوَقَّعِ أَنْ يَضْرِبَ السَّاحِلَ خِلالَ الأَيَّامِ القَادِمَةِ.

The meteorological service issued a warning of a cyclone expected to hit the coast in the coming days.

cyclone impact analysis
تَحْلِيلُ تَأْثِيرِ إِعْصَارٍ

قَامَ العُلَمَاءُ بِتَحْلِيلِ تَأْثِيرِ الإِعْصَارِ عَلَى المِنْطَقَةِ لِتَقْدِيرِ حَجْمِ الأَضْرَارِ وَالتَّخْطِيطِ لِلإِغَاثَةِ.

Scientists analyzed the impact of the cyclone on the area to estimate the extent of damage and plan for relief.

infrastructure damage
تَدْمِيرُ بِنْيَةٍ تَحْتِيَّةٍ

أَدَّى الإِعْصَارُ إِلَى تَدْمِيرِ البِنْيَةِ التَّحْتِيَّةِ الحَيَوِيَّةِ، بِمَا فِي ذَلِكَ الطُّرُقِ وَشَبَكَاتِ الكَهْرَبَاءِ.

The cyclone caused the destruction of vital infrastructure, including roads and electricity networks.

agricultural destruction
تَدْمِيرُ زِرَاعَةٍ

تَسَبَّبَ الإِعْصَارُ فِي تَدْمِيرٍ وَاسِعٍ لِلزِّرَاعَةِ، مِمَّا أَثَّرَ سَلْبًا عَلَى الاِقْتِصَادِ المَحَلِّيِّ.

The cyclone caused widespread destruction of agriculture, negatively affecting the local economy.

coastal destruction

تَدْميرُ ساحِلٍ

خِلالَ الإعْصارِ، تَسَبَّبَتِ الرِّياحُ القَوِيَّةُ وَالأَمْواجُ العاتِيَةُ في تَدْميرِ السَّاحِلِ.

During the cyclone, the strong winds and high waves caused the destruction of the coast.

destruction of homes

تَدْميرُ مَنازِلَ

تَدْميرُ المَنازِلِ كانَ واسِعَ النِّطاقِ في المَناطِقِ المُتَضَرِّرَةِ مِنَ الإعْصارِ.

The destruction of homes was widespread in the areas affected by the cyclone.

to form

تَشَكَّلَ • تَشَكُّلٌ

تَشَكَّلَ الإعْصارُ في المُحيطِ وَبَدَأَ في التَّحَرُّكِ نَحْوَ اليابِسَةِ مَعَ تَزايُدِ قُوَّتِهِ.

The cyclone formed in the ocean and began moving toward land, gaining strength.

cyclone classification

تَصْنيفُ إعْصارٍ

تَمَّ تَصْنيفُ الإعْصارِ كَإعْصارٍ مِنَ الفِئَةِ الرّابِعَةِ، مِمّا يَعْكِسُ قُوَّتَهُ وَخَطَرَهُ المُحْتَمَلَ.

The cyclone was classified as a Category 4, reflecting its strength and potential danger.

to be damaged

تَضَرَّرَ • تَضَرُّرٌ

تَضَرَّرَتِ البِنْيَةُ التَّحْتِيَّةُ بِشَكْلٍ كَبيرٍ بِسَبَبِ الرِّياحِ العاتِيَةِ وَالأَمْطارِ الغَزيرَةِ مِنَ الإعْصارِ.

The infrastructure was significantly damaged due to the cyclone's strong winds and heavy rains.

property damage

تَلَفُ مُمْتَلَكاتٍ

أَدّى الإعْصارُ إلى تَلَفٍ واسِعِ النِّطاقِ لِلْمُمْتَلَكاتِ، بِما في ذَلِكَ المَنازِلِ وَالمَرْكَباتِ.

The cyclone caused widespread property damage, including homes and vehicles.

early warning

تَنْبيهٌ مُبَكِّرٌ

تَمَّ إصْدارُ تَنْبيهٍ مُبَكِّرٍ لِلسُّكّانِ في المَناطِقِ المُعَرَّضَةِ لِخَطَرِ الإعْصارِ لِاتِّخاذِ الاِحْتِياطاتِ اللّازِمَةِ.

An early warning was issued to residents in areas at risk of the cyclone to take necessary precautions.

electrical hazard

خَطَرٌ كَهْرَبائِيٌّ

أَدَّى الإِعْصارُ إِلَى خَطَرٍ كَهْرَبائِيٍّ كَبِيرٍ بِسَبَبِ انْقِطاعِ الكَهْرَباءِ وَسُقوطِ أَعْمِدَةِ الكَهْرَباءِ.

The cyclone posed a significant electrical hazard due to power outages and fallen power poles.

potential destruction

دَمارٌ مُحْتَمَلٌ

حَذَّرَ الخُبَراءُ مِنْ دَمارٍ مُحْتَمَلٍ يُمْكِنُ أَنْ يُسَبِّبَهُ الإِعْصارُ فِي المَناطِقِ السّاحِلِيَّةِ.

Experts warned of potential destruction the cyclone could cause in coastal areas.

cyclone-force winds   pl.

رِياحٌ إِعْصارِيَّةٌ

بَلَغَتْ سُرْعَةُ الرِّياحِ الإِعْصارِيَّةِ أَكْثَرَ مِنْ 150 كيلومتْرًا فِي السّاعَةِ، مِمّا يُشِيرُ إِلَى قُوَّةِ الإِعْصارِ.

The cyclone-force winds reached speeds of over 150 kilometers per hour, indicating the strength of the cyclone.

high winds   pl.

رِياحٌ عاتِيَةٌ

تَسَبَّبَتِ الرِّياحُ العاتِيَةُ فِي اقْتِلاعِ الأَشْجارِ وَتَطايُرِ الأَنْقاضِ، مِمّا زادَ مِنْ مَخاطِرِ الإِصاباتِ.

The fierce winds caused trees to be uprooted and debris to fly, increasing the risk of injuries.

coast, coastline   سَواحِلُ •

ساحِلٌ

تَعَرَّضَ السّاحِلُ لِأَضْرارٍ بالِغَةٍ نَتِيجَةَ العاصِفَةِ القَوِيَّةِ الَّتِي اجْتاحَتِ المِنْطَقَةَ.

The coast suffered severe damage due to the powerful storm that swept through the area.

wind speed

سُرْعَةُ رِياحٍ

بَلَغَتْ سُرْعَةُ الرِّياحِ خِلالَ العاصِفَةِ أَكْثَرَ مِنْ 120 كيلومتْرًا فِي السّاعَةِ، مُنْذِرَةً بِخَطَرٍ كَبِيرٍ.

The wind speed during the storm exceeded 120 kilometers per hour, posing a significant danger.

to hit   ضَرَبَ •

ضَرَبَ

ضَرَبَ الإِعْصارُ المِنْطَقَةَ بِقُوَّةٍ، مِمّا تَسَبَّبَ فِي دَمارٍ واسِعِ النِّطاقِ.

The cyclone struck the area forcefully, causing widespread destruction.

stormy

عَاصِفٌ

كَانَ الطَّقْسُ عَاصِفًا بِشَكْلٍ غَيْرِ مُعْتَادٍ، مِمَّا أَدَّى إِلَى تَعَطُّلِ الرِّحْلَاتِ البَحْرِيَّةِ وَالجَوِّيَّةِ.

The weather was unusually stormy, leading to disruptions in sea and air travel.

storm

عَاصِفَةٌ • عَوَاصِفُ

حَذَّرَتِ الأَرْصَادُ الجَوِّيَّةُ مِنْ عَاصِفَةٍ تَقْتَرِبُ مِنَ السَّاحِلِ، مِمَّا اسْتَدْعَى إِجْرَاءاتٍ احْتِرَازِيَّةً.

The meteorological service warned of a storm approaching the coast, necessitating precautionary measures.

tropical storm

عَاصِفَةٌ اسْتِوَائِيَّةٌ • عَوَاصِفُ

ضَرَبَتْ عَاصِفَةٌ اسْتِوَائِيَّةٌ السَّوَاحِلَ، مِمَّا تَسَبَّبَ فِي أَمْطَارٍ غَزِيرَةٍ وَرِيَاحٍ قَوِيَّةٍ.

A tropical storm hit the coasts, causing heavy rains and strong winds.

rotating storm

عَاصِفَةٌ دَوَّارَةٌ

شَهِدَتِ المِنْطَقَةُ عَاصِفَةً دَوَّارَةً مُدَمِّرَةً، مِمَّا أَدَّى إِلَى تَدْمِيرِ عِدَّةِ بِنَايَاتٍ.

The area experienced a devastating rotating storm, leading to the destruction of several buildings.

dust storm

عَاصِفَةٌ رَمْلِيَّةٌ

اِجْتَاحَتْ عَاصِفَةٌ رَمْلِيَّةٌ المَنَاطِقَ الصَّحْرَاوِيَّةَ، مِمَّا خَلَقَ ظُرُوفًا صَعْبَةً لِلتَّنَقُّلِ وَالرُّؤْيَةِ.

A sandstorm swept through desert areas, creating challenging conditions for travel and visibility.

coastal inundation

غَمْرُ مَنَاطِقَ سَاحِلِيَّةٍ

غَمَرَتِ الأَمْوَاجُ المُرْتَفِعَةُ مَنَاطِقَ سَاحِلِيَّةً بِأَكْمَلِهَا، مِمَّا تَسَبَّبَ فِي أَضْرَارٍ جَسِيمَةٍ.

The high waves inundated entire coastal areas, causing severe damage.

category

فِئَةٌ = دَرَجَةٌ

وَصَلَتْ شِدَّةُ الإِعْصَارِ إِلَى الفِئَةِ الثَّالِثَةِ، مِمَّا يُنْذِرُ بِدَمَارٍ شَدِيدٍ.

The cyclone reached Category 3 intensity, indicating severe destruction.

to overturn

قَلَبَ •

قَلْبٌ

قَلَبَتْ رِياحُ الإِعْصارِ السَّيّاراتِ وَأَلْحَقَتْ أَضْرارًا بِالأَشْجارِ وَاللّافِتاتِ.

The cyclone's winds overturned cars and caused damage to trees and signs.

strength, itensity

قُوَّةُ إِعْصارٍ

بَلَغَتْ قُوَّةُ الإِعْصارِ الفِئَةَ الرّابِعَةَ، مِمّا يُشيرُ إِلى خُطورَةٍ هائِلَةٍ.

The cyclone reached Category 4 strength, indicating immense danger.

strong

قَوِيٌّ

كانَ الإِعْصارُ قَوِيًّا بِشَكْلٍ اسْتِثْنائِيٍّ، مِمّا أَدّى إِلى دَعَواتٍ عاجِلَةٍ لِإِجْلاءِ المَناطِقِ المُعَرَّضَةِ لِلْخَطَرِ.

The cyclone was exceptionally strong, leading to urgent calls for the evacuation of vulnerable areas.

eye of a storm

مَراكِزُ •

مَرْكَزُ إِعْصارٍ

حَدَّدَ العُلَماءُ مَرْكَزَ الإِعْصارِ وَحَذَّروا مِنْ شِدَّتِهِ المُتَزايِدَةِ.

Scientists pinpointed the cyclone's center and warned of its increasing intensity.

storm path

مَسارُ إِعْصارٍ

كانَ مَسارُ الإِعْصارِ غَيْرَ مُتَوَقَّعٍ، مِمّا أَدّى إِلى تَحَدِّياتٍ في التَّخْطيطِ لِلاسْتِجابَةِ لِلطَّوارِئِ.

The cyclone's path was unpredictable, leading to challenges in emergency response planning.

projected path of a cyclone

مَسارٌ مُتَوَقَّعٌ لِإِعْصارٍ

تَمَّ تَحْديدُ المَسارِ المُتَوَقَّعِ لِلإِعْصارِ، مِمّا ساعَدَ في تَوْجيهِ جُهودِ الإِجْلاءِ وَالاسْتِعْدادِ.

The expected path of the cyclone was identified, aiding in directing evacuation and preparedness efforts.

يَتَشَكَّلُ إعْصارٌ اسْتِوائِيٌّ في الأَطْلَسِيِّ مُتَّجِهًا نَحْوَ سَواحِلِ فلوريدا مَعَ تَوَقُّعاتٍ بِأَنْ يَصِلَ إلى الفِئَةِ الثّالِثَةِ حَسْبَ تَصْنيفِ الأَعاصيرِ. أَصْدَرَتِ السُّلُطاتُ تَحْذيرًا مِنَ الإعْصارِ وَبَدَأَتْ في تَجْهيزاتِ إجْلاءٍ لِلْمَناطِقِ الأَكْثَرِ عُرْضَةً لِلْخَطَرِ. وَتُتَوَقَّعُ رِياحٌ عاتِيَةٌ وَأَمْطارٌ غَزيرَةٌ مَعَ انْدِفاعِ مِياهٍ قَدْ يَغْمُرُ المَناطِقَ السّاحِلِيَّةَ.

A tropical hurricane is forming in the Atlantic, heading towards the coasts of Florida with expectations to reach category 3 according to the cyclone classification. Authorities have issued a hurricane warning and started evacuation preparations for the most vulnerable areas. Strong winds and heavy rains are expected, with a surge that may flood coastal areas.

يَتَّجِهُ إعْصارٌ اسْتِوائِيٌّ قَوِيٌّ نَحْوَ سَواحِلِ عُمانَ، مَعَ تَوَقُّعاتٍ بِأَنْ يَصِلَ إلى الفِئَةِ الرّابِعَةِ حَسْبَ تَصْنيفِ الأَعاصيرِ. أَعْلَنَتِ السُّلُطاتُ العُمانِيَّةُ حالَةَ الاسْتِنْفارِ وَبَدَأَتْ في تَنْفيذِ تَجْهيزاتِ إجْلاءٍ واسِعَةِ النِّطاقِ لِلْمَناطِقِ المُعَرَّضَةِ لِلْخَطَرِ، مَعَ تَأْكيدِها عَلى أَهَمِّيَّةِ التَّقَيُّدِ بِتَعْليماتِ السَّلامَةِ. عَمِلَتْ أَنْظِمَةُ التَّنْبيهِ المُبَكِّرِ عَلى نَشْرِ تَحْذيراتٍ مِنَ الإعْصارِ، مُحَذِّرَةً مِنَ انْدِفاعِ مِياهٍ قَدْ يُؤَدّي إلى غَمْرِ المَناطِقِ السّاحِلِيَّةِ وَتَدْميرِ البِنْيَةِ التَّحْتِيَّةِ. يَسْتَعِدُّ المُواطِنونَ لِمُواجَهَةِ الإعْصارِ بِتَخْزينِ المَوادِّ الغِذائِيَّةِ وَالمِياهِ وَتَأْمينِ المُمْتَلَكاتِ.

A powerful tropical cyclone is heading towards the coasts of Oman, with expectations to reach category 4 according to the cyclone classification. The Omani authorities have declared a state of alert and started implementing wide-scale evacuation preparations for the endangered areas, emphasizing the importance of adhering to safety instructions. Early warning systems have issued cyclone warnings, alerting of a surge that could flood coastal areas and destroy infrastructure. Citizens are preparing to face the cyclone by stocking up on food and water and securing properties.

إعْصارٌ مَدارِيٌّ قَوِيٌّ في طَريقِهِ إلى ضَرْبِ الفِلِبّينِ، مَعَ تَوَقُّعاتٍ بِأَنْ يَتَسَبَّبَ في أَضْرارٍ جَسيمَةٍ عَلى السّاحِلِ وَالمَناطِقِ المُجاوِرَةِ. وَقَدْ فَعَّلَتِ الحُكومَةُ تَنْبيهًا مُبَكِّرًا وَتَحْذيرًا مِنَ الإعْصارِ لِلْمَناطِقِ السّاحِلِيَّةِ وَعَزَّزَتْ تَجْهيزاتِ الإجْلاءِ. يَسْتَعِدُّ السُّكّانُ لانْدِفاعِ مِياهٍ وَرِياحٍ إعْصارِيَّةٍ قَدْ تَضْرِبُ المِنْطَقَةَ.

A strong typhoon is on its way to hit the Philippines, with expectations of causing significant damage to the coast and neighboring areas. The government has activated an early warning and typhoon alert for coastal areas and enhanced evacuation preparations. Residents are preparing for storm surges and typhoon-force winds that may hit the area.

اجْتاحَتْ عاصِفَةٌ اسْتِوائِيَّةٌ ساحِلَ بَنْغَلاديش، مُتَسَبِّبَةً في تَدْميرٍ لِلْبِنْيَةِ التَّحْتِيَّةِ وَغَمْرِ مَناطِقَ ساحِلِيَّةٍ بِالْكامِلِ. أَلْحَقَتِ الأَمْطارُ الغَزيرَةُ وَالرِّياحُ العاتِيَةُ أَضْرارًا كَبيرَةً بِالْمُجْتَمَعاتِ السّاحِلِيَّةِ. تَعْمَلُ فِرَقُ البَحْثِ وَالإنْقاذِ عَلى تَقْديمِ المُساعَدَةِ وَتَحْليلِ تَأْثيرِ العاصِفَةِ لِتَقْييمِ الضَّرَرِ البيئِيِّ وَمُساعَدَةِ المُتَضَرِّرينَ.

A tropical storm swept across the coast of Bangladesh, causing infrastructure destruction and completely flooding coastal areas. The heavy rain and strong winds inflicted significant damage on coastal communities. Search and rescue teams are working to provide assistance and analyze the storm's impact to assess environmental damage and help those affected.

شَهِدَتْ وِلايَةُ أُوكْلاهوما الأَمْريكِيَّةُ إعْصارًا قَوِيًّا ضَرَبَ مَناطِقَ عِدَّةٍ، مُسَبِّبًا دَمارًا واسِعَ النِّطاقِ في المَنازِلِ والبِنْيَةِ التَّحْتِيَّةِ. تَسَبَّبَتِ العاصِفَةُ الدَّوَّارَةُ، الَّتي بَلَغَتْ سُرْعَةُ رِياحِها أَكْثَرَ مِنْ 200 كيلومِتْرٍ في السَّاعَةِ، في تَدْميرِ الزِّراعَةِ وانْقِطاعِ التَّيّارِ الكَهْرَبائِيِّ في عِدَّةِ مَناطِقَ. أَصْدَرَتِ السُّلُطاتُ تَحْذيراتٍ مُبَكِّرَةً، مِمّا ساعَدَ في تَقْليلِ عَدَدِ الضَّحايا. هَذا وَتَعْمَلُ فِرَقُ البَحْثِ والإنْقاذِ عَلى مَدارِ السَّاعَةِ لِتَقْديمِ المُساعَدَةِ لِلْمُتَضَرِّرينَ وَتَقْييمِ حَجْمِ الأَضْرارِ.

The state of Oklahoma in the United States experienced a powerful tornado that hit several areas, causing widespread destruction to homes and infrastructure. The twister, with wind speeds of over 200 kilometers per hour, caused agricultural destruction and power outages in several areas. Early warnings were issued, helping to reduce the number of victims. Search and rescue teams are working around the clock to provide assistance to those affected and assess the extent of the damage.

9.2.5 Floods

Track **100**

emergency evacuation

إجْلاءٌ طارِئٌ

نَظَّمَتِ الحُكومَةُ إجْلاءً طارِئًا لِلْمُجْتَمَعاتِ الَّتي تُواجِهُ خَطَرَ الفَيَضاناتِ.

The government organized emergency evacuations for communities facing flood risks.

water removal

إزالَةُ مِياهٍ

قامَتْ فِرَقُ الإنْقاذِ بِإزالَةِ المِياهِ مِنَ المَناطِقِ السَّكَنِيَّةِ لِتَسْهيلِ عَوْدَةِ السُّكّانِ.

Rescue teams removed water from residential areas to facilitate the return of residents.

medical relief

إغاثَةٌ طِبِّيَّةٌ

تَمَّ تَقْديمُ إغاثَةٍ طِبِّيَّةٍ لِلْمُتَضَرِّرينَ مِنَ الفَيَضاناتِ، شَمِلَتِ العِلاجَ والدَّعْمَ النَّفْسِيَّ.

Medical relief was provided to flood victims, including treatment and psychological support.

road closure

إغْلاقُ طَريقٍ

تَمَّ إغْلاقُ الطُّرُقِ الرَّئيسِيَّةِ بِسَبَبِ ارْتِفاعِ مَنْسوبِ المِياهِ والفَيَضاناتِ.

Major roads were closed due to rising water levels and flooding.

water rescue

إِنْقَاذٌ بَحْرِيٌّ

نَفَّذَتْ فِرَقُ الإِنْقَاذِ البَحْرِيِّ عَمَلِيَّاتِ إِنْقَاذٍ حَيَوِيَّةٍ لِلْأَشْخَاصِ العالِقينَ في المَناطِقِ المَغْمورَةِ بِالْمِياهِ.

Marine rescue teams carried out vital rescue operations for people stranded in waterlogged areas.

water level rise

ارْتِفاعُ مَنْسوبِ مِياهٍ

شَهِدَتِ المَدينَةُ ارْتِفاعًا خَطيرًا في مَنْسوبِ المِياهِ، مِمّا تَسَبَّبَ في حالَةِ تَأَهُّبٍ.

The city experienced a dangerous rise in water levels, causing a state of alert.

property retrieval

اسْتِرْجاعُ مُمْتَلَكاتٍ

بَدَأَ السُّكّانُ في اسْتِرْجاعِ مُمْتَلَكاتِهِمْ بَعْدَ انْحِسارِ مِياهِ الفَيَضانِ.

Residents began retrieving their properties after the floodwaters receded.

rush of water

انْدِفاعُ مِياهٍ

حَدَثَ انْدِفاعُ مِياهٍ قَوِيٌّ في الأَنْهارِ، مِمّا أَدّى إلى فَيَضاناتٍ مُفاجِئَةٍ.

There was a strong surge of water in the rivers, leading to sudden floods.

to rush

انْدَفَعَ • انْدِفاعٌ

انْدَفَعَتِ المِياهُ بِقُوَّةٍ إلى المَناطِقِ المُنْخَفِضَةِ، مِمّا تَسَبَّبَ في أَضْرارٍ واسِعَةِ النِّطاقِ.

Water rushed forcefully into low-lying areas, causing extensive damage.

damaged infrastructure

بِنْيَةٌ تَحْتِيَّةٌ مُتَضَرِّرَةٌ • بَنى

أَدّى الفَيَضانُ إلى تَضَرُّرِ البِنْيَةِ التَّحْتِيَّةِ، بِما في ذلِكَ الجُسورِ وَالطُّرُقِ.

The flood damaged infrastructure, including bridges and roads.

floods' impact on agriculture

تَأْثيرُ فَيَضانٍ عَلى الزِّراعَةِ

كانَ لِتَأْثيرِ الفَيَضاناتِ عَلى الزِّراعَةِ تَداعِياتٌ خَطيرَةٌ، حَيْثُ فَقَدَ المُزارِعونَ مَحاصيلَهُمْ.

The impact of the floods on agriculture had serious repercussions, as farmers lost their crops.

flood impact

تَأْثِيرُ فَيَضانٍ

شَهِدَتِ المِنْطَقَةُ تَأْثِيرَ فَيَضانٍ مُدَمِّرٍ، مِمّا تَسَبَّبَ في إِخْلاءِ العَديدِ مِنَ المَنازِلِ.

The area experienced a devastating flood impact, resulting in the evacuation of many homes.

environmental effect of flood

تَأْثِيرُ فَيَضانٍ عَلى البيئَةِ

كانَتْ تَأْثيراتُ الفَيَضانِ عَلى البيئَةِ مَلْحوظَةً، شَمِلَ ذَلِكَ تَلَوُّثَ المِياهِ وَتَدْميرَ البيئاتِ الطَّبيعِيَّةِ.

The environmental impacts of the flood were significant, including water pollution and destruction of natural habitats.

to exceed limits

تَجاوُزٌ • تَجاوَزَ الحُدودَ

تَجاوَزَ مَنْسوبُ المِياهِ الحُدودَ الآمِنَةَ، مِمّا أَدّى إلى فَيَضاناتٍ في المَناطِقِ المُجاوِرَةِ.

Water levels exceeded safe limits, leading to flooding in adjacent areas.

to accumulate

تَجَمَّعَ • تَجَمَّعَ

مَعَ تَفاقُمِ حِدَّةِ الفَيَضانِ، بَدَأَتِ المِياهُ في التَّجَمُّعِ بِكَمِّياتٍ هائِلَةٍ.

With the exacerbation of the floods' severity, the waters began to accumulate in vast quantities.

water accumulation

تَجَمُّعٌ مائِيٌّ

تَشَكَّلَ تَجَمُّعٌ مائِيٌّ كَبيرٌ في المِنْطَقَةِ المُنْخَفِضَةِ بَعْدَ هُطولِ أَمْطارٍ غَزيرَةٍ لِعِدَّةِ أَيّامٍ.

A large water pool formed in the low-lying area after several days of heavy rainfall.

flood warning

تَحْذيرٌ مِنْ فَيَضانٍ

أَصْدَرَتِ السُّلُطاتُ تَحْذيرًا مِنْ فَيَضانٍ مُحْتَمَلٍ نَتيجَةَ ارْتِفاعِ مُسْتَوَياتِ الأَنْهارِ.

Authorities issued a warning of a potential flood due to rising river levels.

water flow

تَدَفُّقُ مِياهٍ

تَسَبَّبَ تَدَفُّقُ المِياهِ القَوِيُّ في تَجاوُزِ الأَنْهارِ لِحُدودِها الطَّبيعِيَّةِ.

The strong water flow caused rivers to exceed their natural boundaries.

تَدَفُّقُ نَهْرٍ

river overflow

شَهِدَتِ المِنْطَقَةُ تَدَفُّقَ النَّهْرِ بِشَكْلٍ غَيْرِ مَسْبوقٍ، مِمّا أَدّى إلى إغْلاقِ الطُّرُقِ وَالجُسورِ.

The region experienced an unprecedented river flow, leading to the closure of roads and bridges.

تَدْميرُ جِسْرٍ

bridge destruction

أَدّى الفَيَضانُ إلى تَدْميرِ جِسْرٍ رَئيسِيٍّ، مِمّا عَطَّلَ حَرَكَةَ النَّقْلِ بِشَكْلٍ كَبيرٍ.

The flood caused the destruction of a major bridge, significantly disrupting transportation.

تَعَرَّضَ لِفَيَضان • تَعَرُّض

to be affected by a flood

تَعَرَّضَتِ المَدينَةُ لِفَيَضانٍ شَديدٍ، مِمّا أَدّى إلى إجْلاءِ السُّكّانِ وَإغْلاقِ العَديدِ مِنَ الطُّرُقِ.

The city was exposed to a severe flood, leading to the evacuation of residents and the closure of many roads.

تَلَوُّثُ مِياهٍ

water contamination

أَدّى الفَيَضانُ إلى تَلَوُّثِ مِياهِ الشُّرْبِ، مِمّا أَثارَ قَلَقًا بِشَأْنِ الصِّحَّةِ العامَّةِ.

The flood caused drinking water pollution, raising concerns about public health.

تَوَقُّعُ فَيَضانٍ

flood forecast

تَوَقَّعَتِ الأَرْصادُ الجَوِّيَّةُ حُدوثَ فَيَضانٍ بِسَبَبِ الأَمْطارِ الغَزيرَةِ المُسْتَمِرَّةِ.

The meteorological service predicted a flood due to ongoing heavy rains.

جَرّاءَ فَيَضانٍ

flood-caused

جَرّاءَ الفَيَضانِ، تَعَطَّلَتِ العَديدُ مِنَ الخِدْماتِ العامَّةِ وَتَأَثَّرَتِ الحَياةُ اليَوْمِيَّةُ لِلسُّكّانِ.

As a result of the flood, many public services were disrupted, and residents' daily lives were affected.

جَرَفَ • جَرْف

to sweep away, carry off

جَرَفَتْ مِياهُ الفَيَضانِ الأَشْجارَ وَالسَّيّاراتِ، مِمّا أَظْهَرَ قُوَّةَ التَّيّاراتِ.

Floodwaters swept away trees and cars, demonstrating the strength of the currents.

stagnant

راكِدٌ

تَسَبَّبَتِ المِياهُ الرّاكِدَةُ بَعْدَ الفَيَضانِ في مَشاكِلَ صِحِّيَّةٍ، شَمِلَتْ تَفَشِّي الأَمْراضِ.

Stagnant water after the flood caused health problems, including the outbreak of diseases.

flash flood

سَيْلٌ مُفاجِئٌ • سُيولٌ

شَهِدَتِ المِنْطَقَةُ سَيْلًا مُفاجِئًا نَتيجَةَ الأَمْطارِ الغَزيرَةِ، مِمّا أَدّى إلى أَضْرارٍ واسِعَةِ النِّطاقِ.

The region experienced a sudden flash flood due to heavy rains, leading to extensive damage.

flood victim

ضَحِيَّةُ فَيَضانٍ • ضَحايا

كانَ هُناكَ ضَحايا لِلفَيَضانِ نَتيجَةً لِلأَحْوالِ الجَوِّيَةِ القاسِيَةِ وَالتَّيّاراتِ القَوِيَّةِ.

There were flood victims due to harsh weather conditions and strong currents.

deluge

طوفانٌ

وَصَفَ السُّكّانُ الفَيَضانَ بِأَنَّهُ طوفانٌ، حَيْثُ غَمَرَتِ المِياهُ المَنازِلَ وَالشَّوارِعَ.

Residents described the flood as a deluge, with water inundating homes and streets.

thunderstorm

عاصِفَةٌ رَعْدِيَّةٌ • عَواصِفُ

ساهَمَتِ العاصِفَةُ الرَّعْدِيَّةُ في زِيادَةِ خَطَرِ الفَيَضاناتِ بِسَبَبِ الأَمْطارِ الغَزيرَةِ المُصاحِبَةِ لَها.

The thunderstorm contributed to the increased risk of flooding due to its accompanying heavy rains.

rainstorm

عاصِفَةٌ مُمْطِرَةٌ • عَواصِفُ

تَحَوَّلَتِ العاصِفَةُ المُمْطِرَةُ إلى سَبَبٍ رَئيسِيٍّ لِلفَيَضاناتِ، مِمّا ضاعَفَ مِنْ حَجْمِ الكارِثَةِ.

The rainstorm turned into a major cause of the floods, magnifying the scale of the disaster.

flood-prone

عُرْضَةٌ لِفَيَضانٍ

تُعْتَبَرُ المَناطِقُ السّاحِلِيَّةُ عُرْضَةً لِلفَيَضاناتِ بِسَبَبِ ارْتِفاعِ مَنْسوبِ المِياهِ البَحْرِيَّةِ وَالأَنْهارِ.

Coastal areas are prone to flooding due to rising sea and river water levels.

عَمَلِيَّةُ إغاثَةٍ

relief operation

نَظَّمَتِ السُّلُطاتُ عَمَلِيَّةَ إغاثَةٍ لِمُساعَدَةِ المُتَضَرِّرينَ مِنَ الفَيَضاناتِ.

Authorities organized a relief operation to help those affected by the floods.

غَرِقَ • غَرَقٌ

to drown

غَرِقَتْ عِدَّةُ مَناطِقَ في المَدينَةِ بَعْدَ ساعاتٍ مِنْ هُطولِ أَمْطارٍ غَزيرَةٍ.

Several areas in the city were submerged after hours of heavy rainfall.

غَمَرَ • غَمْرٌ

to flood, to inundate

غَمَرَتِ المِياهُ الطَّوابِقَ السُّفْلِيَّةَ لِلْمَباني، مِمّا تَسَبَّبَ في أَضرارٍ كَبيرَةٍ.

Water inundated the lower floors of buildings, causing significant damage.

غُمِرَ بِمِياهٍ • غَمْرٌ

to be submerged in water

غُمِرَتِ الشَّوارِعُ بِالمِياهِ، مِمّا جَعَلَ التَّنَقُّلَ صَعْبًا.

The streets were flooded with water, making navigation difficult.

فاضَ • فَيْضٌ / فَيَضانٌ

to overflow

فاضَتِ الأَنْهارُ عَنْ ضِفافِها، مِمّا أَدّى إلى فَيَضاناتٍ في المَناطِقِ المُحيطَةِ.

Rivers overflowed their banks, leading to flooding in the surrounding areas.

فَيَضانٌ

flood

تَسَبَّبَ الفَيَضانُ في خَسائِرَ فادِحَةٍ وَاضطُرَّ السُّكانُ لِلّجوءِ إلى مَلاجِئَ مُؤَقَّتَةٍ.

The flood caused significant losses, and residents had to resort to temporary shelters.

فَيَضانٌ عارِمٌ

massive flood

ضَرَبَ فَيَضانٌ عارِمٌ المِنْطَقَةَ، مِمّا أَدّى إلى غَرَقِ العَديدِ مِنَ القُرى وَالمُدُنِ.

A torrential flood hit the region, resulting in the inundation of many villages and towns.

destructive flood

فَيَضانٌ مُدَمِّرٌ

تَسَبَّبَ الفَيَضانُ المُدَمِّرُ في تَدْميرِ البِنْيَةِ التَّحْتِيَّةِ وَتَشْريدِ الآلافِ مِنَ النّاسِ.

The devastating flood destroyed infrastructure and displaced thousands of people.

flash flood

فَيَضانٌ مُفاجِئٌ

حَدَثَ فَيَضانٌ مُفاجِئٌ بَعْدَ هُطولِ أَمْطارٍ غَزيرَةٍ، مِمّا أَدّى إلى حالَةٍ مِنَ الفَوْضى وَالذُّعْرِ.

A sudden flood occurred after heavy rainfall, leading to chaos and panic.

flood-related

فَيَضانِيٌّ

تَعَرَّضَتِ المِنْطَقَةُ لِحالَةٍ فَيَضانِيَّةٍ خَطيرَةٍ، مِمّا اسْتَدْعى تَدَخُّلَ السُّلُطاتِ لِإِجْلاءِ المُتَضَرِّرينَ.

The area experienced a serious flooding situation, prompting authorities to evacuate those affected.

continuous

مُسْتَمِرٌّ

رَغْمَ جُهودِ الإِجْلاءِ وَالتَّحْذيرِ، إلّا أَنَّ الفَيَضاناتِ مُسْتَمِرَّةٌ، مِما يَجْعَلُ التَّأْثيرَ السَّلْبِيَّ يَتَجَدَّدُ عَلَى البِنْيَةِ التَّحْتِيَّةِ وَالمُجْتَمَعاتِ المُتَأَثِّرَةِ.

Despite evacuation and warning efforts, the floods persist, renewing their negative impact on infrastructure and affected communities.

water level

مُسْتَوى مِياهٍ

بَلَغَ مُسْتَوى مِياهِ الفَيَضانِ ارْتِفاعاتٍ قِياسِيَّةً، مُتَجاوِزًا السُّدودَ وَالحَواجِزَ.

The floodwater level reached record heights, exceeding dams and barriers.

heavy rain

أَمْطارٌ • مَطَرٌ غَزيرٌ

تَسَبَّبَ المَطَرُ الغَزيرُ في تَفاقُمِ الوَضْعِ وَزيادَةِ خَطَرِ حُدوثِ فَيَضاناتٍ في المَناطِقِ المُنْخَفِضَةِ.

The heavy rain exacerbated the situation and increased the risk of flooding in low-lying areas.

seasonal rain

مَطَرٌ مَوْسِمِيٌّ

جَلَبَ المَطَرُ المَوْسِمِيُّ كَمِّياتٍ كَبيرَةً مِنَ المِياهِ، مِمّا أَدّى إلى ارْتِفاعِ مَنْسوبِ الأَنْهارِ.

The seasonal rain brought large amounts of water, leading to rising river levels.

مُعَدّاتُ إغاثَةٍ
relief equipment _pl._

تَمَّ تَوْزِيعُ مُعَدّاتِ الإغاثَةِ بِما في ذَلِكَ الطَّعامِ وَالماءِ وَالأَدْوِيَةِ إلى المَناطِقِ المُتَضَرِّرَةِ مِنَ الفَيَضاناتِ.

Relief equipment, including food, water, and medicine, was distributed to areas affected by the floods.

مَغْمورٌ
submerged

أَصْبَحَتِ العَديدُ مِنَ المَنازِلِ مَغْمورَةً بِالمِياهِ، مِمّا أَجْبَرَ السُّكّانَ عَلى البَحْثِ عَنْ مَأْوى آمِنٍ.

Many homes became submerged in water, forcing residents to seek safe shelter.

مِنْطَقَةٌ عُرْضَةٌ لِلْفَيَضاناتِ • مَناطِقُ
flood-prone area

تُعْتَبَرُ هَذِهِ المِنْطَقَةُ عُرْضَةً لِلْفَيَضاناتِ بِسَبَبِ مَوْقِعِها الجُغْرافِيِّ القَريبِ مِنْ مَجاري المِياهِ.

This region is prone to flooding due to its geographical location near watercourses.

مَنْعُ فَيَضانٍ
flood prevention

نَفَّذَتِ الحُكومَةُ مَشاريعَ هَنْدَسِيَّةً كَبيرَةً لِمَنْعِ الفَيَضاناتِ في المَناطِقِ الأَكْثَرِ عُرْضَةً لِلْخَطَرِ.

The government implemented major engineering projects to prevent flooding in the most vulnerable areas.

مِياهٌ جارِفَةٌ
raging waters _pl._

تَسَبَّبَتِ المِياهُ الجارِفَةُ في إلْحاقِ أَضْرارٍ جَسيمَةٍ بِالْمُنْشَآتِ وَالطُّرُقِ.

The sweeping waters caused significant damage to structures and roads.

مِياهٌ جارِيَةٌ
flowing waters _pl._

تَدَفَّقَتِ المِياهُ الجارِيَةُ بِسُرْعَةٍ عَبْرَ الأَنْهارِ، مِمّا زادَ مِنْ خَطَرِ الفَيَضاناتِ.

Running waters flowed rapidly through the rivers, increasing the risk of flooding.

stagnant water   *pl.*   مِياهٌ راكِدَةٌ

أَدَّتِ المِياهُ الرّاكِدَةُ إلى تَفَشّي الأَمْراضِ وَخَلَقَتْ بيئَةً لِتَكاثُرِ البَعوضِ.

Stagnant waters led to the spread of diseases and created a breeding ground for mosquitoes.

floodwaters   *pl.*   مِياهُ فَيَضانٍ

اِرْتَفَعَتْ مِياهُ الفَيَضانِ فَوْقَ الحُدودِ الطَّبيعِيَّةِ لِلنَّهْرِ، مِمّا تَسَبَّبَ في إغْراقِ المَناطِقِ المُجاوِرَةِ.

Floodwaters rose above the river's natural limits, causing the adjacent areas to be inundated.

river-   نَهْرِيٌّ

أَدَّتِ الظُّروفُ النَّهْرِيَّةُ المُتَغَيِّرَةُ إلى زِيادَةِ التَّحَدِّياتِ في إدارَةِ المَوارِدِ المائِيَّةِ.

Changing riverine conditions increased the challenges in water resource management.

major   هائِلٌ

كانَ الدَّمارُ النّاجِمُ عَنِ الفَيَضانِ هائِلًا، مِمّا أَثَّرَ عَلى الآلافِ مِنَ السُّكّانِ.

The devastation caused by the flood was immense, affecting thousands of people.

dry wadi   • أَوْدِيَةٌ   وادٍ جافٌّ

تَحَوَّلَ الوادي الجافُّ إلى مَجْرى مِياهٍ عارِمٍ بَعْدَ هُطولِ الأَمْطارِ الغَزيرَةِ.

The dry wadi turned into a raging watercourse after heavy rainfall.

9.2.5.1 Mini-Articles

Track **101**

شَهِدَتْ مَدينَةُ الإسْكَنْدَرِيَّةِ فَيَضانًا مُفاجِئًا بَعْدَ عاصِفَةٍ مُمْطِرَةٍ هائِلَةٍ اسْتَمَرَّتْ لِساعاتٍ، مِمّا أَدّى إلى ارْتِفاعِ مَنْسوبِ مِياهِ البَحْرِ وَانْدِفاعِ المِياهِ نَحْوَ المَناطِقِ السَّكَنِيَّةِ. أَعْلَنَتِ السُّلُطاتُ المَحَلِّيَّةُ حالَةَ الطَّوارِئ وَبَدَأَتْ عَمَلِيَّةَ إجْلاءٍ طارِئٍ لِلسُّكّانِ في المَناطِقِ الأَكْثَرِ عُرْضَةً لِلْفَيَضانِ. كانَ تَأْثيرُ الفَيَضانِ عَلى البِنْيَةِ التَّحْتِيَّةِ مُدَمِّرًا، حَيْثُ دُمِّرَتْ جُسورٌ وَأُغْلِقَتْ طُرُقٌ رَئيسِيَّةٌ. هذا وَتَعْمَلُ فِرَقُ الإنْقاذِ البَحْرِيِّ وَفِرَقُ الإغاثَةِ الطِّبِّيَّةِ عَلى مُساعَدَةِ المُتَضَرِّرينَ وَإزالَةِ المِياهِ الجارِفَةِ.

The city of Alexandria witnessed a sudden flood after a massive rainstorm that lasted for hours, leading to a rise in sea levels and water rushing into residential areas. The local authorities declared a state of emergency and started an emergency evacuation process for residents in the most flood-prone areas. The impact of the flood on infrastructure was devastating, with bridges being destroyed and major roads closed. Maritime rescue teams and medical relief teams are working to assist those affected and remove the floodwaters.

تَعَرَّضَتْ عِدَّةُ مَناطِقَ في المَغْرِبِ لِفَيَضاناتٍ عارِمَةٍ جَرّاءَ أَمْطارٍ مَوْسِمِيَّةٍ غَزيرَةٍ، مِمّا أَسْفَرَ عَنْ تَجَمُّعاتٍ مائِيَّةٍ كَبيرَةٍ وَتَدَفُّقٍ نَهْرِيٍّ قَوِيٍّ. أَثَّرَتِ الفَيَضاناتُ بِشَكْلٍ كَبيرٍ عَلَى الزِّراعَةِ وَتَسَبَّبَتْ في تَلَوُّثِ مِياهِ الشُّرْبِ. أَطْلَقَتِ السُّلُطاتُ تَحْذيراتٍ مِنَ الفَيَضانِ وَبَدَأَتْ في تَنْفيذِ اسْتِراتيجِيّاتٍ لِمَنْعِ الفَيَضاناتِ المُسْتَقْبَلِيَّةِ. عَمَلِيّاتُ الإِغاثَةِ وَاسْتِرْجاعِ المُمْتَلَكاتِ جارِيَةٌ، بَيْنَما تَسْتَمِرُّ جُهودُ تَقْييمِ الأَضْرارِ البيئِيَّةِ.

Several areas in Morocco experienced severe flooding due to heavy monsoon rains, resulting in large water accumulations and strong river flows. The floods significantly affected agriculture and caused drinking water contamination. Authorities issued flood warnings and began implementing strategies to prevent future floods. Relief and property recovery operations are underway, while efforts to assess environmental damage continue.

أَصْدَرَتِ الأَرْصادُ الجَوِّيَّةُ في تونِسَ تَحْذيرًا مِنْ فَيَضانٍ مُتَوَقَّعٍ بِسَبَبِ عاصِفَةٍ رَعْدِيَّةٍ قَوِيَّةٍ مَصْحوبَةٍ بِأَمْطارٍ غَزيرَةٍ مِنَ المُتَوَقَّعِ أَنْ تَضْرِبَ المَناطِقَ الشَّمالِيَّةَ. بَدَأَتِ السُّلُطاتُ المَحَلِّيَّةُ في تَجْهيزِ مُعَدّاتِ الإِغاثَةِ وَتَنْظيمِ تَجْهيزاتِ إِجْلاءٍ لِلسُّكّانِ في المَناطِقِ المُعَرَّضَةِ لِلْفَيَضاناتِ. كَما تَمَّ تَعْزيزُ البِنْيَةِ التَّحْتِيَّةِ الَّتي سَبَقَ لَها التَّضَرُّرُ في الماضي لِتَحَمُّلِ الفَيَضاناتِ المُتَوَقَّعَةِ وَتَقْليلِ الأَضْرارِ المُحْتَمَلَةِ عَلَى السُّكّانِ وَالمُمْتَلَكاتِ.

The meteorological service in Tunisia issued a warning of an expected flood due to a strong thunderstorm accompanied by heavy rains expected to hit the northern areas. Local authorities began preparing relief equipment and organizing evacuation preparations for residents in flood-prone areas. Infrastructure that was damaged in the past has been reinforced to withstand the expected floods and minimize potential damage to residents and properties.

9.2.5.2 Article: 2023 Libya Floods

Track **102**

فَيَضاناتٌ عارِمَةٌ تَجْتاحُ ليبيا جَرّاءَ العاصِفَةِ دانيال

في العاشِرِ مِنْ سِبْتَمْبَرَ 2023، ضَرَبَتِ العاصِفَةُ دانيال، وَهِيَ إِعْصارٌ مُتَوَسِّطِيٌّ نادِرٌ، شَرْقَ ليبيا بِفَيَضاناتٍ كارِثِيَّةٍ، مُخَلِّفَةً وَراءَها دَمارًا هائِلًا، وَمُسْفِرَةً عَنْ وَفاةِ أَكْثَرَ مِنْ 4300 شَخْصٍ، بَيْنَما لا يَزالُ أَكْثَرُ مِنْ 8500 في عِدادِ المَفْقودينَ. الرِّياحُ الشَّديدَةُ وَالأَمْطارُ الغَزيرَةُ الَّتي صاحَبَتِ العاصِفَةَ أَدَّتْ إِلَى تَدْميرٍ واسِعِ النِّطاقِ، مُؤَثِّرَةً عَلَى حَوالَيْ 880,000 شَخْصٍ، شَمِلوا 353,000 طِفْلٍ. شَهِدَتْ مُدُنٌ رَئيسِيَّةٌ كالبَيْضاءِ، المَرْجِ، وَدَرْنَةَ تَدْميرًا واسِعًا لِلْبِنْيَةِ التَّحْتِيَّةِ، حَيْثُ يُعْتَقَدُ أَنَّ أَحْياءً كامِلَةً في دَرْنَةَ قَدْ جُرِفَتْ بِالْكامِلِ.

مَوَاطِنُ الضَّعْفِ المَوْجُودَةُ مُسْبَقًا في البِلادِ، وَالَّتي زادَتْ مِنْ حِدَّتِها الأَزَماتُ السِّياسِيَّةُ وَالصِّراعاتُ الماضِيَةُ، عَمَّقَتْ مِنْ تَأْثيرِ الكارِثَةِ، مِمَّا أَثَّرَ بِشَكْلٍ خَطِيرٍ عَلَى الخِدْماتِ الأَساسِيَّةِ كَالصِّحَّةِ، وَالتَّعْليمِ، وَالحِمايَةِ الاِجْتِماعِيَّةِ. كَشَفَتِ الفَيَضاناتُ عَنِ الحاجَةِ الماسَّةِ لِمَتانَةِ البِنْيَةِ التَّحْتِيَّةِ وَالاِسْتِعْدادِ لِلْكَوارِثِ في مُواجَهَةِ تَغَيُّرِ المُناخِ.

إِنَّ العَواصِفَ مِثْلَ العاصِفَةِ دانْيال نادِرَةٌ لَكِنَّها قَوِيَّةٌ، وَيُعْتَقَدُ أَنَّ تَغَيُّرَ المُناخِ يَعْمَلُ عَلَى تَفاقُمِ شِدَّتِها وَالأَمْطارِ المُصاحِبَةِ لَها. وَفْقًا لِلْبُروفيسورَةِ لِيز سْتيفِنز مِنْ مَرْكَزِ الصَّليبِ الأَحْمَرِ وَالهِلالِ الأَحْمَرِ لِلْمُناخِ وَجامِعَةِ ريدينْغ، مِنَ المُرَجَّحِ أَنَّ تَغَيُّرَ المُناخِ يَزيدُ مِنْ تَواتُرِ وَشِدَّةِ هَذِهِ العَواصِفِ، مِمَّا يُشيرُ إلى مُسْتَقْبَلٍ تُصْبِحُ فيهِ مِثْلُ هَذِهِ الأَحْداثِ أَكْثَرَ شُيوعًا.

تُسَلِّطُ مَأْساةُ العاصِفَةِ دانْيال الضَّوْءَ عَلَى الحاجَةِ المُلِحَّةِ لِلاِنْتِباهِ العالَمِيِّ لِتَغَيُّرِ المُناخِ وَتَأْثيراتِهِ عَلَى المَناطِقِ الضَّعيفَةِ. دَعْمُ المُجْتَمَعِ الدَّوْلِيِّ ضَروريٌّ في مُساعَدَةِ ليبيا عَلَى التَّعافي وَالاِسْتِعْدادِ لِلتَّهْديداتِ المُناخِيَّةِ المُسْتَقْبَلِيَّةِ، مِمَّا يُشَدِّدُ عَلَى أَهَمِّيَّةِ الصُّمودِ، وَالتَّكَيُّفِ، وَاسْتِراتيجِيّاتِ إِدارَةِ الكَوارِثِ الشامِلَةِ في التَّخْفيفِ مِنْ تَأْثيرِ هَذِهِ الظَّواهِرِ الطَّبيعِيَّةِ المُدَمِّرَةِ.

Floods Ravage Libya Due to Storm Daniel

On September 10, 2023, Storm Daniel, a rare Mediterranean cyclone, hit eastern Libya with catastrophic floods, leaving behind massive destruction and resulting in the death of more than 4,300 people, while more than 8,500 are still missing. The strong winds and heavy rains accompanying the storm led to widespread destruction, affecting about 880,000 people, including 353,000 children. Major cities such as Al Bayda, Al Marj, and Derna saw significant infrastructure destruction, with entire neighborhoods in Derna believed to have been completely swept away.

The pre-existing vulnerabilities in the country, exacerbated by past political crises and conflicts, deepened the impact of the disaster, severely affecting essential services such as health, education, and social protection. The floods revealed the dire need for infrastructure resilience and disaster preparedness in the face of climate change.

Storms like Storm Daniel are rare but powerful, and climate change is believed to be exacerbating their intensity and the accompanying rainfall. According to Professor Liz Stephens from the Red Cross Red Crescent Climate Centre and the University of Reading, climate change is likely increasing the frequency and intensity of these storms, indicating a future where such events may become more common.

The tragedy of Storm Daniel highlights the urgent need for global attention to climate change and its effects on vulnerable regions. International community support is essential in helping Libya recover and prepare for future climate threats, emphasizing the importance of resilience, adaptation, and comprehensive disaster management strategies in mitigating the impact of these devastating natural phenomena.

9.2.6 Wildfires

أَخْمَدَ حَرِيقًا

put out a fire   • إِخْمَادٌ

تَمَكَّنَتْ فِرْقَةُ الإِطْفَاءِ مِنْ أَخْمَادِ حَرِيقٍ كَبِيرٍ فِي الغَابَةِ بَعْدَ جُهُودٍ مُكَثَّفَةٍ.

The fire brigade successfully extinguished a large forest fire after intensive efforts.

أَرْضٌ مُحْتَرِقَةٌ

scorched earth   • أَرَاضٍ

تَحَوَّلَتْ مِسَاحَاتٌ وَاسِعَةٌ مِنَ الغَابَةِ إِلَى أَرْضٍ مُحْتَرِقَةٍ، مِمّا أَظْهَرَ حَجْمَ الدَّمَارِ.

Large areas of the forest turned into burnt ground, showing the extent of the destruction.

أَشْعَلَ

to ignite   • إِشْعَالٌ

أَشْعَلَ البَرْقُ النَارَ فِي الغَابَةِ، مِمّا أَدَّى إِلَى انْدِلَاعِ حَرِيقٍ سَرِيعِ الِانْتِشَارِ.

Lightning ignited a fire in the forest, leading to a rapidly spreading wildfire.

أَمْنٌ صِحِّيٌّ

health security

اِتَّخَذَتِ السُّلُطَاتُ تَدَابِيرَ لِضَمَانِ الأَمْنِ الصِّحِّيِّ لِلسُّكَّانِ المُتَأَثِّرِينَ بِدُخَانِ الحَرَائِقِ.

Authorities took measures to ensure the health safety of residents affected by the fire smoke.

إِجْلَاءُ حَيَوَانَاتٍ

animal evacuation

تَمَّ إِجْلَاءُ الحَيَوَانَاتِ مِنَ الحَدَائِقِ وَالمَحْمِيَّاتِ الطَّبِيعِيَّةِ كَإِجْرَاءٍ وِقَائِيٍّ ضِدَّ الحَرَائِقِ.

Animals were evacuated from parks and nature reserves as a precaution against the fires.

إِخْلَاءُ مَنْزِلٍ

home evacuation

أُضْطُرَّ العَدِيدُ مِنَ الأَشْخَاصِ إِلَى إِخْلَاءِ مَنَازِلِهِمْ بِسُرْعَةٍ بِسَبَبِ امْتِدَادِ الحَرَائِقِ.

Many people had to quickly evacuate their homes due to the advancing fires.

إِخْمَادُ حَرِيقٍ

fire suppression

رَكَّزَتْ جُهُودُ الِاسْتِجَابَةِ لِلطَّوَارِئِ عَلَى إِخْمَادِ الحَرِيقِ وَالحَدِّ مِنَ انْتِشَارِهِ.

Emergency response efforts focused on extinguishing the fire and preventing its spread.

burning of agricultural land

اِحْتِراقُ أَرْضٍ زِراعِيَّةٍ

أَدَّى اِحْتِراقُ الأَرْضِ الزِّراعِيَّةِ إِلى خَسائِرَ فادِحَةٍ فِي المَحاصيلِ وَالإِنْتاجِ الزِّراعِيِّ.

The burning of agricultural land led to significant losses in crops and agricultural production.

to burn

اِحْتِراقٌ •

اِحْتَرَقَ

اِحْتَرَقَتْ مِساحاتٌ واسِعَةٌ مِنَ الغاباتِ، مِمّا تَسَبَّبَ في تَدْميرِ البيئاتِ الطَّبيعِيَّةِ.

Large areas of forests burned, causing the destruction of natural habitats.

fire containment

اِحْتِواءُ حَريقٍ

تَمَكَّنَتْ فِرَقُ الإِطْفاءِ مِنَ اِحْتِواءِ الحَريقِ بِفَضْلِ تَدابيرِ السَّلامَةِ الَّتي اتُّخِذَتْ.

The fire brigade managed to contain the fire due to the implemented safety measures.

to contain

اِحْتِواءٌ •

اِحْتَوى

اِحْتَوى الإِطْفائِيّونَ الحَريقَ بِنَجاحٍ، مِمّا مَنَعَ اِنْتِشارَهُ إِلى المَناطِقِ المُجاوِرَةِ.

Firefighters successfully contained the fire, preventing it from spreading to neighboring areas.

to spread

اِمْتِدادٌ •

اِمْتَدَّ

اِمْتَدَّ الحَريقُ بِسُرْعَةٍ بِسَبَبِ الرِّياحِ القَوِيَّةِ وَظُروفِ الجَفافِ.

The fire spread quickly due to strong winds and dry conditions.

wildfire expansion

اِنْتِشارُ حَريقِ غاباتٍ

تَسَبَّبَ اِنْتِشارُ حَريقِ الغاباتِ في إِجْلاءِ المَناطِقِ السَّكَنِيَّةِ المُجاوِرَةِ.

The spread of the forest fire caused the evacuation of nearby residential areas.

to spread

اِنْتِشارٌ •

اِنْتَشَرَ

اِنْتَشَرَ الحَريقُ عَلى مَسافَةٍ واسِعَةٍ، مِمّا زادَ مِنْ صُعوبَةِ إِخْمادِهِ.

The fire spread over a wide area, increasing the difficulty of extinguishing it.

fire outbreak

اِنْدِلاعُ حَرِيقٍ

أَدَّى انْدِلاعُ حَرِيقٍ فِي مِنْطَقَةِ الغاباتِ إِلى اسْتِنْفارِ جُهودِ الإطْفاءِ وَالإِنْقاذِ.

A fire outbreak in the forest area led to the mobilization of firefighting and rescue efforts.

to break out, erupt

اِنْدَلَعَ • اِنْدِلاعٌ

اِنْدَلَعَ حَرِيقٌ كَبِيرٌ فِي الغابَةِ، مِمّا تَسَبَّبَ فِي تَحْذِيراتٍ عاجِلَةٍ لِلسُّكّانِ المَحَلِّيِّينَ.

A large fire broke out in the forest, causing urgent warnings to the local residents.

land destruction

تَدْمِيرُ أَرْضٍ

تَسَبَّبَ الحَرِيقُ فِي تَدْمِيرِ الأَرْضِ الزِّراعِيَّةِ، مِمّا أَثَّرَ سَلْبًا عَلى المُزارِعِينَ وَإِنْتاجِهِمْ.

The fire caused the destruction of agricultural land, negatively affecting farmers and their production.

forest destruction

تَدْمِيرُ غابَةٍ

شَهِدَتِ الغابَةُ تَدْمِيرًا واسِعَ النِّطاقِ بِسَبَبِ الحَرِيقِ، مِمّا تَسَبَّبَ فِي خَسارَةِ الغِطاءِ النَّباتِيِّ وَالتَّنَوُّعِ البَيولوجِيِّ.

The forest experienced extensive destruction due to the fire, resulting in the loss of vegetation cover and biodiversity.

to develop

تَطَوَّرَ • تَطَوُّرٌ

تَطَوَّرَ الحَرِيقُ بِسُرْعَةٍ بِسَبَبِ الرِّياحِ القَوِيَّةِ وَالحَرارَةِ الشَّدِيدَةِ.

The fire developed rapidly due to strong winds and intense heat.

firefighting technique

تِقْنِيَّةُ إِخْمادِ حَرِيقٍ

اِسْتَخْدَمَتْ فِرَقُ الإطْفاءِ تِقْنِياتِ إِخْمادِ حَرِيقٍ مُتَقَدِّمَةً لِلسَّيْطَرَةِ عَلى اللَّهَبِ.

Firefighting teams used advanced fire suppression techniques to control the flames.

fire suppression tactic

تَكْتِيكُ إِخْمادِ حَرِيقٍ

تَمَّ تَطْبِيقُ تَكْتِيكاتِ إِخْمادِ حَرِيقٍ اسْتِراتيجِيَّةٍ لِمَنْعِ انْتِشارِ الحَرِيقِ إِلى مَناطِقَ أُخْرى.

Strategic fire extinguishing tactics were applied to prevent the fire from spreading to other areas.

air pollution

تَلَوُّثٌ جَوِّيٌّ

أَدَّى الحَرِيقُ إِلَى تَلَوُّثٍ جَوِّيٍّ بِسَبَبِ دُخانِهِ وانْبِعاثاتِهِ، مِمّا أَثَّرَ عَلَى جَوْدَةِ الهَواءِ.

The fire caused air pollution due to its smoke and emissions, affecting air quality.

intense heat

حَرارَةٌ شَديدَةٌ

تَعَرَّضَتِ المِنْطَقَةُ لِحَرارَةٍ شَديدَةٍ نَتيجَةَ الحَرِيقِ، مِمّا أَدَّى إِلَى زِيادَةِ صُعوبَةِ عَمَلِيّاتِ الإِطْفاءِ.

The area experienced intense heat from the fire, making firefighting operations more challenging.

fire

حَرائِقُ •

حَرِيقٌ

اِنْدَلَعَ حَرِيقٌ كَبِيرٌ فِي المِنْطَقَةِ الصِّناعِيَّةِ، مِمّا اسْتَدْعَى اسْتِجابَةً سَريعَةً مِنْ خَدَماتِ الطَّوارِئِ.

A large fire broke out in the industrial area, necessitating a rapid response from emergency services.

massive fire

حَرِيقٌ ضَخْمٌ = حَرِيقٌ هائِلٌ

اِنْدَلَعَ حَرِيقٌ ضَخْمٌ فِي المِنْطَقَةِ الرّيفِيَّةِ، مِمّا أَدَّى إِلَى تَدْميرٍ واسِعِ النِّطاقِ.

A massive fire broke out in the rural area, leading to extensive destruction.

wildfire, forest fire

حَرِيقُ غابَةٍ

تَسَبَّبَ حَرِيقُ الغابَةِ فِي خَسائِرَ كَبيرَةٍ لِلنِّظامِ البيئِيِّ والحَياةِ البَرِّيَّةِ.

The forest fire caused significant losses to the ecosystem and wildlife.

raging fire

حَرِيقٌ مُسْتَعِرٌ

شَهِدَتِ المِنْطَقَةُ اندِلاعَ حَرِيقٍ مُسْتَعِرٍ، مِمّا دَفَعَ بِفِرَقِ الإِطْفاءِ والدِّفاعِ المَدَنِيِّ إِلَى التَّحَرُّكِ فَوْرًا لِلسَّيْطَرَةِ عَلَى الحَرِيقِ.

The area witnessed the outbreak of a raging fire, prompting the firefighting and civil defense teams to move immediately to control the fire.

to analyze fire impact

تَحْليلٌ •

حَلَّلَ تَأْثيرَ حَرِيقٍ

قَامَ الخُبَرَاءُ بِتَحْلِيلِ تَأْثِيرِ الحَرِيقِ لِفَهْمِ الأَضْرَارِ البِيئِيَّةِ وَالتَّدابِيرِ اللَّازِمَةِ لِلتَّعافِي.

Experts analyzed the impact of the fire to understand the environmental damage and the necessary measures for recovery.

wildlife

حَياةٌ بَرِّيَّةٌ

تَأَثَّرَتِ الحَياةُ البَرِّيَّةُ بِشَكْلٍ كَبِيرٍ جَرَّاءَ الحَرِيقِ، مِمّا أَدَّى إلى فِقْدانِ مَواطِنِ الحَيَواناتِ.

Wildlife was greatly affected by the fire, leading to the loss of animal habitats.

firefighting ammunition

ذَخِيرَةُ إطْفاءٍ • ذَخائِرُ

اسْتَخْدَمَتْ فِرَقُ الإطْفاءِ ذَخِيرَةَ إطْفاءٍ مُتَخَصِّصَةً لِلسَّيْطَرَةِ عَلَى الحَرائِقِ.

Firefighting teams used specialized fire extinguishing agents to control the fires.

to monitor

راقَبَ • مُراقَبَةٌ

تَمَّتْ مُراقَبَةُ تَطَوُّرِ الحَرِيقِ عَنْ كَثَبٍ لِتَقْيِيمِ الخَطَرِ وَتَوْجِيهِ جُهودِ الإطْفاءِ.

The development of the fire was closely monitored to assess the risk and direct firefighting efforts.

dry winds

رِياحٌ جافَّةٌ   pl.

ساهَمَتِ الرِّياحُ الجافَّةُ في زِيادَةِ انْتِشارِ الحَرِيقِ بِسُرْعَةٍ.

The dry winds contributed to the rapid spread of the fire.

increase in wildfires

زِيادَةُ حَرائِقِ غاباتٍ

لوحِظَتْ زِيادَةٌ في حَرائِقِ الغاباتِ بِسَبَبِ التَّغَيُّراتِ المُناخِيَّةِ وَالظُّروفِ الجافَّةِ.

An increase in forest fires was noted due to climate changes and dry conditions.

fast-spreading

سَرِيعُ الانْتِشارِ

كانَ الحَرِيقُ سَرِيعَ الانْتِشارِ، مِمّا أَدَّى إلى إجْلاءِ المَناطِقِ المُحِيطَةِ.

The was fast-spreading, leading to the evacuation of surrounding areas.

burning cigarette

سَجائِرُ • سيجارَةٌ مُشْتَعِلَةٌ

تَسَبَّبَتْ سيجارَةٌ مُشْتَعِلَةٌ في إِشْعالِ حَريقٍ خَطيرٍ في الأَراضي الجافَّةِ.

A lit cigarette caused a dangerous fire in the dry lands.

fire control

سَيْطَرَةٌ عَلى حَريقٍ

نَجَحَتْ فِرَقُ الإِطْفاءِ في السَّيْطَرَةِ عَلى حَرائِقَ عِدَّةٍ في المِنْطَقَةِ.

Firefighting teams successfully controlled several fires in the region.

material damage

أَضْرارٌ • ضَرَرٌ مادِّيٌّ

خَلَّفَ الحَريقُ ضَرَرًا مادِّيًّا هائِلًا، بِما في ذَلِكَ تَدْميرَ المَنازِلِ والمُمْتَلَكاتِ.

The fire left enormous material damage, including the destruction of homes and properties.

firestorm

عَواصِفُ • عاصِفَةٌ نارِيَّةٌ

تَحَوَّلَ الحَريقُ إِلى عاصِفَةٍ نارِيَّةٍ بِسَبَبِ شِدَّةِ الرِّياحِ والحَرارَةِ.

The fire turned into a firestorm due to the intensity of the winds and heat.

firefighting operation

عَمَلِيَّةُ إِطْفاءٍ

تَواصَلَتْ عَمَلِيَّةُ إِطْفاءِ الحَرائِقِ في الغاباتِ المُتَضَرِّرَةِ لِعِدَّةِ أَيّامٍ.

The firefighting operation in the damaged forests continued for several days.

damaged forest

غابَةٌ مُتَضَرِّرَةٌ

أَصْبَحَتِ الغابَةُ مُتَضَرِّرَةً بِشَكْلٍ كَبيرٍ جَرّاءَ الحَريقِ الهائِلِ.

The forest was significantly damaged by the massive fire.

firefighting brigade

فِرَقٌ • فِرْقَةُ إِطْفاءٍ

تَدَخَّلَتْ فِرْقَةُ إِطْفاءٍ مُتَخَصِّصَةٌ لِلسَّيْطَرَةِ عَلى الحَريقِ في المِنْطَقَةِ.

A specialized firefighting team intervened to control the fire in the area.

water bomb

قُنْبُلَةُ ماءٍ • قَنابِلُ

اِسْتَخْدَمَتِ الطَّائِراتُ قَنابِلَ الماءِ لِمُكافَحَةِ الحَرائِقِ فِي المَناطِقِ الوَعِرَةِ.

Aircraft used water bombs to combat fires in rugged areas.

flame tongue

لِسانُ لَهَبٍ • أَلْسِنَةٌ

شُوهِدَ لِسانُ لَهَبٍ يَتَصاعَدُ مِنَ الحَريقِ، مِمّا يُظْهِرُ خُطورَةَ الوَضْعِ.

A tongue of flame was seen rising from the fire, showing the severity of the situation.

smoky

مُحَمَّلٌ بِدُخانٍ

كانَ الهَواءُ مُحَمَّلًا بِدُخانِ الحَريقِ، مِمّا أَثَّرَ عَلى الرُّؤْيَةِ وَجَوْدَةِ الهَواءِ.

The air was laden with smoke from the fire, affecting visibility and air quality.

wind-driven

مَدْفوعٌ بِرِياحٍ

كانَ الحَريقُ مَدْفوعًا بِالرِّياحِ، مِمّا زادَ مِنْ صُعوبَةِ إِخْمادِهِ.

The fire was wind-driven, making it more difficult to extinguish.

raging

مُسْتَعِرٌ

ظَلَّ الحَريقُ مُسْتَعِرًا لِساعاتٍ، مِمّا أَدّى إِلى تَهْديدِ الغاباتِ وَالمَناطِقِ السَّكَنِيَّةِ المُجاوِرَةِ.

The fire remained fiercely burning for hours, threatening the forests and nearby residential areas.

source of the fire

مَصْدَرُ حَريقٍ • مَصادِرُ

تُحَقِّقُ السُّلُطاتُ فِي مَصْدَرِ الحَريقِ لِتَحْديدِ سَبَبِ انْدِلاعِهِ.

Authorities are investigating the source of the fire to determine its cause.

firefighting equipment

مُعَدّاتُ إِطْفاءٍ *pl.*

اِسْتَخْدَمَتْ فِرَقُ الإِطْفاءِ مُعَدّاتِ إِطْفاءٍ مُتَطَوِّرَةً لِلتَّحَكُّمِ فِي الحَرائِقِ وَإِخْمادِها.

Firefighting teams used advanced firefighting equipment to control and extinguish the fires.

firefighting مُكافَحَةُ حَريقٍ

تَعْمَلُ الجِهاتُ المَعْنِيَّةُ عَلى مُكافَحَةِ حَريقِ الغاباتِ بِكُلِّ الوَسائِلِ المُمْكِنَةِ.

The concerned authorities are combating the forest fire by all possible means.

property مُمْتَلَكاتٌ   pl.

تَضَرَّرَتْ مُمْتَلَكاتٌ كَثيرَةٌ نَتيجَةَ الحَريقِ، بِما في ذَلِكَ مَنازِلُ وَمَزارِعُ.

Many properties were damaged by the fire, including homes and farms.

dry area مِنْطَقَةٌ جافَّةٌ   • مَناطِقُ

وَقَعَ الحَريقُ في مِنْطَقَةٍ جافَّةٍ، مِمّا ساهَمَ في سُرْعَةِ انْتِشارِهِ.

The fire occurred in a dry area, contributing to its rapid spread.

fire zone مِنْطَقَةُ حَريقٍ

تَمَّ تَصْنيفُ المِنْطَقَةِ المُحْتَرِقَةِ كَمِنْطَقَةِ حَريقٍ وَجَرى تَحْذيرُ السُّكّانِ لِلابْتِعادِ عَنْها.

The burned area was classified as a fire zone, and residents were warned to stay away.

fire prevention مَنْعُ حَريقٍ

تَتَّبَعُ السُّلُطاتُ إِجْراءاتٍ صارِمَةً لِمَنْعِ الحَرائِقِ في المَناطِقِ المُعَرَّضَةِ لِلْخَطَرِ.

Authorities follow strict procedures to prevent fires in at-risk areas.

9.2.6.1 Mini-Articles

Track 104

انْدَلَعَ حَريقُ غابَةٍ مُسْتَعِرٌ في شَمالِ كاليفورْنِيا، مَدْفوعًا بِرِياحٍ جافَّةٍ وَحَرارَةٍ شَديدَةٍ، مِمّا أَدّى إلى تَدْميرِ غاباتٍ واحْتِراقِ أَراضٍ زِراعِيَّةٍ عَلى نِطاقٍ واسِعٍ. تُكافِحُ فِرَقُ الإِطْفاءِ لِاحْتِواءِ الحَريقِ الضَّخْمِ، مُسْتَخْدِمَةً تَكْتيكاتِ إِخْمادٍ مُتَطَوِّرَةٍ وَقَنابِلَ ماءٍ. تَمَّ إِخْلاءُ مَنازِلَ في المَناطِقِ المُتَضَرِّرَةِ كَإِجْراءٍ وِقائِيٍّ، بَيْنَما جَرَتْ عَمَلِيّاتُ إِجْلاءِ الحَيَواناتِ لِحِمايَتِها مِنَ اللَّهَبِ.

A raging forest fire broke out in northern California, driven by dry winds and extreme heat, leading to the destruction of forests and the burning of agricultural lands on a large scale. Firefighting teams are struggling to contain the massive fire, using advanced extinguishing tactics and water bombs. Homes in the affected areas were evacuated as a precautionary measure, while animal evacuation operations were conducted to protect them from the flames.

حَقَّقَتْ فِرَقُ الإِطْفَاءِ في أُسْتْرَاليا تَقَدُّمًا كَبِيرًا في مُكَافَحَةِ حَرِيقِ غابَةٍ انْدَلَعَ في مِنْطَقَةٍ جافَّةٍ وَسَرِيعَةِ الاِتِّسَاعِ. الحَرِيقُ، الَّذي امْتَدَّ عَلَى مِساحاتٍ شاسِعَةٍ وَتَسَبَّبَ في تَلَوُّثٍ جَوِّيٍّ مُحَمَّلٍ بِالدُّخانِ، بَدَأَ يَخْضَعُ لِلسَّيْطَرَةِ بَعْدَ جُهُودٍ مُكَثَّفَةٍ. اُسْتُخْدِمَتْ ذَخيرَةُ إِطْفاءٍ مِنَ الجَوِّ وَمُعَدّاتُ إِطْفاءٍ حَديثَةٌ لاِحْتِواءِ اللَّهَبِ وَمَنْعِ انْتِشارِهِ إلى مَناطِقَ مَأْهولَةٍ بِالسُّكّانِ.

Firefighting teams in Australia have made significant progress in combating a forest fire that erupted in a dry and rapidly spreading area. The fire, which extended over vast areas and caused smoke-laden air pollution, began to come under control after intensive efforts. Aerial firefighting ammunition and modern firefighting equipment were used to contain the flames and prevent their spread to populated areas.

تُواجِهُ الجَزائِرُ حَريقَ غاباتٍ مُسْتَعِرًا في إِحْدى مَناطِقِها الرّيفِيَّةِ، مِمّا أَجْبَرَ السُّلُطاتِ عَلى إِخْلاءِ العَديدِ مِنَ القُرى كَإِجْراءٍ احْتِرازِيٍّ. الحَريقُ، الَّذي انْدَلَعَ بِسَبَبِ مَصْدَرِ حَريقٍ غَيْرِ مَعْروفٍ وَحَفَّزَتْهُ الرّياحُ الجافَّةُ، تَسَبَّبَ في تَدْميرِ مُمْتَلَكاتٍ وَضَرَرٍ مادِّيٍّ كَبيرٍ. عَمَلِيّاتُ الإِطْفاءِ جارِيَةٌ، مَعَ تَحْليلِ تَأْثيرِ الحَريقِ عَلى البيئَةِ والحَياةِ البَرِّيَّةِ في المِنْطَقَةِ.

Algeria is facing a raging forest fire in one of its rural areas, forcing authorities to evacuate several villages as a precautionary measure. The fire, ignited by an unknown source and accelerated by dry winds, caused property destruction and significant material damage. Firefighting operations are ongoing, with an analysis of the fire's impact on the environment and wildlife in the area.

يَشْهَدُ جَنوبُ إِسْبانِيا سِلْسِلَةً مِنْ حَرائِقِ الغاباتِ العَنيفَةِ، الَّتي احْتَدَمَتْ بِفِعْلِ مَوْجَةِ الحَرِّ الشَّديدَةِ الَّتي تَجْتاحُ البِلادَ. النّيرانُ، الَّتي انْدَلَعَتْ في مَناطِقَ جافَّةٍ وَمُعَرَّضَةٍ لِلحَرائِقِ، أَجْبَرَتِ السُّلُطاتِ عَلى تَنْفيذِ إِجْلاءٍ طارِئٍ لِآلافِ السُّكّانِ وَإِغْلاقِ طُرُقٍ رَئيسِيَّةٍ. فِرَقُ الإِطْفاءِ، مُسَلَّحَةً بِمُعَدّاتِ مُكافَحَةٍ حَديثَةٍ وَتِقْنِيّاتِ إِخْمادٍ فَعّالَةٍ، تُسابِقُ الزَّمَنَ لِإِخْمادِ الحَرائِقِ والسَّيْطَرَةِ عَلى الوَضْعِ قَبْلَ انْتِشارِ النّيرانِ إلى مَناطِقَ أَوْسَعَ.

Southern Spain is witnessing a series of violent forest fires, fueled by the severe heatwave sweeping the country. The flames, which broke out in dry and fire-prone areas, forced authorities to carry out emergency evacuations of thousands of residents and close main roads. Firefighting teams, armed with modern firefighting equipment and effective extinguishing techniques, are racing against time to extinguish the fires and control the situation before the flames spread to broader areas.

تُواجِهُ تُرْكِيا تَحَدِّيًا مُزْدَوَجًا بِسَبَبِ انْدِلاعِ حَريقِ غابَةٍ في مِنْطَقَةٍ تَعَرَّضَتْ مُؤَخَّرًا لِفَيَضاناتٍ عارِمَةٍ، مِمّا أَدّى إلى انْدِفاعِ مِياهٍ وَتَجَمُّعٍ مائِيٍّ في مَناطِقَ كانَتْ تَحْتَرِقُ. الوَضْعُ الاِسْتِثْنائِيُّ خَلَقَ صُعوباتٍ إِضافِيَّةً في عَمَلِيّاتِ الإِطْفاءِ، حَيْثُ تَضَرَّرَتِ البِنْيَةُ التَّحْتِيَّةُ بِشَكْلٍ كَبيرٍ وَأَصْبَحَتِ المَناطِقُ المُحْتَرِقَةُ مَغْمورَةً بِالمِياهِ. تَسْتَعينُ السُّلُطاتُ بِفِرَقِ إِطْفاءٍ مُتَخَصِّصَةٍ وَتِقْنِيّاتٍ مُتَطَوِّرَةٍ لِإِخْمادِ حَريقٍ لاِحْتِواءِ الوَضْعِ وَإِخْمادِ الحَرائِقِ في ظُروفٍ مُعَقَّدَةٍ بيئِيًّا وَجُغْرافِيًّا.

Turkey is facing a dual challenge due to a forest fire in an area recently hit by severe floods, leading to water runoff and accumulation in areas that were burning. The exceptional situation created additional difficulties in firefighting operations, as the infrastructure was significantly damaged and the burned areas became waterlogged. Authorities are using specialized firefighting teams and advanced fire extinguishing techniques to contain the situation and extinguish the fires under environmentally and geographically complex conditions.

9.2.7 Volcanic Eruptions

Track 105

volcanic tornado

إِعْصارٌ بُرْكانِيٌّ

شَهِدَتِ المِنْطَقَةُ إِعْصارًا بُرْكانِيًّا مُصاحِبًا لِلثَّوَرانِ، مِمّا أَدّى إِلى تَدْميرٍ كَبيرٍ.

The area experienced a volcanic cyclone accompanying the eruption, leading to significant destruction.

volcanic eruption likelihood

اِحْتِمالُ ثَوَرَةِ بُرْكانٍ

يَتَزايَدُ احْتِمالُ ثَوَرَةِ البُرْكانِ، مِمّا يَسْتَدْعي تَدابيرَ احْتِرازِيَّةً.

The likelihood of a volcanic eruption is increasing, necessitating precautionary measures.

suffocation

اِخْتِناقٌ

تَعَرَّضَ بَعْضُ السُّكّانِ لِلاخْتِناقِ بِسَبَبِ الغازاتِ البُرْكانِيَّةِ.

Some residents suffered asphyxiation due to volcanic gases.

smoke emission

اِنْبِعاثُ دُخانٍ

تَسَبَّبَ البُرْكانُ في انْبِعاثِ دُخانٍ كَثيفٍ، مِمّا أَثَّرَ عَلى جَوْدَةِ الهَواءِ.

The volcano caused the emission of thick smoke, affecting air quality.

magma surge

اِنْدِفاعُ حُمَمٍ

شَهِدَتِ المِنْطَقَةُ انْدِفاعَ حُمَمٍ مِنَ البُرْكانِ، مِمّا أَدّى إِلى تَدَفُّقِ اللَّهَبِ.

The area witnessed a surge of lava from the volcano, leading to flowing flames.

to erupt

اِنْدَلَعَ • اِنْدِلاع

اِنْدَلَعَ البُرْكانُ بِشَكْلٍ مُفاجِئٍ، مِمّا أَثارَ الذُّعْرَ بَيْنَ السُّكّانِ.

The volcano erupted suddenly, causing panic among the population.

volcanic explosion

اِنْفِجارٌ بُرْكانِيٌّ

حَدَثَ اِنْفِجارٌ بُرْكانِيٌّ كَبِيرٌ، مِمّا أَدّى إلى إِطْلاقِ الرَّمادِ والصُّخورِ.

A major volcanic explosion occurred, releasing ash and rocks.

to explode

اِنْفَجَرَ • اِنْفِجارٌ

اِنْفَجَرَ البُرْكانُ بِقُوَّةٍ، مِمّا أَثَّرَ عَلى المَناطِقِ المُحيطَةِ بِهِ.

The volcano exploded powerfully, affecting the surrounding areas.

volcano

بُرْكانٌ

يُتابِعُ العُلَماءُ نَشاطَ البُرْكانِ عَنْ كَثَبٍ لِتَقْييمِ المَخاطِرِ المُحْتَمَلَةِ.

Scientists closely monitor the volcano's activity to assess potential risks.

dormant volcano

بُرْكانٌ خامِدٌ

يُعْتَبَرُ بُرْكانُ كَراكاتوا في إِنْدونيسْيا بُرْكانًا خامِدًا، حَيْثُ لَمْ يَثُرْ مُنْذُ عُقودٍ.

Krakatoa in Indonesia is considered a dormant volcano, as it hasn't erupted for decades.

extinct volcano

بُرْكانٌ مُنْقَرِضٌ

يُعْرَفُ جَبَلُ كينْيا في كينْيا بِأَنَّهُ بُرْكانٌ مُنْقَرِضٌ، لَمْ يَشْهَدْ أَيَّ نَشاطٍ بُرْكانِيٍّ مُنْذُ آلافِ السِّنينَ.

Mount Kenya in Kenya is known as an extinct volcano, having no volcanic activity for thousands of years.

active volcano

بُرْكانٌ نَشِطٌ • بَراكينُ

تَمَّ تَشْديدُ تَدابيرِ الأَمانِ الشَّخْصِيِّ لِلسُّكّانِ القَريبينَ مِنَ البُرْكانِ النَّشِطِ.

Personal safety measures were intensified for residents near the active volcano.

volcanic eruption impact

تَأْثِيرُ ثَوْرَةٍ بُرْكانِيَّةٍ

أَظْهَرَتِ الدِّراساتُ تَأْثِيرَ ثَوْرَةِ البُرْكانِ عَلى البيئَةِ المُحيطَةِ، بِما في ذَلِكَ الأَنْظِمَةِ البيئِيَّةِ.

Studies showed the impact of the volcanic eruption on the surrounding environment, including ecosystems.

environmental impact

تَأْثِيرٌ عَلى بيئَةٍ

تَأَثَّرَتِ البيئَةُ المَحَلِّيَّةُ بِشَكْلٍ كَبيرٍ بِثَوْرَةِ البُرْكانِ، مِمّا أَدّى إلى تَغْييراتٍ بيئِيَّةٍ.

The local environment was greatly affected by the volcanic eruption, leading to environmental changes.

volcanic eruption analysis

تَحْليلُ ثَوْرَةٍ بُرْكانِيَّةٍ

قامَ العُلَماءُ بِتَحْليلِ الثَّوْرَةِ البُرْكانِيَّةِ لِفَهْمِ ديناميكِيّاتِها وَالتَّأْثيراتِ المُتَرَتِّبَةِ عَلَيْها.

Scientists analyzed the volcanic eruption to understand its dynamics and subsequent impacts.

to flow

تَدَفَّقَ • تَدَفَّقَ

تَدَفُّقُ الحُمَمِ مِنَ البُرْكانِ أَدّى إلى إغْلاقِ الطُّرُقِ وَتَهْديدِ المَناطِقِ المُحيطَةِ.

The flow of lava from the volcano led to the closure of roads and threatened surrounding areas.

lava flow

تَدَفُّقُ حُمَمٍ

شَهِدَ البُرْكانُ تَدَفُّقَ حُمَمٍ شَديدَةِ الحَرارَةِ، مِمّا أَدّى إلى تَدْميرِ النَّباتاتِ وَالأَراضي.

The volcano experienced a flow of intensely hot lava, leading to the destruction of vegetation and land.

volcanic soil

تُرْبَةٌ بُرْكانِيَّةٌ

تَحْتوي التُّرْبَةُ البُرْكانِيَّةُ عَلى مَعادِنَ غَنِيَّةٍ، مِمّا يَجْعَلُها خِصْبَةً لِلزِّراعَةِ.

Volcanic soil contains rich minerals, making it fertile for agriculture.

volcanic tsunami

تْسونامي بُرْكانِيٌّ

أَثارَ الثَّوَرانُ البُرْكانِيُّ مَخاوِفَ مِنْ حُدوثِ تْسونامي بُرْكانِيٍّ في المَناطِقِ المُجاوِرَةِ.

The volcanic eruption raised concerns about a volcanic tsunami in neighboring areas.

volcanic explosion

تَفْجِيرٌ بُرْكانِيٌّ

وَقَعَ تَفْجِيرٌ بُرْكانِيٌّ قَوِيٌّ، مِمَّا أَدَّى إلى انْبِعاثِ كَمِّيّاتٍ هائِلَةٍ مِنَ الرَّمادِ وَالغازاتِ.

A powerful volcanic explosion occurred, emitting large amounts of ash and gases.

magma formation

تَكْوِينُ حُمَم

شاهَدَ العُلَماءُ تَكْوِينَ الحُمَمِ البُرْكانِيَّةِ وَدَرَسوا تَأْثيرَها عَلى البيئَةِ.

Scientists observed the formation of magma and studied its impact on the environment.

volcanic eruption alert

تَنْبِيهٌ مِنْ ثَوَرَةٍ بُرْكانِيَّةٍ

أَصْدَرَتِ السُّلُطاتُ تَنْبيهًا مِنْ ثَوْرَةٍ بُرْكانِيَّةٍ بِناءً عَلى النَّشاطِ الزِّلْزالِيِّ المُتَزايِدِ.

Authorities issued an alert for a volcanic eruption based on increasing seismic activity.

eruption

ثَوَرانٌ

كان الثَّوَرانُ مُميتًا، مِمَّا أَسْفَرَ عَنْ وَفَياتٍ وَإصاباتٍ بَيْنَ السُّكَّانِ.

The eruption was deadly, resulting in fatalities and injuries among the population.

volcanic eruption

ثَوْرَةٌ بُرْكانِيَّةٌ

شَهِدَ البُرْكانُ ثَوْرَةً بُرْكانِيَّةً كَبيرَةً، مِمَّا تَسَبَّبَ في إجْلاءِ السُّكَّانِ المَحَلِّيِّينَ.

The volcano experienced a major eruption, causing the evacuation of local residents.

sudden eruption

ثَوْرَةٌ بُرْكانِيَّةٌ مُفاجِئَةٌ

حَدَثَتْ ثَوْرَةٌ بُرْكانِيَّةٌ مُفاجِئَةٌ، مِمَّا أَدَّى إلى حالَةٍ مِنَ الذُّعْرِ وَالارْتِباكِ.

A sudden volcanic eruption occurred, leading to panic and confusion.

massive volcanic eruption

ثَوْرَةٌ بُرْكانِيَّةٌ هائِلَةٌ

وَقَعَتْ ثَوْرَةٌ بُرْكانِيَّةٌ هائِلَةٌ، مِمَّا أَدَّى إلى إطْلاقِ كَمِّيّاتٍ كَبيرَةٍ مِنَ الرَّمادِ وَالحُمَمِ.

A colossal volcanic eruption occurred, releasing large amounts of ash and lava.

volcanic lava   *pl.*   حُمَمٌ بُرْكانِيَّةٌ

تَدَفَّقَتِ الحُمَمُ البُرْكانِيَّةُ مِنْ فُوَّهَةِ البُرْكانِ، مِمّا أَدّى إلى تَدْميرِ المَناطِقِ المُحيطَةِ.

Volcanic lava flowed from the volcano's crater, leading to the destruction of surrounding areas.

volcanic ash   رَمادٌ بُرْكانِيٌّ

غَطّى الرَّمادُ البُرْكانِيُّ السَّماءَ وَتَراكَمَ عَلى الأَرْضِ، مِمّا أَثَّرَ عَلى الحَياةِ اليَوْمِيَّةِ.

Volcanic ash covered the sky and accumulated on the ground, affecting daily life.

volcanic cloud   سَحابَةٌ بُرْكانِيَّةٌ

تَشَكَّلَتْ سَحابَةٌ بُرْكانِيَّةٌ ضَخْمَةٌ فَوْقَ البُرْكانِ، مِمّا يُشيرُ إلى قُوَّةِ الثَّوَران.

A massive volcanic cloud formed above the volcano, indicating the strength of the eruption.

volcanic gase   غازٌ بُرْكانِيٌّ

انْبَعَثَتْ غازاتٌ بُرْكانِيَّةٌ سامَّةٌ، مِمّا اسْتَدْعى تَحْذيراتٍ لِلسُّكّانِ لاتِّخاذِ احْتِياطاتِ السَّلامَةِ.

Toxic volcanic gases were emitted, prompting warnings for residents to take safety precautions.

plume   غَيْمَةٌ بُرْكانِيَّةٌ

غَطَّتْ غَيْمَةٌ بُرْكانِيَّةٌ السَّماءَ، مِمّا أَدّى إلى تَغَيُّراتٍ في الطَّقْسِ المَحَلِّيِّ.

A volcanic cloud covered the sky, leading to changes in local weather.

volcanic crater   فُوَّهَةٌ بُرْكانِيَّةٌ

أَصْبَحَتْ فُوَّهَةُ البُرْكانِ نَشِطَةً، مِمّا يُشيرُ إلى احْتِمالِ حُدوثِ ثَوَرانٍ بُرْكانِيٍّ إضافيٍّ.

The volcano's crater became active, indicating the possibility of further volcanic eruptions.

volcanic area   مِنْطَقَةٌ بُرْكانِيَّةٌ

تَعيشُ المِنْطَقَةُ البُرْكانِيَّةُ تَحْتَ تَهْديدٍ مُسْتَمِرٍّ بِسَبَبِ النَّشاطِ البُرْكانِيِّ.

The volcanic region lives under constant threat due to volcanic activity.

اِنْدَلَعَ بُرْكانٌ نَشِطٌ في جَزيرَةِ بالي الإِنْدونيسِيَّةِ، مُطْلِقًا انْدِفاعَ حُمَمٍ وَسَحابَةً بُرْكانِيَّةً هائِلَةً. أَصْدَرَتِ السُّلُطاتُ تَنْبيهًا مِنْ ثَوْرَةٍ بُرْكانِيَّةٍ وَبَدَأَتْ عَلى الفَوْرِ في عَمَلِيَّةِ إِجْلاءٍ لِلسُّكّانِ في المَناطِقِ المُعَرَّضَةِ لِلْخَطَرِ. أَدّى الرَّمادُ البُرْكانِيُّ المُنْبَعِثُ إلى تَأْثيراتٍ سَلْبِيَّةٍ عَلى البيئَةِ المَحَلِّيَّةِ وَتَسَبَّبَ في اخْتِناقِ الهَواءِ بِالْمِنْطَقَةِ.

An active volcano erupted on the Indonesian island of Bali, releasing a flow of lava and a massive volcanic cloud. Authorities issued a volcanic eruption alert and immediately began evacuating residents in the danger zones. The emitted volcanic ash had negative effects on the local environment and caused air suffocation in the area.

يُراقِبُ عُلَماءُ الجيولوجيا في الفِلِبّينِ بُرْكانًا خامِدًا أَظْهَرَ مُؤَخَّرًا عَلاماتِ نَشاطٍ مُتَزايِدٍ، مِمّا يَزيدُ مِنَ احْتِمالِ ثَوْرَةٍ بُرْكانِيَّةٍ. جَرى تَحْليلُ ثَوْرَةٍ بُرْكانِيَّةٍ مُحْتَمَلَةٍ وَحَذَّرَتِ السُّلُطاتُ السُّكّانَ في المَناطِقِ المُحيطَةِ بِالْبُرْكانِ لِلْبَقاءِ عَلى أُهْبَةِ الاسْتِعْدادِ لِإِجْراءاتِ الإِخْلاءِ الطّارِئِ.

Geologists in the Philippines are monitoring a dormant volcano that recently showed signs of increasing activity, raising the possibility of a volcanic eruption. A potential eruption was analyzed, and authorities warned residents in the surrounding areas of the volcano to stay alert for emergency evacuation procedures.

شَهِدَ جَنوبُ شيلي ثَوْرَةً بُرْكانِيَّةً هائِلَةً، حَيْثُ انْفَجَرَ بُرْكانٌ نَشِطٌ مُطْلِقًا تَدَفُّقاتِ حُمَمٍ بُرْكانِيَّةٍ وَغَيْمَةً بُرْكانِيَّةً عِمْلاقَةً مُحَمَّلَةً بِالرَّمادِ وَالغازاتِ البُرْكانِيَّةِ. تَسَبَّبَ الانْفِجارُ البُرْكانِيُّ في تَأْثيراتٍ واسِعَةِ النِّطاقِ عَلى البيئَةِ، مِمّا أَدّى إلى تَدْميرِ التُّرْبَةِ البُرْكانِيَّةِ الخِصْبَةِ وَتَلَفٍ في المَناطِقِ الزِّراعِيَّةِ المُجاوِرَةِ.

Southern Chile witnessed a massive volcanic eruption, where an active volcano exploded, releasing volcanic lava flows and a giant ash and volcanic gas-laden cloud. The volcanic explosion had widespread effects on the environment, leading to the destruction of fertile volcanic soil and damage to adjacent agricultural areas.

تَسَبَّبَ ثَوَرانٌ بُرْكانِيٌّ قَوِيٌّ قُبالَةَ ساحِلِ اليابانِ في تَكْوينِ إِعْصارٍ بُرْكانِيٍّ نادِرٍ، مِمّا أَثارَ مَخاوِفَ مِنْ حُدوثِ تسونامي بُرْكانِيٍّ. راقَبَتِ السُّلُطاتُ اليابانِيَّةُ الوَضْعَ عَنْ كَثَبٍ، مُسْتَعِدَّةً لِاتِّخاذِ كافَّةِ التَّدابيرِ اللّازِمَةِ لِحِمايَةِ السُّكّانِ وَالْمُمْتَلَكاتِ في المَناطِقِ السّاحِلِيَّةِ المُعَرَّضَةِ لِلْخَطَرِ.

A powerful volcanic eruption off the coast of Japan caused a rare volcanic typhoon, raising concerns about a volcanic tsunami. The Japanese authorities closely monitored the situation, prepared to take all necessary measures to protect the population and properties in the endangered coastal areas.

تَسَبَّبَتْ ثَوْرَةٌ بُرْكانِيَّةٌ في كوسْتاريكا في انْدِفاعِ حُمَمٍ وَانْبِعاثِ دُخانٍ وَرَمادٍ بُرْكانِيٍّ، مِمّا أَثَّرَ بِشَكْلٍ كَبيرٍ عَلَى الزِّراعَةِ في المَناطِقِ المُحيطَةِ. غَطَّى الرَّمادُ البُرْكانيُّ الأَراضي الزِّراعيَّةَ، مِمّا أَدَّى إِلى تَدْميرِ المَحاصيلِ وَالتَّأْثيرِ سَلْبًا عَلَى الأَمْنِ الغِذائيِّ في المِنْطَقَةِ. بَدَأَتِ الحُكومَةُ وَالمُنَظَّماتُ الدَّوْليَّةُ في تَقْديمِ الإِغاثَةِ وَدَعْمِ جُهودِ اسْتِعادَةِ الإِنْتاجِ الزِّراعيِّ.

A volcanic eruption in Costa Rica led to lava flows and the emission of smoke and volcanic ash, significantly affecting agriculture in the surrounding areas. The volcanic ash covered agricultural lands, leading to crop destruction and a negative impact on food security in the region. The government and international organizations began providing relief and supporting efforts to restore agricultural production.

9.2.8 Droughts

Track **107**

اِحْتِمالُ جَفافٍ

probability of a drought

يَزْدادُ احْتِمالُ حُدوثِ الجَفافِ بِسَبَبِ التَّغَيُّراتِ المُناخيَّةِ وَنَقْصِ الأَمْطارِ.

The likelihood of drought is increasing due to climate changes and lack of rainfall.

اِحْتِياطيُّ مِياهٍ

water reserves

تَمَّ اسْتِنْفاذُ احْتِياطِيّاتِ المِياهِ بِسُرْعَةٍ نَتيجَةَ الاِسْتِخْدامِ المُفْرِطِ وَالجَفافِ.

Water reserves were rapidly depleted due to overuse and drought.

اِسْتِنْزافُ مَصادِرِ مِياهٍ

water source depletion

يُهَدِّدُ اسْتِنْزافُ مَصادِرِ المِياهِ الأَمْنَ الغِذائيَّ وَالاسْتِدامَةَ البيئيَّةَ.

The depletion of water resources threatens food security and environmental sustainability.

اِنْخِفاضُ مَنْسوبِ مِياهٍ

water level drop

أَدَّى انْخِفاضُ مَنْسوبِ المِياهِ في الأَنْهارِ وَالبُحَيْراتِ إِلى مَشاكِلَ في الرَّيِّ وَإِمْداداتِ المِياهِ.

The decrease in water levels in rivers and lakes led to problems in irrigation and water supply.

تَأْثيرُ جَفافٍ

drought impact

كانَ لِتَأْثيرِ الجَفافِ تَداعِياتٌ واسِعَةٌ، بِما في ذَلِكَ نَقْصٌ في المَوارِدِ الطَّبيعيَّةِ.

The impact of the drought had wide-ranging repercussions, including a shortage of natural resources.

water rationing

تَرْشيدُ مِياهٍ

بَدَأَتِ الحُكوماتُ في تَنْفيذِ سِياساتٍ تَرْشيدِ اسْتِهْلاكِ المِياهِ لِلتَّعامُلِ مَعَ الجَفافِ.

Governments began implementing water conservation policies to deal with the drought.

rainfall cessation

تَوَقُّفُ مَطَرٍ

تَسَبَّبَ تَوَقُّفُ الأَمْطارِ في العَديدِ مِنَ المَناطِقِ في تَفاقُمِ الوَضْعِ الجافِّ.

The cessation of rain in many areas exacerbated the dry conditions.

drought

جَفافٌ

يَشْهَدُ الجَفافُ انْتِشارًا في مَناطِقَ مُتَعَدِّدَةٍ، مِمّا يُؤَثِّرُ عَلى الزِّراعَةِ وَالإِمْداداتِ المائِيَّةِ.

Drought is spreading in various regions, affecting agriculture and water supplies.

increased temperature

حَرارَةٌ مُتَزايِدَةٌ

ساهَمَتِ الحَرارَةُ المُتَزايِدَةُ في زِيادَةِ مُعَدَّلاتِ التَّبَخُّرِ، مِمّا أَسْهَمَ في نَقْصِ المِياهِ.

Increasing heat contributed to higher evaporation rates, leading to water shortages.

low humidity

رُطوبَةٌ مُنْخَفِضَةٌ

تَسَبَّبَتِ الرُّطوبَةُ المُنْخَفِضَةُ في زِيادَةِ جَفافِ التُّرْبَةِ وَصُعوبَةِ زِراعَةِ المَحاصيلِ.

Low humidity caused soil dryness and difficulties in crop cultivation.

agriculture, farming

زِراعَةٌ

أَثَّرَ الجَفافُ بِشَكْلٍ كَبيرٍ عَلى الزِّراعَةِ، مِمّا أَدّى إلى تَراجُعِ الإِنْتاجِ الزِّراعِيِّ.

The drought significantly affected agriculture, leading to a decline in agricultural production.

long-term

طَويلُ الأَمَدِ

تَسَبَّبَ الجَفافُ طَويلُ الأَمَدِ في تَفاقُمِ النَّقْصِ في المِياهِ وَالمَحاصيلِ.

The long-term drought exacerbated the shortage of water and crops.

famine مَجاعَةٌ

أَدّى الجَفافُ المُتَواصِلُ إلى مَجاعَةٍ في بَعْضِ المَناطِقِ، مِمّا اسْتَدْعى تَدَخُّلاتٍ إِنْسانِيَّةً.

The prolonged drought led to famine in some areas, necessitating humanitarian interventions.

chronic مُزْمِنٌ

يُعاني المُناخُ في هَذِهِ المِنْطَقَةِ مِنْ مَشاكِلِ الجَفافِ المُزْمِنِ.

The climate in this region suffers from chronic drought issues.

drought mitigation مُكافَحَةُ جَفافٍ

تَتَّخِذُ الحُكوماتُ إِجْراءاتٍ لِمُكافَحَةِ الجَفافِ، بِما في ذَلِكَ بِناءَ السُّدودِ وَتَطْويرَ نُظُمِ الرَّيِّ.

Governments are taking measures to combat drought, including building dams and developing irrigation systems.

drought prevention مَنْعُ جَفافٍ

يَتِمُّ تَنْفيذُ بَرامِجَ لِمَنْعِ الجَفافِ، مِثلِ إِعادَةِ تَدْويرِ المِياهِ وَجَمْعِ مِياهِ الأَمْطارِ.

Programs to prevent drought are being implemented, such as water recycling and rainwater harvesting.

groundwater مِياهٌ جَوْفِيَّةٌ *pl.*

تَعْتَمِدُ المَناطِقُ الزِّراعِيَّةُ بِشَكْلٍ كَبيرٍ عَلى المِياهِ الجَوْفِيَّةِ لِلرَّيِّ.

Agricultural areas heavily rely on groundwater for irrigation.

scarcity نُدْرَةٌ

تُواجِهُ المِنْطَقَةُ نُدْرَةً في المِياهِ بِسَبَبِ الجَفافِ وَالاِسْتِخْدامِ المُفْرِطِ.

The region faces water scarcity due to drought and overuse.

depletion of groundwater

نَفادُ مِياهٍ جَوْفِيَّةٍ

يُمَثِّلُ النَّفادُ المُتَزايِدُ لِلْمِياهِ الجَوْفِيَّةِ تَحَدِّياتٍ جَسيمَةً في تَوْفيرِ المِياهِ لِلسُّكّانِ.

The increasing depletion of groundwater presents significant challenges in providing water for the population.

irrigation shortage

نَقْصُ رَيٍّ

أَثَّرَ نَقْصُ الرَّيِّ نَتيجَةً لِلْجَفافِ بِشَكْلٍ مُباشِرٍ عَلى الزِّراعَةِ وَإِنْتاجِ المَحاصيلِ.

The lack of irrigation due to drought directly affected agriculture and crop production.

rainfall deficiency

نَقْصُ مَطَرٍ

يُعاني المُناخُ مِنْ نَقْصِ مَطَرٍ مُسْتَمِرٍّ، مِمّا يَزيدُ مِنْ خَطَرِ الجَفافِ.

The climate suffers from a continuous lack of rain, increasing the risk of drought.

water shortage

نَقْصُ مِياهٍ

يُواجِهُ المُجْتَمَعُ نَقْصًا حادًّا في المِياهِ، مِمّا يُؤَثِّرُ عَلى جَميعِ جَوانِبِ الحَياةِ.

The community faces a severe water shortage, affecting all aspects of life.

precipitation deficiency

نَقْصُ هُطولِ مَطَرٍ

تُعاني المِنْطَقَةُ مِنْ نَقْصِ هُطولِ المَطَرِ، مِمّا يُؤَدّي إلى تَراجُعِ مُسْتَوَياتِ المِياهِ في السُّدودِ وَالبُحَيْراتِ.

The region suffers from a lack of rainfall, leading to declining water levels in dams and lakes.

9.2.8.1 Mini-Articles

Track **108**

تَشْهَدُ مِصْرُ انْخِفاضًا مَلْحوظًا في مَنْسوبِ مِياهِ نَهْرِ النّيلِ بِسَبَبِ تَوَقُّفِ الأَمْطارِ وَالحَرارَةِ المُتَزايِدَةِ، مِمّا يُهَدِّدُ بِجَفافٍ طَويلِ الأَمَدِ. تَعْمَلُ الحُكومَةُ عَلى تَرْشيدِ اسْتِهْلاكِ المِياهِ وَتَعْزيزِ اسْتِخْدامِ المِياهِ الجَوْفِيَّةِ كاحْتِياطِيٍّ مِياهٍ بَديلٍ لِضَمانِ اسْتِمْرارِيَّةِ الزِّراعَةِ وَمُواجَهَةِ نُدْرَةِ المِياهِ.

Egypt is witnessing a significant decrease in the water levels of the Nile River due to the cessation of rainfall and increasing heat, threatening a long-term drought. The government is working on rationalizing water consumption and enhancing the use of groundwater as an alternative water reserve to ensure the continuity of agriculture and address water scarcity.

في ظِلِّ الِاحْتِمالِ المُتَزايِدِ لِلجَفافِ، بَدَأَتِ المَغرِبُ في تَنْفيذِ سِياساتٍ لِمُكافَحَةِ الجَفافِ تَشْمَلُ إنْشاءَ سُدودٍ جَديدَةٍ وَتَعْزيزَ شَبَكاتِ تَوْزيعِ المِياهِ. أَدَّى الجَفافُ المُزْمِنُ الَّذي يَضْرِبُ مَناطِقَ واسِعَةً مِنَ البِلادِ إلى اسْتِنْزافِ مَصادِرِ المِياهِ وَلَهُ تَأْثيرٌ مُباشِرٌ عَلى الزِّراعَةِ، مِمّا يُهَدِّدُ بِمَجاعَةٍ إذا لَمْ يَتِمَّ التَّعامُلُ مَعَ الأَزْمَةِ بِجِدِّيَّةٍ.

In light of the increasing likelihood of drought, Morocco has started implementing policies to combat drought, including the construction of new dams and strengthening water distribution networks. The chronic drought affecting vast areas of the country has led to the depletion of water sources and has a direct impact on agriculture, threatening famine if the crisis is not seriously addressed.

تُواجِهُ دَوْلَةُ الأُرْدُنِّ، إحْدى الدُّوَلِ الأَكْثَرِ جَفافًا في العالَمِ، نَقْصًا حادًّا في المِياهِ بِسَبَبِ انْخِفاضِ الرُّطوبَةِ وَنَقْصِ هُطولِ الأَمْطارِ لِأَعْوامٍ مُتَتالِيَةٍ. تَعْمَلُ الحُكومَةُ عَلى تَحْسينِ إدارَةِ المِياهِ الجَوْفِيَّةِ وَتَشْجيعِ تِقْنِيّاتِ الرَّيِّ المُوَفِّرِ لِلْمِياهِ لِلْحَدِّ مِنْ تَأْثيراتِ الجَفافِ عَلى سُكّانِها وَقِطاعِها الزِّراعِيِّ.

Jordan, one of the driest countries in the world, is facing a severe water shortage due to low humidity and a lack of rainfall for consecutive years. The government is working on improving the management of groundwater and encouraging water-saving irrigation techniques to mitigate the impacts of drought on its population and agricultural sector.

تَشْهَدُ تونِسُ جَفافًا حادًّا أَدّى إلى انْخِفاضِ مَنْسوبِ المِياهِ في السُّدودِ وَنَفادِ المِياهِ الجَوْفِيَّةِ. يَتَطَلَّبُ الوَضْعُ الرّاهِنُ تَدابيرَ عاجِلَةً لِمَنْعِ جَفافِ الأَراضي الزِّراعِيَّةِ وَضَمانِ الأَمْنِ الغِذائِيِّ. تَدْعو الحُكومَةُ المُواطِنينَ إلى تَرْشيدِ مِياهِ الشُّرْبِ وَالزِّراعَةِ لِلْحِفاظِ عَلى المَوارِدِ المائِيَّةِ المُتاحَةِ.

Tunisia is experiencing a severe drought that has led to a decrease in water levels in dams and the depletion of groundwater. The current situation requires urgent measures to prevent the drying of agricultural lands and ensure food security. The government is urging citizens to rationalize the use of drinking and agricultural water to conserve available water resources.

في ظِلِّ ظُروفِ الجَفافِ المُتَزايِدَةِ وَالحَرارَةِ الشَّديدَةِ، تَعْمَلُ السُّعودِيَّةُ عَلى تَحْسينِ اسْتْراتيجِيّاتِ مُواجَهَةِ نَقْصِ المِياهِ مِنْ خِلالِ تَطْويرِ مَشاريعِ تَحْلِيَةِ المِياهِ وَإعادَةِ اسْتِخْدامِ المِياهِ المُعالَجَةِ. الهَدَفُ هُوَ تَقْليلُ الِاعْتِمادِ عَلى المِياهِ الجَوْفِيَّةِ وَضَمانُ إمْداداتِ مِياهٍ مُسْتَدامَةٍ لِتَلْبِيَةِ احْتِياجاتِها المُتَزايِدَةِ في مُخْتَلِفِ القِطاعاتِ.

Amid increasing drought conditions and extreme heat, Saudi Arabia is working to improve water scarcity strategies through the development of desalination projects and the reuse of treated water. The goal is to reduce dependence on groundwater and ensure sustainable water supplies to meet its growing needs in various sectors.

مُواجَهَةُ التَّحَدِّياتِ: اسْتِراتيجِيّاتُ الدُّوَلِ العَرَبِيَّةِ لِلتَّغَلُّبِ عَلى الجَفافِ

في العُقودِ الأخيرَةِ، شَهِدَتْ مِنطَقَةُ الشَّرقِ الأَوْسَطِ انْخِفاضًا مَلْحوظًا في مَنْسوبِ المِياهِ، مِمّا أدّى إلى ظُروفِ جَفافٍ مُتَزايِدَةٍ وَتَحَدِّياتٍ كَبيرَةٍ في مَجالِ الزِّراعَةِ وَالأَمْنِ الغِذائِيِّ. باتَ احْتِمالُ الجَفافِ طَويلِ الأَمَدِ يُهَدِّدُ اسْتِقْرارَ المِنْطَقَةِ، مِمّا يَسْتَدْعي تَبَنّي اسْتِراتيجِيّاتٍ فَعّالَةٍ لِمُكافَحَةِ هذِهِ الظّاهِرَةِ.

أَحَدُ الحُلولِ المُعْتَمَدَةِ يَتَمَثَّلُ في تَرْشيدِ مِياهِ الشُّرْبِ وَالزِّراعَةِ، حَيْثُ تَعْمَلُ الدُّوَلُ عَلى تَطْويرِ تِقْنِياتِ رَيٍّ مُتَقَدِّمَةٍ تُقَلِّلُ مِنْ نَقْصِ رَيِّ المَحاصيلِ. كَما أنَّ اسْتِنْزافَ مَصادِرِ المِياهِ أَصْبَحَ مَوْضوعًا يَتَطَلَّبُ تَدَخُّلًا عاجِلًا، وَذلِكَ بِإعادَةِ تَوْجيهِ اسْتِخْدامِ المِياهِ الجَوْفِيَّةِ بِشَكْلٍ مُسْتَدامٍ وَالحَدِّ مِنْ نَفادِها.

مِنْ ناحِيَةٍ أُخْرى، يَتَطَلَّبُ تَأْثيرُ الجَفافِ عَلى البيئَةِ وَالزِّراعَةِ تَبَنّي مُمارَساتٍ زِراعِيَّةٍ تَعْتَمِدُ عَلى تَحْليلٍ دَقيقٍ لِاحْتِياطِيِّ المِياهِ وَتَوَقُّعاتِ الأَمْطارِ. كَما تَسْعى الدُّوَلُ أَيْضًا لِمَنْعِ جَفافِ الأراضي مِنْ خِلالِ تَطْبيقِ سِياساتٍ تُحافِظُ عَلى رُطوبَةِ التُّرْبَةِ وَتَحْمي المَحاصيلَ مِنَ التَّأثيراتِ السَّلْبِيَّةِ لِنَقْصِ الهُطولِ.

المَجاعَةُ وَنُدْرَةُ المِياهِ تُشَكِّلانِ خَطَرًا مُحْدِقًا، مِمّا دَفَعَ الدُّوَلَ لِتَكْثيفِ جُهودِها في مُكافَحَةِ الجَفافِ مِنْ خِلالِ بَرامِجِ تَوْعِيَةٍ تَهْدُفُ إلى تَعْزيزِ الوَعْيِ بِأَهَمِّيَّةِ المُحافَظَةِ عَلى المَوارِدِ المائِيَّةِ وَتَعْزيزِ الاسْتِخْدامِ الأَمْثَلِ لَها.

في الخِتامِ، فَإنَّ مُواجَهَةَ تَحَدّي الجَفافِ في الدُّوَلِ العَرَبِيَّةِ يَتَطَلَّبُ جُهْدًا مُشْتَرَكًا وَتَعاوُنًا بَيْنَ جَميعِ الأطرافِ المَعْنِيَّةِ. مِنْ خِلالِ تَبَنّي اسْتِراتيجِيّاتٍ مُبْتَكَرَةٍ وَمُسْتَدامَةٍ، يُمْكِنُ تَعْزيزُ القُدْرَةِ عَلى التَّكَيُّفِ مَعَ التَّغَيُّراتِ المُناخِيَّةِ وَضَمانُ مُسْتَقْبَلٍ أَكْثَرَ أمانًا لِلأَجْيالِ القادِمَةِ.

Facing the Challenges: Arab Countries' Strategies to Overcome Drought

In recent decades, the Middle East region has witnessed a significant decrease in water levels, leading to increasing drought conditions and significant challenges in agriculture and food security. The possibility of long-term drought now threatens the stability of the region, necessitating the adoption of effective strategies to combat this phenomenon.

One of the adopted solutions is the rationalization of drinking and agricultural water, where countries are working on developing advanced irrigation technologies that reduce crop irrigation shortages. Additionally, the depletion of water sources has become an issue requiring urgent intervention, through sustainable redirection of groundwater use and preventing its exhaustion.

On the other hand, the impact of drought on the environment and agriculture requires the adoption of agricultural practices based on precise analysis of water reserves and rainfall forecasts. Countries are also striving to prevent land desiccation through policies that preserve soil moisture and protect crops from the adverse effects of rainfall shortage.

Famine and water scarcity now pose an imminent risk, prompting countries to intensify their efforts to combat drought through awareness programs aimed at enhancing awareness of the importance of conserving water resources and promoting their optimal use.

In conclusion, facing the challenge of drought in Arab countries requires a joint effort and cooperation among all concerned parties. By adopting innovative and sustainable strategies, it is possible to enhance adaptability to climate changes and ensure a safer future for the coming generations.

9.2.9 Landslides

Track 110

erosion

انْجِرافٌ

تَسَبَّبَتِ الأَمْطارُ الغَزيرَةُ في انْجِرافِ التُّرْبَةِ، مِمّا أَدّى إلى غَلْقِ الطُّرُقِ.

Heavy rain caused soil erosion, leading to road blockages.

soil slippage

انْزِلاقُ تُرْبَةٍ

وَقَعَ انْزِلاقُ تُرْبَةٍ كَبيرٌ، مِمّا تَسَبَّبَ في تَدْميرِ البِنْيَةِ التَّحْتِيَّةِ.

A major soil slide occurred, causing destruction to infrastructure.

landslide

انْهِيارٌ أَرْضِيٌّ

شَهِدَتِ المِنْطَقَةُ انْهِيارًا أَرْضِيًّا مُدَمِّرًا، مِمّا أَدّى إلى إِجْلاءِ السُّكّانِ.

The area experienced a devastating landslide, leading to the evacuation of residents.

avalanche

انْهِيارٌ ثَلْجِيٌّ

حَدَثَ انْهِيارٌ ثَلْجِيٌّ في المَناطِقِ الجَبَلِيَّةِ، مِمّا أَثارَ قَلَقًا بَيْنَ المُتَجَوِّلينَ وَالسُّكّانِ المَحَلِّيّينَ.

An avalanche occurred in the mountainous areas, raising concerns among hikers and local residents.

mudflow

تَدَفُّقٌ طينِيٌّ

تَسَبَّبَتِ الأَمْطارُ الغَزيرَةُ في تَدَفُّقٍ طينِيٍّ، مِمّا أَدّى إلى غَمْرِ الطُّرُقِ وَالمُمْتَلَكاتِ.

Heavy rains caused a mudflow, inundating roads and properties.

soil accumulation
تَراكُمُ تُرْبَةٍ

أَدّى تَراكُمُ التُّرْبَةِ بِسَبَبِ الِانْهِياراتِ الأَرْضِيَّةِ إِلى مَشاكِلَ في الصَّرْفِ وَالبِنْيَةِ التَّحْتِيَّةِ.

Soil accumulation due to landslides led to drainage and infrastructure problems.

shift
تَزَحْزُحٌ

تَزَحْزَحَتِ الأَرْضُ في المِنْطَقَةِ المُنْحَدِرَةِ، مِمّا يُشيرُ إِلى خَطَرِ وُقوعِ المَزيدِ مِنَ الِانْهِياراتِ الأَرْضِيَّةِ.

The land in the sloped area shifted, indicating the risk of further landslides.

disintegration
تَفْتيتٌ

تَفْتيتُ الصُّخورِ في المَناطِقِ الجَبَلِيَّةِ يُمْكِنُ أَنْ يُؤَدِّيَ إِلى انْهِياراتٍ أَرْضِيَّةٍ خَطيرَةٍ.

The fragmentation of rocks in mountainous areas can lead to serious landslides.

to pile-up
تَكَدُّسٌ • تَكَدَّسَ

تَسَبَّبَ تَكَدُّسُ المَوادِّ الطّينِيَّةِ عَلى مُنْحَدَراتِ الجِبالِ في زِيادَةِ خَطَرِ حُدوثِ انْهِياراتٍ أَرْضِيَّةٍ.

The accumulation of earth materials on mountain slopes increased the risk of landslides.

to collapse
تَهَدَّمَ = انْهارَ • تَهَدُّمٌ / انْهِيارٌ

اِنْهارَتْ عِدَّةُ مَنازِلَ في المِنْطَقَةِ نَتيجَةَ انْهِيارٍ أَرْضِيٍّ مُفاجِئٍ.

Several houses in the area collapsed due to a sudden landslide.

threat
تَهْديدٌ

تُمَثِّلُ الِانْهِياراتُ الأَرْضِيَّةُ تَهْديدًا كَبيرًا لِلقُرى وَالمُدُنِ القَريبَةِ مِنَ المُنْحَدَراتِ الجَبَلِيَّةِ.

Landslides pose a significant threat to villages and towns near mountain slopes.

subsurface tremor
زِلْزالٌ تَحْتَ السَّطْحِ • زَلازِلُ

أَدّى زِلْزالٌ تَحْتَ السَّطْحِ إِلى تَحْريكِ الأَرْضِ وَزِيادَةِ احْتِمالِيَّةِ حُدوثِ انْهِياراتٍ أَرْضِيَّةٍ.

An underground earthquake caused the ground to move, increasing the likelihood of landslides.

ground fissure — شَقٌّ أَرْضِيٌّ

ظَهَرَ شَقٌّ أَرْضِيٌّ كَبِيرٌ في المِنْطَقَةِ، مِمّا يُشيرُ إلى نَشاطٍ جيولوجيٍّ مُتَزايِدٍ.

A large ground fissure appeared in the area, indicating increased geological activity.

mountain slope — مُنْحَدَرٌ جَبَلِيٌّ

تَقَعُ القَرْيَةُ عَلى مُنْحَدَرٍ جَبَلِيٍّ، مِمّا يَجْعَلُها عُرْضَةً لانْهِياراتٍ أَرْضِيَّةٍ.

The village is located on a mountain slope, making it susceptible to landslides.

landslide-prone area — مَناطِقُ • مِنْطَقَةٌ عُرْضَةٌ لانْهِيارٍ

تُعْتَبَرُ هَذِهِ المِنْطَقَةُ عُرْضَةً لانْهِياراتٍ أَرْضِيَّةٍ بِسَبَبِ طَبيعَتِها الجيولوجيَّةِ.

This area is prone to landslides due to its geological nature.

isolated — مُنْعَزِلٌ

يَقَعُ المُجْتَمَعُ المُتَضَرِّرُ مِنَ الانْهِيارِ الأَرْضِيِّ في مِنْطَقَةٍ مُنْعَزِلَةٍ، مِمّا يُعَقِّدُ جُهودَ الإنْقاذِ.

The community affected by the landslide is located in an isolated area, complicating rescue efforts.

9.2.9.1 Mini-Articles

Track **111**

شَهِدَ مُنْحَدَرٌ جَبَلِيٌّ في المَغْرِبِ انْزِلاقَ تُرْبَةٍ ضَخْمًا بَعْدَ هُطولِ أَمْطارٍ غَزيرَةٍ لِأَيّامٍ، مِمّا أَدّى إلى انْهِيارٍ أَرْضِيٍّ هائِلٍ. تَسَبَّبَ الحادِثُ في تَراكُمِ التُّرْبَةِ وَتَكَدُّسِ الأَنْقاضِ، عازِلًا قُرًى بِأَكْمَلِها وَمُشَكِّلًا تَهْديدًا كَبيرًا لِلسُّكّانِ. تُسابِقُ السُّلُطاتُ الزَّمَنَ لِإيجادِ طُرُقٍ بَديلَةٍ لِلْوُصولِ إلى المَناطِقِ المُتَضَرِّرَةِ.

A mountain slope in Morocco witnessed a massive landslide after days of heavy rain, leading to a huge land collapse. The incident caused soil accumulation and debris pile-up, isolating entire villages and posing a significant threat to the residents. Authorities are racing against time to find alternative routes to reach the affected areas.

أَدّى زِلْزالٌ تَحْتَ السَّطْحِ في اليابانِ إلى تَفْتيتِ التُّرْبَةِ وانْجِرافٍ طينيٍّ كَبيرٍ، مِمّا تَسَبَّبَ في انْهِياراتٍ أَرْضِيَّةٍ في عِدَّةِ مَناطِقَ. أَغْلَقَتْ هَذِهِ الانْهِياراتُ الطُّرُقَ وَدَمَّرَتِ المَنازِلَ، مِمّا جَعَلَ الإغاثَةَ وَعَمَلِيّاتِ الإنْقاذِ تُواجِهُ تَحَدِّياتٍ جَمَّةً. تَعْمَلُ الحُكومَةُ عَلى تَقْييمِ الأَضْرارِ وَتَقْديمِ المُساعَدَةِ لِلْمُتَضَرِّرينَ.

A subsurface earthquake in Japan led to soil fragmentation and significant mudslides, causing landslides in several areas. These landslides closed roads and destroyed homes, making relief and rescue operations face great challenges. The government is working on assessing the damages and providing assistance to the affected.

في إنْجازٍ مَلْحوظٍ، نَجَحَ نِظامُ الإنْذارِ المُبَكِّرِ في نيبالَ في تَحْذيرِ سُكّانِ قَرْيَةٍ جَبَلِيَّةٍ مِنَ احْتِمالِ وُقوعِ انْهِيارٍ ثَلْجيٍّ. تَمَكَّنَ السُّكّانُ مِنَ الإخْلاءِ في الوَقْتِ المُناسِبِ، مِمّا مَنَعَ وُقوعَ ضَحايا. الجُهودُ المُسْتَمِرَّةُ لِتَحْسينِ أَنْظِمَةِ التَّحْذيرِ وَالتَّوْعِيَةُ حَوْلَ المَخاطِرِ الطَّبيعِيَّةِ تُثْبِتُ أَهَمِّيَتَها في حِمايَةِ الأَرْواحِ.

In a notable achievement, the early warning system in Nepal successfully alerted the residents of a mountain village about the possibility of an avalanche. The inhabitants were able to evacuate in time, preventing any casualties. Ongoing efforts to improve warning systems and awareness about natural hazards prove their importance in protecting lives.

تَسَبَّبَتِ انْزِلاقاتُ تُرْبَةٍ وَانْهِياراتٌ أَرْضِيَّةٌ نَتيجَةً لِلْأَمْطارِ المَوْسِمِيَّةِ الغَزيرَةِ في الهِنْدِ في تَهَدُّمِ عِدَّةِ طُرُقٍ رَئيسِيَّةٍ، مِمّا أَدّى إلى عَزْلِ مَناطِقَ بِأَكْمَلِها. تُواجِهُ فِرَقُ الإغاثَةِ صُعوبَةً في الوُصولِ إلى المَناطِقِ المُتَضَرِّرَةِ لِتَقْديمِ المُساعَداتِ الضَّروريَّةِ وَإجْلاءِ السُّكّانِ المُعَرَّضينَ لِلْخَطَرِ.

Landslides and land collapses due to heavy monsoon rains in India caused several main roads to collapse, isolating entire areas. Relief teams are struggling to reach the affected areas to provide necessary aid and evacuate residents at risk.

تُواجِهُ مِنْطَقَةٌ سَكَنِيَّةٌ في إيطاليا تَهْديدًا كَبيرًا بِسَبَبِ تَزَحْزُحِ التُّرْبَةِ، مِمّا يَزيدُ مِنْ خَطَرِ حُدوثِ انْهِياراتٍ أَرْضِيَّةٍ. تَعْمَلُ السُّلُطاتُ عَلى تَعْزيزِ الاسْتِقْرارِ في المِنْطَقَةِ المُعَرَّضَةِ لِلِانْهِيارِ، وَتُنَفِّذُ مَشاريعَ لِتَحْصينِ المُنْحَدَراتِ وَمَنْعِ الِانْزِلاقاتِ المُسْتَقْبَلِيَّةِ لِضَمانِ سَلامَةِ السُّكّانِ وَالمُمْتَلَكاتِ.

A residential area in Italy is facing a significant threat due to soil displacement, increasing the risk of landslides. Authorities are working on enhancing stability in the area prone to collapse and are implementing projects to fortify slopes and prevent future landslides to ensure the safety of residents and properties.

lingualism

Visit our website for information on current and upcoming titles and free language learning resources.

www.lingualism.com